ADVANCED PROCESS CONTROL

McGraw-Hill Chemical Engineering Series

BUILDING THE LITERATURE OF A PROFESSION

Fifteen prominent chemical engineers first met in New York more than 50 years ago to plan a continuing literature for their rapidly growing profession. From industry came such pioneer practitioners as Leo H. Baekeland, Arthur D. Little, Charles L. Reese, John V. N. Dorr, M. C. Whitaker, and R. S. McBride. From the universities came such eminent educators as William H. Walker, Alfred H. White, D. D. Jackson, J. H. James, Warren K. Lewis, and Harry A. Curtis. H. C. Parmelee, then editor of *Chemical and Metallurgical Engineering*, served as chairman and was joined subsequently by S. D. Kirkpatrick as consulting editor.

After several meetings, this committee submitted its report to the McGraw-Hill Book Company in September 1925. In the report were detailed specifications for a correlated series of more than a dozen texts and reference books which have since become the McGraw-Hill Series in Chemical Engineering and which became the cornerstone of the chemical engineering curriculum.

From this beginning there has evolved a series of texts surpassing by far the scope and longevity envisioned by the founding Editorial Board. The McGraw-Hill Series in Chemical Engineering stands as a unique historical record of the development of chemical engineering education and practice. In the series one finds the milestones of the subject's evolution: industrial chemistry, stoichiometry, unit operations and processes, thermodynamics, kinetics, and transfer operations.

Chemical engineering is a dynamic profession, and its literature continues to evolve. McGraw-Hill and its consulting editors remain committed to a publishing policy that will serve, and indeed lead, the needs of the chemical engineering profession during the years to come.

THE SERIES

Bailey and Ollis: *Biochemical Engineering Fundamentals*
Bennett and Myers: *Momentum, Heat, and Mass Transfer*
Beveridge and Schechter: *Optimization: Theory and Practice*
Carberry: *Chemical and Catalytic Reaction Engineering*
Churchill: *The Interpretation and Use of Rate Data—The Rate Concept*
Clarke and Davidson: *Manual for Process Engineering Calculations*
Coughanowr and Koppel: *Process Systems Analysis and Control*
Danckwerts: *Gas Liquid Reactions*
Gates, Katzer, and Schuit: *Chemistry of Catalytic Processes*
Harriott: *Process Control*
Johnson: *Automatic Process Control*
Johnstone and Thring: *Pilot Plants, Models, and Scale-up Methods in Chemical Engineering*
Katz, Cornell, Kobayashi, Poettmann, Vary, Elenbaas, and Weinaug: *Handbook of Natural Gas Engineering*
King: *Separation Processes*
Knudsen and Katz: *Fluid Dynamics and Heat Transfer*
Lapidus: *Digital Computation for Chemical Engineers*
Luyben: *Process Modeling, Simulation, and Control for Chemical Engineers*
McCabe and Smith, J. C.: *Unit Operations of Chemical Engineering*
Mickley, Sherwood, and Reed: *Applied Mathematics in Chemical Engineering*
Nelson: *Petroleum Refinery Engineering*
Perry and Chilton (Editors): *Chemical Engineers' Handbook*
Peters: *Elementary Chemical Engineering*
Peters and Timmerhaus: *Plant Design and Economics for Chemical Engineers*
Ray: *Advanced Process Control*
Reed and Gubbins: *Applied Statistical Mechanics*
Reid, Prausnitz, and Sherwood: *The Properties of Gases and Liquids*
Resnick: *Process Analysis and Design for Chemical Engineers*
Satterfield: *Heterogeneous Catalysis in Practice*
Sherwood, Pigford, and Wilke: *Mass Transfer*
Slattery: *Momentum, Energy, and Mass Transfer in Continua*
Smith, B. D.: *Design of Equilibrium Stage Processes*
Smith, J. M.: *Chemical Engineering Kinetics*
Smith, J. M., and Van Ness: *Introduction to Chemical Engineering Thermodynamics*
Thompson and Ceckler: *Introduction to Chemical Engineering*
Treybal: *Mass Transfer Operations*
Van Winkle: *Distillation*
Volk: *Applied Statistics for Engineers*
Walas: *Reaction Kinetics for Chemical Engineers*
Wei, Russell, and Swartzlander: *The Structure of the Chemical Processing Industries*
Whitwell and Toner: *Conservation of Mass and Energy*

ADVANCED PROCESS CONTROL

W. Harmon Ray

Professor of Chemical Engineering
University of Wisconsin

McGraw-Hill Book Company

New York St. Louis San Francisco Auckland Bogotá Hamburg
Johannesburg London Madrid Mexico Montreal New Delhi
Panama Paris São Paulo Singapore Sydney Tokyo Toronto

ADVANCED PROCESS CONTROL

234567890 FGFG 898765432

This book was set in Times Roman by Science Typographers, Inc.
The editors were Diane D. Heiberg and Madelaine Eichberg;
the production supervisor was John Mancia.
The drawings were done by Burmar.
Fairfield Graphics was printer and binder.

Library of Congress Cataloging in Publication Data

Ray, Willis Harmon, date
Advanced process control.

(McGraw-Hill chemical engineering series)
Includes bibliographical references and index.
1. Chemical process control. I. Title.
TP155.75.R38 660.2'81 79-24791
ISBN 0-07-051250-7

This book is dedicated to my inquisitive students,
who surely have been my best teachers.

CONTENTS

PREFACE

This book is designed to be used as a text for advanced undergraduate and graduate courses in process control as well as to serve as a reference for the practicing control engineer. Bearing in mind the likely background of the reader, the mathematical prerequisites consist of introductory undergraduate process control material, elementary matrix algebra, and an introduction to differential equations. The standard undergraduate chemical engineering curriculum usually provides the necessary background. In spite of these modest mathematical demands, the book strives to provide a broad coverage of applied modern control theory. Although only one or two sections may be devoted to theoretical subjects upon which entire books have been written, the goal is to provide the process control engineer a synopsis of the theory, a clear exposition of the most useful design techniques, and example problems to demonstrate the key features of the computational algorithms. Numerous references are provided so that the interested reader may delve more deeply into the mathematical theory or seek further illustrative examples.

The material has been tested in the classroom over the last five years both at the State University of New York at Buffalo and at the University of Wisconsin. While the bulk of the students have been undergraduate and graduate students in chemical engineering, these classes have also included both electrical and mechanical engineering students interested in process control. Usually these courses have involved laboratory projects through which students are able to implement some of their control system designs.

It is perhaps useful to point out the thrust of each chapter. In Chapter 1 there is a discussion of the engineering and economic incentives for implementation of advanced process control concepts. The key elements of an advanced control scheme are discussed and their integration into a coherent, comprehensive structure is outlined. This is followed by an overview of the different types of process dynamics models normally encountered. This provides a guide for the ensuing chapters, which treat control system design for each type of process model.

Chapter 2 is an introduction to the computer and interfacing technology needed for real-time process control. The basic structure of microcomputers and minicomputers is discussed together with the features of peripheral devices. Both digital and analog data acquisition interfaces are covered, and their essential features are discussed. A substantial number of process sensors, control actuators, and transducers are described in the context of their typical applications. Finally, several actual process control interfacing projects are presented and the ultimate design strategy with regard to sensor selection, multiplexing, signal conditioning, mode of transmission, etc., is discussed. This chapter is designed to provide the reader a good grasp of the considerations necessary to implement computer control schemes. The intention is to give the needed perspective and motivation for the more theoretical material to follow.

Chapter 3 deals with the problem of control system synthesis for lumped parameter systems. Both differential equation state space models and transfer function models are considered, and the equivalence of the two formulations is demonstrated. Standard design procedures for linear multivariable systems are introduced to demonstrate that these "suboptimal" procedures often produce high quality, but simple, designs. Then classical optimal control theory is presented, both to provide a basis for comparison with simpler suboptimal strategies and to lay a theoretical foundation which can be built upon in later discussions of state estimation and stochastic control. Finally, several methods of nonlinear system controller design are presented.

Chapter 4 introduces the reader to distributed parameter systems which are modeled by partial differential or differential-delay equations. As in the previous chapter, there is a discussion of the types of distributed systems commonly encountered in the process industries and the appropriate techniques for control system design. Following this, optimal control theory is presented and optimal controller design illustrated by examples. Where applicable, modal decomposition for linear systems and Galerkin procedures for nonlinear systems are stressed. The chapter ends with a treatment of systems having time delays. The goal of this chapter is to demonstrate that through appropriate analysis, distributed systems are not significantly more difficult to handle than lumped systems.

Chapter 5 is devoted to state estimation and stochastic control. Although the relevant statistical theory can get rather deep at times, particularly for nonlinear systems, the essential features are presented in an operational-intuitive manner suitable for the reader with only a rudimentary background in statistics. This approach is designed to allow the control engineer to see the thrust of the analysis and understand the important results so that useful estimation and control algorithms may be developed.

Chapter 6 consists of a series of detailed case studies of control system design. For each control problem treated, the reader is led through the steps of control system synthesis and then shown the performance of the resulting design when applied to a pilot plant process. It is thought that these exercises in *synthesis*, which draw upon all the techniques covered in the earlier chapters, will demonstrate the power of these sophisticated and useful process control methods in a practical context.

There are many who contributed their efforts to this book. Several generations of students provided example problems, criticism, and testing of the homework assignments; Klavs Jensen and Tunde Ogunnaike were particularly helpful in carrying out computations for example problems. Proofreading help was provided by Klavs Jensen, Tunde Ogunnaike, Joe Schork, and Marvin Schwedock, while Alan Schmidt kindly served as photographer for some of the half-tones. Professors Jay Bailey, Ram Lavie, Manfred Morari, John Seinfeld, and Joe Wright read the manuscript and contributed many helpful suggestions. The detailed comments resulting from the classroom testing of the material by my colleague, Manfred Morari, were especially valuable. Finally there were the typing efforts of Diane Petersen and my wife, Nell. Their skill transformed barely legible scribbling into flawlessly typewritten copy, while their patience allowed numerous revisions of the original manuscript. As usual, this project could not have been completed without the devotion of my wife, Nell, who participated in all aspects of the book (typing, preparation of the index, proofreading, etc.) while keeping up with all her other activities. The author is greatly indebted to all who contributed to this venture.

W. Harmon Ray

ADVANCED PROCESS CONTROL

CHAPTER

ONE

INTRODUCTION

1.1 WHY ADVANCED PROCESS CONTROL

From its beginnings in antiquity [1, 2] until the early 1960s, the field of process control was based almost entirely on mechanical, electrical, or pneumatic analog controllers, which were usually designed using linear single-input single-output considerations. Hardware limitations, economic cost, and the dearth of applicable theory usually precluded anything more complex than these simple schemes. Because many large-scale industrial processes are endowed by nature with large time constants, open-loop stability, and significant damping of fluctuations through mixing and storage tanks, such simple control schemes work well for perhaps 80 percent of the control loops one might encounter. For the remaining 20 percent more difficult control problems, most controllers were considered marginally acceptable during this early period because there were few environmental regulations, product specifications were quite loose, and intermediate blending tanks could cover many of the sins of inadequate control. Thus the costs of even small sophistications in control were high and the economic incentives for improved control were comparatively low.

Over the last 10 to 15 years, there has been a dramatic change in these factors. Industrial processes are now predominantly continuous with large throughputs, highly integrated with respect to energy and material flows, constrained very tightly by high-performance process specifications, and under intense governmental safety and environmental emission regulations. All these

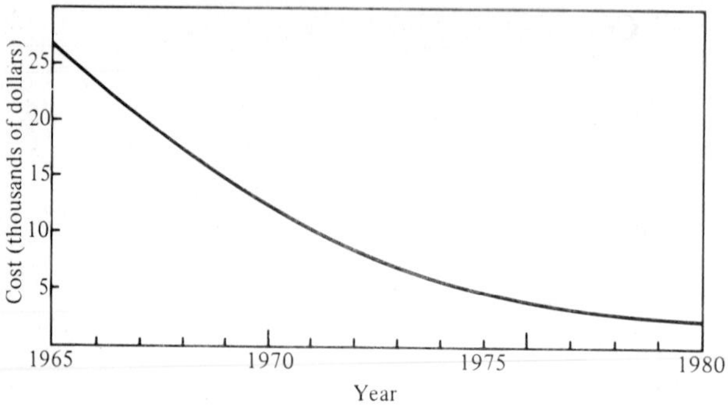

Figure 1.1 An example of price trends for real time minicomputers.

factors combine to produce more difficult process control problems as well as the requirement for better controller performance. Significant time periods with off-specification product, excessive environmental emissions, or process shutdown due to control system failure can have catastrophic economic consequences because of the enormous economic multipliers characteristic of high-throughput continuous processes. This produces large economic incentives for reliable, high-quality control systems in modern industrial plants.

Another recent development in process control is that the performance of real-time digital computers suitable for on-line control has improved significantly, while prices have fallen drastically. Figure 1.1 shows an example of the price trends for small minicomputers in spite of the inclusion of more reliable electronics and increasing inflation. With the process control computer now such a small part of the overall process capital costs, the installation of a fast minicomputer with large amounts of storage can often be easily justified on the basis of improved safety and manpower savings. Once in place, the computer is usually operating in a timesharing mode with large numbers of input/output operations, so that the central processing unit (CPU) is typically in use only about 5 percent of the time. Thus many installations have 95 percent of the computing power of a highly capable minicomputer, programmable in a high-level language such as Fortran, already available for implementing sophisticated computer control schemes.

At the same time, modern control theory has been under intense development, with many successful applications in the aerospace and aircraft industries. Most recently, a number of process control research groups have been applying these ideas to simulated, laboratory, and even a few full-scale plant processes, so that much of the applicable theory needed for sophisticated process control algorithms is at hand. However, there remains the problem of communicating these results, in a readily applicable form, to the process control engineer who must design an economically optimal process control scheme. The present text is directed toward this educational need, and strives to present a comprehensive introduction to the theory and practice of modern computer process control.

1.2 WHAT IS "MODERN" CONTROL THEORY?

In contrast to classical control theory, which is essentially limited to single-input single-output systems described by linear differential equations with constant coefficients (or their corresponding Laplace transforms), so-called *modern* control theory has developed to the point where results are available for a wide range of general multivariable systems, including those described by:

1. Linear, variable-coefficient differential equations
2. Nonlinear differential equations
3. Differential-difference and other hereditary equations
4. Partial differential and integral equations

The results of modern control theory include so-called *optimal control theory*, which allows the design of control schemes which are *optimal* in the sense that the controller performance minimizes some specified cost functional.

In addition to controller design, modern control theory includes methods for process identification and state estimation. *Process identification* algorithms have been developed which determine the model structure and estimate the model parameters, either off-line or adaptively on-line. These are useful both in the initial control system design and in the design of *adaptive control systems* which respond to such changes in the process characteristics as might arise, for example, with the fouling of heating exchanger surfaces or the deactivation of catalyst in chemical reactors. *State estimation* techniques are on-line methods of estimating those system state variables which are not measured and for improving the quality of all the state-variable estimates when there are measurement errors. In processes where numerous sensors are not available or are expensive, on-line state estimation can be of significant practical importance.

It is perhaps useful to demonstrate how all these components of a comprehensive computer process control scheme might fit together for a particular process and to point to where the technical details are discussed in the text. Figure 1.2 outlines such a control scheme which consists of the following:

1. *Process* which responds to control inputs $\mathbf{u}$; natural process disturbances $\mathbf{d}_1$; and special input disturbances $\mathbf{d}_2$ which enhance identification. The true process state $\mathbf{x}$ is produced, but this is seldom measured completely or without error so that one employs
2. *Measurement devices*, which usually are able to measure only a few of the states or some combination of states and are always subject to measurement error. These are discussed in Chap. 2. The measurement device outputs $\mathbf{y}$ are fed to the
3. *State estimator*, which makes use of the noisy measurements $\mathbf{y}$ along with a process model to reconstruct the best possible process state estimates $\hat{\mathbf{x}}$. The state estimator must have parameters $\mathbf{P}$ which are calculated (either off-line

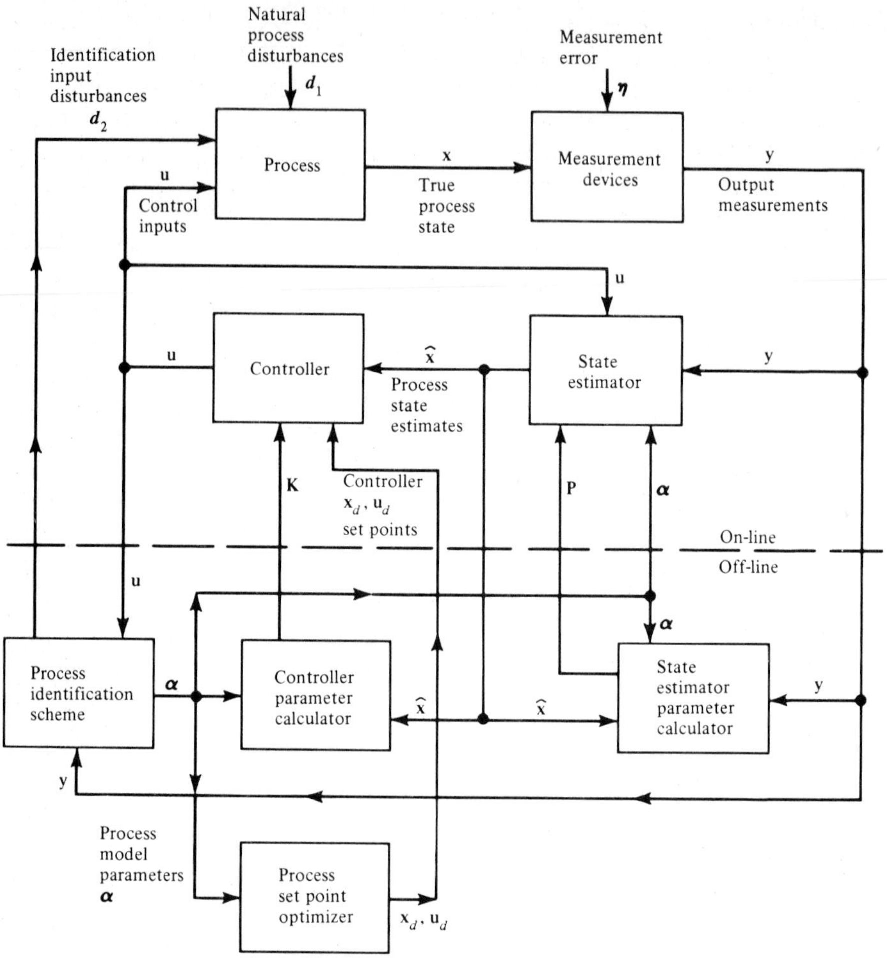

Figure 1.2 A comprehensive computer control scheme.

or periodically updated on-line) by algorithms, possibly requiring the measurement outputs **y** and state estimates $\hat{\mathbf{x}}$ as well as the process model parameters $\boldsymbol{\alpha}$. The details of state estimation are found in Chap. 5. The process state estimates are passed to the

4. *Controller*, which calculates what control actions must be taken based on the state estimates $\hat{\mathbf{x}}$, the set points $\mathbf{u}_d$, $\mathbf{x}_d$ (which themselves may be the subject of process optimization [3]), and the controller parameters **K**. The controller parameters **K** can be calculated either off-line or adaptively on-line based on current estimates of the model parameters $\boldsymbol{\alpha}$ and process state $\hat{\mathbf{x}}$. Techniques for controller designs are discussed in Chap. 3 and 4. The process model parameters must be determined from the

5. *Process identification scheme*, which takes measurements from the process as raw data $\mathbf{y}$ (and may choose to introduce experimentally designed input disturbances $\mathbf{d}_2$) in order to identify the process model parameters $\boldsymbol{\alpha}$. If the parameters are invariant with time, then this need be done only once; however, if the process changes with time, then the process identification scheme may be activated periodically to provide adaptation to changing conditions. Process identification is not treated in great detail in this book because there are many fine existing reference books in this area [4–10].

In most applications only a few of the components of this control structure are required. Chapter 6 describes some control system design case histories which illustrate this point.

1.3 MATHEMATICAL MODELS FOR PROCESS DYNAMICS

For all but the simplest control schemes to be effective, some description of the process to be controlled must be available. Usually this description is a *mathematical model*. In classical single-loop process control theory, this model often takes the form

$$\bar{y}(s) = g(s)\bar{u}(s) + g_d(s)\bar{d}(s) \tag{1.3.1}$$

where $\bar{d}(s)$, $\bar{u}(s)$, $\bar{y}(s)$ are the Laplace transforms of known disturbances $d(t)$, the controller input $u(t)$, and process output $y(t)$, respectively. Here $g(s)$, $g_d(s)$ are the scalar transfer functions relating them as shown in Fig. 1.3. However, many processes are much more complicated and require more complex models. We shall discuss some of the naturally occurring models in what follows.

Linear Multivariable, "Lumped" Models

"Lumped parameter" or "lumped" models refer to process descriptions in which there is no spatial dependence; either *ordinary differential equation* or *Laplace transform* models are employed. The simplest case of a lumped multivariable process model would be a generalization of the single-input single-output transfer function model [Eq. (1.3.1)] to multiple inputs and multiple outputs, as shown in Fig. 1.4. In this case there are k disturbances, m inputs, and l outputs

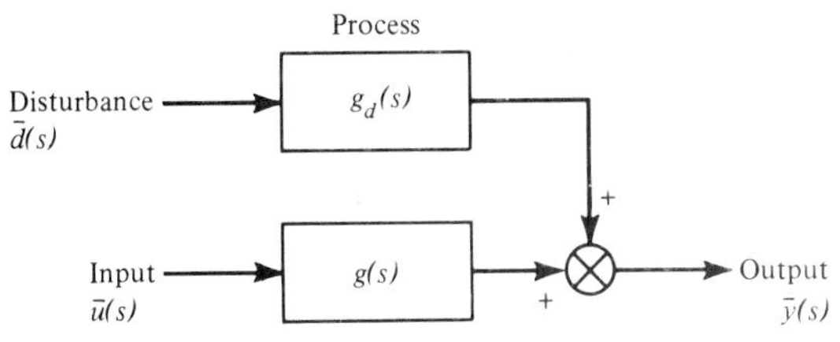

Figure 1.3 Single-input single-output linear system.

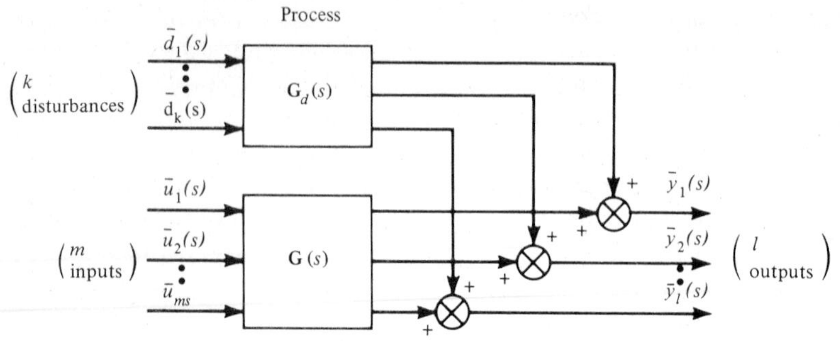

Figure 1.4 Multivariable linear system with k disturbances, m inputs, and ℓ outputs.

related by

$$\bar{\mathbf{y}}(s) = \mathbf{G}(s)\bar{\mathbf{u}}(s) + \mathbf{G}_d\bar{\mathbf{d}}(s) \tag{1.3.2}$$

where $\bar{\mathbf{d}}(s)$, $\bar{\mathbf{u}}(s)$, $\bar{\mathbf{y}}(s)$ are vectors and $\mathbf{G}(s)$ is an $l \times m$ matrix, while $\mathbf{G}_d(s)$ is an $l \times k$ matrix.

$$\bar{\mathbf{d}}(s) = \begin{bmatrix} \bar{d}_1(s) \\ \bar{d}_2(s) \\ \vdots \\ \bar{d}_k(s) \end{bmatrix} \qquad \bar{\mathbf{u}}(s) = \begin{bmatrix} \bar{u}_1(s) \\ \bar{u}_2(s) \\ \vdots \\ \bar{u}_m(s) \end{bmatrix} \qquad \bar{\mathbf{y}}(s) = \begin{bmatrix} \bar{y}_1(s) \\ \bar{y}_2(s) \\ \vdots \\ \bar{y}_l(s) \end{bmatrix} \tag{1.3.3}$$

$$\mathbf{G}_d(s) = \begin{bmatrix} g_{11_d}(s) & g_{12_d}(s) & \cdots & g_{1k_d}(s) \\ g_{21_d}(s) & g_{22_d}(s) & \cdots & g_{2k_d}(s) \\ \cdots & \cdots & \cdots & \cdots \\ g_{l1_d}(s) & & & g_{lk_d}(s) \end{bmatrix}$$

$$\mathbf{G}(s) = \begin{bmatrix} g_{11}(s) & g_{12}(s) & \cdots & g_{1m}(s) \\ g_{21}(s) & g_{22}(s) & \cdots & g_{2m}(s) \\ \cdots & \cdots & \cdots & \cdots \\ g_{l1}(s) & g_{l2}(s) & & g_{lm}(s) \end{bmatrix}$$

An alternative form of linear, lumped parameter models is the *time-domain model*:

$$\frac{d\mathbf{x}(t)}{dt} = \mathbf{A}\mathbf{x}(t) + \mathbf{B}\mathbf{u}(t) + \mathbf{\Gamma}\mathbf{d}(t) \qquad \mathbf{x}(0) = \mathbf{x}_0 \tag{1.3.4}$$

$$\mathbf{y} = \mathbf{C}\mathbf{x}(t) \tag{1.3.5}$$

where the variables $x_i(t)$, $i = 1, 2, \ldots, n$, are the *state variables*; the $y_j(t)$, $j = 1, 2, \ldots, l$, are the *output variables*; the $u_r(t)$, $r = 1, 2, \ldots, m$, are the *input variables* or *control variables*; and the $d_s(t)$, $s = 1, 2, \ldots, k$, are the *disturbance variables*.

The form of the *transform-domain* model [Eq. (1.3.2)] or *time-domain* model [Eqs. (1.3.4), (1.3.5)] may be chosen by convenience because they may be shown to be equivalent if **A**, **B**, **C**, and **D** are constant matrices. The basis of these multivariable models may be determined from the fundamental differential equations of physics or, more often, from empirical fitting of the model equations to measured process dynamics. In either case, there is a wide range of processes which may be approximately modeled in this form. More will be said about these models in Chap. 3.

Nonlinear Lumped Models

Systems described by nonlinear ordinary differential equations are very common in the process industries and have models of the general form

$$\frac{d\mathbf{x}(t)}{dt} = \mathbf{f}(\mathbf{x}(t), \mathbf{u}(t), \mathbf{d}(t)) \qquad \mathbf{x}(0) = \mathbf{x}_0 \tag{1.3.6}$$

$$\mathbf{y}(t) = \mathbf{h}(\mathbf{x}(t), \mathbf{u}(t)) \tag{1.3.7}$$

where as before $\mathbf{x}(t)$ represents a vector of states, $\mathbf{y}(t)$ the outputs, $\mathbf{d}(t)$ the disturbances, and $\mathbf{u}(t)$ the control inputs. The nonlinear functions $\mathbf{f}$ and $\mathbf{h}$ may have a variety of forms and are usually derived from the momentum, energy, and material balances and the type of sensors used for the process under study. As an example, a liquid-phase reaction, $A \rightarrow B$, carried out in a continuous stirred tank reactor will have a nonlinear model of the form

$$\frac{dx_1}{dt} = -x_1 + \mathrm{Da}(1 - x_1)\exp\left(\frac{x_2}{1 + x_2/\gamma}\right) + d_1 \tag{1.3.8}$$

$$\frac{dx_2}{dt} = -(1 + \beta)x_2 + B\,\mathrm{Da}(1 - x_1)\exp\left(\frac{x_2}{1 + x_2/\gamma}\right) + \beta u + d_2 \tag{1.3.9}$$

where x_1 is the conversion of A to product and x_2 is a dimensionless reactor temperature. The quantities Da, γ, B, and β are parameters, and u is the jacket coolant temperature which is manipulated to achieve temperature control. The variables d_1 and d_2 are disturbances in the feed reactant concentration and feed temperature, respectively. The output equation is

$$y = x_2 \tag{1.3.10}$$

which indicates that only reactor temperature is measured. The control of this class of processes is discussed in Chap. 3.

Distributed Parameter Models

A significant number of industrial processes are "distributed" in space so that their behavior depends on spatial position as well as time. These models usually take the form of partial differential equations and are often derived from the fundamental balances of momentum, energy, and material for the process at hand. As an example, many heat conduction, fluid flow, and chemical reactor processes take the form

$$\frac{\partial \mathbf{x}}{\partial t} = \mathbf{f}(\mathbf{x}, \mathbf{u}, \nabla \cdot \mathbf{x}, \nabla^2 \mathbf{x}, \ldots) \tag{1.3.11}$$

where both the state variables $\mathbf{x}$ and control variables $\mathbf{u}$ may depend on time and on a multidimensional spatial position. A simple illustration of this type of distributed model may be found by considering that the liquid-phase reaction $A \rightarrow B$ noted above is now carried out in a tubular reactor with cooling at the wall. A reasonable model of such a reactor is in the form

$$\frac{\partial x_1(r, z, t)}{\partial t} = (r^2 - 1)\frac{\partial x_1}{\partial z} + \frac{1}{\mathrm{Pe}_m}\frac{1}{r}\frac{\partial}{\partial r}\left(r\frac{\partial x_1}{\partial r}\right) + \mathrm{Da}(1 - x_1)\exp\left(\frac{x_2}{1 + x_2/\gamma}\right) \tag{1.3.12}$$

$$\frac{\partial x_2(r, z, t)}{\partial t} = (r^2 - 1)\frac{\partial x_2}{\partial z} + \frac{1}{\mathrm{Pe}_h}\frac{1}{r}\frac{\partial}{\partial r}\left(r\frac{\partial x_2}{\partial r}\right) + B\,\mathrm{Da}(1 - x_1)\exp\left(\frac{x_2}{1 + x_2/\gamma}\right) \tag{1.3.13}$$

with boundary conditions

$$\begin{aligned} z = 0: &\quad x_1 = x_2 = 0 \\ r = 0: &\quad \frac{\partial x_1}{\partial r} = \frac{\partial x_2}{\partial r} = 0 \\ r = 1: &\quad \frac{\partial x_1}{\partial r} = 0 \qquad \frac{\partial x_2}{\partial r} = \mathrm{Bi}_w(u - x_2) \end{aligned} \tag{1.3.14}$$

Here x_1 and x_2 are reactor conversion and temperature, respectively, and u is the wall coolant temperature which can be manipulated. The quantities Pe_m, Pe_h, Da, B, β, γ, and Bi_w are parameters, and the output equations are of the form

$$y_i(t) = x_2(r_i, z_i, t) \qquad i = 1, 2, \ldots N \tag{1.3.15}$$

and represent the thermocouples placed at positions (r_i, z_i) in the reactor. Note that the control variable in this example problem appears in the boundary condition, Eqs. (1.3.14), as often happens in distributed parameter control problems. Chapter 4 will treat the control of this class of processes in some detail.

REFERENCES

1. Fuller, A. T.: "J. Dynamic Systems, Measurement, and Control," *Trans. ASME* **98G**: 109, 224 (1976).
2. Mayr, O.: *Origins of Feedback Control*, MIT Press, Cambridge, Mass., 1970.

3. Ray, W. H., and J. Szekely: *Process Optimization*, Wiley, New York, 1973.
4. Sage, A. P., and J. L. Melsa: *System Identification*, Academic Press, New York, 1971.
5. Box, G. E. P., and G. M. Jenkins: *Time Series Analysis*, Holden-Day, San Francisco, 1970.
6. Seinfeld, J. H., and L. Lapidus: *Mathematical Methods in Chemical Engineering*, vol. 3: *Process Modelling, Estimation, and Identification*, Prentice-Hall, Englewood Cliffs, N.J., 1974.
7. Eykhoff, P.: *System Identification*, Wiley, New York, 1974.
8. Mehra, R. K., and D. G. Lainiotis: *System Identification: Advances and Case Studies*, Academic Press, New York, 1976.
9. Ray, W. H., and D. G. Lainiotis: *Distributed Parameter Systems*, Marcel Dekker, New York, 1978.
10. Stewart, W. E., and J. P. Sørensen: *Collocation and Parameter Estimation in Chemical Reaction Engineering*, Wiley, New York, in press.

CHAPTER

TWO

INTRODUCTION TO ON-LINE DATA ACQUISITION AND COMPUTER CONTROL

2.1 INTRODUCTION

In order to effectively design a modern process control scheme, one must have a basic understanding of the practical means of implementation. For example, computational algorithms suitable for on-line application must be carried out faster than real time on a typical process control minicomputer. Thus sampling frequency, computer computation times, and other factors must be considered in order to design a workable system. The successful installation of a modern control scheme also involves considerations of data links and computer command transmissions. Process variables must be measured and these data provided to the computer, while desired control actions must be computed and transmitted to the process. Figure 2.1 gives the simplified structure of such a computer control scheme. The measured variables are transduced, filtered, and sent by cable to a computer interface for data inputs. This measurement information is then incorporated into the computer control algorithm and control signal outputs generated. These signals are transmitted to local transducers and local controllers (such as valves and heaters), which cause changes in the manipulated variables of the process. The technology which accomplishes these tasks must be generally understood by the control engineer so that the designs are realistic and effective. Thus this chapter shall be devoted to providing the reader an overview of the considerations necessary in actually implementing a computer control scheme.

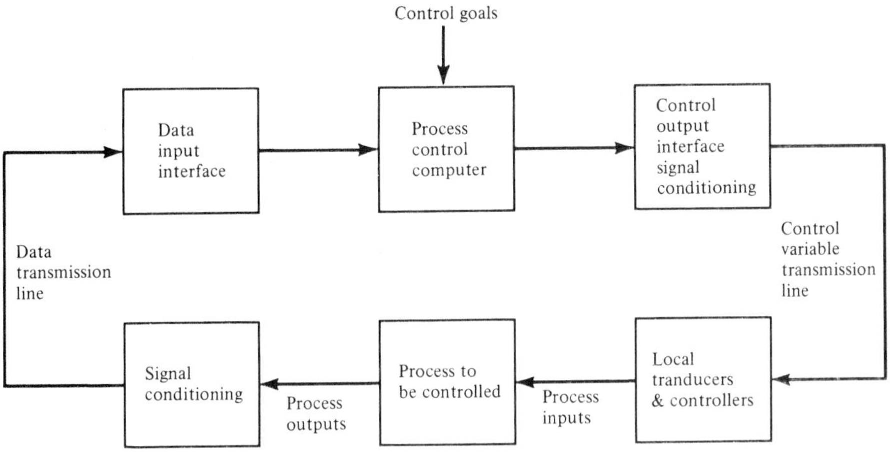

Figure 2.1 Structure of a computer process control scheme.

We shall begin by describing typical minicomputer architecture, capabilities, and peripherals. This should give one an idea of the computer resources which might be typically present in an industrial computer control installation. Secondly, we shall discuss the types of interfaces normally used for data acquisition and control-signal generation. These interfaces put constraints and specifications on the types of signals needed from the measuring devices. Finally, we consider commonly used sensing devices as well as techniques for transducing, multiplexing, and conditioning the data and control signals. This latter material should provide the control system designer with a grasp of the quality of the signals which must be dealt with in design, and can guide the choice of signal mode (e.g., analog voltage, analog current, or digital signal).

While this chapter is important in providing a well-rounded perspective for the reader, it is not crucial to the theory which follows; thus it is possible, if desired, to bypass this material for the moment and return to it later.

2.2 COMPUTER SYSTEM ARCHITECTURE

There are many different manufacturers of minicomputers designed for process control applications (a few of these are listed in Table 2.1) and many different types of architecture. However, the functions of the computer itself are much the same, and peripherals have been standardized to be compatible for most minicomputer mainframes. Thus it is possible to describe generally a typical minicomputer. We choose as our example the minicomputer in the Department of Chemical Engineering at the University of Wisconsin. This system, shown in Figs. 2.2 and 2.3, consists of a PDP 11/55 minicomputer with associated peripherals, interfaces, etc. We shall briefly describe each component of the system.

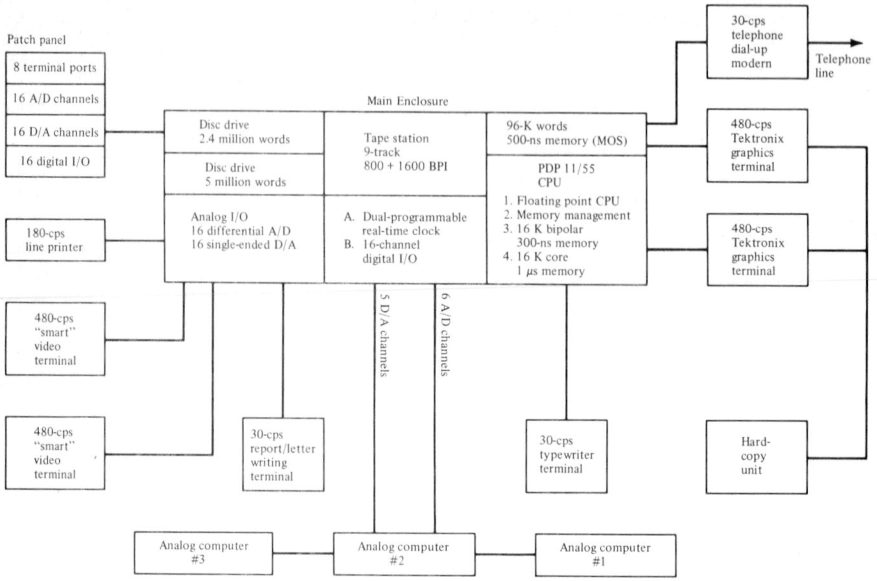

Figure 2.2 Chemical Engineering Minicomputer System, University of Wisconsin.

1. *Central processing unit* (*CPU*)—This is the heart of the minicomputer and has overall control of the system. The computer uses the *binary digits* (0 or 1) as the basic computational and communication code. This is accomplished electronically by manipulating and transmitting pulses which need be interpreted only as a 0 or a 1. The resolution of a machine is dependent on the number of binary digits (abbreviated *bits*) in the basic unit of information, called the *word*. Common minicomputers have 8-, 12-, 16-, or 18-bit words (see Table 2.1). Usually a smaller unit, a *byte* consisting of 8 bits, is used as well, because a byte suffices to specify characters (alphabet letters, numbers, control characters, etc.) according to industry standards (e.g., ASCII Code).

Figure 2.3 PDP 11/55 minicomputer at the University of Wisconsin.

Table 2.1 Some of the commonly encountered minicomputers for real-time applications*

Manufacturer	Computer (word length)	Maximum memory (words)	Speed: fixed-point addition, memory cycle time (μs)	Approximate price†
Data General Corp.	1. Nova (16 bits)	32 K	0.7, 0.7	$10 K
	2. Eclipse S, C (16 bits)	128–512 K	0.6, 0.7	$30 K
Digital Equipment Corp.	1. PDP 8 (12 bits)	128 K	3.0, 1.5	$10 K
	2. PDP 11/03 (16 bits)	32 K	3.5, 1.2	$ 4 K
	3. PDP 11/34 (16 bits)	128 K	2.0, 0.7	$ 9 K
	4. PDP 11/55 (16 bits)	128 K	0.3, 0.3	$40 K
Hewlett-Packard Corp.	HP 1000 (16 bits)	1024 K	0.9, 0.6	$10 K

* Current and comprehensive listings of available minicomputers may be found in trade journals, surveys, etc. (e.g., references [9, 10]).

† Price includes CPU and 32 K words of memory.

Normally 7 bits are used to specify the character and one is used for error checking (parity). Thus $2^7 = 128$ characters may be defined by a byte. Normally the bits in a word will be arranged in *octal* form by grouping them in 3s, e.g.,

110 010 100 001 101

Since 3 bits allows one to obtain the numbers 0 to 7, as shown in Table 2.2, octal integer notation is a convenient shorthand for addresses, machine instructions, etc. For example, the 15 bits shown above represent the octal number 62415, which is a much more efficient notation than the original binary form. A 16-bit machine (the most common type) thus can use 1 bit for sign (+ or −) and 15 bits to represent integer numbers. The maximum integer range then is from −77777 to +77777 octal, which corresponds to −32,767 to +32,768 decimal. These octal numbers are sometimes used to enter elementary computer instructions via switches on the CPU console (Fig. 2.4 shows a photograph of a typical console). Associated with the CPU, and working in parallel, many computers have a *hardware floating-point processor* which performs all floating-point arithmetic operations. For the PDP 11/55 machine shown in Figs. 2.2 and 2.3, which has 16-bit words, these floating-point operations involve numbers whose length is two words (32 bits). If double precision is called for, the floating-point processor uses 4 words (64 bits); however, double-precision operations require substantially more time to execute. The precision of an arithmetic operation depends on the number of bits carried along. For a 32-bit single-precision operation on the PDP 11/55, 24 bits are used for the fractional number and 8 bits for the exponent. In each case 1 bit is reserved for the sign, so that the exponent is limited to floating-point numbers between 2^{-2^7} and 2^{2^7} (approximately 10^{-38} to 10^{+38}

Table 2.2 Binary, octal, and decimal conversion

Binary	Octal	Decimal
000 000	0	0
000 001	1	1
000 010	2	2
000 011	3	3
000 100	4	4
000 101	5	5
000 110	6	6
000 111	7	7
001 000	10	8
001 001	11	9
001 010	12	10
001 011	13	11
001 100	14	12
001 101	15	13
001 110	16	14
001 111	17	15
010 000	20	16
011 000	30	24
100 000	40	32
101 000	50	40
110 000	60	48
111 000	70	56

Octal—binary conversion For 3 bits octal = $b_0 + 2b_1 + 4b_2$, where b_0, b_1, b_2 are binary digits.
Decimal-octal conversion Decimal = $a_0 + 8a_1 + 64a_2 + \cdots + 8^n a_n$, where $a_0, a_1, \ldots, a_n$ are the octal digits.

decimal). The fractional part, of 24 bits, has an error corresponding approximately to the least significant bit. With 1 bit for the sign and 23 for the fractional number, the relative error is approximately $2^{-23} \cong 10^{-7}$, so that a maximum of about 6 decimal digits are reliable in single-precision operations. For double precision, 8 bits are used for the exponent and 56 bits for the fraction, giving an approximate relative error of $2^{-55} \cong 10^{-17}$. This corresponds to a maximum reliability of about 16 decimal digits. For the floating-point processor used on the PDP 11/55, these operations are quite fast (~ 1 μs for addition, ~ 4 μs for division). Such high-performance floating-point processors, coupled with logic which allows operation in parallel with the CPU, make modern, inexpensive minicomputers rather fast in carrying out numerical calculations.

2. *Memory*—The memory devices associated with minicomputers may be of several different types (see Table 2.3). *Core memory*, which uses electromagnetic storage techniques, has a typical cycle time of ~ 1 μs—rather slow in the present context. However, because of its ferromagnetic character, core memory retains stored information even when the electric power fails. *Metal-oxide silicon (MOS) memory*, on the other hand, consists of simple

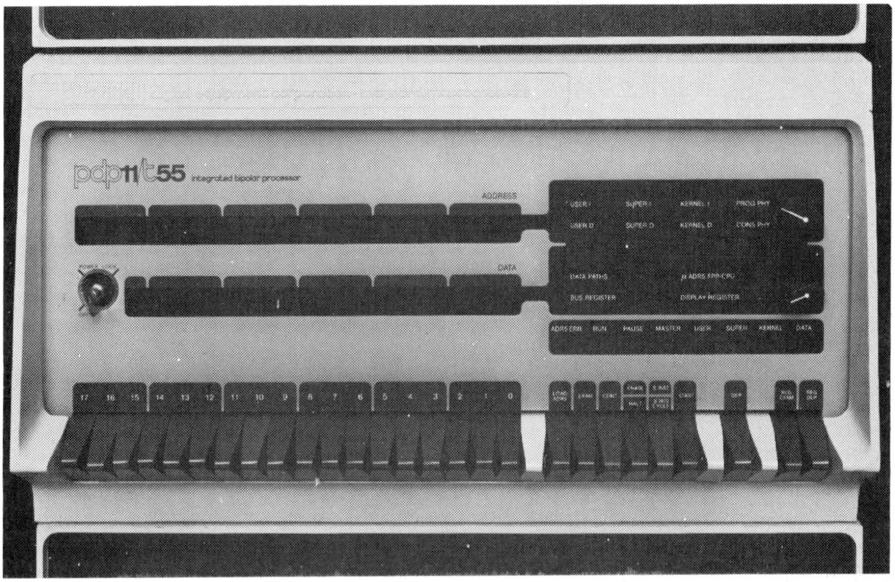

Figure 2.4 The PDP 11/55 CPU operator console (Reproduced by permission of Digital Equipment Corporation).

circuit semiconductor devices, which are both cheaper and faster (~ 500 n s cycle time) than core memory. *Bipolar transistor memory* makes use of more complex integrated circuits which are still faster (~ 300 n s cycle time). Both of these devices, however, lose the stored information in a power failure; thus battery power backup is often available. Special-purpose memory such as *read only memory* (*ROM*) is usually used to permanently store basic instructions for starting up the machine, input/output commands, etc., or for crucial, frequently used data files. These devices require special programming hardware in order to make any changes in the stored information. Memory can be purchased with and without extra *parity bits*. These extra bits are used to double check each byte transfer operation for transmission errors. This feature is useful in crucial computations and in diagnosing the specific locations of any memory failures. For the PDP 11/55 system shown in Figs. 2.2 and 2.3, all four types of memory devices are in use. Although only 64 K bytes (32 K words) of memory can be routinely addressed by a 16-bit machine, the PDP 11 series can make use of as much as 128 K words of memory by using many memory partitions, each of which may be as much as 32 K words in size.

3. *Mass storage devices*—There are a number of different types of mass storage devices available for minicomputers (see Table 2.3). These are used for inexpensive high-capacity storage with access times and transfer rates much slower than memory. *Magnetic tape* is the cheapest bulk storage device, but has the disadvantage that it has very slow access times (due to the time

Table 2.3 Capabilities of storage devices*

Device	Typical capacity/ 16-bit words	Typical access times	Typical transfer rates (words/s)	Approx. cost, $/1000 words
Memory:			(cycle time)	
Core	128 K	0.4 μs	1 μs	50–100
MOS	128 K	0.2 μs	0.5 μs	50–100
Bipolar	128 K	0.1 μs	0.3 μs	500–1000
Mass storage:				
Fixed-head disks	~1 million	~8 μs	10^5	20–50
Moving-head disks	1–100 million	35–70 μs	10^5	0.5–2
Floppy disks	256–512 K	500 ms	3×10^4	5–10
Magnetic tape	10–15 million	Several seconds	2×10^4 to 4×10^4	1

* Figures are for 1980.

required to move back and forth on the tape drive to find the desired files). For sequentially stored files, magnetic tape has reasonably fast transfer rates and is thus suitable for backup storage of large programs, data banks, etc. A much faster mass storage device is the *rotating disk*, which comes in several types (fixed-head, moving-head, and floppy). Most of the disks have removable packs or cartridges so that interchangeable data files, program libraries, etc., are possible. *Fixed-head disks* usually have a small capacity but short access times and high transfer rates. These devices are used for fast swapping of files between memory and disk. *Moving-head disks* have much slower access times but transfer rates comparable to those of fixed-head disks and much higher capacity. *Floppy disks* are low-capital-cost, small-capacity, low-performance mass storage devices in common use with microcomputers. Figure 2.5 shows a photograph of the magnetic tape unit, the movable-head disk and drive, and the floppy-disk drive used with the PDP 11 systems at the University of Wisconsin.

4. *Real-time clock*—The scheduler and timekeeper of the computer system is the *real-time clock*. This allows the computer to schedule tasks to be performed on a regular basis, such as taking data or changing control variables at specified time intervals, and timesharing the CPU's attention between various terminals and other peripherals. Each time the computer is powered up, the correct date and time are entered, and the real-time clock keeps track of chronological time after this initialization. A different means of sharing the CPU's attention is through *interrupts*. Each task running on the computer has a certain *priority* level; when it needs the attention of the CPU (for example, to record a data point), the task generates an *interrupt*, and if this task has a higher priority than the task currently being serviced by the CPU, the new

Figure 2.5*a* Mass storage devices used on PDP 11/55 minicomputer. A: Magnetic tape, B: Moving head disks.

Figure 2.5*b* Mass storage devices used on LSI 11 minicomputer. Floppy disks plus disk drive.

task is immediately serviced. Thus one may establish a hierarchy of priorities and interrupts in the computer and have the most urgent tasks (such as data taking) serviced immediately while those less pressing (such as printing on the line printer) must wait. Typical waiting times are a fraction of a second, so that the user is not usually aware of waiting in a queue.

5. *Input/output interfaces for data*—These interfacing devices deal with either *digital* or *analog* signals. *Digital I/O* interfaces are usually capable of either (*a*) *parallel* two-way simultaneous transmission (for example, 16 bits input and 16 bits output for a 16-bit machine) at speeds comparable to those within the computer system, or (*b*) one-way *serial* transmission (16 bits in only one direction at once for a 16-bit machine) at specified transmission rates. *Parallel-transmission* interfaces are typically used for high-speed communication between minicomputers, to multiplexers, or to other high-speed digital logic devices. *Serial-transmission* interfaces are used for communication with slower digital devices, such as terminals or graphical display units. Serial-transmission rates are indicated as *baud rates*, where baud rate = 10 × (# characters/s). Typical rates range from 30 to 960 characters/s, depending on the device being interfaced (see Table 2.4). Both types of digital interface devices can be put under program control and the information analyzed by individual bits, bytes, or words, depending on the application. Table 2.5 lists some typical applications of digital I/O interfaces.

   Analog I/O interfaces involve *analog-to-digital* (*A/D*) and *digital-to-analog* (*D/A*) *conversion*. A/D converters convert an analog voltage signal lying within a specific range (such as ±10 V, 0 to 5 V, etc.) to an integer number. The maximum size of the integer number, and thus the resolution of the conversion, depends on the number of bits handled by the converter. The range of the integer I is given by $I_{\text{range}} = 2^N$, where N is the number of bits. A 12-bit converter with an input voltage range of $-10\ \text{V} \leq V \leq +10\ \text{V}$ *differential* is shown in Fig. 2.6. The converter handles a *differential* signal because the reference voltage is also measured. A *single-ended input* would have only one voltage converted referenced to the computer ground voltage. The maximum integer range for the 12-bit converter is $2^{12} = 4096$. This

Table 2.4 Some communications peripherals

Peripheral	Communication rates	Typical capital cost
Line printers	150 characters/s–1200 lines/min	\$3000–\$20,000
Typewriter terminals	10–30 characters/s	\$1000–\$4000
Video terminals	240–960 characters/s	\$1000–\$10,000
Storage scope terminals	480–960 characters/s	\$3000–\$8000
Punched cards	250–1200 cards/min	\$3000–\$10,000
Paper tape	10–300 characters/s	\$3000–\$5000
Magnetic tape	10^4–10^5 characters/s	\$5000–\$15,000

Table 2.5 Some typical applications of data I/O interfaces

Type of interface	Typical connections and data
Digital inputs	From other computers Digital instrumentation Communications terminals Switch settings Relay positions Multiplexer status Alarms Counters Logic devices
Digital outputs	To other computers Commands to relays and solenoids Commands to switches Alarm messages Stepping motors Sequencing of multiplexers Logic devices Commands to digital instrumentation Communications terminals Hard copy and graphical output devices Various control signals
Analog inputs	From analog computers Analog instrumentation: Temperatures Pressures Flows Composition
Analog outputs	To analog computers Graphical plotters Oscilloscopes Process parameter changes Control signals: Heater controls Set-point changes Valve drivers

number of integers is chosen to run between $-2048 \leq I \leq +2047$, where $I = 0$ falls between the negative and positive integers. For the positive range (2047), the *resolution* of the converter is the voltage range divided by the intervals between integers, or

$$\text{Resolution} = \frac{10 \text{ V}}{2047} = 0.00489 \text{ V}$$

This gives an *expected error* of $\pm\frac{1}{2}$ the resolution, or ± 0.00244 V. In this case the *relative error* in conversion is approximately given by

$$\text{Relative error} \cong \frac{0.00244\text{ V}}{|\text{measured voltage}|}$$

so that more precision is obtained if the measured voltages are close to the full-scale voltage (10 V in this example). This can be accomplished through *signal conditioning*, which will be discussed in the next section. The throughput speeds of A/D converters are routinely 50,000–100,000 conversions/s, and high-performance models can achieve even higher rates. As an illustration of A/D conversion, suppose the 12-bit converter shown in Fig. 2.6 measures a voltage and reports the integer 1261 as a result of the conversion. To determine the actual measured voltage, one uses the formula

$$V_{\text{measured}} = \frac{10\,I}{2047} = \frac{12{,}610}{2047} = 6.16023\text{ V}$$

where for this input voltage, the relative error is

$$\text{Relative error} = \frac{\pm 0.00244}{6.16023} = \pm 0.000397 = \pm 0.0397\%$$

a rather small value.

D/A converters operate as just the reverse of A/D conversion. An integer with range 2^N is placed in a register and converted to an analog voltage output. The 12-bit D/A converter shown in Fig. 2.6 has a voltage output range of $-10\text{ V} \leq V \leq +10\text{ V}$, corresponding to input integers ranging from $-2048 \leq I \leq +2047$. Thus the resolution and expected error of this D/A converter are the same as those of the A/D converter discussed above. To demonstrate how one programs the converter to obtain a desired voltage output, let us assume we wish to output 3.5 V. To choose the input

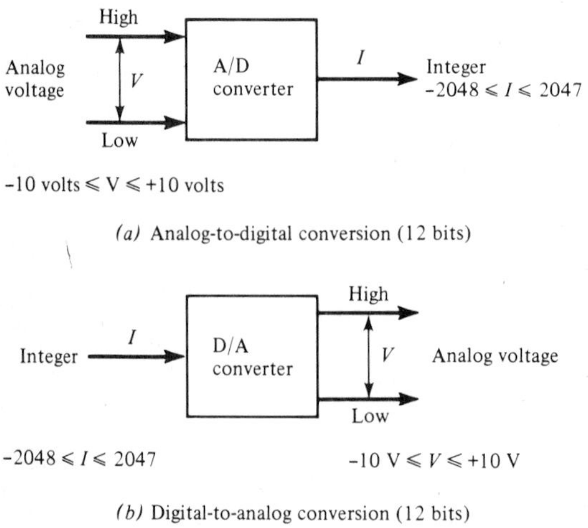

Figure 2.6 12-bit A/D and D/A conversion.

integer, one uses the formula

$$I_{\text{input}} = \frac{2047\,V_{\text{output}}}{10} = \frac{(2047)(3.5)}{10} = 716.45$$

which is rounded to $I_{\text{input}} = 716$. This gives an actual output voltage of

$$V_{\text{output}} = \frac{716}{2047} \times 10 = 3.49780 \text{ V}$$

very close to the desired voltage. Throughput rates for D/A converters are also very high, typically on the order of a million conversions/s.

Most computer installations will have multiple channels of A/D and D/A converters in order to allow several different projects to interface with the computer at any one time. For the computer system at the University of Wisconsin, there are 16 channels of 12-bit differential A/D and 16 channels of 12-bit D/A.

6. *Communications peripherals*—There are many different types of devices for communicating between the user and the computer system (see Table 2.4 and Fig. 2.7). For printed output, there are *line printers*, *typewriter terminals*, and *report-writing terminals*. Line printers can have very high rates of output, while typewriter and report-writing terminals are usually much slower. Graphical output is possible on many devices, but the most common types are *video terminals*, *storage scope terminals*, and *x-y plotters*. Video terminals (or cathode-ray tubes) require either a microprocessor or CPU attention for constantly refreshing the screen in graphical mode, but allow real-time motion of the graphics and even multicolored graphs. Storage scope terminals require no CPU-screen refreshing, but require that all or most of the screen be erased before a new graph can be drawn. Both types of graphics devices

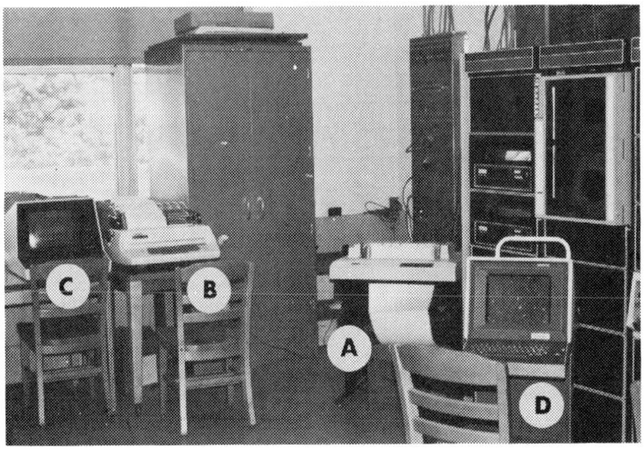

Figure 2.7 Some typical communication peripherals. A: Lineprinter, B: Report-writing terminal, C: Video Terminal, D: Storage scope graphics terminal.

can be linked to hard copy units to provide a paper copy of the screen image. Plotters are of many different types, but most provide report-quality finished graphs.

Input communications devices include *typewriter*, *video*, and *storage scope terminals* as well as *punched cards*, *paper tape*, and *magnetic tape*. Removable disk cartridges, which were discussed above, may also be considered to be I/O communications devices. For long-range I/O, it is possible to communicate with the computer over telephone lines, usually through a terminal at a remote location.

The rates of communication of these various devices are shown in Table 2.4. Modern minicomputers are bypassing the requirements for punched cards (and keypunching) by having large numbers of low-cost terminals on-line in a timeshared mode. In this way, all program input can be made directly into the computer with very small load on the CPU. Similarly, paper tape is losing ground to magnetic tape and disks as an input/output and storage medium, largely due to its very slow transfer rates and mechanical problems.

2.3 DATA ACQUISITION AND CONTROL

In order to use a real-time computer to implement a process control algorithm, one must be concerned with the hardware realization of data acquisition and control. There are many different computer configurations which will accomplish these goals. One may use a large central real-time computer linked to many labs or processes, or have a digital computer network involving many smaller microcomputers, each dedicated to a specific process or lab. We shall begin this section with a discussion of such computer structures.

Computer Data Acquisition and Control Networks

Depending on the specific application, a wide variety of tasks may be required from a data acquisition and control network: control of plant processes or pilot plants, servicing of terminals in various labs and control rooms, logging of data from analytical and/or research laboratories, interfacing with analog computers for hybrid computation, etc. To illustrate some of these applications, let us consider the network used within the department of chemical engineering at the University of Wisconsin and depicted in Fig. 2.8. The hub of the network is the PDP 11/55 minicomputer described earlier, functioning under a multiuser, time-sharing operating system. The links to the various remote stations are basically of two types, either with or without a remote microcomputer. At present the Mössbauer spectroscopy lab, the bioengineering lab, the three pilot plant locations, and the remote terminal links all come directly to the central minicomputer without involvement of a microcomputer. The polymer physics lab and the Raman spectroscopy lab, on the other hand, have PDP 11/LSI

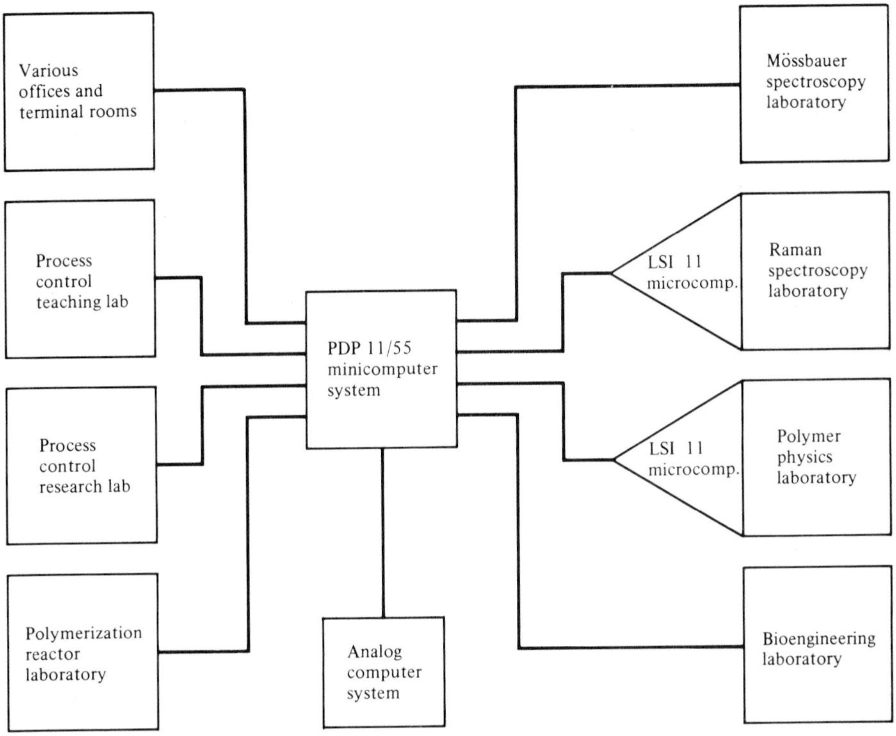

Figure 2.8 The Computer Data Acquisition and Control Network at the University of Wisconsin.

Table 2.6 Capabilities of the computers in the computer network shown in Fig. 2.8

Computer	Memory (words)	Disk storage (words)	Magnetic tape storage (words/tape)	Computing speed	Approximate cost
PDP 11/55 system shown in Fig. 2.2	128 K	2.5 million	15 million	Floating point: add, 1 μs; divide, 4 μs	\$90,000
PDP 11/LSI system shown in Fig. 2.9	32 K	256 K	—	Floating point: add, 60 μs; divide, 160 μs	\$ 9,000

Figure 2.9 LSI 11 microcomputer with video terminal, twin floppy disks, 32 K words memory, A/D and D/A converters, and real time clock.

microcomputers, which provide local control of the instruments and acquire and store the raw data. Through the links to the central minicomputer, these microcomputers are able to call upon the large file storage (disks), permanent data storage (magnetic tape), and computing power of the larger machine for data manipulation. Table 2.6 illustrates the capabilities of the various computers in the network, while Fig. 2.9 shows one of these PDP 11/LSI microcomputers.* Note that while the microcomputer is relatively inexpensive and has a moderate amount of memory and mass storage, computing speed for the LSI 11 is 40 to 60 times slower than that for the 11/55. Thus it is better to use the 11/55 for any substantial numerical calculation. Through different, but compatible, operating systems, the computers in the network are able to transfer programs, data, calculated results, etc., back and forth so as to optimize the performance of the entire computer system.

Through a link between the 11/55 and the analog computer system, hybrid computation may be carried out. As noted in Fig. 2.10, this requires A/D and D/A conversion to handle the analog computer inputs and outputs. Some scaling may also be involved because the voltage ranges of the two computers may be different. For example, the University of Wisconsin network has an analog computer operating over the range -100 V to $+100$ V, while the A/D and D/A converters have the range -10 V to $+10$ V. This means that the analog input signals must be amplified by a factor of 10 and the analog output signals divided by the same factor. The most common application of this hybrid computation facility is for control algorithm testing. A process (distillation column, chemical reactor, etc.) may be readily simulated on the analog computer and will respond in real time in much the same way as the actual process. This allows one to program the computer control algorithm on the digital

* Microcomputers similar to the LSI 11 are often used as industrial process control computers where relatively small numbers of control loops are involved.

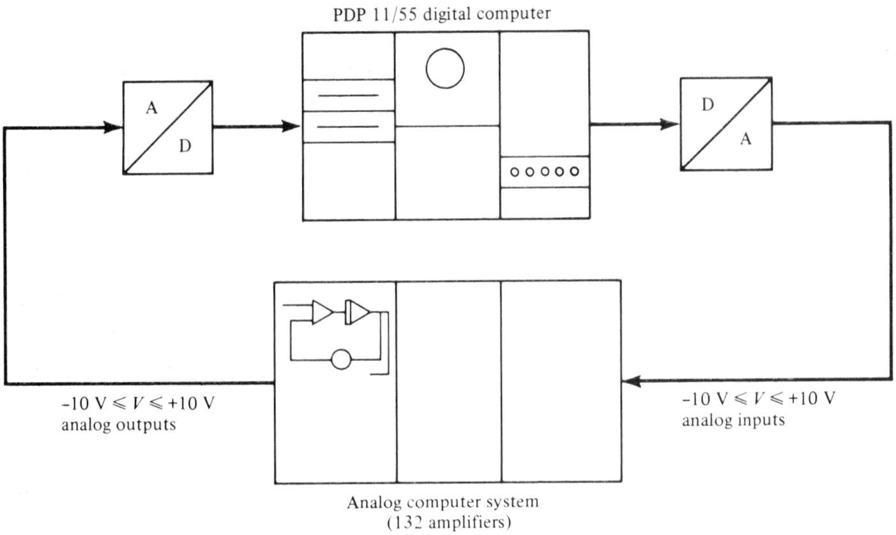

Figure 2.10 Analog-digital links for hybrid computation.

computer and test the performance in real time with the help of the analog computer. Examples of this approach will be given in forthcoming chapters.

Transducers for Data Acquisition and Control Signal Output

It is useful to consider some of the transducers more frequently encountered in the process industries. A representative sample of data acquisition sensors for some of the more common process variables is listed in Table 2.7. Depending on the sensor chosen, the primary output can be either digital, pneumatic (air pressure), current, or voltage. Because the digital computer can receive only voltage or digital signals, the pneumatic and current signals must be converted to one of these acceptable inputs. In practice this involves special transducers for pressure/voltage conversion (P/E transducer) and current/voltage conversion (I/E transducer, which is usually just a high-precision resistor).

In a similar way control system actuators come in several different forms. Table 2.8 includes some of the most common types. Notice that in the process industries, the most frequently seen actuators are for flow control. This is because heating and cooling processes often involve such factors as coolant flow-rate adjustment, steam injection rates, or furnace fuel flow rates. Similarly, pressure adjustments usually require controlling inflow or outflow from a vessel, as does liquid level control. Although the digital computer outputs are limited to digital or voltage signals, some of the control actuators require current or pneumatic inputs. Thus special transducers are needed to provide for voltage/pressure (E/P) and voltage/current (E/I) conversion.

Table 2.7 Some common data acquisition sensors

Process variable	Device	Output	Comments
1. Temperature	Thermocouple	mV	Cheap, rugged
	Resistance sensors (e.g., thermistors)	Resistivity	High sensitivity
	Oscillating quartz crystal	Oscillating frequency	High sensitivity
	Radiation pyrometer	mV	For high-temperature applications
2. Pressure	Diaphragm	Capacitance	Low pressure
	Bellows		
	Bourdon tube	Inductance	Both low and high pressure
		Photoelectric	↓
		Resistance	
		Reluctance	
		Strain gauge	From low to very high pressures
		Piezoelectric	
	Ionization gauge	Emf	Ultra-low pressure
3. Flow	Pitot tube	Differential pressure	
	Orifice	Differential pressure	
	Impaction	Mechanical deflection	
	Turbine	Rotational speed	
	Electromagnetic field	Generated emf	For difficult flow measurements
	Neutron bombardment	Nuclear radiation	For difficult flow measurements
	Ultrasound	Doppler shift	
	Hot-wire anemometry	Resistivity	High precision
4. Liquid level	Float	Mechanical deflection	
	Sonic resonance	Resonant frequency	
	Conductivity	Resistance	
	Dielectric variability	Capacitance	
	Thermoelectric probe	Resistivity	
	Nuclear radiation	Radiation intensity	
	Photoelectric cell	Voltage	
	Head pressure	Differential pressure	

Table 2.7 Some common data acquisition senors (Continued)

Process variable	Device	Output	Comments
5. Composition*	Potentiometry	mV	
	Moisture content:		
	Hygrometry	Resistivity	
	Psychrometry	Wet- and dry-bulb temperatures	
	Chromatography	mV	Long analysis times
	Refractive index	mV	
	Ultrasound	Sound velocity	
	Spectroscopy:		
	UV, visible, IR, Mössbauer, Raman, atomic-emission, x-ray, electron, ion, magnetic resonance	Intensity	Many of these techniques are not yet suitable for on-line applications
	Polarography	mV	
	Conductimetry	Resistance	
	Mass spectrometry	mV	
	Differential thermal analysis	Heat transferred	
	Thermogravimetric analysis	Mass changes	

* There are so many composition detection devices that only a few are noted here.

Table 2.8 Some typical control system actuations

Control action	Device	Input
Electrical heating	Electric furnace	Voltage or current
Flow adjustment	Pneumatic valve	Air pressure
	Solenoid valve	Voltage, current, or digital pulse
	Motor-driven valve	Digital pulses
	Variable-speed pump	Voltage or current
	Fluidic control valve	Pressure
Alarms	Lights, bells	Digital pulse
On-off signals	Relays, switches	Digital pulse

Signal Conditioning

An additional consideration in data acquisition and control is conditioning the sensor or actuator signal so that it will have high accuracy, have low noise levels, and makes efficient use of the interface equipment. Usually the steps involved in signal conditioning are multiplexing and amplification of the signals, suppression of noise on the signal, and selection of a transmitting mode for the signal. We shall discuss each of these considerations in turn.

In some applications, there will be many similar measurements at a remote location, and it is usually most efficient *to multiplex* these at the source and transmit them sequentially over only a few lines. As an example, consider 10 thermocouple measurements from a process, each with a voltage signal of ~ 10 mV. First of all, one would not wish to run 10 lines and use 10 channels of our A/D converters just for these signals, so multiplexing is necessary. In addition, such low-voltage signals will be heavily corrupted by noise in transmission and will have very low resolution when they reach the A/D converter; thus *amplification* as well as *multiplexing* is needed. Figure 2.11 illustrates two possible approaches to solving this problem. Scheme (*a*) involves amplification of each low-level signal (requiring N high-gain amplifiers) up to ~ 5 V, then multiplexing with solid-state relays. By multiplexing high-level signals, one minimizes the effects of noise introduced by the relays; however, this is at the cost of an expensive amplifier for each signal. Scheme (*b*), on the other hand, multiplexes first and then requires only a single high-gain amplifier. This is more efficient, but requires care in selecting a low-noise-level multiplexer. Such a device usually requires relays with mercury-wetted contacts in order to avoid corrupting the low-level voltage signal. Both types of multiplexing schemes are known to be successful, and one of them will be illustrated by an example given below.

Noise suppression, either before or after signal transmission to the computer, is also an important part of signal conditioning. There are times when relatively high-frequency noise, such as 60 Hz coming from power lines or motors, appears on the signal. Fortunately, in the process industries, such high frequencies are very rarely contained in the desired signal; thus *filtering* to remove these frequencies can be a very successful means of noise suppression. A simple *low-pass filter* with frequency response characteristics like those shown in Fig. 2.12*a* will often suffice. Other common types of filters include *high-pass filters*, which reject low frequencies, and *notch filters*, which pass only signals within a specified frequency band. Figure 2.13 shows an example of the performance of a low-pass filter applied to a thermocouple signal afflicted with motor noise.

The last part of signal conditioning involves a decision on how the signal is to be transmitted to the computer. There are several alternatives available for signal transmission:

1. **Voltage signals**—These work well over short distance cables (up to ~ 300 ft) where voltage losses and cable capacitance do not cause signal deterioration.

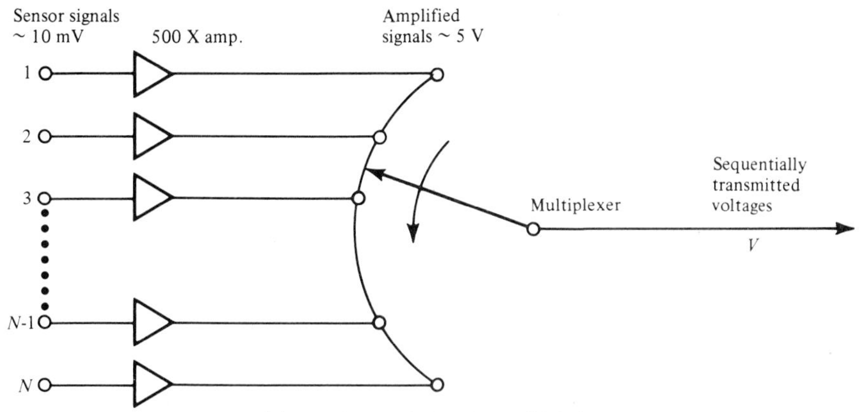

(a) Amplification followed by multiplexing

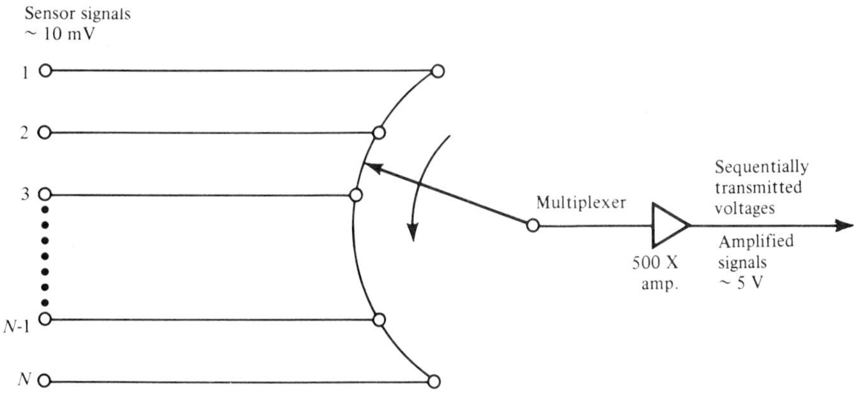

(b) Multiplexing followed by amplification

Figure 2.11 Two different strategies for multiplexing and amplifying low voltage signals.

2. **Current signals**—This method works well with hardwire connections over longer distances but requires special transmitters and I/E conversion at the receiving end.
3. **Digital signals**—These signals can be transmitted most easily and are the natural choice when the original signal is digital. Even voltage signals may be transmitted in a digital mode through D/A conversion at the sending location and A/D conversion at the receiving end. Digital signals have the advantage that they are less susceptible to noise problems and can be transmitted over extremely long distances through telephone connections.

Of course, the selection of transmission mode should be made based on the particular application, noise levels to be encountered, and distances to be covered.

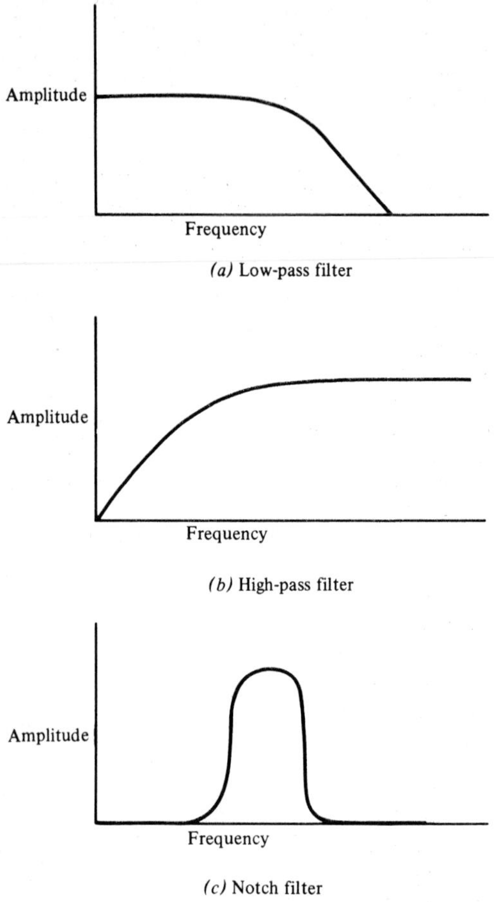

Figure 2.12 Frequency response characteristics of some common filters.

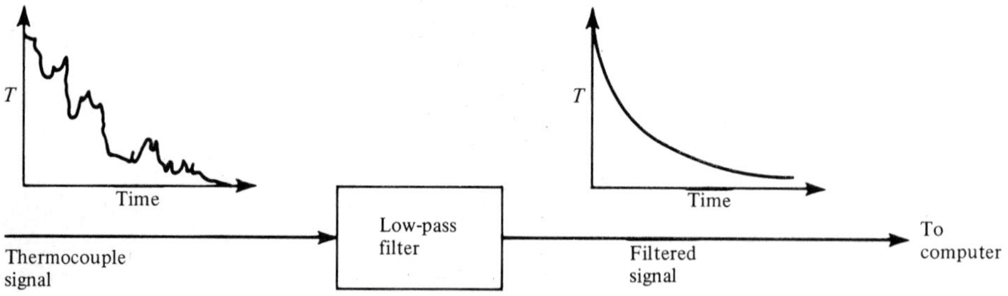

Figure 2.13 Performance of a low-pass filter.

Modes of Computer Control

Computer control is usually carried out in one of two modes: *supervisory control* or *direct digital control* (*DDC*). Supervisory control, illustrated in Fig. 2.14*a*, involves resetting the set point of the local controller according to some computer algorithm. Thus the computer control scheme need only supervise and coordinate the actions of the local controllers. Direct digital control, by contrast, requires that all the controller action be carried out by the digital computer. Measurements are sent to the computer and compared with the set point; then the computed control action is transmitted to the actuator. This is illustrated in Fig. 2.14*b*. For DDC the computer samples the flow measurement at discrete instants of time and sends as control signals step changes in the control valve stem position. The time interval Δt between samples and controller changes must be chosen with care. If Δt is taken too large, the controller performance will deteriorate, while having Δt too small will put an unnecessarily high

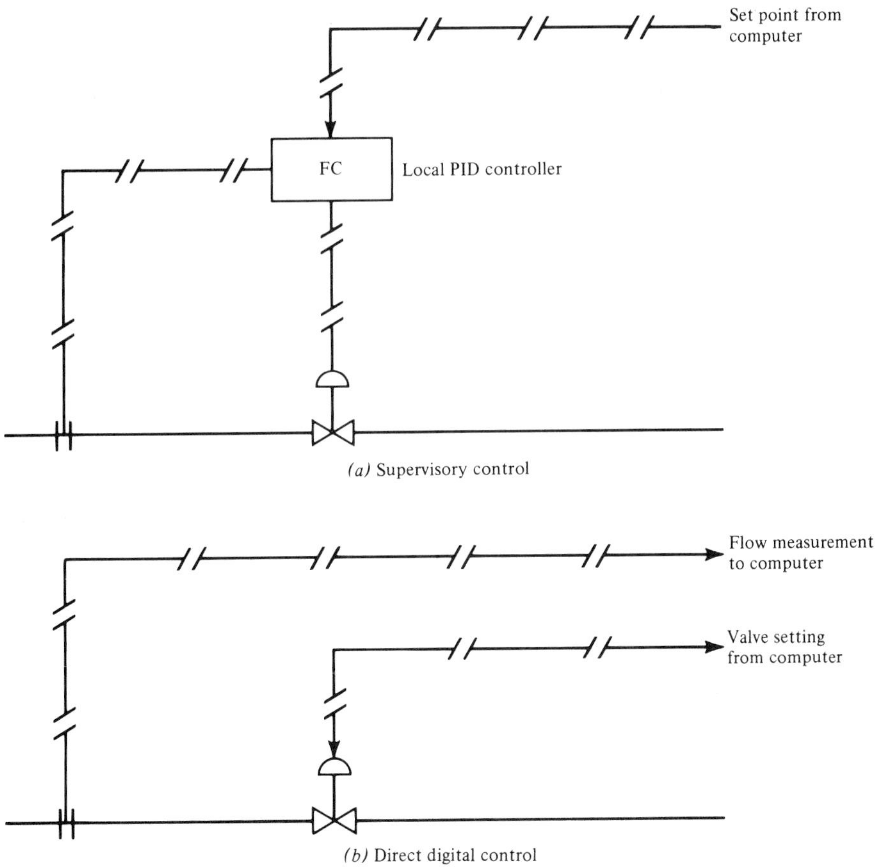

Figure 2.14 Supervisory and direct digital control of a fluid flowrate.

computational load on the computer. Both supervisory control and DDC are in wide use in industrial applications, and both may be readily used to implement modern control strategies. In most processes, the local controller dynamics (whether analog or digital) are short compared with the time constants of the process under control; thus most sophisticated control strategies are implemented in a cascade fashion—involving programmed set-point changes in the local controllers. Hence, it matters little whether these local controllers are analog or digital. As an example, suppose the flow-rate control loop in Fig. 2.14 is a steam flow into a heat exchanger. Suppose further that an optimization algorithm calculates the optimal steam flow-rate program $F(t)$. Clearly this program could be implemented by either supervisory control or DDC when the steam-valve dynamics are fast compared with the heat exchanger time constants. In either case the flow-loop set point would be programmed to follow the function $F(t)$.

Before proceeding to more detailed examples, it is useful to point out that we have provided here only a brief summary of the considerations important in on-line data acquisition and computer control. For more detail, the reader should consult the references at the end of the chapter.

2.4 SOME EXAMPLES

To illustrate some of the principles discussed in the earlier sections, several example case studies shall be presented. It is hoped that these will give the reader a practical grasp of what is involved in interfacing processes to real-time computers.

Computer Control of the Pressure in a Gas Storage Tank

A simple interfacing problem arises for a gas storage tank system which is used in the teaching laboratory at the University of Wisconsin.

A drawing of the interfacing scheme is shown in Fig. 2.15. A bourdon tube transducer is used to measure the pressure in the tank. This transducer is linear and transforms a pressure range of 0 to 60 psig to a voltage range of 0 to 50 mV. This low-voltage signal is then amplified to a voltage range of 0 to 10 V. This high-level voltage is then sent to the computer room (~ 300 ft away) by shielded cable.

The digital computer must be programmed to receive the pressure measurements and calculate control signals based on some controller algorithm. For example, a simple PID controller in discrete form would be

$$u(t_k) = u_0 + K_c\Bigg\{[y_d - y(t_k)] + \frac{\Delta t}{\tau_I}\sum_{n=1}^{k}[y_d - y(t_n)] + \frac{\tau_D}{\Delta t}[y(t_k) - y(t_{k-1})]\Bigg\} \tag{2.4.1}$$

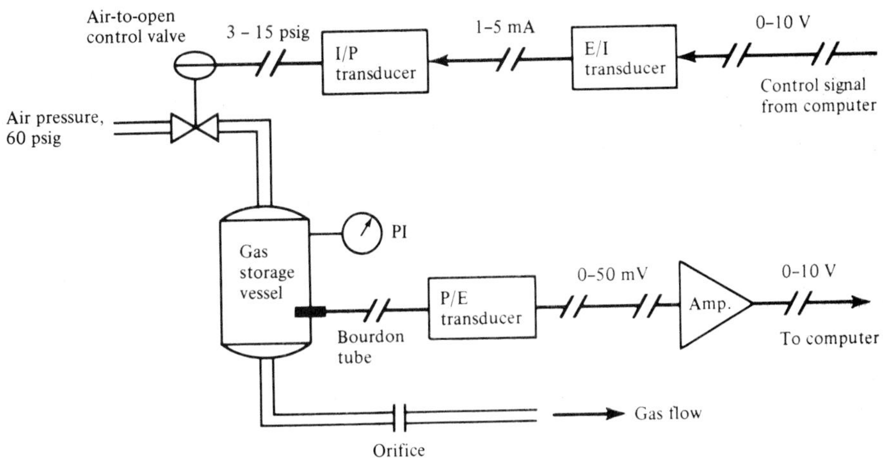

Figure 2.15 Interfacing for the gas storage vessel.

where $u(t_k)$ is the control signal at time t_k, u_0 is the zero-error control signal, K_c is the proportional controller gain, τ_I is the integration time, and τ_D is the derivative time. The measured output (pressure in this case) at time t_k is denoted by $y(t_k)$, and y_d is the controller set point. The quantity Δt is the sampling/control time interval, and is usually selected to be short compared with the time constants of the process.

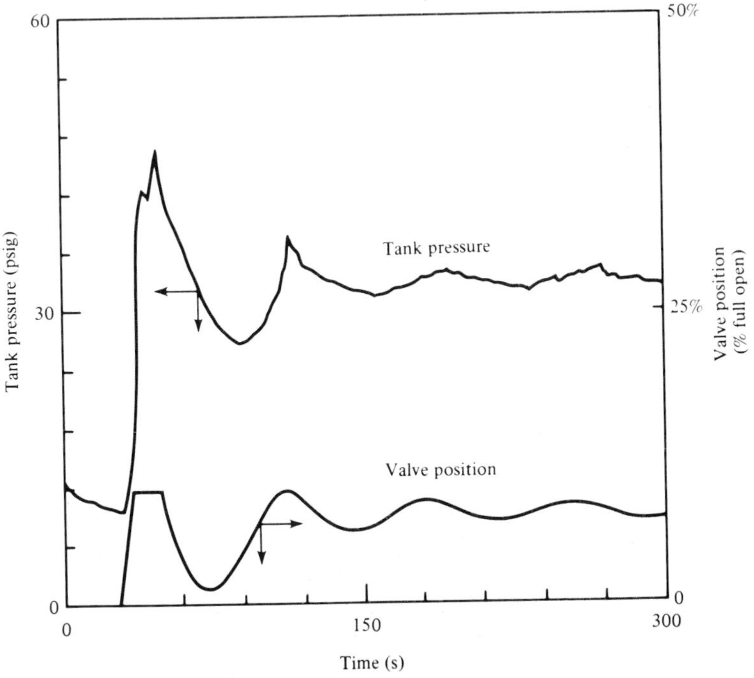

Figure 2.16 Dynamic behavior of the gas storage vessel under DDC control.

The control signal, which is transmitted as an analog voltage, must be converted to a 3- to 15-psig air-pressure signal in order to drive the pneumatic valve. This could be done in one step with an E/P transducer; however, to make use of existing equipment, this conversion is done in two steps, as shown in Fig. 2.15.

After installation, the transducers must be calibrated. For example, 0 to 60 psig corresponds to 0 to 10 V analog voltage for our system, while 0 to 10 V analog control signal corresponds to 3 (full shut) to 15 psig (full open) for the control valve. Because the analog signals were sent over shielded cables for relatively short distances and were not in the vicinity of power lines or motors, no noise suppression devices were needed in this application. Figure 2.16 illustrates the dynamic behavior of the implemented control scheme, showing both the measured tank pressure and the computer-specified control valve position. The control time interval Δt was taken to be only a few seconds, so that the DDC step changes in valve position appear as a continuous curve in the plot. The actual valve stem position does not exactly follow the specified control signal due to the dynamics of the valve itself. Nevertheless, the control system performs adequately, as might be expected.

Computer Control of an Instrumented Steel Ingot

A more complicated scheme of process interfacing can be seen in the following example. It is desired to control the temperature distribution of a cylindrical steel ingot by manipulating the power input to each zone of a three-zone furnace. This is a laboratory model of a metallurgical heating furnace; it is much more heavily instrumented with thermocouples than is possible in practice. This instrumentation is to allow an absolute measure of the temperature distribution in order to evaluate the performance of proposed control algorithms. A photograph of the furnace system is shown in Fig. 2.17. Thirty-two thermocouples are placed axially and radially in the ingot, and each has a 5- to 10-mV voltage

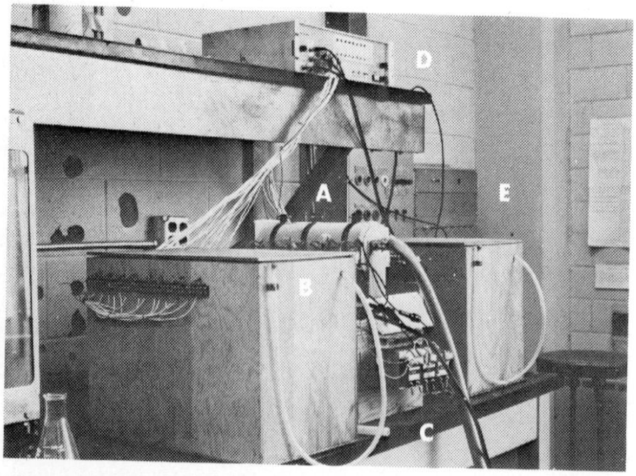

Figure 2.17 An instrumented steel ingot in a three-zone furnace: A, furnace; B, thermocouples; C, furnace heater relays; D, multiplexer and heater controller; E, link to computer.

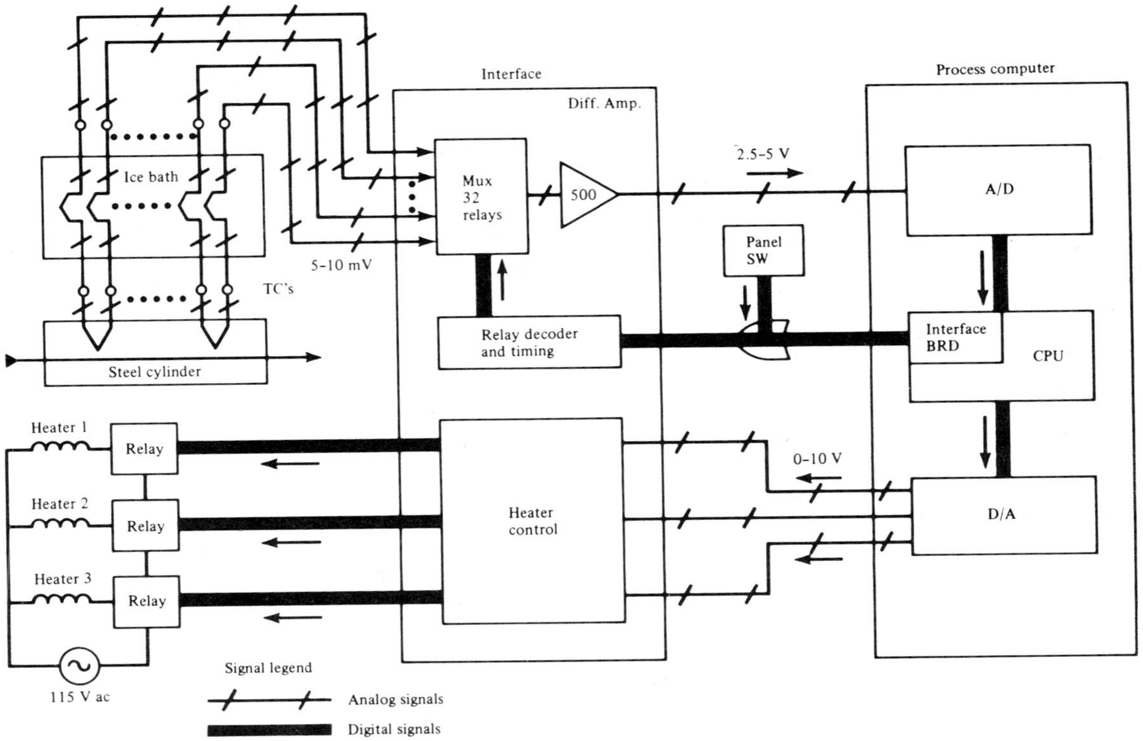

Figure 2.18 Data acquisition and control signal structure for the instrumented steel ingot.

signal. These signals must be multiplexed and amplified before they are sent to the computer. Similarly, the control signal for each zone of the three-zone furnace must be converted to a power input for the electrical heaters.

Figure 2.18 shows the data acquisition and control signal design used for the system. The 32 thermocouples are passed through a reference temperature bath* and then to an interface device. The interface device multiplexes the 32 signals through 32 mercury-wetted relays, which introduce very little noise to the signal. The multiplexing is carried out through digital logic and under digital signal control from the computer. Thus the multiplexing rate and sampling interval are under program control. After multiplexing, the signal passes through a high-quality amplifier with a gain of 500. This brings the 5- to 10-mV signal up to 2.5 to 5 V, and this may be transmitted and processed by the A/D converter without undue error. Through multiplexing, the 32 thermocouple signals require only one channel of the A/D converter—a very efficient use of computing resources. To allow each relay of the multiplexer to properly settle before reading the signal, one must not switch the multiplexer too fast. In the present application it was necessary to allow 1.5 ms per relay for reliable multiplexing. Nevertheless, this allowed all 32 thermocouples to be scanned in less than a tenth of a second. For most process control problems, where the process time constants are minutes to hours, such multiplexing times are negligible.

The control signals for the three-zone furnace are sent through three channels of the D/A converter as analog voltages in the range 0 to 10 V. The interface device has digital logic, which converts the input voltage to an arcless relay controller which controls the power input to the heaters. The conversion is linear, with 0 V control signal corresponding to zero power input and 10 V control signal causing full heater power input.

The interfacing scheme shown in Fig. 2.18 performed well and allowed a detailed study of state estimation and control algorithms for the system. One of the case histories discussed in Chap. 6 demonstrates the performance of this interface design.

REFERENCES

1. Andrew, W. G.: *Applied Instrumentation in the Process Industries*, vols. I, II, III, Gulf Publishing, Houston, 1974.
2. Considine, D. M.: *Process Instruments and Controls Handbook*, 2d ed., McGraw-Hill, New York, 1974.
3. Ewing, G. W.: *Instrumental Methods of Chemical Analysis*, McGraw-Hill, New York, 1975.
4. Finkel, Jules: *Computer-Aided Experimentation*, Wiley, New York, 1975.

*As an alternative to ice baths, there are inexpensive electronic compensators which work equally well.

5. Holman, J. P.: *Experimental Methods for Engineers*, McGraw-Hill, New York, 1971.
6. Korn, G. A.: *Minicomputers for Engineers and Scientists*, McGraw-Hill, New York, 1973.
7. Norton, H. P.: *Handbook of Transducers for Electronic Measuring Systems*, Prentice-Hall, Englewood Cliffs, N.J., 1969.
8. Perone, S. P., and D. O. Jones: *Digital Computers in Scientific Instrumentation*, McGraw-Hill, New York, 1973.
9. Theis, D. J.: *Datamation*, p. 73, (Feb. 1977).
10. *DataPro Reports on Minicomputers*, DataPro Research Corp., October 1978.
11. Harrison, T. J.: *Handbook on Industrial Computer Control*, Wiley, New York, 1972.
12. Harrison, T. J.: *Minicomputers in Industrial Control*, ISA Publ., Pittsburgh, 1978.

PROBLEMS

2.1 Convert the following binary numbers to octal numbers:

(*a*) 100 111 000 111 101
(*b*) 101 010 101 110 011
(*c*) 111 001 110 100 011

2.2 Convert the following octal numbers to decimal numbers:

(*a*) 747 (*c*) 100
(*b*) 440 (*d*) 556

2.3 A Fortran program consists of 100 lines with approximately 25 characters per line. Estimate the number of words of memory in a 16-bit machine required to store this Fortran code.

2.4 In responding to interrupts from various peripheral devices, a computer manufacturer recommends the following priority levels:

Terminal—4 Line printer—4
Real-time clock—7 A/D converter—6
Disk drive—7
Magnetic tape unit—7

Discuss why some of these peripherals are assigned higher priorities than others.

2.5 A computer has a 12-bit A/D converter with −10-V to +10-V span. Determine the analog input voltages and relative error for the following integers coming from the converter:

(*a*) 570 (*c*) −960
(*b*) 2000 (*d*) 25

2.6 Provide the answers to Prob. 2.5 for a 10-bit A/D converter with a −5-V to +5-V span and for the following integers:

(*a*) 450 (*b*) −200 (*c*) 100 (*d*) 25

2.7 It is desired to output the following voltages through a 12-bit D/A converter with a −10-V to +10-V span. Determine the integer that should be loaded into the D/A in each case.

(*a*) −1 V
(*b*) +2.7 V
(*c*) +8.7 V
(*d*) −6 V

2.8 The following analog circuit has been suggested as a simple low-pass filter. Write down the differential equations corresponding to this circuit and indicate how this circuit might accomplish the filtering action. Can you suggest values for *R* and *C* that will eliminate 60-Hz noise without disturbing the 1-Hz signal?

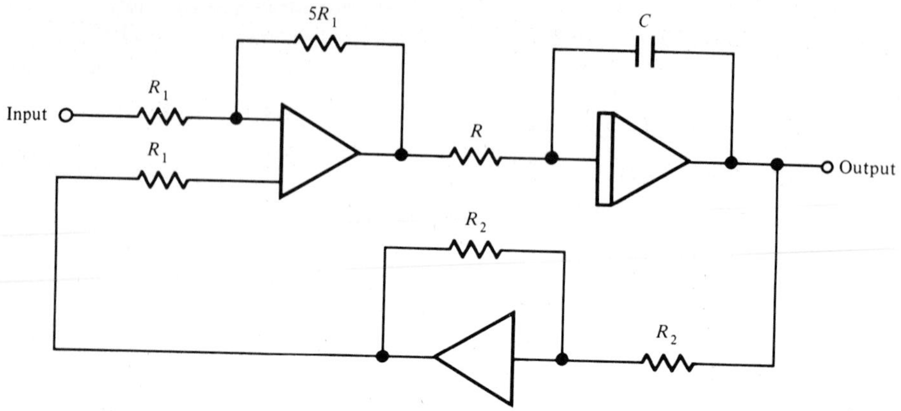

2.9 Two computers are linked over a 300-baud telephone line. One computer would like to transfer a Fortran program to the other computer over this telephone link. The Fortran program in question has about 500 lines of code with approximately 30 characters per line. Estimate how long it will take to transfer this program. An engineer suggests connecting the two computers via a 9600-baud cable link. How long would the program transfer take in this case?

CHAPTER

THREE

CONTROL OF LUMPED PARAMETER SYSTEMS

3.1 INTRODUCTION

In this chapter we shall consider the control of *lumped parameter processes*, i.e., processes described by ordinary differential equations. These include both single-variable and multivariable dynamic systems. We shall begin with a discussion of some of the key concepts and practical difficulties encountered in lumped parameter control system design. Some of the control system design procedures available for linear multivariable systems shall be presented and illustrated with examples. Following this we shall introduce *optimal control theory*, which represents one approach to control system design, and which provides a theoretical foundation helpful in understanding material to be covered later in the book. Finally, we shall discuss special techniques which may be used for nonlinear dynamic systems.

To provide a very simple example of the type of problem we shall be attacking and to clarify a number of concepts, let us consider the simple, well-stirred, steam-heated mixing tank shown in Fig. 3.1. It is used to mix and preheat a recipe of reactants before passing them to a chemical reactor. Now let us suppose that we wish to design a scheme for controlling the effluent temperature $T(t)$ to a desired value T_d by manipulating the steam rate $Q(t)$ with valve v.

An *open-loop control scheme* for such a process would involve programming the steam valve position over time without benefit of *feedback* information, such as a tank effluent temperature measurement. Such a scheme might be useful if a very good *mathematical model* of the process were available, e.g.,

$$\frac{dT}{dt} = \frac{F(T_f - T)}{V} + \frac{Q(t)}{V\rho C_p} \tag{3.1.1}$$

$$T(0) = T_0 \tag{3.1.2}$$

and one had the start-up problem of driving $T(t)$ from the initial condition T_0 to

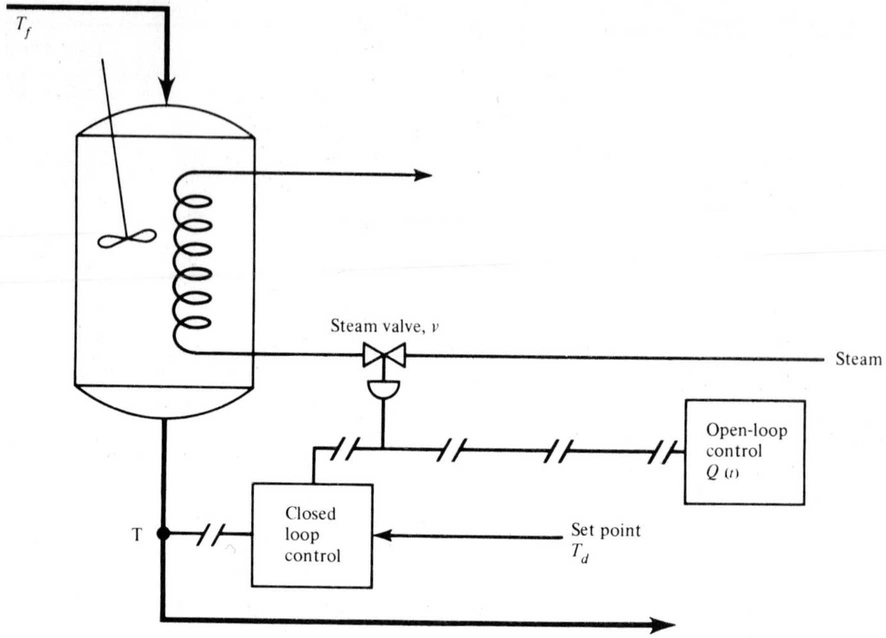

Figure 3.1 A steam-heated mixing tank.

the desired set point T_d. An open-loop control policy $Q(t)$ could be calculated from the model and used to program the steam valve without making use of tank temperature measurements.

In practice, however, most process models contain some error, and *closed-loop control schemes*, which involve process measurements (tank temperature, in this case), have been found necessary for satisfactory controller performance. The choice of the feedback controller structure is left to the designer; for example, a common structure is the three-mode proportional-integral-derivative (PID) controller given by

$$Q(t) = Q_s + K_c\left[(T_d - T) + \frac{1}{\tau_I}\int (T_d - T)\,dt' + \tau_D\frac{d(T_d - T)}{dt}\right] \quad (3.1.3)$$

where K_c, τ_I, and τ_D are the controller parameters. However, in what follows we shall not restrict ourselves to this limited class of controllers, but shall show, in a more general way, how one may design both *open-loop* and *closed-loop* control schemes for processes described by ordinary differential equations.

3.2 LINEAR MULTIVARIABLE CONTROL SYSTEMS

Perhaps the most commonly encountered control system design problem in the process industries is the design of multivariable control systems. If the process under study is linear, a very general model in the time domain (so-called *state variable* notation) is

$$\frac{d\mathbf{x}}{dt} = \mathbf{Ax} + \mathbf{Bu} + \mathbf{\Gamma d} \qquad \mathbf{x}(t_0) = \mathbf{x}_0 \tag{3.2.1}$$

$$\mathbf{y} = \mathbf{Cx} \tag{3.2.2}$$

where

$$\mathbf{d} = \begin{bmatrix} d_1 \\ d_2 \\ \vdots \\ d_k \end{bmatrix}$$

is a k vector of disturbances,

$$\mathbf{x} = \begin{bmatrix} x_1 \\ x_2 \\ \vdots \\ x_n \end{bmatrix}$$

is an n vector of states,

$$\mathbf{u} = \begin{bmatrix} u_1 \\ u_2 \\ \vdots \\ u_m \end{bmatrix}$$

is an m vector of controls (manipulated variables), and

$$\mathbf{y} = \begin{bmatrix} y_1 \\ y_2 \\ \vdots \\ y_l \end{bmatrix}$$

is an l vector of outputs (those states or combination of states which can be measured). The matrices

$$\mathbf{A} = \begin{bmatrix} a_{11} & a_{12} & \cdots & a_{1n} \\ a_{21} & a_{22} & \cdots & a_{2n} \\ \cdots & \cdots & \cdots & \cdots \\ a_{n1} & \cdots & & a_{nn} \end{bmatrix} \qquad \mathbf{B} = \begin{bmatrix} b_{11} & b_{12} & \cdots & b_{1m} \\ b_{21} & b_{22} & \cdots & b_{2m} \\ \cdots & \cdots & \cdots & \cdots \\ b_{n1} & \cdots & & b_{nm} \end{bmatrix}$$

$$\mathbf{C} = \begin{bmatrix} c_{11} & c_{12} & \cdots & c_{1n} \\ c_{21} & c_{22} & \cdots & c_{2n} \\ \cdots & \cdots & \cdots & \cdots \\ c_{l1} & \cdots & & c_{ln} \end{bmatrix} \qquad \mathbf{\Gamma} = \begin{bmatrix} \gamma_{11} & \gamma_{12} & \cdots & \gamma_{1k} \\ \gamma_{21} & \gamma_{22} & \cdots & \gamma_{2k} \\ \cdots & \cdots & \cdots & \cdots \\ \gamma_{n1} & \cdots & & \gamma_{nk} \end{bmatrix}$$

can be either constant or time-varying. This very general model shall be used as a basis for much of the discussion which follows.

It is important to note that Eqs. (3.2.1) and (3.2.2) have analytical solutions which are useful to know. In the case of an *autonomous system* (i.e., where **A**, **B**, **C**, and **Γ** are constant matrices), one may take the Laplace transform of Eq. (3.2.1) to yield

$$s\mathbf{I}\bar{\mathbf{x}}(s) - \mathbf{x}_0 = \mathbf{A}\bar{\mathbf{x}}(s) + \mathbf{B}\bar{\mathbf{u}}(s) + \mathbf{\Gamma}\bar{\mathbf{d}}(s)$$

$$\bar{\mathbf{y}}(s) = \mathbf{C}\bar{\mathbf{x}}(s)$$

Solving for $\bar{\mathbf{x}}(s)$, we obtain

$$\bar{\mathbf{x}}(s) = (s\mathbf{I} - \mathbf{A})^{-1}\left[\mathbf{x}_0 + \mathbf{B}\bar{\mathbf{u}}(s) + \mathbf{\Gamma}\bar{\mathbf{d}}(s)\right] \tag{3.2.3}$$

Now, using the convolution theorem of Laplace transforms to invert this expression, the analytical solution takes the form

$$\mathbf{x}(t) = e^{\mathbf{A}(t-t_0)}\mathbf{x}_0 + \int_{t_0}^{t} e^{\mathbf{A}(t-r)}\left[\mathbf{B}\mathbf{u}(r) + \mathbf{\Gamma}\mathbf{d}(r)\right] dr \tag{3.2.4}$$

where the exponential matrix $e^{\mathbf{A}\tau}$ must be evaluated. Let us note that $\mathbf{X} = e^{\mathbf{A}\tau}$ is the solution to the simple homogeneous matrix differential equation

$$\frac{d\mathbf{X}}{d\tau} = \mathbf{A}\mathbf{X} \qquad \mathbf{X}(0) = \mathbf{I} \tag{3.2.5}$$

where **X** is an $n \times n$ matrix. If the eigenvalues of **A** are distinct, then there is a canonical transformation [1]

$$\mathbf{A} = \mathbf{M}\mathbf{\Lambda}\mathbf{M}^{-1} \tag{3.2.6}$$

relating the matrix **A** to its diagonal matrix of eigenvalues

$$\mathbf{\Lambda} = \begin{bmatrix} \lambda_1 & & & \mathbf{0} \\ & \lambda_2 & & \\ & & \ddots & \\ \mathbf{0} & & & \lambda_n \end{bmatrix} \tag{3.2.7}$$

and matrix of eigenvectors **M**. Substituting Eq. (3.2.6) into Eq. (3.2.5) yields

$$\frac{d(\mathbf{M}^{-1}\mathbf{X})}{d\tau} = \mathbf{\Lambda}(\mathbf{M}^{-1}\mathbf{X}) \qquad \mathbf{M}^{-1}\mathbf{X}(0) = \mathbf{M}^{-1} \tag{3.2.8}$$

which has the solution

$$\mathbf{M}^{-1}\mathbf{X} = e^{\mathbf{\Lambda}\tau}\mathbf{M}^{-1}$$

or

$$\mathbf{X} = e^{\mathbf{A}\tau} = \mathbf{M}e^{\mathbf{\Lambda}\tau}\mathbf{M}^{-1} \tag{3.2.9}$$

where $e^{\Lambda\tau}$ is the diagonal $n \times n$ matrix

$$e^{\Lambda\tau} = \begin{bmatrix} e^{\lambda_1\tau} & & & \mathbf{0} \\ & e^{\lambda_2\tau} & & \\ & & \ddots & \\ \mathbf{0} & & & e^{\lambda_n\tau} \end{bmatrix} \tag{3.2.10}$$

Thus one direct way to evaluate $e^{\mathbf{A}\tau}$ is through Eq. (3.2.9).

In the event that the matrices **A**, **B**, **C**, and **Γ** are time-varying, the system represented by Eqs. (3.2.1) and (3.2.2) is *nonautonomous*, and an alternative solution must be used. In this case, the analytical solution takes the form [2]

$$\mathbf{x}(t) = \mathbf{\Phi}(t, t_0)\mathbf{x}_0 + \mathbf{\Phi}(t, t_0)\int_{t_0}^{t}\mathbf{\Phi}(r, t_0)^{-1}\left[\mathbf{B}(r)\mathbf{u}(r) + \mathbf{\Gamma}(r)\mathbf{d}(r)\right] dr \tag{3.2.11}$$

where $\mathbf{\Phi}(t, t_0)$ is an $n \times n$ time-varying matrix known as *the fundamental matrix solution*. The fundamental matrix solution arises from the solution of the equation

$$\frac{d\mathbf{\Phi}(t, t_0)}{dt} = \mathbf{A}(t)\mathbf{\Phi}(t, t_0) \qquad \mathbf{\Phi}(t_0, t_0) = \mathbf{I} \tag{3.2.12}$$

Example 3.2.1 To illustrate how these general results apply to a particular multivariable system, let us consider the stirred mixing tank in Fig. 3.2 with cross-sectional area A_c. There are three streams entering the tank: (1) a hot

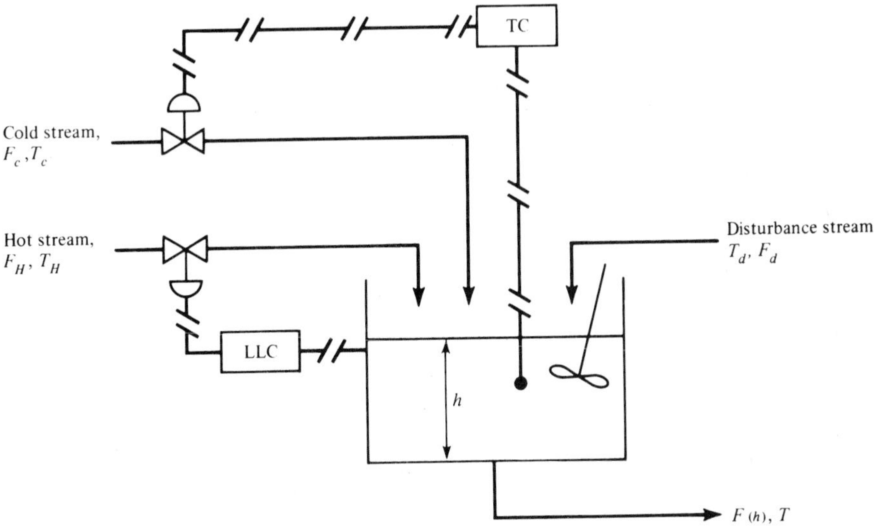

Figure 3.2 Stirred mixing tank requiring level and temperature control.

stream at temperature T_H with adjustable flow F_H, (2) a cold stream at temperature T_C with adjustable flow F_C, and (3) a disturbance stream from another process unit with variable temperature T_d and flow F_d. The tank is well stirred, with liquid outflow determined by the liquid height in the tank, h, i.e., $F(h) = Kh^{1/2}$. The modeling equations arise from material and energy balances:

$$A_c \frac{dh}{dt} = F_H + F_C + F_d - F(h)$$

$$\rho C_p A_c \frac{d(hT)}{dt} = \rho C_p [F_H T_H + F_C T_C + F_d T_d - F(h)T] \quad (3.2.13)$$

Clearly the tank model is nonlinear; however, it is possible to linearize the equations about the desired operating point h_s, T_s by using Taylor series expansions truncated after the first-order terms:

$$F(h) \cong F(h_s) + \frac{1}{2}\frac{K}{h_s^{1/2}}(h - h_s) + \cdots$$

$$F(h)T \cong F(h_s)T_s + F(h_s)(T - T_s) + \frac{1}{2}\frac{T_s K(h - h_s)}{h_s^{1/2}} + \cdots$$

$$hT \cong h_s T_s + h_s(T - T_s) + T_s(h - h_s) + \cdots \quad (3.2.14)$$

$$F_d T_d \cong F_{ds} T_{ds} + F_{ds}(T_d - T_{ds}) + T_{ds}(F_d - F_{ds}) + \cdots$$

If we then define F_{Hs}, F_{Cs}, F_{ds}, T_{ds} as the steady-state values of F_H, F_C, F_d, T_d corresponding to $h = h_s$, $T = T_s$, that is, satisfying

$$0 = F_{Hs} + F_{Cs} + F_{ds} - F(h_s)$$

$$0 = F_{Hs} T_H + F_{Cs} T_C + F_{ds} T_{ds} - F(h_s) T_s \quad (3.2.15)$$

then one can use the deviation variables

$$x_1 = h - h_s \qquad x_2 = T - T_s \qquad u_1 = F_H - F_{Hs}$$

$$u_2 = F_C - F_{Cs} \qquad d_1 = F_d - F_{ds} \qquad d_2 = T_d - T_{ds} \quad (3.2.16)$$

to obtain the linearized modeling equations

$$A_c \frac{dx_1}{dt} = u_1 + u_2 + d_1 - \frac{1}{2}\frac{K}{h_s^{1/2}} x_1$$

$$A_c \left[h_s \frac{dx_2}{dt} + T_s \frac{dx_1}{dt} \right] = T_H u_1 + T_C u_2 + T_{ds} d_1 + F_{ds} d_2$$

$$- \frac{T_s}{2}\frac{K}{h_s^{1/2}} x_1 - F(h_s) x_2 \quad (3.2.17)$$

or rearranging,

$$\frac{dx_1}{dt} = \frac{1}{A_c}\left[u_1 + u_2 + d_1 - \frac{1}{2}\frac{F(h_s)}{h_s}x_1\right]$$

$$\frac{dx_2}{dt} = \frac{1}{A_c h_s}[(T_H - T_s)u_1 + (T_C - T_s)u_2 + (T_{ds} - T_s)d_1 + F_{ds}d_2 - F(h_s)x_2] \tag{3.2.18}$$

Thus, if we define the vectors

$$\mathbf{x} = \begin{bmatrix} x_1 \\ x_2 \end{bmatrix} \qquad \mathbf{u} = \begin{bmatrix} u_1 \\ u_2 \end{bmatrix} \qquad \mathbf{d} = \begin{bmatrix} d_1 \\ d_2 \end{bmatrix}$$

and the matrices

$$\mathbf{A} = \begin{bmatrix} -\dfrac{1}{2}\dfrac{F(h_s)}{A_c h_s} & 0 \\ 0 & -\dfrac{F(h_s)}{A_c h_s} \end{bmatrix} \qquad \mathbf{B} = \begin{bmatrix} \dfrac{1}{A_c} & \dfrac{1}{A_c} \\ \dfrac{T_H - T_s}{A_c h_s} & \dfrac{T_C - T_s}{A_c h_s} \end{bmatrix}$$

$$\mathbf{\Gamma} = \begin{bmatrix} \dfrac{1}{A_c} & 0 \\ \dfrac{T_{ds} - T_s}{A_c h_s} & \dfrac{F_{ds}}{A_c h_s} \end{bmatrix} \tag{3.2.19}$$

then the model for this system is in the form of Eq. (3.2.1). If both the state variables are measured, then

$$\mathbf{y} = \begin{bmatrix} y_1 \\ y_2 \end{bmatrix} = \begin{bmatrix} x_1 \\ x_2 \end{bmatrix} \qquad \text{and} \qquad \mathbf{C} = \begin{bmatrix} 1 & 0 \\ 0 & 1 \end{bmatrix}$$

To use the analytical solution, Eq. (3.2.4), for this example problem, let us note that the matrix **A** is diagonal and that the characteristic equation

$$|\mathbf{A} - \lambda \mathbf{I}| = 0$$

yields the eigenvalues

$$\lambda_1 = -\frac{1}{2}\frac{F(h_s)}{A_c h_s} \qquad \lambda_2 = -\frac{F(h_s)}{A_c h_s} \tag{3.2.20}$$

Hence **A** is already in canonical form and

$$e^{\mathbf{A}\tau} = \begin{bmatrix} e^{\lambda_1 \tau} & 0 \\ 0 & e^{\lambda_2 \tau} \end{bmatrix} \tag{3.2.21}$$

Let us now evaluate the response of the system to a unit step change in u_1 and u_2 at $t = 0$, that is $u_1 = 1$, $u_2 = 1$. Further, let us assume

$$\mathbf{x}(0) = \mathbf{x}_0 = \begin{bmatrix} x_{10} \\ x_{20} \end{bmatrix} \qquad \text{and} \qquad d_1 = d_2 = 0$$

In this case Eq. (3.2.4) becomes

$$\mathbf{x}(t) = e^{\mathbf{A}t}\mathbf{x}_0 + \int_0^t e^{\mathbf{A}(t-s)}\mathbf{B}\mathbf{u}(s)\,ds \tag{3.2.22}$$

or

$$\mathbf{x}(t) = \begin{bmatrix} x_1 \\ x_2 \end{bmatrix} = \begin{bmatrix} e^{\lambda_1 t}x_{10} + \displaystyle\int_0^t e^{\lambda_1(t-s)}\frac{2}{A_c}\,ds \\ e^{\lambda_2 t}x_{20} + \displaystyle\int_0^t e^{\lambda_2(t-s)}\left(\frac{T_H + T_C - 2T_s}{A_c h_s}\right)ds \end{bmatrix}$$

Evaluation of the integrals yields the analytical solution:

$$x_1(t) = \exp\left[-\frac{1}{2}\frac{F(h_s)}{A_c h_s}t\right]x_{10} + \frac{4h_s}{F(h_s)}\left\{1 - \exp\left[-\frac{1}{2}\frac{F(h_s)}{A_c h_s}t\right]\right\}$$

$$x_2(t) = \exp\left[-\frac{F(h_s)}{A_c h_s}t\right]x_{20} + \frac{T_H + T_C - 2T_s}{F(h_s)}\left\{1 - \exp\left[\frac{-F(h_s)t}{A_c h_s}\right]\right\} \tag{3.2.23}$$

Time-Domain versus Transform-Domain Representation

In considering the dynamics of multivariable linear systems with constant coefficients, one may choose to do the analysis either in the time domain, with models of the form

$$\frac{d\mathbf{x}}{dt} = \mathbf{A}\mathbf{x} + \mathbf{B}\mathbf{u} + \mathbf{\Gamma}\mathbf{d} \qquad \mathbf{x}(t_0) = \mathbf{x}_0 \tag{3.2.24}$$

$$\mathbf{y} = \mathbf{C}\mathbf{x} \tag{3.2.25}$$

or in the Laplace transform domain, involving transfer functions in the form

$$\bar{\mathbf{y}}(s) = \mathbf{G}(s)\bar{\mathbf{u}}(s) + \mathbf{G}_d(s)\bar{\mathbf{d}}(s) \tag{3.2.26}$$

Here the overbar denotes the Laplace-transformed variable and the matrices $\mathbf{G}(s)$, $\mathbf{G}_d(s)$ are the multivariable transfer functions relating the system control variables $\bar{\mathbf{u}}(s)$ and disturbances $\bar{\mathbf{d}}(s)$ to the system output, i.e.,

$$\mathbf{G}(s) = \begin{bmatrix} g_{11}(s) & g_{12}(s) & \cdots & g_{1m}(s) \\ g_{21}(s) & g_{22}(s) & \cdots & g_{2m}(s) \\ \cdots & \cdots & \cdots & \cdots \\ g_{l1}(s) & \cdots & & g_{lm}(s) \end{bmatrix}$$

$$\mathbf{G}_d(s) = \begin{bmatrix} g_{11}^d(s) & g_{12}^d(s) & \cdots & g_{1k}^d(s) \\ g_{21}^d(s) & g_{22}^d(s) & \cdots & g_{2k}^d(s) \\ \cdots & \cdots & \cdots & \cdots \\ g_{l1}^d(s) & \cdots & & g_{lk}(s) \end{bmatrix} \quad (3.2.27)$$

Note that the state variables $\mathbf{x}$ are not used in the Laplace-domain representation.

Some control system design procedures are easiest in the first representation, while other algorithms are more convenient using the second. Thus the control system designer should have the capability to quickly switch back and forth between the two formulations. Let us discuss how this may be easily done.

The transformation from the state space [Eqs. (3.2.1) and (3.2.2)] to the transform space is unique and simply done by taking the Laplace transform of Eqs. (3.2.1) and (3.2.2) with $\mathbf{x}_0 = 0$, to yield

$$\bar{\mathbf{y}} = \mathbf{C}(s\mathbf{I} - \mathbf{A})^{-1}\mathbf{B}\bar{\mathbf{u}}(s) + \mathbf{C}(s\mathbf{I} - \mathbf{A})^{-1}\boldsymbol{\Gamma}\bar{\mathbf{d}}(s) \quad (3.2.28)$$

Hence

$$\mathbf{G}(s) = \mathbf{C}(s\mathbf{I} - \mathbf{A})^{-1}\mathbf{B} \quad (3.2.29)$$

$$\mathbf{G}_d(s) = \mathbf{C}(s\mathbf{I} - \mathbf{A})^{-1}\boldsymbol{\Gamma} \quad (3.2.30)$$

There exist standard computer programs (see Appendix A) which can efficiently perform the operations in Eq. (3.2.28).

The reverse transformation from the transform domain to the time domain is more difficult for several reasons:

1. Because there is more information contained in the time-domain representation than in the simple input/output transfer function, the transformation from the transform domain is not unique. There are many sets of Eqs. (3.2.1), (3.2.2) equivalent to Eq. (3.2.28).
2. Among the many possible transformations, one wishes to choose one which provides the *minimal realization* of the transfer function. This means the smallest set of state variables necessary to match the transfer-function relationship. Even so, there are many possible choices of a minimal realization.

Among the several different algorithms for finding the minimal realization of a transfer function (see [3-5] for a more detailed discussion) is a most useful technique which works when all the poles of the transfer function matrix are real and distinct. The procedure may be outlined in the following way.

Let us consider the transfer function matrix $\mathbf{G}(s)$ which can be expanded in a partial fraction expansion of the form

$$\mathbf{G}(s) = \sum_{i=1}^{p} \frac{\mathbf{M}_i}{s + \lambda_i} \tag{3.2.31}$$

where the $-\lambda_i$, $i = 1, 2, \ldots p$, are the poles and the $l \times m$ matrix $\mathbf{M}_i$ is the matrix of residues for the pole $-\lambda_i$, defined by

$$\mathbf{M}_i = \lim_{s \to -\lambda_i} \left[(s + \lambda_i)\mathbf{G}(s) \right] \tag{3.2.32}$$

If n_i is the rank of the ith matrix of residues, then the minimal state space realization must consist of n state variables, where

$$n = \sum_{i=1}^{p} n_i \tag{3.2.33}$$

The construction of the matrices $\mathbf{A}$, $\mathbf{B}$, and $\mathbf{C}$ can be done in many different ways, and, as noted above, the selection is not unique. One procedure is to make $\mathbf{A}$ diagonal and of the form

$$\mathbf{A} = \begin{bmatrix} \mathbf{A}_{11} & & & \mathbf{0} \\ & \mathbf{A}_{22} & & \\ & & \ddots & \\ \mathbf{0} & & & \mathbf{A}_{pp} \end{bmatrix} \tag{3.2.34}$$

where the diagonal submatrices are given by

$$\mathbf{A}_{ii} = -\lambda_i \mathbf{I}_{n_i}$$

and $\mathbf{I}_{n_i}$ is an identity matrix of dimension n_i. To determine the elements of $\mathbf{B}$ and $\mathbf{C}$, note that with $\mathbf{A}$ in diagonal form, the quantity $(s\mathbf{I} - \mathbf{A})^{-1}$ is also diagonal, so that Eq. (3.2.29) may be rewritten in the form of Eq. (3.2.31), where $\mathbf{M}_i$ will be composed only of the elements of **C** and **B**:

$$\mathbf{M}_i = \sum_{j=1}^{n_i} \mathbf{c}_{ij}\mathbf{b}_{ij}^T \qquad i = 1, 2, \ldots, p \tag{3.2.35}$$

where $\mathbf{c}_{ij}$ is an l vector and $\mathbf{b}_{ij}$ is an m vector. Then the vectors $\mathbf{c}_{ij}$, $\mathbf{b}_{ij}$ are one possible choice for the columns of **C** and $\mathbf{B}^T$, respectively, and these would take the form

$$\mathbf{B} = \begin{bmatrix} \mathbf{b}_{11}^T \\ \vdots \\ \mathbf{b}_{1n_1}^T \\ \hdashline \mathbf{b}_{21}^T \\ \vdots \\ \mathbf{b}_{2n_2}^T \\ \hdashline \vdots \\ \mathbf{b}_{p1}^T \\ \vdots \\ \mathbf{b}_{pn_p}^T \end{bmatrix} \qquad \mathbf{C} = \left[\, \mathbf{c}_{11} \cdots \mathbf{c}_{1n_1} \,\vdots\, \mathbf{c}_{21} \cdots \mathbf{c}_{2n_2} \,\vdots\, \cdots \,\vdots\, \mathbf{c}_{p1} \cdots \mathbf{c}_{pn_p} \right] \tag{3.2.36}$$

where, of course, **B** is an $n \times m$ matrix and **C** is an $l \times n$ matrix.

If in addition we must invert the disturbance transfer function

$$\mathbf{G}_d = \mathbf{C}(s\mathbf{I} - \mathbf{A})^{-1}\boldsymbol{\Gamma} \tag{3.2.30}$$

we must now choose the $n \times k$ matrix $\boldsymbol{\Gamma}$ to obtain the proper transformation. This can be done by expanding $\mathbf{G}_d$ in the form of Eq. (3.2.29), where the poles of **G** and $\mathbf{G}_d$ must be the same:*

$$\mathbf{G}_d = \sum_{i=1}^{p} \frac{\mathbf{M}_i^d}{s + \lambda_i} \tag{3.2.37}$$

Here the matrix of residues $\mathbf{M}_i^d$ may be expanded as

$$\mathbf{M}_i^d = \sum_{j=1}^{n_i} \mathbf{c}_{ij}\boldsymbol{\gamma}_{ij}^T \tag{3.2.38}$$

* This is not really a restriction because a common denominator may be defined which contains all the poles of **G** and $\mathbf{G}_d$.

where the elements $\mathbf{c}_{ij}$ have already been determined and the k vector $\boldsymbol{\gamma}_{ij}$ must be selected to form the matrix

$$\boldsymbol{\Gamma} = \begin{bmatrix} \boldsymbol{\gamma}_{11}^T \\ \boldsymbol{\gamma}_{12}^T \\ \vdots \\ \boldsymbol{\gamma}_{1n_1}^T \\ \hdashline \boldsymbol{\gamma}_{21}^T \\ \vdots \\ \boldsymbol{\gamma}_{2n_2}^T \\ \hdashline \vdots \\ \boldsymbol{\gamma}_{1n_p}^T \\ \vdots \\ \boldsymbol{\gamma}_{pn_p} \end{bmatrix} \tag{3.2.39}$$

Let us illustrate these procedures by examples.

Example 3.2.2 Let us consider the dynamic modeling of a liquid-phase chemical reaction for reacting species A to products. Assume that the rate of reaction is independent of temperature and that the reactor chosen is an adiabatic stirred tank. Composition and energy balances yield the modeling equations

$$\frac{dc_A}{dt} = \frac{1}{\theta}(c_{Af} - c_A) - kc_A$$

$$\frac{dT}{dt} = \frac{1}{\theta}(T_f - T) + Jkc_A$$

Here we assume T_f is the manipulated variable and T the output, so that by letting $x_1 = c_A$, $x_2 = T$, $u_1 = c_{Af}$, $u_2 = T_f$, and $y = T$, one obtains

$$\frac{d\mathbf{x}}{dt} = \mathbf{Ax} + \mathbf{b}u$$

$$y = \mathbf{Cx} \tag{3.2.40}$$

where

$$\mathbf{A} = \begin{bmatrix} -\left(\frac{1}{\theta} + k\right) & 0 \\ Jk & -\frac{1}{\theta} \end{bmatrix} \qquad \mathbf{B} = \begin{bmatrix} \frac{1}{\theta} & 0 \\ 0 & \frac{1}{\theta} \end{bmatrix} \qquad \mathbf{C} = [0 \quad 1]$$

Then, by application of Eq. (3.2.28), one obtains

$$\mathbf{G}(s) = \mathbf{C}(s\mathbf{I} - \mathbf{A})^{-1}\mathbf{B}$$

where

$$(s\mathbf{I} - \mathbf{A}) = \begin{bmatrix} s + \dfrac{1}{\theta} + k & 0 \\ -Jk & s + \dfrac{1}{\theta} \end{bmatrix}$$

and

$$(s\mathbf{I} - \mathbf{A})^{-1} = \frac{1}{(s + 1/\theta + k)(s + 1/\theta)} \begin{bmatrix} s + \dfrac{1}{\theta} & 0 \\ Jk & s + \dfrac{1}{\theta} + k \end{bmatrix}$$

Thus

$$\mathbf{G}(s) = \frac{1}{(s + 1/\theta + k)(s + 1/\theta)} \begin{bmatrix} \dfrac{Jk}{\theta} & \dfrac{s + \dfrac{1}{\theta} + k}{\theta} \end{bmatrix} \tag{3.2.41}$$

is the unique transfer function required.

Example 3.2.3 Let us now determine a minimal state space realization for the transfer function, Eq. (3.2.41), derived in the previous example. Clearly the poles are $-(1/\theta + k)$ and $-1/\theta$. Thus a partial fraction expansion of the form of Eq. (3.2.31) gives

$$\mathbf{G}(s) = \frac{1}{s + 1/\theta + k} \begin{bmatrix} -\dfrac{J}{\theta} & 0 \end{bmatrix} + \frac{1}{s + \dfrac{1}{\theta}} \begin{bmatrix} \dfrac{J}{\theta} & \dfrac{1}{\theta} \end{bmatrix}$$

Since the rank of each of the $\mathbf{M}_i$, $i = 1, 2$, is 1, a minimal realization requires two state variables. Let us now determine a set of $\mathbf{A}$, $\mathbf{B}$, $\mathbf{C}$ for this realization using the algorithm suggested above. In diagonal form,

$$\mathbf{A} = \begin{bmatrix} -\left(\dfrac{1}{\theta} + k\right) & 0 \\ 0 & -\dfrac{1}{\theta} \end{bmatrix} \tag{3.2.42}$$

and we can choose $\mathbf{M}_1$ and $\mathbf{M}_2$ according to Eq. (3.2.35), i.e.,

$$\mathbf{M}_1 = \begin{bmatrix} -\dfrac{J}{\theta} & 0 \end{bmatrix} = [1] \begin{bmatrix} -\dfrac{J}{\theta} & 0 \end{bmatrix}$$

$$\mathbf{M}_2 = \begin{bmatrix} \dfrac{J}{\theta} & \dfrac{1}{\theta} \end{bmatrix} = [1] \begin{bmatrix} \dfrac{J}{\theta} & \dfrac{1}{\theta} \end{bmatrix}$$

Thus

$$\mathbf{B} = \begin{bmatrix} -\dfrac{j}{\theta} & 0 \\ \dfrac{J}{\theta} & \dfrac{1}{\theta} \end{bmatrix} \qquad \mathbf{C} = \begin{bmatrix} 1 & 1 \end{bmatrix} \tag{3.2.43}$$

is an acceptable choice. Note that this leads to the state space model

$$\frac{dx_1}{dt} = -\left(\frac{1}{\theta} + k\right)x_1 - \frac{J}{\theta}u_1$$

$$\frac{dx_2}{dt} = -\frac{1}{\theta}x_2 + \frac{J}{\theta}u_1 + \frac{1}{\theta}u_2$$

$$y = x_1 + x_2$$

Clearly y, u_1, and u_2 have the same physical meaning as in the previous example, but x_1 and x_2 here are not the same. In fact, $x_1 = Jc_A + T$, $x_2 = -Jc_A$ here.

This example clearly illustrates the nonuniqueness of the minimal state space realization, since the transfer function of Eq. (3.2.41) has been shown to be equivalent to two different state space models, Eqs. (3.2.40) and (3.2.42), (3.2.43).

More complicated transformations will be illustrated in the next example problem.

Example 3.2.4 In this example we illustrate the state space representation of a more complicated transfer function relationship,

$$\bar{\mathbf{y}} = \mathbf{G}\bar{\mathbf{u}}(s) + \mathbf{G}_d\bar{d}(s) \tag{3.2.44}$$

where

$$\mathbf{G}(s) = \begin{bmatrix} \dfrac{0.7}{1+9s} & 0 \\ \dfrac{2.0}{1+8s} & \dfrac{0.4}{1+9s} \end{bmatrix}$$

$$\mathbf{G}_d(s) = \begin{bmatrix} 0 & 0 \\ \dfrac{0.5}{1+8s} & \dfrac{1.0}{1+9s} \end{bmatrix}$$

Making use of Eq. (3.2.31), one obtains

$$\mathbf{G}(s) = \frac{1}{s+\frac{1}{9}}\begin{bmatrix} 0.078 & 0 \\ 0 & 0.044 \end{bmatrix} + \frac{1}{s+\frac{1}{8}}\begin{bmatrix} 0 & 0 \\ 0.25 & 0 \end{bmatrix}$$

where $\lambda_1 = -\frac{1}{9}$, $\lambda_2 = -\frac{1}{8}$ are the poles. Evaluating the ranks of the residue matrices, one obtains $n_1 = 2$, $n_2 = 1$, so that the minimal realization must be of order 3. By using the diagonal form,

$$\mathbf{A} = \begin{bmatrix} -\frac{1}{9} & 0 & 0 \\ 0 & -\frac{1}{9} & 0 \\ 0 & 0 & -\frac{1}{8} \end{bmatrix}$$

and expanding $\mathbf{M}_1$, $\mathbf{M}_2$ in the form of Eq. (3.2.35), then

$$\mathbf{M}_1 = \begin{bmatrix} 1 \\ 0 \end{bmatrix} \begin{bmatrix} 0.078 & 0 \end{bmatrix} + \begin{bmatrix} 0 \\ 1 \end{bmatrix} \begin{bmatrix} 0 & 0.044 \end{bmatrix}$$

$$\mathbf{M}_2 = \begin{bmatrix} 0 \\ 1 \end{bmatrix} \begin{bmatrix} 0.25 & 0 \end{bmatrix}$$

Thus $\mathbf{B}$ and $\mathbf{C}$ can take the form

$$\mathbf{B} = \begin{bmatrix} 0.078 & 0 \\ 0 & 0.044 \\ 0.25 & 0 \end{bmatrix} \qquad \mathbf{C} = \begin{bmatrix} 1 & 0 & 0 \\ 0 & 1 & 1 \end{bmatrix}$$

Now expanding $\mathbf{G}_d(s)$, one obtains

$$\mathbf{G}_d(s) = \frac{1}{s + \frac{1}{9}} \begin{bmatrix} 0 & 0 \\ 0 & 0.111 \end{bmatrix} + \frac{1}{s + \frac{1}{8}} \begin{bmatrix} 0 & 0 \\ 0.0625 & 0 \end{bmatrix}$$

and expanding the matrix of residues $\mathbf{M}_i^d$ according to Eq. (3.2.38), one obtains

$$\mathbf{M}_1^d = \begin{bmatrix} 1 \\ 0 \end{bmatrix} \begin{bmatrix} 0 & 0 \end{bmatrix} + \begin{bmatrix} 0 \\ 1 \end{bmatrix} \begin{bmatrix} 0 & 0.111 \end{bmatrix}$$

$$\mathbf{M}_2^d = \begin{bmatrix} 0 \\ 1 \end{bmatrix} \begin{bmatrix} 0.0625 & 0 \end{bmatrix}$$

Thus

$$\mathbf{\Gamma} = \begin{bmatrix} 0 & 0 \\ 0 & 0.111 \\ 0.0625 & 0 \end{bmatrix}$$

Summarizing, the state space model takes the form

$$\frac{d}{dt}\begin{bmatrix} x_1 \\ x_2 \\ x_3 \end{bmatrix} = \begin{bmatrix} -\frac{1}{9} & 0 & 0 \\ 0 & -\frac{1}{9} & 0 \\ 0 & 0 & -\frac{1}{8} \end{bmatrix} \begin{bmatrix} x_1 \\ x_2 \\ x_3 \end{bmatrix} + \begin{bmatrix} 0 & 0.078 \\ 0 & 0.044 \\ 0.25 & 0 \end{bmatrix} \begin{bmatrix} u_1 \\ u_2 \end{bmatrix}$$

$$+ \begin{bmatrix} 0 & 0 \\ 0 & 0.111 \\ 0.0625 & 0 \end{bmatrix} \begin{bmatrix} d_1 \\ d_2 \end{bmatrix} \qquad \begin{bmatrix} y_1 \\ y_2 \end{bmatrix} = \begin{bmatrix} 1 & 0 & 0 \\ 0 & 1 & 1 \end{bmatrix} \begin{bmatrix} x_1 \\ x_2 \\ x_3 \end{bmatrix}$$

and is an equivalent minimal realization of the transfer function relationship, Eq. (3.2.44).

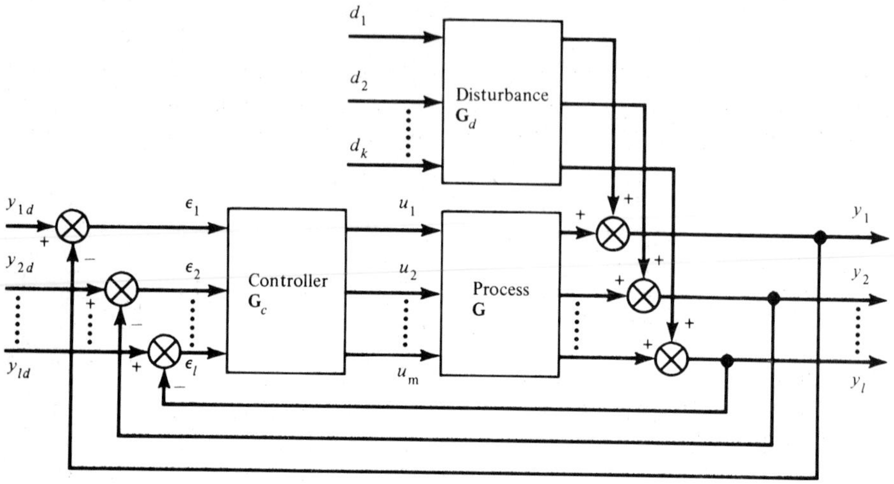

Figure 3.3 Multivariable block diagram.

Multivariable Block Diagrams

Having developed the facility to readily convert linear constant-coefficient systems between the time domain and the transform domain, it is now useful to consider multivariable feedback control loops. As a preliminary, let us discuss the meaning of the simple multivariable block diagram shown in Fig. 3.3. In the transform domain, $\mathbf{G}(s)$ and $\mathbf{G}_d(s)$ are the plant transfer functions relating the control variables and disturbances to the process outputs,

$$\bar{\mathbf{y}}(s) = \mathbf{G}(s)\bar{\mathbf{u}}(s) + \mathbf{G}_d(s)\bar{\mathbf{d}}(s) \tag{3.2.45}$$

Here $\mathbf{G}(s)$ and $\mathbf{G}_d(s)$ are defined by Eq. (3.2.27), where the elements take the form*

$$g_{ij}(s) = \frac{K_{ij}\prod_p (1 + h_{ij}^p s)}{\prod_p (1 + e_{ij}^p s)} \tag{3.2.46}$$

for lumped parameter systems. The parameters are

K_{ij}—transfer-function gain	$(-h_{ij}^p)^{-1}$ — transfer-function zeros
	$(-e_{ij}^p)^{-1}$ — transfer-function poles

It is interesting to realize that these block diagrams may also be represented in the *time domain*. In this case, $\mathbf{G}$ and $\mathbf{G}_d$ may be thought of as integral operators. For the linear system equation (3.2.1) with initial condition $\mathbf{x}_0 = \mathbf{0}$, $\mathbf{G}$ is defined as

$$\mathbf{y}(t) = \langle \mathbf{G}(t), \mathbf{u}(t) \rangle \tag{3.2.47}$$

* As described in Chap. 4, sometimes time delays also appear in the transfer function.

where

$$\mathbf{G}(t) = \mathbf{C}\boldsymbol{\Phi}(t)\int_0^t \boldsymbol{\Phi}(r)^{-1}\mathbf{B}(r)(\cdot)\, dr \tag{3.2.48}$$

and the brackets $\langle \mathbf{L}, \mathbf{w} \rangle$ represent a general inner product operation of the operator $\mathbf{L}$ operating on the variable $\mathbf{w}$. This result comes directly from the analytical solution to Eq. (3.2.1):

$$\mathbf{x}(t) = \boldsymbol{\Phi}(t, t_0)\mathbf{x}_0 + \boldsymbol{\Phi}(t, t_0)\int_{t_0}^t \boldsymbol{\Phi}(r, t_0)^{-1}[\mathbf{B}(r)\mathbf{u}(r)]\, dr \tag{3.2.49}$$

$$\mathbf{y}(t) = \mathbf{C}\mathbf{x}(t) \tag{3.2.2}$$

where we recall that $\boldsymbol{\Phi}(t, t_0)$ is the $n \times n$ *fundamental matrix solution* defined by

$$\dot{\boldsymbol{\Phi}} = \mathbf{A}(t)\boldsymbol{\Phi} \qquad \boldsymbol{\Phi}(t_0, t_0) = \mathbf{I} \tag{3.2.12}$$

The block diagram in Fig. 3.3 also includes a multivariable controller $\mathbf{G}_c$ which can be written in either the transform or state space domain. Although $\mathbf{G}_c$ can have entries in all elements, it is very common to have multiple single-loop controllers where $\mathbf{G}_c$ takes the diagonal form

$$\mathbf{G}_c = \begin{bmatrix} g_{11_c} & & & \mathbf{0} \\ & g_{22_c} & & \\ & & \ddots & \\ \mathbf{0} & & & g_{ll_c} \end{bmatrix} \tag{3.2.50}$$

Here the single-loop controllers could be of the simple linear proportional-integral-derivative type. In the Laplace transform domain, these take the form

$$g_{ii_c}(s) = K_{c_i}\left(1 + \frac{1}{\tau_{I_i} s} + \tau_{D_i} s\right) \qquad i = 1, 2, \ldots, l \tag{3.2.51}$$

In the time domain, the single-loop controller action $u_i(t)$ is

$$u_i(t) = \langle \mathbf{G}_c, \boldsymbol{\varepsilon} \rangle_i = K_{c_i}\left[\varepsilon_i + \frac{1}{\tau_{I_i}}\int \varepsilon_i(t)\, dt + \tau_{D_i}\frac{d\varepsilon_i}{dt}\right] \tag{3.2.52}$$

where the output error signal is

$$\varepsilon_i(t) = y_{d_i}(t) - y_i(t) \tag{3.2.53}$$

Thus block diagrams such as Fig. 3.3 can represent linear systems in either the transform or state space domain.

The closed-loop operator equations for the block diagram shown in Fig. 3.3 can be found in the standard way by writing

$$\mathbf{y} = \mathbf{G}\mathbf{G}_c\boldsymbol{\varepsilon} + \mathbf{G}_d\mathbf{d} \tag{3.2.54}$$

$$\boldsymbol{\varepsilon} = \mathbf{y}_d - \mathbf{y} \tag{3.2.55}$$

where $\boldsymbol{\varepsilon}$ is the l vector of deviations from the set-point vector $\mathbf{y}_d$ and $\mathbf{d}$ is the process disturbance. Substituting Eq. (3.2.55) into Eq. (3.2.54) yields the closed-loop expression

$$\mathbf{y} = (\mathbf{I} + \mathbf{G}\mathbf{G}_c)^{-1}(\mathbf{G}\mathbf{G}_c\mathbf{y}_d + \mathbf{G}_d\mathbf{d}) \tag{3.2.56}$$

where for the transform domain, the inverse operation denotes matrix inversion. This expression may be simplified to

$$\mathbf{y} = \mathbf{T}\mathbf{y}_d + \mathbf{T}_d\mathbf{d} \tag{3.2.57}$$

where the closed-loop transfer functions $\mathbf{T}$ and $\mathbf{T}_d$ are defined by

$$\mathbf{T} = (\mathbf{I} + \mathbf{G}\mathbf{G}_c)^{-1}\mathbf{G}\mathbf{G}_c \tag{3.2.58}$$

$$\mathbf{T}_d = (\mathbf{I} + \mathbf{G}\mathbf{G}_c)^{-1}\mathbf{G}_d \tag{3.2.59}$$

We shall discuss methods of designing these multivariable controllers in the latter part of this chapter. However, we must first introduce some important concepts.

Let us recall the time-domain representation of our system,

$$\frac{d\mathbf{x}}{dt} = \mathbf{A}\mathbf{x} + \mathbf{B}\mathbf{u} + \mathbf{\Gamma}\mathbf{d} \qquad x(t_0) = x_0 \tag{3.2.1}$$

$$\mathbf{y} = \mathbf{C}\mathbf{x} \tag{3.2.2}$$

and consider some important properties of this system.

Controllability

One notion which is very useful in analyzing control systems is *controllability* [2, 6, 7]. Loosely speaking, a system may be said to be *controllable* if there exists a control policy $\mathbf{u}(t)$ which will steer the system from *any* given initial state $\mathbf{x}_0$ to *any other* desired state $\mathbf{x}_d$ in finite time. A more precise definition may be given as follows:

If every initial state $\mathbf{x}_0(t_0)$ *can be taken to any other state* $\mathbf{x}_d(t)$ *in some finite time* $t > t_0$, *then the system is completely controllable.* It is also possible to have systems which are only partially controllable, i.e., in which there are some subsets of initial states $\mathbf{x}_0(t_0)$ which cannot reach every other state in finite time.

It is possible to define conditions of controllability for specific classes of systems [2]. For example, if the matrices $\mathbf{A}$ and $\mathbf{B}$ are constant, then it can be shown [2, 7] that the system of Eqs. (3.2.1) and (3.2.2) is *completely controllable* if and only if the rank of an $n \times nm$ "controllability matrix" $\mathbf{L}_c$ is n, where

$$\mathbf{L}_c \equiv \left[\mathbf{B} \,\vdots\, \mathbf{A}\mathbf{B} \,\vdots\, \mathbf{A}^2\mathbf{B} \,\vdots\, \cdots \,\vdots\, \mathbf{A}^{n-1}\mathbf{B}\right] \tag{3.2.60}$$

An informal derivation of this result may be seen by considering the analytical solution to Eqs. (3.2.1) and (3.2.2).*

$$\mathbf{x}(t) = e^{\mathbf{A}t}\mathbf{x}_0 + \int_0^t e^{\mathbf{A}(t-s)}\mathbf{B}\mathbf{u}(s)\,ds \tag{3.2.61}$$

* We neglect the disturbances $\mathbf{d}(t)$ because *controllability* is a property of the system itself.

where the exponential matrix may be written [1]

$$e^{\mathbf{A}t} = \mathbf{I} + \mathbf{A}t + \tfrac{1}{2}\mathbf{A}^2t^2 + \cdots \tag{3.2.62}$$

which when combined with the Hamilton-Cayley theorem* [1] leads to the finite series representation

$$e^{\mathbf{A}t} = c_0\mathbf{I} + c_1\mathbf{A}t + c_2(\mathbf{A}t)^2 + \cdots + c_{n-1}(\mathbf{A}t)^{n-1} \tag{3.2.63}$$

Upon substitution of this into Eq. (3.2.61), one obtains

$$\mathbf{x}(t) = e^{\mathbf{A}t}\mathbf{x}_0 + \int_0^t \Big[c_0\mathbf{B} + c_1(t-s)\mathbf{AB} + \cdots + c_{n-1}(t-s)^{n-1}\mathbf{A}^{n-1}\mathbf{B}\Big]\mathbf{u}(s)\, ds \tag{3.2.64}$$

or

$$\mathbf{x}(t) = e^{\mathbf{A}t}\mathbf{x}_0 + \int_0^t \left[\, \mathbf{B} \,\vdots\, \mathbf{AB} \,\vdots\, \cdots \,\vdots\, \mathbf{A}^{n-1}\mathbf{B} \,\right] \begin{bmatrix} c_0\mathbf{u}(s) \\ \cdots\cdots \\ c_1(t-s)\mathbf{u}(s) \\ \cdots\cdots \\ \vdots \\ \cdots\cdots \\ c_{n-1}(t-s)^{n-1}\mathbf{u}(s) \end{bmatrix} ds \tag{3.2.65}$$

Now the concept of controllability means that the control $\mathbf{u}$ is capable of influencing all the states $\mathbf{x}$ through the integral in Eq. (3.2.65). Therefore the system is controllable if and only if the integrand in Eq. (3.2.65) allows the influence of $\mathbf{u}(t)$ to reach all the states $\mathbf{x}(t)$. This requires the $n \times nm$ matrix transformation

$$\left[\, \mathbf{B} \,\vdots\, \mathbf{AB} \,\vdots\, \cdots \,\vdots\, \mathbf{A}^{n-1}\mathbf{B} \,\right]$$

to have rank n.

Note that *output controllability* conditions can be found by multiplying Eq. (3.2.64) by $\mathbf{C}$ to yield

$$\mathbf{y}(t) = \mathbf{Cx} = \mathbf{C}e^{\mathbf{A}t}\mathbf{x}_0 + \int_0^t \Big[c_0\mathbf{CB} + c_1(t-s)\mathbf{CAB} + \cdots + c_{n-1}(t-s)^{n-1}\mathbf{CA}^{n-1}\mathbf{B}\Big]\mathbf{u}(s)\, ds \tag{3.2.66}$$

Thus, by the same arguments, the controls $\mathbf{u}(t)$ must influence all the l outputs $\mathbf{y}(t)$ for *output controllability*. This means that the outputs $\mathbf{y}$ are *completely controllable* if and only if the rank of the $l \times nm$ controllability matrix $\mathbf{L}_c^\circ$ is l, where

$$\mathbf{L}_c^\circ = \left[\, \mathbf{CB} \,\vdots\, \mathbf{CAB} \,\vdots\, \cdots \,\vdots\, \mathbf{CA}^{n-1}\mathbf{B} \,\right] \tag{3.2.67}$$

* This theorem states that every matrix satisfies its own characteristic equation; thus every infinite series can be reduced to an n-term series.

Controllability conditions for the case of a *linear nonautonomous system* of the form of Eq. (3.2.1), when $\mathbf{A}(t)$, $\mathbf{B}(t)$ are known functions of time, specify that the nonsingularity of the $n \times n$ matrix

$$\mathbf{M}(t_0, t_f) = \int_{t_0}^{t_f} \mathbf{\Phi}(t, t_0)^{-1}\mathbf{B}(t)\mathbf{B}^T(t)\left[\mathbf{\Phi}(t, t_0)^T\right]^{-1} dt \qquad (3.2.68)$$

is necessary and sufficient for controllability. Here the $n \times n$ matrix $\mathbf{\Phi}(t, t_0)$ is the *fundamental matrix solution* defined by

$$\dot{\mathbf{\Phi}}(t, t_0) = \mathbf{A}(t)\mathbf{\Phi}(t, t_0) \qquad \mathbf{\Phi}(t_0, t_0) = \mathbf{I} \qquad (3.2.12)$$

The proof is straightforward [2], but shall not be given here. Note that since the integrand of Eq. (3.2.68) is positive semidefinite, it is sufficient for controllability that the integrand be nonsingular for any instant of time $t_0 < t < t_f$.

Let us illustrate these points with a few examples.

Example 3.2.5 Let us consider an isothermal continuous-stirred tank reactor CSTR with the irreversible first-order reactions $A \overset{k_1}{\to} B \overset{k_3}{\to} C$ taking place.

The rates of reactions are given by

$$r_1 = k_1 c_A$$

$$r_2 = k_3 c_B$$

where k_1 and k_3 are constants.

The modeling equations for this system take the form

$$V\frac{dc_A}{dt'} = F(c_{Af} - c_A) - V(k_1 c_A) \qquad c_A(0) = c_{A0}$$

$$V\frac{dc_B}{dt'} = F(c_{Bf} - c_B) + V(k_1 c_A - k_3 c_B) \qquad c_B(0) = c_{B0}$$

It is required to control c_A, c_B as close as possible to a desired set point c_{Ad}, c_{Bd} by adjusting c_{Af} and c_{Bf}, the feed concentrations of A and B. Let us now define

$$\mathrm{Da}_1 = \frac{k_1 V}{F} \qquad \mathrm{Da}_3 = \frac{k_3 V}{F} \qquad t = \frac{t'F}{V}$$

$$x_1 = \frac{c_A}{c_{A\,\mathrm{ref}}} \qquad x_2 = \frac{c_B}{c_{A\,\mathrm{ref}}} \qquad u_1 = \frac{c_{Af}}{c_{A\,\mathrm{ref}}} \qquad u_2 = \frac{c_{Bf}}{c_{A\,\mathrm{ref}}}$$

where $c_{A\,\mathrm{ref}}$ is an arbitrary reference concentration of A. In this instance, the modeling equations take the form

$$\frac{dx_1}{dt} = -(1 + \mathrm{Da}_1)x_1 + u_1 \qquad x_1(t_0) = x_{10}$$

$$\frac{dx_2}{dt} = \mathrm{Da}_1 x_1 - (1 + \mathrm{Da}_3)x_2 + u_2 \qquad x_2(t_0) = x_{20}$$

Thus one wishes to control the reactor outlet concentration x_1, x_2 by adjusting the feed concentrations u_1, u_2. By putting these equations into the general form of Eq. (3.2.1), the controllability criterion may be tested by noting that

$$\mathbf{A} = \begin{bmatrix} -(1 + \mathrm{Da}_1) & 0 \\ \mathrm{Da}_1 & -(1 + \mathrm{Da}_3) \end{bmatrix} \qquad \mathbf{B} = \begin{bmatrix} 1 & 0 \\ 0 & 1 \end{bmatrix}$$

and the "controllability matrix" is

$$\mathbf{L}_c = \left[\begin{array}{cc:cc} 1 & 0 & -(1 + \mathrm{Da}_1) & 0 \\ 0 & 1 & \mathrm{Da}_1 & -(1 + \mathrm{Da}_3) \end{array}\right]$$

Clearly the rank of $\mathbf{L}_c$ is two for this second-order system, so that the system is completely controllable.

Example 3.2.6 Let us now consider the question of *controllability* of the reactor in Example 3.2.5 with the modification that $u_2 = c_{Bf}/c_{A\,\mathrm{ref}} \equiv 0$ and only u_1, the feed concentration of A, may be manipulated to control the reactor. In this case $\mathbf{A}$ is given as before, but $\mathbf{B}$ and $\mathbf{L}_c$ take the form

$$\mathbf{b} = \begin{bmatrix} 1 \\ 0 \end{bmatrix} \qquad \mathbf{L}_c = \left[\begin{array}{c:c} 1 & -(1 + \mathrm{Da}_1) \\ 0 & \mathrm{Da}_1 \end{array}\right]$$

Again the rank of $\mathbf{L}_c$ is two, so that the reactor is completely controllable with only control variable u_1. However, the controller performance would surely be poorer than for the case when both u_1 and u_2 are available.

Stabilizability

A much weaker condition than *controllability* for a system is the property of *stabilizability* [2]. *Stabilizability is the property that all the unstable modes of the system Eq.* (3.2.1), *can be made stable by controller action.* This means that any positive eigenvalues of $\mathbf{A}$ may be made negative by controller action. Clearly then, any system with $\mathbf{A}$ having all negative eigenvalues is stabilizable (in fact, even without controller action). In addition, any system which is controllable is automatically stabilizable.

In the case of the constant-gain proportional feedback controller on the state variables

$$\mathbf{u}(t) = -\mathbf{K}\mathbf{x}(t) \tag{3.2.69}$$

where $\mathbf{K}$ is an $m \times n$ feedback matrix of controller gains, the system of Eq. (3.2.1) becomes

$$\frac{d\mathbf{x}}{dt} = (\mathbf{A} - \mathbf{BK})\mathbf{x} \tag{3.2.70}$$

The system would then be *stabilizable* with such a feedback controller if and only if there existed a combination of feedback gains k_{ij} which would cause the real parts of all the eigenvalues of $(\mathbf{A} - \mathbf{BK})$ to be negative.

With a proportional controller on the output variables

$$\mathbf{u}(t) = -\mathbf{K}\mathbf{y}(t) \tag{3.2.71}$$

the system of Eq. (3.2.1) takes the form

$$\frac{d\mathbf{x}}{dt} = (\mathbf{A} - \mathbf{BKC})\mathbf{x} \tag{3.2.72}$$

In this case, stabilizability requires that the real parts of all the eigenvalues of $(\mathbf{A} - \mathbf{BKC})$ be negative for some selection of the feedback gains k_{ij}.

We shall illustrate these points with an example problem.

Example 3.2.7 Let us consider the reactor problem of Example 3.2.5 except now c_{Af} is fixed and only c_{Bf} may be adjusted to control c_A and c_B. In this case let us define

$$x_1 = \frac{c_A}{c_{Af}} - \frac{1}{1 + \mathrm{Da}_1} \qquad x_2 = \frac{c_B}{c_{Af}} \qquad t = \frac{t'F}{V} \qquad \mathrm{Da}_1 = \frac{k_1 V}{F}$$

$$\mathrm{Da}_3 = \frac{k_3 V}{F} \qquad u_1 = \frac{c_{Bf}}{c_{Af}} + \frac{\mathrm{Da}_1}{1 + \mathrm{Da}_1}$$

so that the modeling equations take the form

$$\frac{dx_1}{dt} = -(1 + \mathrm{Da}_1)x_1 \qquad x_1(t_0) = x_{10} \tag{3.2.73}$$

$$\frac{dx_2}{dt} = \mathrm{Da}_1 x_1 - (1 + \mathrm{Da}_3)x_2 + u_1 \qquad x_2(t_0) = x_{20} \tag{3.2.74}$$

In this instance, the **A** matrix is given as before and

$$\mathbf{b} = \begin{bmatrix} 0 \\ 1 \end{bmatrix} \qquad \mathbf{L}_c = \left[\begin{array}{c:c} 0 & 0 \\ 1 & -(1 + \mathrm{Da}_3) \end{array}\right]$$

Here the controllability matrix $\mathbf{L}_c$ is singular and the system is *not* completely controllable. Only the state x_2 can be controlled by u_1, and x_1 is completely free. However, from the solution of Eq. (3.2.73), one sees that

$$x_1(t) = x_{10}\exp[-(1 + \mathrm{Da}_1)(t - t_0)]$$

so that the eigenvalue associated with x_1 is always negative and x_1 is stable. Thus the system of Eqs. (3.2.73) and (3.2.74) is stabilizable. In practical terms, this means that while both concentrations A and B *cannot* be controlled by adjusting the feed rate of B (only B can be controlled in this manner), the concentration of A is stable and will approach the steady state unaffected by whatever control action is taken. Thus one could successfully design a control system for Eqs. (3.2.73) and (3.2.74) even though the system is not controllable.

Let us review the implications of *controllability* and *stabilizability* in the light of these three examples. First, a control system can always be designed for a *completely controllable system* and is *sometimes* impossible to design for one which is not *completely controllable*. If the system is *stabilizable* (but not completely controllable) and the uncontrollable eigenvalues of the system are sufficiently large and negative, then an acceptable control system design is possible. However, if the system is *not stabilizable*, then control is generally impossible.

For Examples 3.2.5 to 3.2.7, the use of control variables c_{Af}, c_{Bf} together or c_{Af} alone will allow the CSTR to be completely controlled, but c_{Bf} alone cannot completely control the reactor. Physically this is due to the fact that there is kinetic coupling from c_A to c_B but not in reverse, i.e., the rate of formation of B depends on c_A, and thus the control of c_A by c_{Af} is sufficient to control c_B as well. In contrast, the rate of formation of A is independent of c_B, and thus controlling c_B exercises no control over c_A. Had the first reaction been reversible in Example 3.2.7, then the reverse coupling would exist and the system would have been controllable with c_{Bf} alone.

Normality

A stronger form of controllability is called *normality* [2]. A system is said to be *normal* if each element of the control vector **u** *alone* will achieve controllability. This will be true if and only if the *normality matrix* $\mathbf{L}_{c_i}$,

$$\mathbf{L}_{c_i} \equiv \left[\mathbf{b}_i \vdots \mathbf{A}\mathbf{b}_i \vdots \mathbf{A}^2\mathbf{b}_i \vdots \cdots \vdots \mathbf{A}^{n-1}\mathbf{b}_i\right] \tag{3.2.75}$$

has rank n *for all* i, where $\mathbf{b}_i$, $i = 1, 2, \ldots, m$, are the columns of the matrix $\mathbf{B}$. Thus the CSTR control system discussed in Example 3.2.5 is *completely controllable* but not *normal* because u_2 alone will not cause the system to be controllable. For scalar control variables, normality and controllability are identical properties.

The Interaction Problem

The fundamental problem in designing multivariable feedback controllers lies in the steady-state and dynamic interactions which occur between the various input and output variables. If the system had no coupling between variables and the number of control variables equaled the number of outputs to be controlled, then the linear system of Eq. (3.2.1) in the transform domain would have a diagonal open-loop transfer function

$$\mathbf{G}(s) = \mathbf{C}(s\mathbf{I} - \mathbf{A})^{-1}\mathbf{B} = \begin{bmatrix} g_{11}(s) & & \mathbf{0} \\ & g_{22}(s) & \\ & & \ddots \\ \mathbf{0} & & g_{ll}(s) \end{bmatrix} \tag{3.2.76}$$

and for $\mathbf{G}_c$ in the diagonal form, Eq. (3.2.50), the closed-loop transfer function, Eq. (3.2.58), relating $\mathbf{y}$ to $\mathbf{y}_d$ would then be diagonal and each control loop could be tuned separately by classical methods.

Unfortunately, most multivariable systems have significant coupling between outputs and controls, and these pose great difficulties in control system design. To illustrate these problems, consider the following example.

Example 3.2.8 You are working for XYZ Chemical Co. in their engineering department and the plant supervisor comes to you with a control problem. In the plant is a large binary distillation column, sketched schematically in Fig. 3.4. There are four product streams drawn from this tower, with concentrations of the heavier component in the top three sidestreams denoted by y_1, y_2, and y_3. The bottoms must satisfy an overall material balance. The compositions of these products at each drawoff point have specifications y_{1d}, y_{2d}, and y_{3d} and are controlled by adjusting the drawoff rates, u_1, u_2, and u_3. Currently the tower is run by manual control because the present single-loop PID controllers do not work well. They produce considerable offset and occasionally cause the sidestream compositions to continuously oscillate. Under manual operation there are no oscillations, but there are still significant deviations from the set point which require hours of time and many trial-and-error manual adjustments to eliminate. As an indication of the problem, the plant supervisor asks you to consider Fig. 3.5, where the operator successfully adjusts y_2 to a new set point by increasing flow rate u_2 and decreasing flow rate u_1 by an equal amount. This causes the concentration of the less volatile component at sidestream 2, y_2,

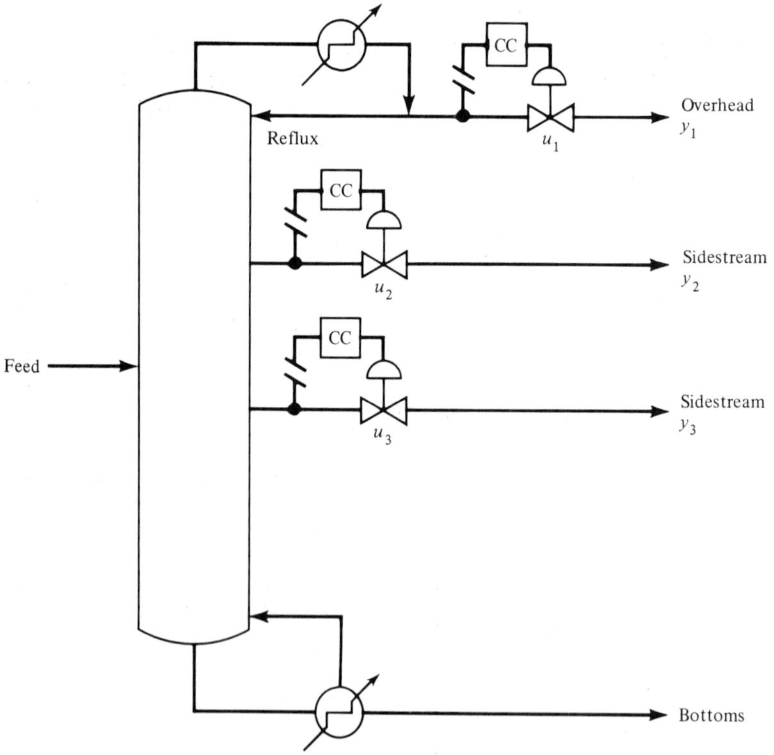

Figure 3.4 Multi-sidestream distillation column.

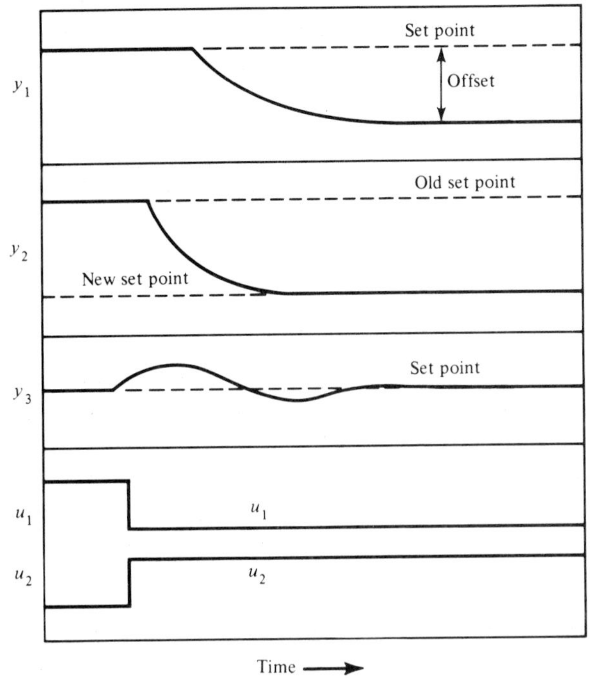

Figure 3.5 Open-loop response of the distillation column to manual adjustments of u_1 and u_2.

to decrease to the new set-point value.* However as can be seen, the concentration drawn overhead does not remain constant but decreases also. The concentration y_3 at sidestream 2 first increases and finally decreases to approximately the old operating point. Thus, by successfully meeting the new specification on y_2, the operator has thrown y_1 off specification and must now work on correcting this by adjusting u_1. This begins a whole new round of detrimental interactions, and meanwhile the column is making many tons per hour of off-specification product.

Note that because of dynamic interactions which can cause temporary deviations in the wrong direction, after each adjustment, the operator must wait for the transients to die out to determine if this action is a success. The plant engineer asks for your help to develop a better controller for this tower.†

As a good control engineer, you first request that some modeling work be carried out on the column. Thus step input test data are fit to a rather simple transfer function relating the flow rates $\mathbf{u}$ to the sidestream composition $\bar{\mathbf{y}}(s)$, i.e.,

$$\bar{\mathbf{y}}(s) = \mathbf{G}\bar{\mathbf{u}}(s)$$

* The operator uses this approach because he has learned that this usually doesn't cause y_3 to be thrown too far off specification.

† Chapter 6 contains a further treatment of this example problem.

where **G**(*s*) has been found as

$$\mathbf{G}(s) = \begin{bmatrix} \dfrac{0.7}{1+9s} & 0 & 0 \\ \dfrac{2.0}{1+8s} & \dfrac{0.4}{1+6s} & 0 \\ \dfrac{2.3}{1+10s} & \dfrac{2.3}{1+8s} & \dfrac{2.1}{1+7s} \end{bmatrix} \tag{3.2.77}$$

Some interpretation of this model shows that all the responses between flow rates u_j and sidestream compositions y_i can be considered first-order. However, one should note that in actuality the system is of much higher order (order $\simeq$ number of trays between drawoffs). In practice, time delay terms $e^{-\alpha_{ij}s}$ would often appear, but for smaller columns, these delays may be negligible and have been neglected here. The model shows that there are significant interactions between variables, and in fact, the diagonal terms are not even dominant. Note that the interactions are one way, i.e., the adjustment of a drawoff rate affects all stream concentrations below it, but none above. This is the easiest type of process interaction to deal with.

Let us try to understand the difficulties encountered by the operators. The present column feedback control scheme, which was taken out of service, is of the form shown in Fig. 3.3, where

$$\mathbf{G}_c = \begin{bmatrix} g_{11_c}(s) & 0 & 0 \\ 0 & g_{22_c}(s) & 0 \\ 0 & 0 & g_{33_c}(s) \end{bmatrix}$$

represents three single-loop PI controllers. From Eq. (3.2.56), the closed-loop transfer function for the column is

$$\bar{\mathbf{y}} = \mathbf{T}\bar{\mathbf{y}}_d \tag{3.2.78}$$

where

$$\mathbf{T} = (\mathbf{I} + \mathbf{G}\mathbf{G}_c)^{-1}\mathbf{G}\mathbf{G}_c = \mathbf{I} - (\mathbf{I} + \mathbf{G}\mathbf{G}_c)^{-1} \tag{3.2.58}$$

and

$$\mathbf{G}\mathbf{G}_c = \begin{bmatrix} \dfrac{0.7g_{11_c}}{1+9s} & 0 & 0 \\ \dfrac{2.0g_{11_c}}{1+8s} & \dfrac{0.4g_{22_c}}{1+6s} & 0 \\ \dfrac{2.3g_{11_c}}{1+10s} & \dfrac{2.3g_{22_c}}{1+8s} & \dfrac{2.1g_{33_c}}{1+7s} \end{bmatrix} \tag{3.2.79}$$

Thus

$$\mathbf{T} = \begin{bmatrix} \dfrac{0.7g_{11_c}}{1+9s+0.7g_{11_c}} & 0 & 0 \\ \dfrac{2.0g_{11_c}(1+9s)(1+6s)}{(1+8s)(1+9s+0.7g_{11_c})(1+6s+0.4g_{22_c})} & \dfrac{0.4g_{22_c}}{1+6s+0.4g_{22_c}} & 0 \\ \dfrac{\left[\dfrac{2.3g_{11_c}}{1+10s}\left(\dfrac{0.4g_{22_c}}{1+6s}+1\right) - \dfrac{4.6g_{11_c}g_{22_c}}{(1+8s)^2}\right](1+9s)(1+6s)(1+7s)}{(1+9s+0.7g_{11_c})(1+6s+0.4g_{22_c})(1+7s+2.1g_{33_c})} & \dfrac{2.3g_{22_c}(1+6s)(1+7s)}{(1+8s)(1+6s+0.4g_{22_c})(1+7s+2.1g_{33_c})} & \dfrac{2.1g_{33_c}}{1+7s+2.1g_{33_c}} \end{bmatrix} \tag{3.280}$$

Observe that there are significant off-diagonal terms in **T** corresponding to strong dynamic and steady-state interactions in the system. This easily explains how operating difficulties with the present control scheme could arise if the controllers were not carefully tuned. Note that because the interactions are only one way, the controllers could, in principle, be tuned one at a time, starting at the top of the column. Nevertheless, the control system performance could be greatly improved by a better control system design which would minimize the effects of interaction.

Let us now consider another example problem where the transfer function is full and interactions occur in both directions.

Example 3.2.9 Recall the simple mixing tank control problem shown in Fig. 3.2 and discussed in Example 3.2.1. If we assume that both the liquid level and tank temperature are measured, then the state variables and output variables are identical. Using Eq. (3.2.28) to convert to the Laplace domain,

$$\mathbf{G}(s) = \mathbf{C}(s\mathbf{I} - \mathbf{A})^{-1}\mathbf{B}$$

$$\mathbf{G}_d(s) = \mathbf{C}(s\mathbf{I} - \mathbf{A})^{-1}\mathbf{\Gamma}$$

or

$$\mathbf{G}(s) = \begin{bmatrix} 1 & 0 \\ 0 & 1 \end{bmatrix} \begin{bmatrix} s + \frac{1}{2}\frac{F(h_s)}{A_c h_s} & 0 \\ 0 & s + \frac{F(h_s)}{A_c h_s} \end{bmatrix}^{-1} \begin{bmatrix} \frac{1}{A_c} & \frac{1}{A_c} \\ \frac{T_H - T_s}{A_c h_s} & \frac{T_C - T_s}{A_c h_s} \end{bmatrix}$$

$$\mathbf{G}(s) = \begin{bmatrix} \dfrac{1}{A_c\left(s + \frac{1}{2}\frac{F(h_s)}{A_c h_s}\right)} & \dfrac{1}{A_c\left(s + \frac{1}{2}\frac{F(h_s)}{A_c h_s}\right)} \\ \dfrac{T_H - T_s}{A_c h_s\left(s + \frac{F(h_s)}{A_c h_s}\right)} & \dfrac{T_C - T_s}{A_c h_s\left(s + \frac{F(h_s)}{A_c h_s}\right)} \end{bmatrix}$$

$$\mathbf{G}_d(s) = \begin{bmatrix} 1 & 0 \\ 0 & 1 \end{bmatrix} \begin{bmatrix} s + \frac{1}{2}\frac{F(h_s)}{A_c h_s} & 0 \\ 0 & s + \frac{F(h_s)}{A_c h_s} \end{bmatrix}^{-1} \begin{bmatrix} \frac{1}{A_c} & 0 \\ \frac{T_{ds} - T_s}{A_c h_s} & \frac{F_{ds}}{A_c h_s} \end{bmatrix}$$

$$\mathbf{G}_d(s) = \begin{bmatrix} \dfrac{1}{A_c\left(s + \frac{1}{2}\frac{F(h_s)}{A_c h_s}\right)} & 0 \\ \dfrac{T_{ds} - T_s}{A_c h_s\left(s + \frac{F(h_s)}{A_c h_s}\right)} & \dfrac{F_{ds}}{A_c h_s\left(s + \frac{F(h_s)}{A_c h_s}\right)} \end{bmatrix}$$

Thus changing either tank inlet flow rate, u_1 or u_2, influences both the level and the temperature; hence coupling is in both directions.

Efforts have been made to establish measures of interaction in multivariable processes. Perhaps the most widely used measure is the Bristol array [8], which measures the degree of steady-state interaction. To illustrate the application of the Bristol array, consider the 2×2 multivariable system shown in Fig. 3.6. The conventional method of tuning the control system would be to first open loop 2 and tune loop 1 so that y_1 has a good response, then open loop 1 and tune loop 2 until y_2 has a good response. If there were *no interaction* ($g_{12} = g_{21} = 0$), one could then close both loops and expect the control system to work well. However, in the presence of interactions, the overall control system performance could be quite poor when both loops are closed. Bristol [8] developed a general measure of this interaction in the steady state in a form of the so-called *Bristol*

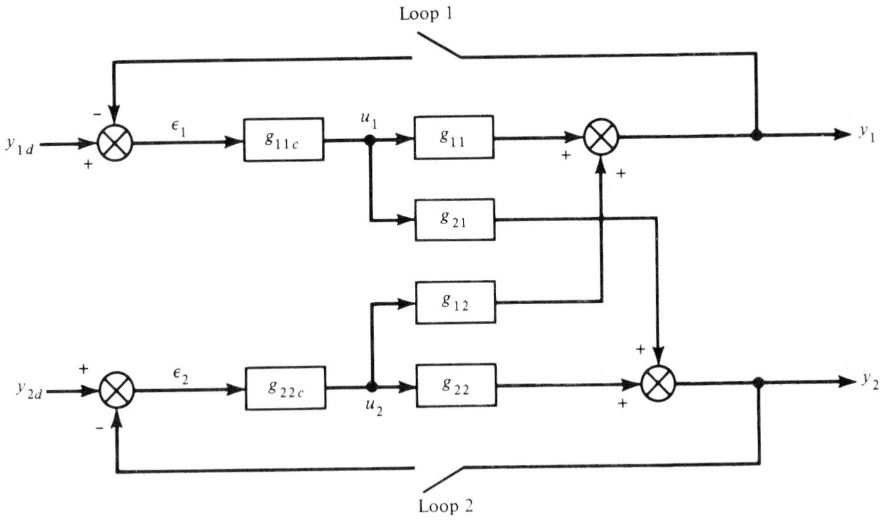

Figure 3.6 2 × 2 multivariable system undergoing sequential tuning of conventional controllers.

array:

$$\Lambda = \begin{bmatrix} \lambda_{11} & \lambda_{12} & \cdots & \lambda_{1m} \\ \lambda_{21} & \cdots & \cdots & \cdots \\ \cdots & \cdots & \cdots & \cdots \\ \lambda_{m1} & \cdots & \cdots & \lambda_{mm} \end{bmatrix}$$

whose elements are defined as the steady-state ratio:

$$\lambda_{ij} \equiv \frac{\left\{\dfrac{\partial y_i}{\partial u_j}\right\}_{\text{all loops open}}}{\left\{\dfrac{\partial y_i}{\partial u_j}\right\}_{\substack{\text{all loops closed}\\ \text{except for } u_j}}} \qquad i, j = 1, 2, \ldots, m$$

The elements of the Bristol array are then the ratio of the steady-state open-loop response and the steady-state closed-loop response when a particular manipulated variable is adjusted. It is straightforward to determine the elements of the Bristol array, for the numerator is simply the i, jth element of the open-loop steady-state transfer function, i.e., $\lim_{s \to 0} g_{ij}(s)$. The denominator is calculated assuming that all the closed loops work perfectly, so that y_k is constant for $k \neq j$. Thus

$$\left\{\frac{\partial y_i}{\partial u_j}\right\}_{\substack{\text{all loops closed}\\ \text{except for } u_j}} \equiv \left\{\frac{\partial y_i}{\partial u_j}\right\}_{y_k \text{ constant}, i \neq k} = \left\{\frac{\partial u_j}{\partial y_k}\right\}^{-1}_{y_k \text{ constant}, i \neq k}$$

However, $\{\partial u_j/\partial y_i]$ is just the j, ith element of the inverse of the steady-state process transfer function, i.e.,

$$\frac{\partial u_j}{\partial y_i} = \lim_{s \to 0} \left[\mathbf{G}^{-1}(s) \right]_{ji}$$

Thus

$$\lambda_{ij} \equiv \left[\mathbf{G}(0) \right]_{ij} \left[\mathbf{G}(0)^{T-1} \right]_{ij}$$

where $[\ ]_{ij}$ denotes the i, jth element of the matrix in question.

To illustrate the application of the Bristol array, consider the 2×2 system shown in Fig. 3.6 with

$$\lim_{s \to 0} \mathbf{G}(s) = \begin{bmatrix} k_{11} & k_{12} \\ k_{21} & k_{22} \end{bmatrix}$$

Then

$$\left[\mathbf{G}(0)^T \right]^{-1} = \frac{\begin{bmatrix} k_{22} & -k_{21} \\ -k_{12} & k_{11} \end{bmatrix}}{k_{11}k_{22} - k_{12}k_{22}}$$

and

$$\mathbf{\Lambda} = \frac{\begin{bmatrix} k_{11}k_{22} & -k_{21}k_{12} \\ -k_{21}k_{12} & k_{11}k_{22} \end{bmatrix}}{k_{11}k_{22} - k_{12}k_{21}}$$

Several things can be noted from this example which are general properties of the Bristol array:

1. The sum of any row or any column in the Bristol array is unity.
2. When the transfer function matrix is diagonal or is triangular, the Bristol array is the identity matrix.

From the definition of the interaction measure, it is clear that the best possible situation is to have all the off-diagonal terms near zero and the diagonal terms close to unity, i.e.,

$$\mathbf{\Lambda}_{\text{ideal}} = \begin{bmatrix} 1 & & & & \mathbf{0} \\ & 1 & & & \\ & & 1 & & \\ & & & \ddots & \\ \mathbf{0} & & & & 1 \end{bmatrix}$$

This means that there is little interaction and that the closed-loop behavior is similar to the open-loop behavior. As the off-diagonal terms increase in absolute magnitude and the diagonal terms depart from 1.0, more and more interaction is indicated.

Positive interaction arises when all elements of $\mathbf{\Lambda}$ are positive: this means that there is some interaction, and one must choose the loop pairings (u_i, y_i) to make the diagonal terms as close to unity as possible.

Negative interaction occurs when some of the elements of $\mathbf{\Lambda}$ are negative. This means that changing u_j in the closed-loop situation has just the opposite effect from changing u_j in the open-loop case—a potentially dangerous situation.

The Bristol array can be used as a guide in choosing the pairing of control and output variables. Some general rules for this pairing are:

1. From examining $\mathbf{G}(0)$, pair $\mathbf{u}$, $\mathbf{y}$ such that diagonal elements are largest relative to off-diagonal elements.
2. From examining $\mathbf{\Lambda}$, pair $\mathbf{u}$, $\mathbf{y}$ such that diagonal terms are dominant and close to unity in absolute value. If some diagonal terms are negative, then all must be negative for good performance.

Example 3.2.10 Let us consider the pairing of control loops for the distillation column in Example 3.2.8, where

$$\mathbf{G}(0) = \begin{bmatrix} 0.7 & 0 & 0 \\ 2.0 & 0.4 & 0 \\ 2.3 & 2.3 & 2.1 \end{bmatrix} \qquad \mathbf{G}(0)^{-1} = \begin{bmatrix} 1.43 & 0 & 0 \\ -7.14 & 2.5 & 0 \\ 6.26 & -2.74 & 0.48 \end{bmatrix}$$

Thus

$$\mathbf{\Lambda} = \begin{bmatrix} 1.0 & 0 & 0 \\ 0 & 1.0 & 0 \\ 0 & 0 & 1.0 \end{bmatrix}$$

and the Bristol array predicts no serious steady-state intereactions because the coupling is only in one direction. Tuning can be carried out one loop at a time, i.e., loop 1 (u_1 versus y_1) can be tuned, then loop 2 (u_2 versus y_2), and then loop 3 (u_3 versus y_3). This procedure should, in principle, allow reasonable control system performance when all loops are closed. However, as shown in Chap. 6, there are still interaction problems with these columns, and more sophisticated multivariable controller designs can be helpful.

Example 3.2.11 Let us now consider the stirred tank of Example 3.2.1 where we pair the control and output variables as shown in Fig. 3.2; i.e., the level is controlled by adjusting the hot stream, and the tank temperature by manipulating the cold stream. Recall from Example 3.2.9 that

$$\bar{\mathbf{y}} = \mathbf{G}(s)\bar{\mathbf{u}}$$

where

$$\mathbf{G}(s) = \begin{bmatrix} \dfrac{1}{A_c\left[s + \dfrac{1}{2}\dfrac{F(h_s)}{A_c h_s}\right]} & \dfrac{1}{A_c\left[s + \dfrac{1}{2}\dfrac{F(h_s)}{A_c h_s}\right]} \\ \dfrac{T_H - T_s}{A_c h_s\left[s + \dfrac{F(h_s)}{A_c h_s}\right]} & \dfrac{T_C - T_s}{A_c h_s\left[s + \dfrac{F(h_s)}{A_c h_s}\right]} \end{bmatrix}$$

and

$$\mathbf{y} = \begin{bmatrix} y_1 \\ y_2 \end{bmatrix} \qquad \mathbf{u} = \begin{bmatrix} u_1 \\ u_2 \end{bmatrix}$$

where y_1 represents the tank level and y_2 the tank temperature. Here u_1 is the flow rate of the hot stream and u_2 the flow rate of the cold stream. If we pair u_1 with y_1 and u_2 with y_2, as shown, it is interesting to calculate the Bristol array to check the interaction. Note that

$$\mathbf{G}(0) = \frac{1}{F(h_s)}\begin{bmatrix} 2h_s & 2h_s \\ T_H - T_s & T_C - T_s \end{bmatrix}$$

$$\mathbf{G}^T(0)^{-1} = \frac{F(h_s)}{2h_s(T_C - T_H)}\begin{bmatrix} T_C - T_s & -(T_H - T_s) \\ -2h_s & 2h_s \end{bmatrix}$$

so that the Bristol array becomes

$$\mathbf{\Lambda} = \begin{bmatrix} \dfrac{T_C - T_s}{T_C - T_H} & \dfrac{-(T_H - T_s)}{T_C - T_h} \\ \dfrac{-(T_H - T_s)}{T_C - T_H} & \dfrac{T_C - T_s}{T_C - T_H} \end{bmatrix}$$

where we recall that T_C, T_H, and T_s are the temperatures of the cold inlet stream, the hot inlet stream, and the steady-state exit temperature, respectively. Note that since $T_C \leq T_s \leq T_H$, all the elements of $\mathbf{\Lambda}$ are positive, so that only *positive interactions* are possible. Furthermore, if the steady-state operating temperature T_s is close to the hot-stream temperature T_H, the Bristol array predicts diagonal elements close to unity, and the present loop pairing will be good.

If, on the other hand, the steady-state temperature T_s is close to the cold-stream temperature T_C, then the diagonal elements in the Bristol array are almost zero and the loop pairing should be switched for good performance. In the event that T_s is midway between T_C and T_H, then

$$\mathbf{\Lambda} = \begin{bmatrix} 0.5 & 0.5 \\ 0.5 & 0.5 \end{bmatrix}$$

and neither loop pairing will be very good. Very difficult interactions will be present. This example illustrates the fact that the amount of interaction can depend on the steady-state operating condition in some problems.

It should be emphasized that the Bristol array is only a measure of *steady-state interactions*. Although a great deal of work has been devoted to the study of *dynamic interactions*, there is, as yet, no generally accepted measure of dynamic interaction comparable to the Bristol array. Such a measure would be useful because it is sometimes possible to have significant dynamic interactions in the absence of important steady-state interactions.

Noninteracting Control

The performance of a multivariable control system can often be significantly improved by some type of compensation which accounts for interactions. Such improvement is possible even for systems which appear to have only weak interactions according to the Bristol array. There are numerous techniques for designing multivariable feedback controllers with compensation for interactions. One of the classical approaches to the problem is to design a *noninteracting controller* [9, 10]. To illustrate noninteracting control, let us assume that it is desired to control the process outputs $\mathbf{y}(t)$ by adjusting the controls $\mathbf{u}(t)$. The feedback control structure, making use of single-loop controllers and a *noninteraction compensator* $\mathbf{G}_I$, may be seen in Fig. 3.7. These single-loop controllers give $\mathbf{G}_c$ the diagonal form

$$\mathbf{G}_c = \begin{bmatrix} g_{11_c} & & & \mathbf{0} \\ & g_{22_c} & & \\ & & \ddots & \\ \mathbf{0} & & & g_{ll_c} \end{bmatrix} \tag{3.2.50}$$

The closed-loop transfer function for the noninteracting control scheme shown in Fig. 3.7 is

$$\bar{\mathbf{y}} = (\mathbf{I} + \mathbf{G}\mathbf{G}_I\mathbf{G}_c)^{-1}(\mathbf{G}\mathbf{G}_I\mathbf{G}_c\bar{\mathbf{y}}_d + \mathbf{G}_d\bar{\mathbf{d}}) \tag{3.2.81}$$

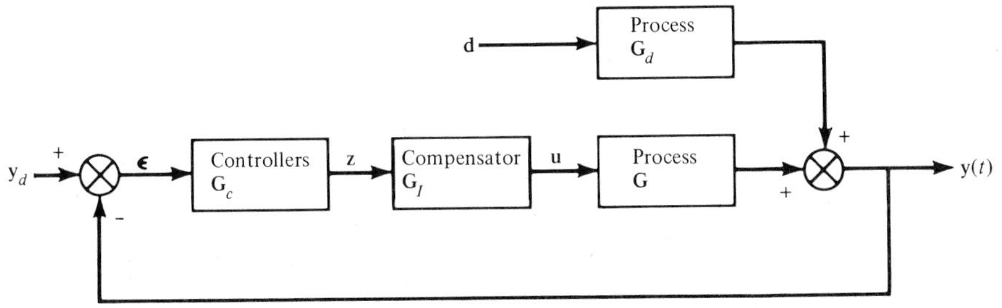

Figure 3.7 Multivariable controller structure which includes interaction compensator.

or

$$\bar{\mathbf{y}} = \mathbf{T}\bar{\mathbf{y}}_d + \mathbf{T}_d\bar{\mathbf{d}} \tag{3.2.57}$$

Here $\mathbf{G}_I$ is a compensator which must be designed to eliminate as much interaction as possible. Ideally $\mathbf{G}_I(s)$ should be chosen to make

$$\mathbf{T} = (\mathbf{I} + \mathbf{G}\mathbf{G}_I\mathbf{G}_c)^{-1}\mathbf{G}\mathbf{G}_I\mathbf{G}_c \tag{3.2.82}$$

diagonal and drive $\mathbf{T} \to \mathbf{I}$ for $s = 0$ ($t \to \infty$) for some choice of the controller tuning parameters (such as controller gain). Obviously noninteracting control only makes sense when $\mathbf{G}$, $\mathbf{G}_I$, $\mathbf{G}_c$ are square matrices (i.e., when the number of controls and outputs are the same).*

Recalling that $\mathbf{G}_c$ is diagonal, a sufficient condition for $\mathbf{T}$ to be diagonal and have $\mathbf{T}(0) \to \mathbf{I}$ as the controller gains increase is to require

$$\mathbf{G}\mathbf{G}_I = \text{diag } \mathbf{G}(s)$$

or

$$\mathbf{G}_I = \mathbf{G}^{-1} \text{ diag } \mathbf{G}(s) \tag{3.2.83}$$

where diag $\mathbf{G}(s)$ is a diagonal matrix having the diagonal elements of $\mathbf{G}(s)$ along the main diagonal, i.e.,

$$\text{diag } \mathbf{G}(s) = \begin{bmatrix} g_{11}(s) & & & \mathbf{0} \\ & g_{22}(s) & & \\ & & \ddots & \\ \mathbf{0} & & & g_{ll}(s) \end{bmatrix}$$

If this compensation were done perfectly, the closed-loop transfer function would take the form

$$\bar{\mathbf{y}}(s) = (\mathbf{I} + \mathbf{G}\mathbf{G}^{-1} \text{ diag } \mathbf{G}\mathbf{G}_c)^{-1}(\mathbf{G}\mathbf{G}^{-1} \text{ diag } \mathbf{G}\mathbf{G}_c\bar{\mathbf{y}}_d + \mathbf{G}_d\bar{\mathbf{d}})$$

or

$$\bar{y}_i(s) = \frac{g_{ii_c}(s)g_{ii}(s)}{1 + g_{ii_c}(s)g_{ii}(s)}\bar{y}_{id}(s)$$

$$+ \frac{1}{1 + g_{ii_c}(s)g_{ii}(s)} \sum_{j=1}^{k} g_{ij_d}(s)\bar{d}_j(s) \qquad i = 1, 2, \ldots, l \tag{3.2.84}$$

Notice that there is total decoupling for set-point changes, and that even though each disturbance may influence all the outputs, the effect of the disturbances on any output $\bar{y}_i$ is damped by a single controller g_{ii_c}.

* If there are more controls than outputs, $m > l$, then a subset of controls may be chosen to accomplish decoupling, while if there are more outputs than controls, $l > m$, then only partial decoupling is possible.

Sometimes it is difficult or impossible to accomplish perfect dynamic compensation of the form of Eq. (3.2.83); however, one may always carry out *steady-state decoupling*, which eliminates the steady-state interactions. This requires $\lim_{s\to 0} \mathbf{T}(s)$ in Eq. (3.2.82) to be diagonal. The *steady-state compensator* is given by

$$\mathbf{G}_{I_{ss}} = \lim_{s\to 0} \mathbf{G}_I(s) = \lim_{s\to 0} \left[\mathbf{G}(s)^{-1} \operatorname{diag} \mathbf{G}(s)\right] = \mathbf{G}_{ss}^{-1} \operatorname{diag} \mathbf{G}_{ss} \qquad (3.2.85)$$

In this case the closed-loop transfer functions takes the form

$$\bar{\mathbf{y}} = \left(\mathbf{I} + \mathbf{G}\mathbf{G}_{ss}^{-1} \operatorname{diag} \mathbf{G}_{ss}\mathbf{G}_c\right)^{-1}\left(\mathbf{G}\mathbf{G}_{ss}^{-1} \operatorname{diag} \mathbf{G}_{ss}\mathbf{G}_c\bar{\mathbf{y}}_d + \mathbf{G}_d\bar{\mathbf{d}}\right) \qquad (3.2.86)$$

With such *steady-state decoupling*, the steady-state interactions are eliminated, so that by increasing the controller gains, steady-state offset may more easily be decreased. Even so, there is still a period of dynamic interaction which could cause single-loop controllers to fight each other if they were too tightly tuned. For the same reasons, significant integral action in the controllers is usually not desired, for this often leads to controllers fighting with each other in an attempt to eliminate offset.

In our discussion, we have presented noninteracting control via *output feedback*. It is also possible to use *state feedback control* to accomplish decoupling if all the state variables can be measured or inferred [11].

We shall illustrate noninteracting controller design with an example problem.

Example 3.2.12 Let us consider the distillation column control problem discussed in Example 3.2.8 and design both static and dynamic noninteracting controllers for the column. For *steady-state decoupling*, $\mathbf{G}_{I_{ss}} = \mathbf{G}_{ss}^{-1} \operatorname{diag} \mathbf{G}_{ss}$, where we recall

$$\mathbf{G}(s) = \begin{bmatrix} \dfrac{0.7}{1+9s} & 0 & 0 \\ \dfrac{2.0}{1+8s} & \dfrac{0.4}{1+6s} & 0 \\ \dfrac{2.3}{1+10s} & \dfrac{2.3}{1+8s} & \dfrac{2.1}{1+7s} \end{bmatrix} \qquad (3.2.87)$$

$$\mathbf{G}_{ss} = \begin{bmatrix} 0.7 & 0 & 0 \\ 2.0 & 0.4 & 0 \\ 2.3 & 2.3 & 2.1 \end{bmatrix} \qquad \operatorname{diag} \mathbf{G}_{ss} = \begin{bmatrix} 0.7 & 0 & 0 \\ 0 & 0.4 & 0 \\ 0 & 0 & 2.1 \end{bmatrix} \qquad (3.2.88)$$

and thus

$$\mathbf{G}_{I_{ss}} = \begin{bmatrix} 1.43 & 0 & 0 \\ -7.14 & 2.50 & 0 \\ 6.26 & -2.74 & 0.48 \end{bmatrix} \begin{bmatrix} 0.7 & 0 & 0 \\ 0 & 0.4 & 0 \\ 0 & 0 & 2.1 \end{bmatrix} = \begin{bmatrix} 1 & 0 & 0 \\ -7.14 & 1 & 0 \\ 6.26 & -2.74 & 1 \end{bmatrix}$$

If we neglect disturbances for the moment, the noninteracting control scheme for the distillation column is shown in Fig. 3.8, where for static

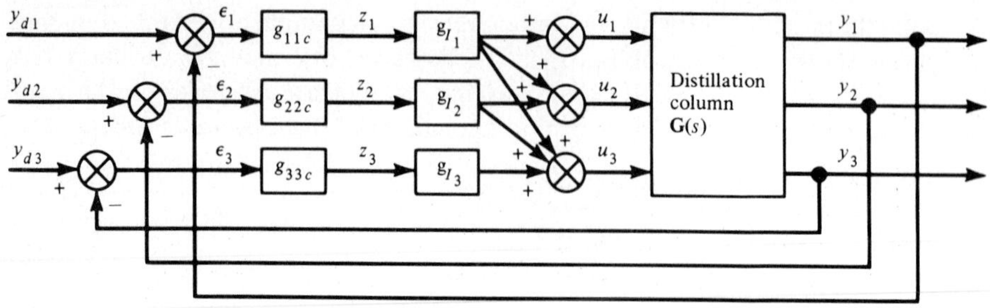

Figure 3.8 Noninteracting control of a distillation column.

decoupling,

$$\mathbf{g}_{I_1} = \begin{bmatrix} 1.00 \\ -7.14 \\ 6.26 \end{bmatrix} \qquad \mathbf{g}_{I_2} = \begin{bmatrix} 0 \\ 1.0 \\ -2.74 \end{bmatrix} \qquad \mathbf{g}_{I_3} = \begin{bmatrix} 0 \\ 0 \\ 1.0 \end{bmatrix} \tag{3.2.89}$$

Thus u_1 responds only to errors in y_1, while u_2 responds to errors in both y_1 and y_2, and u_3 responds to errors in all three output variables.

The *dynamic compensator design* for the column is of the form

$$\mathbf{G}_I = \mathbf{G}(s)^{-1} \operatorname{diag} \mathbf{G}(s) \tag{3.2.83}$$

where

$$\mathbf{G}^{-1}(s) = \begin{bmatrix} 1.43(1+9s) & 0 & 0 \\ -7.14\dfrac{(1+9s)(1+6s)}{1+8s} & 2.50(1+6s) & 0 \\ \left[\dfrac{7.82(1+9s)(1+6s)(1+7s)}{(1+8s)^2} - 1.56\dfrac{(1+9s)(1+7s)}{(1+10s)}\right] & \dfrac{-2.74(1+6s)(1+7s)}{(1+8s)} & 0.48(1+7s) \end{bmatrix}$$

(3.2.90)

and

$$\operatorname{diag} \mathbf{G}(s) = \begin{bmatrix} \dfrac{0.7}{1+9s} & 0 & 0 \\ 0 & \dfrac{0.4}{1+6s} & 0 \\ 0 & 0 & \dfrac{2.1}{1+7s} \end{bmatrix}$$

Hence

$$
\mathbf{G}_I(s) = \begin{bmatrix} 1 & 0 & 0 \\ \dfrac{-7.14(1+9s)(1+6s)}{1+8s} & 1 & 0 \\ \left[\dfrac{7.82(1+9s)(1+6s)(1+7s)}{(1+8s)^2} - \dfrac{-1.56(1+9s)(1+7s)}{1+10s}\right] & \dfrac{-2.74(1+6s)(1+7s)}{1+8s} & 1 \end{bmatrix}
$$

and the compensator blocks in Fig. 3.8 take the form

$$
\mathbf{g}_{I_1} = \begin{bmatrix} 1.0 \\ -7.14\dfrac{(1+9s)(1+6s)}{1+8s} \\ \dfrac{7.82(1+9s)(1+6s)(1+7s)}{(1+8s)^2} - 1.56\dfrac{(1+9s)(1+7s)}{1+10s} \end{bmatrix} \tag{3.2.91}
$$

$$
\mathbf{g}_{I_2} = \begin{bmatrix} 0 \\ 1.0 \\ \dfrac{-2.74(1+6s)(1+7s)}{(1+8s)} \end{bmatrix} \qquad \mathbf{g}_{I_3} = \begin{bmatrix} 0 \\ 0 \\ 1.0 \end{bmatrix}
$$

Note that for this example problem dynamic compensation requires differentiation of the signal coming from the single-loop controllers. The actual performance of steady-state and dynamic noninteracting control designs for this example problem will be described in Chap. 6.

Noninteracting controller design does not always work out as well as it did for the previous example. There can be conditions where implementation is difficult or impossible. For example, if the transfer function $\mathbf{G}(s)$ contains *time delays*, then the dynamic compensator will often contain *time leads*, requiring a knowledge of the outputs at some future time. Clearly this is impossible to implement exactly. However, in some cases, such a control scheme involving a predictor can yield reasonable results.

A problem encountered even more frequently results from the fact that perfect compensation requires a perfect transfer function model. Because the process model is often only approximate, the actual control scheme implemented will have the closed-loop transfer function

$$
\bar{\mathbf{y}} = \left(\mathbf{I} + \mathbf{G}^*\mathbf{G}^{-1} \operatorname{diag} \mathbf{G}\mathbf{G}_c\right)^{-1}\mathbf{G}^*\mathbf{G}^{-1} \operatorname{diag} \mathbf{G}\mathbf{G}_c\bar{\mathbf{y}}_d \tag{3.2.92}
$$

where $\mathbf{G}^*$ is the actual process and $\mathbf{G}^{-1}$ is the inverse of the process model. If the differences between the model and the process are too large, the control scheme behaves badly and can even become unstable.

These stability problems are most serious if there are right-half-plane zeros in the transfer function. These zeros become unstable poles in $\mathbf{G}_I$, and imperfect cancellation of these elements due to imperfections in the model can result in unstable poles in the transfer function.

Another potential disadvantage of noninteracting control is that a great deal of the control flexibility is used to achieve noninteraction, sometimes at the expense of overall dynamic response. In cases where some of the interactions greatly aid dynamic response, another type of controller design which takes advantage of these beneficial interactions (and only eliminates the most troublesome couplings) might be a better choice. We shall describe some alternative methods in what follows.

Set-Point Compensation

As an alternative means of eliminating *steady-state interactions* due to set-point changes, one may use *set-point compensation*. This scheme, which can be applied either directly to analog controllers by the operator or through supervisory computer control, compensates for steady-state offset due to set-point adjustments. Recall that for the control scheme shown in Fig. 3.3,

$$\bar{\mathbf{y}} = \mathbf{T}\bar{\mathbf{y}}_d + \mathbf{T}_d\bar{\mathbf{d}} \tag{3.2.57}$$

where $\mathbf{G}_c$ is a diagonal controller matrix and

$$\mathbf{T} = (\mathbf{I} + \mathbf{G}\mathbf{G}_c)^{-1}\mathbf{G}\mathbf{G}_c \tag{3.2.58}$$

is, in general, not diagonal. However, suppose Fig. 3.3 is altered to Fig. 3.9 by

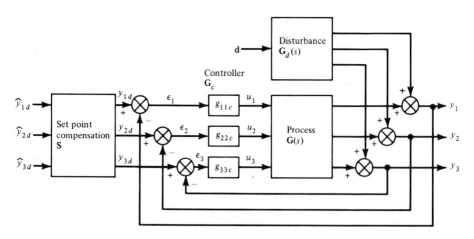

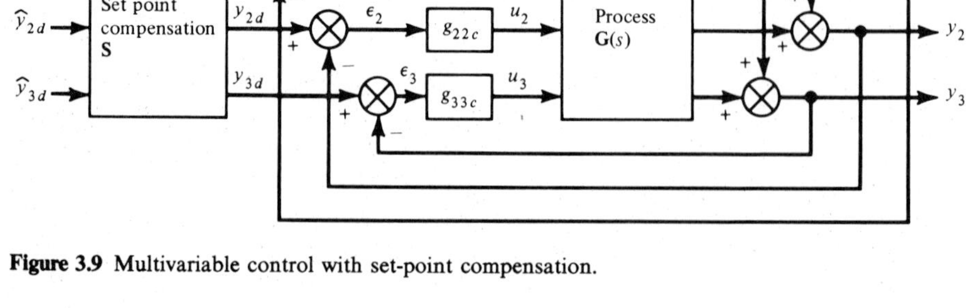

Figure 3.9 Multivariable control with set-point compensation.

the addition of the set-point compensator

$$\mathbf{y}_d = \mathbf{S}\hat{\mathbf{y}}_d \tag{3.2.93}$$

where $\hat{\mathbf{y}}_d$ is the actual set point desired and $\mathbf{S}$ is the set-point compensation matrix. For example, for the three-input, three-output system in Fig. 3.9,

$$\mathbf{S} = \begin{bmatrix} S_{11} & S_{12} & S_{13} \\ S_{21} & S_{22} & S_{23} \\ S_{31} & S_{32} & S_{33} \end{bmatrix}$$

Substitution of Eq. (3.2.93) into Eq. (3.2.57) yields

$$\bar{\mathbf{y}} = (\mathbf{I} + \mathbf{G}\mathbf{G}_c)^{-1}(\mathbf{G}\mathbf{G}_c\mathbf{S}\hat{\mathbf{y}}_d + \mathbf{G}_d\bar{\mathbf{d}}) \tag{3.2.94}$$

and $\mathbf{S}$ must be chosen so that

$$\hat{\mathbf{T}} = (\mathbf{I} + \mathbf{G}\mathbf{G}_c)^{-1}\mathbf{G}\mathbf{G}_c\mathbf{S} \tag{3.2.95}$$

is diagonal and approaches the identity matrix at steady state. Thus by the ultimate value theorem of Laplace transforms,

$$\mathbf{S} = \lim_{s \to 0}\left[(\mathbf{I} + \mathbf{G}\mathbf{G}_c)^{-1}\mathbf{G}\mathbf{G}_c\right]^{-1} \tag{3.2.96}$$

The application of the set-point compensator shall be illustrated by the following example.

Example 3.2.13 Let us consider the distillation column control problem of Example 3.2.12 and apply the set-point compensation scheme shown in Figure 3.9. If the controller matrix $\mathbf{G}_c$ consists of three proportional controllers

$$\mathbf{G}_c = \begin{bmatrix} k_{c_1} & 0 & 0 \\ 0 & k_{c_2} & 0 \\ 0 & 0 & k_{c_3} \end{bmatrix} \tag{3.2.97}$$

and $\mathbf{G}_{ss}$ is given by Eq. (3.2.88), then

$$\mathbf{S} = (\mathbf{G}_{ss}\mathbf{G}_c)^{-1}(\mathbf{I} + \mathbf{G}_{ss}\mathbf{G}_c) = (\mathbf{G}_{ss}\mathbf{G}_c)^{-1} + \mathbf{I} \tag{3.2.98}$$

Now

$$(\mathbf{G}_{ss}\mathbf{G}_c)^{-1} \equiv \mathbf{G}_c^{-1}\mathbf{G}_{ss}^{-1}$$

where

$$\mathbf{G}_c^{-1} = \begin{bmatrix} 1/k_{c_1} & 0 & 0 \\ 0 & 1/k_{c_2} & 0 \\ 0 & 0 & 1/k_{c_3} \end{bmatrix} \tag{3.2.99}$$

and

$$\mathbf{G}_{ss}^{-1} = \begin{bmatrix} 1.43 & 0 & 0 \\ -7.14 & 2.5 & 0 \\ 6.26 & -2.74 & 0.48 \end{bmatrix} \tag{3.2.100}$$

Thus the set-point compensator is

$$\mathbf{S} = \begin{bmatrix} \dfrac{1.43}{k_{c_1}} + 1 & 0 & 0 \\ \dfrac{-7.14}{k_{c_2}} & \dfrac{2.5}{k_{c_2}} + 1 & 0 \\ \dfrac{6.26}{k_{c_3}} & \dfrac{-2.74}{k_{c_3}} & \dfrac{0.48}{k_{c_3}} + 1 \end{bmatrix} \tag{3.2.101}$$

Note that for sufficiently high controller gains (i.e., $k_{c_i} \to \infty$), $\mathbf{S} \to \mathbf{I}$ and no steady-state compensation is necessary.

As an exercise, show that the set-point compensator $\mathbf{S}$ is the identity matrix $\mathbf{I}$ if PI control is used; i.e., if

$$\mathbf{G}_c = \begin{bmatrix} k_{c_1}\left(1 + \dfrac{1}{\tau_{I_1} s}\right) & & \mathbf{0} \\ & k_{c_2}\left(1 + \dfrac{1}{\tau_{I_2} s}\right) & \\ \mathbf{0} & & k_{c_3}\left(1 + \dfrac{1}{\tau_{I_3} s}\right) \end{bmatrix} \tag{3.2.102}$$

Explain why this must be true.

One obvious drawback of the set-point compensator is that it will not improve the response to disturbances because it does not appear in the feedback control loop. However, in making new set-point changes to compensate for sustained disturbances, a set-point compensator will minimize the effects of steady-state interactions. This is especially valuable if one is using supervisory control with local analog controllers in order to minimize the effects of interaction. In this case set-point compensation is rather easy to implement.

Modal Feedback Control

Another approach to multivariable controller design is to use *modal feedback control*. This technique makes use of the linear nature of the system model to design a control scheme which allows one to specify the closed-loop eigenvalues of the system. To illustrate this technique, let us consider the system described in state space by

$$\dot{\mathbf{x}} = \mathbf{Ax} + \mathbf{Bu} + \mathbf{\Gamma d} \tag{3.2.1}$$

$$\mathbf{y} = \mathbf{Cx} \tag{3.2.2}$$

where for this discussion let us assume the number of controls, and the number of outputs, are the same as the number of states. Thus **A**, **B**, **C** are constant $n \times n$ matrices, and we shall assume **A** has real, distinct eigenvalues. These limitations are not crucial to the method (see [12]), but make the explanations to follow easier.

Let us further assume a proportional controller on the output

$$\mathbf{u}(t) = -\mathbf{G}_c\mathbf{y} = -\mathbf{G}_c\mathbf{Cx} \tag{3.2.103}$$

Now let us review the concepts of eigenvectors and eigenvalues. If $\mathbf{\Lambda}$ is a diagonal matrix of eigenvalues of the $n \times n$ matrix

$$\mathbf{\Lambda} = \begin{bmatrix} \lambda_1 & & & \mathbf{0} \\ & \lambda_2 & & \\ & & \ddots & \\ \mathbf{0} & & & \lambda_n \end{bmatrix} \tag{3.2.104}$$

then

$$\mathbf{R\Lambda} = \mathbf{AR} \tag{3.2.105}$$

$$\mathbf{\Lambda L} = \mathbf{LA} \tag{3.2.106}$$

where **R** and **L** are the normalized right and left eigenvectors for the matrix. This means that **R**, **L** are the matrices of the n solutions of the equations

$$\mathbf{Ar}_i = \lambda_i\mathbf{r}_i \qquad i = 1, 2, \ldots, n \tag{3.2.107}$$

$$\mathbf{l}_i^T\mathbf{A} = \lambda_i\mathbf{l}_i \qquad i = 1, 2, \ldots, n \tag{3.2.108}$$

where the eigenvalues λ_i, $i = 1, \ldots, n$, are solutions of the equations

$$|\mathbf{A} - \lambda_i\mathbf{I}| = 0 \qquad i = 1, 2, \ldots, n \tag{3.2.109}$$

The n vectors $\mathbf{l}_i$, $\mathbf{r}_i$ are each divided by a constant to make them orthonormal, i.e.,

$$\mathbf{l}_i^T\mathbf{r}_j = \delta_{ij} \qquad \mathbf{r}_i^T\mathbf{l}_j = \delta_{ij} \tag{3.2.110}$$

or

$$\mathbf{LR} = \mathbf{RL} = \mathbf{I} \tag{3.2.111}$$

where

$$\mathbf{R} = \left[\mathbf{r}_1 \,\vdots\, \mathbf{r}_2 \,\vdots\, \cdots \,\vdots\, \mathbf{r}_n\right] \qquad \mathbf{L} = \left[\mathbf{l}_1 \,\vdots\, \mathbf{l}_2 \,\vdots\, \cdots \,\vdots\, \mathbf{l}_n\right]^T \tag{3.2.112}$$

Thus the properties in Eqs. (3.2.105) and (3.2.106) follow directly from Eqs. (3.2.107) and (3.2.111).

Making use of Eqs. (3.2.105) and (3.2.106), one can show that

$$\mathbf{\Lambda} = \mathbf{LAR} \tag{3.2.113}$$

and

$$\mathbf{R\Lambda L} = \mathbf{A} \tag{3.2.114}$$

Thus substituting Eqs. (3.2.103) and (3.2.114) into Eqs. (3.2.1), one obtains

$$\dot{\mathbf{x}} = (\mathbf{R\Lambda L} - \mathbf{BG}_c\mathbf{C})\mathbf{x} \tag{3.2.115}$$

Now if we choose the control matrix $\mathbf{G}_c$ to be

$$\mathbf{G}_c = \mathbf{B}^{-1}\mathbf{RK} \tag{3.2.116}$$

where **K** is a diagonal proportional controller matrix

$$\mathbf{K} = \begin{bmatrix} k_1 & & & \mathbf{0} \\ & k_2 & & \\ & & \ddots & \\ \mathbf{0} & & & k_n \end{bmatrix} \tag{3.2.117}$$

and choose the output matrix $\mathbf{C} = \mathbf{L}$, then Eq. (3.2.115) becomes

$$\dot{\mathbf{x}} = \mathbf{R}(\mathbf{\Lambda} - \mathbf{K})\mathbf{Lx} \tag{3.2.118}$$

By noting that

$$\mathbf{y} = \mathbf{Lx} \tag{3.2.119}$$

Eq. (3.2.118) takes the form

$$\dot{\mathbf{y}} = (\mathbf{\Lambda} - \mathbf{K})\mathbf{y} \tag{3.2.120}$$

and clearly $(\mathbf{\Lambda} - \mathbf{K})$ is a diagonal matrix, so the outputs have no interaction and

$$y_i = \alpha_i e^{(\lambda_i - k_i)t} \qquad i = 1, 2, \ldots, l \tag{3.2.121}$$

In addition the closed-loop solution to the state equations takes the form

$$\mathbf{x} = \sum_{i+1}^{n} \alpha_i \mathbf{r}_i e^{(\lambda_i - k_i)t} \tag{3.2.122}$$

where α_i is a constant determined from the initial conditions. Note that by adjusting k_i we can make the closed-loop eigenvalues as large and negative as we wish, and there is no interaction between the y_i. Adjusting the ith controller constant k_i affects only the ith mode. This means we can control the modes of the process, and even though there is state interaction, the output **y** has no interaction. The disadvantages of this control scheme are that only proportional control is possible, freedom is needed to choose $\mathbf{C} = \mathbf{L}$, and experience seems to indicate that tuning is a problem [10]. The block diagram for the control scheme is shown in Fig. 3.10.

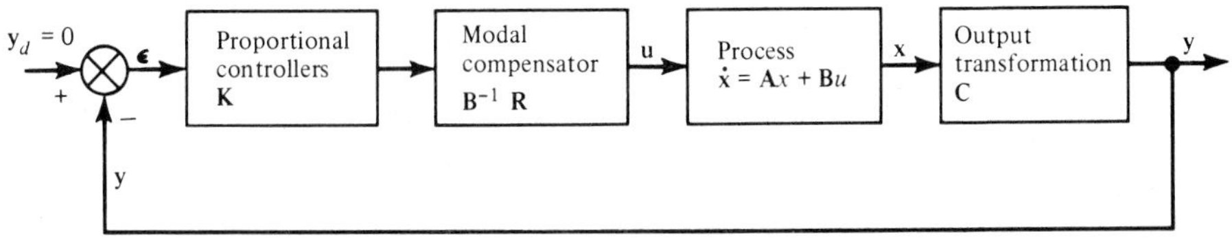

Figure 3.10 Block diagram for modal feedback control.

In the case where there are more states than controls, it is possible to apply modal control to the first m eigenvectors (where m is the number of control variables) with zero output interaction [12].

Example 3.2.14 Let us illustrate the concepts of modal control through consideration of the simple CSTR of Example 3.2.5, in which the reaction $A \rightarrow B \rightarrow C$ is taking place. It is desired to control the outlet concentration of A and B through manipulation of feed concentrations c_{Af}, c_{Bf}. In dimensionless form (see Example 3.2.5) the modeling equations become

$$\frac{dx_1}{dt} = -(1 + \mathrm{Da}_1)x_1 + u_1 \tag{3.2.123}$$

$$\frac{dx_2}{dt} = \mathrm{Da}_1 x_1 - (1 + \mathrm{Da}_3)x_2 + u_2 \tag{3.2.124}$$

where we recall that x_1 and x_2 are the dimensionless forms of c_A, c_B and u_1, u_2 are dimensionless feed concentrations. The Da_i are the Damköhler numbers for each of the reaction steps. Let us suppose that both x_1 and x_2 are available as outputs, so any output of the form

$$\mathbf{y} = \mathbf{C}\mathbf{x} \tag{3.2.2}$$

is possible.

Now if we apply simple single-loop proportional feedback control on the states (where we assume the problem has been scaled to let $\mathbf{x}_d = \mathbf{0}$ be the set point)

$$u_1 = -k_{11}x_1$$
$$u_2 = -k_{22}x_2 \tag{3.2.125}$$

then the system equations are

$$\frac{dx_1}{dt} = -(1 + \mathrm{Da}_1 + k_{11})x_1 \tag{3.2.126}$$

$$\frac{dx_2}{dt} = \mathrm{Da}_1 x_1 - (1 + \mathrm{Da}_3 + k_{22})x_2 \tag{3.2.127}$$

Even though k_{11} may be used to control x_1, there is a strong influence of x_1 on the state x_2.

Let us now apply modal control to the problem. We begin by determining the eigenvalues and eigenvectors of the state matrix **A**, where

$$\mathbf{A} = \begin{bmatrix} -(1 + \mathrm{Da}_1) & 0 \\ \mathrm{Da}_1 & -(1 + \mathrm{Da}_3) \end{bmatrix} \tag{3.2.128}$$

Thus

$$|\mathbf{A} - \lambda\mathbf{I}| = \left\| \begin{bmatrix} -(1 + \mathrm{Da}_1 + \lambda) & 0 \\ \mathrm{Da}_1 & -(1 + \mathrm{Da}_3 + \lambda) \end{bmatrix} \right\| = 0 \tag{3.2.129}$$

yields

$$\lambda^2 + (2 + \mathrm{Da}_1 + \mathrm{Da}_3)\lambda + (1 + \mathrm{Da}_1)(1 + \mathrm{Da}_3) = 0 \tag{3.2.130}$$

or

$$\lambda_1, \lambda_2 = -(1 + \mathrm{Da}_1), \; -(1 + \mathrm{Da}_3) \tag{3.2.131}$$

Now from standard references on matrix algebra (e.g., [1]), one obtains the right and left eigenvectors as the nontrivial solutions to

$$(\mathbf{A} - \lambda\mathbf{I})\mathbf{x} = \mathbf{0} \tag{3.2.132}$$

which from standard solutions to homogeneous algebraic equations becomes the nontrivial columns of the adjoint of $(\mathbf{A} - \lambda\mathbf{I})$; i.e.,

$$\mathrm{adj}(\mathbf{A} - \lambda\mathbf{I}) = \begin{bmatrix} (1 + \mathrm{Da}_3 + \lambda) & 0 \\ -\mathrm{Da}_1 & -(1 + \mathrm{Da}_1 + \lambda) \end{bmatrix} \tag{3.2.133}$$

so that for

$$\lambda_1 = -(1 + \mathrm{Da}_1) \qquad \mathbf{r}_1 = \begin{bmatrix} \mathrm{Da}_1 - \mathrm{Da}_3 \\ -\mathrm{Da}_1 \end{bmatrix} \tag{3.2.134}$$

$$\lambda_2 = -(1 + \mathrm{Da}_3) \qquad \mathbf{r}_2 = \begin{bmatrix} 0 \\ \mathrm{Da}_1 \end{bmatrix} \tag{3.2.135}$$

Similarly, the left-hand eigenvectors (or eigenrows) are the nontrivial rows of adj $(\mathbf{A} - \lambda\mathbf{I})$; i.e., for

$$\lambda_1 = -(1 + \mathrm{Da}_1) \qquad \mathbf{l}_1 = \begin{bmatrix} \mathrm{Da}_1 \\ 0 \end{bmatrix} \tag{3.2.136}$$

$$\lambda_2 = -(1 + \mathrm{Da}_3) \qquad \mathbf{l}_2 = \begin{bmatrix} \mathrm{Da}_1 \\ \mathrm{Da}_1 - \mathrm{Da}_3 \end{bmatrix} \tag{3.2.137}$$

Now because each eigenvector is uniquely determined only up to a multiplicative constant, one can divide $\mathbf{r}_1$ and $\mathbf{r}_2$ by $\mathrm{Da}_1(\mathrm{Da}_1 - \mathrm{Da}_3)$ to make the matrix of right- and left-hand eigenvectors orthonormal [i.e., satisfy

Eq. (3.2.111)]. Thus

$$\mathbf{R} = \begin{bmatrix} \dfrac{1}{\mathrm{Da}_1} & 0 \\ \dfrac{-1}{\mathrm{Da}_1 - \mathrm{Da}_3} & \dfrac{1}{\mathrm{Da}_1 - \mathrm{Da}_3} \end{bmatrix} \tag{3.2.138}$$

$$\mathbf{L} = \begin{bmatrix} \mathrm{Da}_1 & 0 \\ \mathrm{Da}_1 & \mathrm{Da}_1 - \mathrm{Da}_3 \end{bmatrix} \tag{3.2.139}$$

and one may verify that $\mathbf{LR} = \mathbf{I}$. Now if we let $\mathbf{C} = \mathbf{L}$ and choose $\mathbf{G}_c$ from Eq. (3.2.102), then

$$\begin{aligned} y_1 &= \mathrm{Da}_1 x_1 \\ y_2 &= \mathrm{Da}_1 x_1 + (\mathrm{Da}_1 - \mathrm{Da}_3) x_2 \end{aligned} \tag{3.2.140}$$

and the feedback control law becomes

$$\mathbf{u} = -\mathbf{RKLx} \tag{3.2.141}$$

where

$$\mathbf{RKL} = \begin{bmatrix} k_{11} & 0 \\ \dfrac{\mathrm{Da}_1(k_{22} - k_{11})}{\mathrm{Da}_1 - \mathrm{Da}_3} & k_{22} \end{bmatrix} \tag{3.2.142}$$

or

$$\frac{dx_1}{dt} = -(1 + \mathrm{Da}_1 + k_{11}) x_1 \tag{3.2.143}$$

$$\frac{dx_2}{dt} = \mathrm{Da}_1 \left(1 + \frac{k_{11} - k_{22}}{\mathrm{Da}_1 - \mathrm{Da}_3} \right) x_1 - (1 + \mathrm{Da}_3 + k_{22}) x_2 \tag{3.2.144}$$

where one may note that the outputs given by

$$\frac{dy_1}{dt} = -(1 + \mathrm{Da}_1 + k_{11}) y_1 \tag{3.2.145}$$

$$\frac{dy_2}{dt} = -(1 + \mathrm{Da}_3 + k_{22}) y_2 \tag{3.2.146}$$

show no interactions.

Let us now discuss the features of modal feedback control for this problem. First of all, the outputs [Eq. (3.2.140)] can be controlled independently without any interaction, and this is an advantage if a meaningful output set point could be devised. However, this is not a problem, because in general $\mathbf{y}_d = \mathbf{L}\mathbf{x}_d$ and $\mathbf{x}_d = \mathbf{R}\mathbf{y}_d$; thus one may change back and forth with no difficulties.

Another advantage of the controller matrix [Eq. (3.2.128)] is that if k_{11} and k_{22} are chosen so that

$$k_{22} - k_{11} = \mathrm{Da}_1 - \mathrm{Da}_3 \tag{3.2.147}$$

then Eq. (3.2.144) shows that the state interactions can be eliminated entirely. This is not generally a property of modal control, but is due to the particular structure of this example problem.

Because the matrix **A** must be known and all the states accessible, modal control design in the transform domain is a little artificial. However, one may obviously use it if one desires [10]. For a more complex example of modal control, see the paper by Davison and Chadha [13].

Further Design Techniques

There are a whole host of multivariable controller design techniques available (see [10] and [14] for an overview). These methods, usually implemented in an interactive mode with a computer, allow the iterative design of the feedback gains until good multivariable controller response is obtained. In addition to optimal control (to be discussed in the next section) and the modal control and noninteractive control design procedures already discussed, other proposed methods include:

1. The *commutative-controller* technique [10]
2. The *inverse Nyquist array* technique [10, 14]
3. The *characteristic locus* technique [10]

The reader is urged to consult these references for the details of the design procedure. A very nice series of case studies showing the performance of some of these designs when applied to the control of a double-effect evaporator may be found in Ref. [15].

3.3 OPTIMAL CONTROL THEORY AND PRACTICE*

Another major class of lumped parameter controller design methods involves optimal control. We shall begin our discussion of optimal control theory with the consideration of optimal *open-loop* control policies. The general class of problems we wish to consider can be represented by the nonlinear modeling equation

$$\frac{d\mathbf{x}(t)}{dt} = \mathbf{f}(\mathbf{x}(t), \mathbf{u}(t)) \qquad 0 \le t \le t_f \tag{3.3.1}$$

* Part of the material in this section is adapted from Ref. [16]. Reprinted by permission of John Wiley & Sons, Inc.

where $\mathbf{x}(t)$ is an n-dimensional vector of the state variables and $\mathbf{u}(t)$ is an m-dimensional vector of control variables which we wish to choose optimally.

The initial and terminal conditions will depend on the physical nature of the problem. If we specify only the initial state, then

$$\mathbf{x}(0) = \mathbf{x}_0 \tag{3.3.2}$$

An example of such an initial condition would be to specify the initial composition charged to a batch chemical reactor. Thus, if we were to fix the initial conditions only, the result would be a straightforward initial-value problem.

In other practical systems we may also desire to specify the final state

$$\mathbf{x}(t_f) = \mathbf{x}_f \tag{3.3.3}$$

(an example of which would be the requirement that the final product be of a given composition in the batch reactor); then we have a two-point boundary-value problem. Thus, we must find an optimal control $\mathbf{u}(t)$ which also causes $\mathbf{x}(t_f) = \mathbf{x}_f$.

Other possible conditions may require that some components of $\mathbf{x}$ be specified at the initial time and others at the final time. Alternatively, one may wish that some transversality conditions

$$\psi(\mathbf{x}(t_f)) = 0 \tag{3.3.4}$$

be satisfied at the final time. In physical terms, such a transversality condition may mean that rather than requiring a given final state of the process, we may wish to specify some relationship between the final states. This might correspond to the situation where there are tradeoffs possible in the final product specifications for a chemical reactor or other process.

In order to specify what is meant by optimal, we must select an objective functional* $I[\mathbf{u}(t)]$,

$$I[\mathbf{u}(t)] = G(\mathbf{x}(t_f)) + \int_0^{t_f} F(\mathbf{x}, \mathbf{u})\, dt \tag{3.3.5}$$

which we wish to maximize or minimize. We shall see that Eq. (3.3.5) is sufficiently general to allow the treatment of a wide class of practical problems.

Although the definitions of $G(\mathbf{x}(t_f))$ and $\int_0^{t_f} F(\mathbf{x}, \mathbf{u})\, dt$ have been given implicitly above, it may be helpful to illustrate the form that these functions can take for a given application.

If we were to consider the control of a batch chemical reactor, then the first component of the objective functional might take the following form:

$$G(\mathbf{x}(t_f)) = [\mathbf{x}(t_f) - \mathbf{x}_s]^T[\mathbf{x}(t_f) - \mathbf{x}_s] \tag{3.3.6}$$

where $\mathbf{x}_s$ is a vector describing the desired end composition; thus in this instance

* It is perhaps helpful to make clear that our objective is a functional (the transformation of a function into a value for I) rather than a function (the transformation of a parameter into a value for I).

the function $G(\mathbf{x}(t_f))$ is just the square deviation from the desired end composition. The second term in the objective $\int_0^{t_f} F(\mathbf{x}, \mathbf{u})\, dt$, might be used to describe the sum of the loss of reactant or product due to side reactions, the cost of control action (e.g., steam input), etc.; thus we may write

$$\int_0^{t_f} F(\mathbf{x}, \mathbf{u})\, dt = C_1 \int_0^{t_f} \begin{pmatrix}\text{rate of reactant}\\ \text{loss}\end{pmatrix} dt + C_2 \int_0^{t_f} \begin{pmatrix}\text{rate of product}\\ \text{loss}\end{pmatrix} dt + C_3 \int_0^{t_f} (\text{cost of control})\, dt \tag{3.3.7}$$

Here C_1, C_2, and C_3 are the appropriate cost factors. It is noted that the influence of the modeling Eq. (3.2.1) appears implicitly in the three integrals appearing on the right-hand side of Eq. (3.3.7).

For this example, the chemical compositions, together with the temperature, would constitute the state variables, whereas the heating rate, together with the rate of addition of catalyst or reactants, would constitute the control variables.

As an alternative form that

$$\int_0^{t_f} F(\mathbf{x}, \mathbf{u})\, dt$$

might take, let us leave $\mathbf{x}(t_f)$ in Eq. (3.3.3) unspecified and use the objective functional to force $\mathbf{x}$ to a given, desired final value. For example, the minimization of

$$\int_0^{t_f} (x - x_s)^2\, dt$$

will cause x to approach x_s in a very short time and will minimize the integral squared error.

In some optimal control problems, there also arise constraints of the form

$$\mathbf{g}(\mathbf{x}, \mathbf{u}) \leq \mathbf{0} \tag{3.3.8}$$

$$\mathbf{h}(\mathbf{x}, \mathbf{u}) = \mathbf{0} \tag{3.3.9}$$

and there are techniques for handling these.† However, because of the tremendous complexity that constraints of this form add, and because a great many practical problems only involve constraints of the form

$$\mathbf{u}_* \leq \mathbf{u} \leq \mathbf{u}^* \tag{3.3.10}$$

we shall only be concerned with upper and lower bounds on our control for the present.

In many practical problems, one may wish to choose t_f (e.g., the batch time) optimally as well. As seen in the next section, this presents no theoretical difficulties.

† For example, see the text by Bryson and Ho [6].

Necessary Conditions for Optimality

In this section we shall derive in a formal manner the necessary conditions for optimality for the lumped parameter system (3.3.1). This section is important not only for the useful final result, but also because the essence of variational methods is introduced in the derivation.

Let us consider the system with n state variables $x_i(t)$, m control variables $u_j(t)$, $j = 1, 2, \ldots, m$, and with dynamic behavior described by the ordinary differential equations*

$$\frac{d\mathbf{x}}{dt} = \mathbf{f}(\mathbf{x}, \mathbf{u}) \qquad \mathbf{x}(0) = \mathbf{x}_0 \tag{3.3.11}$$

We wish to find the control vector $\mathbf{u}(t)$, $0 \leq t \leq t_f$, such that the objective functional given by Eq. (3.3.5) is maximized.† Suppose that we have a set of nominal values for the control variables

$$\bar{\mathbf{u}}(t) = \begin{bmatrix} \bar{u}_1(t) \\ \bar{u}_2(t) \\ \vdots \\ \bar{u}_m(t) \end{bmatrix}$$

which we think may be optimal. Let us express any other control as a perturbation about $\bar{\mathbf{u}}(t)$,

$$\mathbf{u}(t) = \bar{\mathbf{u}}(t) + \delta\mathbf{u}(t) \tag{3.3.12}$$

and represent the state $\mathbf{x}(t)$ resulting from $\mathbf{u}(t)$ as a perturbation about the state $\bar{\mathbf{x}}(t)$ caused by the control $\bar{\mathbf{u}}(t)$; that is,

$$\mathbf{x}(t) = \bar{\mathbf{x}}(t) + \delta\mathbf{x}(t) \tag{3.3.13}$$

By checking the value of I in Eq. (3.3.5) for all perturbations $\delta\mathbf{u}(t)$, we could determine whether $\bar{\mathbf{u}}(t)$ is optimal. However, there are variations $\delta\mathbf{x}(t)$ which are produced by the perturbations $\delta\mathbf{u}(t)$, so that one must consider whether Eq. (3.3.11) is satisfied. If the perturbations $\delta\mathbf{u}(t)$ are chosen small enough, that is, if

$$|\delta\mathbf{u}(t)| \leq \varepsilon_1$$

then a first-order expansion about $\bar{\mathbf{u}}(t)$ would be adequate to represent the system. Thus we linearize Eqs. (3.3.11) and (3.3.5) about the nominal controls $\bar{\mathbf{u}}$

* It is straightforward to show (e.g., [2]) that any set of higher-order ordinary differential equations can be reduced to a set of first-order equations such as Eqs. (3.3.11).

† It is perhaps helpful to note that if we wished to *minimize* the objective I in Eq. (3.3.5), it is only necessary to maximize $-I$. This is due to the happy relationship

$$\min_{\mathbf{u}(t)} (I) \equiv -\max_{\mathbf{u}(t)} (-I)$$

to obtain Eqs. (3.3.14) and (3.3.15), respectively:

$$\frac{d(\delta\mathbf{x})}{dt} = \left(\frac{\partial\mathbf{f}}{\partial\mathbf{x}}\right)_{\cdot}\delta\mathbf{x} + \left(\frac{\partial\mathbf{f}}{\partial\mathbf{u}}\right)_{\cdot}\delta\mathbf{u} \qquad \delta\mathbf{x}(0) = \delta\mathbf{x}_0 \tag{3.3.14}$$

$$\begin{aligned}\delta I &= I[\bar{\mathbf{u}}(t) + \delta\mathbf{u}(t)] - I[\bar{\mathbf{u}}(t)] \\ &= \left(\frac{\partial G}{\partial\mathbf{x}}\right)_{\cdot}\delta\mathbf{x}(t_f) + \int_0^{t_f}\left[\left(\frac{\partial F}{\partial\mathbf{x}}\right)_{\cdot}\delta\mathbf{x} + \left(\frac{\partial F}{\partial\mathbf{u}}\right)_{\cdot}\delta\mathbf{u}\right]dt \\ &\quad + \left[F(t_f) + \frac{\partial G}{\partial\mathbf{x}}\mathbf{f}(t_f)\right]_{\cdot}\delta t_f\end{aligned} \tag{3.3.15}$$

where the notation $(\ )_{\cdot}$ reminds us that the partial derivatives are evaluated along the nominal trajectory $\bar{\mathbf{u}}(t)$, $\bar{\mathbf{x}}(t)$.

The last term in Eq. (3.3.15) arises because we may wish to choose t_f optimally; thus variations δt_f are allowed as well as variations $\delta\mathbf{u}(t)$.

Let us now adjoin to the objective functional the linearized constraint [Eqs. (3.3.14) and (3.3.15)] by using the n-dimensional adjoint variables (i.e., time-dependent Lagrange multipliers) $\boldsymbol{\lambda}(t)$. If we require that Eq. (3.3.14) be satisfied everywhere, then the subtraction of

$$\int_0^{t_f}\boldsymbol{\lambda}^T(t)\left[\frac{d(\delta\mathbf{x}(t))}{dt} - \left(\frac{\partial\mathbf{f}}{\partial\mathbf{x}}\right)_{\cdot}\delta\mathbf{x} - \left(\frac{\partial\mathbf{f}}{\partial\mathbf{u}}\right)_{\cdot}\delta\mathbf{u}\right]dt = 0 \tag{3.3.16}$$

from Eq. (3.3.15) yields

$$\begin{aligned}\delta I &= \left(\frac{\partial G}{\partial\mathbf{x}}\right)_{\cdot}\delta\mathbf{x}(t_f) + \left[F(t_f) + \frac{\partial G}{\partial\mathbf{x}}\mathbf{f}(t_f)\right]_{\cdot}\delta t_f \\ &\quad + \int_0^{t_f}\left[\left(\frac{\partial F}{\partial\mathbf{x}} + \boldsymbol{\lambda}^T\frac{\partial\mathbf{f}}{\partial\mathbf{x}}\right)_{\cdot}\delta\mathbf{x}\right. \\ &\quad \left. + \left(\frac{\partial F}{\partial\mathbf{u}} + \boldsymbol{\lambda}^T\frac{\partial\mathbf{f}}{\partial\mathbf{u}}\right)_{\cdot}\delta\mathbf{u}\right]dt - \int_0^{t_f}\boldsymbol{\lambda}^T(t)\frac{d(\delta\mathbf{x})}{dt}\,dt\end{aligned} \tag{3.3.17}$$

By integrating the last term by parts, we obtain

$$\begin{aligned}\delta I &= \left[F(t_f) + \frac{\partial G}{\partial\mathbf{x}}\mathbf{f}(t_f)\right]_{\cdot}\delta t_f + \boldsymbol{\lambda}^T(0)\delta\mathbf{x}_0 + \left[\left(\frac{\partial G}{\partial\mathbf{x}}\right)_{\cdot} - \boldsymbol{\lambda}^T(t_f)\right]\delta\mathbf{x}(t_f) \\ &\quad + \int_0^{t_f}\left\{\left[\left(\frac{\partial H}{\partial\mathbf{x}}\right)_{\cdot} + \frac{d\boldsymbol{\lambda}^T}{dt}\right]\delta\mathbf{x} + \left(\frac{\partial H}{\partial\mathbf{u}}\right)_{\cdot}\delta\mathbf{u}\right\}dt\end{aligned} \tag{3.3.18}$$

where H (sometimes called the Hamiltonian) is defined by

$$H \equiv F(x, u) + \boldsymbol{\lambda}^T\mathbf{f}(\mathbf{x}, \mathbf{u}) \tag{3.3.19}$$

Equation (3.3.18) represents the influence of variations $\delta\mathbf{u}(t)$ on δI, both directly and through $\delta\mathbf{x}(t)$. In order to express the direct influence of $\delta\mathbf{u}(t)$ alone, let us define the heretofore arbitrary functions $\boldsymbol{\lambda}(t)$ such that they satisfy

$$\frac{d\boldsymbol{\lambda}^T}{dt} = -\left(\frac{\partial H}{\partial\mathbf{x}}\right)_{\cdot} \tag{3.3.20}$$

In effect, this allows the influence of the system equations [Eq. (3.3.11)] to be transmitted by $\boldsymbol{\lambda}(t)$ and is felt in $(\partial H/\partial \mathbf{u})$, which carries $\boldsymbol{\lambda}(t)$.

The remaining terms outside the integral in Eq. (3.3.18) will depend on the boundary conditions of the physical system. Let us first consider the case where t_f is specified (so that $\delta t_f = 0$), x_0 is fixed, and $\mathbf{x}(t_f)$ is unspecified. In this case the variation $\delta \mathbf{x}_0 = \mathbf{0}$, and $\delta \mathbf{x}(t_f)$ is completely arbitrary. However, the condition

$$\lambda_i(t_f) = \left(\frac{\partial G}{\partial x_i}\right) \tag{3.3.21}$$

will shift the influence of $\delta \mathbf{x}(t)$ to $\boldsymbol{\lambda}(t)$ and cause it to arise in $(\partial H/\partial \mathbf{u})$. Notice that Eq. (3.3.21) completes the definition of $\boldsymbol{\lambda}(t)$ when combined with Eq. (3.3.20). If only some of the components of $\mathbf{x}(t_f)$ are unspecified, then $\delta x_i(t_f) = 0$ for those specified, and Eq. (3.3.21) holds for those unspecified. Similarly, if some components of $\mathbf{x}_0$ were to be unspecified, then $\lambda_i(0) = 0$ would hold for those components.

If in addition we wish to choose t_f optimally, then the first term in Eq. (3.3.18) remains. Now if all the $x_i(t_f)$ are unspecified, then Eq. (3.3.21) must hold, and in addition

$$H(t_f) = F(t_f) + \frac{\partial G}{\partial \mathbf{x}}\mathbf{f}(t_f) \tag{3.3.22}$$

must vanish when t_f is chosen optimally.

In the case where some of the $x_i(t_f)$ are fixed at x_{if}, then by a Taylor series expansion

$$x_i(t_f + \delta t_f) = x_i(t_f) + \left(f_i(t_f)\right)\delta t_f = \bar{x}_i(t_f) = x_{if} \tag{3.3.23}$$

as shown in Fig. 3.11. Thus the difference between $x_i(t_f)$ and $\bar{x}_i(t_f)$ to a first-order approximation is given by

$$\delta x_i(t_f) = x_i(t_f) - \bar{x}_i(t_f) = -\left(f_i(t_f)\right)\delta t_f \tag{3.3.24}$$

and again we see that

$$H(t_f) = F(t_f) + \boldsymbol{\lambda}^T(t_f)\mathbf{f}(t_f) \tag{3.3.25}$$

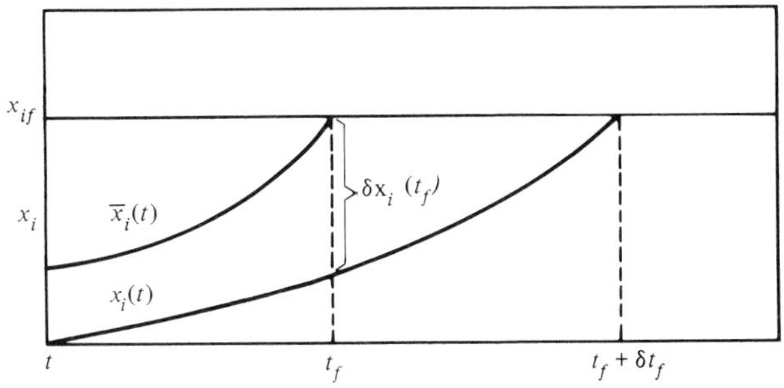

Figure 3.11 The expansion of $x_i(t)$ about t_f.

must vanish for t_f to be optimal. Notice that in this case the $\lambda_i(t_f)$ associated with fixed $x_i(t_f)$ are unspecified, while those associated with unspecified $x_i(t_f)$ are given by Eq. (3.3.21).

Having removed the boundary condition terms from Eq. (3.3.18), we obtain

$$\delta I = \int_0^{t_f} \left[\left(\frac{\partial H}{\partial \mathbf{u}} \right)_{.} \delta \mathbf{u}(t) \right] dt \tag{3.3.26}$$

and we now see the direct influence of variations $\delta \mathbf{u}(t)$ on δI. A necessary condition for optimality of $\bar{\mathbf{u}}(t)$ is that $\delta I \leq 0$ for all possible small variations $\delta \mathbf{u}(t)$. It is clear from Eq. (3.3.26) that the only way this can be true is that

$$\left(\frac{\partial H}{\partial \mathbf{u}} \right)_{.} = 0 \tag{3.3.27}$$

at every t.

Suppose that some components of $\bar{\mathbf{u}}(t)$ include segments along the constraints u_i^*, u_{i*}. Obviously, variations $\delta u_i(t)$ can only be negative at the upper bound u_i^* and only positive along lower bounds u_{i*}. An examination of Eq. (3.3.26) shows that a necessary condition for optimality at upper and lower bounds is

$$\begin{aligned} &\text{for} \qquad \bar{u}_i(t) = u_i^* \qquad \left(\frac{\partial H}{\partial u_i} \right)_{.} \geq 0 \\ &\text{and for} \qquad \bar{u}_i(t) = u_{i*} \qquad \left(\frac{\partial H}{\partial u_i} \right)_{.} \leq 0 \end{aligned} \tag{3.3.28}$$

Equations (3.3.28) can be reduced to the requirement that H have a local maximum at the constraints.

The results derived here may now be summarized as follows:

Theorem 3.1: Weak maximum principle In order for a control $\bar{\mathbf{u}}(t)$, $\mathbf{u}_* \leq \bar{\mathbf{u}}(t) \leq \mathbf{u}^*$, to be optimal in the sense that it maximizes the objective I in Eq. (3.3.5) while satisfying the system Eqs. (3.3.11), it is necessary that Eq. (3.3.27) be satisfied for unconstrained portions of the path and H as defined by Eq. (3.3.19) be maximized along constrained portions of the control trajectory.

Thus, given

$$\frac{d\mathbf{x}}{dt} = \mathbf{f}(\mathbf{x}, \mathbf{u}) \qquad \mathbf{x}(0) = \mathbf{x}_0 \tag{3.3.11}$$

and

$$I[\mathbf{u}(t)] = G(\mathbf{x}(t_f)) + \int_0^{t_f} F(\mathbf{x}, \mathbf{u})\, dt \tag{3.3.5}$$

the necessary condition for $\bar{\mathbf{u}}(t)$ to maximize

$$I[\mathbf{u}(t)]$$

is that

$$\frac{\partial H}{\partial \mathbf{u}} = 0 \tag{3.3.27}$$

on the unconstrained portion of the path and

$$H \equiv F(\mathbf{x}, \mathbf{u}) + \boldsymbol{\lambda}^T \mathbf{f}(\mathbf{x}, \mathbf{u}) \tag{3.3.19}$$

be a maximum on the constrained portion of the path. Here H is the Hamiltonian defined by Eq. (3.2.19), and $\boldsymbol{\lambda}$ is the time-dependent Lagrange multiplier, which is defined by

$$\frac{d\boldsymbol{\lambda}^T}{dt} = -\frac{\partial H}{\partial \mathbf{x}} \tag{3.3.20}$$

and

$$\lambda_i(t_f) = \frac{\partial G}{\partial x_i} \tag{3.3.21}$$

for those state variables unspecified at $t = t_f$.

In addition it is necessary that the Hamiltonian $H(t)$ remain constant along the optimal trajectory, and that $H(t)$ take the constant value of zero when the terminal time t_f is unspecified [see Eq. (3.3.25)].

A much stronger version of these necessary conditions, whose derivation is available elsewhere [17, 2] is summarized in the following theorem.

Theorem 3.2: Strong maximum principle In order for a control $\mathbf{u}(t)$ (constrained to lie in some constraint set Ω) to be optimal for the problem given by Eqs. (3.3.5) and (3.3.11), it is necessary that H be maximized by $\mathbf{u}(t)$ almost everywhere.

This much stronger result can also be shown sufficient for optimality under certain convexity assumptions. For further details, see the work of Lee and Markus [2].

The results developed in this section are very similar to those arising from dynamic programming or the classical calculus of variations. While the relationship can be made quite explicit, we shall not pursue the discussion further here. The reader is referred to Dreyfus [18] and Leitman [19] for a treatment of these relationships.

Example 3.3.1 Consider the radiant heating of a small billet or slab having a uniform temperature distribution so that the modeling equations are

$$\frac{dT}{dt'} = C_1(T_s^4 - T^4) \qquad T(0) = T_0 \tag{3.3.29}$$

where T_s is the radiant source temperature bounded by $T_* \le T_s \le T^*$, and T_0 is the initial temperature. Let us determine the optimal source temperature $T_s(t')$ so as to bring the billet to temperature T_1 in minimum time while minimizing the heat losses. This objective can be expressed as

$$\min_{T_s(t')} I[T_s(t')] = t_f' + C\int_0^{t_f'} T_s(t')^4 \, dt' \tag{3.3.30}$$

where t_f' is left free and C denotes the relative value of heat losses to operating time.

SOLUTION Let us define the variables

$$x_0 = T_0 \qquad x = T \qquad u = T_s^4 \qquad t = C_1 t'$$

$$x_s = T_1 \qquad u_* = T_*^4 \qquad u^* = T^{*4}$$

so that our problem becomes

$$\min_{u(t)} \left\{ I[u] = \int_0^{t_f} [1 + Cu(t)] \, dt \right\} \tag{3.3.31}$$

subject to

$$\frac{dx}{dt} = u - x^4 \qquad x(0) = x_0 \qquad x(t_f) = x_s \tag{3.3.32}$$

and

$$u_* \le u \le u^* \tag{3.3.33}$$

We can now define the Hamiltonian

$$H = 1 + Cu(t) + \lambda(u - x^4) = 1 - \lambda x^4 + (\lambda + C)u \tag{3.3.34}$$

and adjoint variables $\lambda(t)$ by

$$\frac{d\lambda}{dt} = 4\lambda x^3 \tag{3.3.35}$$

From the fact that H is linear in u, it is clear that

$$u(t) = \begin{cases} u^* & \text{if} \quad \lambda + C < 0 \\ u_* \le u \le u^* & \text{if} \quad \lambda + C = 0 \\ u_* & \text{if} \quad \lambda + C > 0 \end{cases} \tag{3.3.36}$$

because this is the only policy which minimizes H and thus satisfies the maximum principle. We note at this juncture that had our objective been to maximize rather than minimize H, then Eq. (3.3.36) would have taken the following form:

$$u(t) = \begin{cases} u_* & \text{if} \quad \lambda + C < 0 \\ u_* \le u \le u^* & \text{if} \quad \lambda + C = 0 \\ u^* & \text{if} \quad \lambda + C > 0 \end{cases}$$

Let us now deduce the exact optimal policy. If $u_* < u < u^*$ somewhere on the optimal policy, say, the region $0 \le t \le t_1$ in Fig. 3.12*a* (which indicates a slow increase in source temperature with time until the final

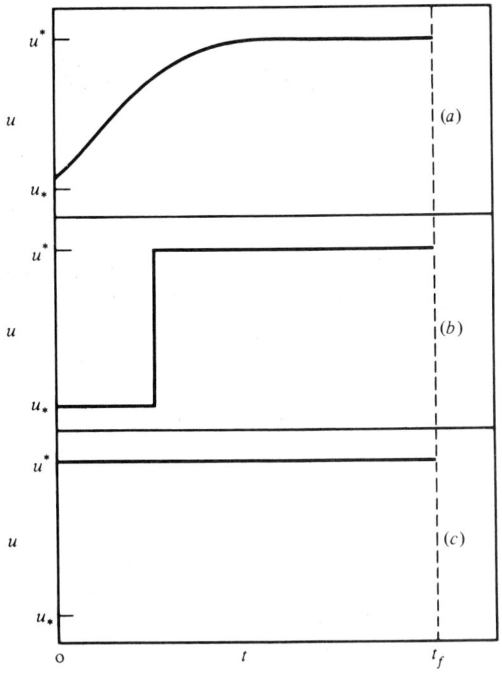

Figure 3.12 Possible optimal control policies for the billet reheating problem: (*a*) gradual increase of u from u_* to u^*; (*b*) stepwise increase from the lower bound to the upper bound; and (*c*) optimum at the upper bound.

value is reached), then from Eq. (3.3.36), $\lambda + C = 0$ and $d\lambda/dt = 0$ on $0 \le t \le t_1$. However, Eq. (3.3.35) does not allow this, because $d\lambda/dt = 0$ implies $\lambda = 0$, a contradiction because $C \neq 0$. Thus the policy shown in Fig. 3.12*a* (as well as any other policy where $u_* < u < u^*$) is not optimal.

Examination of Eq. (3.3.35) shows that $\lambda + C$ can change sign only once and that is when $\lambda(0) + C > 0$ and $\lambda(0) < 0$. This would produce the "optimal" policy shown in Fig. 3.12*b*. However, the fact that H must be identically zero along the optimal trajectory when t_f is unspecified, leads to

$$u_{\text{opt}} = \frac{-1 + \lambda x^4}{C + \lambda} \tag{3.3.37}$$

Clearly if $\lambda < 0$ and $\lambda + C > 0$, then $u_{\text{opt}} < 0$ which is physically impossible. Therefore, the policy given in Fig. 3.12*b* cannot be optimal. The policy $u = u_*$ is not optimal because for the temperature to increase, $u_{\text{opt}} > x^4$ must be true; however when $u = u_*$, then both $\lambda > 0$ and $\lambda + C > 0$ are satisfied everywhere, and $u_{\text{opt}} = -1/(\lambda + C) + \lambda x^4/(\lambda + C)$ and $u_{\text{opt}} < x^4$.

The only remaining possibility for the optimal policy is shown in Fig. 3.12*c*, in which the radiant heat source is kept at its maximum value until the billet reaches the desired temperature. In this case both $\lambda < 0$ and $\lambda + C < 0$ for all times. All that remains is to evaluate Eq. (3.3.29) with $T_s = T^*$ in order to determine the actual minimum time.

Although this problem may be a simple one, it shows that in some cases the optimal control may be deduced without performing any calculations.

Computational Techniques

There are a large variety of computational methods available for determining the optimal *open-loop* and *closed-loop* control policy. Some of the methods are based on numerically satisfying the necessary conditions of optimality derived in the last section, while others involve more direct search algorithms. In this section we shall discuss a few of the more commonly used algorithms.

Control vector iteration procedures for open-loop optimal control synthesis are very similar in philosophy to techniques used for parameter optimization [16]. Basically one makes use of Eq. (3.3.26).

$$\delta I = \int_0^{t_f} \left[\sum_{i=1}^{m} \left(\frac{\partial H}{\partial u_i} \right) \delta u_i(t) \right] dt \tag{3.3.38}$$

Suppose that $\bar{u}_i(t)$ is not optimal, so that $\partial H/\partial u_i \neq 0$; how can we determine a correction $\delta u_i(t)$ so as to improve I (i.e., cause $\delta I > 0$)? It can be shown [2] that choosing $\delta u_i(t)$ corrected in the gradient direction at each time t produces the greatest local improvement in I. Thus on selecting

$$\delta u_i(t) = \varepsilon \left(\frac{\partial H}{\partial u_i} \right) \qquad \varepsilon > 0 \tag{3.3.39}$$

one obtains

$$\delta I = \varepsilon \int_0^{t_f} \sum_{i=1}^{m} \left(\frac{\partial H}{\partial u_i} \right)^2 dt > 0 \tag{3.3.40}$$

which guarantees $\delta I > 0$ for ε small enough that the linear approximation is not violated.

These results can be incorporated in the following modified gradient method:

1. Guess $\bar{\mathbf{u}}(t)$, $0 \leq t \leq t_f$.
2. With this value of $\bar{\mathbf{u}}(t)$, integrate the state Eqs. (3.3.1) forward in time to produce $\bar{\mathbf{x}}(t)$, $0 \leq t \leq t_f$.
3. With these values of $\bar{\mathbf{x}}(t)$, $\bar{\mathbf{u}}(t)$, integrate the adjoint Eqs. (3.3.20) backward in time, $0 \leq t \leq t_f$.
4. Correct $\bar{\mathbf{u}}(t)$ by Eqs. (3.3.39) where ε is chosen arbitrarily. Evaluate I for this new control $\mathbf{u}(t)$.
5. If $I[\mathbf{u}(t)] > I[\bar{\mathbf{u}}(t)]$ double ε and repeat step 4: If $I[\mathbf{u}(t)] < I[\bar{\mathbf{u}}(t)]$, halve ε and repeat step 4. Do this until a concave function $I(\varepsilon)$ is formed (see Fig. 3.13).
6. Fit a quadratic $I(\varepsilon)$ to these results and predict the optimal value of ε, i.e., ε_{opt}.

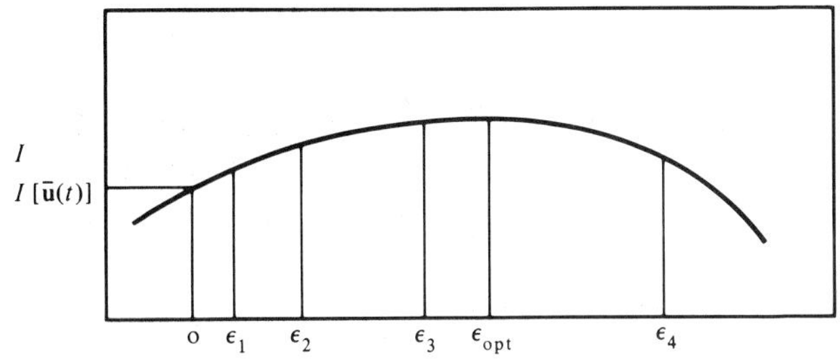

Figure 3.13 Determination of the optimal ε by a quadratic approximation.

7. Let

$$\bar{\mathbf{u}}^{\text{new}} = \bar{\mathbf{u}}^{\text{old}} + \varepsilon_{\text{opt}}\left(\frac{\partial H}{\partial \mathbf{u}}\right). \tag{3.3.41}$$

   and return to step 2.
8. Iterate until convergence is attained.

Experience has shown that these methods will lead to rapid progress in the first few iterations, but tend to become very slow as the optimum is approached. Even though convergence to the optimum can be proved theoretically, the rate of convergence can be so slow that the exact optimum is never found in a finite number of iterations. For this reason, several second-order methods have been proposed (e.g., [20–21]) which are similar to those for parameter optimization. In addition, conjugate gradient procedures have been developed [22, 23] which showed improved convergence properties over the standard gradient methods.

As an illustration of the application of control vector iteration techniques, let us consider an example of chemical reactor control.

Example 3.3.2 Let us consider a batch chemical reactor in which we can control the reaction temperature exactly* and in which we wish to carry out the following reaction:

$$A \overset{k_1}{\rightarrow} B \overset{k_2}{\rightarrow} C \tag{3.3.42}$$

We consider the kinetics and the temperature dependence of the rate constants known, and our objective is to find the optimal temperature control policy, for a fixed batch time, which will maximize the production of the intermediate B. We note that this is one of the classical batch reactor control problems and that the general scheme given by Eq. (3.3.42) is of considerable practical importance in a number of chemical processing operations, e.g., the oxidation of hydrocarbons or the chlorination of aromatics. In all these cases we may wish to maximize the production of an intermediate and thus wish to prevent the reaction from going to completion.

* In many practical situations such close temperature control is, in fact, quite feasible.

In order to define the problem, let us assume that the reaction is of second order with respect to the first step and of first order with respect to the second step. Thus the material balance on the reacting species may be written as

$$\frac{dc_1}{dt} = -k_1(T)c_1^2 \qquad c_1(0) = 1.0 \tag{3.3.43}$$

$$\frac{dc_2}{dt} = k_1(T)c_1^2 - k_2(T)c_2 \qquad c_2(0) = 0 \tag{3.3.44}$$

where

$$c_1 = [\mathrm{A}] \qquad c_2 = [\mathrm{B}] \qquad k_i(T) = \mathrm{A}_{i0}e^{-E_i/RT} \qquad i = 1, 2$$

Let us consider that the temperature is bounded by

$$T_* \leq T(t) \leq T^* \tag{3.3.45}$$

The object is to find the open-loop temperature control $T(t)$ which maximizes the amount of species B present after 1 h of reaction. Thus our objective becomes

$$\max_{T(t)} [I = c_2(1)] \tag{3.3.46}$$

The additional parameters of the system required to define the problem are given as follows:

$$A_{10} = 4000.0 \text{ L/(mol)(s)}$$
$$A_{20} = 6.2 \times 10^5\text{/s}$$
$$E_1 = 5000 \text{ cal/(g)(mol)}$$
$$E_2 = 10{,}000 \text{ cal/(g)(mol)}$$
$$T_* = 298^\circ\text{K}$$
$$T^* = 398^\circ\text{K}$$

batch time: 1 h

SOLUTION For this problem, the Hamiltonian is

$$H = (\lambda_2 - \lambda_1)k_1(T)c_1^2 - \lambda_2 k_2(T)c_2 \tag{3.3.47}$$

where the adjoint variables λ_1, λ_2 are given by

$$\frac{d\lambda_1}{dt} = -\frac{\partial H}{\partial c_1} = 2(\lambda_1 - \lambda_2)k_1(T)c_1 \qquad \lambda_1(1) = 0 \tag{3.3.48}$$

$$\frac{d\lambda_2}{dt} = -\frac{\partial H}{\partial c_2} = \lambda_2 k_2(T) \qquad \lambda_2(1) = 1 \tag{3.3.49}$$

and the gradient $\partial H/\partial T$ is

$$\frac{\partial H}{\partial T} = \frac{1}{RT^2}[(\lambda_2 - \lambda_1)E_1 k_1 c_1^2 - E_2\lambda_2 k_2(T)c_2] \tag{3.3.50}$$

The modified gradient algorithm was applied to the problem from two different initial guesses of $T(t)$. The resulting optimal temperature program is shown in Fig. 3.14 together with some of the intermediate iterations. Figure 3.15 shows the optimal yield $c_2(1)$ as a function of the number of iterations—for two initial guesses of the temperature program. As can be seen, the same optimal temperature program is found in both cases within three to four iterations. An inspection of the graph shows quite clearly that the optimal policy would produce very marked improvements in the yield of the desired intermediate species B. This improvement is found to be ~ 30 percent and 300 percent compared with operation of constant temperatures corresponding to the initial guesses of 398 °K and 298 °K, respectively. This example is thus an illustration of situations in which optimal control may produce significant improvements in performance.

Another approach to the problem of numerically solving the necessary conditions of optimality is to convert the control problem to a two-point boundary-value problem (TPBVP) through the elimination of the control variable. These are called *indirect* or *direct substitution* methods. The first step in such a procedure is to eliminate the control vector $\mathbf{u}(t)$ by solving Eq. (3.3.27)

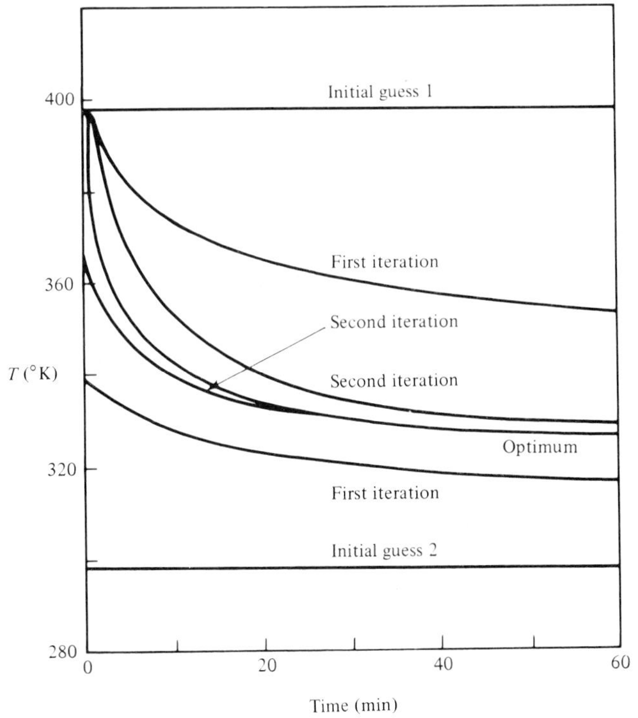

Figure 3.14 The optimal temperature program in Example 3.3.1.

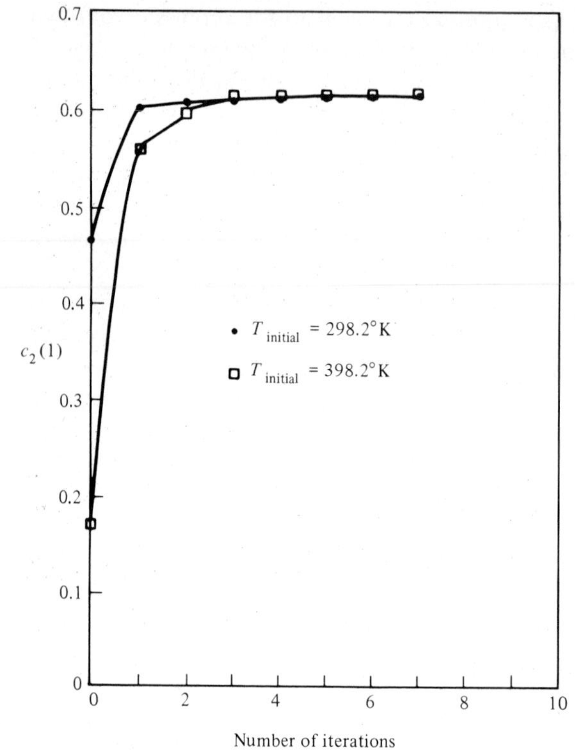

Figure 3.15 Plot of $c_2(1)$ against the number of iterations.

for $\mathbf{u}(t)$ explicitly:

$$u_i(t) = g_i(\mathbf{x}, \boldsymbol{\lambda}) \qquad i = 1, 2, \ldots, m \tag{3.3.51}$$

It is clear that this may not always be possible; however, it can be done for simple problems. If Eq. (3.3.51) is then substituted into Eqs. (3.3.11) and (3.3.20), the result is a set of $2n$ equations

$$\frac{d\mathbf{x}}{dt} = \mathbf{f}_1(\mathbf{x}, \boldsymbol{\lambda}) \qquad \mathbf{x}(0) = \mathbf{x}_0 \tag{3.3.52}$$

$$\frac{d\boldsymbol{\lambda}}{dt} = \mathbf{f}_2(\mathbf{x}, \boldsymbol{\lambda}) \qquad \boldsymbol{\lambda}(t_f) = \left(\frac{\partial G}{\partial \mathbf{x}}\right)_{t_f} \tag{3.3.53}$$

with split boundary conditions.* This problem, having boundary conditions at two values of the independent variables [a two-point boundary-value problem (TPBVP)], has a solution which produces the optimal values of $\mathbf{x}(t)$, $\boldsymbol{\lambda}(t)$. When these are substituted into Eq. (3.3.51), one obtains the optimal control $\mathbf{u}(t)$.

What has been effected by the elimination of $\mathbf{u}(t)$ is the trading of a trajectory optimization problem for a TPBVP. TPBVPs are notoriously difficult

* The boundary conditions for $\lambda(t_f)$ given here assume that all the $x(t_f)$ are unspecified. In some instances we may end up with two sets of boundary conditions for Eqs. (3.3.52) and none for Eqs. (3.3.53), as will be illustrated by the example given at the end of the end of the section. However, these problems, too, are two-point boundary-value problems.

to solve, even numerically, and thus most of the techniques associated with this approach are techniques for solving TPBVPs. Let us discuss several types of these techniques.

One technique for solving TPBVPs is the method of *boundary-condition iteration*. This approach tries to find, by some iterative procedure, the missing boundary conditions $\mathbf{x}(t_f)$ or $\boldsymbol{\lambda}(0)$ so that Eqs. (3.3.52) and (3.3.53) can be integrated together in the same direction of time. For simple scalar cases a mapping can be done of guessed values of $\boldsymbol{\lambda}(0)$ versus the resulting values of $\boldsymbol{\lambda}(t_f)_{\text{calc}} - (\partial G/\partial \mathbf{x})_{t_f}$ as sketched in Fig. 3.16. Obviously this graphical technique will not work well for multivariable problems. However, a number of techniques have been proposed for solving these problems [24] by perturbation methods or by minimizing the error in the boundary conditions by a direct search.

There is a basic difficulty with the boundary-condition-iteration approach which often arises in practical problems. The numerical integration of Eqs. (3.3.52) and (3.3.53) in the same direction is very often unstable. The reason for this behavior is that the state equations are usually stable when integrated forward, but unstable in the reverse direction. Similarly, the adjoint equations are usually unstable when integrated forward, but stable in the reverse direction. This can cause great numerical difficulties which are quite independent of the choice of the proper boundary conditions. Nevertheless, the method has been used successfully for some problems. The reader is urged to refer to standard references (e.g., [24 to 26]) for further methods of solving TPBVPs.

Let us illustrate the direct-substitution–boundary-condition-iteration approach by considering a slight variation on the problem posed in Example 3.3.1.

Example 3.3.3 As before, let us consider the radiant heating of a small billet, as described in Eq. (3.3.29).

$$\frac{dT}{dt} = C_1(T_s^4 - T^4) \qquad T(0) = T_0 \tag{3.3.29}$$

where T_s is the source temperature, T_0 is the initial temperature of the billet, and T_1 is the final desired temperature.

Our objective is to find the optimal source temperature $T_s(t)$ so as to bring the billet to the desired temperature in a minimum time, while minimizing the rate of wear of the refractory roof.

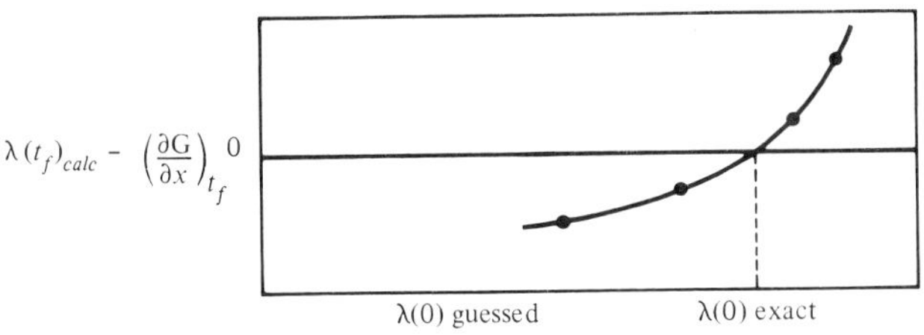

Figure 3.16 Solution of a two-point boundary value problem by a mapping procedure.

The rate of wear may be expressed as

$$C_2 e^{T_s^4} \tag{3.3.54}$$

where C_2 is a constant.

Thus the optimality criterion may be written as

$$\min_{T_s(t')} \left\{ I[T_s(t')] = t_f' + C_2 \int_0^{t_f'} e^{T_s^4(t')} dt' \right\} \tag{3.3.55}$$

where, as before, t_f' is left free and C_2 denotes the relative value of the roof erosion to operating time.

Let us define the variables:

$$x_0 = T_0 \qquad x = T \qquad u(t) \equiv u = T_s^4 \qquad t = C_1 t' \qquad C = \frac{C_2}{C_1}$$

$$x_1 = T_1 \qquad \text{and} \qquad u_* = T_*^4 \qquad u^* = T^{*4}$$

where, as before, u^* and u_* denote the upper and lower limits of the operating temperature, respectively.

The problem may now be written as

$$\min_{u(t)} \left[I(u) = \int_0^{t_f} 1 + Ce^u \, dt \right] \tag{3.3.56}$$

subject to

$$\frac{dx}{dt} = u - x^4 \qquad x(0) = x_0 \qquad x(t_f) = x_1 \tag{3.3.57}$$

Let us follow the procedure set out in Eqs. (3.3.51) to (3.3.53).

The Hamiltonian is given as

$$H = \lambda(u - x^4) + Ce^u + 1 \tag{3.3.58}$$

Thus, from Eq. (3.3.27) we have that

$$\frac{\partial H}{\partial u} = 0 \tag{3.3.27}$$

that is,

$$\lambda + Ce^u = 0$$

$$u = \ln\left(-\frac{\lambda}{C}\right) \tag{3.3.59}$$

On recalling Eq. (3.3.20), i.e.,

$$\frac{d\lambda}{dt} = -\frac{\partial H}{\partial x}$$

by differentiation we obtain

$$\frac{d\lambda}{dt} = 4\lambda x^3 \tag{3.3.60}$$

Thus the optimal $u(t)$ is defined by

$$-\frac{dx}{dt} = x^4 - \ln\left(-\frac{\lambda}{C}\right) \tag{3.3.61}$$

$$x = x_0 \qquad t = 0$$

$$x = x_1 \qquad t = t_f$$

and Eq. (3.3.60). Equations (3.3.60) and (3.3.61) may be solved numerically, e.g., by the boundary-condition-iteration technique described above. The result would then be

$$x = x(t)$$

$$\lambda = \lambda(t)$$

from which $u = u(t)$ is readily obtained from Eq. (3.3.59). While in general one would have to iterate to determine the optimal t_f from the condition $H(t) = 0$, in this simple problem Eq. (3.3.58) may be combined with Eq. (3.3.59) algebraically to yield

$$\lambda\left[\ln\left(-\frac{\lambda}{C}\right) - x^4 - 1\right] + 1 = 0$$

This expression may be solved together with Eq. (3.3.61) from $x = x_0$ to $x = x_1$ to yield the solution in one integration.

We note that the applicability of the direct-substitution technique depends critically on the types of functional relationships involved. Had the rate of wear, Eq. (3.3.54), been given by an alternative expression, such as

$$\text{Rate of wear} = C_2' e^{T_s} \tag{3.3.62}$$

then H would have taken the following form:

$$H = \lambda(u - x^4) + C\exp(u^{1/4}) \tag{3.3.63}$$

thus

$$\frac{\partial H}{\partial u} = 0 = \lambda + \tfrac{1}{4} C u^{-3/4} \exp(u^{1/4}) \tag{3.3.64}$$

Clearly, Eq. (3.3.64) cannot be solved explicitly for u. While one could proceed with solving the problem for certain parametric relationships between u and λ, this is likely to be cumbersome in the majority of cases.

An alternative approach which uses direct search methods is termed *control vector parameterization*. For open-loop control, one could represent $u_i(t)$ by a set of trial functions $\phi_{ij}(t)$, that is,

$$u_i(t) = \sum_{j=1}^{s} a_{ij}\phi_{ij}(t) \tag{3.3.65}$$

and use parameter optimization techniques to determine the optimal set of coefficients a_{ij}. A second approach, which allows a type of optimal closed-loop control, involves generating u_i in a feedback form, i.e., by expanding in a set of trial functions of the state variables

$$u_i(t) = \sum_{j=1}^{p} b_{ij}\phi_{ij}(x_1, x_2, \ldots, x_n) \tag{3.3.66}$$

and determining the optimal constants b_{ij}. Limited computational experience [16, 27] has shown that this feedback control scheme has much better convergence properties than the open-loop version. However, the resulting feedback controller parameters may not be generally optimal; they have been computed for only *one* initial condition. To be a good set for controller design, they must give good feedback controller performance for a wide range of initial conditions.

Both of these parameterization approaches have the advantages that no adjoint equations need to be solved, and standard parameter optimization techniques such as those discussed in [16] can be used to determine the coefficients. An even greater advantage, as demonstrated in Fig. 3.17, is the ability of the technique to optimize complex process models by allowing a parameter optimization scheme to select the experiments to be performed on this model. This avoids having to modify existing process models in order to perform optimal control calculations—a significant practical advantage.

The principal disadvantage of parameterization methods is that the functional form of the optimal control must be specified in advance. This requires much more physical insight than is needed for the previous methods discussed. In the absence of a physical feeling for the general shape of the optimal control, a very general functional form [Eq. (3.3.65)] must be used and the optimization performed with respect to a large number of coefficients. On the other hand, if

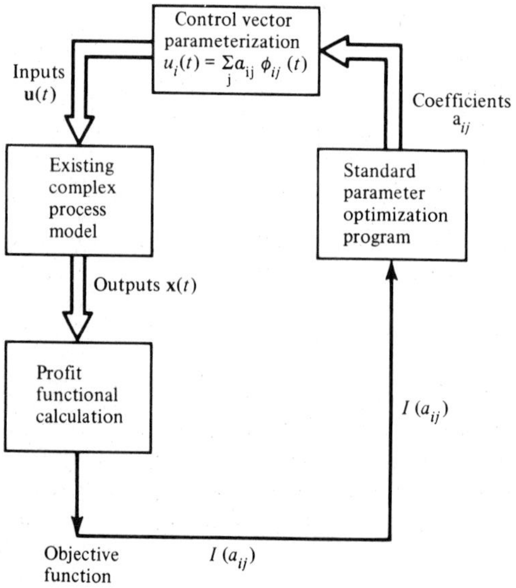

Figure 3.17 The use of control vector parameterization with an existing complex process model.

one has good reason to suspect a particular form of the optimal policy (e.g., a falling temperature profile in Example 3.3.2), then a simple functional form with only a few coefficients should be adequate. A word of caution is in order, however: surprises do arise from optimal control studies (that is why we do them), and in practical problems one should use several types of functional forms to ensure that the functional form chosen is, in fact, general enough. Several other parameterization approaches have been reported and seem to have some merit. See Ref. [27] for a discussion and comparison of these methods.

Let us illustrate this method with an example problem.*

Example 3.3.4 Consider the problem of determining the optimal start-up control scheme for a nonlinear CSTR in which the exothermic, first-order reaction $A \to B$ is taking place. The modeling equations take the form

$$\frac{dc}{dt} = \frac{1}{\theta}(c_f - c) - k_0 e^{(-E/RT)} c \qquad 0 < t < t_f$$

$$\frac{dT}{dt} = \frac{1}{\theta}(T_f - T) + \frac{(-\Delta H)}{\rho C_p} k_0 e^{(-E/RT)} c - \alpha u (T - T_c) \qquad 0 < t < t_f$$

where c is the reactant composition, T the reactor temperature, and u the reactor jacket heat-transfer coefficient, which is influenced by adjusting the coolant flow rate. In this problem, the control variable u is bounded by $u_* \le u \le u^*$ and can be parameterized in time by letting

$$u = u_* + (u^* - u_*) \sum_{j=1}^{6} (-1)^{j+1} H(t - b_j) + \sum_{i=1}^{3} a_i (t - b_6)^i$$

where $H(t)$ is the Heaviside step function

$$H(t) = \begin{Bmatrix} 1 & t > 0 \\ 0 & t < 0 \end{Bmatrix}$$

This expression for $u(t)$ allows as many as six switches between the upper and lower bounds on u, followed by a smooth cubic trajectory whose shape is determined by the a_i. This produces an open-loop start-up program.

Alternatively, one can parameterize in a feedback controller form

$$u(t) = u_d + K_1(c - c_d) + K_2(T - T_d)$$

and search for the two parameters K_1, K_2.

The objective to be minimized is

$$I = 10^6 \int_0^{t_f} \left[(c - c_d)^2 + 2 \times 10^{-5} (T - T_d)^2 + 10^{-9} (u - u_s)^2 \right] dt$$

where $c_d = 0.408$, $T_d = 330°\text{K}$, and $u_s = 370$ represent the set-point values for composition, temperature, and control.

For both schemes, the control variable parameterization procedure then searches for the parameters (a_i, b_j for time parameterization or K_1, K_2 for

* This example is taken from Ref. [27] and adapted with permission of the Canadian Journal of Chemical Engineering.

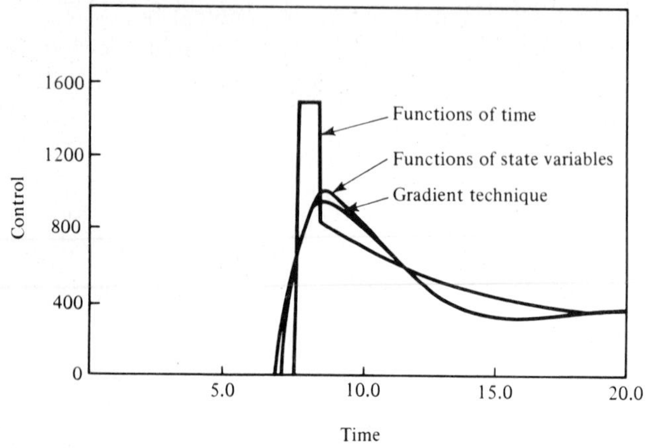

Figure 3.18 Optimal stirred tank reactor start-up [27]; (a) Hamiltonian gradient method (I_{min} = 987,502); (b) open-loop time parameterization (I_{min} = 987,955); (c) closed-loop state feedback parameterization (I_{min} = 987,436).

state feedback) which minimize the objective I. The resulting control trajectories are shown in Fig. 3.18 and compared with the optimal control found from Hamiltonian gradient techniques based on the maximum principle. Note that the value of the objective is almost identical for the three methods even though the control policy varies slightly. The resulting concentration and temperature responses, seen in Fig. 3.19, indicate that the start-up procedure is quite good from a practical point of view.

Let us now discuss briefly the advantages and disadvantages of these various computational approaches. The control vector iteration procedure has the advantage that it can be applied with little algebraic manipulation to even the most complex problems. In addition, because the state equations are solved

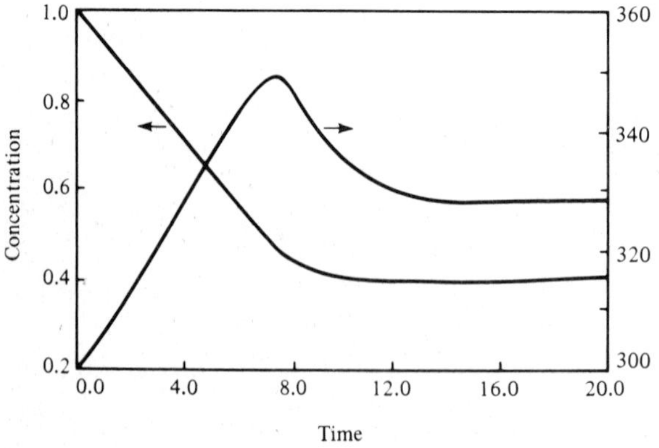

Figure 3.19 CSTR concentration and temperature responses to optimal start-up control [27].

exactly at each stage, each iteration produces a feasible solution. This has the attraction that one may stop at any iteration with a suboptimal, but reasonably good, usable solution.

The direct-substitution procedures have the disadvantage that a fair amount of algebraic manipulation is required to produce the TPBVP, and then sophisticated procedures are needed for solution. The complexity of these methods makes them difficult for the novice to apply. One advantage of the boundary-condition-iteration approach is that every iteration produces an optimum solution—to the wrong problem. If $\mathbf{x}(t_f)$ is the boundary condition to be adjusted so that Eqs. (3.3.52) and (3.3.53) are integrated backward together, then a calculated value of $\mathbf{x}(0)$ is produced at each iteration. Thus each iteration produces the optimal solution for that calculated initial condition $\mathbf{x}(0)$. This property would be useful if one wished to obtain the optimal policies for a variety of initial conditions.

The control vector parameterization procedure seems to be the most attractive for the novice. Very little sophistication is required, and standard techniques for parameter optimization may be applied. The one major disadvantage seems to be that there is no guarantee that the parameterized optimal control will be very close to the *exact* optimum unless the trial functions are chosen in a sufficiently general way. The number of trial functions needs to be as small as possible to minimize the number of coefficients to be optimized, and yet the functional form must be capable of representing the exact optimum. Thus care must be exercised in the choice of trial functions.

A final word on the practical problems of convergence is in order. As in parameter optimization problems, trajectory optimization algorithms always stop progressing before the exact optimum is reached. However, efficient algorithms will usually stop very close to the true optimum. Thus, to ensure that the optimum has indeed been found, one must be able to produce the same "optimal policy" from several initial guesses. This would seem to ensure that, at least, a local optimum has been found. One should be aware that multiple optima are possible, and in rare cases these have been found in real problems. Thus, even though several starting points must always be used to ensure that the algorithm has converged, this is not an absolute guarantee that the global optimum has been found.

Problems Linear in the Control

There are a number of classes of optimal control problems which allow special techniques to be used. One such case is systems which have Hamiltonians linear in the control; i.e.,

$$H = h_0(\mathbf{x}, \boldsymbol{\lambda}) + \sum_{i=1}^{m} h_i(\mathbf{x}, \boldsymbol{\lambda}) u_i(t) \tag{3.3.67}$$

then the structure of the optimal control policy is clear without further computation. For example, if $u(t)$ is constrained by $\mathbf{u}_* \le \mathbf{u} \le \mathbf{u}^*$, then from the *strong*

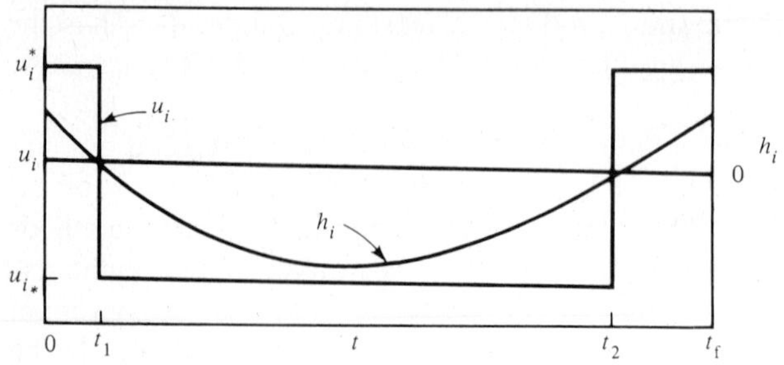

Figure 3.20 Bang-bang control policy.

maximum principle we see that the optimal control has the form

$$u_i(t) = \begin{cases} u_i^* & \text{if } h_i > 0 \\ u_{i*} & \text{if } h_i < 0 \end{cases} \tag{3.3.68}$$

This behavior, plotted in Fig. 3.20, is called a *bang-bang control policy*. The points t_1, t_2 where $h_i(t)$ changes sign are called switching times.

There is another special situation which occurs when $h_i = 0$ over some interval of time. An examination of Fig. 3.21 shows us that $h_i = 0$ over $t_1 \leq t \leq t_2$. Since this causes the control to vanish from H in that interval, it is not clear how we can determine the optimal value of $u_i(t)$ over $t_1 \leq t \leq t_2$. The control over this interval is called a *singular arc*, and these especially difficult problems are called *singular control problems*. Whenever one encounters a problem such that the Hessian matrix

$$\mathbf{H} = \frac{\partial^2 H}{\partial \mathbf{u}^2} \tag{3.3.69}$$

is singular over some interval $t_1 < t < t_2$, then one has encountered a singular optimal control problem and must exercise special caution. The reader is referred to [6] and [28] for a deeper discussion of these problems and the techniques available for their solution.

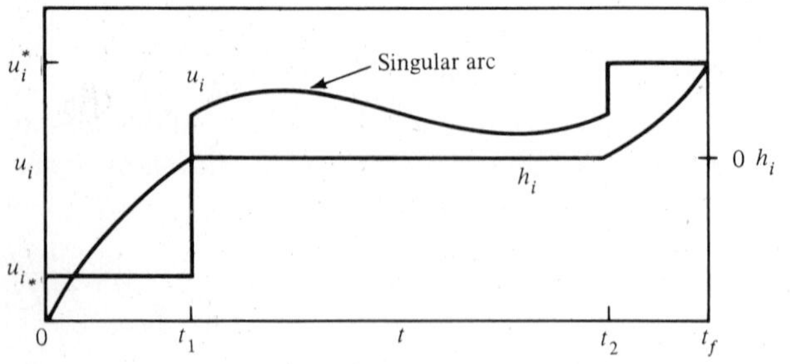

Figure 3.21 Control policy with a singular arc.

Optimal State Feedback Control of Linear Systems—Linear Quadratic Problem

Let us now consider a special classical problem in optimal control theory—the *linear-quadratic problem*—which leads to an optimal state feedback control law. There have been numerous papers written on this problem (see [6] and [29]). The problem may be posed as follows: We assume that the state of the system $\mathbf{x}$ can be represented by the linear differential equation

$$\frac{d\mathbf{x}}{dt} = \mathbf{Ax} + \mathbf{Bu} \qquad \mathbf{x}(t_0) = \mathbf{x}_0 \tag{3.3.70}$$

and that it is desired to control the system at the set point* $\mathbf{x}_d = \mathbf{0}$ without excessive control action. The quadratic objective functional is

$$I = \tfrac{1}{2}\mathbf{x}^T\mathbf{S}_f\mathbf{x}\big|_{t_f} + \tfrac{1}{2}\int_{t_0}^{t_f}(\mathbf{x}^T\mathbf{Fx} + \mathbf{u}^T\mathbf{Eu})\,dt \tag{3.3.71}$$

where $\mathbf{A}(t)$, $\mathbf{B}(t)$ are system matrices, $\mathbf{S}_f$, $\mathbf{F}(t)$ are symmetric, positive semidefinite weighting matrices, and $\mathbf{E}(t)$ is a symmetric positive definite matrix.

Now if optimal control theory is applied to this problem, one obtains as the Hamiltonian

$$H = \tfrac{1}{2}(\mathbf{x}^T\mathbf{Fx} + \mathbf{u}^T\mathbf{Eu}) + \boldsymbol{\lambda}^T(\mathbf{Ax} + \mathbf{Bu})$$

with conditions

$$\dot{\boldsymbol{\lambda}}^T = -\frac{\partial H}{\partial \mathbf{x}} \qquad \boldsymbol{\lambda}(t_f) = \mathbf{S}_f\mathbf{x}(t_f) \tag{3.3.72}$$

$$\frac{\partial H}{\partial \mathbf{u}} = \mathbf{0} \tag{3.3.73}$$

Equation (3.3.73) becomes

$$\mathbf{Eu} + \mathbf{B}^T\boldsymbol{\lambda} = \mathbf{0}$$

or

$$\mathbf{u} = -\mathbf{E}^{-1}\mathbf{B}^T\boldsymbol{\lambda} \tag{3.3.74}$$

Thus Eqs. (3.3.70) and (3.3.72) become

$$\left.\begin{aligned} \dot{\mathbf{x}} &= \mathbf{Ax} - \mathbf{BE}^{-1}\mathbf{B}^T\boldsymbol{\lambda} \qquad & \mathbf{x}(t_0) &= \mathbf{x}_0 \\ \dot{\boldsymbol{\lambda}} &= -\mathbf{Fx} - \mathbf{A}^T\boldsymbol{\lambda} \qquad & \boldsymbol{\lambda}(t_f) &= \mathbf{S}_f\mathbf{x}(t_f) \end{aligned}\right\} \tag{3.3.75}$$

Now this linear TPBVP can be solved in several ways. However, the solution can be conveniently represented by the form

$$\boldsymbol{\lambda}(t) = \mathbf{S}(t)\mathbf{x}(t) \tag{3.3.76}$$

which has been termed the *Riccati transformation* [29]. Here $\mathbf{S}(t)$ is a symmetric positive definite $n \times n$ matrix. Substitution of Eq. (3.3.76) into Eqs. (3.3.75)

* If we wish to achieve any nonzero state set point $\mathbf{x} = \mathbf{x}_d$, then defining $\check{\mathbf{x}} = \mathbf{x} - \mathbf{x}_d$ will convert the problem to this form. See Example 3.3.5 below.

yields

$$\dot{\mathbf{x}} = \mathbf{A}\mathbf{x} - \mathbf{B}\mathbf{E}^{-1}\mathbf{B}^T\mathbf{S}\mathbf{x} \tag{3.3.77}$$

$$(\dot{\mathbf{S}}\mathbf{x} + \mathbf{S}\dot{\mathbf{x}}) = -\mathbf{F}\mathbf{x} - \mathbf{A}^T\mathbf{S}\mathbf{x} \tag{3.3.78}$$

The elimination of $\dot{\mathbf{x}}$ by substituting Eq. (3.3.77) into Eq. (3.3.78) yields

$$(\dot{\mathbf{S}} + \mathbf{S}\mathbf{A} + \mathbf{A}^T\mathbf{S} - \mathbf{S}\mathbf{B}\mathbf{E}^{-1}\mathbf{B}^T\mathbf{S} + \mathbf{F})\mathbf{x}(t) = \mathbf{0} \tag{3.3.79}$$

Now for Eq. (3.3.79) to hold for all nonzero $\mathbf{x}(t)$, the coefficient matrix of $\mathbf{x}(t)$ must vanish, yielding the *Riccati equation*

$$\frac{d\mathbf{S}}{dt} = -\mathbf{S}\mathbf{A} - \mathbf{A}^T\mathbf{S} + \mathbf{S}\mathbf{B}\mathbf{E}^{-1}\mathbf{B}^T\mathbf{S} - \mathbf{F} \qquad \mathbf{S}(t_f) = \mathbf{S}_f \tag{3.3.80}$$

for $\mathbf{S}(t)$. Note that the boundary conditions on $\mathbf{S}$ follow directly from a comparison of Eqs. (3.3.76) and (3.3.72). By making use of Eq. (3.3.74), one obtains the *state feedback control law*

$$\mathbf{u}(t) = -\mathbf{K}(t)\mathbf{x}(t) \tag{3.3.81}$$

where

$$\mathbf{K}(t) = \mathbf{E}^{-1}\mathbf{B}^T\mathbf{S}(t) \tag{3.3.82}$$

To summarize, a proportional state feedback controller with time-varying gain has been derived which will control the system [Eq. (3.3.70)] so that the objective [Eq. (3.3.71)] is minimized. Some points to note are:

1. The time-varying gain $\mathbf{K}(t)$ can be determined offline [by solving for $\mathbf{S}(t)$ beginning at $t = t_f$] because $\mathbf{K}(t)$ does not depend on $\mathbf{x}(t)$ or $\mathbf{u}(t)$.
2. If we let $t_f \to \infty$, and $\mathbf{A}$, $\mathbf{B}$, $\mathbf{F}$, $\mathbf{E}$ are constant, then $\mathbf{S}(t)$ becomes a constant and is the solution of

$$\mathbf{S}\mathbf{B}\mathbf{E}^{-1}\mathbf{B}^T\mathbf{S} - \mathbf{S}\mathbf{A} - \mathbf{A}^T\mathbf{S} - \mathbf{F} = \mathbf{0} \tag{3.3.83}$$

   Thus $\mathbf{K}(t)$ is also a constant. In this case the controller is a constant-gain proportional controller.
3. The precise physical meaning of the objective [Eq. (3.3.71)] is somewhat vague. Clearly the quadratic weighting of the state leads to desirable controller performance when I is minimized; however, the quadratic weighting of the control has less justification, particularly if controller power is not costly. Sometimes the quadratic weighting can be used in place of explicit control constraints in order to yield a feedback controller, but it is difficult to say in what sense this is optimal. Additionally, weighting $\mathbf{E}$ too large causes the state performance to decline, and weighting $\mathbf{E}$ too small causes the control $\mathbf{u}(t)$ to take on extremely large values. The crucial limitations of this controller are that $\mathbf{E}$ must stay positive definite and $\mathbf{x}$, $\mathbf{u}$ must be unconstrained.
4. If one makes the objective functional [Eq. (3.3.71)] more general to include cross terms between the state and the control, one can write Eq. (3.3.71) as

$$I = \tfrac{1}{2}\mathbf{x}^T\mathbf{S}_f\mathbf{x}\big|_{t_f} + \frac{1}{2}\int_{t_0}^{t_f}(\mathbf{x}^T, \mathbf{u}^T)\begin{bmatrix} \mathbf{F}(t) & \mathbf{N}(t) \\ \mathbf{N}^T(t) & \mathbf{E}(t) \end{bmatrix}\begin{bmatrix} \mathbf{x} \\ \mathbf{u} \end{bmatrix} dt \tag{3.3.84}$$

In this case it is straightforward to show that the feedback control law takes the form of Eq. (3.3.81), where

$$\mathbf{K}(t) = \mathbf{E}^{-1}(\mathbf{N}^T + \mathbf{B}^T\mathbf{S}) \tag{3.3.85}$$

and

$$\begin{aligned} \frac{d\mathbf{S}}{dt} &= -\mathbf{SA} - \mathbf{A}^T\mathbf{S} + (\mathbf{SB} + \mathbf{N})\mathbf{E}^{-1}(\mathbf{N}^T + \mathbf{B}^T\mathbf{S}) - \mathbf{F} \\ \mathbf{S}(t_f) &= \mathbf{S}_f \end{aligned} \tag{3.3.86}$$

This more general form will be useful in the derivation of nonlinear optimal feedback controllers.

Example 3.3.5 Determine the optimal feedback control law for a process described by Eq. (3.3.70) with the objective to minimize

$$\begin{aligned} I = \tfrac{1}{2}(\mathbf{x} - \mathbf{x}_d)^T\mathbf{S}_f(\mathbf{x} - \mathbf{x}_d)|_{t_f} + \frac{1}{2}\int_{t_0}^{t_f}\big[(\mathbf{x} - \mathbf{x}_d)^T\mathbf{F}(\mathbf{x} - \mathbf{x}_d) \\ + (\mathbf{u} - \mathbf{u}_d)^T\mathbf{E}(\mathbf{u} - \mathbf{u}_d)\big]\, dt \end{aligned} \tag{3.3.87}$$

where $\mathbf{x}_d$, $\mathbf{u}_d$ correspond to a desired *steady-state* position.

Let us define

$$\check{\mathbf{x}} = \mathbf{x} - \mathbf{x}_d \qquad \check{\mathbf{u}} = \mathbf{u} - \mathbf{u}_d \tag{3.3.88}$$

then Eq. (3.3.87) takes the form of Eq. (3.3.71) in the variables $\check{\mathbf{x}}$, $\check{\mathbf{u}}$ and Eq. (3.3.70) becomes

$$\frac{d\check{\mathbf{x}}}{dt} = \mathbf{A}\check{\mathbf{x}} + \mathbf{B}\check{\mathbf{u}} + \cancelto{0}{\mathbf{A}\mathbf{x}_d + \mathbf{B}\mathbf{u}_d} \tag{3.3.89}$$

However, the last two terms in Eq. (3.3.88) vanish because they represent a steady state. Therefore we have the control law

$$\check{\mathbf{u}} = -\mathbf{K}(t)\check{\mathbf{x}} \tag{3.3.90}$$

where $\mathbf{K}(t)$ is given by Eq. (3.3.82). In terms of the original variables, this is

$$\mathbf{u}(t) = \mathbf{u}_d - \mathbf{K}(t)(\mathbf{x} - \mathbf{x}_d) \tag{3.3.91}$$

Example 3.3.6 Let us consider the CSTR in which an isothermal multicomponent chemical reaction is being carried out. The chemical reaction system is

$$A \underset{k_2}{\overset{k_1}{\rightleftarrows}} B \overset{k_3}{\rightarrow} C$$

with the rates of reaction given by

$$\begin{aligned} r_1 &= k_1 c_A - k_2 c_B \\ r_2 &= k_3 c_B \end{aligned}$$

where k_1, k_2, k_3 are constants.

The modeling equations for this system take the form

$$V\frac{dc_A}{dt'} = F(c_{Af} - c_A) - V(k_1 c_A - k_2 c_B) \qquad c_A(0) = c_{A0}$$

$$V\frac{dc_B}{dt'} = F(c_{Bf} - c_B) + V[k_1 c_A - (k_2 + k_3)c_B] \qquad c_B(0) = c_{B0}$$

It is desired to control c_A, c_B as close as possible to a desired set point c_{Ad}, c_{Bd} by adjusting c_{Bf}. At the same time, there is a target steady-state value of c_{Bf}, i.e., c_{Bfd}, which we would like to achieve as well. The feed concentration of c_{Af} is considered fixed.

By defining the dimensionless variables

$$t = \frac{t'F}{V} \qquad u = \frac{c_{Bf}}{c_{Af}} \qquad x_1 = \frac{c_A}{c_{Af}} \qquad x_2 = \frac{c_B}{c_{Af}}$$

$$\mathrm{Da}_1 = \frac{k_1 V}{F} \qquad \mathrm{Da}_2 = \frac{k_2 V}{F} \qquad \mathrm{Da}_3 = \frac{k_3 V}{F}$$

one obtains the model

$$\frac{dx_1}{dt} = 1 - (1 + \mathrm{Da}_1)x_1 + \mathrm{Da}_2 x_2$$

$$\frac{dx_2}{dt} = \mathrm{Da}_1 x_1 - (1 + \mathrm{Da}_2 + \mathrm{Da}_3)x_2 + u$$

Now let us define the quadratic objective

$$I = \frac{1}{2}\int_0^{t_f}\left[(x_1 - x_{1d})^2 + \alpha(x_2 - x_{2d})^2 + \beta(u - u_d)^2\right] dt$$

where x_{1d}, x_{2d}, u_d satisfy the steady-state equations

$$0 = 1 - (1 + \mathrm{Da}_1)x_{1d} + \mathrm{Da}_2 x_{2d}$$

$$0 = \mathrm{Da}_1 x_{1d} - (1 + \mathrm{Da}_2 + \mathrm{Da}_3)x_{2d} + u_d$$

By defining $\check{x}_1 = x_1 - x_{1d}$, $\check{x}_2 = x_2 - x_{2d}$, $\check{u} = u - u_d$, one obtains the linear quadratic problem having a model

$$\frac{d\check{x}_1}{dt} = -(1 + \mathrm{Da}_1)\check{x}_1 + \mathrm{Da}_2\check{x}_2$$

$$\frac{d\check{x}_2}{dt} = \mathrm{Da}_1\check{x}_1 - (1 + \mathrm{Da}_2 + \mathrm{Da}_3)\check{x}_2 + \check{u}$$

and an objective to be minimized

$$I = \frac{1}{2}\int_0^{t_f}(\check{x}_1^2 + \alpha\check{x}_2^2 + \beta\check{u}^2)\, dt$$

The solution then can be found from Eqs. (3.3.91), (3.3.82), and (3.3.86),

where

$$\mathbf{A} = \begin{bmatrix} -(1 + \mathrm{Da}_1) & \mathrm{Da}_2 \\ \mathrm{Da}_1 & -(1 + \mathrm{Da}_2 + \mathrm{Da}_3) \end{bmatrix} \qquad \mathbf{B} = \begin{bmatrix} 0 \\ 1 \end{bmatrix}$$

$$\mathbf{F} = \begin{bmatrix} 1 & 0 \\ 0 & \alpha \end{bmatrix} \qquad E = \beta$$

Thus

$$\mathbf{S} = \begin{bmatrix} S_{11} & S_{12} \\ S_{21} & S_{22} \end{bmatrix}$$

is given by the solution of

$$\dot{S}_{11} = 2S_{11}(1 + \mathrm{Da}_1) - 2S_{12}\,\mathrm{Da}_1 + \frac{1}{\beta}S_{12}^2 - 1 \qquad S_{11}(t_f) = 0$$

$$\dot{S}_{12} = -S_{11}\,\mathrm{Da}_2 + S_{12}(2 + \mathrm{Da}_1 + \mathrm{Da}_2 + \mathrm{Da}_3) - S_{22}\,\mathrm{Da}_1 + \frac{1}{\beta}S_{12}S_{22} \qquad S_{12}(t_f) = 0$$

$$\dot{S}_{22} = 2S_{22}(1 + \mathrm{Da}_2 + \mathrm{Da}_3) - 2S_{12}\,\mathrm{Da}_2 + \frac{1}{\beta}S_{22}^2 - \alpha \qquad S_{22}(t_f) = 0$$

and $S_{21} = S_{12}$. Also, $\mathbf{K}(t)$ is

$$\mathbf{K}(t) = \frac{1}{\beta}[S_{12}S_{22}]$$

Thus the final controller is of the form

$$u(t) = u_d - \{K_1(t)[x_1(t) - x_{1d}] + K_2(t)[x_2(t) - x_{2d}]\}$$

Note that the Riccati equations for S_{11}, S_{12}, and S_{22} may be solved offline and $K_1(t)$, $K_2(t)$ stored in the computer for real-time use.

To illustrate the performance of the linear quadratic controller for this problem, computational results shall be presented for the parameter values:

$$\mathrm{Da}_1 = 3.0 \quad \mathrm{Da}_2 = 0.5 \quad \mathrm{Da}_3 = 1.0 \quad x_{1d} = 0.3 \quad x_{2d} = 0.4 \quad u_{1d} = 1.0$$

$$x_1(0) = 1.0 \quad x_2(0) = 0.0 \quad t_f = 2.0 \quad \alpha = 1.0 \quad \beta = 0.25$$

Solving the Riccati equations for $\mathbf{S}(t)$ by solving backward from $\mathbf{S}_f = \mathbf{0}$ gives the time-dependent controller gains $K_1(t)$, $K_2(t)$ shown in Fig. 3.22. Notice that K_1 and K_2 are constant over much of the time period and only change significantly as t approaches t_f. The linear-quadratic optimal feedback controller response is shown in Fig. 3.23, where it is seen that the controller does cause the system to approach the desired set points $x_{1d} = 0.3$, $x_{2d} = 0.4$ rather closely within the time period $0 < t < 2$. Also note that β has been chosen large enough so that $u(t)$ does not violate the physical

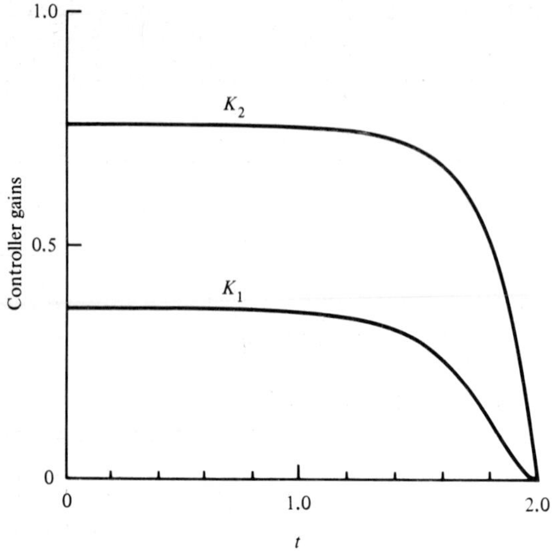

Figure 3.22 Optimal time-dependent controller gains for Example 3.3.6.

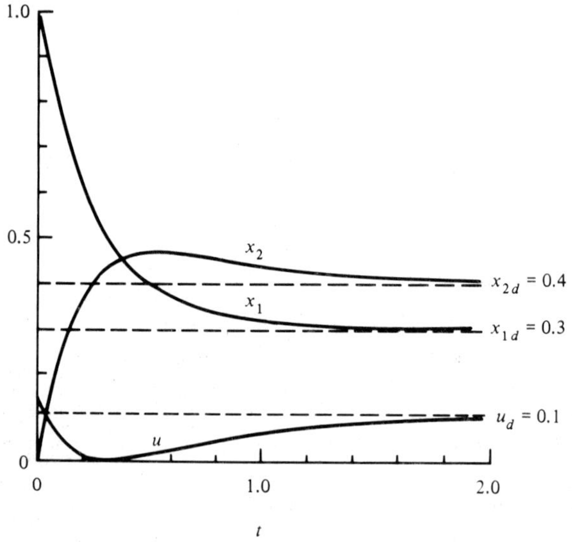

Figure 3.2.3 Linear-quadratic optimal feedback controller performance for Example 3.3.6.

constraint $u(t) > 0$. For values of β too small, $u(t)$ can become negative, violating this constraint, while for β too large, little dynamic control action is possible because $K_1(t)$, $K_2(t)$ remain close to zero. Thus for good optimal linear-quadratic controller design, one must tune the weighting parameters (such as α and β here) in order to obtain the desired controller response.

From the previous example one may note that the linear-quadratic formulation produces a proportional state feedback controller. From classical control theory one recognizes that proportional controllers lead to offset when there are set-point changes or load changes in the process; thus, it would be desirable to formulate the optimal feedback control problem so as to allow *integral control action* which would eliminate these offsets. There are several possible ways of doing this.

One method of including integral action is to include $d\mathbf{u}/dt$ terms in the objective functional so that Eq. (3.3.71) becomes

$$I = \tfrac{1}{2}\mathbf{x}^T\mathbf{S}_f\mathbf{x}\big|_{t_f} + \frac{1}{2}\int_{t_0}^{t_f}(\mathbf{x}^T\mathbf{F}\mathbf{x} + \dot{\mathbf{u}}^T\mathbf{E}\dot{\mathbf{u}})\,dt \tag{3.3.92}$$

where the state equation (3.3.70) must be differentiated to yield (for constant matrices **A**, **B**)

$$\ddot{\mathbf{x}} = \mathbf{A}\dot{\mathbf{x}} + \mathbf{B}\dot{\mathbf{u}}$$

Then the problem may be reformulated by letting

$$\mathbf{v}(t) = \dot{\mathbf{u}} \qquad \mathbf{w}_1 = \mathbf{x} \qquad \mathbf{w}_2 = \dot{\mathbf{x}} \qquad \mathbf{w} = \left[\begin{array}{c}\mathbf{w}_1\\ \hdashline \mathbf{w}_2\end{array}\right] \tag{3.3.93}$$

so that

$$\dot{\mathbf{w}} = \left[\begin{array}{c:c}0 & \mathbf{I}\\ \hdashline 0 & \mathbf{A}\end{array}\right]\mathbf{w} + \left[\begin{array}{c}\mathbf{0}\\ \hdashline \mathbf{B}\end{array}\right]\mathbf{v} \tag{3.3.94}$$

and the objective becomes

$$I = \frac{1}{2}\left\{\mathbf{w}^T\left[\begin{array}{c:c}\mathbf{S}_f & \mathbf{0}\\ \hdashline \mathbf{0} & \mathbf{0}\end{array}\right]\mathbf{w}\right\}_{t=t_f} + \frac{1}{2}\int_{t_0}^{t_f}\left\{\mathbf{w}^T\left[\begin{array}{c:c}\mathbf{F} & \mathbf{0}\\ \hdashline \mathbf{0} & \mathbf{0}\end{array}\right]\mathbf{w} + \mathbf{v}^T\mathbf{E}\mathbf{v}\right\}dt \tag{3.3.95}$$

By applying the feedback control law [Eq. (3.3.82)] to this reformulated problem, we obtain

$$\mathbf{v} = -\mathbf{K}(t)\mathbf{w} = -\left[\mathbf{K}_1 \,\vdots\, \mathbf{K}_2\right]\left[\begin{array}{c}\mathbf{w}_1\\ \hdashline \mathbf{w}_2\end{array}\right] \tag{3.3.96}$$

which, upon integration, takes the form

$$\mathbf{u}(t) = -\mathbf{K}_2\mathbf{x}(t) - \int_{t_0}^{t_f}(\mathbf{K}_1 - \dot{\mathbf{K}}_2)\mathbf{x}(t)\,dt \tag{3.3.97}$$

which has somewhat complicated integral action. If one allows $t_f \to \infty$, then $\mathbf{K}_1$ and $\mathbf{K}_2$ are constants and the feedback control law is

$$\mathbf{u}(t) = -\mathbf{K}_2\mathbf{x}(t) - \mathbf{K}_1\int_{t_0}^{t_f}\mathbf{x}(t)\,dt \tag{3.3.98}$$

an "optimal" proportional-integral controller.*

One may justifiably question the physical meaning of minimizing the time derivative of the control action in Eq. (3.3.92) and how this relates to reducing offset in the state variables. At the moment this relation is unclear.

* Through a slightly different transformation of states, derivative action may be obtained as well (see [30]).

A second means of incorporating integral action into the controller [31, 32] is to augment the state variables to include p new variables $\mathbf{z}(t)$ where

$$\dot{\mathbf{z}} = \mathbf{C}^*\mathbf{x} \tag{3.3.99}$$

are those state variables for which integral action is desired. Thus the new state $\hat{\mathbf{x}}$ of dimension $n + p$ is

$$\hat{\mathbf{x}} = \begin{bmatrix} \mathbf{x} \\ \hline \mathbf{z} \end{bmatrix} \tag{3.3.100}$$

When the objective functional is also modified to accommodate the new state variable, i.e.,

$$I = \tfrac{1}{2}\hat{\mathbf{x}}^T\hat{\mathbf{S}}_f\mathbf{x} + \frac{1}{2}\int_0^{t_f}(\hat{\mathbf{x}}\hat{\mathbf{F}}\hat{\mathbf{x}} + \mathbf{u}^T\mathbf{E}\mathbf{u})\,dt \tag{3.3.101}$$

the linear-quadratic optimal control law takes the form

$$\mathbf{u} = -\mathbf{K}\hat{\mathbf{x}} = -\mathbf{K}_1\mathbf{x} - \mathbf{K}_2\mathbf{z} = -\mathbf{K}_1\mathbf{x} - \mathbf{K}_2\mathbf{C}^*\int\mathbf{x}\,dt \tag{3.3.102}$$

which naturally includes integral action. Note that necessarily $p < m$, that is, the number of state variables for which integral action is desired cannot be larger than the number of control variables.

Another derivation of proportional and integral "optimal" feedback control is given in Sec. 5.4, where stochastic control is discussed. There integral action arises naturally as a means of dealing with random process disturbances.

Optimal Linear-Quadratic Feedback Control of Nonlinear Systems

It is possible to extend the results of the linear-quadratic problem to nonlinear systems so as to produce an optimal feedback control law. Let us consider the nonlinear optimal control problem given by the modeling equations

$$\frac{d\mathbf{x}}{dt} = \mathbf{f}(\mathbf{x}, \mathbf{u}) \qquad \mathbf{x}(t_0) = \mathbf{x}_0 \tag{3.3.103}$$

and the control objective functional

$$I[\mathbf{u}(t)] = G(\mathbf{x}(t_f)) + \int_{t_0}^{t_f} F(\mathbf{x}, \mathbf{u})\,dt \tag{3.3.104}$$

Now if one expands the objective functional to second-order about a nominal control and state trajectory $\bar{\mathbf{u}}(t)$, $\bar{\mathbf{x}}(t)$ while adjoining the state constraints, the variation in I is

$$\begin{aligned}\delta I = {} & \left(\frac{\partial G}{\partial \mathbf{x}}\right)_{\cdot t_f}\delta\mathbf{x}(t_f) + \frac{1}{2}\delta\mathbf{x}^T(t_f)\left(\frac{\partial^2 G}{\partial \mathbf{x}^2}\right)_{\cdot t_f}\delta\mathbf{x}(t_f) - \boldsymbol{\lambda}^T(t_f)\,\delta\mathbf{x}(t_f) \\ & + \boldsymbol{\lambda}^T(t_0)\,\delta\mathbf{x}(t_0) + \int_{t_0}^{t_f}\left[\left(\frac{\partial H}{\partial \mathbf{u}}\right)_{\cdot}\delta\mathbf{u} + \frac{1}{2}\delta\mathbf{u}^T\left(\frac{\partial^2 H}{\partial \mathbf{u}^2}\right)_{\cdot}\delta\mathbf{u} + \left(\frac{\partial H}{\partial \mathbf{x}}\right)_{\cdot}\delta\mathbf{x}\right. \\ & \left. + \frac{1}{2}\delta\mathbf{x}^T\left(\frac{\partial^2 H}{\partial \mathbf{x}^2}\right)_{\cdot}\delta\mathbf{x} + \delta\mathbf{x}^T\left(\frac{\partial^2 H}{\partial \mathbf{x}\,\partial \mathbf{u}}\right)_{\cdot}\delta\mathbf{u} + \frac{d\boldsymbol{\lambda}^T}{dt}\delta\mathbf{x}\right]dt\end{aligned} \tag{3.3.105}$$

where it is useful to recall that

$$\delta\mathbf{x} = \mathbf{x} - \bar{\mathbf{x}} \qquad \delta\mathbf{u} = \mathbf{u} - \bar{\mathbf{u}} \qquad \text{and} \qquad H = F + \boldsymbol{\lambda}^T\mathbf{f}$$

Now let us suppose our nominal trajectory $\bar{\mathbf{u}}(t)$, $\bar{\mathbf{x}}(t)$ satisfies the first-order necessary conditions for open-loop optimality, i.e.,

$$\frac{\partial H}{\partial \bar{\mathbf{u}}} = 0 \qquad \frac{d\boldsymbol{\lambda}^T}{dt} = -\left(\frac{\partial H}{\partial \mathbf{x}}\right)_. \qquad \boldsymbol{\lambda}^T(t_f) = \left(\frac{\partial G}{\partial \mathbf{x}(t_f)}\right)_. \tag{3.3.106}$$

where we assume $\mathbf{x}(t_0)$ is specified ($\mathbf{x}(t_0) = \bar{\mathbf{x}}_0$) and $\mathbf{x}(t_f)$ is unspecified. Thus $\bar{\mathbf{x}}(t)$, $\bar{\mathbf{u}}(t)$ are the open-loop optimal controls for a particular initial condition $\mathbf{x}(t_0) = \bar{\mathbf{x}}_0$. In this case Eq. (3.3.105) has only the remaining terms:

$$\delta I = \int_{t_0}^{t_f}\left[\frac{1}{2}\delta\mathbf{u}^T\left(\frac{\partial^2 H}{\partial \mathbf{u}^2}\right)_.\delta\mathbf{u} + \delta\mathbf{x}^T\left(\frac{\partial^2 H}{\partial \mathbf{x}\,\partial \mathbf{u}}\right)_.\delta\mathbf{u} + \frac{1}{2}\delta\mathbf{x}^T\left(\frac{\partial^2 H}{\partial \mathbf{x}^2}\right)_.\delta\mathbf{x}\right]dt$$

$$+ \frac{1}{2}\delta\mathbf{x}^T(t_f)\left(\frac{\partial^2 G}{\partial \mathbf{x}^2}\right)_{.t_f}\delta\mathbf{x}(t_f) \tag{3.3.107}$$

Now let us note that if we change the initial condition $\mathbf{x}(t_0)$, the entire nonlinear open-loop optimal control policy must be recalculated, because unlike linear problems, in which superposition may be used to quickly adjust for changes in initial conditions, nonlinear optimal control problems depend nonlinearly on the initial conditions. However, it is possible to develop a perturbation approach to solve this problem. If we consider the system equations linearized about the open-loop optimal policy $\bar{\mathbf{x}}(t)$, $\bar{\mathbf{u}}(t)$ for a fixed initial condition $\mathbf{x}(t_0) = \bar{\mathbf{x}}_0$, we obtain the *perturbation equations*

$$\frac{d(\delta\mathbf{x}(t))}{dt} = \left(\frac{\partial \mathbf{f}}{\partial \mathbf{x}}\right)_.\delta\mathbf{x} + \left(\frac{\partial \mathbf{f}}{\partial \mathbf{u}}\right)_.\delta\mathbf{u} \qquad \delta\mathbf{x}(t_0) = \delta\mathbf{x}_0 \tag{3.3.108}$$

which represent the system behavior for initial conditions in some domain close to the nominal value $\bar{\mathbf{x}}_0$, i.e., for $|\delta\mathbf{x}(t_0)| < \varepsilon$. The degradation in the system performance due to the deviations is given by Eq. (3.3.107). Thus Eqs. (3.3.107) and (3.3.108) represent a *linear-quadratic* optimal control problem whose solution $\delta\mathbf{u}^*(t)$, $\delta\mathbf{x}^*(t)$ represents the optimal feedback corrections to the nominal open-loop control. This is illustrated graphically for a single control–single state process in Fig. 3.24. There the nominal open-loop optimal control trajectory $\bar{\mathbf{x}}(t)$, $\bar{\mathbf{u}}(t)$ originating from $\bar{\mathbf{x}}_0$, and the perturbation feedback corrections $\delta\mathbf{u}(t)$, $\delta\mathbf{x}(t)$ resulting from another initial disturbance $\mathbf{x}_0$, are shown.

The solution to the perturbation feedback control law follows directly from the results of the last section if we define

$$\mathbf{A}(t) = \left(\frac{\partial \mathbf{f}}{\partial \mathbf{x}}\right)_. \qquad \mathbf{B}(t) = \left(\frac{\partial \mathbf{f}}{\partial \mathbf{u}}\right)_. \qquad \mathbf{F}(t) = \left(\frac{\partial^2 H}{\partial \mathbf{x}^2}\right)_.$$

$$\mathbf{E}(t) = \left(\frac{\partial^2 H}{\partial \mathbf{u}^2}\right)_. \qquad \mathbf{N}(t) = \left(\frac{\partial^2 H}{\partial \mathbf{x}\,\partial \mathbf{u}}\right)_. \qquad \mathbf{S}_f = \left(\frac{\partial^2 G}{\partial \mathbf{x}^2}\right)_{.t_f} \tag{3.3.109}$$

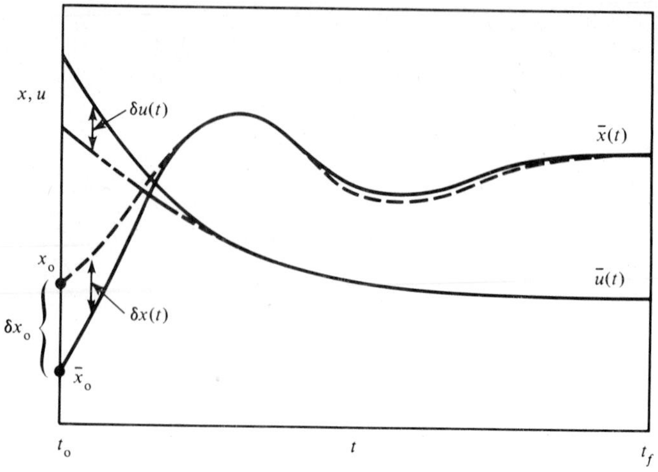

Figure 3.24 Optimal perturbation feedback control of a nonlinear system.

and use the results of Eqs. (3.3.84) to (3.3.86). Thus

$$\delta\mathbf{u}(t) = -\mathbf{K}(t)\,\delta\mathbf{x}(t) \tag{3.3.110}$$

where

$$\mathbf{K}(t) = \mathbf{E}^{-1}(\mathbf{N}^T + \mathbf{B}^T\mathbf{S}) \tag{3.3.85}$$

or

$$\mathbf{u}(t) = \bar{\mathbf{u}}(t) + \mathbf{K}(t)[\mathbf{x}(t) - \bar{\mathbf{x}}(t)] \tag{3.3.111}$$

The implementation of such a feedback control scheme could be carried out as follows:

1. Calculate and store a set of optimal open-loop control policies $\bar{\mathbf{u}}(t)$, $\bar{\mathbf{x}}(t)$ corresponding to a very coarse grid of nominal initial conditions $\bar{\mathbf{x}}_0$.
2. Also precalculate and store the controller gains $\mathbf{K}(t)$ for each nominal initial condition.
3. The on-line control can then be carried out by identifying the closest nominal initial condition in the stored grid and using that corresponding $\mathbf{K}(t)$ in the control law {Eq. (3.3.111)].

Let us illustrate this technique with the following example.

Example 3.3.7 Consider the simple problem of the control, by cooling-rate manipulation, of the temperature of a continuous-stirred tank reactor (CSTR) in which a zero-order reaction is taking place. The mathematical model for the reactor temperature is

$$\rho C_p V \frac{dT}{dt'} = \rho C_p F(T_f - T) + (-\Delta H) V k_0 e^{-E/RT} - Q' \quad (3.3.112)$$

$$T(0) = T_0$$

Let

$$x = \frac{T}{T_f} \qquad t = \frac{t'F}{V} \qquad a = \frac{(-\Delta H) k_0 V}{\rho C_p T_f F} \qquad \gamma = \frac{E}{RT_f} \qquad u = \frac{Q'}{\rho C_p F T_f}$$

$$x_0 = \frac{T_0}{T_f} \qquad x_d = \frac{T_d}{T_f}$$

so that the dimensionless model equation is

$$\frac{dx}{dt} = 1 - x + ae^{-\gamma/x} - u \qquad x(0) = x_0 \quad (3.3.113)$$

Our objective is to minimize the objective functional

$$I = \frac{1}{2} \int_0^{t_f} \left[(x - x_d)^2 + \alpha u^2 \right] dt \quad (3.3.114)$$

by designing an optimal feedback controller.

Let us assume that the open-loop optimal control policy $\bar{u}(t)$, $\bar{x}(t)$ has been determined for a given initial condition, $\bar{x}_0$ by a control vector iteration procedure:

1. Guess $u(t)$.
2. Integrate Eq. (3.3.102) from x_0 to x_f to yield $x(t)$.
3. Integrate

$$\frac{d\lambda}{dt} = -(x - x_d) + \lambda \left(1 - \frac{a\gamma e^{-\gamma/x}}{x^2} \right) \quad (3.3.115)$$

   backwards from $\lambda(t_f) = 0$.
4. Correct u by

$$u^{\text{new}} = u^{\text{old}} + \varepsilon \frac{\partial H}{\partial u} \qquad \varepsilon < 0$$

   where

$$H = \tfrac{1}{2} \left[(x - x_d)^2 + \alpha u^2 \right] + \lambda (1 - x + ae^{-\gamma/x} - u)$$

   and

$$\frac{\partial H}{\partial u} = \alpha u - \lambda \quad (3.3.116)$$

   and go back to step 2.

Let the result of this iterative calculation be denoted $\bar{x}(t)$, $\bar{u}(t)$. Repeat this open-loop optimal control calculation for a grid of x_0 values over the expected range of disturbances.

Now we can compute the linearized "matrices"

$$A = \left(\frac{\partial f}{\partial x}\right)_{\cdot} = \left(-1 + \frac{a\gamma}{\bar{x}^2} e^{-\gamma/\bar{x}}\right)$$

$$B = \left(\frac{\partial f}{\partial u}\right)_{\cdot} = -1$$

$$F = \left(\frac{\partial^2 H}{\partial x^2}\right)_{\cdot} = 1 + \bar{\lambda}\left(\frac{a\gamma^2}{\bar{x}^4} - \frac{2a\gamma}{\bar{x}^3}\right)e^{-\gamma/\bar{x}}$$

$$E = \left(\frac{\partial^2 H}{\partial u^2}\right)_{\cdot} = \alpha$$

$$N = 0$$

Thus $S(t)$ satisfies

$$\frac{dS}{dt} = -2S\left(-1 + \frac{a\gamma}{\bar{x}^2} e^{-\gamma/\bar{x}}\right) - \left[1 + \bar{\lambda}\left(\frac{a\gamma^2}{\bar{x}^4} - \frac{2a\gamma}{\bar{x}^3}\right)e^{-\gamma/\bar{x}}\right] + \frac{S^2}{\alpha}$$

$$S(t_f) = 0$$

or recognizing from Eq. (3.3.105) that $\bar{\lambda} = \alpha\bar{u}$, one obtains

$$\frac{dS}{dt} = -2\left[\frac{a\gamma}{\bar{x}^2} e^{-\gamma/\bar{x}} - 1\right]S + \frac{S^2}{\alpha} - 1 - \alpha\bar{u}\left(\frac{a\gamma^2}{\bar{x}^4} - \frac{2a\gamma}{\bar{x}^3}\right)e^{-\gamma/\bar{x}}$$

$$S(t_f) = 0 \tag{3.3.117}$$

and

$$K(t) = -\frac{S(t)}{\alpha} \tag{3.3.118}$$

Thus the optimal feedback controller is

$$u(t) = \bar{u}(t) - K(t)[x(t) - \bar{x}(t)] \tag{3.3.119}$$

3.4 NONLINEAR MULTIVARIABLE CONTROL

Although most of existing control theory only applies to linear systems with constant coefficients, the great majority of practical process control problems involve nonlinear systems. Thus there is a need to explore the useful theory for nonlinear multivariable control problems. For systems described by nonlinear differential equations, the general form of the modeling equations is

$$\frac{d\mathbf{x}}{dt} = \mathbf{f}(\mathbf{x}, \mathbf{u}, \mathbf{d}) \qquad \mathbf{x}(t_0) = \mathbf{x}_0 \tag{3.4.1}$$

$$\mathbf{y} = \mathbf{h}(\mathbf{x}, \mathbf{u}) \tag{3.4.2}$$

where, as in the previous section, $\mathbf{x}(t)$ is an n vector of states, $\mathbf{u}(t)$ is an m vector of controls, $\mathbf{d}(t)$ is a k vector of disturbances, and $\mathbf{y}(t)$ is an l vector of measured outputs. Clearly when

$$\mathbf{f} = \mathbf{Ax} + \mathbf{Bu} + \boldsymbol{\Gamma}\mathbf{d} \tag{3.4.3}$$

$$\mathbf{h} = \mathbf{C} \tag{3.4.4}$$

the nonlinear system [Eqs. (3.4.1) and (3.4.2)] reduces to the linear problem treated in the last section.

General strategies of nonlinear multivariable controller design seem to fall into two major categories:

1. Linearization of the nonlinear equations so that the linear design procedures (such as those described in Secs. 3.2 and 3.3) may be applied.
2. Special-purpose methods which may be applied directly to the nonlinear system.

Both approaches to control system design have their merits and shall be discussed in more detail in what follows.

Linearization

The easiest and most common approach to the design of control schemes for nonlinear multivariable systems is to linearize the modeling equations and apply standard linear design procedures. Although this approach is straightforward, it is useful to outline the essential features.

Rigorous conditions for *controllability*, *stabilizability*, etc., for nonlinear systems have been derived only for rather limited special cases (e.g., [2]). However, in most cases a good practical answer to such questions may be found through linearization of the nonlinear equations (3.4.1) and (3.4.2) and application of the linear theory to these linearized equations. The details of this approach are best illustrated by an example.

Example 3.4.1 Let us consider the isothermal CSTR described in Example 3.2.6 *except* that here the reaction $A \to B$ is second-order and the reaction $B \to C$ is $\frac{1}{2}$-order. In this case the modeling equations are

$$V\frac{dc_A}{dt'} = F(c_{A_f} - c_A) - Vk_1c_A^2 \tag{3.4.5}$$

$$V\frac{dc_B}{dt'} = F(c_{B_f} - c_B) + V(k_1c_A^2 - k_3c_B^{1/2}) \tag{3.4.6}$$

and may be put in the form of Eqs. (3.4.1) and (3.4.2) by defining

$$x_1 = \frac{c_A}{c_{A_{\text{ref}}}} \qquad x_2 = \frac{c_B}{c_{A_{\text{ref}}}} \qquad u_1 = \frac{c_{A_f}}{c_{A_{\text{ref}}}} \qquad u_2 = \frac{c_{B_f}}{c_{A_{\text{ref}}}}$$

$$\text{Da}_1 = \frac{k_1c_{A_{\text{ref}}}V}{F} \qquad \text{Da}_3 = \frac{k_3V}{F(c_{A_{\text{ref}}})^{1/2}} \qquad t = \frac{t'F}{V} \tag{3.4.7}$$

Thus the nonlinear model becomes

$$\frac{dx_1}{dt} = -x_1 - \mathrm{Da}_1 x_1^2 + u_1 \tag{3.4.8}$$

$$\frac{dx_2}{dt} = \mathrm{Da}_1 x_1^2 - x_2 - \mathrm{Da}_3 (x_2)^{1/2} + u_2 \tag{3.4.9}$$

Let us linearize these equations around the steady state defined by $u_{1s} = 1$, $u_{2s} = 0$ and make use of deviation variables $\hat{x}_i = x_i - x_{is}$, $\hat{u}_i = u_i - u_{is}$, $i = 1, 2$. Expanding Eqs. (3.4.8) and (3.4.9) in a first-order Taylor series, one obtains the linearized model

$$\frac{d\hat{x}_1}{dt} = -(1 + 2\,\mathrm{Da}_1 x_{1s})\hat{x}_1 + \hat{u}_1 \tag{3.4.10}$$

$$\frac{d\hat{x}_2}{dt} = (2\,\mathrm{Da}_1 x_{1s})\hat{x}_1 - \left(1 + \frac{1}{2}\frac{\mathrm{Da}_3}{(x_{2s})^{1/2}}\right)\hat{x}_2 + \hat{u}_2 \tag{3.4.11}$$

where x_{1s}, x_{2s} are solutions to the steady-state equations

$$\begin{aligned} 0 &= -x_{1s} - \mathrm{Da}_1 x_{1s}^2 + 1 \\ 0 &= \mathrm{Da}_1 x_{1s}^2 - x_{2s} - \mathrm{Da}_3 (x_{2s})^{1/2} \end{aligned} \tag{3.4.12}$$

The linearized equations (3.4.10) and (3.4.11) may now be written in the form of Eq. (3.2.1), where

$$\mathbf{A} = \begin{bmatrix} -(1 + 2\,\mathrm{Da}_1 x_{1s}) & 0 \\ (2\,\mathrm{Da}_1 x_{1s}) & -\left(1 + \frac{1}{2}\frac{\mathrm{Da}_3}{(x_{2s})^{1/2}}\right) \end{bmatrix} \tag{3.4.13}$$

$$\mathbf{B} = \begin{bmatrix} 1 & 0 \\ 0 & 1 \end{bmatrix} \tag{3.4.14}$$

and the test for controllability [Eq. (3.2.60)] applied. This requires that the controllability matrix

$$\mathbf{L}_c = [\mathbf{B} \vdots \mathbf{AB}] = \left[\begin{array}{cc|cc} 1 & 0 & -(1 + 2\,\mathrm{Da}_1 x_{1s}) & 0 \\ 0 & 1 & 2\,\mathrm{Da}_1 x_{1s} & -\left(1 + \frac{1}{2}\frac{\mathrm{Da}_3}{(x_{2s})^{1/2}}\right) \end{array}\right]$$

have rank 2. Clearly this is satisfied for all steady states. Thus we may say that this nonlinear system [Eqs. (3.4.8) and (3.4.9)] is controllable.

Example 3.4.2 Let us now determine the controllability of the problem in the previous example when we define $u_1 = c_{B_f}/c_{A_{\mathrm{ref}}}$ and $d_1 = c_{A_f}/c_{A_{\mathrm{ref}}}$, i.e., we have only one control and one disturbance. In this case the nonlinear equations are

$$\frac{dx_1}{dt} = -x_1 - \mathrm{Da}_1 x_1^2 + d_1 \tag{3.4.15}$$

$$\frac{dx_2}{dt} = \mathrm{Da}_1 x_1^2 - x_2 - \mathrm{Da}_3 (x_2)^{1/2} + u_1 \tag{3.4.16}$$

When one linearizes around the steady state defined by $d_{1s} = 1$, $u_{1s} = 0$, the linearized equations take the form of Eq. (3.3.1), with **A** given by Eq. (3.4.13) and

$$\mathbf{B} = \begin{bmatrix} 0 \\ 1 \end{bmatrix} \tag{3.4.17}$$

The controllability matrix [Eq. (3.2.60)] becomes

$$\mathbf{L}_c = [\mathbf{B} \vdots \mathbf{AB}] = \begin{bmatrix} 0 & \vdots & 0 \\ 1 & \vdots & -\left(1 + \dfrac{1}{2} \dfrac{\mathrm{Da}_3}{(x_{2s})^{1/2}}\right) \end{bmatrix}$$

which clearly has only rank one. Therefore the nonlinear system [Eqs. (3.4.15) and (3.4.16)] is *not* controllable.

One should note that these two examples are completely similar in structure to Examples 3.2.5 and 3.2.7, and the conclusions regarding controllability are the same for both the linear and nonlinear systems. This emphasizes the fact that the dominant factor determining controllability is the system structure, not whether the system is linear or nonlinear. Thus, in practical problems, one may usually use "linearized" controllability tests with confidence.

As a final comment, one should note that we linearized about a *steady state* to produce linear *constant coefficient* linearized equations. Had we linearized about some nominal time-varying path $\mathbf{x}_s(t)$ (such as might be necessary in batch processes or other processes not having a steady state), then the linearized equations would have had time-varying coefficients and a nonautonomous test of controllability [Eq. (3.2.68)] would have been necessary.

Having linearized the nonlinear system and tested for controllability as illustrated above, one may now directly apply one of the multivariable controller design procedures discussed in Secs. 3.2 and 3.3. To illustrate, we shall apply modal control to a nonlinear example.

Example 3.4.3 Let us design a modal feedback controller for the nonlinear CSTR described in Example 3.4.1. Notice that this is a nonlinear analog to the linear system discussed in Example 3.2.14. The nonlinear model is given by Eqs. (3.4.8) and (3.4.9), while the linearized state equations are given by Eqs. (3.4.10) and (3.4.11) and the output equation is

$$\mathbf{y} = \mathbf{C}\hat{\mathbf{x}} \tag{3.4.18}$$

where **C** must be chosen to provide modal decoupling. Analyzing the matrix

A, Eq. (3.4.13), one sees that the eigenvalues of the linearized system are

$$\lambda_1 = -(1 + 2\,\mathrm{Da}_1 x_{1s})$$
$$\lambda_2 = -\left[1 + \frac{1}{2}\frac{\mathrm{Da}_3}{(x_{2s})^{1/2}}\right] \tag{3.4.19}$$

and by noting the similarity to Example 3.2.14, one may immediately write down an orthonormal set of right and left eigenvectors of **A**:

$$\mathbf{R} = \frac{1}{2\,\mathrm{Da}_1 x_{1s} - \dfrac{1}{2}\dfrac{\mathrm{Da}_3}{(x_{2s})^{1/2}}}\begin{bmatrix} \dfrac{2\,\mathrm{Da}_1 x_{1s} - (1/2)\left[\mathrm{Da}_3/(x_{2s})^{1/2}\right]}{2\,\mathrm{Da}_1 x_{1s}} & 0 \\ -1 & 1 \end{bmatrix} \tag{3.4.20}$$

$$\mathbf{L} = \begin{bmatrix} 2\,\mathrm{Da}_1 x_{1s} & 0 \\ 2\,\mathrm{Da}_1 x_{1s} & 2\,\mathrm{Da}_1 x_{1s} - \dfrac{1}{2}\dfrac{\mathrm{Da}_3}{(x_{2s})^{1/2}} \end{bmatrix} \tag{3.4.21}$$

Recalling the modal design procedure of Sec. 3.2, the feedback controller must take the form

$$\hat{\mathbf{u}} = -\mathbf{B}^{-1}\mathbf{R}\mathbf{K}\mathbf{y} \tag{3.4.22}$$

where **B** is given by Eq. (3.4.14), **K** is a proportional controller given by

$$\mathbf{K} = \begin{bmatrix} k_{11} & 0 \\ 0 & k_{22} \end{bmatrix}$$

and the outputs are given by

$$\mathbf{y} = \mathbf{L}\hat{\mathbf{x}} \tag{3.4.23}$$

In component form the controller design is

$$\hat{u}_1 = -\frac{k_{11}}{2\,\mathrm{Da}_1 x_{1s}} y_1 = -k_{11}\hat{x}_1$$

$$\hat{u}_2 = \frac{1}{2\,\mathrm{Da}_1 x_{1s} - (1/2)\left[\mathrm{Da}_3/(x_{2s})^{1/2}\right]}\left[k_{11} y_1 - k_{22} y_2\right]$$
$$= \frac{2(k_{11} - k_{22})\mathrm{Da}_1 x_{1s}}{2\,\mathrm{Da}_1 x_{1s} - (1/2)\left[\mathrm{Da}_3/(x_{2s})^{1/2}\right]}\hat{x}_1 - k_{22}\hat{x}_2 \tag{3.4.24}$$

where the outputs must be chosen as

$$y_1 = 2\,\mathrm{Da}_1 x_{1s}\hat{x}_1$$
$$y_2 = 2\,\mathrm{Da}_1 x_{1s}\hat{x}_1 + \left[2\,\mathrm{Da}_1 x_{1s} - \frac{1}{2}\frac{\mathrm{Da}_3}{(x_{2s})^{1/2}}\right]\hat{x}_2 \tag{3.4.25}$$

Although this modal feedback control does decouple the outputs of the *linearized* system, the actual system is *nonlinear*, with closed-loop dynamics given by

$$\frac{dx_1}{dt} = -x_1 - \mathrm{Da}_1 x_1^2 + 1 - k_{11}(x_1 - x_{1s}) \tag{3.4.26}$$

$$\frac{dx_2}{dt} = \mathrm{Da}_1 x_1^2 - x_2 - \mathrm{Da}_3 (x_2)^{1/2}$$
$$+ \frac{2(k_{11} - k_{22})\mathrm{Da}_1 x_{1s}}{2\mathrm{Da}_1 x_{1s} - (1/2)\left[\mathrm{Da}_3/(x_{2s})^{1/2}\right]}(x_1 - x_{1s}) - k_{22}(x_2 - x_{2s}) \tag{3.4.27}$$

$$y_1 = 2\,\mathrm{Da}_1 x_{1s}(x_1 - x_{1s})$$
$$y_2 = 2\,\mathrm{Da}_1 x_{1s}(x_1 - x_{1s}) + \left[2\,\mathrm{Da}_1 x_{1s} - \frac{1}{2}\frac{\mathrm{Da}_3}{(x_{2s})^{1/2}}\right](x_2 - x_{2s}) \tag{3.4.28}$$

The controller performance can be illustrated by simulation of these nonlinear equations. Some results may be seen in Figs. 3.25 and 3.26 for the parameters $\mathrm{Da}_1 = 1.0$, $\mathrm{Da}_3 = 2.0$, $u_{1s} = 1.0$, and $u_{2s} = 0$, which from the solution of Eq. (3.4.12) yield $x_{1s} = 0.618$, $x_{2s} = 0.0308$. The initial conditions are $x_1 = 1.0$, $x_2 = 0$. Two cases were run: Case 1 with $k_{11} = 0.5$, $k_{22} = 1.5$, and Case 2 with $k_{11} = 5.0$, $k_{22} = 10.0$. The state variables are shown in Fig. 3.25, while the output variables are plotted in Fig. 3.26. Note

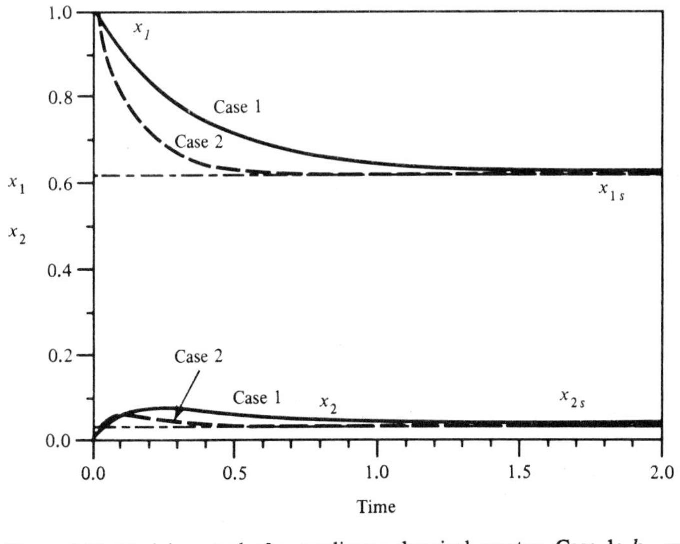

Figure 3.25 Modal control of a nonlinear chemical reactor. Case 1: $k_{11} = 0.5$. $k_{22} = 1.5$; Case 2: $k_{11} = 5.0$, $k_{22} = 10.0$.

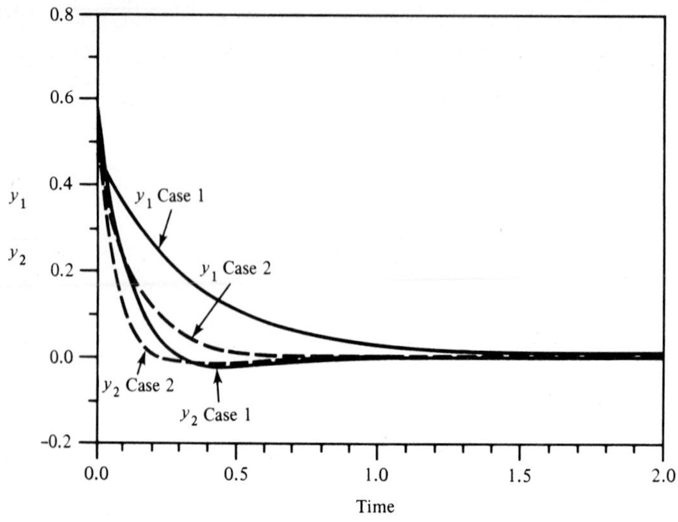

Figure 3.26 Modal control of a nonlinear chemical reactor. Case 1: $k_{11} = 0.5$; $k_{22} = 1.5$. Case 2: $k_{11} = 5.0$; $k_{22} = 10.0$.

that the controller performs well in both cases even though the design is based on the linearized equations. As might be expected, the larger controller gains provide faster system response.

Feedback Controller Parameterization

Although there are many special-purpose nonlinear system controller design procedures, most of these have very limited applicability and usually result from accumulated experience with a special type of nonlinear system. There is, however, one approach, termed *feedback controller parameterization*, which can be applied directly to any nonlinear system and has been found to perform well [27, 33].* The basic approach has been described previously in Sec. 3.3, and Example 3.3.4 illustrates things for a single control variable.

By defining a feedback control law

$$\mathbf{u} = \mathbf{g}(\mathbf{y}, \mathbf{b}) \tag{3.4.29}$$

with a specific structure and undetermined parameters $\mathbf{b}$, one can search for the optimal set of parameters which minimizes some objective functional such as

$$I = \mathbf{G}(\mathbf{y}(t_f)) + \int_0^{t_f} F(\mathbf{y}(t), \mathbf{u}(t))\, dt \tag{3.4.30}$$

Even though in principle there will be a different optimal set of parameters for each system initial condition, experience has shown that this dependence is often weak, and in practice one can determine a global set of optimal controller parameters. It is perhaps best to illustrate this type of control scheme by an example.

* In the control literature this approach is sometimes referred to as "specific optimal control."

Example 3.4.4 Let us apply feedback control parameterization to the design of a multivariable proportional controller for the isothermal CSTR system treated in Example 3.4.1. We shall assume that set points are on both x_1 and x_2, and we wish a state feedback controller of the form

$$\hat{\mathbf{u}} = \mathbf{K}(\mathbf{x} - \mathbf{x}_s) \tag{3.4.31}$$

where

$$\mathbf{K} = \begin{bmatrix} k_{11} & k_{12} \\ k_{21} & k_{22} \end{bmatrix} \tag{3.4.32}$$

is the multivariable proportional controller having four parameters k_{ij} to be chosen optimally. The objective to be minimized is

$$I = \int_0^{t_f} \left[(x_1 - x_{1s})^2 + \alpha(x_2 - x_{2s})^2 + \beta(\hat{u}_2)^2 \right] dt \tag{3.4.33}$$

where the last term arises because it is expensive to feed species B to the reactor to achieve good control. The controls u_1, u_2 are bounded by $0 \le u_1 \le 2.0$, $0 \le u_2 \le 1.0$.

The control system synthesis involves the following steps:

1. Guess the elements of **K**.
2. Solve Eqs. (3.4.8), (3.4.9), (3.4.31), and (3.4.33).
3. Send the resultant value of I to a parameter search routine and receive a new set of elements of **K**.
4. Return to step 2 and iterate.

For the parameters $\alpha = 2$, $\beta = 5$, $\mathrm{Da}_1 = 1.0$, $\mathrm{Da}_2 = 2.0$, $u_{1s} = 1.0$, $u_{2s} = 0$, $x_{1s} = 0.618$, $x_{2s} = 0.0308$, the optimal values of **K** found from the initial state $x_1 = 1.0$, $x_2 = 0$ were

$$\mathbf{K} = \begin{bmatrix} 3.0 & 0.35 \\ 0.2 & 2.0 \end{bmatrix}$$

while from the initial state $x_1 = 0.0$, $x_2 = 0.0$, the optimal proportional controller gains were

$$\mathbf{K} = \begin{bmatrix} 3.5 & 0.4 \\ 0 & 2.0 \end{bmatrix}$$

Note that there is little variation in **K** even though the initial start-up conditions are vastly different. The control system performance may be seen in Fig. 3.27. Clearly this design procedure is effective for this problem.

One disadvantage of this design procedure is that one must perform a complete dynamic simulation in order to compute I at each iteration of the parameter search. Because 50 to 100 iterations are not atypical, large-scale problems could require long computing times. As yet there does not appear to be sufficient practical experience with this design procedure to determine if this is a serious limitation.

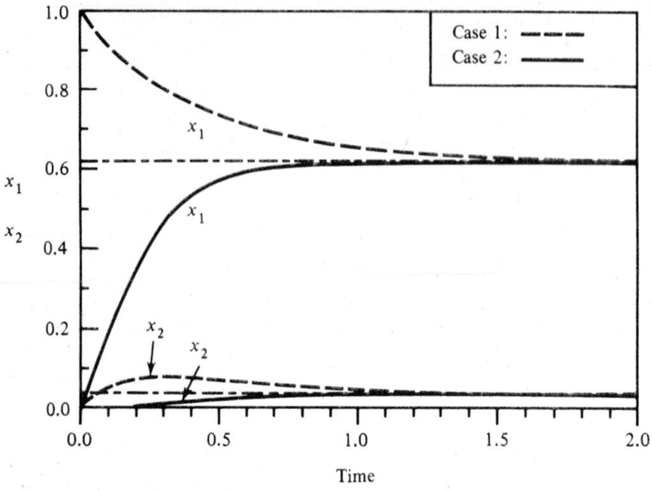

Figure 3.27 Parameterized feedback controller performance. Case 1: $x_1(0) = 1.0$; $x_2(0) = 0$. Case 2: $x_1(0) = 0$; $x_2(0) = 0$.

3.5 DISCRETE TIME SYSTEMS

Although the natural process model for most dynamic systems takes the form of differential equations, there are instances when discrete time models are convenient to use. In this case the model is a difference equation, which for linear systems may be written

$$\mathbf{x}[(k+1)\,\Delta t] = \mathbf{\Phi}(k\,\Delta t)\mathbf{x}(k\,\Delta t) + \boldsymbol{\beta}\mathbf{u}(k\,\Delta t) \tag{3.5.1}$$

$$\mathbf{y}(k\,\Delta t) = \mathbf{C}\mathbf{x}(k\,\Delta t) \tag{3.5.2}$$

Discrete time models are particularly useful when implementing direct digital control (DDC) because the measurements $\mathbf{y}(k\,\Delta t)$ are taken at discrete times $t_k = k\,\Delta t$, $k = 1, 2, \ldots,$ and the controls are held piecewise constant over the interval Δt. In this case the difference equations (3.5.1) and (3.5.2) may be derived from the original differential equation

$$\dot{\mathbf{x}} = \mathbf{A}\mathbf{x} + \mathbf{B}\mathbf{u} \qquad \mathbf{x}(0) = \mathbf{x}_0 \tag{3.5.3}$$

$$\mathbf{y} = \mathbf{C}\mathbf{x} \tag{3.5.4}$$

where **A**, **B**, **C**, are constant matrices. By recalling the solution to Eq. (3.5.3),

$$\mathbf{x}(t) = e^{\mathbf{A}t}\mathbf{x}_0 + \int_0^t e^{\mathbf{A}(t-\tau)}\mathbf{B}\mathbf{u}(\tau)\,d\tau \tag{3.5.5}$$

we may solve for $\mathbf{x}(k\,\Delta t)$ by repeated application of Eq. (3.5.5) for piecewise constant controls to yield

$$\begin{aligned} \mathbf{x}(\Delta t) &= e^{\mathbf{A}\,\Delta t}\mathbf{x}_0 + \int_0^{\Delta t} e^{\mathbf{A}(\Delta t-\tau)}\,d\tau\;\mathbf{B}\mathbf{u}(0) \\ \mathbf{x}(2\,\Delta t) &= e^{\mathbf{A}\,\Delta t}\mathbf{x}(\Delta t) + \int_{\Delta t}^{2\,\Delta t} e^{\mathbf{A}(2\,\Delta t-\tau)}\,d\tau\;\mathbf{B}\mathbf{u}(\Delta t) \\ \mathbf{x}[(k+1)\,\Delta t] &= e^{\mathbf{A}\,\Delta t}\mathbf{x}(k\,\Delta t) + \int_{k\,\Delta t}^{(k+1)\,\Delta t} e^{\mathbf{A}[(k+1)\,\Delta t-\tau]}\,d\tau\;\mathbf{B}\mathbf{u}(k\,\Delta t) \end{aligned} \tag{3.5.6}$$

Thus comparing Eqs. (3.5.6) and (3.5.1), one sees that defining

$$\mathbf{\Phi} = e^{\mathbf{A}\,\Delta t} \tag{3.5.7}$$

$$\boldsymbol{\beta} = \int_0^{\Delta t} e^{\mathbf{A}(\Delta t - \tau)}\, d\tau\, \mathbf{B} \tag{3.5.8}$$

gives the equivalent difference equation for implementation of DDC. By rearrangement of Eqs. (3.5.6), the discrete analog to Eq. (3.5.5) is

$$\mathbf{x}(k\,\Delta t) = \mathbf{\Phi}^k \mathbf{x}_0 + \boldsymbol{\beta} \sum_{i=0}^{k-1} \mathbf{\Phi}^{k-1-i} \mathbf{u}(i\,\Delta t) \tag{3.5.9}$$

The discrete equations (3.5.1) can also arise by taking the finite difference form of Eq. (3.5.3). This leads to

$$\frac{\mathbf{x}[(k+1)\,\Delta t] - \mathbf{x}(k\,\Delta t)}{\Delta t} = \mathbf{A}\mathbf{x}(k\,\Delta t) + \mathbf{B}\mathbf{u}(k\,\Delta t) \tag{3.5.10}$$

which by defining

$$\mathbf{\Phi} = (\mathbf{I} + \mathbf{A}\,\Delta t) \tag{3.5.11}$$

$$\boldsymbol{\beta} = \mathbf{B}\,\Delta t \tag{3.5.12}$$

reduces to Eq. (3.5.1). For the finite difference formulation to be valid, Δt must be small compared with the smallest time constant of the system. By contrast, the DDC formulation [Eqs. (3.5.7) and (3.5.8)] is valid for any size Δt.

Although there is a full theory of discrete systems, involving difference equations in the time domain [34] and z transforms in the transform space [35], we shall not go deeper in this direction here. The results parallel those already discussed for continuous systems, and the details are readily available to the interested reader (e.g., [6, 34, 35]).

REFERENCES

1. Amundson, N. R.: *Mathematical Methods in Chemical Engineering*, Prentice-Hall, New York, 1966.
2. Lee, E. B., and L. Markus: *Foundations of Optimal Control*, Wiley, New York, 1967.
3. Athans, M., and P. L. Falb: *Optimal Control*, McGraw-Hill, New York, 1966.
4. Brogan, W. L.: *Modern Control Theory*, Quantum Publishers, Inc., 1974.
5. Fossard, A. J.: *Multivariable System Control*, North-Holland, Amsterdam, 1977.
6. Bryson, A. E., and Y. C. Ho: *Applied Optimal Control*, 2d ed., Blaisdell, Waltham, Mass., 1976.
7. Brockett, R. W.: *Finite Dimensional Linear Systems*, Wiley, New York, 1970.
8. Bristol, E. H.: *IEEE Trans. Auto. Control AC-11*, 133 (1966).
9. Gilbert, E. G., and J. R. Pivnichny: *IEEE Trans. Auto. Control AC-14*, 652 (1969).
10. MacFarlane, A. G. J.: *Automatica* **8**:455 (1972).
11. Fossard, A., and C. Gueguen: *Multivariable System Control*, North-Holland, Amsterdam, 1977.
12. Gould, L.: *Chemical Process Control*, Addison-Wesley, Reading, Mass., 1969.
13. Davison, E. J., and K. J. Chadha: *Automatica* **8**:263 (1972).
14. Rosenbrock, H. H.: *Computer-aided Control System Design*, Wiley, New York, 1974.
15. Fisher, D. G., and D. E. Seborg: *Multivariable Computer Control*, American Elsevier, New York, 1976.

16. Ray, W. H., and J. Szekely: *Process Optimization*, Wiley, New York, 1973.
17. Pontryagin, L. S.: *Mathematical Theory of Optimal Processes*, Wiley, New York, 1962.
18. Dreyfus, S. E.: *Dynamic Programming and the Calculus of Variations*, Academic Press, New York, 1965.
19. Leitman, G.: *An Introduction to Optimal Control*, McGraw-Hill, New York, 1966.
20. Jacobson, D. H.: *Int. J. Cont.* 7:175 (1969).
21. Padmanabhan, L., and D. G. Bankoff: *Automatica* **8**:65 (1972).
22. Lasdon, L. S., S. K. Mitter, and A. D. Waren: *IEEE Trans. Aut. Cont.* **AC-12**:132 (1967).
23. Pagurek, B., and C. M. Woodside: *Automatica* **4**:337 (1968).
24. Fox, L.: *The Numerical Solution of TPBVP's*, Oxford, 1957.
25. Lee, E. S.: *Quasilinearization and Invariant Imbedding*, Academic Press, New York, 1968.
26. Keller, H. B.: *Numerical Methods for TPBVP's*, Blaisdell, Waltham, Mass., 1968.
27. Hicks, G.A., and W. H. Ray: *Can. J. ChE.* **49**:522 (1971).
28. Johnson, C. D.: *Adv. Control systems* **2** (1964).
29. Special Issue of *IEEE Trans. Auto. Control*, December 1971.
30. Douglas, J. M.: *Process Dynamics and Control*, vol. II, Prentice-Hall, Englewood Cliffs, N.J., 1972, p. 288.
31. Newell, R. B., and D. G. Fisher: *Automatica* **8**:247 (1972).
32. Johnson, C. D.: *Automatica* **9**:137 (1973).
33. Sage, A. P.: *Optimum Systems Control*, Prentice-Hall, Englewood Cliffs, N.J., 1968.
34. Dorf, R. C.: *Time Domain Analysis and Design of Control Systems*, Addison-Wesley, Reading, Mass., 1964.
35. Kuo, B. J.: *Analysis and Synthesis of Sampled Data Control Systems*, Prentice-Hall, Englewood Cliffs, N.J., 1963.

PROBLEMS

3.1 A high-priced specialty chemical is made in a batch reactor. The reactions of interest are

$$R \xrightarrow{k_1} P \tag{1}$$

$$R \xrightarrow{k_2} W \tag{2}$$

where R is an expensive raw material, P is the product, and W is a waste byproduct. Both reactions (1) and (2) are irreversible and first-order in species R. The velocity constants k_1 and k_2 are given by

$$k_i = A_i e^{-E_i/RT} \qquad i = 1, 2$$

Material balances on species R and P in the batch reactor are

$$\frac{dR}{dt} = -(k_1 + k_2)R \qquad R(0) = R_0$$

$$\frac{dP}{dt} = k_1 R \qquad P(0) = 0$$

$$W = R_0 - R - P$$

As a control engineer you have been asked to design a temperature control program for the batch reactor to be carried out over a 1-h batch time and which maximizes the amount of P produced at the end of the run. The mathematics can be simplified by letting

$$x_1 = \frac{R}{R_0} \qquad x_2 = \frac{P}{R_0} \qquad u = k_1 \qquad p = \frac{E_2}{E_1}$$

$$\alpha = \frac{A_2}{(A_1)^p}$$

so that $k_2 = \alpha u^p$. With these substitutions, the optimal control problem is to choose $u(t)$, $0 \le t \le 1$, such that $x_2|_{t=1}$ is maximized and

$$\frac{dx_1}{dt} = -(u + \alpha u^p)x_1 \qquad x_1(0) = 1$$

$$\frac{dx_2}{dt} = ux_1 \qquad x_2(0) = 0$$

Note that it is permissible to use u as the control variable, because

$$u = k_1 = A_1 e^{-E_1/RT}$$

yields a monotonic relationship between $u(t)$ and $T(t)$.

For the parameters $p = 2.0$, $\alpha = 0.5$, $A_1 = 10^6\ \mathrm{s}^{-1}$, $E_1 = 10{,}000$ cal/(g)(mol), and for temperature constraints of the form $0 \le u(t) \le 5$, determine the optimal open-loop temperature program $u(t) \Leftrightarrow T(t)$ in three different ways:

(*a*) Apply the maximum principle in order to calculate the optimal control using a gradient procedure. Determine the optimal program from two initial guesses of $u(t)$.

(*b*) Apply the control vector parameterization procedure to the problem by finding the optimal set of coefficients a_0, a_1, a_2 in the expression

$$u(t) = a_0 + a_1 t + a_2 t^2$$

Use a multivariable search routine (see Ref. [16]) to determine the optimal values of a_0, a_1, and a_2. Compare your results with those found by the gradient method.

(*c*) Determine an optimal feedback control law of the form

$$u(x_1) = b_0 + b_1 x_1 + b_2 x_1^2$$

by using a multivariable search routine to determine the optimal controller parameters b_0, b_1, b_2. Compare with the results of parts (*a*) and (*b*).

3.2 A simple suspension system is to be designed for a high-speed rapid transit vehicle. A simple laboratory model of the system is sketched in the figure below, where springs (spring constant K') are used to cushion the vertical motions in the absence of feedback control. However, it is desired to design a feedback controller to improve the stability and performance of the suspension system. To accomplish this, a force $u'(t)$ may be applied to the bouncing system.

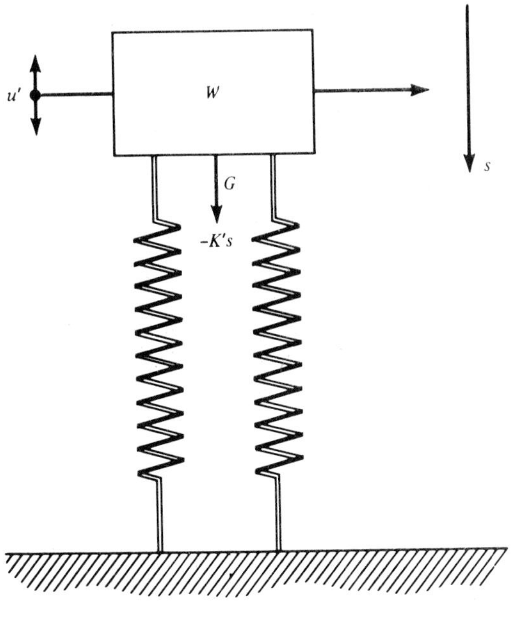

The modeling equations are

$$W\frac{ds^2}{dt} = -K's + G + u'$$

where G is the force of gravity and W is the mass of the system. By noting that at steady state ($u' = 0$)

$$0 = -K's_s + G$$

we may define normalized deviation variables and parameters

$$x_1 = s - s_s \qquad x_2 = \dot{s} \qquad u = \frac{u'}{W} \qquad K = \frac{K'}{W}$$

to yield the model

$$\frac{dx_1}{dt} = x_2$$

$$\frac{dx_2}{dt} = -Kx_1 + u$$

Based on this information:

(*a*)Make use of the results in Sec. 3.3 to find the optimal linear quadratic feedback control law which minimizes

$$I = \int_0^{t_f} (x_1^2 + \alpha x_2^2 + \beta u^2)\, dt$$

Carry out the computations for $\alpha = 1$, $\beta = 0.25$, $K = 3$, $t_f = 2.0$, $x_1(0) = 1.0$, $x_2(0) = 1.0$.

(*b*) The traditional feedback controller for suspension systems is the shock absorber, which has the form $u = -C\dot{x}_1$ (pure derivative action). Compare your "optimal controller" with this traditional one.

3.3 Carry out the computations to determine the near-optimal linear quadratic feedback controller for the problem discussed in Example 3.3.7. Use the following parameters: $a = 1000$, $\gamma = 10$, $x_d = 1.3$, $\bar{x}(0) = 1.5$, $t_f = 2.0$, and $\alpha = 0.25$. After the optimal open-loop policy has been found for $x(0) = 1.5$, determine the near-optimal feedback controller performance for $x(0) = 1.4$ and $x(0) = 1.6$. How does the controller perform for this highly nonlinear system?

3.4 Consider the tank network shown in the figure below. Liquid flows from one tank to the next, with the outflow of each tank assumed to be proportional to the level in that tank. The outlet of the second tank is split, with a fraction F exiting and the remainder pumped back to the first tank. The modeling equations can be assumed as

$$\frac{dh_1}{dt} = u_1 - \alpha h_1 + \beta h_2$$

$$\frac{dh_2}{dt} = u_2 + \alpha h_1 - (\beta + \gamma)h_2$$

It is desired to control the liquid levels in these tanks by choosing a controlled inlet flow position (either u_1 or u_2) as shown. As a means of aiding your choice,

(*a*) Determine if the controllability conditions are satisfied for u_1 alone (valve u_2 at constant flow rate) and for u_2 along (valve u_1 at constant flow rate).

(*b*) Are there other practical conditions to be considered which are not treated by formal controllability conditions, but which may influence your choice? Discuss these.

(*c*) If the recycle loop were removed, modify the modeling equations, and reevaluate controllability as in part (*a*).

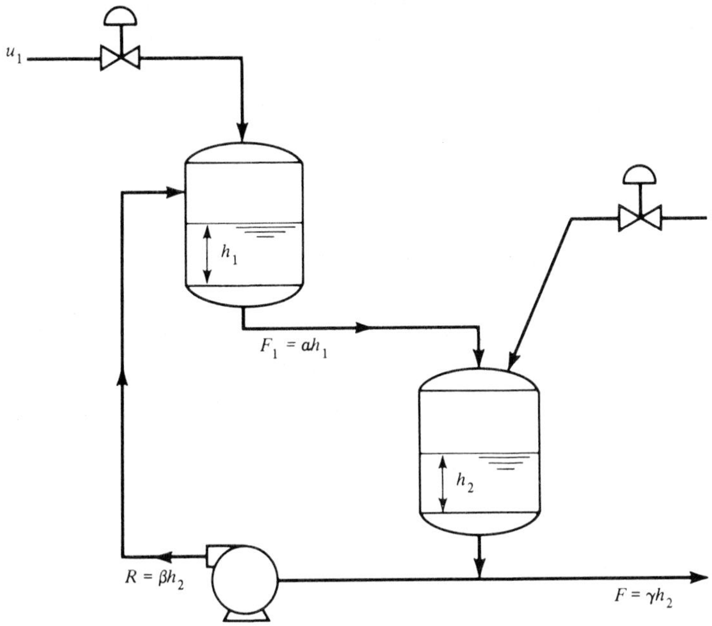

3.5 For the vehicle suspension problem discussed in Prob. 3.2, develop a transform-domain representation between the measured vertical height $y = x_1$ and control force u, i.e.,

$$\bar{y}(s) = g(s)\bar{u}(s)$$

Determine $g(s)$. [Hint: See Eq. (3.3.50) and the accompanying discussion.]

3.6 You have been given the multivariable control system

$$\bar{\mathbf{y}}(s) = \begin{bmatrix} \bar{y}_1 \\ \bar{y}_2 \end{bmatrix} \qquad \bar{\mathbf{u}}(s) = \begin{bmatrix} \bar{u}_1 \\ \bar{u}_2 \end{bmatrix} \qquad \mathbf{G}(s) = \begin{bmatrix} \dfrac{3}{1+10s} & \dfrac{1}{1+20s} \\ \dfrac{2}{1+25s} & \dfrac{4}{1+5s} \end{bmatrix}$$

in the Laplace domain. Convert this to an equivalent set of ordinary differential equations of the form

$$\frac{d\mathbf{x}}{dt} = \mathbf{Ax} + \mathbf{Bu}$$

$$\mathbf{y} = \mathbf{Cx}$$

3.7 Consider the water tank system of Prob. 3.4 with both control valves u_1, u_2 available. Carry out the following types of controller designs:

(*a*) Two single-loop proportional controllers.

(*b*) Modal feedback control.

(*c*) Set-point compensation for the controller in part (*a*).

(*d*) Complete dynamic noninteracting control. Compare the controller responses (interaction, offset, etc.) and the relative ease of implementation of the controllers.

As test disturbances, consider a unit step change in the h_1 set point while endeavoring to keep h_2 constant. Conversely, consider a unit step change in h_2 while h_1 is held constant. Make use of the following parameters: $\alpha = 3$, $\beta = 2$, $\gamma = 2$. For each design, choose the more convenient system representation (i.e., time domain or transform domain).

3.8 Pulse testing of a distillation column yields the following dynamic model between product concentrations y_1, y_2 and product drawoff rates u_1, u_2:

$$\bar{\mathbf{y}}(s) = \mathbf{G}(s)\bar{\mathbf{u}}(s)$$

where

$$\mathbf{y} = \begin{bmatrix} y_1 \\ y_2 \end{bmatrix} \qquad \mathbf{u} = \begin{bmatrix} u_1 \\ u_2 \end{bmatrix} \qquad \mathbf{G}(s) = \begin{bmatrix} \dfrac{1.0}{1+10s} & \dfrac{0.3}{1+8s} \\ \dfrac{0.2}{1+7s} & \dfrac{0.5}{1+5s} \end{bmatrix}$$

(*a*) Convert the above *transform state space model* to a *time-domain model* in the form

$$\mathbf{x} = \mathbf{Ax} + \mathbf{Bu}$$

$$\mathbf{y} = \mathbf{Cx}$$

Is this a minimal realization in state space?

(*b*) Is the distillation column *output controllable*? Why?

(*c*) Write down the block diagram and the design equations for a noninteracting proportional feedback controller which eliminates *steady-state* interactions. What is the closed-loop transfer function between $\mathbf{y}$ and set point $\mathbf{y}_d$?

3.9 Extend the linear quadratic optimal feedback control law of Sec. 3.3 to include *optimal feedforward control* when measured disturbances are included in the model; i.e., find the optimal feedback-feedforward control law for the system

$$\frac{d\mathbf{x}}{dt} = \mathbf{Ax} + \mathbf{Bu} + \mathbf{Dd} \qquad \mathbf{x}(t_0) = \mathbf{x}_0$$

where $\mathbf{D}$ is an $n \times k$ matrix and $\mathbf{d}$ is a k vector of disturbances. (*Hint:* see Ref. [15]).

3.10 Consider the nonisothermal CSTR in which the exothermic reaction $A \to B$ is being carried out. The modeling equations in dimensionless form may be written

$$\frac{dx_1}{dt} = -x_1 + \mathrm{Da}(1 - x_1)e^{x_2} + u_1$$

$$\frac{dx_2}{dt} = -(1+\beta)x_2 + B\,\mathrm{Da}(1 - x_1)e^{x_2} + \beta u_2$$

(*a*) Determine if this system is controllable when operated around the steady state x_{1s}, x_{2s} resulting from $u_{1s} = u_{2s} = 0$.

(*b*) Design a proportional feedback control system which contains a steady-state noninteracting compensator. Begin by linearization around the steady-state noted in (*a*).

(*c*) Simulate the reactor for the parameters $\mathrm{Da} = 0.1$, $\beta = 3.0$, $B = 19$, and demonstrate your controller performance when applied to the nonlinear system.

3.11 Consider the CSTR described in Example 3.2.5 with continuous modeling equations

$$\frac{dx_1}{dt} = -(1 + \mathrm{Da}_1)x_1 + u_1$$

$$\frac{dx_2}{dt} = \mathrm{Da}_1 x_1 - (1 + \mathrm{Da}_3)x_2 + u_2$$

It is planned to implement $P + I$ control relating u_1 to $x_{1d} - x_1$ and u_2 to $x_{2d} - x_2$ under DDC mode with sampling time Δt. Here x_{1d}, x_{2d}, are the state set points. Convert the continuous model to the equivalent discrete model necessary for DDC design. Draw the block diagram and specify final controller design equations.

CHAPTER

FOUR

CONTROL OF DISTRIBUTED PARAMETER SYSTEMS

4.1 INTRODUCTION

Distributed parameter systems are distinguished by the fact that the states, controls, and outputs may depend on spatial position. Thus the natural form of the system model is the partial differential equation, integral equation, or transcendental transfer function. One particularly important class of distributed parameter systems consists of those having pure time delays. There exists a wide range of industrially important distributed parameter control problems (see [1–4] for a selection); however, we shall choose two simple example problems to illustrate some of the fundamental concepts.

Example 4.1.1* Consider the problem of reheating a steel slab by thermal radiation (for rolling) in a batch furnace as sketched in Fig. 4.1. For proper rolling characteristics, it is necessary for the slab to have a specified temperature distribution $T_d(z)$. Thus our problem is to control the heat flux to the surface of the slab in such a way as to approach this desired temperature distribution in some optimal fashion.

* This example is taken from [5] and reprinted by permission of John Wiley and Sons, Inc.

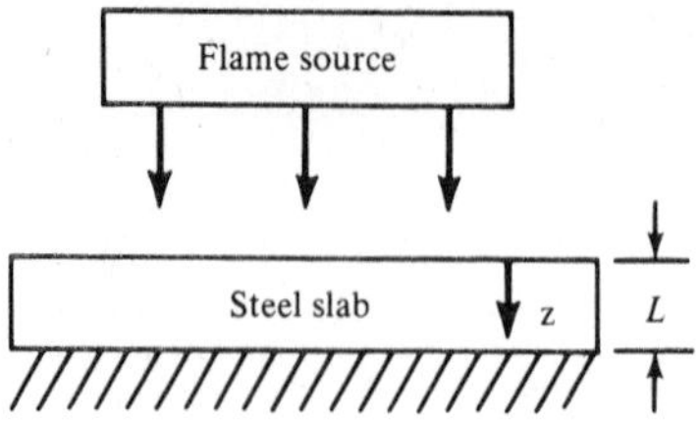

Figure 4.1 Radiant heating of a slab.

To be more precise, let us consider the modeling equations for the slab

$$\frac{\partial T(z,t)}{\partial t} = \frac{1}{\beta(T)} \frac{\partial[\alpha(T)\,\partial T(z,t)/\partial z]}{\partial z} \qquad \begin{matrix} 0 \le z \le L \\ 0 \le t \le t_f \end{matrix} \tag{4.1.1}$$

$$\frac{\partial T(0,t)}{\partial z} = v(t) \tag{4.1.2}$$

$$\frac{\partial T(L,t)}{\partial z} = 0 \tag{4.1.3}$$

$$T(z,0) = T_0(z) \tag{4.1.4}$$

which reflect the fact that negligible heat is lost at the sides and bottom of the slab; by adjusting the flame, one can control the heat flux at the upper surface between bounds

$$v_* \le v(t) \le v^* \tag{4.1.5}$$

Note that the state variables $T(z, t)$ are spatially dependent, but that the control $v(t)$ is only time-dependent and is applied at the boundary. For distributed parameter systems one often must consider control variables appearing in the boundary conditions as well as those appearing in the differential equations.

The set points in such a control problem are also spatially dependent. For example, here one wishes to manipulate $v(t)$ so as to achieve a certain set point $T_d(z)$. If one wished to apply *optimal control* to this example problem, then the objective functional

$$I[v(t)] = \int_0^{t_f}\int_0^L [T(z,t) - T_d(z)]^2\, dt\, dz \tag{4.1.6}$$

if minimized, would cause $T(z, t)$ to be quickly driven toward the set point $T_d(z)$. This is an example of *open-loop control* applied at the boundary of a distributed process.

Example 4.1.2 Let us consider the problem of controlling the temperature in a stirred mixing tank such as that shown in Fig. 4.2. The temperature is regulated by a feedback controller which adjusts the fraction of hot stream $\lambda(t)$ which is fed to the tank. The tank level is controlled by an overflow weir, and the total inlet flow is kept constant by a flow regulator even when the ratio of hot- and cold-stream flow rates varies. Unfortunately, by poor

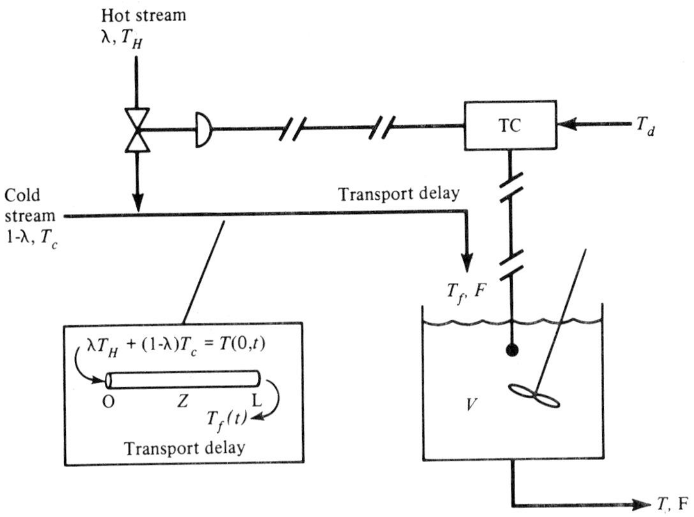

Figure 4.2 Control of the temperature in a stirred mixing tank with transport delays in the inlet piping.

design, the hot and cold streams are mixed some distance from the mixing tank, so that there is a transport delay in the inlet feed line.

An energy balance on the tank (assuming no heat losses to the environment) yields

$$\rho C_p V \frac{dT}{dt} = \rho C_p \big(F T_f(t) - F T \big) \tag{4.1.7}$$

where $T_f(t)$ represents the feed temperature at the mixing tank itself. It is necessary to calculate $T_f(t)$ in terms of the cold-stream temperature T_C, hot-stream temperature T_H, and fraction of hot-stream feed $\lambda(t)$. Also one must account for the fact that a transport delay occurs due to fluid flowing at flow rate F in a well-insulated pipe of length L and cross-sectional area a_c. An energy balance over this pipe [6] yields a model for the temperature profile in the pipe, $T_p(z, t)$,

$$\rho C_p \frac{\partial T_p(z, t)}{\partial t} + \rho C_p \frac{F}{a_c} \frac{\partial T_p(z, t)}{\partial z} = 0 \qquad 0 < z < L \tag{4.1.8}$$

The inlet to the pipe is

$$T_p(0, t) = \lambda(t) T_H + \big[1 - \lambda(t) \big] T_C \tag{4.1.9}$$

and the exit of the pipe is the inlet temperature to the mixing tank, given by

$$T_f(t) \equiv T_p(L, t) \tag{4.1.10}$$

Equation (4.1.8) is a first-order hyperbolic equation which models a pure transport delay. Fortunately it has a very simple solution,

$$T_p(L, t) = T(0, t - \alpha) \tag{4.1.11}$$

where $\alpha = La_c/F$ is the time required for the fluid to travel in the pipe. Thus making use of Eqs. (4.1.9) and (4.1.10), one obtains an expression for $T_f(t)$:

$$T_f(t) = T_C + (T_H - T_C)\lambda(t - \alpha) \tag{4.1.12}$$

If this expression is used in Eq. (4.1.7), one obtains

$$\theta\frac{dT}{dt} = [T_C + (T_H - T_C)\lambda(t - \alpha) - T] \tag{4.1.13}$$

where $\theta = V/F$ is the mean residence time in the tank. If one converts Eq. (4.1.13) to the transform domain by first defining deviation variables about some steady state

$$T = T_s \qquad \lambda = \lambda_s$$

that is,

$$y = T - T_s \qquad u = \lambda - \lambda_s$$

then

$$\frac{dy}{dt} = (T_H - T_C)u(t - \alpha) - y \qquad y(0) = 0 \tag{4.1.14}$$

and transforming, one obtains

$$\bar{y}(s) = \frac{(T_H - T_C)e^{-\alpha s}}{\theta s + 1}\bar{u}(s) \tag{4.1.15}$$

Note that except for the time delay, Eqs. (4.1.14) and (4.1.15) would be simple lumped parameter models. However, the presence of the time delay causes both theoretical and practical complications in control system design. Design procedures for this class of important problems shall be discussed in Sec. 4.5.

In the next section we shall introduce some basic concepts which are important in understanding the dynamics of distributed parameter systems. Then some simple controller design strategies for linear systems will be considered. Following this introductory material, the underlying theory and control system synthesis for the optimal control of distributed parameter systems will be presented. Finally, control system design procedures for nonlinear distributed parameter systems and for systems having pure time delays are discussed.

4.2 FEEDBACK CONTROL OF LINEAR DISTRIBUTED PARAMETER SYSTEMS

In carrying out the design of feedback controllers for distributed parameter systems, one can call on the optimal linear-quadratic controllers of the previous section as well as on a whole host of "suboptimal" design procedures similar to those discussed for lumped parameter systems in Chap. 3. There is a significant division of philosophy in the approaches taken to distributed parameter systems control. This is illustrated in Fig. 4.3. The easiest, most straightforward approach, termed *early lumping*, simply discretizes the distributed parameter system at the earliest opportunity into an approximate model consisting of a set of ordinary differential equations in time. Then the design methods of Chap. 3 are applied directly to accomplish controller design without recourse to distributed parameter systems theory at all. This approach has several disadvantages. First, conditions for controllability, stabilizability, etc., which should depend only on the placement of control actuators, can also depend on the method of lumping and the location of discretization points if early lumping is used. Second, one quickly loses the physical features of the problem through early lumping, and the ultimate controller design may be naïve and fail to take advantage of natural properties of the system.

The alternative approach, *late lumping*, takes full advantage of the available distributed parameter control theory and analyzes the full PDE model for controllability, stabilizability, best controller structure, etc. It is only at the last stages, after the controller design has been made, that the resulting process and control system equations are lumped for reasons of numerical integration in implementation. Late lumping allows the designer to take advantage of all the natural features of the problem and to understand the system structure much more completely. However, this approach requires a greater knowledge of distributed parameter systems control theory; hence this section shall be devoted to illustrating how late lumping may be applied to systems of engineering interest.

Because the properties of distributed parameter systems depend so strongly on the type of equations (parabolic, hyperbolic, elliptic, etc.), we shall discuss

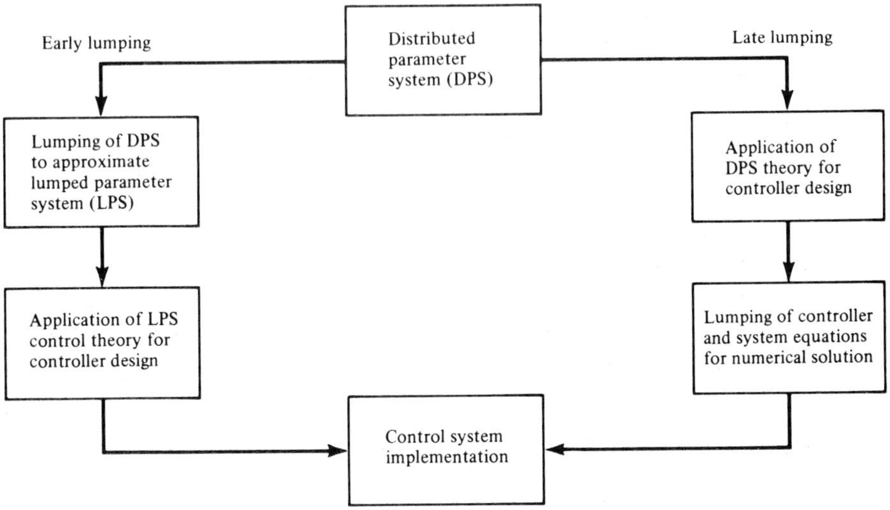

Figure 4.3 Design procedures via *early lumping* and *late lumping*.

those classes of equations that arise most often in process control and the applications of distributed parameter control theory to each.

First-Order Hyperbolic Systems

Let us consider the class of systems described by

$$\frac{\partial \mathbf{x}(z,t)}{\partial t} = \mathbf{A}_1 \frac{\partial \mathbf{x}}{\partial z} + \mathbf{A}_0 \mathbf{x}(z,t) + \mathbf{B}\mathbf{u}(z,t) \tag{4.2.1}$$

$$\mathbf{x}(0,t) = \mathbf{B}_0 \mathbf{u}_0(t) \tag{4.2.2}$$

$$\mathbf{y}(z,t) = \int_0^1 \mathbf{C}(z,r,t)\mathbf{x}(r,t)\,dr \tag{4.2.3}$$

Examples of this class of problems arise in the control of heat exchangers, chemical reactors, and other tubular processes [7]. Recall that Example 4.1.2 illustrates a very simple hyperbolic system.

There are several ways in which one can proceed in analyzing these processes. One approach is to use Laplace transforms in space,

$$\bar{\mathbf{x}}(p,t) = \int_0^\infty e^{-pz}\mathbf{x}(z,t)\,dz \tag{4.2.4}$$

so that for $\mathbf{A}_1$, $\mathbf{A}_0$, $\mathbf{B}$, and $\mathbf{B}_0$ constant, one obtains the *transform equations in space*

$$\frac{d\bar{\mathbf{x}}(p,t)}{dt} = p\mathbf{A}_1\bar{\mathbf{x}}(p,t) - \mathbf{A}_1\mathbf{B}_0\mathbf{u}_0(t) + \mathbf{A}_0\bar{\mathbf{x}}(p,t) + \mathbf{B}\bar{\mathbf{u}}(p,t) \tag{4.2.5}$$

or

$$\frac{d\bar{\mathbf{x}}(p,t)}{dt} = (p\mathbf{A}_1 + \mathbf{A}_0)\bar{\mathbf{x}}(p,t) - \mathbf{A}_1\mathbf{B}_0\mathbf{u}_0(t) + \mathbf{B}\bar{\mathbf{u}}(p,t) \tag{4.2.6}$$

In this manner the equations are reduced to ODEs in time. Now if one defines some set point $\mathbf{x}_d(z)$ and its transform

$$\bar{\mathbf{x}}_d(p) = \int_0^\infty e^{-pz}\mathbf{x}_d(z)\,dz \tag{4.2.7}$$

then one possible feedback control law would be

$$\bar{\mathbf{u}}(p,t) = -\mathbf{K}\bar{\mathbf{x}}(p,t) \tag{4.2.8}$$

$$\mathbf{u}_0(t) = -\mathbf{K}_0\bar{\mathbf{x}}(p,t) \tag{4.2.9}$$

so as to drive $\bar{\mathbf{x}}(p,t)$ to $\bar{\mathbf{x}}_d(p)$.

A second approach, which is probably easier, is to make use of the *Laplace transform in time*

$$\bar{\mathbf{x}}(z,s) = \int_0^\infty e^{-st}\mathbf{x}(z,t)\,dt \tag{4.2.10}$$

Then Eq. (4.2.1) becomes

$$\frac{d\bar{\mathbf{x}}}{dz} = \mathbf{A}_1^{-1}\{(s\mathbf{I} - \mathbf{A}_0)\bar{\mathbf{x}} - [\mathbf{x}_0(z) + \mathbf{B}\bar{\mathbf{u}}(z,s)]\} \tag{4.2.11}$$

$$\bar{\mathbf{x}}(0,s) = \mathbf{B}_0\bar{\mathbf{u}}_0(s) \tag{4.2.12}$$

This first-order ODE in the transformed variables then can be solved to yield

$$\bar{\mathbf{x}}(z, s) = \mathbf{\Phi}(z, s)\mathbf{B}_0\bar{\mathbf{u}}_0(s) - \mathbf{\Phi}(z, s)\int_0^z \mathbf{\Phi}^{-1}(r, s)\left[\mathbf{x}_0(r) + \mathbf{B}\bar{\mathbf{u}}(r, s)\right] dr \tag{4.2.13}$$

where $\mathbf{\Phi}(z, s)$ is the *fundamental matrix solution* found from the solution

$$\frac{d\mathbf{\Phi}(z, s)}{dz} = \mathbf{A}_1^{-1}(sI - \mathbf{A}_0)\mathbf{\Phi}(z, s) \tag{4.2.14}$$

$$\mathbf{\Phi}(0, s) = \mathbf{I} \tag{4.2.15}$$

Thus Eq. (4.2.13) is a linear input-output relation

$$\bar{\mathbf{x}}(z, s) = \mathbf{G}_0\bar{\mathbf{u}}_0(s) + \int_0^z \mathbf{G}(z, r, s)\bar{\mathbf{u}}(r, s)\, dr + \int_0^z \mathbf{G}_i(z, r, s)\mathbf{x}_0(r)\, dr \tag{4.2.16}$$

where

$$\begin{aligned}\mathbf{G}_0 &= \mathbf{\Phi}(z, s)\mathbf{B}_0\\ \mathbf{G}(z, r, s) &= -\mathbf{\Phi}(z, s)\mathbf{\Phi}^{-1}(r, s)\mathbf{B}\\ \mathbf{G}_i(z, r, s) &= -\mathbf{\Phi}(z, s)\mathbf{\Phi}^{-1}(r, s)\end{aligned} \tag{4.2.17}$$

In the event that the control action is applied at a discrete number of points z_i or is independent of z, then Eq. (4.2.16) loses the integral signs and simple transfer functions arise.

A third approach to first-order hyperbolic PDE systems is through the *method of characteristics*. To illustrate this technique, let us assume that $\mathbf{A}_1$ in Eq. (4.2.1) has the simple form

$$\mathbf{A}_1 = -a\mathbf{I} \tag{4.2.18}$$

Thus Eq. (4.2.1) becomes

$$\frac{\partial \mathbf{x}(z, t)}{\partial t} + a\frac{\partial \mathbf{x}}{\partial z} = \mathbf{A}_0\mathbf{x} + \mathbf{B}\mathbf{u} \tag{4.2.19}$$

$$\mathbf{x}(0, t) = \mathbf{B}_0\mathbf{u}_0(t) \tag{4.2.2}$$

Then by defining lines given by

$$\frac{dz}{dt} = a \tag{4.2.20}$$

or

$$t - \frac{1}{a}z = \text{const} \tag{4.2.21}$$

one obtains the solution of Eq. (4.2.19) as

$$\left.\frac{d\mathbf{x}}{dt}\right|_0 = \mathbf{A}_0\mathbf{x} + \mathbf{B}\mathbf{u} \tag{4.2.22}$$

where the notation $|_0$ denotes the fact that the solution is taken along a characteristic line defined by Eq. (4.2.21). Therefore the repeated solution of

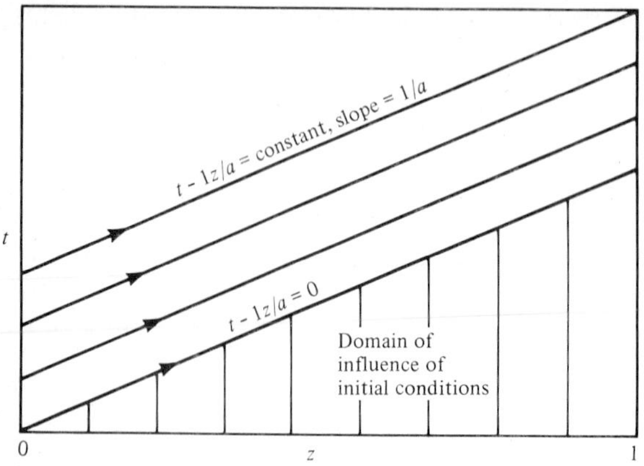

Figure 4.4 Characteristic lines of constant slope.

Eq.(4.2.22) at different values of t_0 will give the entire solution (see Fig. 4.4). If $\mathbf{A}_1$ is not of the form of Eq. (4.2.18), there will be characteristic lines for each element of $\mathbf{x}$, but the procedure can still be used.

The method of characteristics allows one to see several things very clearly. First, the initial conditions only have the domain of influence (shown in Fig. 4.4) below the line $t - z/a = 0$. For times greater than this, only the inlet conditions $\mathbf{x}(0, t)$ and the controls influence the solution. As a second point, note that solving the equations along a characteristic line corresponds to following the changes in an element of material moving from 0 to 1 with velocity a. Also note that discontinuities in the state variables arise in first-order hyperbolic systems when step changes are made at the boundary $z = 0$.

We shall now present an example problem to illustrate the methods discussed.

Example 4.2.1 Let us consider the feedback control of the steam-jacketed tubular heat exchanger shown in Fig. 4.5. Thermocouples measure the tube fluid temperature at four points, $T(0.25, t)$, $T(0.5, t)$, $T(0.75, t)$, and $T(1, t)$. These are used to determine the adjustment in the steam-jacket temperature $T_w(t)$ (through a steam inlet valve) in order to control the exchanger.

The mathematical model for the process takes the form

$$\frac{\partial T}{\partial t} + v\frac{\partial T}{\partial z} = \frac{-hA}{\rho C_p}(T - T_w) \qquad T(0, t) = T_f \tag{4.2.23}$$

Now if we define the deviation variables

$$x = T - T_d(z) \qquad u = T_w - T_{wd} \qquad x_f = T_f - T_{f_d}$$

and parameters

$$a_0 = \frac{hA}{\rho C_p} \qquad a_1 = -v$$

where $T_d(z)$ is the desired temperature profile, T_{wd} is the steady-state steam-jacket temperature required to keep $T = T_d(z)$, and T_{f_d} is the nominal

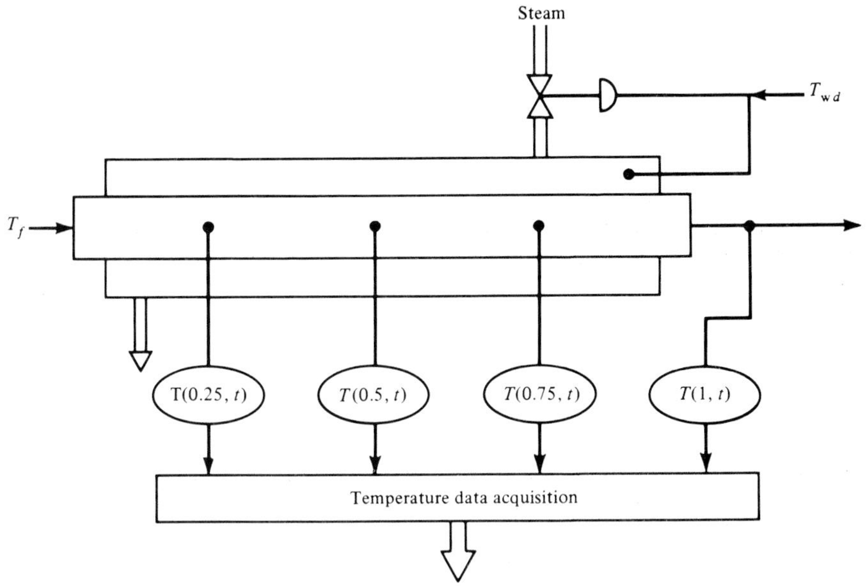

Figure 4.5 Control of a tubular heat exchanger with steam-jacket temperature control.

heat exchanger inlet temperature, then T_{wd}, T_d, and T_{f_d} satisfy

$$v\frac{\partial T_d}{\partial z} = \frac{-hA}{\rho C_p}(T_d - T_{wd}) \qquad T_d(0) = T_{f_d} \tag{4.2.24}$$

and the heat exchanger model is

$$\frac{\partial x}{\partial t} = a_1\frac{\partial x}{\partial z} - a_0 x + a_0 u \qquad x(0, t) = x_f(t) \tag{4.2.25}$$

For this system, we wish to design a feedback controller which measures the temperatures at four points, $T(0.25, t)$, $T(0.5, t)$, $T(0.75, t)$, and $T(1, t)$, and adjusts the steam-jacket temperature $T_w(t)$ to control the outlet temperature $T(1, t)$. The measured output variables are given by

$$\mathbf{y}(t) = \int_0^1 \mathbf{C}(r, t)x(r, t)\,dr \tag{4.2.26}$$

$$\mathbf{y} = \begin{bmatrix} x(0.25, t) \\ x(0.5, t) \\ x(0.75, t) \\ x(1, t) \end{bmatrix} \tag{4.2.27}$$

and

$$\mathbf{C}(r, t) = \begin{bmatrix} \delta(r - 0.25) \\ \delta(r - 0.5) \\ \delta(r - 0.75) \\ \delta(r - 1.0) \end{bmatrix} \tag{4.2.28}$$

Here $\delta(x)$ is the Dirac delta function. Let us now apply the *Laplace transform in time* to Eq. (4.2.25) to yield

$$s\bar{x}(z, s) - x_0(z) - a_1 \frac{d\bar{x}(z, s)}{dz} = -a_0\bar{x}(z, s) + a_0\bar{u}(s)$$

or, applying Eq. (4.2.16),

$$\bar{x}(z, s) = G(z, s)\bar{u}(s) + \int_0^z G_i(z, r, s)x_0(r)\,dr + G_0(z, s)\bar{x}_f(s) \tag{4.2.29}$$

where

$$G_0(z, s) = \exp\left[\frac{(s + a_0)z}{a_1}\right]$$

$$G(z, s) = -\exp\left[\frac{(s + a_0)z}{a_1}\right]\left\{\int_0^z \exp\left[\frac{-(s + a_0)r}{a_1}\right] dr\right\}\frac{a_0}{a_1}$$

$$= \frac{a_0}{s + a_0}\left[1 - \exp\left[\frac{(s + a_0)z}{a_1}\right]\right] \tag{4.2.30}$$

$$G_i(z, r, s) = -\frac{1}{a_1}\exp\left[\left(\frac{s + a_0}{a_1}\right)(z - r)\right]$$

Thus one has a transfer function representation, and we may now use the design procedures of Chap. 3. Generally speaking, our control law should have the form

$$\bar{u}(s) = \mathbf{G}_c(s)\varepsilon(s) \tag{4.2.31}$$

relating control action to our measured output variables. For a proportional controller this would take the form

$$\bar{u}(s) = \mathbf{K}(\mathbf{y} - \mathbf{y}_d) \tag{4.2.32}$$

where the designer must choose the individual components of $\mathbf{K}$. Such a controller structure is sketched in Fig. 4.6 for the case where $x_0(r) = 0$ and

$$\mathbf{K} = (K_{1/4}, K_{1/2}, K_{3/4}, K_1) \tag{4.2.33}$$

Let us note a few things about the transfer function for the heat exchanger. Assuming $x_f = 0$, $x_0(z) = 0$, let us look at the response of $x(1, t)$ to steam-jacket temperature

$$\bar{x}(1, s) = G(1, s)\bar{u}(s) \tag{4.2.34}$$

where the transfer function is

$$G(1, s) = \frac{a_0}{s + a_0}\left(1 - e^{a_0/a_1}e^{+s/a_1}\right) \tag{4.2.35}$$

Here there is a pure time delay* of magnitude $-1/a_1 = 1/v$ appearing in

* Recall that $a_1 = -v$.

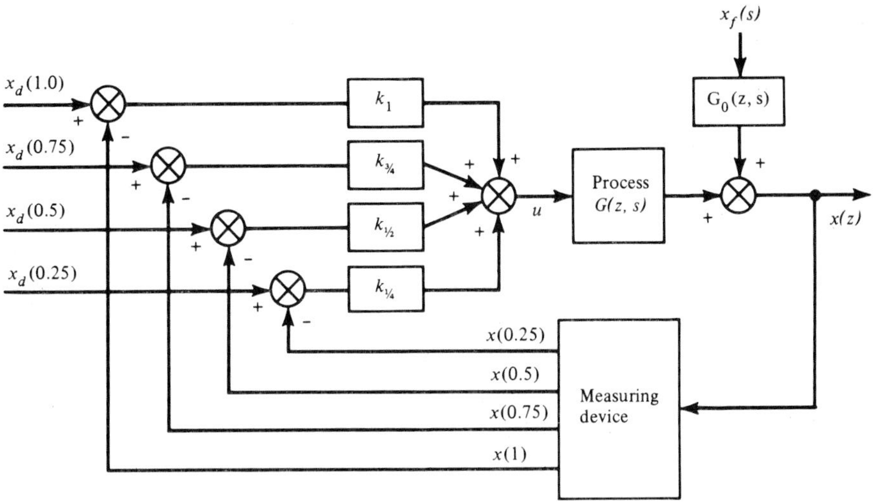

Figure 4.6 Proportional feedback control scheme for a tubular heat exchanger.

the transfer function. We shall discuss such delay problems further in Sec. 4.5.

Let us now consider the conditions for *controllability* and *stabilizability* for first-order hyperbolic partial differential equations. This question is much more complicated than for lumped parameter systems [8, 9], and complete results are not yet available. However, the basic requirement for controllability of first-order hyperbolic equations is that a control actuator intersect each characteristic line (see Fig. 4.4) and that a controllability condition along these characteristics be satisfied.

Second-Order Partial Differential Equations

Linear second-order PDEs can be classified according to values of the coefficients of the highest derivatives.* The linear scalar second-order PDE in variables t, z takes the form

$$a_{11}x_{tt} + 2a_{12}x_{tz} + a_{22}x_{zz} = F(x_t, x_z, x, t, z) \tag{4.2.36}$$

where the a_{ij} may be functions of t, z. One may form a *characteristic equation* by replacing all z derivatives on the left-hand side by $(-\lambda)$. Then one obtains

$$a_{11} - 2a_{12}\lambda + a_{22}\lambda^2 = 0 \tag{4.2.37}$$

which has roots

$$\lambda_1, \lambda_2 = \frac{a_{12} \pm \sqrt{a_{12}^2 - a_{11}a_{22}}}{a_{22}} \tag{4.2.38}$$

* A particularly readable description of this may be found in [7, 10].

Table 4.1

Δ	Type	Characteristics
$\Delta < 0$	Elliptic	Complex
$\Delta = 0$	Parabolic	$\lambda_1 = \lambda_2$, real
$\Delta > 0$	Hyperbolic	$\lambda_1 \neq \lambda_2$, real

Now depending on the nature of the roots, the PDE will be *hyperbolic*, *parabolic*, or *elliptic*. If we recall that the nature of the roots is determined by the sign of the discriminant

$$\Delta = a_{12}^2 - a_{11}a_{22} \tag{4.2.39}$$

we are let to the classifications in Table 4.1.

These classifications also apply to first-order PDEs such as

$$a_1 x_t + a_2 x_z = F(\bar{x}, t, z) \tag{4.2.40}$$

which has the characteristic equation

$$a_1 - a_2\lambda = 0 \tag{4.2.41}$$

yielding a unique, real value for λ. Thus *all first-order equations are hyperbolic*. In addition, *all systems of first-order equations are hyperbolic*,* and *all second-order hyperbolic equations can be reduced to systems of first-order equations*. We have seen examples of first-order hyperbolic equations in the previous section.

Second-order hyperbolic equations arise in wave propagation problems. For example, the propagation of sound is modeled by

$$\frac{\partial^2 \zeta}{\partial t^2} = v_s^2 \frac{\partial^2 \zeta}{\partial z^2} \tag{4.2.42}$$

where v_s is the speed of sound and ζ is the sound amplitude. The characteristics of Eq. (4.2.42) are found from

$$v_s^2 \lambda^2 = 1 \Rightarrow \lambda = \pm \frac{1}{v_s} \tag{4.2.43}$$

Thus there are two sets of characteristic lines in the t, z space for Eq. (4.2.42), one with slope $1/v_s$ and another with slope $-1/v_s$. These lines, shown in Fig. 4.7, represent the motion of sound waves being reflected from the boundaries. By making the substitution

$$\begin{aligned} x_1 &= \frac{\partial \zeta}{\partial t} \\ x_2 &= v_s \frac{\partial \zeta}{\partial z} \end{aligned} \tag{4.2.44}$$

* The only exception is if a_2/a_1 is the same in each equation, in which case the roots of the characteristic equation (4.2.41) are identical, and the system becomes *parabolic*.

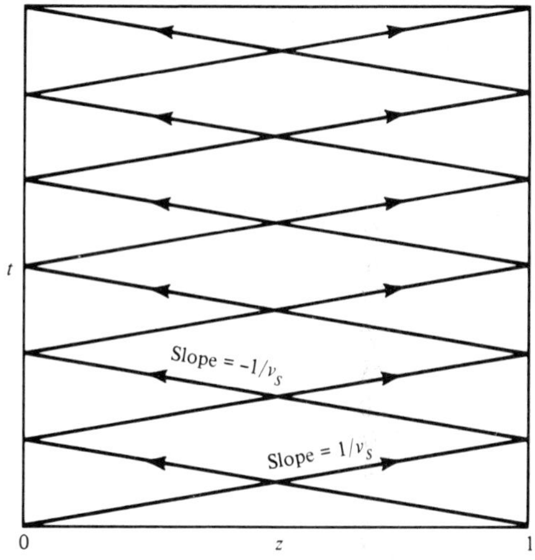

Figure 4.7 Characteristic lines for the sound propagation equation.

we can convert Eq. (4.2.42) to the first-order system

$$\frac{\partial x_1}{\partial t} + v_s \frac{\partial x_1}{\partial z} = 0$$

$$\frac{\partial x_2}{\partial t} - v_s \frac{\partial x_2}{\partial z} = 0 \tag{4.2.45}$$

Thus any higher-order hyperbolic equations can be converted to a system of first-order equations and handled by the techniques of the last section.

Parabolic equations arise in processes with diffusion or heat conduction. For example, heat conduction in a one-dimensional solid is governed by the equation

$$\rho C_p \frac{\partial T}{\partial t} = k \frac{\partial^2 T}{\partial z^2} \tag{4.2.46}$$

This has the characteristic equation

$$\lambda^2 = 0 \Rightarrow \lambda_1 = \lambda_2 = 0 \tag{4.2.47}$$

We shall discuss the treatment of parabolic equations in more detail in a later section.

Elliptic equations occur in multidimensional diffusion or heat transport problems such as steady-state conduction in a two-dimensional slab:

$$k\left(\frac{\partial^2 T}{\partial z^2} + \frac{\partial^2 T}{\partial y^2}\right) = 0 \tag{4.2.48}$$

This problem has two space variables, so it does not fit our model, Eq. (4.2.36), exactly. However, the *characteristic equation* is

$$\lambda^2 + 1 = 0 \tag{4.2.49}$$

and λ is definitely complex. In practice, elliptic equations involving *time* and a spatial variable rarely occur because physical systems seldom (if ever) have these modeling equations.

Classifications of second-order equations involving more than two independent variables are slightly more involved [10], but can be found by straightforward tests of the coefficients of the highest derivatives.

As in the case of first-order equations, the thrust of the analysis for second-order systems is to use an *exact* reduction of a distributed system to a lumped one and to take advantage of all the theory for lumped parameter systems. There are several means of doing this.

1. *The Laplace transform in time* can be used for second-order processes just as for first-order ones. These result in transfer functions involving spatial variables, often in infinite series form. In principle the lumped parameter design techniques can be applied to these transfer functions, although in practice there are difficulties. We shall discuss these points below.
2. *The method of characteristics* can be used with all hyperbolic equations and with some parabolic equations which have nonzero characteristics.* All these systems reduce to first-order equations and can be treated by the methods of the previous section.
3. *Modal analysis* is a very attractive method of treating PDEs which have a real, discrete spectrum of eigenvalues and which can be made self-adjoint. It is the natural reduction technique and works well with only a few modes if the eigenvalues are not bunched together.

Let us now discuss in more detail some of these exact lumping techniques.

Laplace Transform Methods

We have discussed the Laplace transform technique applied to first-order equations. Let us now show the form that this representation takes for parabolic equations. To illustrate this, let us consider the heat equation in a slab.

* Parabolic equations with nonzero characteristics are really degenerate cases of hyperbolic problems. For example, the parabolic system

$$\frac{\partial^2 x_1}{\partial t^2} + 2v\frac{\partial^2 x_1}{\partial t\,\partial z} = v^2\frac{\partial^2 x_1}{\partial z^2} = F \tag{4.2.50}$$

can be reduced to

$$\frac{\partial x_1}{\partial t} + v\frac{\partial x_1}{\partial z} = f_1$$

$$\frac{\partial x_2}{\partial t} + v\frac{\partial x_2}{\partial z} = f_2 \tag{4.2.51}$$

by defining x_2 appropriately. These equations could represent a tubular reactor in plug flow. For example, if $f_1 = x_2$, then the substitution

$$x_2 = \frac{\partial x_1}{\partial t} + v\frac{\partial x_1}{\partial z} \tag{4.2.52}$$

leads to Eq. (4.2.50).

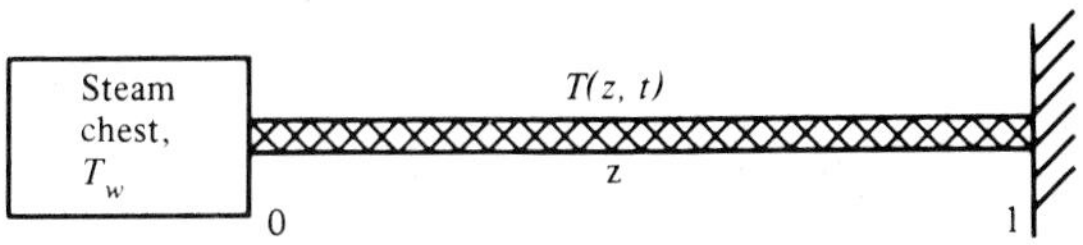

Figure 4.8 A one-dimensional heated rod.

Example 4.2.2 Let us consider the one-dimensional rod shown in Fig. 4.8. Heat is added from a steam chest at $z = 0$, and the $z = 1$ end is perfectly insulated. Let us define variables

$$x(z, t) = T - T_d$$
$$u(t) = T_w - T_{wd}$$

which represent deviations from the set-point values. In this case the model takes the form

$$\frac{\partial x(z, t)}{\partial t} = \frac{\partial^2 x(z, t)}{\partial z^2} \tag{4.2.53}$$

$$z = 0 \qquad \frac{\partial x}{\partial z} = \beta(x - u) \tag{4.2.54}$$

$$z = 1 \qquad \frac{\partial x}{\partial z} = 0 \tag{4.2.55}$$

If one takes the Laplace transform with respect to time and assumes $x(z, 0) = 0$, then

$$s\bar{x}(z, s) = \frac{d^2\bar{x}}{dz^2} \tag{4.2.56}$$

$$z = 0 \qquad \frac{d\bar{x}}{dz} = \beta(\bar{x} - \bar{u}) \tag{4.2.57}$$

$$z = 1 \qquad \frac{d\bar{x}}{dz} = 0 \tag{4.2.58}$$

Equation (4.2.56) has the general solution

$$\bar{x}(z, s) = A \sinh\sqrt{s}\, z + B \cosh\sqrt{s}\, z \tag{4.2.59}$$

and the boundary condition of Eq. (4.2.58) yields

$$A + B \tanh\sqrt{s} = 0 \tag{4.2.60}$$

and Eq. (4.2.57) yields

$$\sqrt{s}\, A = \beta[B - \bar{u}(s)] \tag{4.2.61}$$

or

$$B = \frac{(\beta/\sqrt{s})\bar{u}(s)}{(\beta/\sqrt{s}) + \tanh\sqrt{s}} \tag{4.2.62}$$

Thus the solution is

$$\bar{x}(z, s) = \frac{\bar{u}(s)}{1 + (\sqrt{s}/\beta)\tanh\sqrt{s}}(-\tanh\sqrt{s}\,\sinh\sqrt{s}\,z + \cosh\sqrt{s}\,z) \tag{4.2.63}$$

Now as an example let us consider the control of the left-hand-side end temperature $x(0, t)$ by the steam-chest temperature $u(t)$. The system transfer function takes the form

$$\bar{x}(0, s) = \frac{\bar{u}(s)}{1 + (\sqrt{s}/\beta)\tanh\sqrt{s}} \tag{4.2.64}$$

and in principle, standard lumped parameter system controller design techniques may be used. However, there is no simple inversion of this complex transfer function. In fact, Eq. (4.2.64) can be expanded in an infinite series to yield

$$\bar{x}(z, s) = \bar{u}(s) \sum_{i=1}^{\infty} \frac{a_i}{s - \lambda_i} \tag{4.2.65}$$

where the λ_i are an infinite series of eigenvalues arising from the roots of the denominator of Eq. (4.2.64). The coefficients a_i are given by

$$a_i = \frac{2\beta\sqrt{\lambda_i}\cosh^2\sqrt{\lambda_i}}{\sqrt{\lambda_i} + \sinh\sqrt{\lambda_i}\cosh\sqrt{\lambda_i}} = \frac{2\beta\lambda_i}{\lambda_i - \beta(\beta + 1)} \tag{4.2.66}$$

Thus we see that for parabolic PDEs one obtains transcendental transfer functions which in general must be expanded into an infinite series of exponentials. However, if this series can be approximated by the first few terms, then normal lumped parameter transfer function design techniques may be directly applied.

Modal Analysis

A convenient and useful form of analysis of second-order equations is through modal decomposition. This form of analysis is possible when the second-order equation

$$\frac{\partial \mathbf{x}}{\partial t} = \mathbf{A}\mathbf{x} + \mathbf{B}\mathbf{u} \tag{4.2.67}$$

has a spatial operator $\mathbf{A}$ which can be made self-adjoint and which has a real, discrete spectrum of eigenvalues. For example, in one dimension the operator

$$\mathbf{A}\mathbf{x}(z, t) = \mathbf{A}_2(z)\frac{\partial^2 \mathbf{x}}{\partial z^2} + \mathbf{A}_1(z)\frac{\partial \mathbf{x}}{\partial z} + \mathbf{A}_0(z)\mathbf{x} \tag{4.2.68}$$

would lead to a parabolic set of equations. It is also possible to extend these ideas to two space dimensions. For example,

$$\mathbf{A}\mathbf{x}(z, r, t) = \mathbf{A}_2(z)\frac{\partial^2 \mathbf{x}}{\partial z^2} + \mathbf{A}_1(z)\frac{\partial \mathbf{x}}{\partial z} + \mathbf{A}_0(z)\mathbf{x} + \mathbf{D}_2(r)\frac{\partial^2 \mathbf{x}}{\partial r^2} + \mathbf{D}_1(r)\frac{\partial \mathbf{x}}{\partial r} \tag{4.2.69}$$

would be one possible two-dimensional operator amenable to modal analysis. A wider discussion of these techniques may be found in Refs. [11–16].

Perhaps the best means of discussing the modal reduction of distributed systems is by considering a series of example problems. Let us begin by studying the control of the temperature distribution in a long, thin rod being heated in a multizone furnace, and shown in Fig. 4.9. The heating rate is defined as $q(z', t')$, and the modeling equation becomes

$$\rho C_p \frac{\partial T}{\partial t'} = k\frac{\partial^2 T}{\partial z'^2} + q(z', t') \qquad \begin{array}{l} t' > 0 \\ 0 < z' < l \end{array}$$

If one assumes negligible heat flux at the ends of the rod, the boundary conditions become

$$\frac{\partial T}{\partial z'} = 0 \qquad z' = 0, l$$

By putting the variables in dimensionless form,

$$t = \frac{t'k}{\rho C_p l^2} \qquad z = \frac{z'}{l} \qquad u(z, t) = \frac{q(z', t')l^2}{kT_0} \qquad x(z, t) = \frac{T(z, t)}{T_0}$$

where T_0 is some reference initial temperature, such as $T(0, 0)$, one obtains the equation

$$\frac{\partial x(z, t)}{\partial t} = \frac{\partial^2 x(z, t)}{\partial z^2} + u(z, t) \qquad \begin{array}{l} t > 0 \\ 0 < z < 1 \end{array} \tag{4.2.70}$$

$$z = 0 \qquad \frac{\partial x}{\partial z} = 0 \tag{4.2.71}$$

$$z = 1 \qquad \frac{\partial x}{\partial z} = 0 \tag{4.2.72}$$

$$x(z, 0) = x_0(z) \tag{4.2.73}$$

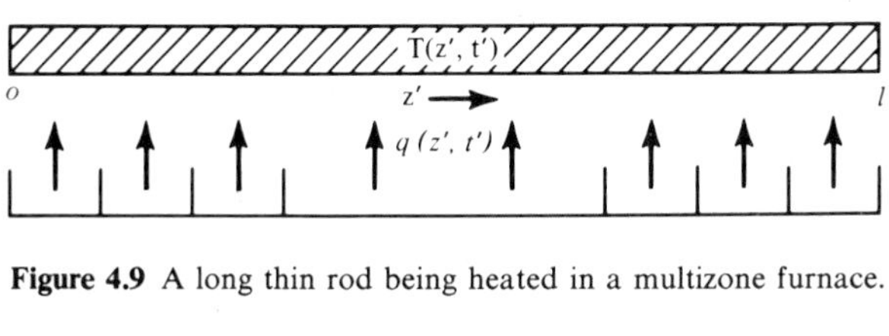

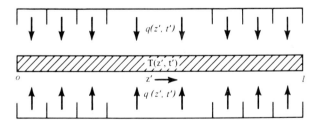

Figure 4.9 A long thin rod being heated in a multizone furnace.

Note that Eq. (4.2.70) is separable and can be treated by the technique of separation of variables. Thus we assume a solution of the form

$$x(z, t) = \sum_{n=0}^{\infty} a_n(t)\phi_n(z) \tag{4.2.74}$$

where $a_n(t)$, $\phi_n(z)$ are a set of functions to be determined. We also assume that $u(z, t)$ can be represented in a separable fashion with the same functions $\phi_n(z)$.

$$u(z, t) = \sum_{n=0}^{\infty} b_n(t)\phi_n(z) \tag{4.2.75}$$

This will always be possible if $\phi_n(z)$, $n = 0, 1, \ldots,$ represent a complete set of basis functions.

Substituting Eqs. (4.2.74) and (4.2.75) into Eqs. (4.2.70) to (4.2.72) yields

$$\phi_n(z)\frac{da_n(t)}{dt} = a_n(t)\frac{d^2\phi_n(z)}{dz^2} + b_n(t)\phi_n(z) \qquad n = 0, 1, 2, \ldots \tag{4.2.76}$$

$$z = 0 \qquad \frac{d\phi_n}{dz} = 0 \tag{4.2.77}$$

$$z = 1 \qquad \frac{d\phi_n}{dz} = 0 \tag{4.2.78}$$

Dividing Eq. (4.2.76) by $a_n(t)\phi_n(z)$ produces

$$\frac{1}{a_n}\frac{da_n}{dt} = \frac{1}{\phi_n}\frac{d^2\phi_n}{dz^2} + \frac{b_n(t)}{a_n(t)}$$

which may be separated into only functions of t and only functions of z as follows:

$$\frac{1}{a_n}\frac{da_n}{dt} - \frac{b_n}{a_n} = -\lambda_n \tag{4.2.79}$$

$$\frac{1}{\phi_n}\frac{d^2\phi_n}{dz^2} = -\lambda_n \tag{4.2.80}$$

where λ_n is a constant. Let us now rewrite these as

$$\frac{da_n}{dt} + \lambda_n a_n = b_n(t) \qquad n = 0, 1, 2, \ldots \tag{4.2.81}$$

$$\frac{d^2\phi_n}{dz^2} + \lambda_n\phi_n = 0 \qquad n = 0, 1, 2, \ldots \tag{4.2.82}$$

Clearly, Eq. (4.2.81) allows us to calculate $a_n(t)$ if $b_n(t)$ and λ_n are known. Equation (4.2.82) is a *self-adjoint* differential equation. Let us now take a short excursion and discuss some basic concepts of differential equations.

The second-order differential operator defined over $0 < z < 1$

$$L(\cdot) = a_2(z)\frac{d^2(\cdot)}{dz^2} + a_1(z)\frac{d(\cdot)}{dz} + a_0(z)(\cdot) \tag{4.2.83}$$

has an adjoint operator $L^*(\cdot)$ defined [16, 17] so that for any two functions $y(z)$, $w(z)$, the relation

$$\int_0^1 y(z) L(w(z))\, dz = \int_0^1 w(z) L^*(y(z))\, dz \tag{4.2.84}$$

holds. For the differential operator, Eq. (4.2.83), the adjoint operator so defined is

$$L^*(\cdot) = \frac{d^2(a_2(z)(\cdot))}{dz^2} - \frac{d(a_1(z)(\cdot))}{dz} + a_0(z)(\cdot) \tag{4.2.85}$$

Now an operator which is identical to its adjoint is termed *self-adjoint*. Self-adjoint operators have some very nice properties, as we shall see shortly; thus, very often it is useful to put equations into self-adjoint form. For Eq. (4.2.83), this amounts to a change of variable [17]. If we define

$$r(z) = \exp\left[\int \frac{1}{a_2}(a_1 - \dot{a}_2)\, dz\right] \tag{4.2.86}$$

and change variables as

$$\hat{\Phi}_n = \Phi_n r(z) \tag{4.2.87}$$

then the operator $L\hat{\Phi}(z)$ in Eq. (4.2.83) will become self-adjoint.

Having established these concepts, let us now continue with the rod heat conduction problem. Recall that Eq. (4.2.82) is already self-adjoint and, together with the boundary condition, Eq. (4.2.77), yields the solution

$$\phi_n(z) = A_n \cos\sqrt{\lambda_n}\, z \tag{4.2.88}$$

Application of the boundary condition, Eq. (4.2.77), yields the condition

$$\sqrt{\lambda_n} \sin\sqrt{\lambda_n} = 0 \tag{4.2.89}$$

The only possible solutions to this are

$$\sqrt{\lambda_n} = n\pi \qquad n = 0, \pm 1, \pm 2, \ldots$$

or

$$\lambda_n = n^2\pi^2 \qquad n = 0, 1, 2, \ldots \tag{4.2.90}$$

Here the λ_n are the *eigenvalues* of the system and the ϕ_n are the *eigenfunctions* or *modes* of the system. Because Eq. (4.2.82) is a homogeneous *self-adjoint* differential equation with homogeneous boundary conditions, the eigenfunctions are *orthogonal*. That is,

$$\int_0^1 \phi_n(z)\phi_m(z)\, dz = 0 \qquad \text{for } n \neq m \tag{4.2.91}$$

It is useful to choose the constant A_n in Eq. (4.2.88) to make the eigenfunctions *orthonormal*, i.e.,

$$\int_0^1 \phi_n(z)^2\, dz = 1 \tag{4.2.92}$$

To do this we simply substitute Eq. (4.2.88) into Eq. (4.2.91) to obtain

$$A_n^2 = \left[\int_0^1 \left(\cos \sqrt{\lambda_n}\, z \right)^2 dz \right]^{-1}$$

or

$$A_n = \begin{cases} 1 & n = 0 \\ \sqrt{2} & n = 1, 2, \ldots \end{cases} \tag{4.2.93}$$

Now due to the orthogonality of the eigenfunctions, one can immediately write down the following relationships:

$$\int_0^1 \phi_m(z) x(z, t)\, dz = \sum_{n=0}^{\infty} a_n(t) \int_0^1 \phi_n(z) \phi_m(z)\, dz$$

$$= a_m(t) \tag{4.2.94}$$

Thus, given any temperature distribution $x(z, t)$, it is possible to immediately determine the eigencoefficient $a_n(t)$. In particular, we can immediately represent the initial conditions $x_0(z)$ in the form of Eq. (4.2.74) by determining the coefficients

$$a_n(0) = \int_0^1 \phi_n(z) x_0(z)\, dz \tag{4.2.95}$$

By similar equations the coefficients $b_n(t)$ for the series representation of $u(z, t)$ in Eq. (4.2.75) are given by

$$b_n(t) = \int_0^1 \phi_n(z) u(z, t)\, dz \tag{4.2.96}$$

Thus the temperature distribution $x(z, t)$ resulting from some heat flux distribution $u(x, t)$ is given by the expression

$$x(z, t) = a_0(t) + \sqrt{2} \sum_{n=1}^{N} a_n(t) \cos n\pi z$$

Here $a_n(t)$ is determined from the solution of

$$\frac{da_n}{dt} = -n^2\pi^2 a_n + b_n(t)$$

where $a_n(0)$ is given by Eq. (4.2.95) and $b_n(t)$ by Eq. (4.2.96). The quantity N is the actual number of terms in the eigenfunction expansion necessary to provide a good approximation to the exact solution.

It is possible to use this modal representation in several ways.

1. *Simulation* The modal representation is a very efficient means of simulating the process when there is time-varying control action. Because the eigenvalues $\lambda_n = n^2\pi^2$ increase rapidly with increasing n, only a few eigenfunctions N are required for representing the the system behavior.

   For simulation, only N ordinary differential equations of the form of Eq. (4.2.81) must be solved sequentially (not simultaneously) for $a_n(t)$. In practice, $N = 2$ or 3 is often found to suffice, so that there is very little computational effort involved in simulation. As an example of the form of this solution, in the case where the heating rate $u(z, t)$ is constant in time (but possibly spatially varying), the problem in Eqs. (4.2.70) to (4.2.73) may be solved analytically to yield

$$a_n(t) = e^{-n^2\pi^2 t} a_n(0) + \frac{b_n}{n^2\pi^2}\left(1 - e^{-n^2\pi^2 t}\right) \qquad n = 0, 1, \ldots N$$

and

$$x(z, t) = a_0(0) + \sqrt{2} \sum_{n=1}^{N} \left[e^{-n^2\pi^2 t} a_n(0) + \frac{b_n}{n^2\pi^2}\left(1 - e^{-n^2\pi^2 t}\right) \right] \cos n\pi z$$

2. *Control* A second valuable use of modal decomposition is in the design of control structures. These applications have been discussed by Gilles [11], Gould [12], Wang [13], and Ajinkya et al. [15]. Let us consider the controller structure in Fig. 4.10, where we assume state variable outputs.

   The control $u(z, t)$ is applied to the plant, yielding the state $x(z, t)$. The actual state $x(z, t)$ and the desired state $x_d(z, t)$ are compared and the error fed to a *modal analyzer* consisting of Eq. (4.2.94). The resulting coefficients of the error signal

$$\varepsilon_n = a_{nd} - a_n \qquad n = 0, 1, \ldots, N$$

   are fed to an $N + 1$ lumped parameter variable feedback control scheme. The outputs of this are the controller coefficients $b_n(t)$. These are then fed to a modal synthesizer consisting of Eq. (4.2.75). This produces the control signal $u(z, t)$ which is fed to the plant. Notice that the multivariable controller for this linear problem consists of $N + 1$ single-loop controllers. This is because *there are no interactions* in the modal formulation for linear problems, i.e., the coefficient b_n only influences coefficient a_n.

In principle, this control scheme requires that the complete state $x(z, t)$ must be available as an output. In practice, of course, this is impossible. However, one can provide this information in several ways.

1. One can measure $x(z_i, t)$, $i = 1, 2, \ldots l$, at a large number of points and simply smooth these data to get $x(z, t)$.
2. One can measure $x(z_i, t)$ at only a few points (possibly only one) and use a

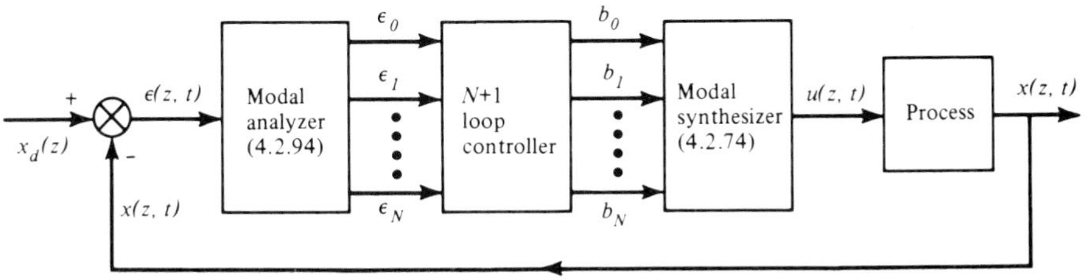

Figure 4.10 A distributed parameter modal feedback controller for distributed control $u(z, t)$.

state estimator to provide estimates of $x(z, t)$ (see Chap. 5 for a discussion of state estimation).

3. One can use a technique suggested by Gould [12] and replace Eq. (4.2.94) in the modal analyzer by the scheme described below.

First, measure $x(z_i, t)$ at $N + 1$ spatial positions; then

$$x(z_i, t) = \sum_{n=0}^{N} a_n(t)\phi_n(z_i) \qquad i = 1, 2, \ldots, N + 1 \tag{4.2.97}$$

If we define

$$\mathbf{x} = \begin{bmatrix} x(z_1, t) \\ x(z_2, t) \\ \vdots \\ x(z_{N+1}, t) \end{bmatrix} \qquad \mathbf{\Phi} = \begin{bmatrix} \phi_0(z_1) & \phi_0(z_2) & \cdots & \phi_0(z_{N+1}) \\ \phi_1(z_1) & \phi_1(z_2) & \cdots & \phi_1(z_{N+1}) \\ \cdots & \cdots & \cdots & \cdots \\ \phi_N(z_1) & \cdots & \cdots & \phi_N(z_{N+1}) \end{bmatrix}$$

$$\mathbf{a} = \begin{bmatrix} a_0 \\ a_1 \\ \vdots \\ a_N \end{bmatrix}$$

then Eq. (4.2.97) becomes

$$\mathbf{x} = \mathbf{\Phi a} \tag{4.2.98}$$

and if the sampling locations are well chosen, $\mathbf{\Phi}$ will not be singular and

$$\mathbf{a} = \mathbf{\Phi}^{-1}\mathbf{x} \tag{4.2.99}$$

This relation may be used in place of Eq. (4.2.94) in the modal analyzer. If measurements at more than $N + 1$ spatial positions are available, then one could use a least squares fit for $\mathbf{a}$ using

$$\mathbf{a} = (\mathbf{\Phi}^T\mathbf{\Phi})^{-1}\mathbf{\Phi}^T\mathbf{x}$$

in place of Eq. (4.2.99).

Schemes 1 and 2 have been tested experimentally and found to work well, but no experimental testing of scheme 3 seems to have been performed.

Example 4.2.3 Let us illustrate the application of modal feedback control by applying a proportional plus integral modal controller to the rod-heating problem. This means that in Eq. (4.2.81) the control law

$$b_n(t) = K_n\left(\varepsilon_n + \frac{1}{\tau_{I_n}}\int \varepsilon_n \, dt\right) \qquad n = 0, 1, 2, \ldots, N$$

would be applied to the Fourier coefficients, where

$$\varepsilon_n = a_{nd} - a_n \qquad n = 0, 1, 2, \ldots, N$$

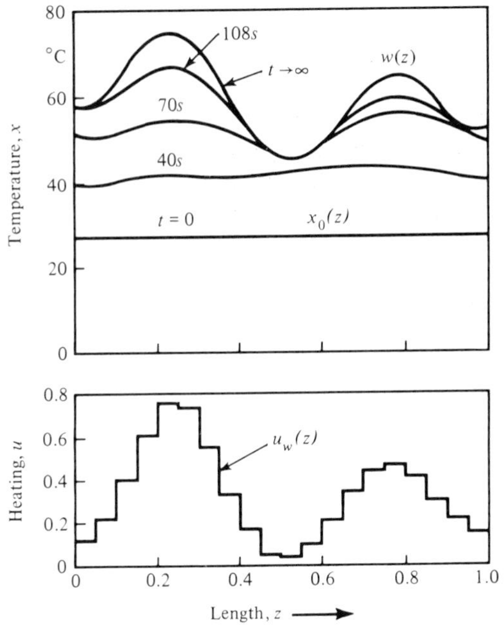

Figure 4.11 Experimental results of modal feedback PI control of a heated billet in a multizone furnace [18]. (*Reproduced by permission of Oldenbourg Verlag, G.M.B.H.*)

Mäder [18] has applied this control law experimentally to such a problem using the controller structure shown in Fig. 4.10. Some of his experimental results are shown in Fig. 4.11, where the modal PI controller takes the metal temperature from $x_0(z)$ at $t = 0$ to the desired profile $w(z)$ very quickly. He found that six eigenfunctions $\phi_n(z)$ were sufficient to provide a good representation of both the state and control variables.

Sometimes the control appearing in the differential equation will depend only on time, i.e., $u(t)$. In this case, the modal feedback control scheme shown in Fig. 4.10 must be modified to the form shown in Fig. 4.12, where a single controller of the form

$$u(t) = g(\varepsilon_0, \varepsilon_1, \ldots, \varepsilon_N) \tag{4.2.100}$$

must be determined. There are many different ways of determining this control law; however, one simple way is to drive the instantaneous integral squared deviation

$$\varepsilon(t) = \int_0^1 [x_d(z) - x(z, t)]^2 \, dz \tag{4.2.101}$$

toward zero. Expanding Eq. (4.2.101) in the modal expansion, one obtains

$$\varepsilon(t) = \int_0^1 \left(\sum_{n=0}^{N} \varepsilon_n(t)\phi_n(z) \right)^2 dz \tag{4.2.102}$$

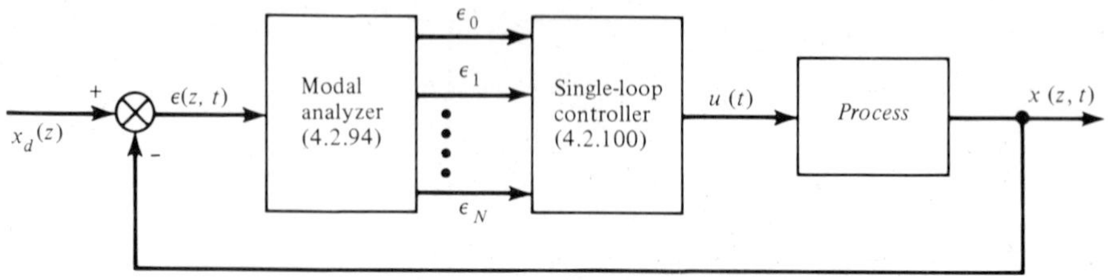

Figure 4.12 A distributed parameter modal feedback controller for time dependent control $u(t)$.

or by orthogonality,

$$\varepsilon(t) = \sum_{n=0}^{N} \varepsilon_n^2(t) \tag{4.2.103}$$

Hence a possible design would be a PI controller of the form

$$u(t) = K\left[\varepsilon(t) + \frac{1}{\tau_I}\int \varepsilon(t)\, dt\right] \tag{4.2.104}$$

Thus making $\varepsilon(t)$ as small as possible will cause $x(z, t)$ to approach $x_d(z)$ with minimal error in the least squares sense.

Let us now consider another example problem in which the differential operator is *non-self-adjoint* and the control is applied at the boundary. We shall discuss the control of a cylindrical ingot being heated in a furnace as shown in Fig. 4.13. We shall assume the top and bottom of the ingot receive negligible heating and the heating rate at the surface is uniform and may be controlled as a function of time. In addition, axial variations in temperature are neglected, and the problem is described by the one-dimensional, cylindrical heat equation

$$\rho C_p \frac{\partial T}{\partial t'} = \frac{k}{r'}\frac{\partial}{\partial r'}\left(r'\frac{\partial T}{\partial r'}\right) \qquad \begin{matrix} 0 \le r' \le R \\ t' > 0 \end{matrix} \tag{4.2.105}$$

with boundary conditions

$r' = 0$:
$$\frac{\partial T}{\partial r'} = 0 \tag{4.2.106}$$

$r' = R$:
$$k\frac{\partial T}{\partial r'} = q(t') \tag{4.2.107}$$

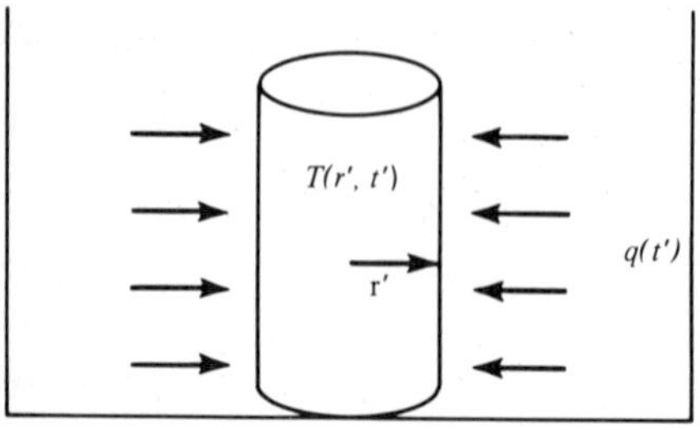

Figure 4.13 A cylindrical ingot being heated in a furnace.

The control problem is to adjust $q(t')$ so that the ingot achieves the desired temperature distribution $T(r', t')$. Note, however, two complications: (1) the operator in r is *non-self-adjoint*, and (2) the control is applied at the boundary.

First let us discuss how to treat *non-self-adjoint* systems. In general, one may invoke a change of variable, such as in Eq. (4.2.86). However, for equations of the form

$$L(\cdot) = \frac{1}{\rho(z)} \frac{d}{dz}\left[p(z)\frac{d(\cdot)}{dz}\right] + q(z)(\cdot) \qquad 0 \le z \le 1 \qquad (4.2.108)$$

such as arise in cylindrical and spherical diffusion and heat conduction problems, it is possible to use Sturm-Liouville theory [16, 17]. This theory allows one to state that the system

$$Lx = \lambda x \qquad (4.2.109)$$

[where L is defined in Eq. (4.2.108)] coupled with homogeneous boundary conditions, will have a discrete spectrum of eigenvalues λ_n and a corresponding set of eigenfunctions $\phi_n(z)$ which are orthogonal with respect to $\rho(z)$, i.e.,

$$\int_0^1 \rho(z)\phi_n(z)\phi_m(z)\, dz = 0 \qquad n \ne m \qquad (4.2.110)$$

Now let us discuss the situation when the control is applied at the boundary, as in Eq. (4.2.107). This causes the boundary conditions to become nonhomogeneous and could lead to great theoretical complications. However, it is possible to make some transformations to eliminate this problem. Generally speaking, one may introduce the boundary control into the differential equation through the use of a Dirac delta function. For a general discussion of this, see [19–21]. To illustrate this approach, let us now proceed with our cylindrical ingot heating problem. Let us put the problem in more convenient form by defining

$$x = \frac{T}{T_0} \qquad t = \frac{t'k}{\rho C_p R^2} \qquad r = \frac{r'}{R} \qquad u(t) = \frac{q(t')R}{T_0 k} \qquad (4.2.111)$$

where T_0 is some reference initial temperature [for example, $T_0 = T(R, 0)$, the initial surface temperature]. With these dimensionless variables the problem takes the form

$$\frac{\partial x(r,t)}{\partial t} = \frac{1}{r}\frac{\partial}{\partial r}\left(r\frac{\partial x(r,t)}{\partial r}\right) \qquad \begin{array}{l} 0 \le r \le 1 \\ t > 0 \end{array} \qquad (4.2.112)$$

with boundary conditions

$$r = 0 \qquad \frac{\partial x}{\partial r} = 0 \qquad (4.2.113)$$

$$r = 1 \qquad \frac{\partial x}{\partial r} = u(t) \qquad (4.2.114)$$

$$t = 0 \qquad x = x_0(r) \qquad (4.2.115)$$

Now it is possible to construct the solution to this problem in terms of the *Green's function* [10, 16, 17] and to show that there is an equivalent problem to

Eqs. (4.2.112) to (4.2.115) with $u(t)$ appearing on the right-hand side of the differential equation (see Olivei [21] for an example). Let us now show a less rigorous shortcut to that equivalent problem. Let us add $u(t)$ to Eq. (4.2.112) with a Dirac delta function $\delta(r-1)$ so that

$$\frac{\partial x}{\partial t} = \frac{1}{r}\frac{\partial}{\partial r}\left(r\frac{\partial x(r,t)}{\partial r}\right) + \delta(r-1)u(t) \tag{4.2.116}$$

with boundary conditions

$$r = 0 \qquad \frac{\partial x}{\partial r} = 0 \tag{4.2.113}$$

$$r = 1^+ \qquad \frac{\partial x}{\partial r} = 0 \tag{4.2.117}$$

$$t = 0 \qquad x = x_0(r) \tag{4.2.115}$$

Now we can prove that this change is rigorous by integrating Eq. (4.2.116) across the infinitesimal interval $1^- < r < 1^+$:

$$\int_{1^-}^{1^+} r\frac{\partial x}{\partial t}\nearrow^{0}\, dr = \int_{1^-}^{1^+} \frac{\partial}{\partial r}\left(r\frac{\partial x}{\partial r}\right) dr + \int_{1^-}^{1^+} r\,\delta(r-1)u(t)\, dr \tag{4.2.118}$$

$$0 = \frac{\partial x}{\partial r}\bigg]_{1^-}^{1^+} + u(t) \tag{4.2.119}$$

but invoking Eq. (4.2.117), we see that Eq. (4.2.119) yields

$$\frac{\partial x}{\partial r} = u(t)$$

at $r = 1^-$, so the *formulations are equivalent*.

Let us now proceed to use separation of variables to solve Eqs. (4.2.113) and (4.2.115) to (4.2.117). If one assumes a solution of the form

$$x(r,t) = \sum_{n=0}^{\infty} a_n(t)\phi_n(r) \tag{4.2.120}$$

$$\delta(r-1)u(t) = \sum_{n=0}^{\infty} b_n(t)\phi_n(r) \tag{4.2.121}$$

and substitutes into Eqs. (4.2.113), and (4.2.115) to (4.2.117), the equations become

$$\phi_n(r)\frac{da_n}{dt} = \frac{a_n(t)}{r}\frac{\partial}{\partial r}\left(r\frac{\partial \phi_n}{\partial r}\right) + b_n(t)\phi_n(r) \qquad n = 0, 1, 2, \ldots \tag{4.2.122}$$

with boundary conditions

$$r=0 \qquad \frac{d\phi_n}{dr} = 0 \tag{4.2.123}$$

$$r=1 \qquad \frac{d\phi_n}{dr} = 0 \tag{4.2.124}$$

By separation of variables we are led to the eigenvalue problem (where we choose the separation constant $-\lambda_n$ for convenience)

$$\frac{da_n}{dt} + \lambda_n a_n = b_n \qquad n = 0, 1, \ldots \tag{4.2.125}$$

$$\frac{1}{r}\frac{d}{dr}\left(r\frac{d\phi_n}{dr}\right) + \lambda_n \phi_n = 0 \qquad n = 0, 1, \ldots \tag{4.2.126}$$

Now Eq. (4.2.126) is *non-self-adjoint*; however, it is in the Sturm-Liouville form [Eq. (4.2.108)], and Sturm-Liouville theory tells us that

$$\int_0^1 r\phi_n(r)\phi_m(r)\, dr = 0 \qquad n \neq m \tag{4.2.127}$$

so that $\phi_n^* = r\phi_n(r)$ are the eigenfunctions of the adjoint equation to Eq. (4.2.126), that is, of

$$\frac{d^2\phi_n^*}{dr^2} - \frac{1}{r}\frac{d\phi_n^*}{dr} + \left(\frac{1}{r^2} + \lambda_n\right)\phi_n^* = 0 \tag{4.2.128}$$

because in general the eigenfunctions of the operator and its adjoint operator are orthogonal,

$$\int_0^1 \phi_n^*(r)\phi_m(r)\, dr = 0 \qquad n \neq m \tag{4.2.129}$$

With this as background, let us proceed to solve Eq. (4.2.126) with the boundary conditions of Eqs. (4.2.123) and (4.2.124). Equation (4.2.126) can be put in the form of Bessel's equation [22],

$$r^2\frac{d^2\phi_n}{dr^2} + r\frac{d\phi_n}{dr} + r^2\lambda_n\phi_n = 0 \tag{4.2.130}$$

which has the general solution

$$\phi_n = A_n J_0\left(\sqrt{\lambda_n}\, r\right) + B_n Y_0\left(\sqrt{\lambda_n}\, r\right) \tag{4.2.131}$$

where $J_n(y)$ is a Bessel function of the first kind and of nth order and $Y_n(y)$ is a Bessel function of the second kind and nth order. If we apply the boundary condition of Eq. (4.2.123), we obtain

$$r = 0 \qquad \frac{d\phi_n}{dr} = -A_n\sqrt{\lambda_n}\, \cancelto{0}{J_1(0)} - B_n\sqrt{\lambda_n}\, Y_1(0) = 0 \tag{4.2.132}$$

which requires $B_n = 0$ because $Y_1(0) \neq 0$. Applying the boundary condition of Eq. (4.2.124) yields

$$r = 1 \qquad \frac{d\phi_n}{dr} = -A_n\sqrt{\lambda_n}\, J_1\left(\sqrt{\lambda_n}\right) = 0 \tag{4.2.133}$$

which leads to a definition of the constant λ_n.

$$J_1\left(\sqrt{\lambda_n}\right) = 0 \tag{4.2.134}$$

This has roots $\lambda_0 = 0$, $\sqrt{\lambda_1} = 3.83$, $\sqrt{\lambda_2} = 7.01$, $\sqrt{\lambda_3} = 10.17$, $\sqrt{\lambda_4} = 13.33$, etc. Thus one can calculate λ_n for n as large as desired from Eq. (4.2.134). We can now choose A_n so that the eigenfunctions are *orthonormal*, i.e.,

$$A_n^2 = \left[\int_0^1 r J_0\left(\sqrt{\lambda_n}\, r\right)^2 dr \right]^{-1} \qquad n = 0, 1, 2, \ldots \tag{4.2.135}$$

or using Bessel function identities (as in [22]),

$$A_n = \left[\frac{J_0^2\left(\sqrt{\lambda_n}\right)}{2} \right]^{-1/2} = \frac{\sqrt{2}}{J_0\left(\sqrt{\lambda_n}\right)} \qquad n = 0, 1, \ldots \tag{4.2.136}$$

Thus

$$\phi_n(r) = \frac{\sqrt{2}\, J_0\left(\sqrt{\lambda_n}\, r\right)}{J_0\left(\sqrt{\lambda_n}\right)} \qquad n = 0, 1, 2, \ldots \tag{4.2.137}$$

Hence the solution to Eq. (4.2.112) takes the form of Eq. (4.2.120), where $\phi_n(r)$ is given by Eq. (4.2.137) and Eq. (4.2.125) must be solved for the $a_n(t)$.

Because of the orthogonality relationships, Eq. (4.2.127), one obtains inversion relations

$$a_n(t) = \int_0^1 \phi_n^*(r) x(r, t)\, dr = \int_0^1 r \phi_n(r) x(r, t)\, dr \tag{4.2.138}$$

and in particular, the initial conditions are

$$a_n(0) = \int_0^1 r \phi_n(r) x_0(r)\, dr \tag{4.2.139}$$

Also, the coefficients $b_n(t)$ can be found from

$$b_n(t) = \int_0^1 r\, \delta(r - 1) \phi_n(r) u(t)\, dr = \phi_n(1) u(t) \tag{4.2.140}$$

$$b_n(t) = \sqrt{2}\, u(t) \qquad n = 0, 1, 2, \ldots \tag{4.2.141}$$

Thus the boundary control $u(t)$ affects all the modes in the same way, and Eq. (4.2.125) becomes

$$\frac{da_n}{dt} + \lambda_n a_n = \sqrt{2}\, u(t) \tag{4.2.142}$$

The modal control scheme for this problem will have the same form as Fig. 4.12, and the feedback control law is

$$u(t) = g(\varepsilon_0, \varepsilon_1, \varepsilon_2, \ldots, \varepsilon_N(t)) \tag{4.2.143}$$

This means that some weighting of the ε_i is necessary in the feedback control law, and some of the methods of Chap. 3 would be useful in that regard.

More detailed applications of these modal approaches are presented in Chap. 6.

Controllability and Stabilizability

As in the case of first-order hyperbolic PDE systems, controllability and stabilizability results are complex and depend strongly on the exact definition of what is meant by *controllability* or *stabilizability* [2, p. 138; 9; 23; 24]. For example, *exact* controllability requires the *exact* achievement of some final distributed state $x_d(z)$ from any initial distributed state $\mathbf{x}_0(z)$, and the requirements for exact controllability are quite stringent [9]. By contrast, *approximate controllability* only requires that the null initial state $\mathbf{x}_0(z) = \mathbf{0}$ be taken to within an arbitrarily small neighborhood of the final desired state $\mathbf{x}_d(z)$. For essentially all practical process control problems of interest, *approximate controllability* is sufficient for the adequate design of a controller. Thus we shall be concerned here with approximate controllability conditions.

Another difference between distributed parameter systems and lumped parameter systems is in controllability conditions when the control is applied at the boundary of a distributed parameter system. However, detailed consideration of the various controllability conditions is beyond the purpose of this book, and we shall simply illustrate the fundamental concepts through several examples. The approach we shall use is to develop *approximate controllability* and *approximate stabilizability* results by lumping the system through N-eigenfunction decomposition and then applying lumped parameter *controllability* and *stabilizability* theorems to the N ODEs in the eigencoefficients. This *N-mode controllability* can usually be extended to approximate controllability by letting $N \to \infty$. This approach is best discussed in terms of specific example systems. Thus let us consider the control of the axial temperature distribution in the long, thin rod with modeling equations given by Eqs. (4.2.70) to (4.2.72).

$$\frac{\partial x(z, t)}{\partial t} = \frac{\partial^2 x(z, t)}{\partial z^2} + u(z, t) \tag{4.2.70}$$

$$z = 0 \qquad \frac{\partial x}{\partial z} = 0 \tag{4.2.71}$$

$$z = 1 \qquad \frac{\partial x}{\partial z} = 0 \tag{4.2.72}$$

The modal decomposition using N eigenfunctions produces the solution

$$x(z, t) = \sum_{n=0}^{N} a_n(t)\phi_n(z) \tag{4.2.74}$$

where

$$\phi_n(z) = \begin{cases} 1 & n = 0 \\ \sqrt{2} \quad \cos n\pi z & n = 1, 2, \ldots, N \end{cases} \tag{4.2.144}$$

and

$$\dot{a}_n(t) = -n^2\pi^2 a_n + b_n(t) \qquad n = 0, 1, 2, \ldots, N \tag{4.2.145}$$

Now define the state variables

$$\mathbf{w} = \begin{bmatrix} a_0 \\ a_1 \\ \vdots \\ a_N \end{bmatrix} \quad \mathbf{A} = \begin{bmatrix} 0 & & & & \mathbf{0} \\ & -\pi^2 & & & \\ & & -4\pi^2 & & \\ & & & \ddots & \\ & \mathbf{0} & & & -N^2\pi^2 \end{bmatrix} \quad \mathbf{v} = \begin{bmatrix} b_0 \\ b_1 \\ b_2 \\ \vdots \\ b_N \end{bmatrix} \tag{4.2.146}$$

$$\mathbf{B} = \mathbf{I}$$

Then we can put Eq. (4.2.145) in the form

$$\dot{\mathbf{w}} = \mathbf{A}\mathbf{w} + \mathbf{v}$$

and applying the lumped parameter controllability criterion, we get the controllability matrix

$$\mathbf{L}_c = [\mathbf{I} \vdots \mathbf{A} \vdots \ldots \vdots \mathbf{A}^N] \tag{4.2.147}$$

which must have rank $N + 1$ for *approximate controllability*. However, the $(N + 1) \times (N + 1)$ identity matrix $\mathbf{I}$ has rank $N + 1$, so this system is *approximately controllable* for any number of eigenfunctions.

Now let us consider the cylindrical ingot heating problem with control on the boundary considered earlier. The modeling equations are

$$\frac{\partial x(r, t)}{\partial t} = \frac{1}{r}\frac{\partial}{\partial r}\left(r\frac{\partial x}{\partial r}\right) \qquad \begin{matrix} 0 \le r \le 1 \\ t > 0 \end{matrix} \tag{4.2.112}$$

with boundary conditions

$$r = 0 \qquad \frac{\partial x}{\partial r} = 0 \tag{4.2.113}$$

$$r = 1 \qquad \frac{\partial x}{\partial r} = u(t) \tag{4.2.114}$$

The solution is

$$x(r, t) = \sum_{n=0}^{N} a_n(t)\phi_n(r) \tag{4.2.74}$$

where

$$\phi_n(r) = \frac{\sqrt{2}\, J_0(\sqrt{\lambda_n}\, r)}{J_0(\sqrt{\lambda_n}\,)} \tag{4.2.137}$$

and $a_n(t)$ comes from the solution to

$$\dot{a}_n = -\lambda_n a_n + \sqrt{2}\, u(t) \qquad n = 0, 1, 2, \ldots \tag{4.2.148}$$

If as before we define

$$\mathbf{w} = \begin{bmatrix} a_0 \\ a_1 \\ \vdots \\ a_N \end{bmatrix} \qquad \mathbf{A} = \begin{bmatrix} -\lambda_0 & & & & \mathbf{0} \\ & -\lambda_1 & & & \\ & & -\lambda_2 & & \\ & & & \ddots & \\ & \mathbf{0} & & & -\lambda_N \end{bmatrix} \qquad \mathbf{b} = \begin{bmatrix} \sqrt{2} \\ \sqrt{2} \\ \sqrt{2} \\ \vdots \\ \sqrt{2} \end{bmatrix}$$

then

$$\dot{\mathbf{w}} = \mathbf{A}\mathbf{w} + \mathbf{b}u \tag{4.2.149}$$

and the $(N + 1) \times (N + 1)$ controllability matrix is

$$\mathbf{L}_c = \begin{bmatrix} \sqrt{2} & 0 & 0 & 0 & 0 \\ \sqrt{2} & -\sqrt{2}\,\lambda_1 & \sqrt{2}\,\lambda_1^2 & \cdots & \sqrt{2}\,(-\lambda_1)^N \\ \cdots & \cdots & \cdots & \cdots & \cdots \\ \sqrt{2} & -\sqrt{2}\,\lambda_N & \sqrt{2}\,\lambda_N^2 & \cdots & \sqrt{2}\,(-\lambda_N)^N \end{bmatrix} \tag{4.2.150}$$

and the system is *approximately controllable* so long as the eigenvalues are simple. Simple eigenvalues are a consequence of the Sturm-Liouville character of this example problem. This result is somewhat surprising when one thinks about achieving any given temperature profile with only surface heat flux control. However, having simple eigenvalues means that each mode is excited at a different rate by $u(t)$, and by suitable adjustment of $u(t)$, each $a_n(t)$ can be taken to the set-point value.

Feedback Control with Discrete Control Actuators

In all the discussions so far we have considered controls which acted either at boundaries or continuous in space. However, in a number of practical problems, control actuators can only be placed at a finite number of discrete points or zones along the length of the distributed system. As examples, consider the problem of heating a rod in a furnace with a small number of local heaters or the control of a packed-bed chemical reactor through interstage cooling. In such problems, the performance of the control system is strongly influenced by the location of these control actuators. In fact, it is possible to choose locations for which the system is *uncontrollable*, or, alternatively, locations which are *optimal* in some sense [25–29]. Let us illustrate these points through an example problem.

Example 4.2.4 Let us consider the rod heating problem modeled by Eq. (4.2.70) and shown in Fig. 4.9. Here let us assume that the heating control takes the form

$$u(z, t) = \sum_{k=1}^{M} g_k(z) u_k(t) \tag{4.2.151}$$

where the choice

$$g_k(z) = \delta(z - z_k^*) \tag{4.2.152}$$

corresponds to pointwise control at positions $z_1^*, z_2^*, \ldots, z_M^*$. Note that other functional forms $g_k(z)$ will lead to other forms of local control, for example,

$$g_k(z) = H(z - z_k^*) - H(z - z_{k+1}^*) \tag{4.2.153}$$

[where $H(z)$ is the Heaviside step function] would produce M zones of piecewise uniform heating in the interval $z_k^* < z < z_{k+1}^*$. These cases are illustrated in Fig. 4.14.

If we apply the controller [Eq. (4.2.151)], then the model equations become

$$\frac{\partial x(z, t)}{\partial t} = \frac{\partial^2 x(z, t)}{\partial z^2} + \sum_{k=1}^{M} g_k(z) u_k(t) \tag{4.2.154}$$

$$\frac{\partial x}{\partial z} = 0 \qquad z = 0, 1 \tag{4.2.155}$$

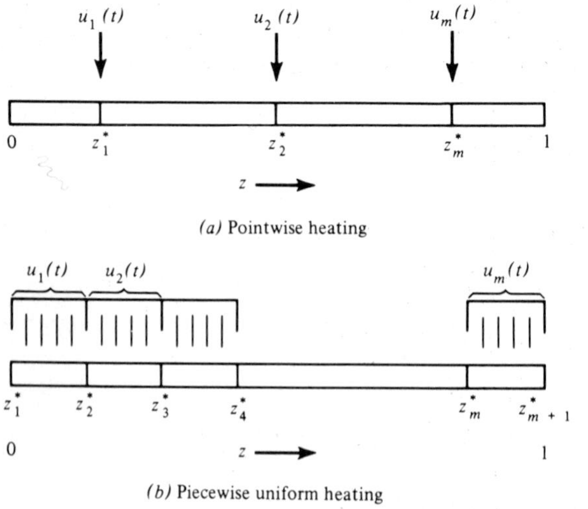

Figure 4.14 Examples of discrete control actuators.

Now let us illustrate how the selection of the location of the actuators influences the *controllability* of the system. Equations (4.2.154) and (4.2.155) may be reduced to the set of eigencoefficient equations

$$\dot{a}_n(t) = -n^2\pi^2 a_n + b_n(t) \qquad n = 0, 1, \ldots, N \qquad (4.2.145)$$

where $b_n(t)$ is the eigencoefficient of the control

$$b_n(t) = \sum_{k=1}^{M} u_k(t) \int_0^1 \phi_n(z) g_k(z)\, dz \qquad (4.2.156)$$

For the case where discrete pointwise actuators, Eq. (4.2.152), are used, then

$$b_n(t) = \sum_{k=1}^{M} \phi_n(z_k^*) u_k(t) \qquad (4.2.157)$$

By defining **w**, **A** from Eq. (4.2.146) and

$$\mathbf{B} = \begin{bmatrix} \phi_0(z_1^*) & \phi_0(z_2^*) & \cdots & \phi_0(z_M^*) \\ \phi_1(z_1^*) & \phi_1(z_2^*) & \cdots & \phi_1(z_M^*) \\ \cdots & \cdots & \cdots & \cdots \\ \phi_N(z_1^*) & \cdots & \cdots & \phi_N(z_M^*) \end{bmatrix} \qquad (4.2.158)$$

one obtains

$$\dot{\mathbf{w}} = \mathbf{A}\mathbf{w} + \mathbf{B}\mathbf{u} \qquad (4.2.159)$$

as an N-eigenfunction representation of the system. The $(N+1)M \times (N+1)$ controllability matrix for this system is

$$\mathbf{L}_c = \begin{bmatrix} 1 & \cdots & 1 & 0 & \cdots & 0 & \cdots \\ \phi_1(z_1^*) & \cdots & \phi_1(z_M^*) & -\pi^2\phi_1(z_1^*) & \cdots & -\pi^2\phi_1(z_M^*) & \cdots \\ \cdots & \cdots & \cdots & \cdots & \cdots & \cdots & \cdots \\ \phi_N(z_1^*) & \cdots & \phi_N(z_M^*) & -N^2\pi^2\phi_N(z_1^*) & \cdots & -N^2\pi^2\phi_N(z_M^*) & \cdots \end{bmatrix} \qquad (4.2.160)$$

and must have the rank $N + 1$ for controllability. Now if the z_k^* are chosen badly, one of the rows of $\mathbf{L}_c$ might vanish identically and the system would be uncontrollable. For example, if $N = 2$, $M = 2$, then

$$\mathbf{L}_c = \left[\begin{array}{cc:cc:cc} 1 & 1 & 0 & 0 & 0 & 0 \\ \phi_1(z_1^*) & \phi_1(z_2^*) & -\pi^2\phi_1(z_1^*) & -\pi^2\phi_1(z_2^*) & \pi^4\phi_1(z_1^*) & \pi^4\phi_1(z_2^*) \\ \phi_2(z_1^*) & \phi_2(z_2^*) & -4\pi^2\phi_2(z_1^*) & -4\pi^2\phi_2(z_2^*) & 16\pi^4\phi_2(z_1^*) & 16\pi^4\phi_2(z_2^*) \end{array}\right] \qquad (4.2.161)$$

must have rank 3. Here ϕ_1 and ϕ_2 are given by

$$\phi_1 = \sqrt{2}\cos \pi z$$
$$\phi_2 = \sqrt{2}\cos 2\pi z \qquad (4.2.162)$$

Now if one chooses $z_1^* = \frac{1}{4}$, $z_2^* = \frac{3}{4}$, then

$$\phi_2(z_1^*) = \phi_2(z_2^*) = 0 \tag{4.2.163}$$

and $\mathbf{L}_c$ has only rank 2. Thus this choice of heater positions causes the system, Eqs. (4.2.154) and (4.2.155), to be *uncontrollable*. This example illustrates the rough rule of thumb that *for controllability one should avoid placing the control actuators at the zeros of the system eigenfunctions*. More will be said about optimal actuator placement in the next section.

4.3 OPTIMAL CONTROL THEORY AND PRACTICE*

One particularly important class of distributed parameter control system design procedures is *optimal control*. As in the case of lumped parameter systems, we shall begin our discussion of the optimal control of distributed parameter systems with the consideration of *open-loop* optimal control strategies. A very general class of such problems can be modeled by the partial differential equations

$$\mathbf{A}\frac{\partial \mathbf{x}}{\partial t} = \mathbf{f}\left(\mathbf{x}, \frac{\partial \mathbf{x}}{\partial z}, \frac{\partial^2 \mathbf{x}}{\partial z^2}, \mathbf{u}\right) \qquad 0 \le t \le t_f \qquad 0 \le z \le L \tag{4.3.1}$$

where $\mathbf{x}(t, z)$ is an n vector of state variables, $\mathbf{u}(t, z)$ is a m vector of control variables, and $\mathbf{A}$ is an $n \times n$ matrix. To prevent matters from becoming too complex, we shall restrict ourselves to two independent variables, $0 \le t \le t_f$ and $0 \le z \le L$, although the analysis could be extended to more independent variables in a straightforward way [30, 31].

Equation 4.3.1 is the general representation of a very large number of practical problems. The drying of porous materials, the behavior of chemical reactor systems, and heat transfer problems like those described in the last section are only a few examples of problems having this form.

The boundary conditions associated with Eq. (4.3.1) depend on the particular problem being considered; however, normally there is an initial state

$$\mathbf{x}(z, 0) = \mathbf{w}(z) \tag{4.3.2}$$

which may be available as a control variable. For example, the initial temperature distribution in the slab of the previous section might be subject to control by preheat. The system boundary conditions are usually split (for obvious physical reasons) and can take a variety of forms. We shall consider three separate cases of boundary conditions here.

Case 1 Some state variables x_s may have boundary conditions of the form

$$\frac{\partial x_s}{\partial z} = g_s(\mathbf{x}, \mathbf{v}(t)) \qquad \text{at } z = 0 \tag{4.3.3a}$$

$$\frac{\partial x_s}{\partial z} = h_s(\mathbf{x}, \mathbf{y}(t)) \qquad \text{at } z = L \tag{4.3.4a}$$

* Parts of this section are adapted from [5] with permission of John Wiley and Sons, Inc.

as, for example, when there is convective or radiant heat transfer at the surface.

Case 2 Other state variables x_r may have boundary conditions of the form

$$x_r(0, t) = \text{const} \tag{4.3.3b}$$

$$x_r(L, t) = \text{const} \tag{4.3.4b}$$

Case 3 Still others x_p may take the form

$$x_p(0, t) = v_p(t) \tag{4.3.3c}$$

$$x_p(L, t) = y_p(t) \tag{4.3.4c}$$

which allows the surface conditions to be controlled in an optimal fashion.

Here $\mathbf{v}(t)$ is a control operating at $z = 0$, and $\mathbf{y}(t)$ is a control operating at $z = L$. It can be seen that the boundary conditions given by Eqs. (4.1.2) and (4.1.3) are just special cases of this general form.

The optimal control problem for this system can be stated, in the most general way, as the desire to maximize the functional

$$I[\mathbf{u}(z, t), \mathbf{v}(t), \mathbf{y}(t), \mathbf{w}(z)] = \int_0^L G_1(\mathbf{x}(t_f, z), \mathbf{w}(z))\, dz + \int_0^{t_f} G_2(\mathbf{x}(L, t), \mathbf{x}(0, t), \mathbf{y}, \mathbf{v})\, dt + \int_0^L \int_0^{t_f} G\left(\mathbf{x}, \mathbf{u}, \frac{\partial \mathbf{x}}{\partial z}, \frac{\partial^2 \mathbf{x}}{\partial z^2}\right) dt\, dz \tag{4.3.5}$$

by choosing the controls $\mathbf{u}(z, t)$, $\mathbf{v}(t)$, $\mathbf{y}(t)$, $\mathbf{w}(z)$.

Necessary Conditions for Optimality

For the optimal control problem given by Eqs. (4.3.1) to (4.3.5), we shall now develop an informal derivation of the necessary conditions for optimality. As in the case of the maximum principle for ordinary differential equations, let us assume that we have a nominal set of optimal control trajectories $\bar{\mathbf{u}}(z, t)$, $\bar{\mathbf{v}}(t)$, $\bar{\mathbf{y}}(t)$, $\bar{\mathbf{w}}(z)$, and let us consider the effect of variations $\delta\mathbf{u}$, $\delta\mathbf{v}$, $\delta\mathbf{y}$, $\delta\mathbf{w}$ about these nominal trajectories. We shall begin by expanding Eq. (4.3.1) about the nominal trajectories to yield the perturbation equations

$$A_{ij}\frac{\partial(\delta x_j)}{\partial t} = \left(\frac{\partial f_i}{\partial x_j}\right)_{.} \delta x_j + \left(\frac{\partial f_i}{\partial u_k}\right)_{.} \delta u_k + \left(\frac{\partial f_i}{\partial(\dot{x}_j)}\right)_{.} \delta(\dot{x}_j) + \left(\frac{\partial f_i}{\partial(\ddot{x}_j)}\right)_{.} \delta(\ddot{x}_j) \tag{4.3.6}$$

where $(\ )_.$ signifies that the quantity is evaluated along the nominal trajectory. In addition,

$$\dot{x}_j \equiv \frac{\partial x_j}{\partial z} \qquad \ddot{x}_j \equiv \frac{\partial^2 x_j}{\partial z^2}$$

and we use the convention that a repeated subscript denotes a sum over that index; for example,

$$\frac{\partial f_i}{\partial x_k}\,\delta x_k \equiv \sum_{k=1}^{n} \frac{\partial f_i}{\partial x_k}\,\delta x_k = \frac{\partial f_i}{\partial x_1}\,\delta x_1 + \frac{\partial f_i}{\partial x_2}\,\delta x_2 + \cdots + \frac{\partial f_i}{\partial x_n}\,\delta x_n$$

Equation (4.3.6) can be rewritten as

$$A_{ij}\frac{\partial(\delta x_j)}{\partial t} = \left(\frac{\partial f_i}{\partial x_k}\right)_. \delta x_k + \left(\frac{\partial f_i}{\partial u_k}\right)_. \delta u_k + \left[\frac{\partial f_i}{\partial(\dot{x}_j)}\right]_. \frac{\partial(\delta x_j)}{\partial z} + \left[\frac{\partial f_i}{\partial(\ddot{x}_j)}\right]_. \frac{\partial^2(\delta x_j)}{\partial z^2} \tag{4.3.7}$$

Expanding the objective [Eq. (4.3.5)] in the same way yields

$$\begin{aligned}
\delta I = &\int_0^L \left\{\left[\frac{\partial G_1}{\partial x_k(z, t_f)}\right]_. \delta x_k(z, t_f) + \left[\frac{\partial G_1}{\partial w_j(z)}\right]_. \delta w_j(z)\right\} dz \\
&+ \int_0^{t_f} \left\{\left[\frac{\partial G_2}{\partial x_k(L, t)}\right]_. \delta x_k(L, t) + \left[\frac{\partial G_2}{\partial x_k(0, t)}\right]_. \delta x_k(0, t)\right. \\
&+ \left.\left[\frac{\partial G_2}{\partial y_j(t)}\right]_. \delta y_j(t) + \left[\frac{\partial G_2}{\partial v_j(t)}\right]_. \delta v_j(t)\right\} dt \\
&+ \int_0^{t_f}\int_0^L \left\{\left(\frac{\partial G}{\partial x_k}\right)_. \delta x_k + \left(\frac{\partial G}{\partial u_i}\right)_. \delta u_i\right. \\
&+ \left.\left[\frac{\partial G}{\partial(\dot{x}_j)}\right]_. \frac{\partial(\delta x_j)}{\partial z} + \left[\frac{\partial G}{\partial(\ddot{x}_j)}\right]_. \frac{\partial^2(\delta x_i)}{\partial z^2}\right\} dz\,dt
\end{aligned} \tag{4.3.8}$$

Now let us use a distributed Lagrange multiplier (called an adjoint variable) $\lambda_k(z, t)$ to form the quantity

$$\begin{aligned}
\int_0^{t_f}\int_0^L \Bigg(\lambda_i(z, t)\Bigg\{ &A_{ij}\frac{\partial(\delta x_j)}{\partial t} - \left(\frac{\partial f_i}{\partial x_k}\right)_. \delta x_k - \left(\frac{\partial f_i}{\partial u_k}\right)_. \delta u_k \\
&- \left[\frac{\partial f_i}{\partial(\dot{x}_j)}\right]_. \frac{\partial(\delta x_j)}{\partial z} - \left[\frac{\partial f_i}{\partial(\ddot{x}_j)}\right]_. \frac{\partial^2(\delta x_j)}{\partial z^2}\Bigg\}\Bigg)\, dz\,dt = 0
\end{aligned} \tag{4.3.9}$$

which can be subtracted from Eq. (4.3.8) to yield

$$\delta I = \int_0^{t_f} \left\{ \left[\frac{\partial G_2}{\partial x_k(L, t)} \right]_. \delta x_k(L, t) + \left[\frac{\partial G_2}{\partial x_k(0, t)} \right]_. \delta x_k(0, t) \right.$$

$$\left. + \left[\frac{\partial G_2}{\partial y_j(t)} \right]_. \delta y_j(t) + \left[\frac{\partial G_2}{\partial v_j(t)} \right]_. \delta v_j(t) \right\} dt$$

$$+ \int_0^L \left\{ \left[\frac{\partial G_1}{\partial x_k(z, t_f)} \right]_. \delta x_k(z, t_f) + \left[\frac{\partial G_1}{\partial w_j(z)} \right]_. \delta w_j(z) \right\} dz$$

$$+ \int_0^{t_f} \int_0^L \left\{ \left(\frac{\partial H}{\partial x_k} \right)_. \delta x_k + \left(\frac{\partial H}{\partial u_i} \right)_. \delta u_i + \left[\frac{\partial H}{\partial (\dot{x}_j)} \right]_. \frac{\partial (\delta x_j)}{\partial z} \right.$$

$$\left. + \left[\frac{\partial H}{\partial (\ddot{x}_j)} \right]_. \frac{\partial^2 (\delta x_j)}{\partial z^2} - \lambda_i \left[A_{ij} \frac{\partial (\delta x_j)}{\partial t} \right] \right\} dz\, dt \tag{4.3.10}$$

where the quantity H (known as the Hamiltonian) is defined as

$$H = G + \lambda_i f_i \tag{4.3.11}$$

If we integrate the last three terms by parts so that

$$\int_0^{t_f} \int_0^L \left[\frac{\partial H}{\partial \dot{x}_j} \frac{\partial (\delta x_j)}{\partial z} \right] dz\, dt = \int_0^{t_f} \left\{ \frac{\partial H}{\partial \dot{x}_j} \delta x_j \Big]_0^L - \int_0^L \frac{\partial}{\partial z} \left(\frac{\partial H}{\partial \dot{x}_j} \right) \delta x_j \, dz \right\} dt \tag{4.3.12}$$

$$\int_0^{t_f} \int_0^L \left[\frac{\partial H}{\partial (\ddot{x}_j)} \frac{\partial^2 (\delta x_j)}{\partial z^2} \right] dz\, dt = \int_0^{t_f} \left\{ \frac{\partial H}{\partial (\ddot{x}_j)} \frac{\partial (\delta x_j)}{\partial z} \Big]_0^L - \frac{\partial}{\partial z} \left(\frac{\partial H}{\partial \ddot{x}_j} \right) \delta x_j \Big]_0^L \right.$$

$$\left. + \int_0^L \frac{\partial^2 (\partial H / \partial \ddot{x}_j)}{\partial z^2} \delta x_j \, dz \right\} dt \tag{4.3.13}$$

$$\int_0^{t_f} \int_0^L \lambda_i \left[A_{ij} \frac{\partial (\delta x_j)}{\partial t} \right] dt\, dz = \int_0^L \left\{ \lambda_i A_{ij}\, \delta x_j \Big]_0^{t_f} - \int_0^{t_f} \frac{\partial (\lambda_i A_{ij})}{\partial t} \delta x_j \, dt \right\} dz \tag{4.3.14}$$

then Eq. (4.3.10) becomes

$$\delta I = \int_0^{t_f}\int_0^L \left\{ \left[\left(\frac{\partial H}{\partial x_k} \right)_{.} - \frac{\partial(\partial H/\partial \dot{x}_k)_{.}}{\partial z} + \frac{\partial^2(\partial H/\partial \ddot{x}_k)_{.}}{\partial z^2} + \frac{\partial(\lambda_i A_{ik})}{\partial t} \right] \delta x_k \right.$$

$$\left. + \left(\frac{\partial H}{\partial u_i} \right)_{.} \delta u_i \right\} dz\, dt + \int_0^{t_f} \left(\left\{ \left[\frac{\partial G_2}{\partial x_k(L, t)} \right]_{.} + \left(\frac{\partial H}{\partial \dot{x}_k} \right)_{.} - \frac{\partial(\partial H/\partial \ddot{x}_k)_{.}}{\partial z} \right\} \delta x_k(L, t) \right.$$

$$+ \left(\frac{\partial G_2}{\partial y_j} \right)_{.} \delta y_j(t) + \left[\frac{\partial G_2}{\partial v_j(t)} \right]_{.} \delta v_j(t) + \left[\frac{\partial H}{\partial (\ddot{x}_j)} \right]_{.} \left[\frac{\partial(\delta x_j)}{\partial z} \right]_0^L$$

$$\left. + \left\{ \left[\frac{\partial G_2}{\partial x_j(0, t)} \right]_{.} - \left(\frac{\partial H}{\partial \dot{x}_j} \right)_{.} + \frac{\partial}{\partial z} \left(\frac{\partial H}{\partial \ddot{x}_j} \right)_{.} \right\} \delta x_j(0, t) \right) dt$$

$$+ \int_0^L \left(\left\{ \left[\frac{\partial G_1}{\partial x_k(t_f, z)} \right]_{.} - \lambda_i A_{ik} \right\} \delta x_k(z, t_f) + \left\{ \left[\frac{\partial G_1}{\partial w_k(z)} \right]_{.} + \lambda_i A_{ik} \right\} \delta w_k(z) \right) dz$$

(4.3.15)

To remove the explicit dependence of δI on $\delta x(z, t)$, let us define the adjoint variables $\lambda_i(z, t)$ by

$$\boxed{\frac{\partial(\lambda_i A_{ik})}{\partial t} = -\left[\left(\frac{\partial H}{\partial x_k} \right)_{.} - \frac{\partial(\partial H/\partial \dot{x}_k)_{.}}{\partial z} + \frac{\partial^2(\partial H/\partial \ddot{x}_k)_{.}}{\partial z^2} \right] \qquad k = 1, 2, \ldots, n}$$

(4.3.16)

which causes the first term in Eq. (4.3.15) to vanish.

Now let us consider the three separate cases that can arise from the boundary conditions [Eqs. (4.3.3) and (4.3.4)].

Case 1 For those state variables having boundary conditions Eqs. (4.3.3*a*) and (4.3.4*a*), the boundary condition variations become

$$\frac{\partial(\delta x_i(0, t))}{\partial z} = \left\{ \left[\frac{\partial g_i}{\partial x_j(0, t)} \right]_{.} \delta x_j(0, t) + \left[\frac{\partial g_i}{\partial v_j(t)} \right]_{.} \delta v_j(t) \right\} \quad (4.3.17)$$

$$\frac{\partial(\delta x_i(L, t))}{\partial z} = \left\{ \left[\frac{\partial h_i}{\partial x_j(L, t)} \right]_{.} \delta x_j(L, t) + \left[\frac{\partial h_i}{\partial y_j(t)} \right]_{.} \delta y_j(t) \right\} \quad (4.3.18)$$

Case 2 For those state variables with boundary conditions of the form of Eqs. (4.3.3*b*) and (4.3.4*b*), the variations

$$\left. \frac{\partial(\delta x_i)}{\partial z} \right]_0^L$$

are free and the variations

$$\delta x_i(0, t) \qquad \delta x_i(L, t)$$

vanish.

Case 3 For those state variables with boundary conditions Eqs. (4.3.3*c*) and (4.3.4*c*), the variations

$$\left.\frac{\partial(\delta x_i)}{\partial z}\right]_0^L$$

are free and

$$\delta x_i(0, t) = \delta v_i(t), \qquad \delta x_i(L, t) = \delta y_i(t) \tag{4.3.19}$$

If we denote the state variables in Case 1 by index s, those in Case 2 by index r, and those in Case 3 by index p, we can rewrite Eq. (4.3.15) as

$$\begin{aligned}
\delta I = & \int_0^{t_f}\int_0^L \left(\frac{\partial H}{\partial u_i}\right)_. \delta u_i\, dz\, dt + \int_0^L \left(\left\{ \left[\frac{\partial G_1}{\partial x_k(z, t_f)}\right]_. - \lambda_i A_{ik} \right\} \delta x_k(z, t_f) \right. \\
& + \left. \left\{ \left[\frac{\partial G_1}{\partial w_k(z)}\right]_. + \lambda_i A_{ik} \right\} \delta w_k(z) \right) dz + \int_0^{t_f} \left(\left(\frac{\partial H_2}{\partial v_s}\right)_. \delta v_s(t) + \left(\frac{\partial H_3}{\partial y_s}\right)_. \delta y_s \right. \\
& + \left\{ \left[\frac{\partial H_2}{\partial x_s(0, t)}\right]_. - \left[\frac{\partial H(0, t)}{\partial \dot{x}_s}\right]_. + \frac{\partial}{\partial z}\left(\frac{\partial H}{\partial \ddot{x}_s}\right)_. \right\} \delta x_s(0, t) \\
& + \left. \left\{ \left[\frac{\partial H_3}{\partial x_s(L, t)}\right]_. + \left[\frac{\partial H(L, t)}{\partial \dot{x}_s}\right]_. - \frac{\partial}{\partial z}\left(\frac{\partial H}{\partial \ddot{x}_s}\right)_. \right\} \delta x_s(L, t) \right) dt \\
& + \int_0^{t_f} \left(\left\{ \left[\frac{\partial G_2}{\partial x_r(0, t)}\right]_. - \left(\frac{\partial H}{\partial \dot{x}_r}\right)_. + \left(\frac{\partial H}{\partial \ddot{x}_r}\right)_. \right\} \delta x_r(0, t) \right. \\
& + \left. \left\{ \left[\frac{\partial G_2}{\partial x_r(L, t)}\right]_. + \left(\frac{\partial H}{\partial \dot{x}_r}\right)_. - \frac{\partial(\partial H/\partial \ddot{x}_r)_.}{\partial z} \right\} \delta x_r(L, t) + \left(\frac{\partial H}{\partial \ddot{x}_r}\right)_. \frac{\partial(\delta x_r)}{\partial z}\right]_0^L \right) dt \\
& + \int_0^{t_f} \left\{ \left[\left(\frac{\partial G_2}{\partial v_p}\right)_. - \left(\frac{\partial H}{\partial \dot{x}_p}\right)_. + \frac{\partial}{\partial z}\left(\frac{\partial H}{\partial \ddot{x}_p}\right)_. \right] \delta v_p(t) \right. \\
& + \left. \left[\left(\frac{\partial G_2}{\partial y_p}\right)_. + \left(\frac{\partial H}{\partial \dot{x}_p}\right)_. - \frac{\partial(\partial H/\partial \ddot{x}_p)_.}{\partial z} \right] \delta y_p(t) + \left(\frac{\partial H}{\partial(\ddot{x}_p)}\right)_. \frac{\partial(\delta x_p)}{\partial z}\right]_0^L \right\} dt
\end{aligned} \tag{4.3.20}$$

where we have defined additional Hamiltonians as

$$H_1 \equiv G_1 + \lambda_i A_{ik} w_k \tag{4.3.21}$$

$$H_2 \equiv G_2 - \frac{\partial H}{\partial \ddot{x}_i}(0, t) g_i \tag{4.3.22}$$

$$H_3 \equiv G_2 + \frac{\partial H(L, t)}{\partial \ddot{x}_i} h_i \tag{4.3.23}$$

Now to cause the coefficients of the arbitrary variations

$$\delta x_s(0, t) \qquad \delta x_s(L, t) \qquad \frac{\partial(\delta x_r)}{\partial z}\Bigg]_0^L \qquad \frac{\partial(\delta x_p)}{\partial z}\Bigg]_0^L$$

to vanish, we must specify the following boundary conditions on the adjoint variables.

For Case 1 boundary conditions:

$$\left\{ \frac{\partial H_2}{\partial x_s(0, t)} - \frac{\partial H(0, t)}{\partial \dot{x}_s} + \frac{\partial}{\partial z}\left[\frac{\partial H(0, t)}{\partial \ddot{x}_s} \right] \right\} = 0 \tag{4.3.24}$$

$$\left\{ \frac{\partial H_3}{\partial x_s(L, t)} + \frac{\partial H(L, t)}{\partial \dot{x}_s} - \frac{\partial}{\partial z}\left[\frac{\partial H(L, t)}{\partial \ddot{x}_s} \right] \right\} = 0 \tag{4.3.25}$$

For Cases 2 and 3 boundary conditions:

$$\frac{\partial H}{\partial \ddot{x}_r}\Bigg]_0^L = \frac{\partial H}{\partial \ddot{x}_p}\Bigg]_0^L = 0 \tag{4.3.26}$$

In addition, if the terminal state $\mathbf{x}(z, t_f)$ is completely unspecified, the terminal conditions on $\boldsymbol{\lambda}$ become

$$\lambda_i(z, t_f) A_{ik} = \frac{\partial G_1}{\partial x_k(z, t_f)} \qquad k = 1, 2, \ldots, n \tag{4.3.27}$$

It should be noted that if the partial differential equations are not second-order in some of the state variables $x_q(z, t)$, then $\partial H / \partial \ddot{x}_q \equiv 0$, and Case 2 or 3 boundary conditions are possible only at one side. If, for example, $x_q(L, t)$ was unspecified, then the coefficient of $\delta x_q(L, t)$ in Eq. (4.3.20) must vanish. The boundary condition on $\lambda_q(L, t)$ would then be

$$\frac{\partial G_2}{\partial x_q(L, t)} + \frac{\partial H}{\partial \dot{x}_q} = 0 \tag{4.3.28}$$

Thus these results apply to both first- and second-order partial differential equations. Applying these results reduces the variation in I to

$$\delta I = \int_0^{t_f}\int_0^L \left(\frac{\partial H}{\partial u_i}\right)_{.} \delta u_i \, dz \, dt + \int_0^{t_f}\left\{\left[\frac{\partial H_2}{\partial v_s(t)}\right]_{.} \delta v_s(t) + \left[\frac{\partial H_3}{\partial y_s(t)}\right]_{.} \delta y_s(t)\right\} dt$$

$$+ \int_0^{t_f}\left\{\left[\left(\frac{\partial G_2}{\partial v_p}\right)_{.} - \left(\frac{\partial H}{\partial \dot{x}_p}\right)_{.} + \frac{\partial}{\partial z}\left(\frac{\partial H}{\partial \ddot{x}_p}\right)_{.}\right] \delta v_p(t)\right.$$

$$\left. + \left[\left(\frac{\partial G_2}{\partial y_p}\right)_{.} + \left(\frac{\partial H}{\partial \dot{x}_p}\right)_{.} - \frac{\partial(\partial H/\partial \ddot{x}_p)_{.}}{\partial z}\right] \delta y_p(t)\right\} dt$$

$$+ \int_0^{L}\left\{\left[\frac{\partial H_1}{\partial w_i(z)}\right]_{.} \delta w_i(z)\right\} dz \tag{4.3.29}$$

where the influence of the variations $\delta \mathbf{u}$, $\delta \mathbf{v}$, $\delta \mathbf{y}$, $\delta \mathbf{w}$ on the objective δI is now clear. Since the variations δu_i, δv_j, δy_k, δw_i are all arbitrary, a necessary condition for $\delta I \le 0$ and the nominal policies $\bar{\mathbf{u}}$, $\bar{\mathbf{v}}$, $\bar{\mathbf{y}}$, $\bar{\mathbf{w}}$ to be optimal is that the coefficients of the variations vanish. Thus we can collect our results into the following weak maximum principle:

Theorem In order for the control trajectories $\bar{\mathbf{u}}$, $\bar{\mathbf{v}}$, $\bar{\mathbf{y}}$, and $\bar{\mathbf{w}}$ to be optimal for the problem defined by Eqs. (4.3.1) to (4.3.5) and subject to the upper- and lower-bound constraints

$$\begin{aligned} u_{i*} &\le u_i \le u_i^* \\ v_{j*} &\le v_j \le v_j^* \\ y_{k*} &\le y_k \le y_k^* \\ w_{l*} &\le w_l \le w_l^* \end{aligned} \tag{4.3.30}$$

it is necessary that

$$\left(\frac{\partial H}{\partial u_i}\right)_{.} = 0 \tag{4.3.31}$$

for $\bar{u}_i(z, t)$ unconstrained and H be a maximum when $\bar{u}_i(z, t)$ is constrained. If $\bar{u}_i$ is only a function of z, then

$$\int_0^{t_f}\left(\frac{\partial H}{\partial u_i}\right)_{.} dt = 0 \tag{4.3.32}$$

must hold for unconstrained $\bar{u}_i(z)$ and $\int_0^{t_f} H\, dt$ must be maximized with respect to constrained $\bar{u}_i(z)$. Similarly, if $\bar{u}_i$ is only a function of t, then

$$\int_0^{L}\left(\frac{\partial H}{\partial u_i}\right)_{.} dz = 0 \tag{4.3.33}$$

must hold for unconstrained $\bar{u}_i(t)$ and $\int_0^L H\, dz$ must be a maximum with respect to constrained $\bar{u}_i(t)$.

Furthermore, it is necessary that

$$\left(\frac{\partial H_1}{\partial w_l}\right) = 0 \qquad (4.3.34)$$

$$\left(\frac{\partial H_2}{\partial v_s}\right) = 0 \qquad (4.3.35)$$

$$\left\{\frac{\partial G_2}{\partial v_p} - \frac{\partial H(0,t)}{\partial \dot{x}_p} + \frac{\partial}{\partial z}\left[\frac{\partial H(0,t)}{\partial \ddot{x}_p}\right]\right\} = 0 \qquad (4.3.36)$$

$$\left(\frac{\partial H_3}{\partial y_s}\right) = 0 \qquad (4.3.37)$$

$$\left[\frac{\partial G_2}{\partial y_p} + \frac{\partial H(L,t)}{\partial \dot{x}_p} - \frac{\partial(\partial H(L,t)/\partial \ddot{x}_p)}{\partial z}\right] = 0 \qquad (4.3.38)$$

must hold for unconstrained $w_l(z)$, $v_s(t)$, $v_p(t)$, $y_s(t)$, $y_p(t)$, respectively, and these quantities must be nonnegative at the upper bounds on the controls and nonpositive at the lower bounds. If any of the w_l, v_s, v_p, y_s, y_p are unconstrained constant parameters, then the necessary conditions become

$$\int_0^L \left(\frac{\partial H_1}{\partial w_l}\right) dz = 0 \qquad (4.3.39)$$

$$\int_0^{t_f} \left(\frac{\partial H_2}{\partial v_s}\right) dt = 0 \qquad (4.3.40)$$

$$\int_0^{t_f} \left\{\frac{\partial G_2}{\partial v_p} - \frac{\partial H(0,t)}{\partial \dot{x}_p} + \frac{\partial}{\partial z}\left[\frac{\partial H(0,t)}{\partial \ddot{x}_p}\right]\right\} dt = 0 \qquad (4.3.41)$$

$$\int_0^{t_f} \left(\frac{\partial H_3}{\partial y_s}\right) dt = 0 \qquad (4.3.42)$$

$$\int_0^{t_f} \left[\frac{\partial G_2}{\partial y_p} + \frac{\partial H(L,t)}{\partial \dot{x}_p} - \frac{\partial(\partial H(L,t)/\partial \ddot{x}_p)}{\partial z}\right] dt = 0 \qquad (4.3.43)$$

The adjoint variables $\lambda_i(z, t)$ are defined by Eqs. (4.3.16) and (4.3.24) to (4.3.28), and H, H_1, H_2, H_3 by Eqs. (4.3.11) and (4.3.21) to (4.3.23).

We hope that the reader was not unduly intimidated by the apparent complexity of the theorem. The rather involved nature of these expressions is caused by the fact that we wish to present a fairly general statement of the necessary conditions for optimality for the system described by Eq. (4.3.1). The hope is that the reader can apply the results of the theorem directly to many real problems and will have to derive the necessary conditions only for very unusual problems not falling within this framework.

In order to illustrate the application of these general results to a particular problem, we shall produce the necessary conditions for optimality for the slab-heating problem discussed in Sec. 4.1.

Example 4.3.1 From the general formulation, produce the necessary conditions for optimality of the heat flux program $v(t)$ for the optimization problem described by Eqs. (4.1.1) to (4.1.6). Let us assume for the moment that the coefficients α and β are constant.

SOLUTION First we shall define the needed Hamiltonians:

$$H = [T - T_d(z)]^2 + \lambda(z, t)\frac{\alpha}{\beta}\frac{\partial^2 T}{\partial z^2}$$

$$H_2 = -\frac{\alpha}{\beta}\lambda(0, t)v(t)$$

$$H_3 = 0$$

Then the necessary condition [from Eq. (4.3.35)] for $v(t)$ to be optimal is that

$$v(t) = \begin{cases} v^* & \text{for } \dfrac{\alpha}{\beta}\lambda(0, t) > 0 \\ v_* \le v \le v^* & \text{for } \dfrac{\alpha}{\beta}\lambda(0, t) = 0 \\ v_* & \text{for } \dfrac{\alpha}{\beta}\lambda(0, t) < 0 \end{cases}$$

where the adjoint equation [from Eq. (4.3.16)] is

$$\frac{\partial \lambda(z, t)}{\partial t} = -\left[2(T - T_d) + \frac{\alpha}{\beta}\frac{\partial^2 \lambda(z, t)}{\partial z^2}\right]$$

Clearly the terminal state $\lambda(z, t_f)$ is unspecified and the boundary conditions are Case 1, so that the boundary conditions on λ [from Eqs. (4.3.24), (4.3.25), and (4.3.27)] become

$$\frac{\alpha}{\beta}\frac{\partial}{\partial z}[\lambda(0, t)] = 0$$

$$\frac{\alpha}{\beta}\frac{\partial}{\partial z}[\lambda(L, t)] = 0$$

$$\lambda(z, t_f) = 0$$

Thus we have specified the necessary conditions for $v(t)$ to be optimal by simply plugging into the general equations given in the theorem. We note the fact, which is of considerable practical interest, that the optimal heat flux must either correspond to the upper bound (the maximum allowable value) or be zero. The only exception to this stipulation is the case when $\lambda(0, t) = 0$. Thus we have learned the form of the optimal program without performing any calculations. One could readily test likely candidates for the optimal program $v(t)$ by solving the given adjoint partial differential equations and examining the behavior of $\lambda(0, t)$.

Some Computational Procedures

Just as Pontryagin's maximum principle formed the basis of computational approaches to the solution of lumped parameter optimal control problems in Chap. 3, the distributed maximum principle of this section forms the basis of a number of computational procedures for distributed parameter optimal control problems. The most commonly applied method is the *control vector iteration technique*. This procedure is very similar to the one described in Chap. 3 and makes use of the fact that if the initial estimates $\bar{\mathbf{u}}$, $\bar{\mathbf{v}}$, $\bar{\mathbf{y}}$, and $\bar{\mathbf{w}}$ are nonoptimal, then a gradient correction

$$\delta u_i(z, t) = \varepsilon_0\left(\frac{\partial H}{\partial u_i}\right). \tag{4.3.44}$$

$$\delta w_l(z) = \varepsilon_1\left(\frac{\partial H_1}{\partial w_l}\right). \tag{4.3.45}$$

$$\delta v_s(t) = \varepsilon_2\left(\frac{\partial H_2}{\partial v_s}\right). \tag{4.3.46}$$

$$\delta v_p(t) = \varepsilon_3\left[\frac{\partial G_2}{\partial v_p} - \frac{\partial H}{\partial \dot{x}_p} + \frac{\partial}{\partial z}\left(\frac{\partial H}{\partial \ddot{x}_p}\right)\right]. \tag{4.3.47}$$

$$\delta y_s(t) = \varepsilon_4\left(\frac{\partial H_3}{\partial y_s}\right). \tag{4.3.48}$$

$$\delta y_p(t) = \varepsilon_5\left[\frac{\partial G_2}{\partial y_p} + \frac{\partial H}{\partial \dot{x}_p} - \frac{\partial(\partial H/\partial \ddot{x}_p)}{\partial z}\right]. \tag{4.3.49}$$

will show the greatest local improvement in δI for sufficiently small positive ε_0, ε_1, ε_2, ε_3, ε_4, ε_5. The detailed algorithm then is

1. Guess $u_i(z, t)$, $v_j(t)$, $y_k(t)$, $w_l(z)$, $0 \le t \le t_f$, $0 \le z \le L$.
2. Solve the state Eq. (4.3.1) together with the boundary conditions [Eqs. (4.3.2) to (4.3.4)]. Compute I from Eq. (4.3.5).
3. Solve the adjoint Eqs. (4.3.16) together with the boundary condition [Eqs. (4.3.24) to (4.3.28)].
4. Correct $u_i(z, t)$, $v_j(t)$, $y_k(t)$, $w_l(z)$ by Eqs. (4.3.44) to (4.3.49), where the ε_i are so chosen as to maximize I. A multivariable search may be used, or alternatively we may assume $\varepsilon_i = a_i\varepsilon_0$, $i = 1, 2, \ldots, 5$, and perform an initial scaling of the a_i followed by a single variable search on ε_0 at each iteration.
5. Return to step 2 and iterate.

Just as in the lumped parameter optimal control problems, these procedures progress very rapidly in the initial stages, but slow down considerably as the optimum is approached. Thus efforts are being made to extend second-order ascent procedures as well as conjugate gradient methods to these problems.

From a practical standpoint, computational difficulties would arise (caused largely by inadequate computer memory) if we were to tackle problems in several dimensions with a large number of control and state variables using this technique. We note, however, that it is quite feasible to carry out the optimal control of systems modeled by partial differential equations and having a number of state and control variables. Indeed, a host of such problems have been tackled by chemical and control engineers; some references will be made to such work in subsequent sections of this chapter.

For practical reasons we shall restrict ourselves, in the illustrative examples to be presented, to systems described by partial differential equations with relatively few state and control variables.

To demonstrate this control vector iteration procedure, we shall determine the optimal inlet temperature control for a train of packed bed reactors whose catalyst is subject to deactivation (see [32, 33] for the treatment of similar problems).

Example 4.3.2 Let us consider the problem of disposing of exhaust gases from a smelting or other ore-processing operation. One solution which has been employed to avoid the air pollution resulting from SO_2 and other noxious components in the stack gases is to oxidize the material (e.g., transform SO_2 to SO_3 for the production of sulfuric acid). Let us consider, furthermore, that this oxidation is to be carried out over some catalyst which is subject to deactivation with time. Because the reaction is exothermic and is assumed to be reversible, a number of adiabatic stages are employed with interstage cooling, as shown in Fig. 4.15. We assume that species A is the reactant and B is the oxidation product. Thus the reaction

$$A \underset{k_2}{\overset{k_1}{\rightleftarrows}} B$$

is to be carried out in the three adiabatic packed bed reactors sketched in

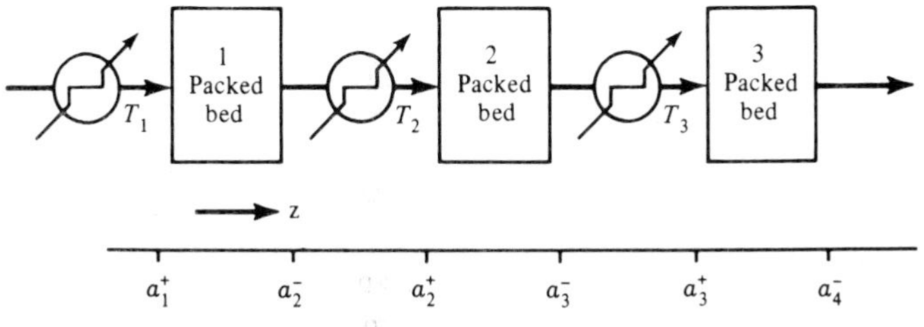

Figure 4.15 Optimization of the reactors used for SO_2 oxidation.

Fig. 4.15. The modeling equations are given as

$$u\frac{\partial C_B}{\partial z'}(z', t') = \psi(z', t')[k_1(T)(C_T - C_B) - k_2(T)C_B]$$

$$\text{(Mass balance on the product)} \qquad \begin{matrix} 0 \le t' \le t_f \\ 0 \le z' \le L \end{matrix} \qquad (4.3.50)$$

$$\rho C_p u\frac{\partial T(z', t')}{\partial z'} = (-\Delta H)\psi(z', t')[k_1(T)(C_T - C_B) - k_2(T)C_B]$$

$$\text{(Heat balance)} \qquad \begin{matrix} 0 \le t' \le t_f \\ 0 \le z' \le L \end{matrix} \qquad (4.3.51)$$

$$T(\alpha_1'^+, t') = T_1 \qquad T(\alpha_2'^+, t') = T_2$$

$$T(\alpha_3'^+, t') = T_3 \qquad C_B(0, t') = C_{Bf} \qquad (4.3.52)$$

which represent steady-state material and heat balances in the reactor train. The quantities α_i' denote the points of separation between the beds, C_T is the total feed concentration, and C_{Bf} is the feed concentration of B. The total catalyst lifetime is t_f, and the total reactor length is L. The reaction rate constants are given by $k_i = A_{i0}e^{-E_i/RT}$, $i = 0, 1, 2$. The decline in catalyst activity $\psi(z', t')$ at each point in the bed can be described by

$$\frac{\partial \psi(z', t')}{\partial t'} = -k_0(T)\psi^2 \qquad \begin{matrix} 0 \le t' \le t_f \\ 0 \le z' \le L \end{matrix} \qquad (4.3.53)$$

where the initial activity is taken to be unity for fresh catalyst, that is,

$$\psi(z', 0) = 1.0 \qquad (4.3.54)$$

Thus if the time scale for catalyst decay is much longer than the time scale for the dynamics of the reactor, then Eqs. (4.3.50) to (4.3.54) are the modeling equations for the system.

Let us suppose that we wish to control the interstage coolers (i.e., the inlet temperatures T_1, T_2, T_3) so as to maximize the conversion of A over the catalyst lifetime t_f. However, due to heat exchange constraints, it is assumed that the possible inlet temperatures are bounded by $T_* \le T_i \le T^*$. This is a practical optimal control problem because by raising the inlet temperature, we both increase the conversion of A from Eqs. (4.3.50) and (4.3.51) and hasten the deactivation of the catalyst through Eq. (4.3.53). Thus there is an optimal inlet temperature control strategy $T_1(t')$, $T_2(t')$, $T_3(t')$ which must be determined, and we do this by applying the control vector iteration technique to the problem.

SOLUTION Let us first recognize that Eqs. (4.3.50) and (4.3.51) are not independent, but can be related by the transformation

$$T(z', t') = T_i + \left(\frac{-\Delta H}{\rho C_p}\right)[C_B(z, t) - C_B(\alpha_i', t)] \qquad i = 1, 2, 3 \qquad (4.3.55)$$

because of the adiabatic operation.

Now we define the new variables

$$x_1(z, t) = \frac{C_B}{C_T} \qquad x_2(z, t) = \psi(z, t) \qquad u_1 = \frac{RT_1}{E_1} \qquad u_2 = \frac{RT_2}{E_1}$$

$$u_3 = \frac{RT_3}{E_1} \qquad p = \frac{E_1}{E_0} \qquad p_1 = \frac{E_2}{E_1} \tag{4.3.56}$$

$$\tau_k = \frac{RT}{E_1} \qquad \beta_i = \frac{A_{i0}LC_T}{u} \qquad i = 1, 2 \qquad \rho = A_0 t_f \qquad z = \frac{z'}{L} \qquad t = \frac{t'}{t_f}$$

$$\alpha_i = \frac{\alpha_i'}{L} \qquad x_{1f} = \frac{C_{Bf}}{C_T} \qquad J = \frac{(-\Delta H)RC_T}{\rho C_p E_1} \qquad u_{k*} = \frac{RT_*}{E_1} \qquad u_k^* = \frac{RT^*}{E_1}$$

so that the modeling equations become

$$0 = -\frac{\partial x_1(z, t)}{\partial z} + x_2(z, t)\left[\beta_1 e^{-1/\tau_k}(1 - x_1) - \beta_2 e^{-p_1/\tau_k} x_1\right] \qquad \begin{array}{l} 0 \le t \le 1 \\ 0 \le z \le 1 \end{array} \tag{4.3.57}$$

or

$$0 = -\frac{\partial x_1(z, t)}{\partial z} + \hat{f}(x_1, x_2, u_k)$$

which describes the reactor conversion. The catalyst activity can be determined from

$$\frac{\partial x_2(z, t)}{\partial t} = -\rho (x_2)^2 e^{-(p\tau_k)^{-1}} = \hat{g}(x_1, x_2, u_k) \qquad \begin{array}{l} 0 \le t \le 1 \\ 0 \le z \le 1 \end{array} \tag{4.3.58}$$

where

$$x_1(0, t) = x_{1f} \qquad x_2(z, 0) = 1.0 \tag{4.3.59}$$

and Eq. (4.3.55) becomes

$$\tau_k(z, t) = u_k(t) + J[x_1(z, t) - x_1(\alpha_k, t)] \qquad k = 1, 2, 3 \tag{4.3.60}$$

The objective functional, which is the cumulative conversion of A over a catalyst lifetime, now becomes

$$I = \int_0^1 x_1(1, t)\, dt \tag{4.3.61}$$

The Hamiltonians of interest, H and H_3, become

$$H = \lambda_1(z, t)\left[-\frac{\partial x_1(z, t)}{\partial z} + \hat{f}(x_1, x_2, u_k)\right] + \lambda_2(z, t)\hat{g}(x_1, x_2, u_k) \tag{4.3.62}$$

$$H_3 = x_1(1, t) \tag{4.3.63}$$

where the adjoint variables are given [see Eq. (4.3.16)] by

$$0 = -\left[\frac{\partial \lambda_1(z, t)}{\partial z} + \lambda_1 \frac{\partial \hat{f}}{\partial x_1} + \lambda_2 \frac{\partial \hat{g}}{\partial x_1}\right] \tag{4.3.64}$$

$$\frac{\partial \lambda_2(z, t)}{\partial t} = -\lambda_1 \frac{\partial \hat{f}}{\partial x_2} - \lambda_2 \frac{\partial \hat{g}}{\partial x_2} \tag{4.3.65}$$

with boundary conditions [see Eqs. (4.3.27) and (4.3.28)]

$$\lambda_1(1, t) = 1 \tag{4.3.66}$$

$$\lambda_2(z, 1) = 0 \tag{4.3.67}$$

The computational procedure then is as follows:

1. Guess $u_k(t)$, $0 \le t \le 1$, $k = 1, 2, 3$.
2. Solve the state Eqs. (4.3.57) and (4.3.58) forward in z, t using the method of characteristics (or finite differences); compute I.
3. Solve the adjoint Eqs. (4.3.64) and (4.3.65) backward in z, t.
4. Correct the controls $u_k(t)$ by

$$\underset{\text{new}}{u_k(t)} = \underset{\text{old}}{u_k(t)} + \varepsilon_0 \int_{\alpha_k}^{\alpha_{k+1}} \left(\frac{\partial H}{\partial u_k} \right) dz \tag{4.3.68}$$

   where $k = 1, 2, 3$, $\alpha_1 = 0$, $\alpha_2 = \frac{1}{3}$, $\alpha_3 = \frac{2}{3}$, $\alpha_4 = 1$, and ε_0 is determined by a one-dimensional search.
5. Return to step 2 and iterate.

It is important to note that because there are three beds, control u_1 only applies over $0 \le z < \frac{1}{3}$, u_2 over $\frac{1}{3} \le z < \frac{2}{3}$, and u_3 over $\frac{2}{3} \le z < 1$. This explains the limits on the integral in Eq. (4.3.68). This computational algorithm was applied for the set of parameters $\beta_1 = 5.244 \times 10^5$, $\beta_2 = 2.28 \times 10^9$, $\rho = 1300$, $u_{k*} = 0.070$, $u_k^* = 0.080$, $p = 1.648$, $p_1 = 1.666$, $J = 0.005$, $x_{if} = 0$, and the result after five iterations is shown in Fig. 4.16. The

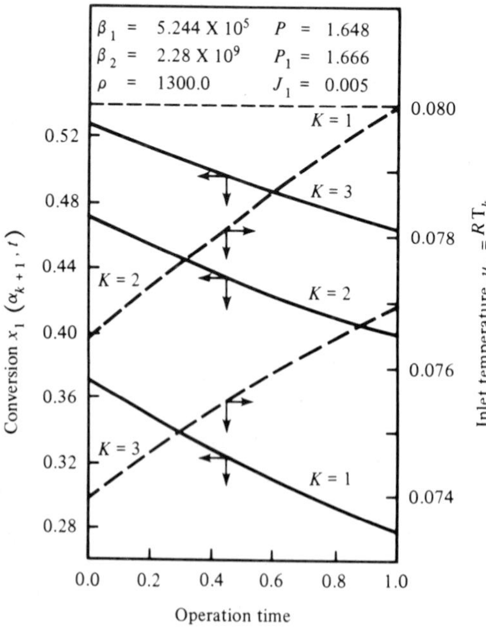

Figure 4.16 Optimal inlet temperature progression for Example 4.3.2, an oxidation reaction.

convergence of the algorithm was checked by successfully producing the same optimal temperature control strategy from two starting points. The inlet temperature is seen to be at the upper bound always for the first bed, and it rises to compensate for catalyst decay in the other beds. The low conversion (~ 50 percent) of A is due to the fact that the reaction is equilibrium limiting, which even the falling temperature from bed to bed cannot overcome. The optimal temperature controls shown in Fig. 4.16 produce about a 10 percent improvement in the objective over a constant inlet temperature policy of $u_k = 0.080$, $k = 1, 2, 3$.

The fact that this optimal control was found from two starting points in about 5 minutes of computing time (IBM 360/75) illustrates the practicality of this control vector iteration procedure for complex problems. More detailed descriptions of this approach may be found in Refs. [32, 33].

Another computational approach which has definite advantages for distributed parameter systems is the *control vector parameterization method.* This technique has essentially the same form for distributed parameter as for lumped parameter problems, discussed in Chap. 3. To apply the method, one represents the controls in terms of trial functions

$$u_i(z, t) = \sum_{j=1}^{s_1} a_{ij}\phi_{ij}(z, t) \tag{4.3.69}$$

$$v_j(t) = \sum_{k=1}^{s_2} b_{jk}\eta_{jk}(t) \tag{4.3.70}$$

$$y_j(t) = \sum_{k=1}^{s_3} c_{jk}\xi_{jk}(t) \tag{4.3.71}$$

$$w_i(z) = \sum_{k=1}^{s_4} e_{ik}\nu_{ik}(z) \tag{4.3.72}$$

and then parameter optimization techniques are used to determine the optimal values for the coefficients a_{ij}, b_{jk}, c_{jk}, e_{ik}. We note that parameterization in terms of state variables may be done as well in order to develop a feedback control law. The computational experience available [5] indicates that these methods are reasonably efficient.

A number of other computational techniques have been suggested for the solution of distributed parameter optimal control problems. Sage [30] gives several examples in which the partial differential equations have been discretized in the spatial direction and the resulting set of ordinary differential equations then treated in the standard way. Zahradnik and Lynn [34] and Bosarge [35] suggest the use of approximate methods in which all the variables $\mathbf{x}(z, t)$, $\boldsymbol{\lambda}(z, t)$, $\mathbf{u}$, $\mathbf{v}$, $\mathbf{y}$, $\mathbf{w}$ are expanded in trial functions and then the method of weighted residuals is used to evaluate the coefficients; however, there has been little computational experience to date on nonlinear problems.

In principle a direct substitution approach similar to that discussed in Chap. 3 could be used for these problems. However, the uncoupling problem of explicitly representing the optimal control in terms of the state and adjoint variables can rarely be done in practice; thus direct-substitution methods usually cannot be applied.

There have been a large number of applications of these computational procedures to practical problems. The reader is directed to Refs. [1, 2, 36–40] for general surveys.

Optimal Feedback Control of Linear Distributed Parameter Systems—The Linear-Quadratic Problem

Just as the linear-quadratic problem led to an optimal feedback control law for lumped parameter systems in Chap. 3, there are similar results for distributed parameter systems. To illustrate this *general result* [2, 3], we shall explicitly consider an example of parabolic second-order partial differential equations.*

Let us consider the linear state equations

$$\frac{\partial \mathbf{x}}{\partial t} = \mathbf{A}_2 \frac{\partial^2 \mathbf{x}}{\partial z^2} + \mathbf{A}_1 \frac{\partial \mathbf{x}}{\partial z} + \mathbf{A}_0 \mathbf{x} + \mathbf{B}\mathbf{u}(z, t) \tag{4.3.73}$$

with boundary conditions

$$\frac{\partial \mathbf{x}}{\partial z} + \mathbf{D}_0 \mathbf{x} = \mathbf{B}_0 \mathbf{u}_0(t) \qquad z = 0 \tag{4.3.74}$$

$$\frac{\partial \mathbf{x}}{\partial z} + \mathbf{D}_1 \mathbf{x} = \mathbf{B}_1 \mathbf{u}_1(t) \qquad z = 1 \tag{4.3.75}$$

Now the quadratic objective functional has the form

$$\begin{aligned} I = {} & \tfrac{1}{2}\int_0^1\int_0^1 \mathbf{x}(r, t_f)^T \mathbf{S}_f(r, s)\mathbf{x}(s, t_f)\, dr\, ds \\ & + \tfrac{1}{2}\int_0^{t_f}\int_0^1\int_0^1 \left[\mathbf{x}(r, t)^T \mathbf{F}(r, s, t)\mathbf{x}(s, t) + \mathbf{u}(r, t)^T \mathbf{E}(r, s, t)\mathbf{u}(s, t)\right] dr\, ds\, dt \\ & + \tfrac{1}{2}\int_0^{t_f}\left[\mathbf{u}_0^T(t)\mathbf{E}_0(t)\mathbf{u}_0(t) + \mathbf{u}_1^T(t)\mathbf{E}_1(t)\mathbf{u}_1(t)\right] dt \end{aligned} \tag{4.3.76}$$

Now let us apply the maximum principle of the previous section to this problem. Let

$$\begin{aligned} H(r, t) = {} & \tfrac{1}{2}\int_0^1 (\mathbf{x}^T\mathbf{F}\mathbf{x} + \mathbf{u}^T\mathbf{E}\mathbf{u})\, ds + \boldsymbol{\lambda}^T(r, t)\left[\mathbf{A}_2\ddot{\mathbf{x}}(r, t)\right. \\ & \left. + \mathbf{A}_1\dot{\mathbf{x}}(r, t) + \mathbf{A}_0\mathbf{x}(r, t) + \mathbf{B}\mathbf{u}(r, t)\right] \end{aligned} \tag{4.3.77}$$

$$H_2(t) = \tfrac{1}{2}\mathbf{u}_0^T\mathbf{E}_0\mathbf{u}_0 - \boldsymbol{\lambda}^T(0, t)\mathbf{A}_2\left[-\mathbf{D}_0\mathbf{x}(0, t) + \mathbf{B}_0\mathbf{u}_0(t)\right] \tag{4.3.78}$$

$$H_3(t) = \tfrac{1}{2}\mathbf{u}_1^T\mathbf{E}_1\mathbf{u}_1 + \boldsymbol{\lambda}^T(1, t)\mathbf{A}_2\left[-\mathbf{D}_1\mathbf{x}(1, t) + \mathbf{B}_1\mathbf{u}_1(t)\right] \tag{4.3.79}$$

$$H_1(r) = \tfrac{1}{2}\int_0^1 \mathbf{x}(r, t_f)^T \mathbf{S}_f(r, s)\mathbf{x}(s, t_f)\, ds \tag{4.3.80}$$

* As we shall show, these results also apply to hyperbolic first-order PDE systems.

Then the necessary conditions for optimality become

$$\frac{\partial H(r, t)}{\partial \mathbf{u}(r, t)} = \int_0^1 \mathbf{Eu}(s, t)\, ds + \mathbf{B}^T \boldsymbol{\lambda}(r, t) = \mathbf{0} \tag{4.3.81}$$

$$\frac{\partial H_2}{\partial \mathbf{u}_0} = \mathbf{E}_0 \mathbf{u}_0 - \mathbf{B}_0^T \mathbf{A}_2^T \boldsymbol{\lambda}(0, t) = \mathbf{0} \tag{4.3.82}$$

$$\frac{\partial H_3}{\partial \mathbf{u}_1} = \mathbf{E}_1 \mathbf{u}_1 + \mathbf{B}_1^T \mathbf{A}_2^T \boldsymbol{\lambda}(1, t) = \mathbf{0} \tag{4.3.83}$$

If **u** depends only on time, then the necessary conditions for optimality become

$$\int_0^1 \frac{\partial H(r, t)}{\partial \mathbf{u}(t)}\, dr = \int_0^1 \left[\int_0^1 \mathbf{E}(r, s, t)\mathbf{u}(t)\, ds + \mathbf{B}^T \boldsymbol{\lambda}(r, t) \right] dr = \mathbf{0} \tag{4.3.84}$$

For $\mathbf{u}(r, t)$, inverting Eq. (4.3.81) leads to

$$\mathbf{u}(r, t) = -\int_0^1 \mathbf{E}^*(r, s, t)\mathbf{B}^T \boldsymbol{\lambda}(s, t)\, ds \tag{4.3.85}$$

where $\mathbf{E}^*(r, s, t)$ is the inverse of $\mathbf{E}(r, s, t)$, defined by

$$\int_0^1 \mathbf{E}^*(r, s, t)\mathbf{E}(s, \rho, t)\, ds = \delta(r - \rho)\mathbf{I} \tag{4.3.86}$$

For $\mathbf{u}(t)$, Eq. (4.3.84) leads to

$$\mathbf{u}(t) = -\left[\int_0^1 \int_0^1 \mathbf{E}(r, s, t)\, ds\, dr \right]^{-1} \int_0^1 \mathbf{B}^T \boldsymbol{\lambda}(r, t)\, dr \tag{4.3.87}$$

Similarly,

$$\mathbf{u}_0(t) = \mathbf{E}_0^{-1} \mathbf{B}_0^T \mathbf{A}_2^T \boldsymbol{\lambda}(0, t) \tag{4.3.88}$$

$$\mathbf{u}_1(t) = -\mathbf{E}_1^{-1} \mathbf{B}_1^T \mathbf{A}_2^T \boldsymbol{\lambda}(1, t) \tag{4.3.89}$$

Now the adjoint variable $\boldsymbol{\lambda}(r, t)$ is given by

$$\frac{d\boldsymbol{\lambda}(r, t)}{dt} = -\int_0^1 \mathbf{F}(r, s, t)\mathbf{x}(s, t)\, ds - \mathbf{A}_0^T \boldsymbol{\lambda} + \mathbf{A}_1^T \frac{\partial \boldsymbol{\lambda}}{\partial z} - \mathbf{A}_2^T \frac{\partial^2 \boldsymbol{\lambda}}{\partial z^2} \tag{4.3.90}$$

with boundary conditions

$$\boldsymbol{\lambda}(t_f, r) = \int_0^1 \mathbf{S}_f(r, s)\mathbf{x}(s, t_f)\, ds$$

$$\mathbf{D}_0^T \mathbf{A}_2^T \boldsymbol{\lambda}(0, t) - \mathbf{A}_1^T \boldsymbol{\lambda}(0, t) + \mathbf{A}_2^T \frac{\partial \boldsymbol{\lambda}(0, t)}{\partial z} = 0 \tag{4.3.91}$$

$$-\mathbf{D}_1^T \mathbf{A}_2^T \boldsymbol{\lambda}(1, t) + \mathbf{A}_1^T \boldsymbol{\lambda}(1, t) - \mathbf{A}_2^T \frac{\partial \boldsymbol{\lambda}(1, t)}{\partial z} = 0$$

Now if we *define* a variable $\mathbf{S}(r, s, t)$ by the Riccati transformation

$$\boldsymbol{\lambda}(r, t) = \int_0^1 \mathbf{S}(r, s, t)\mathbf{x}(s, t)\, ds \tag{4.3.92}$$

we can substitute Eq. (4.3.92) into Eq. (4.3.90) to yield

$$\int_0^1 \left[\dot{\mathbf{S}}\mathbf{x}(s,t) + \mathbf{S}\dot{\mathbf{x}}(s,t) \right] ds = \text{LHS} \tag{4.3.93}$$

$$\text{RHS} = \int_0^1 \{ [-\mathbf{F}(r,s,t)\mathbf{x}(s,t) - \mathbf{A}_0^T \mathbf{S}\mathbf{x}(s,t) + \mathbf{A}_1^T \mathbf{S}_r \mathbf{x}(s,t) - \mathbf{A}_2^T \mathbf{S}_{rr} \mathbf{x}(s,t)] \} \, ds \tag{4.3.94}$$

$$\text{LHS} = \int_0^1 \left\{ \dot{\mathbf{S}}\mathbf{x} + \mathbf{S}\left[\mathbf{A}_2 \frac{\partial^2 \mathbf{x}}{\partial s^2} + \mathbf{A}_1 \frac{\partial \mathbf{x}}{\partial s} + \mathbf{A}_0 \mathbf{x} + \mathbf{B}\mathbf{u}(s,t) \right] \right\} ds \tag{4.3.95}$$

Now

$$\begin{aligned} \int_0^1 \mathbf{S}(r,s,t)\mathbf{A}_2 \frac{\partial x^2}{\partial s^2} \, ds &= \mathbf{S}(r,s,t)\mathbf{A}_2 \frac{\partial \mathbf{x}}{\partial s}\bigg]_0^1 - \int_0^1 \mathbf{S}_s \mathbf{A}_2 \frac{\partial \mathbf{x}}{\partial s} \, ds \\ &= \mathbf{S}(r,1,t)\mathbf{A}_2[\mathbf{B}_1\mathbf{u}_1 - \mathbf{D}_1 x(1,t)] \\ &\quad - \mathbf{S}(r,0,t)\mathbf{A}_2[\mathbf{B}_0\mathbf{u}_0 \\ &\quad - \mathbf{D}_0\mathbf{x}(0,t)] - \mathbf{S}_s A_2 \mathbf{x}]_0^1 + \int_0^1 \mathbf{S}_{ss}\mathbf{A}_2\mathbf{x}(s,t) \, ds \end{aligned} \tag{4.3.96}$$

Similarly

$$\int_0^1 \mathbf{S}\mathbf{A}_1 \frac{\partial \mathbf{x}}{\partial s} \, ds = \mathbf{S}\mathbf{A}_1\mathbf{x}]_0^1 - \int_0^1 \mathbf{S}_s \mathbf{A}_1 \mathbf{x}(s,t) \, ds \tag{4.3.97}$$

Thus

$$\begin{aligned} \text{LHS} = \int_0^1 & [(\dot{\mathbf{S}} + \mathbf{S}_{ss}\mathbf{A}_2 - \mathbf{S}_s\mathbf{A}_1 + \mathbf{S}\mathbf{A}_0)\mathbf{x}(s,t) + \mathbf{S}\mathbf{B}\mathbf{u}(s,t)] \, ds \\ & - [\mathbf{S}(r,1,t)\mathbf{A}_2\mathbf{D}_1 - \mathbf{S}(r,1,t)\mathbf{A}_1 + \mathbf{S}_s(r,1,t)\mathbf{A}_2]\mathbf{x}(1,t) \\ & + [\mathbf{S}(r,0,t)\mathbf{A}_2\mathbf{D}_0 - \mathbf{S}(r,0,t)\mathbf{A}_1 + \mathbf{S}_s(r,0,t)\mathbf{A}_2]\mathbf{x}(0,t) \\ & + \mathbf{S}(r,1,t)\mathbf{A}_2\mathbf{B}_1\mathbf{u}_1 - \mathbf{S}(r,0,t)\mathbf{A}_2\mathbf{B}_0\mathbf{u}_0 \end{aligned} \tag{4.3.98}$$

Now

$$\begin{aligned} \int_0^1 \mathbf{S}\mathbf{B}\mathbf{u}(s,t) \, ds &= -\int_0^1 \int_0^1 \mathbf{S}(r,s,t)\mathbf{B}\mathbf{E}^*(s,\rho,t)\mathbf{B}^T \boldsymbol{\lambda}(\rho,t) \, ds \, d\rho \\ &= -\int_0^1 \int_0^1 \int_0^1 \mathbf{S}(r,s,t)\mathbf{B}\mathbf{E}^*(s,\rho,t)\mathbf{B}^T \mathbf{S}(\rho,z,t)\mathbf{x}(z,t) \, dz \, ds \, d\rho \\ &= -\int_0^1 \left[\int_0^1 \int_0^1 \mathbf{S}(r,z,t)\mathbf{B}\mathbf{E}^*(z,\rho,t)\mathbf{B}^T \mathbf{S}(\rho,s,t) \, dz \, d\rho \right] \mathbf{x}(s,t) \, ds \end{aligned} \tag{4.3.99}$$

$$\mathbf{S}(r,1,t)\mathbf{A}_2\mathbf{B}_1\mathbf{u}_1 = -\int_0^1 \mathbf{S}(r,1,t)\mathbf{A}_2\mathbf{B}_1\mathbf{E}_1^{-1}\mathbf{B}_1^T\mathbf{A}_2^T\mathbf{S}(1,s,t)\mathbf{x}(s,t) \, ds \tag{4.3.100}$$

$$\mathbf{S}(r,0,t)\mathbf{A}_2\mathbf{B}_0\mathbf{u}_0 = \int_0^1 \mathbf{S}(r,0,t)\mathbf{A}_2\mathbf{B}_0\mathbf{E}_0^{-1}\mathbf{B}_0^T\mathbf{A}_2^T\mathbf{S}(0,s,t)\mathbf{x}(s,t) \, ds \tag{4.3.101}$$

Now combining RHS and LHS and collecting coefficients of $\mathbf{x}(s, t)$, one obtains the Riccati equation:

$$\begin{aligned}\mathbf{S}_t(r, s, t) = & -\mathbf{S}_{ss}\mathbf{A}_2 - \mathbf{A}_2^T\mathbf{S}_{rr} + \mathbf{S}_s\mathbf{A}_1 + \mathbf{A}_1^T\mathbf{S}_r \\ & -\mathbf{S}\mathbf{A}_0 - \mathbf{A}_0^T\mathbf{S} + \int_0^1\int_0^1 \mathbf{S}(r, z, t)\mathbf{B}\mathbf{E}^*(z, \rho, t)\mathbf{B}^T\mathbf{S}(\rho, s, t)\, dz\, d\rho \\ & +\mathbf{S}(r, 1, t)\mathbf{A}_2\mathbf{B}_1\mathbf{E}_1^{-1}\mathbf{B}_1^T\mathbf{A}_2^T\mathbf{S}(1, s, t) \\ & +\mathbf{S}(r, 0, t)\mathbf{A}_2\mathbf{B}_0\mathbf{E}_0^{-1}\mathbf{B}_0^T\mathbf{A}_2^T\mathbf{S}(0, s, t) - \mathbf{F}(r, s, t) \end{aligned} \tag{4.3.102}$$

With the coefficients of $\mathbf{x}(1, t)$, $\mathbf{x}(0, t)$ in Eq. (4.3.98) yielding the boundary conditions

$$\mathbf{S}_s(r, 1, t)\mathbf{A}_2 + \mathbf{S}(r, 1, t)(\mathbf{A}_2\mathbf{D}_1 - \mathbf{A}_1) = \mathbf{0} \tag{4.3.103}$$

$$\mathbf{S}_s(r, 0, t)\mathbf{A}_2 + \mathbf{S}(r, 0, t)(\mathbf{A}_2\mathbf{D}_0 - \mathbf{A}_1) = \mathbf{0} \tag{4.3.104}$$

and the terminal condition [see Eqs. (4.3.91) and (4.3.92)]

$$\mathbf{S}(r, s, t_f) = \mathbf{S}_f(r, s) \tag{4.3.105}$$

one can show that the symmetry conditions

$$\mathbf{S}(r, s, t) = \mathbf{S}(s, r, t)^T \tag{4.3.106}$$

must hold. Thus we now have the feedback control law for $\mathbf{u}(z, t)$ as

$$\mathbf{u}(z, t) = -\int_0^1\int_0^1 \mathbf{E}^*(z, s, t)\mathbf{B}^T\mathbf{S}(s, \rho, t)\mathbf{x}(\rho, t)\, ds\, d\rho \tag{4.3.107}$$

and for $\mathbf{u}(t)$ from

$$\mathbf{u}(t) = -\left[\int_0^1\int_0^1 \mathbf{E}(r, s, t)\, ds\, dr\right]^{-1}\int_0^1\int_0^1 \mathbf{B}^T\mathbf{S}(s, \rho, t)\mathbf{x}(\rho, t)\, ds\, d\rho \tag{4.3.108}$$

The boundary controls take the form

$$\mathbf{u}_0(t) = \mathbf{E}_0^{-1}\mathbf{B}_0^T\mathbf{A}_2^T\int_0^1 \mathbf{S}(0, s, t)\mathbf{x}(s, t)\, ds \tag{4.3.109}$$

$$\mathbf{u}_1(t) = -\mathbf{E}_1^{-1}\mathbf{B}_1^T\mathbf{A}_2^T\int_0^1 \mathbf{S}(1, s, t)\mathbf{x}(s, t)\, ds \tag{4.3.110}$$

where $\mathbf{S}(s, \rho, t)$ can be precomputed off-line from Eqs. (4.3.102) to (4.3.106).

Thus the linear quadratic problem leads to an optimal feedback control law even in the case of PDE systems.

Let us now illustrate the specific form of the optimal control law with more detailed examples.

Example 4.3.3 Let us consider the control of the temperature distribution in a long, thin rod being heated in a multizone furnace. This is similar to the example problem discussed in the last section. The modeling equations are

$$\rho C_p \frac{\partial T(z', t')}{\partial t'} = k\frac{\partial^2 T}{\partial z'^2} + q(z', t') \qquad T(z', 0) = T_0 \tag{4.3.111}$$

where $q(z', t')$ represents the heat flux from the different zones of the furnace and the boundary conditions

$$z' = 0 \qquad z' = l \qquad \frac{\partial T}{\partial z'} = 0$$

arise when we assume negligible heat loss at the ends of the rod. Defining dimensionless variables

$$t = \frac{t'k}{\rho C_p} \qquad z = \frac{z'}{l} \qquad u'(z, t) = \frac{q(z', t')l^2}{kT_0} \qquad x'(z, t) = \frac{T(z', t')}{T_0}$$

where T_0 is the initial uniform temperature in the rod, one obtains

$$\frac{\partial x'(z, t)}{\partial t} = \frac{\partial^2 x'(z, t)}{\partial z^2} + u'(z, t) \tag{4.3.112}$$

$$z = 0 \qquad \frac{\partial x'}{\partial z} = 0 \tag{4.3.113}$$

$$z = 1 \qquad \frac{\partial x'}{\partial z} = 0 \tag{4.3.114}$$

$$t = 0 \qquad x' = 1 \tag{4.3.115}$$

If we define the objective functional (to be minimized) as

$$I = \tfrac{1}{2}\int_0^1 \left[x'(z, t_f) - x'_d(z)\right]^2 S_f \, dz + \tfrac{1}{2}\int_0^{t_f}\int_0^1 \left\{F\left[x'(z, t) - x'_d(z)\right]^2 + E\left[u'(z, t) - u'_d(z)\right]^2\right\} dt\, dz \tag{4.3.116}$$

where $x'_d(z)$ is the desired final temperature profile and $u'_d(z)$ is the final steady-state control profile required to hold $x'_d(z)$, i.e.,

$$u'_d(z) \equiv -\frac{\partial^2 x'_d(z)}{\partial z^2} \tag{4.3.117}$$

and defining $x = x' - x'_d$, $u = u' - u'_d$, then Eqs. (4.3.112) to (4.3.116) become

$$\frac{\partial x(z, t)}{\partial t} = \frac{\partial^2 x(z, t)}{\partial z^2} + u(z, t) \tag{4.3.118}$$

$$z = 0 \qquad \frac{\partial x}{\partial z} = 0 \tag{4.3.119}$$

$$z = 1 \qquad \frac{\partial x}{\partial z} = 0 \tag{4.3.120}$$

$$x(z, 0) = 1 - x'_d(z) \tag{4.3.121}$$

$$I = \tfrac{1}{2} S_f \int_0^1 x^2(z, t_f)\, dz + \tfrac{1}{2}\int_0^{t_f}\int_0^1 \left[Fx^2(z, t) + Eu^2(z, t)\right] dt\, dz \tag{4.3.122}$$

This is the same form as the linear-quadratic problem posed above, where

$$\begin{aligned} S_f(r, s) &= S_f\, \delta(r - s) \\ F(r, s, t) &= F\, \delta(r - s) \\ E(r, s, t) &= E\, \delta(r - s) \Rightarrow E^*(r, s, t) = E^{-1}\, \delta(r - s) \qquad (4.3.123) \\ A_2 = 1 \qquad A_1 &= 0 \qquad A_0 = 0 \qquad B = 1 \\ D_0 = B_0 &= D_1 = B_1 = 0 \end{aligned}$$

Thus the optimal feedback control law for this problem is

$$u(z, t) = -\int_0^1 E^{-1} S(z, \rho, t) x(\rho, t)\, d\rho \qquad (4.3.124)$$

where $S(r, s, t)$ is given by

$$S_t(r, s, t) = -S_{ss} - S_{rr} + \int_0^1 S(r, \rho, t) E^{-1} S(\rho, s, t)\, d\rho - F\, \delta(r - s) \qquad (4.3.125)$$

with boundary conditions

$$S_s(r, 1, t) = S_s(r, 0, t) = S_r(1, s, t) = S_r(0, s, t) = 0 \qquad (4.3.126)$$

and

$$S(r, s, t_f) = S_f\, \delta(r - s) \qquad (4.3.127)$$

Thus one can precompute $S(r, s, t)$ from Eqs. (4.3.125) to (4.3.127) and use it in the optimal feedback law, Eq. (4.3.124).

Example 4.3.4 Let us now consider the feedback control of the steam-jacketed tubular heat exchanger shown in Fig. 4.5 and discussed in Example 4.2.1. Thermocouples measure the tube fluid temperature at four points, $T(0.25, t)$, $T(0.5, t)$, $T(0.75, t)$, and $T(1, t)$, and adjust the steam-jacket temperature $T_w(t)$ (through a steam inlet valve) in order to control the exchanger.

Recall that the mathematical model for the process takes the form

$$\frac{\partial T}{\partial t} + v\frac{\partial T}{\partial z} = \frac{hA}{\rho C_p}(T - T_w) \qquad T(0, t) = T_f \qquad (4.3.128)$$

Now if we define the deviation variables

$$x = T - T_d(z) \qquad u = T_w - T_{wd} \qquad a_0 = \frac{hA}{\rho C_p}$$

where $T_d(z)$ is the desired temperature profile and T_{wd} is the steady-state steam jacket temperature required to keep $T = T_d(z)$; i.e., T_{wd} satisfies

$$v\frac{\partial T_d}{\partial z} = \frac{hA}{\rho C_p}(T_d - T_{wd}) \qquad T_d(0) = T_f \qquad (4.3.129)$$

then the linear quadratic problem takes the form

$$\min_{u(t)}\left(I = \tfrac{1}{2}\int_0^1 x(z, t_f)^2 S_f\, dz + \tfrac{1}{2}\int_0^{t_f}\left\{\int_0^1 \left[x(z, t)^2 F\right] dz + Eu(t)^2\right\} dt\right) \tag{4.3.130}$$

where

$$\frac{\partial x}{\partial t} = -v\frac{\partial x}{\partial z} + a_0 x - a_0 u \qquad x(0, t) = 0 \tag{4.3.131}$$

Again, this is in the linear-quadratic form of Eqs. (4.3.73) to (4.3.76) where

$$\begin{aligned} S_f(r, s) &= S_f\, \delta(r - s) \\ F(r, s, t) &= F\, \delta(r - s) \\ E(r, s, t) &= E \Rightarrow E^*(r, s, t) = E^{-1} \\ A_2 = 0 \qquad & A_1 = -v \qquad A_0 = -a_0 \qquad B = +a_0 \\ D_0 \to \infty \qquad & B_0 = 0 \end{aligned} \tag{4.3.132}$$

Thus the optimal feedback control law is

$$u(t) = -E^{-1}a_0 \int_0^1\int_0^1 S(s, \rho, t)x(\rho, t)\, ds\, d\rho \tag{4.3.133}$$

where $S(r, s, t)$ is given by

$$S_t(r, s, t) = -S_s v - S_r v + 2Sa_0 + a_0^2 E^{-1}\left[\int_0^1 S(r, z, t)\, dz\right] \times\left[\int_0^1 S(\rho, s, t)\, d\rho\right] - F\, \delta(r - s) \tag{4.3.134}$$

with boundary conditions

$$S(r, 0, t) = S(0, s, t) = 0 \tag{4.3.135}$$

$$S(r, s, t_f) = S_f\, \delta(r - s) \tag{4.3.136}$$

Thus the optimal feedback control can be implemented if $x(z, t)$ can be estimated from the four measurements $x(0.25, t)$, $x(0.5, t)$, $x(0.75, t)$, and $x(1.0, t)$. More shall be said about this estimation problem in Chap. 5.

A fuller discussion of the linear-quadratic problem applied to first-order partial differential equations such as these may be found in [41, 42].

Example 4.3.5 Let us now consider the optimal feedback control of the heated rod problem of Example 4.2.4 with discrete spatial actuators. Recall that the model equations take the form

$$\frac{\partial x(z, t)}{\partial t} = \frac{\partial^2 x(z, t)}{\partial z^2} + \sum_{k=1}^{M} g_k(z)u_k(t) \tag{4.3.137}$$

$$\frac{\partial x}{\partial z} = 0 \qquad z = 0, 1 \tag{4.3.138}$$

and the linear-quadratic control problem (Example 4.3.3) is to minimize*

$$I = \tfrac{1}{2}\int_0^1 S_f x^2(z, t_f)\, dz + \tfrac{1}{2}\int_0^{t_f}\int_0^1 \left[Fx^2(z, t) + \sum_{k=1}^{M} E_k g_k(z)(u_k(t))^2 \right] dz\, dt \tag{4.3.139}$$

Thus by choosing

$$\mathbf{E}(r, s, t) = \begin{bmatrix} \int_0^1 E_1 g_1\, dz & & & \mathbf{0} \\ & \int_0^1 E_2 g_2\, dz & & \\ & & \ddots & \\ \mathbf{0} & & & \int_0^1 E_M g_M\, dz \end{bmatrix} = \hat{\mathbf{E}} \tag{4.3.140}$$

and applying the general results of Eq. (4.3.86), one obtains

$$\mathbf{E}^*(r, s, t) = \begin{bmatrix} \left(\int_0^1 E_1 g_1\, dz\right)^{-1} & & & \mathbf{0} \\ & \left(\int_0^1 E_2 g_2\, dz\right)^{-1} & & \\ & & \ddots & \\ \mathbf{0} & & & \left(\int_0^1 E_M g_M\, dz\right)^{-1} \end{bmatrix} = \hat{\mathbf{E}}^{-1} \tag{4.3.141}$$

and the feedback control law

$$\mathbf{u}(t) = \hat{\mathbf{E}}^{-1}\int_0^1\int_0^1 \mathbf{g}(s) S(s, \rho, t) x(\rho, t)\, ds\, d\rho \tag{4.3.142}$$

where

$$\mathbf{u}(t) \equiv \begin{bmatrix} u_1(t) \\ \vdots \\ u_M(t) \end{bmatrix} \qquad \mathbf{g} = \begin{bmatrix} g_1(z) \\ \vdots \\ g_M(z) \end{bmatrix} \tag{4.3.143}$$

The Riccati equation then becomes

$$S_t(r, s, t) = -S_{ss} - S_{rr} + \left[\int_0^1 S(r, z, t)\mathbf{g}^T(z)\, dz\right]\hat{\mathbf{E}}^{-1}\left[\int_0^1 S(\rho, s, t)\mathbf{g}(\rho)\, d\rho\right] - F\,\delta(r - s) \tag{4.3.144}$$

with boundary conditions given by Eqs. (4.3.126) and (4.3.127).

* Notice that we use only the first power of $g_k(x)$ in the objective. This is done to avoid mathematical complexities when delta functions such as in Eq. (4.2.152) are used.

To illustrate, the form of the control for discrete pointwise controllers, Eq. (4.2.152), is

$$u_k(t) = E_k^{-1} \int_0^1 S(z_k^*, \rho, t) x(\rho, t)\, d\rho \qquad k = 1, 2, \ldots, M \quad (4.3.145)$$

where $S(r, s, t)$ is the solution of

$$S_t(r, s, t) = -S_{ss} - S_{rr} + \sum_{k=1}^{M} S(r, z_k^*, t) E_k^{-1} S(z_k^*, s, t) - F\,\delta(r - s) \quad (4.3.146)$$

In the case of zone heating, Eq. (4.2.153), the control law is

$$u_k(t) = \left[E_k(z_{k+1}^* - z_k^*) \right]^{-1} \int_0^1 \left[\int_{z_k^*}^{z_{k+1}^*} S(s, \rho, t)\, ds \right] x(\rho, t)\, d\rho \quad (4.3.147)$$

where $S(r, s, t)$ arises from

$$S_t(r, s, t) = -S_{ss} - S_{rr} + \sum_{k=1}^{M} \left\{ \int_{z_k^*}^{z_{k+1}^*} S(r, z, t)\, dz \left[E_k(z_{k+1}^* - z_k^*) \right]^{-1} \times \int_{z_k^*}^{z_{k+1}^*} S(\rho, s, t)\, d\rho \right\} - F\,\delta(r - s) \quad (4.3.148)$$

In order to determine the *optimal* location and shape of the actuator signal $g_k(z)$, it is necessary to define a suitable objective functional. For example, the linear quadratic objective, Eq. (4.3.139), could be modified to

$$\min_{u_k(t),\, g_k(z)} \left\{ I = \tfrac{1}{2} \int_0^1 S_f x^2(z, t_f)\, dz + \tfrac{1}{2} \int_0^{t_f} \int_0^1 \left[F x^2(z, t) + \sum_{k=1}^{M} E_k g_k(z) u_k^2(t) \right] dt\, dz \right\} \quad (4.3.149)$$

where one must optimize both with respect to $u_k(t)$ and to the function $g_k(z)$. Note that having *complete* freedom in the choice of $g_k(z)$ is equivalent to choosing the continuous control $u(z, t)$ optimally. Thus Eq. (4.3.149) is most useful when $g_k(z)$ is restricted in form. For a detailed discussion of the optimal shape and location of discrete controllers, see Refs. [25–29].

It is possible to extend the linear-quadratic optimal feedback control problem to *nonlinear* partial differential equation systems by linearizing about some nominal optimal open-loop trajectory, just as was done for lumped parameter systems in Chap. 3. However, this extension is straightforward and shall not be discussed further here.

Some more detailed examples of the application of optimal feedback control are given in Chap. 6.

4.4 FEEDBACK CONTROLLER DESIGN FOR NONLINEAR DISTRIBUTED PARAMETER SYSTEMS

Just as for lumped parameter systems, nonlinear distributed parameter processes are difficult to analyze because most of the powerful tools of linear analysis fail to apply. In addition, many of the exact lumping methods of the last section also are not applicable. Thus one must resort to a host of ad hoc methods for controller design similar to those employed for lumped parameter systems, and some new lumping methods must be used. In this section we shall begin with a brief discussion of some nonlinear controller design methods and then proceed to a more detailed treatment of efficient lumping techniques for distributed parameter systems.

Controller Design Methods

The design methods available for nonlinear distributed parameter systems are essentially of the same type as for lumped parameter systems. They are principally:

1. Linearized linear-quadratic optimal feedback control
2. Feedback controller parameterization
3. Linearization and application of linear design methods (e.g., Sec. 4.2) to the linearized equations
4. Lumping the system to ODEs and application of the lumped parameter design methods of Sec. 3.2

Linearized linear-quadratic feedback control was discussed in Sec. 4.3 and is similar in approach and philosophy to the design procedure for lumped systems.

Feedback controller parameterization is conceptually the same procedure as discussed in Sec. 3.4 for lumped parameter systems. Basically one defines a feedback controller structure, e.g.,

$$\mathbf{u}(z, t) = \int_0^1 \mathbf{F}_B(z, r, t, \boldsymbol{\alpha}, \mathbf{x}(r, t), \mathbf{x}_d(r, t))\, dr \tag{4.4.1}$$

with parameters $\boldsymbol{\alpha}$, and then chooses the controller parameters to minimize some desired objective functional. Some examples of this design procedure may be found in [43, 44].

Linearization of the distributed parameter system about some steady state is possible in some instances. However, there can be some difficulties when the linearization is about a nonhomogeneous steady state because the coefficients become spatially dependent. Example 4.4.1 below illustrates these points.

Lumping of the distributed system and then applying lumped parameter design methods is the most straightforward approach. However, one must be aware of the potential loss of information in the lumping process, as discussed in Sec. 4.2.

Various approaches to this problem are illustrated in what follows.

Example 4.4.1 Let us consider the nonlinear problem of the control of a short, homogeneous chemical reactor in which a zero-order exothermic reaction is taking place. A mathematical model for such a system is the axial dispersion model

$$\rho_f C_{p_f} \frac{\partial T}{\partial t'} = -\rho_f C_{p_f} v \frac{\partial T}{\partial z'} + k \frac{\partial^2 T}{\partial z'^2} + (-\Delta H) k_0 e^{-E/RT} - hA_s (T - T_w) \qquad \begin{matrix} 0 < z' < l \\ t' > 0 \end{matrix} \tag{4.4.2}$$

with boundary conditions

$$z' = 0 \qquad \rho_f C_{p_f} v (T - T_f) = k \frac{\partial T}{\partial z'} \tag{4.4.3}$$

$$z' = l \qquad \frac{\partial T}{\partial z'} = 0 \tag{4.4.4}$$

where $T_f(t)$, $T_w(t)$ may be considered the manipulated variables. Let us now put the model in dimensionless form by defining

$$t = \frac{t'v}{l} \qquad z = \frac{z'}{l} \qquad \text{Pe} = \frac{\rho_f C_{p_f} v_l}{k}$$

$$B = \frac{(-\Delta H) k_0 e^{-E/RT_0}}{\rho_f C_{p_f} T_0} \frac{l}{v} \qquad \gamma = \frac{E}{RT_0} \qquad \beta = \frac{hA_s l}{\rho_f C_{p_f} v}$$

$$x(z, t) = \frac{T - T_0}{T_0} \qquad u = \frac{T_w - T_0}{T_0} \qquad u_0 = \frac{T_f - T_0}{T_0} \tag{4.4.5}$$

where T_0 is a reference temperature. The system then becomes

$$\frac{\partial x(z, t)}{\partial t} = -\frac{\partial x}{\partial z} + \frac{1}{\text{Pe}} \frac{\partial^2 x}{\partial z^2} + B e^{\gamma x/(1+x)} - \beta x + \beta u(t) \tag{4.4.6}$$

$$z = 0 \qquad \frac{\partial x}{\partial z} = \text{Pe}\, x - \text{Pe}\, u_0(t) \tag{4.4.7}$$

$$z = 1 \qquad \frac{\partial x}{\partial z} = 0 \tag{4.4.8}$$

Now we shall indicate how one may linearize this system about some steady state $x_s(z)$, u_s, u_{0s}, satisfying

$$0 = -\frac{\partial x_s}{\partial z} + \frac{1}{\text{Pe}} \frac{\partial^2 x_s}{\partial z^2} + B e^{\gamma x_s/(1+x_s)} - \beta x_s + \beta u_s \tag{4.4.9}$$

$$z = 0 \qquad \frac{\partial x_s}{\partial z} = \text{Pe}\, x_s - \text{Pe}\, u_{0s} \tag{4.4.10}$$

$$z = 1 \qquad \frac{\partial x_s}{\partial z} = 0 \tag{4.4.11}$$

Subtracting Eqs. (4.4.9) to (4.4.11) from (4.4.6) to (4.4.8) and linearizing, one may obtain the linearized equation in $\check{x}(z, t) = x(z, t) - x_s(z)$, $\check{u} = u(t) - u_s$, $\check{u}_0 = u_0(t) - u_{0s}$

$$\frac{\partial \check{x}(z,t)}{\partial t} = -\frac{\partial \check{x}(z,t)}{\partial z} + \frac{1}{\text{Pe}}\frac{\partial^2 \check{x}(z,t)}{\partial z^2} + J(z)\check{x} + \beta\check{u} \qquad (4.4.12)$$

$$z = 0 \qquad \frac{\partial \check{x}}{\partial z} = \text{Pe}\,\check{x} - \text{Pe}\,\check{u}_0 \qquad (4.4.13)$$

$$z = 1 \qquad \frac{\partial \check{x}}{\partial z} = 0 \qquad (4.4.14)$$

where J is the Jacobian of the nonlinear term evaluated at $x_s(z)$

$$J(z) = \frac{B\gamma}{(1 + x_s)^2} e^{\gamma x_s/(1+x_s)} - \beta \qquad (4.4.15)$$

Note that it is this nonlinear term which makes the analysis difficult—due to the fact that J depends on $x_s(z)$ and is thus a function of z. However, let us proceed to show how one, in some instances, may be able to use *modal* decomposition and control on these linearized equations. Let us first make the boundary condition, Eq. (4.4.13), homogeneous by inserting the homogeneous part into the differential equation with a delta function to generate the equivalent system of equations [and let us suppress the ($\check{\ }$) notation]:

$$\frac{\partial x(z,t)}{\partial t} = -\frac{\partial x(z,t)}{\partial z} + \frac{1}{\text{Pe}}\frac{\partial^2 x(z,t)}{\partial z^2} + J(z)x + \beta u + \delta(z)u_0 \qquad (4.4.16)$$

$$z = 0 \qquad \frac{\partial x}{\partial z} = \text{Pe}\,x \qquad (4.4.17)$$

$$z = 1 \qquad \frac{\partial x}{\partial z} = 0 \qquad (4.4.18)$$

This system of equations is now amenable to modal decomposition. Thus let us assume that a solution to Eqs. (4.4.16) to (4.4.18) is in the form

$$x(z, t) = \sum_{n=1}^{\infty} a_n(t)\phi_n(z) \qquad (4.4.19)$$

$$u(t) = \sum_{n=1}^{\infty} b_n(t)\phi_n(z) = u(t)\left[\sum_{n=1}^{\infty} b_n\phi_n(z)\right] \qquad (4.4.20)$$

$$\delta(z)u_0(t) = \sum_{n=1}^{\infty} c_n(t)\phi_n(z) = u_0(t)\left[\sum_{n=1}^{\infty} c_n\phi_n(z)\right] \qquad (4.4.21)$$

which means

$$\sum_{n=1}^{\infty} b_n\phi_n(z) = 1 \qquad \sum_{n=1}^{\infty} c_n\phi_n(z) = \delta(z) \qquad (4.4.22)$$

Applying separation of variables leads to

$$\frac{1}{a_n}\frac{da_n}{dt} = \frac{\beta b_n}{a_n}u(t) - \frac{c_n u_0(t)}{a_n}$$

$$= \frac{1}{\phi_n(z)}\left[-\frac{d\phi_n}{dz} + \frac{1}{\text{Pe}}\frac{d^2\phi_n}{dz^2} + J(z)\phi_n(z)\right] = -\lambda_n \tag{4.4.23}$$

and the equations

$$\frac{da_n}{dt} + \lambda_n a_n = \beta b_n u(t) + c_n u_0(t) \tag{4.4.24}$$

$$\frac{1}{\text{Pe}}\frac{d^2\phi_n}{dz^2} - \frac{d\phi_n}{dz} + [J(z) + \lambda_n]\phi_n(z) = 0 \tag{4.4.25}$$

$$\frac{d\phi_n(0)}{dz} = \text{Pe}\ \phi_n(0) \tag{4.4.26}$$

$$\frac{d\phi_n(1)}{dz} = 0 \tag{4.4.27}$$

Notice that the presence of $J(z)$ in Eq. (4.4.25) is a problem because it prevents a general analytical solution to the eigenvalue problem of Eqs. (4.4.25) to (4.4.27). To surmount this problem, there are several ways to proceed.

1. If the steady-state temperature profiles of interest are essentially uniform, then one may linearize about a uniform temperature $x_s(z) = \text{const}$, and $J(z)$ becomes a constant. In this case, the separation of variables solution proceeds in a straightforward way.
2. A second approach is to assume that the $J(z)x(z, t)$ term in Eq. (4.4.16) may be expanded as follows:

$$J(z)x(z, t) = \sum_{n=1}^{\infty} f_n(t)\phi_n(z) \tag{4.4.28}$$

where $f_n(t)$ is to be determined.

In this instance the separation of variables procedure leads to

$$\frac{da_n}{dt} + \lambda_n a_n(t) = \beta b_n u(t) + c_n u_0(t) + f_n(t) \tag{4.4.29}$$

$$\frac{1}{\text{Pe}}\frac{d^2\phi_n}{dz^2} - \frac{d\phi_n}{dz} + \lambda_n\phi_n(z) = 0 \tag{4.4.30}$$

with boundary conditions (4.4.26) and (4.4.27). Now this equation may be put into Sturm-Liouville form

$$L(\cdot) = \frac{1}{\rho(z)}\frac{d}{dz}\left[p(z)\frac{d(\cdot)}{dz}\right] + q(z)(\cdot) \tag{4.2.108}$$

by noting that

$$\frac{p(z)}{\rho(z)} = \frac{1}{\text{Pe}} \qquad \frac{1}{\rho}\frac{dp(z)}{dz} = -1 \tag{4.4.31}$$

$$q(z) = \lambda_n$$

which immediately leads to

$$p(z) = e^{-\text{Pe}\,z} \qquad \rho(z) = \frac{1}{\text{Pe}} e^{-\text{Pe}\,z} \qquad q = \lambda_n \tag{4.4.32}$$

and Eq. (4.4.30) becomes

$$\text{Pe}\, e^{\text{Pe}\,z} \frac{d}{dz}\left(e^{-\text{Pe}\,z} \frac{d\phi_n}{dz}\right) + \lambda_n \phi_n(z) = 0 \tag{4.4.33}$$

with the orthogonality relation

$$\int_0^1 e^{-\text{Pe}\,z} \phi_n(z)\phi_m(z)\,dz = 0 \qquad n \neq m \tag{4.4.34}$$

Thus $\phi_n(z)$ is the system eigenfunction and $\phi_n^*(z) = e^{-\text{Pe}\,z}\phi_n(z)$ is the adjoint eigenfunction.

To solve Eq. (4.4.30) for $\phi_n(z)$, let us make the substitution

$$\phi_n(z) = e^{\text{Pe}\,z/2}\, w_n(z) \tag{4.4.35}$$

to yield

$$\frac{1}{\text{Pe}} \ddot{w}_n + \left(\lambda_n - \frac{\text{Pe}}{4}\right) w_n = 0 \tag{4.4.36}$$

subject to

$$\frac{dw_n(0)}{dz} = \frac{\text{Pe}}{2} w_n(0) \tag{4.4.37}$$

$$\frac{dw_n(1)}{dz} = -\frac{\text{Pe}}{2} w_n(1) \tag{4.4.38}$$

Now this has the solution

$$w_n = A_n \sin \alpha_n z + B_n \cos \alpha_n z \tag{4.4.39}$$

where

$$\alpha_n^2 = \text{Pe}\left(\lambda_n - \frac{\text{Pe}}{4}\right) \tag{4.4.40}$$

Now application of Eq. (4.4.37) yields

$$\frac{A_n}{B_n} = \frac{\text{Pe}}{2\alpha_n} \tag{4.4.41}$$

and Eq. (4.4.38) gives

$$\alpha_n(A_n \cos \alpha_n - B_n \sin \alpha_n) = -\frac{\text{Pe}}{2}(A_n \sin \alpha_n + B_n \cos \alpha_n) \tag{4.4.42}$$

or substituting Eq. (4.4.41) and collecting terms,

$$\cos \alpha_n = \left[\alpha_n - \left(\frac{\text{Pe}}{2} \right)^2 \frac{1}{\alpha_n} \right] \sin \alpha_n \qquad (4.4.43)$$

which may be simplified to the transcendental equation

$$\tan \alpha_n = \frac{\text{Pe}\, \alpha_n}{\alpha_n^2 - (\text{Pe}/2)^2} \qquad n = 1, 2, \ldots \qquad (4.4.44)$$

Thus

$$w_n = B_n \left(\cos \alpha_n z + \frac{\text{Pe}}{2\alpha_n} \sin \alpha_n z \right) \qquad n = 1, 2, \ldots \qquad (4.4.45)$$

where α_n is determined from the roots of Eq. (4.4.44). In terms of the system eigenfunctions, the solution to Eq. (4.4.30) is

$$\phi_n(z) = B_n e^{\text{Pe}\, z/2} \left(\cos \alpha_n z + \frac{\text{Pe}}{2\alpha_n} \sin \alpha_n z \right) \qquad n = 1, 2, \ldots \qquad (4.4.46)$$

We shall choose B_n to make the eigenfunctions orthonormal to the adjoint eigenfunctions [see Eq. (4.4.34)]:

$$B_n = \left[\int_0^1 \left(\cos \alpha_n z + \frac{\text{Pe}}{2\alpha_n} \sin \alpha_n z \right)^2 dz \right]^{-1/2} \qquad (4.4.47)$$

Thus we have accomplished the *exact modal* decomposition, where the lumped system equations are given by Eq. (4.4.29). This can be used directly in a control synthesis scheme. The coefficients c_n, d_n, $f_n(t)$ are given from the orthogonality relations

$$b_n = \int_0^1 \phi_n \, dz \qquad n = 1, 2, \ldots \qquad (4.4.48)$$

$$c_n = \phi_n(0) = B_n \qquad n = 1, 2, \ldots \qquad (4.4.49)$$

$$f_n(t) = \int_0^1 \left[J(z)\phi_n(z) \sum_{m=1}^{\infty} a_m(t)\phi_m(z) \right] dz \qquad (4.4.50)$$

Note that in practice only N terms in the eigenfunction expansion will be retained, and this means the evaluation of N integrals for $f_n(t)$, i.e.,

$$f_n(t) = \sum_{m=1}^{N} a_m(t) I_{nm} \qquad (4.4.51)$$

where

$$I_{nm} = \int_0^1 J(z)\phi_n(z)\phi_m(z)\, dz \qquad (4.4.52)$$

Thus one can effectively linearize nonlinear PDEs and perform *exact* modal analysis. However, the equations for $a_n(t)$ are now coupled [due to the $f_n(t)$ term], so that the problem is multivariable in $a_n(t)$ with interactions.

Even more complex nonlinear distributed parameter systems have been analyzed through such modal decomposition using the eigenfunctions of the associated linear operator (e.g., [45, 46]). This shall be illustrated through an example.

Example 4.4.2 Let us consider a packed bed reactor with jacket temperature cooling. It is assumed that the exothermic gas phase reaction $A \to B$ is carried out in the reactor and that the reaction is zero order. Furthermore, the thermal time constants of the packing are dominant, so that we assume the gas temperature is always at quasi-steady state (i.e., the gas residence time is much shorter than the packing thermal time constant). Thus the gas temperature is given by

$$u\rho_f C_{pf} \frac{\partial T_g}{\partial z} = h_c S_c (T - T_g) - h_g S_h (T_g - T_w) \tag{4.4.53}$$

with boundary conditions

$$z' = 0 \qquad T_g = T_f \tag{4.4.54}$$

Now the catalyst packing has the equation

$$\rho_s C_{p_s} \frac{\partial T}{\partial t'} - k_e \frac{\partial^2 T}{\partial z'^2} = (-\Delta H) k_0 e^{-E/RT} - h_c S_c (T - T_g)$$
$$- h_p S_h [T - T_w(t)] \tag{4.4.55}$$

where S_c is the pellet surface area/volume and S_h is the surface area for wall heat transport/unit volume, and with boundary conditions

$$z' = 0 \qquad \frac{\partial T}{\partial z'} = 0 \tag{4.4.56}$$

$$z' = l \qquad \frac{\partial T}{\partial z'} = 0 \tag{4.4.57}$$

Now if we put this problem in dimensionless form by defining

$$x_g = \frac{T_g - T_f}{T_f} \qquad x = \frac{T - T_f}{T_f} \qquad \alpha_c = \frac{h_c S_c l}{u\rho_f C_{pf}} \qquad \alpha_g = \frac{h_g S_h l}{u\rho_f C_{pf}}$$

$$z = \frac{z'}{l} \qquad t = \frac{t' k_e}{\rho_s C_{p_s} l^2} \qquad \gamma = \frac{E}{RT_f}$$

$$B = \frac{(-\Delta H) k_0 e^{-\gamma} l^2}{k_e T_f} \qquad \beta_c = \frac{h_c S_c l^2}{k_e} \qquad \beta_p = \frac{h_p S_h l^2}{k_e} \tag{4.4.58}$$

$$u(t) = \frac{T_w}{T_f} \qquad \frac{E}{RT} = \gamma \frac{1}{x+1} \qquad \frac{E}{RT_f} - \frac{E}{RT} = \gamma \frac{x}{x+1}$$

then we get

$$\frac{\partial x_g}{\partial z} = \alpha_c(x - x_g) - \alpha_g(x_g - u) \tag{4.4.59}$$

$$x_g(0, t) = 0 \tag{4.4.60}$$

$$\frac{\partial x(z, t)}{\partial t} - \frac{\partial^2 x(z, t)}{\partial z^2} = Be^{\gamma[x/(x+1)]} - \beta_c(x - x_g) - \beta_p(x - u) \tag{4.4.61}$$

$$z = 0 \qquad \frac{\partial x}{\partial z} = 0 \tag{4.4.62}$$

$$z = 1 \qquad \frac{\partial x}{\partial z} = 0 \tag{4.4.63}$$

Now the equation for x_g can be solved as

$$x_g(z, t) = \int_0^1 e^{-(\alpha_c + \alpha_g)(z-r)}\left[\alpha_c x(r, t) + \alpha_g u(t)\right] dr$$

$$= \frac{\alpha_g u(t)}{\alpha_c + \alpha_g}\left(1 - e^{-(\alpha_c + \alpha_g)z}\right) + \alpha_c \int_0^1 e^{-(\alpha_c + \alpha_g)(z-r)} x(r, t)\, dr \tag{4.4.64}$$

If we assume that the solution can be found in terms of

$$x_g(z, t) = \sum_{n=0}^{N} c_n(t)\phi_n(z)$$

$$x(z, t) = \sum_{n=0}^{N} a_n(t)\phi_n(z) \tag{4.4.65}$$

$$u(t) = \sum_{n=0}^{N} b_n(t)\phi_n(z) \tag{4.4.66}$$

and assume the nonlinear terms can be expanded in terms of the complete set of functions $\phi_n(z)$:

$$F(x, x_g) = Be^{\gamma[x/(x+1)]} - \beta_c(x - x_g) - \beta_p x = \sum_{n=0}^{N} f_n(t)\phi_n(z) \tag{4.4.67}$$

then Eq. (4.4.61) becomes

$$\phi_n(z)\frac{da_n(t)}{dt} - a_n\frac{d^2\phi_n}{dz^2} = \left[\beta_p b_n(t) + f_n(t)\right]\phi_n(z) \tag{4.4.68}$$

with the boundary conditions

$$z = 0 \qquad \frac{d\phi_n}{dz} = 0 \tag{4.4.69}$$

$$z = 1 \qquad \frac{d\phi_n}{dz} = 0 \tag{4.4.70}$$

By separating variables we are led to the equations

$$\frac{da_n(t)}{dt} + \lambda_n a_n(t) = \beta_p b_n(t) + f_n(t) \tag{4.4.71}$$

$$\frac{d^2\phi_n(z)}{dz^2} + \lambda_n \phi_n(z) = 0 \tag{4.4.72}$$

Now the eigenvalue problem [Eqs. (4.4.69) to (4.4.72)] is the same one treated in Sec. 4.2 and has the solution

$$\phi_n(z) = \begin{cases} 1 & n = 0 \\ \sqrt{2}\cos n\pi z & n = 1, 2, \ldots, N \end{cases} \tag{4.4.73}$$

and

$$\lambda_n = n^2\pi^2 \qquad n = 0, 1, 2, \ldots, N \tag{4.4.74}$$

From the orthogonality relations

$$a_n(t) = \int_0^1 \phi_n(z)x(z, t)\, dz \tag{4.4.75}$$

$$b_n(t) = \int_0^1 \phi_n(z)u(t)\, dz = \begin{cases} u(t) & n = 0 \\ 0 & n = 1, 2, \ldots, N \end{cases} \tag{4.4.76}$$

$$c_n(t) = \int_0^1 \phi_n(z)x_g(z, t)\, dz \tag{4.4.77}$$

$$f_n(t) = \int_0^1 \phi_n(z)F(x, x_g)\, dz \tag{4.4.78}$$

Thus the control scheme has the structure shown in Fig. 4.17. Notice that a nonlinear function generator is needed to determine the coefficients f_n and that the controller must deal with nonlinear behavior $f_n(\mathbf{a}, \mathbf{c})$. The resulting lumped system, Eq. (4.4.71), is a nonlinear multivariable lumped parameter system with interactions because Eq. (4.4.67) leads to a nonlinear relation between f_n and a_n, c_n; i.e., substituting Eq. (4.4.65) into Eq. (4.4.67) and applying Eq. (4.4.78) yields

$$\int_0^1 \phi_n(z)\left\{ B \exp\left[\gamma\left(\frac{\sum a_n\phi_n}{1 + \sum a_n\phi_n}\right)\right] - \beta_c \sum (a_n - c_n)\phi_n - \beta_p \sum a_n\phi_n \right\} dz = f_n \tag{4.4.79}$$

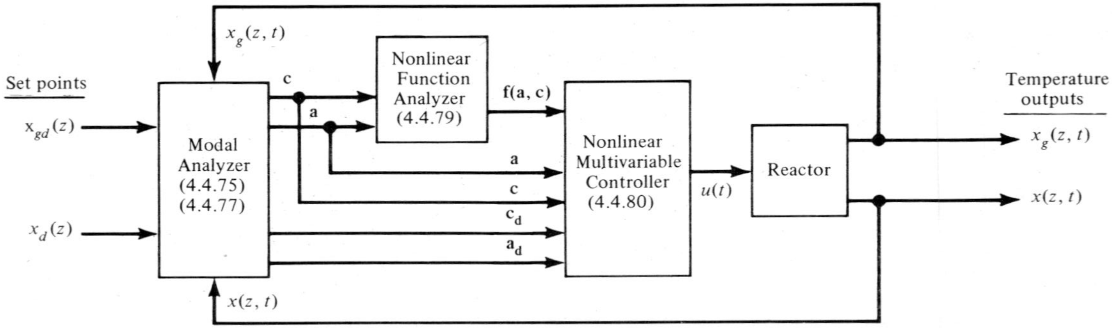

Figure 4.17 Nonlinear distributed parameter control scheme for packed bed reactor example.

Thus the lumped controller design equation takes the form

$$\frac{da_n(t)}{dt} = -n^2\pi^2 a_n(t) + f_n(a_0, a_1, \ldots, a_N, c_1, c_2, \ldots, c_N) + \beta_p b_n(t) \tag{4.4.80}$$

and we must appeal to the nonlinear design techniques of Sec. 3.4. This Galerkin modal decomposition procedure should converge for sufficient number of eigenfunctions. This method can be applied whenever the nonlinearity appears as a forcing function in the partial differential equation—a very frequent situation.

Lumping Methods

If one wishes to "lump" the partial differential equations (either before control system design or after the design in order to numerically solve the design equations), there are a large number of very efficient methods available. Therefore classical finite difference methods should be used only after several of the more efficient methods have been considered. The most efficient lumping methods may be viewed as *pseudo-modal methods*; that is, one expands the solution into a set of known basis functions $\phi_n(z)$; for example,

$$x_a(z, t) = \sum_{n=1}^{N} a_n(t)\phi_n(z) \tag{4.4.81}$$

Then one uses some goodness-of-fit criterion to determine the coefficients $a_n(t)$ which yield the best approximation to $x(z, t)$. Notice that this is simply an extension of the modal decomposition method with the difference that *pseudo-modal* methods may use any set of basis functions, while eigenfunction expansions use the eigenfunctions of the linear operator. It is possible to treat both linear and nonlinear partial differential equation systems by pseudo-modal methods such as the *method of weighted residuals* [47–51]. Given a nonlinear system, for example,

$$\frac{\partial x(z, t)}{\partial t} = A_2(z, t, x)\frac{\partial^2 x}{\partial z^2} + A_1(z, t, x)\frac{\partial x}{\partial z} + A_0(z, t, x)x + f(x, u, z, t)$$

$$0 \le z \le 1 \qquad t > 0 \tag{4.4.82}$$

with boundary conditions

$$z = 0 \qquad b_1(t, x)\frac{\partial x}{\partial z} + b_0(t, x)x = f_0(x, u_0, t) \tag{4.4.83}$$

$$z = 1 \qquad c_1(t, x)\frac{\partial x}{\partial z} + c_0(t, x)x = f_1(x, u_1, t) \tag{4.4.84}$$

one can proceed to reduce the system to a set of ODEs by pseudo-modal methods. To do this, one takes a set of *basis functions* $\phi_n(z)$, which are analogous to the eigenfunctions for the linear problem. These functions $\phi_n(z)$ should be *complete* and preferably orthogonal with some weighting function $\rho(z)$:

$$\int_0^1 \rho(z)\phi_n(z)\phi_m(z)\,dz = 0 \qquad \text{for } n \neq m \tag{4.4.85}$$

The choice of the $\phi_n(z)$ is arbitrary, but it is helpful to try the eigenfunctions of a related linear problem—particularly if Eqs. (4.4.82) to (4.4.84) are only slightly nonlinear.

The approximate solution to the problem is then expressed in terms of N basis functions, Eq. (4.4.81), where the coefficients $a_n(t)$ must be determined in such a way that $x_a(z, t)$ is a good approximation to the solution to Eqs. (4.4.82) to (4.4.84). Many criteria are possible for measuring a good approximation, and each criterion chosen leads to a different technique. *The method of weighted residuals* (MWR) is one class of methods. One often chooses the $\phi_n(z)$ so that the boundary conditions, Eqs. (4.4.83) and (4.4.84), are satisfied exactly* and the *residual* (let us assume u, u_0, $u_1 = 0$ for the moment)

$$R(z, t) = \frac{\partial \hat{x}}{\partial t} - \hat{A}_2\frac{\partial^2 \hat{x}}{\partial z^2} - \hat{A}_1\frac{\partial \hat{x}}{\partial z} - \hat{A}_0\hat{x} - \hat{f} \tag{4.4.86}$$

must be made small in the sense that

$$\int_0^1 w_i(z)R(z, t)\,dz = 0 \qquad i = 0, 1, 2, \ldots, N \tag{4.4.87}$$

where the $w_i(z)$ are a set of weighting functions to be chosen. The choice of weighting functions can lead to several different criteria. Let us discuss some of the types of criteria possible.

1. *Galerkin's method* If the weighting functions are chosen to be the basis functions themselves,

$$w_n(z) = \phi_n(z) \qquad n = 0, 1, 2, \ldots, N \tag{4.4.88}$$

then the technique is called Galerkin's method. This has the advantage that the residual is made orthogonal to each basis function and is, therefore, the best solution possible in the space made up of the $N + 1$ functions $\phi_n(z)$. Thus as $N \to \infty$, $R(z, t) \to 0$ because it will be orthogonal to every function in a complete set of functions.

2. *Method of subdomains* If we choose the w_n to be a set of Heaviside functions breaking the region $0 \leq z \leq 1$ into subdomains, i.e.,

$$w_n(z) = \begin{cases} 1 & z_n < z < z_{n+1} \\ 0 & \text{elsewhere} \end{cases} \tag{4.4.89}$$

then Eq. (4.4.87) becomes

$$\int_{z_n}^{z_{n+1}} R(z, t)\,dz = 0 \qquad n = 0, 1, 2, \ldots, N \tag{4.4.90}$$

* Cases where the boundary conditions are not satisfied exactly are also possible (e.g., [47], [51]), but usually it is more convenient to satisfy them a priori.

and the average value of the residual must vanish over each of $N + 1$ subdomains. For $N = 0$ (zeroth approximation), $z_0 = 0$, $z_1 = 1$, and we have

$$\int_0^1 R(z, t)\, dz = 0 \tag{4.4.91}$$

This special case is called the *integral method* and is used widely in boundary-layer problems.

3. *Method of moments*. If the w_n are chosen to be powers of z, then Eq. (4.4.87) becomes

$$\int_0^1 z^n R(z, t)\, dz = 0 \qquad n = 0, 1, 2, \ldots, N \tag{4.4.92}$$

and the first N moments of $R(z, t)$ are required to vanish.

4. *Collocation methods*. If the w_n are chosen to be delta functions $\delta(z - z_n)$, then Eq. (4.4.87) becomes

$$R(z_n, t) = 0 \qquad n = 0, 1, 2, \ldots, N \tag{4.4.93}$$

and the differential equation is required to be solved exactly at N points on the spatial domain. The collocation method has been refined greatly [47, 49, 51] and has been shown to be extremely powerful. The recent versions are called *orthogonal collocation* because orthogonal polynomials are used as the basis functions and the collocation points are specified automatically.

There are other pseudo-modal methods which can be considered as MWR techniques. For example, finite element methods [50], the use of spline functions [47], and other approaches may be shown to fall within this framework. Results on the convergence of pseudo-modal methods are not abundant. Galerkin methods may be shown to be uniformly convergent for a rather broad class of problems (see [47, 52]), but general convergence results have not been proved at present for most other methods.

Although pseudo-modal methods have been known for more than fifty years, it has only been recently that extensive computational experience has been available. The most popular approaches appear to be Galerkin's method (e.g., [47], [53–56]), collocation methods [47, 49, 51], and finite element methods [50]. We shall illustrate the application of some of these methods with examples.

Example 4.4.3 Let us consider the heating of a thin metal rod in a furnace as in Example 4.3.3. However, in this case, the temperature range of interest is so wide that ρC_p and k depend strongly on temperature. Thus modeling equations take the form

$$\rho C_p \frac{\partial T}{\partial t'} = \frac{\partial(k(T)\, \partial T/\partial z')}{\partial z'} + q(z', t') \tag{4.4.94}$$

with boundary conditions

$$\frac{\partial T}{\partial z'} = 0 \qquad \text{at } z = 0, l \tag{4.4.95}$$

In this instance the differential spatial operator is nonlinear and given by

$$\frac{\partial T}{\partial t'} = \frac{k}{\rho C_p}\frac{\partial^2 T}{\partial z'^2} + \frac{1}{\rho C_p}\frac{\partial k}{\partial T}\left(\frac{\partial T}{\partial z'}\right)^2 + q(z', t) \tag{4.4.96}$$

Now let us suppose that it is possible to neglect the second term and represent the nonlinearity in the first term by the form

$$\alpha = \frac{k}{\rho C_p} = \alpha_0 + \alpha_1 T \tag{4.4.97}$$

Furthermore, let us put the problem in dimensionless form by setting

$$z = \frac{z'}{l} \qquad x = \frac{T}{T_0} \qquad t' = \frac{\alpha_0 t}{l^2} \qquad \beta = \frac{\alpha_1}{\alpha_0}T_0 \qquad u = \frac{ql^2}{\alpha_0 T_0} \tag{4.4.98}$$

then we get

$$\frac{\partial x(z, t)}{\partial t} = (1 + \beta x)\frac{\partial^2 x(z, t)}{\partial z^2} + u(z, t) \tag{4.4.99}$$

with boundary conditions

$$z = 0 \qquad \frac{\partial x}{\partial z} = 0 \tag{4.4.100}$$

$$z = 1 \qquad \frac{\partial x}{\partial z} = 0 \tag{4.4.101}$$

Now if we choose as basis functions the eigenfunctions of the problem when $\beta = 0$, we obtain

$$x(z, t) = \sum_{n=0}^{N} a_n(t)\phi_n(z) \tag{4.4.102}$$

$$u(z, t) = \sum_{n=0}^{N} b_n(t)\phi_n(z) \tag{4.4.103}$$

where

$$\phi_n(z) = \begin{cases} 1 & n = 0 \\ \sqrt{2}\cos n\pi z & n = 1, 2, \ldots, N \end{cases} \tag{4.4.104}$$

Now if we substitute Eqs. (4.4.102) and (4.4.103) into Eqs. (4.4.99) to (4.4.101), we see that the boundary conditions are satisfied exactly and the residual becomes

$$R(z, t) = \sum_{n=0}^{N} \phi_n(z)\left\{\frac{da_n}{dt} - \sum_{m=0}^{N}\left[\beta a_n a_m (m\pi)^2 \phi_m(z)\right] - b_n(t) + a_n(t)(n\pi)^2\right\} \tag{4.4.105}$$

Now if we apply Galerkin's method to the problem, we must have

$$\int_0^1 \phi_n(z)R(z, t)\,dz = 0 \qquad n = 0, 1, 2, \ldots, N \tag{4.4.106}$$

which becomes

$$\frac{da_n}{dt} + (n\pi)^2 a_n - b_n(t) - \beta \int_0^1 \sum_{m=0}^{N} \sum_{k=0}^{N} \phi_n(z)\phi_m(z)\phi_k(z) a_m a_k (m\pi)^2 \, dz$$

or

$$\frac{da_n}{dt} + (n\pi)^2 a_n - b_n(t) - \beta \sum_{m=0}^{N} \sum_{k=0}^{N} a_m a_k (m\pi)^2 \int_0^1 \phi_n(z)\phi_m(z)\phi_k(z)\, dz = 0$$

$$n = 0, 1, 2, \ldots, N \qquad (4.4.107)$$

Now let us denote

$$I_{nmk} = \int_0^1 \phi_n \phi_m \phi_k \, dz \qquad (4.4.108)$$

Although it requires some algebra, this integral I_{nmk} can be evaluated analytically in the following way:

$$I_{n,m,k} = 2\sqrt{2} \int_0^1 \cos n\pi z \cos m\pi z \cos k\pi z \, dz = \sqrt{2} \int_0^1 [\cos (n + m)\pi z + \cos(n - m)\pi z] \cos k\pi z \, dz \qquad (4.4.109)$$

Now using integral tables (e.g., [57], p. 105), one obtains

$$I_{n,m,k} = 0 \qquad \text{if } n - m \neq k,\ m + n \neq k \qquad (4.4.110)$$

Also if $n - m = k$ or $n + m = k$ ([48], p. 101), then

$$I_{n,m,k} = \frac{\sqrt{2}}{2} \qquad (4.4.111)$$

and for $n = m = k$ ([48], p. 102),

$$I_{n,m,k} = 0 \qquad (4.4.112)$$

Thus in summary

$$I_{n,m,k} = \begin{cases} 0 & \text{if } n = m = k \text{ or } (n - m \neq k \text{ and } n + m \neq k) \\ \delta_{pq} & \text{if one of the indices } n, m, k = 0 \\ & \text{and } p, q \text{ are the remaining indices} \\ \dfrac{\sqrt{2}}{2} & \text{if } n + m = k \text{ or } n - m = k \end{cases} \qquad (4.4.113)$$

Therefore Eq. (4.4.107) becomes

$$\frac{da_n}{dt} + (n\pi)^2 a_n - b_n(t) - \beta \sum_{m=0}^{N} \sum_{k=0}^{N} a_m a_k (m\pi)^2 I_{n,m,k} = 0$$

$$n = 0, 1, 2, \ldots, N \qquad (4.4.114)$$

To illustrate this lumping, let us look at the first few terms

$$\frac{da_0}{dt} - b_0 - \beta(\pi^2 a_1^2 + 4\pi^2 a_2^2 + \cdots) = 0 \tag{4.4.115}$$

$$\frac{da_1}{dt} + \pi^2 a_1 - b_1 - \beta\left[a_1\pi^2\left(a_0 + \frac{a_2\sqrt{2}}{2}\right)\right.$$
$$\left. + a_2 4\pi^2\left(a_1\frac{\sqrt{2}}{2} + a_3\frac{\sqrt{2}}{2}\right) + \cdots\right] = 0 \tag{4.4.116}$$

$$\frac{da_2}{dt} + 4\pi^2 a_2 - b_2 - \beta\left[a_0 4\pi^2 a_2 + \frac{a_1^2\sqrt{2}}{2}\pi^2\right.$$
$$\left. + a_1 a_3\left(\frac{\sqrt{2}}{2}9\pi^2 + \frac{\sqrt{2}}{2}\pi^2\right) + \cdots\right] = 0$$

$$\text{etc.} \tag{4.4.117}$$

Thus the coefficients are coupled and nonlinear, and the controller design requires the use of nonlinear lumped parameter design techniques. The control structure will be very similar to that shown in Fig. 4.17.

It should be noted that Galerkin's method leads to *exact modal* analysis when the system becomes linear (e.g., when $\beta = 0$ here), and thus is to be recommended on that basis. Also if we choose an orthonormal basis, the orthogonality relations allow us to synthesize $u(z, t)$ from Eq. (4.4.102) and to obtain $a_n(t)$ from the data from

$$a_n(t) = \int_0^1 x(z, t)\phi_n(z)\, dz \tag{4.4.118}$$

Thus Galerkin's method when used with a set of orthonormal basis functions has all the properties of exact modal analysis *except*:

1. The solution to the system is only approximate, and the smallness of the residual $R(z, t)$ will depend on the type and number of basis functions chosen.
2. The lumped parameter controller design, Eq. (4.4.114), in the coefficients $a_n(t)$, $b_n(t)$ is a coupled, nonlinear multivariable design problem of order N so that simple PID single-loop controllers will not suffice, but some control design compensating for interaction must be used.

It is useful to compare the eigenfunction expansion method of Examples 4.4.1 and 4.4.2 with the approximate Galerkin method of Example 4.4.3. The principal differences in the first two examples were that the spatially dependent coefficients of the forcing function in Example 4.4.1 and the nonlinear forcing function of Example 4.4.2 are assumed to be exactly expandable in the eigenfunctions of the linear differential operator. In this case uniform convergence of the Galerkin aproximation can be shown.* In contrast, for Example 4.4.3, there is the requirement that the second spatial derivative be exactly expandable in the eigenfunctions of the linear operator for the separation of variables method to apply. However, the second space derivative of the solution will, in general, not be uniformly convergent in the basis functions (see [47], pp. 373–379), and thus the Galerkin method will not necessarily converge uniformly for this example.

It should be emphasized that Galerkin's method is not the only technique one may use for this example. In fact, collocation techniques would also seem to have some advantages, particularly if the control were applied at discrete points in space $u(z_i, t)$, $i = 1, 2, m$. If the collocation points were chosen at these points, then the control could be incorporated directly.

The detailed application of these methods to example nonlinear distributed systems is discussed in Chap. 6.

4.5 CONTROL OF SYSTEMS HAVING TIME DELAYS

An especially important class of distributed parameter systems is *hereditary systems*, or *systems having time delays*. This class of dynamic systems arises in a wide range of applications, including paper making, chemical reactors, and distillation. Example 4.1.2 serves to illustrate a very simple single-loop control problem with a transport time delay. The principal difficulty with time delays in the control loop is the increased phase lag, which leads to unstable control system behavior at relatively low controller gains. This limits the amount of control action possible in the presence of time delays.

In multivariable time-delay systems with multiple delays, these problems are even more complex. In these problems, the normal control difficulties due to loop interactions (see Chap. 3) are complicated by the additional effects of time delays. A good example of this type of problem is in *distillation column* control. To illustrate, let us consider the problem discussed in Example 3.2.8, where the column output compositions y_i are related to the sidestream flow rates u_j by a transfer function matrix

$$\bar{\mathbf{y}}(s) = \mathbf{G}(s)\bar{\mathbf{u}}(s) \tag{4.5.1}$$

Now in practice, the transfer function matrix often has elements in the form

$$g_{ij}(s) = \frac{K_{ij}e^{-\beta_{ij}s}\prod_{p=1}^{l}(a_{ijp}s+1)}{\prod_{q=1}^{l}(b_{ijq}s+1)} \tag{4.5.2}$$

or rewriting,

$$g_{ij}(s) = \frac{e^{-\beta_{ij}s}\left(e_{ijl}s^{l} + e_{ijl-1}s^{l-1} + \cdots + e_{ij0}\right)}{s^{l} + d_{ijl-1}s^{l-1} + \cdots + d_{ij0}} \tag{4.5.3}$$

* For convergence in Example 4.4.1, see [47], p. 371; for Example 4.4.2, see [47], pp. 373, 374.

Here the factor $e^{-\beta_{ij}s}$ denotes a time delay associated with the ijth element of $\mathbf{G}(s)$. Hence the transfer function for the distillation column of Example 3.2.8 would more often in practice have the form

$$\mathbf{G}(s) = \begin{bmatrix} \dfrac{0.7e^{-2s}}{1+9s} & 0 & 0 \\ \dfrac{2.0e^{-5s}}{1+8s} & \dfrac{0.4e^{-2s}}{1+6s} & 0 \\ \dfrac{2.3e^{-6s}}{1+10s} & \dfrac{2.3e^{-4s}}{1+8s} & \dfrac{2.1e^{-2s}}{1+7s} \end{bmatrix} \tag{4.5.4}$$

where the time delays in each element of the matrix will be different.

The time-domain realization of transfer functions such as Eqs. (4.5.1) to (4.5.3) will have a slightly different form from that discussed in Chap. 3. In terms of Eq. (4.5.3), the time-domain representation is given by

$$\frac{d\mathbf{z}_{ij}(t)}{dt} = \mathbf{A}_{ij}\mathbf{z}_{ij}(t) + \mathbf{h}_{ij}u_j(t-\beta_{ij}) \qquad \begin{matrix} i = 1, 2, \ldots, n \\ j = 1, 2, \ldots, m \end{matrix} \tag{4.5.5}$$

where

$$x_i(t) = \sum_{j=1}^{m} \left[z_{ij1}(t) + h_{ij0}u_j(t-\beta_{ij}) \right] \tag{4.5.6}$$

$$\mathbf{z}_{ij} = \begin{bmatrix} z_{ij1} \\ z_{ij2} \\ \vdots \\ z_{ijl} \end{bmatrix} \qquad \mathbf{A}_{ij} = \begin{bmatrix} 0 & 1 & 0 & \cdots & 0 \\ 0 & 0 & 1 \quad 0 & \cdots & 0 \\ \cdots & \cdots & \cdots & \cdots & \cdots \\ 0 \ldots & \ldots & & \ldots & 1 \\ -d_{ij0} & -d_{ij1} & & \ldots & -d_{ijl-1} \end{bmatrix} \tag{4.5.7}$$

$$\mathbf{h}_{ij} = \begin{bmatrix} h_{ij1} \\ h_{ij2} \\ \vdots \\ h_{ijl} \end{bmatrix} \tag{4.5.8}$$

and

$$h_{kj0} = e_{ijl}$$

$$h_{ijl-p} = e_{ijp} - \sum_{q=0}^{l-p-1} h_{ijq}d_{ijq+p} \qquad p = 0, 1, 2, \ldots, l-1 \tag{4.5.9}$$

Thus transfer functions of the form of Eqs. (4.5.1) to (4.5.3) when converted to state space take the form of ODEs with delays in the control. Other realizations of time delay systems are discussed by Ogunnaike [58].

In this section we shall first present a rather general formulation of time-delay control problems and then consider some relatively simple design procedures for this class of problem. Finally, optimal control theory and practice for time-delay systems shall be discussed.

A General Formulation

A very general representation of systems having delays in the control variables $\mathbf{u}(t)$, state variables $\mathbf{x}(t)$, or output variables $\mathbf{y}(t)$ is illustrated in Fig. 4.18. Each type of delay can be thought of as a transport lag in a pipe modeled by a first-order hyperbolic equation (see Example 4.1.2). The inlet to these pipes can be either the state variable $\mathbf{x}(t)$ or control $\mathbf{u}(t)$. If we further allow integral hereditary terms, the general formulation is given as follows:

$$\frac{d\mathbf{x}(t)}{dt} = \mathbf{f}\big(\mathbf{x}(t), \mathbf{w}_1(r_1, t), \mathbf{w}_1(r_2, t), \ldots \mathbf{w}_1(r_\delta, t), \mathbf{u}(t), \mathbf{w}_2(\hat{r}_1, t),$$

$$\mathbf{w}_2(\hat{r}_2, t), \ldots, \mathbf{w}_2(\hat{r}_\mu, t)\big) + \int_0^1 \mathbf{K}(\mathbf{w}_1(r, t), r, \mathbf{u}(t))\, dr \qquad (4.5.10)$$

$$\frac{\partial \mathbf{w}_1(r, t)}{\partial t} = -\mathbf{M}_1(r, t)\frac{\partial \mathbf{w}_1(r, t)}{\partial r} + \mathbf{g}_1(\mathbf{w}_1(r, t), \mathbf{w}_2(r, t), \mathbf{x}(t), \mathbf{u}(t)) \qquad (4.5.11)$$

$$\frac{\partial \mathbf{w}_2(r, t)}{\partial t} = -\mathbf{M}_2(r, t)\frac{\partial \mathbf{w}_2(r, t)}{\partial r} + \mathbf{g}_2(\mathbf{w}_1(r, t), \mathbf{w}_2(r, t), \mathbf{x}(t), \mathbf{u}(t)) \qquad (4.5.12)$$

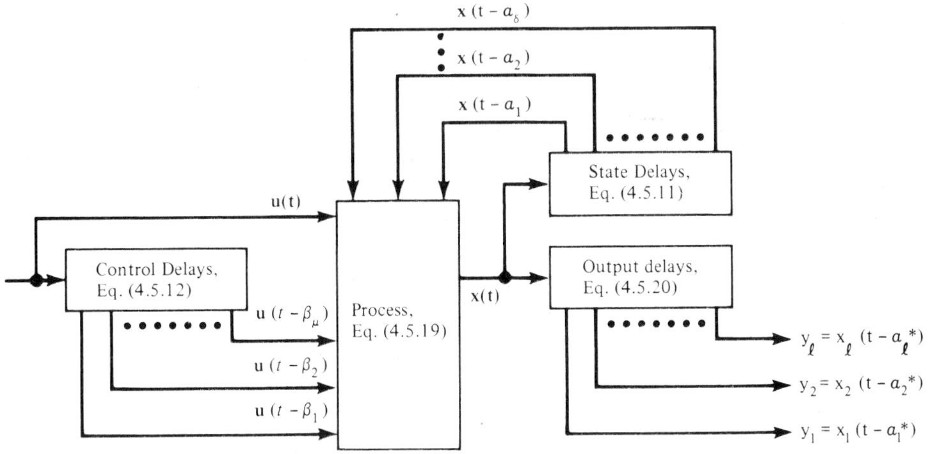

Figure 4.18 Example of transport lag models for systems having state, control, and output delays.

with initial and boundary conditions

$$\mathbf{x}(0) = \mathbf{x}_0 \tag{4.5.13}$$

$$\mathbf{w}_1(r, 0) = \mathbf{w}_{10}(r) \tag{4.5.14}$$

$$\mathbf{w}_2(r, 0) = \mathbf{w}_{20}(r) \tag{4.5.15}$$

$$\mathbf{w}_1(0, t) = \mathbf{b}_1(\mathbf{x}(t)) \tag{4.5.16}$$

$$\mathbf{w}_2(0, t) = \mathbf{b}_2(\mathbf{u}(t)) \tag{4.5.17}$$

The outputs take the form

$$\mathbf{y}(t) = \mathbf{h}\big(\mathbf{x}(t), \mathbf{w}_1(r_1^*, t), \mathbf{w}_1(r_2^*, t), \ldots, \mathbf{w}_1(r_\gamma^*, t)\big) + \int_0^1 H(\mathbf{w}_1(r, t), r)\, dr \tag{4.5.18}$$

It is possible to show that this coupled set of ODEs and first-order hyperbolic PDEs have as special cases all the commonly encountered time-delay problems [59, 60].

As an example, if one allows that $\mathbf{K} = \mathbf{H} = \mathbf{g}_1 = \mathbf{g}_2 = 0$, $\mathbf{b}_1(\mathbf{x}(t)) = \mathbf{x}(t)$, $\mathbf{b}_2(\mathbf{u}(t)) = \mathbf{u}(t)$, $\mathbf{M}_1 = \mathbf{I}\alpha_{\max}^{-1}$, $\mathbf{M}_2 = \mathbf{I}\beta_\mu^{-1}$, $r_i = \alpha_i/\alpha_{\max}$, $r_j^* = \alpha_j^*/\alpha_{\max}$, $\hat{r}_i = \beta_i/\beta_\mu$, $\mathbf{w}_1(r, 0) = \boldsymbol{\Phi}(-r\beta_\mu)$, $\mathbf{w}_2(r, 0) = \phi(-r\alpha_{\max})$, then $\mathbf{w}_1(r_i, t) = \mathbf{x}(t - \alpha_i)$, $\mathbf{w}_1(r_i^*, t) = \mathbf{x}(t - \alpha_i^*)$, $\mathbf{w}_2(\hat{r}_i, t) = \mathbf{u}(t - \beta_i)$. Thus Eqs. (4.5.10) to (4.5.18) reduce to a *nonlinear ODE system having constant time delays*:

$$\frac{d\mathbf{x}(t)}{dt} = \mathbf{f}\big(\mathbf{x}(t), \mathbf{x}(t - \alpha_1), \ldots, \mathbf{x}(t - \alpha_\delta), \mathbf{u}(t), \mathbf{u}(t - \beta_1), \ldots, \mathbf{u}(t - \beta_\mu)\big) \tag{4.5.19}$$

$$\mathbf{y}(t) = \mathbf{h}\big(\mathbf{x}(t), \mathbf{x}(t - \alpha_1^*), \mathbf{x}(t - \alpha_2^*), \ldots, \mathbf{x}(t - \alpha_\gamma^*)\big) \tag{4.5.20}$$

$$\mathbf{x}(t) = \phi(t) \qquad -\alpha_{\max} \le t \le 0 \qquad \alpha_{\max} = \max(\alpha_\delta, \alpha_\gamma^*) \tag{4.5.21}$$

$$\mathbf{u}(t) = \boldsymbol{\Phi}(t) \qquad -\beta_\mu \le t \le 0 \tag{4.5.22}$$

Another important class of problems arises if one allows

$$\mathbf{K} = \mathbf{H} = \mathbf{g}_1 = \mathbf{g}_2 = \mathbf{0} \qquad \delta = \gamma = \lambda = 1 \qquad r_1 = r_1^* = \hat{r}_1 = 1$$

$$\mathbf{b}_1(\mathbf{x}(t)) = \left[\mathbf{x}^T(t), \mathbf{x}^T(t), \mathbf{x}^T(t), \ldots, \mathbf{x}^T(t)\right]^T$$

$$\mathbf{b}_2(\mathbf{u}(t)) = \left[\mathbf{u}^T(t), \mathbf{u}^T(t), \mathbf{u}^T(t), \ldots, \mathbf{u}^T(t)\right]^T$$

$$\mathbf{M}_1(r, t) = \left[M_{1ij}(r, t)\right] = \begin{cases} 0 & i \ne j \\ \dfrac{1 - r\dot{\alpha}_i}{\alpha_i}\mathbf{I} & i = 1, 2, \ldots, \rho \qquad i = j \\ \left(\dfrac{1 - r\dot{\alpha}_{i-\rho}^*}{\alpha_{i-\rho}^*}\right)\mathbf{I} & i = \rho + 1, \ldots, \rho + w \end{cases}$$

$$\mathbf{M}_2(r, t) = \left[M_{2ij}(r, t)\right] = \begin{cases} 0 & i \ne j \\ \dfrac{i - r\dot{\beta}_i}{\beta_i}\mathbf{I} & i = 1, 2, \ldots, \eta \end{cases}$$

Then
$$\mathbf{w}_1(r,t) = \left[\mathbf{w}_{11}^T(r,t), \mathbf{w}_{12}(r,t)^T, \ldots, \mathbf{w}_{1,\rho}(r,t)^T, \mathbf{w}_{11}^*(r,t), \mathbf{w}_{12}^*(r,t), \ldots, \mathbf{w}_{1w}^*(r,t)\right]^T$$
$$\mathbf{w}_2(r,t) = \left[\mathbf{w}_{21}^T(r,t)\, \mathbf{w}_{22}^T(r,t), \ldots, \mathbf{w}_{2\eta}^T(r,t)\right]$$
$$\mathbf{w}_{1i}(r,0) = \boldsymbol{\phi}(-r\alpha_i(0)),\ \mathbf{w}_{1j}^*(r,0) = \boldsymbol{\phi}(-r\alpha_j^*(0))$$
$$\mathbf{w}_{2i}(r,0) = \boldsymbol{\Phi}(-r\beta_i(0)),$$
then
$$\mathbf{w}_{1i}(1,t) = \mathbf{x}(t-\alpha_i(t)),\ \mathbf{w}_{1j}^*(1,t) = \mathbf{x}(t-\alpha_i^*(t))$$
$$\mathbf{w}_{2i}(1,t) = \mathbf{u}(t-\beta_i(t))$$

In this case we obtain a *nonlinear system of ODEs with time-varying time delays*

$$\frac{d\mathbf{x}(t)}{dt} = \mathbf{f}(\mathbf{x}(t), \mathbf{x}(t-\alpha_1(t)), \ldots, \mathbf{x}(t-\alpha_\rho(t)), \mathbf{u}(t), \mathbf{u}(t-\beta_1(t)), \ldots, \mathbf{u}(t-\beta_\eta(t))) \tag{4.5.23}$$
$$\mathbf{y}(t) = \mathbf{h}(\mathbf{x}(t), \mathbf{x}(t-\alpha_1^*(t)), \ldots, \mathbf{x}(t-\alpha_\omega^*(t))) \tag{4.5.24}$$
$$\dot{\alpha}_i(t) < 1 \tag{4.5.25}$$
$$\dot{\alpha}_j^*(t) < 1 \tag{4.5.26}$$
$$\dot{\beta}_i(t) < 1 \tag{4.5.27}$$
$$\mathbf{x}(t) = \boldsymbol{\phi}(t) \qquad -\alpha_{\max} \le t \le 0 \tag{4.5.28}$$
$$\mathbf{u}(t) = \boldsymbol{\Phi}(t) \qquad -\beta_{\max} \le t \le 0 \tag{4.5.29}$$
$$\alpha_{\max} = \max\left[\alpha_1(0), \ldots, \alpha_\rho(0), \alpha_1^*(0), \ldots, \alpha_\omega^*(0)\right] \tag{4.5.30}$$
$$\beta_{\max} = \max\left[\beta_1(0), \ldots, \beta_\eta(0)\right] \tag{4.5.31}$$

The conditions of Eqs. (4.5.25) to (4.5.27) are necessary to ensure that the time delays do not increase faster than time itself.

Many other time-delay problems of interest may be extracted from the general formulation, Eqs. (4.5.10) to (4.5.18), but we shall not treat all of them here. The reader is referred to [59, 60] for a fuller discussion of these.

Time-Delay Compensation Methods

Aside from optimal control design methods to be discussed later in this section, controller design procedures for time-delay systems usually involve using a prediction device in the control loop to compensate for the time delays. If this is done, then often the standard ODE multivariable controller design procedures of Chap. 3 may be used. There are several methods which may be used to compensate for delays in the states, outputs, or controls. One may use one of the statistical state-estimation procedures of Chap. 5 or much simpler procedures such as the Smith predictor [61–63], which has been applied with success to processes having delays in both the outputs and the controls. Other methods which have been proposed involve the use of cascade control [64], feedforward control [65], or noninteracting control [66] to compensate for the time delays. Our emphasis in the discussion here will be on time-delay compensation procedures and will highlight recent results on multivariable, multidelay compensators [67].

Let us begin by considering the design of compensators for single-loop control problems with time delays. In the late 1950s Smith [61] developed a time-delay compensator for a single delay in a single control loop which eliminated the delay from the feedback loop, allowing higher controller gains to be used. This compensator, termed the Smith predictor, is shown in the block diagram in Fig. 4.19. Here the compensator

$$g_k(s) = h(s)g(s)(1 - e^{-\alpha s}) \tag{4.5.32}$$

acts to eliminate the time delay α from the system characteristic equation. To see this, note that when $g_k(s) = 0$, the closed-loop response of the system shown in Fig. 4.19 is given by

$$\bar{y}(s) = \left[1 + h(s)g(s)g_c(s)e^{-\alpha s}\right]^{-1}\left[g(s)e^{-\alpha s}g_c(s)\bar{y}_d(s) + g_d(s)\bar{d}(s)\right] \tag{4.5.33}$$

Thus the characteristic equation

$$1 + h(s)g(s)g_c(s)e^{-\alpha s} = 0 \tag{4.5.34}$$

contains the time delay α. When the Smith predictor, Eq. (4.5.32), is added to the loop as shown in Fig. 4.19, the closed-loop response becomes

$$\bar{y}(s) = \left[1 + h(s)g(s)g_c(s)\right]^{-1}\left[g(s)g_c(s)e^{-\alpha s}\bar{y}_d(s) + g_d(s)\bar{d}(s)\right] \tag{4.5.35}$$

and the time delay has been removed from the control loop characteristic equation,

$$1 + h(s)g(s)g_c(s) = 0 \tag{4.5.36}$$

so that higher controller gains are allowed before the system becomes unstable.

Moore et al. [68], working with a scalar state-space model, used the analytic solution of the modeling equation to predict the value of the state one delay time ahead. This analytical predictor was developed primarily for sampled data systems and hence included in its structure corrections for the effect of sam-

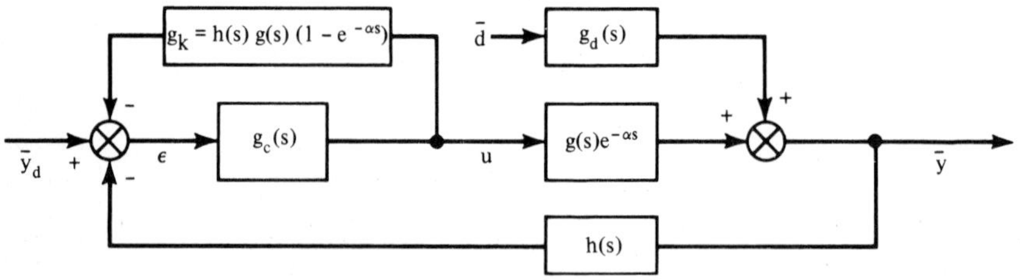

Figure 4.19 Single-loop control system including a Smith predictor for a system having a single delay.

pling, and the zero-order hold. It can be shown that the Smith and Moore predictors are equivalent [67].

Example 4.5.1 To illustrate these compensators, let us consider the control problem described in Example 4.1.2 and Fig. 4.2. Recall that the relation between the fraction of hot stream fed to the tank $u(t)$ and the tank outlet temperature $y(t)$ was given by

$$\theta \frac{dy}{dt} = (T_H - T_C)u(t - \alpha) - y \tag{4.1.14}$$

in the time domain and by the transfer function

$$\bar{y}(s) = \frac{(T_H - T_C)e^{-\alpha s}}{\theta s + 1}\bar{u}(s) \tag{4.1.15}$$

in the Laplace transform domain. If we assume a perfect measuring device $h = 1$ and a proportional feedback controller $g_c = k_c$, then the closed-loop transfer function, Eq. (4.5.33), takes the form

$$\bar{y}(s) = \left[1 + \frac{k_c(T_H - T_C)e^{-\alpha s}}{\theta s + 1}\right]^{-1}\left[\frac{k_c(T_H - T_C)e^{-\alpha s}}{\theta s + 1}\bar{y}_d(s)\right] \tag{4.5.37}$$

By application of the Smith predictor, Eq. (4.5.32),

$$g_k(s) = \frac{T_H - T_C}{\theta s + 1}(1 - e^{-\alpha s}) \tag{4.5.38}$$

the closed-loop response of the compensated system becomes

$$\bar{y}(s) = \left[1 + \frac{k_c(T_H - T_C)}{\theta s + 1}\right]^{-1}\left[\frac{k_c(T_H - T_C)e^{-\alpha s}}{\theta s + 1}\bar{y}_d(s)\right] \tag{4.5.39}$$

Note that the characteristic equation of the compensated system, Eq. (4.5.39),

$$1 + \frac{k_c(T_H - T_C)}{\theta s + 1} = 0 \tag{4.5.40}$$

has stable roots for all positive controller gains, so that stability is not a problem. By contrast, the characteristic equation for the uncompensated control system, Eq. (4.5.37),

$$1 + \frac{k_c(T_H - T_C)}{\theta s + 1}e^{-\alpha s} = 0 \tag{4.5.41}$$

has unstable roots for sufficiently large values of controller gain. For example, if $\theta = 10$, $\alpha = 2$, the uncompensated system becomes unstable for $k_c(T_H - T_C) > 7.04$.

The practical value of this compensator may be seen by comparing the control system response both with and without the compensator when Ziegler-Nichols controller tuning [i.e., $k_c(T_H - T_C) = 3.52$] is used with the

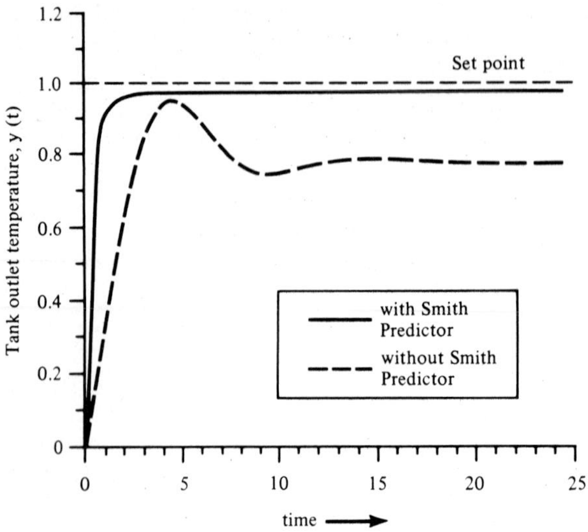

Figure 4.20 Response of heated mixing tank to set-point change in outlet temperature; dashed lines show the response without the Smith predictor, $k_c(T_H - T_C) = 3.52$; solid lines show the response with the Smith predictor, $k_c(T_H - T_C) = 30$.

uncompensated system and $k_c(T_H - T_C) = 30$ is used with the compensated system. The response of the system to a unit set point change may be seen in Fig. 4.20. Note the much slower response and much greater offset with the uncompensated system.

For the more general case of multivariable systems with multiple delays, the design of a compensator becomes more complex. Let us consider the general form of a multivariable transfer function such as described in Eqs. (4.5.1) to (4.5.3). Recall that the transfer function between outputs y and controls u is

$$\bar{\mathbf{y}}(s) = \mathbf{G}(s)\bar{\mathbf{u}}(s) \tag{4.5.1}$$

where $\mathbf{y}$ is an l vector of outputs and $\mathbf{u}$ is an m vector of controls. Similarly, the transfer function between the outputs and disturbances $\mathbf{d}$ is

$$\bar{\mathbf{y}}(s) = \mathbf{G}_d(s)\bar{\mathbf{d}}(s) \tag{4.5.42}$$

where $\mathbf{d}$ is a k vector of disturbances. The transfer functions $\mathbf{G}(s)$, $\mathbf{G}_d(s)$ are matrices of the form

$$\mathbf{G}(s) = \begin{bmatrix} g_{11} & g_{12} & \cdots & g_{1m} \\ g_{21} & \cdots & \cdots & \cdots \\ \cdots & \cdots & \cdots & \cdots \\ g_{l1} & \cdots & \cdots & g_{lm} \end{bmatrix} \quad \mathbf{G}_d(s) = \begin{bmatrix} g_{11}^d & g_{12}^d & \cdots & g_{1k}^d \\ g_{21}^d & \cdots & \cdots & \cdots \\ \cdots & \cdots & \cdots & \cdots \\ g_{l1}^d & \cdots & \cdots & g_{lk}^d \end{bmatrix} \tag{4.5.43}$$

In many practical applications where the transfer functions are fitted to experimental data, $g_{ij}(s)$ or $g_{ij}^d(s)$ have the rather simple form of Eq. (4.5.2). However, more complex transfer functions sometimes arise as illustrated below.

The block diagram for the system under conventional feedback control may be seen in Fig. 4.21, where $\mathbf{G}_c$ represents the feedback controller, $\mathbf{H}$ the output measurement device, and $\mathbf{y}_d$ the output set point. The closed-loop response for the conventional controller is then given by

$$\bar{\mathbf{y}}(s) = (\mathbf{I} + \mathbf{G}\mathbf{G}_c\mathbf{H})^{-1}\left[\mathbf{G}\mathbf{G}_c\bar{\mathbf{y}}_d(s) + \mathbf{G}_d\bar{\mathbf{d}}(s)\right] \tag{4.5.44}$$

in the Laplace domain. In the absence of time delays, there are many multivariable control design procedures available (see Chap. 3) for choosing the elements $\mathbf{G}_c$ in order to achieve good control system performance. However, when there are multiple delays in the transfer function, as in Eq. (4.5.2), the choice of design algorithm is more limited. Thus it is advantageous to use time-delay compensation methods in combination with the conventional controller design methods of Chap. 3. These compensation techniques can largely eliminate the effects of the time delays and allow conventional multivariable controller design procedures to be used for systems with multiple time delays. The multidelay compensator can be formulated so as to apply in either a continuous time or in a discrete time (DDC) mode [67].

There are many different forms that linear systems with time delays may take. For constant delays, a general formulation for linear multivariable systems in the time domain is

$$\dot{\mathbf{x}} = \sum_i \mathbf{A}_i\mathbf{x}(t - \rho_i) + \sum_j \mathbf{B}_j\mathbf{u}(t - \beta_j) + \sum_k \mathbf{D}_k\mathbf{d}(t - \delta_k) \tag{4.5.45}$$

$$\mathbf{y} = \sum_i \mathbf{C}_i\mathbf{x}(t - \gamma_i) + \sum_j \mathbf{E}_j\mathbf{u}(t - \varepsilon_j) \tag{4.5.46}$$

where $\mathbf{x}$ is an n vector of state variables and the ρ_i, β_j, δ_k, γ_i, ε_j are constant time delays. By taking Laplace transforms of Eqs. (4.5.45) and (4.5.46), transfer functions of the form

$$\bar{\mathbf{y}}(s) = \mathbf{G}(s)\bar{\mathbf{u}}(s) + \mathbf{G}_d\bar{\mathbf{d}}(s) \tag{4.5.47}$$

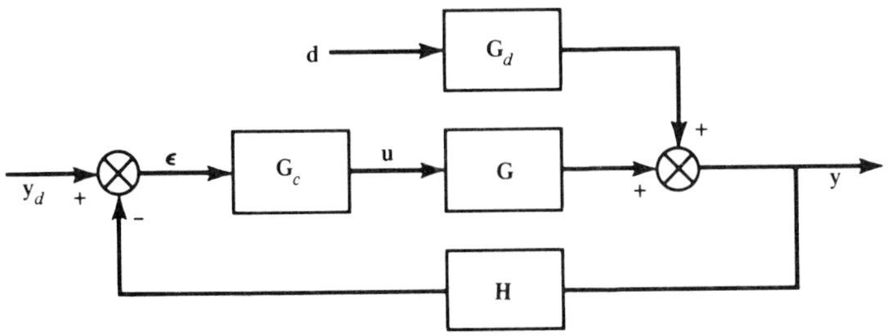

Figure 4.21 Block diagram for conventional feedback control of a multivariable system.

arise, where

$$\mathbf{G}(s) = \sum_j \mathbf{E}_j e^{-\varepsilon_j s} + \left[\left(\sum_i \mathbf{C}_i e^{-\gamma_i s}\right)\left(s\mathbf{I} - \sum_i \mathbf{A}_i e^{-\rho_i s}\right)^{-1}\right]\left(\sum_j \mathbf{B}_j e^{-\beta_j s}\right) \tag{4.5.48}$$

$$\mathbf{G}_d(s) = \left[\left(\sum_i \mathbf{C}_i e^{-\gamma_i s}\right)\left(s\mathbf{I} - \sum_i \mathbf{A}_i e^{-\rho_i s}\right)^{-1}\right]\left(\sum_k \mathbf{D}_k e^{-\delta_k s}\right) \tag{4.5.49}$$

Note that $\mathbf{G}(s)$ and $\mathbf{G}_d(s)$ in Eqs. (4.5.48) and (4.5.49) are very much more general than the more commonly encountered forms of $\mathbf{G}(s)$ and $\mathbf{G}_d(s)$ given by Eq. (4.5.2). However, in normal engineering practice, the usual modeling procedure is to carry out step, pulse, or frequency response measurements on the actual process to obtain an approximate transfer function model in the simpler form of Eqs. (4.5.2) and (4.5.42). The more complex forms [Eqs. (4.5.48) and (4.5.49)] usually arise when the model is formulated as differential equations and transformed to the Laplace domain.

For the case of multivariable systems in the general form [Eqs. (4.5.48) and (4.5.49)] that have multiple delays in the transfer functions $\mathbf{G}$, $\mathbf{G}_d$, $\mathbf{H}$, it is possible to design a compensator analogous to the Smith predictor which eliminates the time delays in the characteristic equation. As we show [67], this is *not equivalent* to predicting the output variable at some single time in the future but corresponds to the prediction of certain *state* variables at various specific times in the future. By analogy with the philosophy of the original Smith predictor, the corresponding multivariable multidelay compensator would have the structure shown in Fig. 4.22, where the compensator $\mathbf{G}_K$ could have many forms. Let us demonstrate that with the particular choice

$$\mathbf{G}_K = \mathbf{H}^*\mathbf{G}^* - \mathbf{H}\mathbf{G} \tag{4.5.50}$$

(where $\mathbf{H}^*$, $\mathbf{G}^*$ are the transfer functions $\mathbf{H}$, $\mathbf{G}$ without the delays), the compensator eliminates both the delays in the output variable signal sent to the

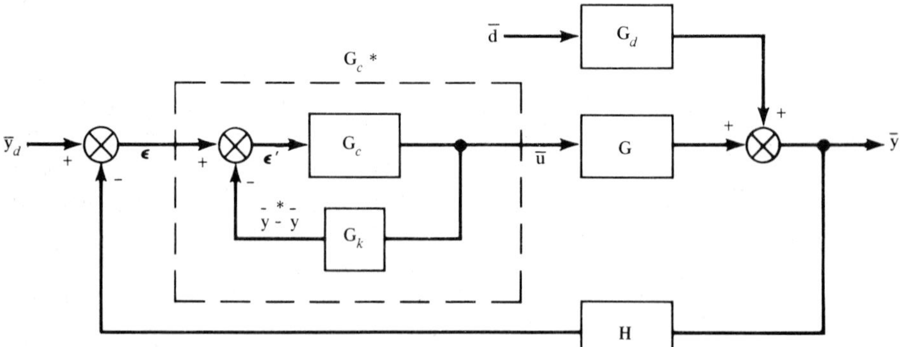

Figure 4.22 Block diagram of feedback control of a multivariable system with time-delay compensation.

controller and the delays in the characteristic equation. To see this, let us evaluate the inner loop $\mathbf{G}_c^*$ in Fig. 4.22. Here

$$\bar{\mathbf{u}} = \mathbf{G}_c^* \bar{\varepsilon}$$

or

$$\mathbf{G}_c^* = (\mathbf{I} + \mathbf{G}_c\mathbf{G}_k)^{-1}\mathbf{G}_c \tag{4.5.51}$$

Thus the entire transfer function including the multidelay compensator is

$$\bar{\mathbf{y}} = (\mathbf{I} + \mathbf{G}\mathbf{G}_c^*\mathbf{H})^{-1}(\mathbf{G}\mathbf{G}_c^*\bar{\mathbf{y}}_d + \mathbf{G}_d\bar{\mathbf{d}}) \tag{4.5.52}$$

One of the principal goals of time delay compensation is to eliminate the time delay from the characteristic equation of the closed-loop transfer function so that higher controller gains and standard multivariable controller design algorithms may be used. Let us show that the multidelay compensator noted above achieves this goal. Substituting Eqs. (4.5.5) and (4.5.51) into (4.5.52) yields

$$\bar{\mathbf{y}} = (\mathbf{I} + \mathbf{G}\mathbf{R}^{-1}\mathbf{G}_c\mathbf{H})^{-1}(\mathbf{G}\mathbf{R}^{-1}\mathbf{G}_c\bar{\mathbf{y}}_d + \mathbf{G}_d\bar{\mathbf{d}}) \tag{4.5.53}$$

where

$$\mathbf{R} = \mathbf{I} + \mathbf{G}_c(\mathbf{H}^*\mathbf{G}^* - \mathbf{H}\mathbf{G}) \tag{4.5.54}$$

Now it is easy to show that if $\mathbf{G}$ is square and nonsingular* then the following identity holds:

$$(\mathbf{I} + \mathbf{G}\mathbf{R}^{-1}\mathbf{G}_c\mathbf{H})^{-1} = \mathbf{G}(\mathbf{R} + \mathbf{G}_c\mathbf{H}\mathbf{G})^{-1}\mathbf{R}\mathbf{G}^{-1}$$

Now, from Eq. (4.5.54),

$$\mathbf{R} + \mathbf{G}_c\mathbf{H}\mathbf{G} = \mathbf{I} + \mathbf{G}_c\mathbf{H}^*\mathbf{G}^*$$

Thus Eq. (4.5.53) becomes

$$\bar{\mathbf{y}} = \mathbf{G}(\mathbf{I} + \mathbf{G}_c\mathbf{H}^*\mathbf{G}^*)^{-1}\mathbf{G}_c\bar{\mathbf{y}}_d + \mathbf{G}(\mathbf{I} + \mathbf{G}_c\mathbf{H}^*\mathbf{G}^*)^{-1}\mathbf{R}\mathbf{G}^{-1}\mathbf{G}_d\bar{\mathbf{d}} \tag{4.5.55}$$

Hence the stability of the closed-loop system including the compensator (Fig. 4.22) is determined by the characteristic equation

$$|\mathbf{I} + \mathbf{G}_c\mathbf{H}^*\mathbf{G}^*| = 0 \tag{4.5.56}$$

and the compensator has indeed removed the time delays from the characteristic equation. Thus the delays do not influence the closed-loop stability if the model matches the plant exactly. In practice, modeling errors usually allow some delays to remain in the system, so that one should be conservative in controller tuning. However, even with very conservative gains chosen for the compensated system, the control system response will be much better than in the case with no compensation.

It is useful to note that the Smith predictor [61] and the Alevisakis and Seborg predictor [62, 63] all become special cases of this general multidelay

* This is by no means restrictive, since we can always construct pseudo-inverses or generalized inverses of the matrix **G**. We note, however, that in most cases the number of inputs and outputs used in a feedback control scheme are equal; hence **G** is square.

compensator. It is also important to realize that any type of delay can be dealt with through the use of this compensator, even the very complex types shown in Eqs. (4.5.48) and (4.5.49). In addition, it can be shown that the feedback law resulting from using the multidelay compensator has exactly the same structure as that obtained from the optimal feedback controller (to be discussed below), and can therefore be made an optimal controller with proper tuning.

Let us demonstrate the multidelay compensator with some illustrative examples.

Example 4.5.2 Some physical interpretation of the effective action of this compensator is useful and can be illustrated by the following 2 × 2 example system with **H** = **H*** = **I** and

$$\mathbf{G} = \begin{bmatrix} a_{11}(s)e^{-\alpha_{11}s} & a_{12}(s)e^{-\alpha_{12}s} \\ a_{21}(s)e^{-\alpha_{21}s} & a_{22}(s)e^{-\alpha_{22}s} \end{bmatrix} \tag{4.5.57}$$

By definition,

$$\mathbf{G}^* = \begin{bmatrix} a_{11}(s) & a_{12}(s) \\ a_{21}(s) & a_{22}(s) \end{bmatrix} \tag{4.5.58}$$

and for $\mathbf{G}_c$ consisting of two proportional controllers,

$$\mathbf{G}_c = \begin{bmatrix} k_{c_{11}} & 0 \\ 0 & k_{c_{22}} \end{bmatrix}$$

then

$$\mathbf{I} + \mathbf{G}_c\mathbf{H}^*\mathbf{G}^* = \begin{bmatrix} 1 + k_{c_{11}}a_{11} & k_{c_{11}}a_{12} \\ k_{c_{22}}a_{21} & 1 + k_{c_{22}}a_{22} \end{bmatrix} \tag{4.5.59}$$

and the characteristic equation is

$$|\mathbf{I} + \mathbf{G}_c\mathbf{H}^*\mathbf{G}^*| = 1 + k_{c_{11}}a_{11} + k_{c_{22}}a_{22} + k_{c_{11}}k_{c_{22}}(a_{11}a_{22} - a_{12}a_{21}) = 0 \tag{4.5.60}$$

which contains no time delays.

Further, because of the compensator (see Fig. 4.22), the error signal fed to the controller is

$$\bar{\boldsymbol{\varepsilon}}' = \bar{\mathbf{y}}_d - \bar{\mathbf{y}}^*$$

Here

$$\bar{\mathbf{y}}^* = \mathbf{G}^*\bar{\mathbf{u}} \tag{4.5.61}$$

is the output variable without delays in **G**. Now it is interesting to note that $\bar{\mathbf{y}}^*$ does not correspond to the actual value of $\bar{\mathbf{y}}$ at any specific time, but is a totally fictitious value composed of certain predicted "state" variables. To illustrate, let us define variables x_{ij} by

$$\bar{x}_{ij}(s) = a_{ij}(s)e^{-\alpha_{ij}s}\bar{u}_j(s) \tag{4.5.62}$$

Thus the system with delays

$$\bar{\mathbf{y}}(s) = \mathbf{G}(s)\bar{\mathbf{u}}(s)$$

may be written

$$\bar{y}_1(s) = \bar{x}_{11}(s) + \bar{x}_{12}(s)$$
$$\bar{y}_2(s) = \bar{x}_{21}(s) + \bar{x}_{22}(s) \tag{4.5.63}$$

or in the time domain

$$y_1(t) = x_{11}(t) + x_{12}(t)$$
$$y_2(t) = x_{21}(t) + x_{22}(t) \tag{4.5.64}$$

By adding the compensator to the loop, the controller receives $\bar{\mathbf{y}}^*(s)$ defined by Eq. (4.5.61), which may be written as

$$\bar{y}_1^*(s) = e^{\alpha_{11}s}\bar{x}_{11}(s) + e^{\alpha_{12}s}\bar{x}_{12}(s)$$
$$\bar{y}_2^*(s) = e^{\alpha_{21}s}\bar{x}_{21}(s) + e^{\alpha_{22}s}\bar{x}_{22}(s) \tag{4.5.65}$$

where $\bar{x}_{ij}(s)$ is defined by Eq. (4.5.62). Thus in the time domain

$$y_1^*(t) = x_{11}(t + \alpha_{11}) + x_{12}(t + \alpha_{12})$$
$$y_2^*(t) = x_{21}(t + \alpha_{21}) + x_{22}(t + \alpha_{22}) \tag{4.5.66}$$

and the compensated output $\mathbf{y}^*(t)$ is composed of predictions of the "state" variables x_{ij}. Because the time delays in all the state variables are different, $\mathbf{y}^*(t)$ is a totally fictitious output never attained in reality. However, if the control system is stable, then $\mathbf{y}^* \to \mathbf{y}$ as $t \to \infty$ and the fictitious value $\mathbf{y}^*$ is a good "aiming point" for the controller.

Example 4.5.3 As a means of illustrating the case of state variable delays combined with output delays, consider the two-stage chemical reactor with recycle shown in Fig. 4.23. The irreversible reaction $A \to B$ with negligible heat effect is carried out in the two-stage reactor system. Reactor temperature is maintained constant so that only c_1 and c_2, the composition of product streams from the two reactors, need to be controlled. However, there is substantial analysis delay. The manipulated variables are the feed compositions to the two reactors c_{1f} and c_{2f}, and the process disturbance is an extra feed stream F_d whose composition c_d varies because it comes from another processing unit. The flow rates to the reactor system are fixed, and only the compositions vary. The state delay arises due to the transient lags in the recycle stream.

A material balance on the reactor train yields

$$V_1\frac{dc_1}{dt} = F_1c_{1f} + Rc_2(t - \alpha) + F_dc_d - (F_1 + R + F_d)c_1 - V_1k_1c_1$$

$$V_2\frac{dc_2}{dt} = (F_1 + R + F_d - F_{p_1})c_1 + F_2c_{2f} - (F_{p_2} + R)c_2 - V_2k_2c_2 \tag{4.5.67}$$

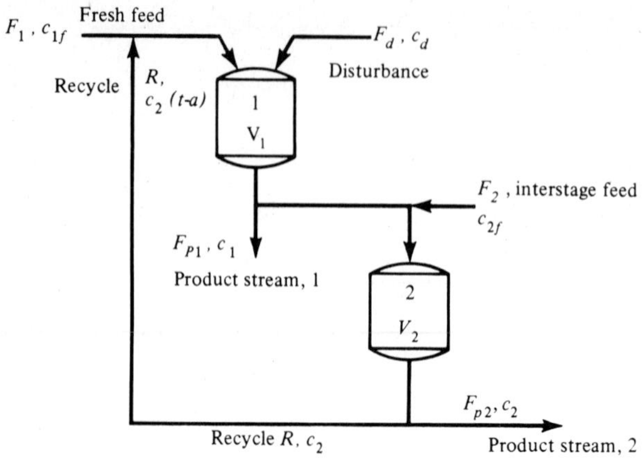

Figure 4.23 Two-stage chemical reactor train with delayed recycle.

where the second product stream F_{p_2} is given by

$$F_{p_2} = F_1 + F_d - F_{p_1} + F_2$$

Defining the variables

$$\theta_1 = \frac{V_1}{F_1 + R + F_d} \qquad \theta_2 = \frac{V_2}{F_{p_2} + R}$$

$$\lambda_R = \frac{R}{F_1 + R + F_d} \qquad \mu = \frac{F_{p_2} - F_2 + R}{F_{p_2} + R}$$

$$\lambda_d = \frac{F_d}{F_1 + R + F_d} \qquad \text{Da}_1 = k_1\theta \qquad \text{Da}_2 = k_2\theta_2$$

$$u_1 = c_{1f} - c_{1f_s} \qquad u_2 = c_{2f} - c_{2f_s}$$

$$x_1 = c_1 - c_{1s} \qquad x_2 = c_2 - c_{2s} \qquad d = c_d - c_{d_s}$$

(where c_{1f_s}, c_{2f_s}, c_{1s}, c_{2s}, c_{d_s} denote steady-state values) allows one to use vector-matrix notation, so that Eq. (4.5.67) becomes

$$\frac{d\mathbf{x}}{dt} = \mathbf{A}_0\mathbf{x}(t) + \mathbf{A}_1\mathbf{x}(t - \alpha) + \mathbf{Bu}(t) + \mathbf{D}d \tag{4.5.68}$$

$$\mathbf{y}(t) = \mathbf{x}(t)$$

$$\mathbf{y}_m(t) = \mathbf{Hx}(t) \tag{4.5.69}$$

where $y_m(t)$ is the measured output and

$$\mathbf{A}_0 = \begin{bmatrix} -\dfrac{1+\mathrm{Da}_1}{\theta_1} & 0 \\ \dfrac{\mu}{\theta_2} & -\dfrac{1+\mathrm{Da}_2}{\theta_2} \end{bmatrix} \qquad \mathbf{A}_1 = \begin{bmatrix} 0 & \dfrac{\lambda R}{\theta_1} \\ 0 & 0 \end{bmatrix}$$

$$\mathbf{H} = \begin{bmatrix} e^{-\tau_1 s} & 0 \\ 0 & e^{-\tau_2 s} \end{bmatrix} \tag{4.5.70}$$

$$\mathbf{B} = \begin{bmatrix} \dfrac{1+\lambda_R-\lambda_d}{\theta_1} & 0 \\ 0 & \dfrac{1-\mu}{\theta_2} \end{bmatrix} \qquad \mathbf{D} = \begin{bmatrix} \dfrac{\lambda_d}{\theta_1} \\ 0 \end{bmatrix}$$

Here τ_1 and τ_2 are the delays in analyzing c_1 and c_2, respectively. Taking Laplace transforms, one obtains a transfer function model of the form

$$\bar{\mathbf{y}}(s) = \mathbf{G}(s)\bar{\mathbf{u}}(s) + \mathbf{G}_d(s)\bar{\mathbf{d}}(s) \tag{4.5.47}$$

or, since what we observe is $\bar{\mathbf{y}}_m$,

$$\bar{\mathbf{y}}_m(s) = \mathbf{H}(s)\mathbf{G}(s)\bar{\mathbf{u}}(s) + \mathbf{H}(s)\mathbf{G}_d(s)\bar{\mathbf{d}}(s) \tag{4.5.71}$$

where

$$\mathbf{G}(s) = \frac{\begin{bmatrix} \dfrac{1-\lambda_R-\lambda_d}{\theta_1}\left(s+\dfrac{1+\mathrm{Da}_2}{\theta_2}\right) & \dfrac{\lambda_R(1-\mu)}{\theta_1\theta_2}e^{-\alpha s} \\ \dfrac{1-\lambda_R-\lambda_d}{\theta_1\theta_2}\mu & \dfrac{1-\mu}{\theta_2}\left(s+\dfrac{1+\mathrm{Da}_1}{\theta_1}\right) \end{bmatrix}}{s^2+\left(\dfrac{1+\mathrm{Da}_1}{\theta_1}+\dfrac{1+\mathrm{Da}_2}{\theta_2}\right)s+\dfrac{(1+\mathrm{Da}_1)(1+\mathrm{Da}_2)}{\theta_1\theta_2}-\dfrac{\lambda_R\mu e^{-\alpha s}}{\theta_1\theta_2}} \tag{4.5.72}$$

$$\mathbf{G}_d(s) = \frac{\begin{bmatrix} \dfrac{\lambda_d}{\theta_1} & \left(s+\dfrac{1+\mathrm{Da}_1}{\theta_2}\right) \\ \dfrac{\lambda_d}{\theta_1} & \dfrac{\mu}{\theta_2} \end{bmatrix}}{s^2+\left(\dfrac{1+\mathrm{Da}_1}{\theta_1}+\dfrac{1+\mathrm{Da}_2}{\theta_2}\right)s+\dfrac{(1+\mathrm{Da}_1)(1+\mathrm{Da}_2)}{\theta_1\theta_2}-\dfrac{\lambda_R\mu e^{-\alpha s}}{\theta_1\theta_2}} \tag{4.5.73}$$

and if we let

$$\mathbf{G}_0(s) = \mathbf{H}(s)\mathbf{G}(s) \qquad \mathbf{G}_{d0}(s) = \mathbf{H}(s)\mathbf{G}_d(s)$$

then the working transfer functions are

$$\mathbf{G}_0(s) = \frac{\begin{bmatrix} \dfrac{1-\lambda_R-\lambda_d}{\theta_1}\left(s+\dfrac{1+\mathrm{Da}_2}{\theta_2}\right)e^{-\tau_1 s} & \dfrac{\lambda_R(1-\mu)}{\theta_1\theta_2}e^{-(\tau_1+\alpha)s} \\ \dfrac{(1-\lambda_R-\lambda_d)\mu e^{-\tau_2 s}}{\theta_1\theta_2} & \dfrac{1-\mu}{\theta_2}\left(s+\dfrac{1+\mathrm{Da}_1}{\theta_1}\right)e^{-\tau_2 s} \end{bmatrix}}{s^2+\left(\dfrac{1+\mathrm{Da}_1}{\theta_1}+\dfrac{1+\mathrm{Da}_2}{\theta_2}\right)s+\dfrac{(1+\mathrm{Da}_1)(1+\mathrm{Da}_2)}{\theta_1\theta_2}-\dfrac{\lambda_R\mu e^{-\alpha s}}{\theta_1\theta_2}} \tag{4.5.74}$$

$$\mathbf{G}_{d0}(s) = \frac{\begin{bmatrix} \dfrac{\lambda_d}{\theta_1}\left(s+\dfrac{1+\mathrm{Da}_2}{\theta_2}\right)e^{-\tau_1 s} \\ \dfrac{\lambda_d}{\theta_1}\dfrac{\mu}{\theta_2}e^{-\tau_2 s} \end{bmatrix}}{s^2+\left(\dfrac{1+\mathrm{Da}_1}{\theta_1}+\dfrac{1+\mathrm{Da}_2}{\theta_2}\right)s+\dfrac{(1+\mathrm{Da}_1)(1+\mathrm{Da}_2)}{\theta_1\theta_2}-\dfrac{\lambda_R\mu e^{-\alpha s}}{\theta_1\theta_2}} \tag{4.5.75}$$

Now, using the multidelay compensator shown in Fig. 4.22, $\mathbf{H}^*$ becomes $\mathbf{I}$ and

$$\mathbf{G}^* = \mathbf{G}_0^* = \frac{\begin{bmatrix} \dfrac{1-\lambda_R-\lambda_d}{\theta_1}\left(s+\dfrac{1+\mathrm{Da}_2}{\theta_2}\right) & \dfrac{\lambda_R(1-\mu)}{\theta_1\theta_2} \\ \dfrac{(1-\lambda_R-\lambda_d)\mu}{\theta_1\theta_2} & \dfrac{1-\mu}{\theta_2}\left(s+\dfrac{1+\mathrm{Da}_1}{\theta_1}\right) \end{bmatrix}}{s^2+\left(\dfrac{1+\mathrm{Da}_1}{\theta_1}+\dfrac{1+\mathrm{Da}_2}{\theta_2}\right)s+\dfrac{(1+\mathrm{Da}_1)(1+\mathrm{Da}_2)}{\theta_1\theta_2}-\dfrac{\lambda_R\mu}{\theta_1\theta_2}} \tag{4.5.76}$$

and by choosing two single-loop proportional controllers for $\mathbf{G}_c$, i.e.,

$$\mathbf{G}_c = \begin{bmatrix} k_{c_{11}} & 0 \\ 0 & k_{c_{22}} \end{bmatrix} \tag{4.5.77}$$

we may compare the control system performance both with and without the compensator. To illustrate, let us choose

$\theta_1 = 1 \quad \theta_2 = 1 \quad \mathrm{Da}_1 = 1 \quad \mathrm{Da}_2 = 1 \quad \lambda_R = 0.5 \quad \lambda_d = 0.1$

$\mu = 0.5$

with time delays $\alpha = 1$, $\tau_1 = 3$, $\tau_2 = 2$.

In this case

$$\mathbf{G}_0(s) = \mathbf{H}(s)\mathbf{G}(s) = \begin{bmatrix} \dfrac{0.4(s+2)e^{-3s}}{(s+2)^2 - 0.25e^{-s}} & \dfrac{0.25e^{-4s}}{(s+2)^2 - 0.25e^{-s}} \\ \dfrac{0.2e^{-2s}}{(s+2)^2 - 0.25e^{-s}} & \dfrac{0.5(s+2)e^{-2s}}{(s+2)^2 - 0.25e^{-s}} \end{bmatrix}$$

$$\mathbf{G}_0^*(s) = \mathbf{H}^*(s)\mathbf{G}^*(s) = \begin{bmatrix} \dfrac{0.4(s+2)}{(s+2.5)(s+1.5)} & \dfrac{0.25}{(s+2.5)(s+1.5)} \\ \dfrac{0.2}{(s+2.5)(s+1.5)} & \dfrac{0.5(s+2)}{(s+2.5)(s+1.5)} \end{bmatrix}$$

$$\mathbf{G}_d(s) = \begin{bmatrix} \dfrac{0.1(s+2)e^{-3s}}{(s+2)^2 - 0.25e^{-s}} \\ \dfrac{0.05e^{-2s}}{(s+2)^2 - 0.25e^{-s}} \end{bmatrix} \tag{4.5.78}$$

so that the closed-loop system *without the compensator* is

$$\mathbf{y} = (\mathbf{I} + \mathbf{G}\mathbf{G}_c\mathbf{H})^{-1}\mathbf{G}\mathbf{G}_c\mathbf{y}_d + (\mathbf{I} + \mathbf{G}\mathbf{G}_c\mathbf{H})^{-1}\mathbf{G}_d\mathbf{d} \tag{4.5.79}$$

or equivalently, since $\mathbf{y}_m$ is observed and $\mathbf{y}_m = \mathbf{H}\mathbf{y}$,

$$\mathbf{y}_m = (\mathbf{I} + \mathbf{H}\mathbf{G}\mathbf{G}_c)^{-1}\mathbf{H}\mathbf{G}\mathbf{G}_c\mathbf{y}_d + (\mathbf{I} + \mathbf{H}\mathbf{G}\mathbf{G}_c)^{-1}\mathbf{H}\mathbf{G}_d\mathbf{d}$$

or in terms of $\mathbf{G}_0$, $\mathbf{G}_{d0}$,

$$\mathbf{y}_m = (\mathbf{I} + \mathbf{G}_0\mathbf{G}_c)^{-1}\mathbf{G}_0\mathbf{G}_c\mathbf{y}_d + (\mathbf{I} + \mathbf{G}_0\mathbf{G}_c)^{-1}\mathbf{G}_{d0}\mathbf{d} \tag{4.5.80}$$

Now *with the compensator* the closed-loop expressions are

$$\mathbf{y} = \mathbf{G}(\mathbf{I} + \mathbf{G}_c\mathbf{H}^*\mathbf{G}^*)^{-1}\mathbf{G}_c\mathbf{y}_d + \mathbf{G}(\mathbf{I} + \mathbf{G}_c\mathbf{H}^*\mathbf{G}^*)^{-1}\mathbf{R}\mathbf{G}^{-1}\mathbf{G}_d\mathbf{d}$$

or in terms of $\mathbf{G}_0$, $\mathbf{G}_{d0}$,

$$\mathbf{y}_m = \mathbf{G}_0(\mathbf{I} + \mathbf{G}_c\mathbf{G}_0^*)^{-1}\mathbf{G}_c\mathbf{y}_d + \mathbf{G}_0(\mathbf{I} + \mathbf{G}_c\mathbf{G}_0^*)\mathbf{R}\mathbf{G}^{-1}\mathbf{G}_d\mathbf{d} \tag{4.5.81}$$

where

$$\mathbf{R} = \mathbf{I} + \mathbf{G}_c(\mathbf{G}_0^* - \mathbf{G}_0)$$

The control system performance for set-point changes $y_{1d} = 0.5$, $y_{2d} = 1.0$ is shown in Fig. 4.24. The dashed lines represent the performance without the compensator for controller gains $k_{c_{11}} = 3.0$, $k_{c_{22}} = 3.5$. In the neighborhood of $k_{c_{11}} = 5.0$ serious instabilities set in due to the presence of the time delays.

The application of the multidelay compensator permits the use of higher controller gains $k_{c_{11}} = k_{c_{22}} = 20.0$, and as seen in Fig. 4.24 (solid lines), greatly improved performance is obtained.

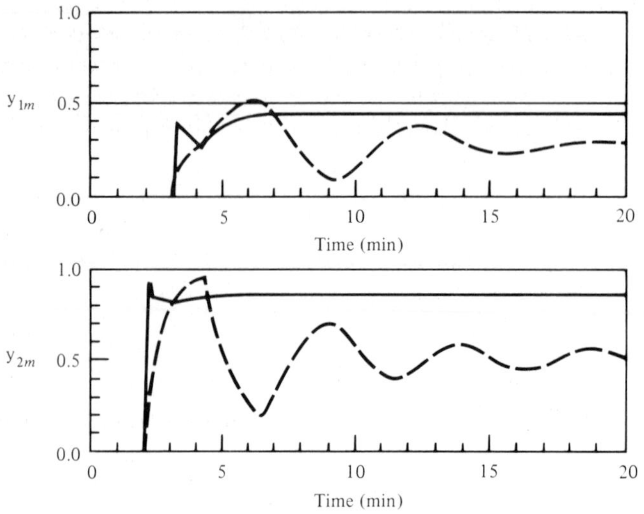

Figure 4.24 Chemical reactor response to set-point changes. Dashed lines: proportional control without compensator; solid lines: proportional control with compensator.

In Fig. 4.25 the response to a step input in disturbance $d = 5.0$ is shown. The dashed lines show the response without the compensator. Again, controller gains $k_{c_{11}} = 3.0$, $k_{c_{22}} = 3.5$ are used, these being the largest before the onset of serious instabilities. The continuous lines show the performance using the compensator with gains $k_{c_{11}} = 45.0$, $k_{c_{22}} = 20.0$.

This example serves to illustrate the improvements in control with the multidelay compensator for a problem having both state and measurement delays.

Example 4.5.4 To illustrate the effects of multiple delays in the control and output variables, let us consider the binary distillation column studied by Wood and Berry [69], Shah and Fisher [70], and Meyer et al. [71, 72]. The column, shown in schematic in Fig. 4.26, was used for methanol-water separation and was found to be well modeled by the transfer function model

$$\bar{\mathbf{y}}(s) = \mathbf{G}(s)\bar{\mathbf{u}}(s) + \mathbf{G}_d(s)\bar{d}(s) \tag{4.5.47}$$

where, in terms of deviation variables,

y_1 = overhead mole fraction methanol

y_2 = bottoms mole fraction methanol

u_1 = overhead reflux flow rate

u_2 = bottom steam flow rate

d = column feed flow rate

After pulse testing of the column, the transfer functions determined from

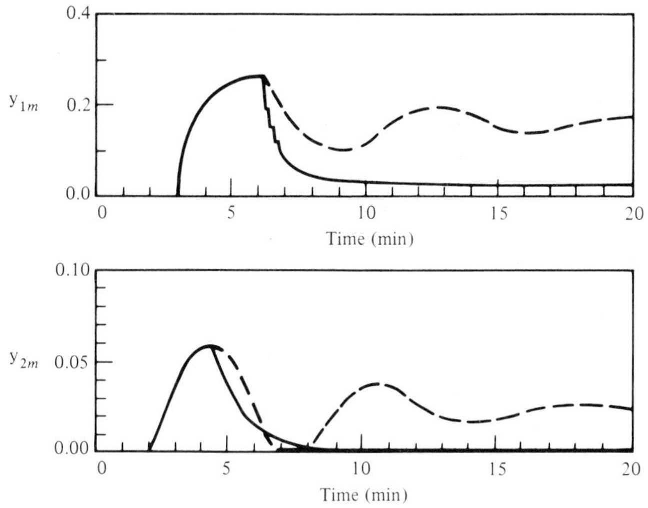

Figure 4.25 Chemical reactor response to a step change disturbance. Dashed lines: proportional control without compensator; solid lines: proportional control with compensator.

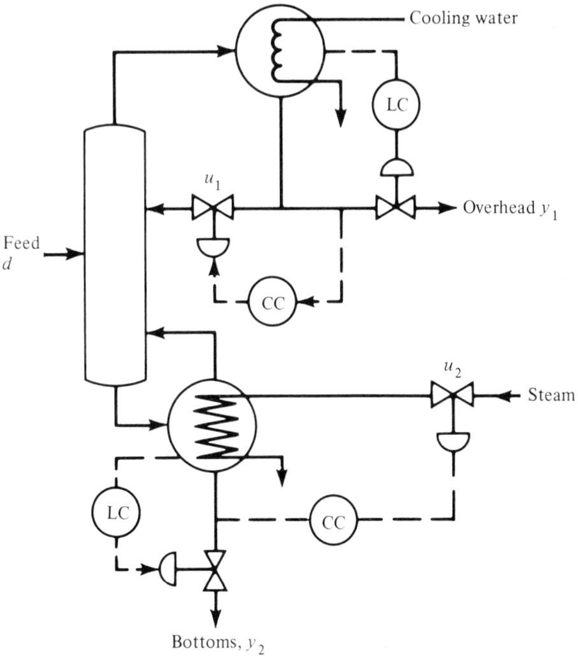

Figure 4.26 Schematic diagram of the methanol distillation column with conventional two-point column control system, Wood and Berry [69].

the data were [69]

$$\mathbf{G}(s) = \begin{bmatrix} \dfrac{12.8e^{-s}}{16.7s + 1} & \dfrac{-18.9e^{-3s}}{21.0s + 1} \\ \dfrac{6.6e^{-7s}}{10.9s + 1} & \dfrac{-19.4e^{-3s}}{14.4s + 1} \end{bmatrix}$$

$$G_d(s) = \begin{bmatrix} \dfrac{3.8e^{-8.1s}}{14.9s + 1} \\ \dfrac{4.9e^{-3.4s}}{13.2s + 1} \end{bmatrix} \tag{4.5.82}$$

where the time constants and time delays are given in minutes.* Here we take $\mathbf{H} = \mathbf{H}^* = \mathbf{I}$ because any measurement delays may be included in $\mathbf{G}$ for this problem.

We shall illustrate the performance of the system under conventional PI control (Fig. 4.26) both with and without the compensator. The steady-state values for the overhead and bottoms compositions are taken to be 96.25 percent and 0.5 percent methanol, respectively, (see [69]) for this simulation. With the "tuned" conventional controller settings which were originally used experimentally by Wood and Berry [69], reported in their Table 1,† i.e.,

Overhead		Bottoms	
K_p	K_I	K_p	K_I
0.20	0.045	−0.040	−0.015

the control system response is shown in dashed lines in Figs. 4.27 and 4.28. Figure 4.27 is the response to the same positive disturbance, 0.34 lb/min in feed flow rate, as that used in the experimental study. Figure 4.28 is the response to the negative disturbance, −0.36 lb/min in feed flow rate.

This simulated response is seen to be essentially identical to the experimental response reported by Wood and Berry [69] for conventional control. Larger controller gains cannot be taken because the characteristic equation

$$\begin{aligned} |\mathbf{I} + \mathbf{G}\mathbf{G}_c| = {} & 55{,}045s^4 + 14{,}698s^3 + 1219s^2 + 62s + 1 \\ & + (228.9s^2 + 31.9s + 1)\left[g_{c_1}(12 + 172.8s)e^{-s} \right. \\ & \left. - g_{c_2}(19.4 + 323.8s)e^{-3s} - 232.8g_{c_1}g_{c_2}e^{-4s} \right] \\ & + 124.7(240.5s^2 + 31.1s + 1)g_{c_1}g_{c_2}e^{-10s} = 0 \end{aligned}$$

* The time unit of minutes was used here in place of the appropriate SI unit (seconds) to avoid confusing the reader who may refer to the original articles from which this example was taken.

† Private communications with Professor R. K. Wood confirmed that the signs of the controller gains reported in the original publication should be corrected as shown here.

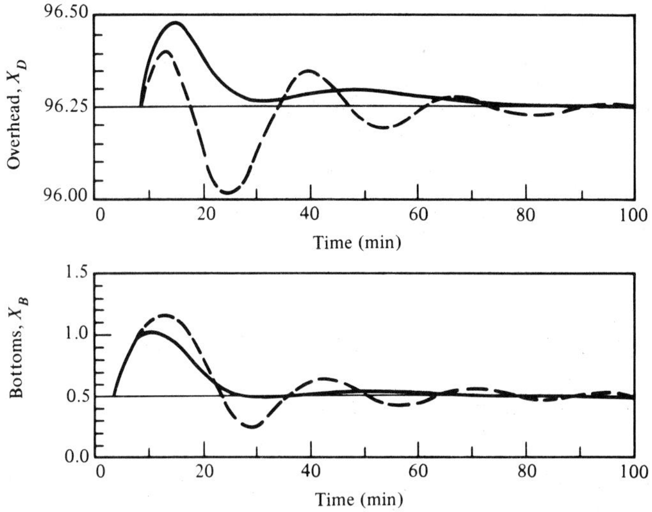

Figure 4.27 Comparison of column performance with and without the multidelay compensator (positive feed-rate disturbance). Dashed line: without compensator; solid line: with compensator.

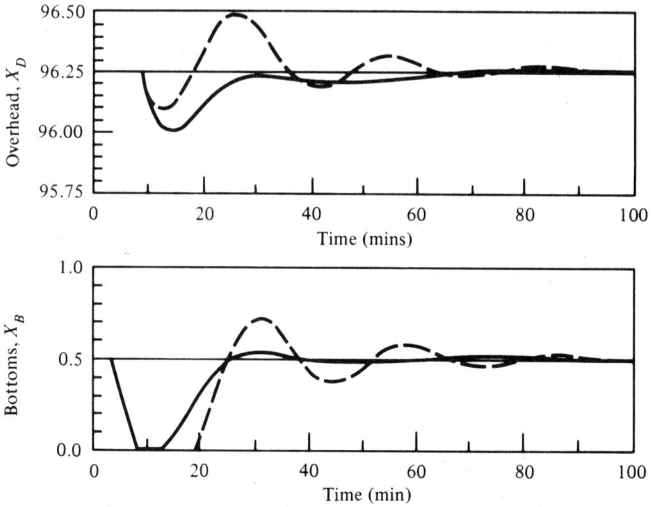

Figure 4.28 Comparison of column performance with and without the multidelay compensator (negative feed-rate disturbance). Dashed line: without compensator; solid line: with compensator.

contains time delays which cause stability problems. Here we have taken

$$\mathbf{G}_c = \begin{bmatrix} g_{c_{11}} & 0 \\ 0 & g_{c_{22}} \end{bmatrix} \tag{4.5.83}$$

with

$$g_{c_{ii}} = K_{p_i} + \frac{K_{I_i}}{s}$$

in keeping with the notation of Wood and Berry.

When the multidelay compensator is applied to the control loop as in Fig. 4.22, with

$$\mathbf{G}^* = \begin{bmatrix} \dfrac{12.8}{16.7s + 1} & \dfrac{-18.9}{21.0s + 1} \\ \dfrac{6.6}{10.9s + 1} & \dfrac{-19.4}{14.4s + 1} \end{bmatrix}$$

and $\mathbf{G}_c$ as in Eq. (4.5.83), the characteristic equation becomes

$$\begin{aligned} |\mathbf{I} + \mathbf{G}_c\mathbf{G}^*| = {} & 55{,}045s^4 + (14{,}698s + 39{,}553g_{c_{11}} - 74{,}117g_{c_{22}})s^3 \\ & + (1219 + 8259g_{c_{11}} - 14{,}769g_{c_{22}} - 23{,}290g_{c_{11}}g_{c_{22}})s^2 \\ & + (62 + 555g_{c_{11}} - 942g_{c_{22}} - 3546g_{c_{11}}g_{c_{22}})s \\ & + (1 - 108g_{c_{11}}g_{c_{22}}) = 0 \end{aligned}$$

which contains no time delays. The improved response obtained with the compensator is shown as continuous lines in Figs. 4.27 and 4.28 for precisely the same controller settings specified in the table. Apart from noting that there are no serious oscillations, observe that the bottoms composition benefits more from the use of the multidelay compensator. That this should indeed be so can be readily seen by merely inspecting the transfer function $\mathbf{G}(s)$ and noting that the time delays associated with the bottoms are substantially larger than those associated with the overhead.

One interesting feature of this distillation column is the appreciable amount of interactions existing between the system variables. This is due to the presence of off-diagonal elements in $\mathbf{G}(s)$, with the result that y_1 is affected by u_2, and y_2 by u_1. The system performance is most affected by this coupling when set-point changes are made. For example, when a set-point change from 96.25 to 97.0 is made in the overhead composition, the multidelay compensated system responds as shown in dashed lines in Fig. 4.29. The interesting point to note is the resulting effect on the bottoms composition. Were there no coupling between the overheads and bottoms compositions, such a set-point change would not have perturbed the bottoms composition.

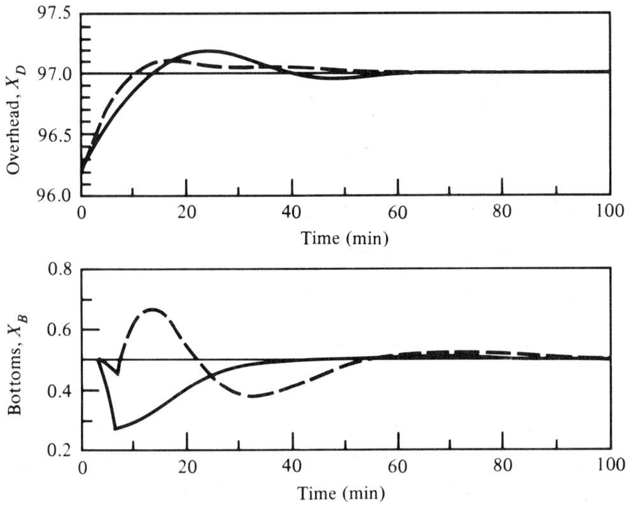

Figure 4.29 Column response to a positive set-point change in overhead composition using the multidelay compensator. Dashed line: without steady-state decoupling; solid line: with steady-state decoupling.

To illustrate how the multidelay compensator may be used in conjunction with the conventional multivariable control design techniques of Chap. 3, we shall attempt to eliminate some of the interaction effects through the use of steady-state decoupling along with the multidelay compensator. This combined control scheme is illustrated in Fig. 4.29 by the solid lines. Note the improvements in the bottoms response resulting from this very simple additional design change.

Optimal Control of Time-Delay Systems

Optimal control is one approach to controller design which can be used either in an open-loop fashion (such as in start-up) or as a closed-loop feedback control system. Here we shall outline the essence of optimal control theory and present some examples to demonstrate how the control schemes might be implemented. General fundamental results on the optimal control of time-delay systems are discussed in [60, 73]; however, here we shall discuss only the case for *constant time delays*, i.e., for the system

$$\frac{d\mathbf{x}(t)}{dt} = \mathbf{f}(\mathbf{x}(t), \mathbf{x}(t-\alpha_1), \ldots, \mathbf{x}(t-\alpha_\delta), \mathbf{u}(t), \mathbf{u}(t-\beta_1), \ldots, \mathbf{u}(t-\beta_\mu)) \tag{4.5.19}$$

$$\begin{aligned} \mathbf{x}(t) &= \boldsymbol{\phi}(t) \qquad -\alpha_\delta \le t \le 0 \\ \mathbf{u}(t) &= \boldsymbol{\Phi}(t) \qquad -\beta_\mu \le t \le 0 \end{aligned} \tag{4.5.22}$$

where the α_i, $i = 1, 2, \ldots, \delta$, and β_j, $j = 1, 2, \ldots, \mu$ are constant state and control delays, respectively. The maximum principle, which provides necessary conditions for optimality, takes the following form:

Theorem For the optimal control problem given by the system equations (4.5.19) to (4.5.22) with the objective

$$I = G(\mathbf{x}(t_f)) + \int_0^{t_f} F(\mathbf{x}(t), \mathbf{x}(t - \alpha_1), \ldots, \mathbf{x}(t - \alpha_\delta), \mathbf{u}(t),$$

$$\mathbf{u}(t - \beta_1), \ldots, \mathbf{u}(t - \beta_\mu))\, dt \tag{4.5.84}$$

to be maximized, and where $\mathbf{u}(t)$ belongs to a constraint set Ω, the optimal control $\bar{\mathbf{u}}(t)$ must satisfy the conditions

$$\frac{\partial H(t)}{\partial \mathbf{u}(t)} + \sum_{j=1}^{\mu} \left[\frac{\partial H(\tau)}{\partial \mathbf{u}(\tau - \beta_j)} \right]_{\tau = t + \beta_j} = \mathbf{0} \qquad 0 < t < t_f - \beta_\mu$$

$$\frac{\partial H(t)}{\partial \mathbf{u}(t)} + \sum_{j=1}^{\mu - k} \left[\frac{\partial H(\tau)}{\partial \mathbf{u}(\tau - \beta_j)} \right]_{\tau = t + \beta_j} = \mathbf{0} \qquad t_f - \beta_{\mu+1-k} < t < t_f - \beta_{\mu-k}$$

$$\frac{\partial H(t)}{\partial \mathbf{u}(t)} = \mathbf{0} \qquad t_f - \beta_1 < t < t_f \tag{4.5.85}$$

for $\bar{\mathbf{u}}(t)$ in the interior of Ω (**u** unconstrained), while at constraints the quantities

$$H(t) + \sum_{j=1}^{\mu} H(t + \beta_j) \qquad 0 < t < t_f - \beta_\mu$$

$$H(t) + \sum_{j=1}^{\mu - k} H(t + \beta_j) \qquad \begin{array}{l} t_f - \beta_{\mu+1-k} < t < t_f - \beta_{\mu-k} \\ k = 1, 2, \ldots, \mu - 1 \end{array}$$

$$H(t) \qquad t_f - \beta_1 < t < t_f \tag{4.5.86}$$

must be a maximum with respect to $\mathbf{u}(t)$. In addition, it is necessary that this last maximum condition hold even on unconstrained portions of the control trajectory. The Hamiltonian is given by

$$H(t) = F + \boldsymbol{\lambda}^T(t)\mathbf{f} \tag{4.5.87}$$

and the adjoint variables $\boldsymbol{\lambda}$ must satisfy:

$$\frac{d\boldsymbol{\lambda}^T(t)}{dt} = \begin{cases} -\left\{\dfrac{\partial H(t)}{\partial \mathbf{x}(t)} + \displaystyle\sum_{i=1}^{\delta}\left[\dfrac{\partial H(\tau)}{\partial \mathbf{x}(\tau - \alpha_i)}\right]_{\tau = t+\alpha_i}\right\} & 0 < t < t_f - \alpha_\delta \\ -\left\{\dfrac{\partial H(t)}{\partial \mathbf{x}(t)} + \displaystyle\sum_{i=1}^{\delta-k}\left[\dfrac{\partial H(\tau)}{\partial \mathbf{x}(\tau - \alpha_i)}\right]_{\tau = t+\alpha_i}\right\} & \begin{array}{l} t_f - \alpha_{\delta+1-k} \\ \quad < t < t_f - \alpha_{\delta-k} \\ k = 1, 2, \ldots, \delta - 1 \end{array} \\ -\dfrac{\partial H}{\partial \mathbf{x}(t)} & t_f - \alpha_1 < t < t_f \end{cases} \tag{4.5.88}$$

$$\boldsymbol{\lambda}(t_f - \alpha_i^{+}) = \boldsymbol{\lambda}(t_f - \alpha_i^{-}) \qquad i = 1, 2, \ldots, \delta \tag{4.5.89}$$

$$\boldsymbol{\lambda}(t_f - \beta_j^{+}) = \boldsymbol{\lambda}(t_f - \beta_j^{-}) \qquad j = 1, 2, \ldots, \mu \tag{4.5.90}$$

and for $\mathbf{x}(t_f)$ unspecified,

$$\boldsymbol{\lambda}^T(t_f) = \frac{\partial G}{\partial \mathbf{x}(t_f)} \tag{4.5.91}$$

The proof of this maximum principle and more general results may be found in [73]. Let us now proceed to illustrate the application of control vector iteration computational procedures through an example problem.

Example 4.5.5* To demonstrate the application of the theory we have developed, we shall treat an example of the open-loop control of a continuous stirred tank reactor (CSTR). Suppose we would like to optimally move from one steady state to another in the CSTR shown in Fig. 4.30. The describing equations are

$$V\frac{dc}{dt'} = u_3'(c_f - c) - K_0 V e^{-E/RT}\hat{c}c \qquad c(0) = c_0 \tag{4.5.92}$$

$$V\frac{dc}{dt'} = (1-\gamma)u_2'(t' - \beta_1') + \gamma u_2'(t') - \hat{c}u_3' \qquad \hat{c}(0) = \hat{c}_0 \tag{4.5.93}$$

$$\rho C_p V\frac{dT}{dt'} = \rho C_p u_3'(T_f - T) + (-\Delta H)K_0 V e^{-E/RT}\hat{c}c - \{hA + u_1'(t')[T(t' - \alpha_1') - T_s]\}(T - T_c)$$
$$T(0) = T_0 \tag{4.5.94}$$

where it is assumed that:

1. The chemical reaction $A_1 \rightarrow A_2$ is first-order in both the catalyst $\hat{c}$ and reactant c.

* This example is taken from [73] with permission of Pergamon Press Ltd.

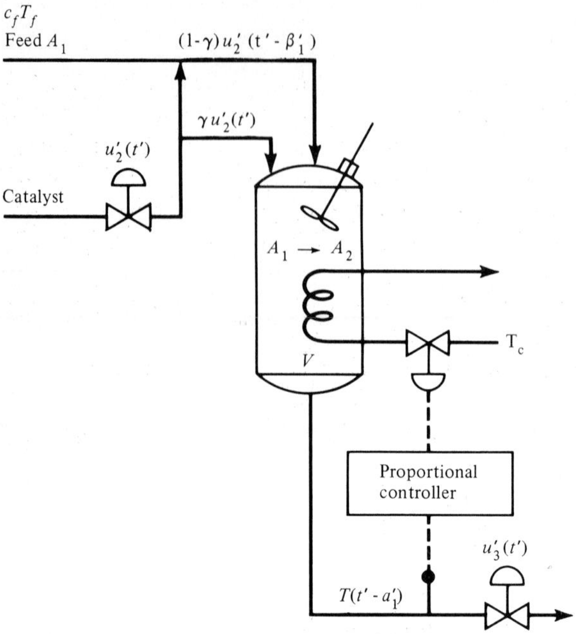

Figure 4.30 The CSTR system [73]. (*Reproduced by permission of Pergamon Press Ltd.*)

2. The catalyst feed u_2' is made up of two parts (see Fig. 4.30): a fraction γ entering the reactor directly, and $(1-\gamma)$ mixed with the feed a time β_1' upstream of the reactor.
3. The temperature is controlled by a feedback controller which uses continuous temperature measurements at time $t' - \alpha_1'$ to adjust the coolant flow rate, where $u_1'(t')$ is a time-variable proportional gain.
4. The molar feed rate of catalyst u_2' is negligible compared with the reactants feed rate $u_3' c_f$, so that the physical properties are unaffected by catalyst addition.

If we wish to move from the state $(c_0, \hat{c}_0, T_0)$ to $(c_s, \hat{c}_s, T_s)$, then it is convenient to define the dimensionless variables

$$
\begin{gathered}
x_1 = \frac{c - c_s}{c_s} \qquad x_2 = \frac{\hat{c} - \hat{c}_s}{\hat{c}_s} \qquad x_3 = \frac{T - T_s}{T_s} \qquad \theta_h = \frac{V}{F_s} \\
t = \frac{t'}{\theta_h} \qquad u_1 = \frac{u_1' T_s}{F_s} \qquad u_2 = \frac{u_2'}{\hat{c}_s F_s} \qquad u_3 = \frac{u_3'}{F_s} \qquad (4.5.95) \\
\Theta = \frac{E}{RT_s} \qquad \beta_1 = \frac{\beta_1'}{\theta_h} \qquad \alpha_1 = \frac{\alpha_1'}{\theta_h} \qquad Q = \frac{hA}{\rho C_p F_s} \\
P = K_0 \theta_h e^{-\Theta} \hat{c}_s \qquad J = \frac{(-\Delta H)\hat{c}_s}{\rho C_p T_s} \qquad x_{3c} = \frac{T_c - T_s}{T_s}
\end{gathered}
$$

so that

$$\frac{dx_1}{dt} = -u_3 x_1 - P\left[(1 + x_1)(1 + x_2)e^{\Theta x_3/(x_3+1)} - u_3\right] \qquad x_1(0) = x_{10} \tag{4.5.96}$$

$$\frac{dx_2}{dt} = (1 - \gamma)u_2(t - \beta_1) + \gamma u_2(t) - u_3(x_2 + 1) \qquad x_2(0) = x_{20} \tag{4.5.97}$$

$$\frac{dx_3}{dt} = -u_3 x_3 + JP\left[(1 + x_1)(1 + x_2)e^{x_3\theta/(1+x_3)} - u_3\right]$$
$$- Q\left[x_3(t) - x_{3c}(1 - u_3)\right] - u_1(t)x_3(t - \alpha_1)\left[x_3(t) - x_{3c}\right]$$

$$x_3(0) = x_{30} \tag{4.5.98}$$

We shall apply our maximum principle to this system so that we find the controls which minimize the functional

$$I = \int_0^{t_f} \left[x_1^2 + x_2^2 + x_3^2 + \eta_2(u_2 - 1)^2 + \eta_3(u_3 - 1)^2\right] dt \tag{4.5.99}$$

subject to the constraints

$$u_{i*} \le u_i \le u_i^* \qquad i = 1, 2, 3 \tag{4.5.100}$$

We will choose the set of parameters

$$\begin{array}{llll} \Theta = 25 & Q = 1 & x_{3c} = -0.125 & P = 1 \quad J = 0.25 \\ \beta_{1s} = 0.020 & \theta = 0.4 & \gamma = 0.1 & u_{1*} = -500 \\ u_1^* = 500 & u_{2*} = 0 & u_{3*} = 0.01 & u_2^* = u_3^* = 2 \\ x_{10} = 0.49 & x_{20} = 0.0002 & x_{30} = -0.02 & \alpha_{1s} = 0.015 \end{array} \tag{4.5.101}$$

and the initial functions

$$\begin{array}{ll} x_3(t) = -0.02 & -\alpha_1 \le t \le 0 \\ u_2(t) = 1 & -\beta_1 \le t < 0 \\ u_3(t) = 1 & -\max(\alpha_{1s}, \beta_{1s}) \le t < 0 \end{array} \tag{4.5.102}$$

and apply a control vector iteration method to the problem to find the optimum. The detailed algorithm is described in [73].

We shall assume that the flow rate u_3 is not a control but is held constant at the steady-state value. Hence, our time delays are constants. The results of applying the control vector iteration procedure from two initial guesses of u_1, u_2 are shown in Figs. 4.31 and 4.32. We see that $\eta_2 = 1$ is too large to allow any control action in u_2 and all the control is being done by u_1. Note that the same optimal state trajectories $x_1(t)$, $x_2(t)$, $x_3(t)$ are found from both starting guesses, which suggests adequate convergence of the algorithm. The differences in u_1 for large t are due to the fact that $x_3 \cong 0$, so

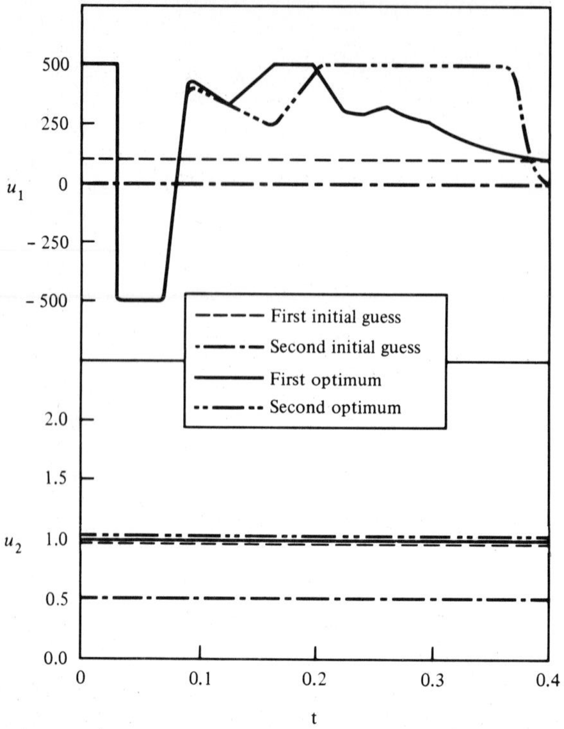

Figure 4.31 Optimal open-loop control policy for Example 4.5.5 when $\eta_2 = 1.0$ [73]. (*Reproduced by permission of Pergamon Press, Ltd.*)

that any gain $u_1(t)$ gives good results. If we remove the penalty on the control u_2 from the objective by setting $\eta_2 = 0$, the u_2 does exercise some control, but gives only a slight improvement in the state trajectories and the objective functional.

Linear-Quadratic Feedback Control

As in other distributed parameter systems, it is possible to design an optimal feedback controller by considering the linear problem with constant time delays:

$$\frac{d\mathbf{x}(t)}{dt} = \mathbf{A}_0\mathbf{x}(t) + \sum_{i=1}^{\delta} \mathbf{A}_i\mathbf{x}(t - \alpha_i) + \mathbf{B}_0\mathbf{u}(t) + \sum_{j=1}^{\mu} \mathbf{B}_j\mathbf{u}(t - \beta_j) \qquad (4.5.103)$$

$$\mathbf{x}(t) = \phi(t) \qquad -\alpha_\delta \le t \le 0 \qquad (4.5.104)$$

$$\mathbf{u}(t) = \Phi(t) \qquad -\beta_\mu \le t \le 0 \qquad (4.5.105)$$

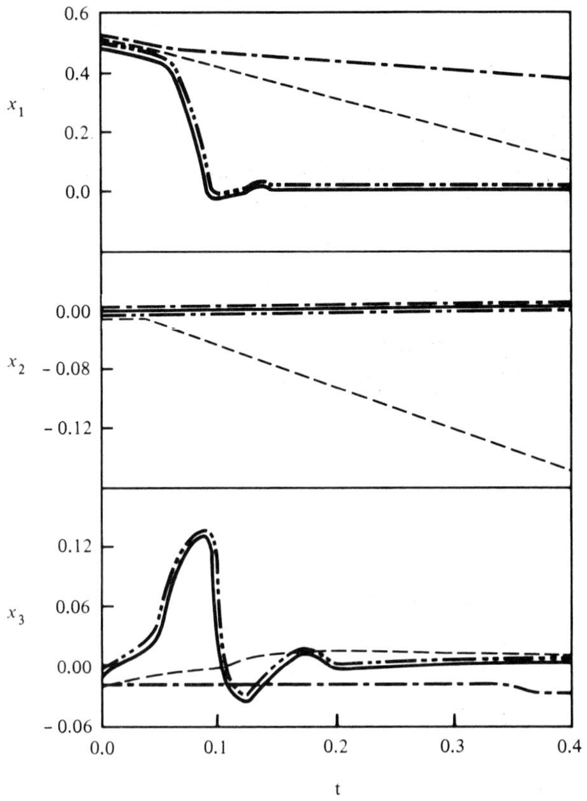

Figure 4.32 Optimal open-loop state trajectories for Example 4.5.5 when $\eta_2 = 1.0$ [73]. (*Reproduced by permission of Pergamon Press, Ltd.*)

with the quadratic objective

$$I = \tfrac{1}{2}\mathbf{x}^T(t_f)\mathbf{S}_f\mathbf{x}(t_f) + \tfrac{1}{2}\int_0^{t_f}\left[\mathbf{x}^T(t)\mathbf{F}\mathbf{x}(t) + \mathbf{u}^T(t)\mathbf{E}\mathbf{u}(t)\right] dt \qquad (4.5.106)$$

The optimal feedback control law has been derived by many routes [60, 74, 75] and takes the form

$$\begin{aligned}\mathbf{u}(t) = -\mathbf{E}^{-1}\Big\{&\left[\mathbf{B}_0^T\mathbf{E}_0(t) + \mathbf{E}_3^T(t, 0)\right]\mathbf{x}(t)\\ &+ \int_{-\alpha_\delta}^{0}\left[\mathbf{B}_0^T\mathbf{E}_1(t, s) + \mathbf{E}_5^T(t, s, 0)\right]\mathbf{x}(t + s)\, ds\\ &+ \int_{-\beta_\mu}^{0}\left[\mathbf{B}_0^T\mathbf{E}_3(t, s) + \mathbf{E}_4(t, 0, s)\right]\mathbf{u}(t + s)\, ds\Big\}\end{aligned} \qquad (4.5.107)$$

where the controller parameters may be precomputed from

$$\frac{d\mathbf{E}_0(t)}{dt} = -\mathbf{E}_0(t)\mathbf{A}_0 - \mathbf{A}_0^T\mathbf{E}_0(t) - \mathbf{E}_1^T(t,0) - \mathbf{E}_1(t,0)$$

$$+\left[\mathbf{E}_0(t)\mathbf{B}_0 + \mathbf{E}_3(t,0)\right]\mathbf{E}^{-1}\left[\mathbf{B}_0^T\mathbf{E}_0(t) + \mathbf{E}_3^T(t,0)\right] - \mathbf{F} \tag{4.5.108}$$

$$\frac{\partial \mathbf{E}_1(t,s)}{\partial t} = \frac{\partial \mathbf{E}_1(t,s)}{\partial s} - \mathbf{A}_0^T\mathbf{E}_1(t,s) - \mathbf{E}_2(t,0,s) + \left[\mathbf{E}_0(t)\mathbf{B}_0 + \mathbf{E}_3(t,0)\right]$$

$$\times\, \mathbf{E}^{-1}\left[\mathbf{B}_0^T\mathbf{E}_1(t,s) + \mathbf{E}_5^T(t,s,0)\right] \qquad -\alpha_\delta \le s \le 0 \tag{4.5.109}$$

$$\frac{\partial \mathbf{E}_2(t,r,s)}{\partial t} = \frac{\partial \mathbf{E}_2(t,r,s)}{\partial r} + \frac{\partial \mathbf{E}_2(t,r,s)}{\partial s} + \left[\mathbf{E}_1^T(t,r)\mathbf{B}_0 + \mathbf{E}_5(t,r,0)\right]$$

$$\times\, \mathbf{E}^{-1}\left[\mathbf{B}_0^T\mathbf{E}_1(t,s) + \mathbf{E}_5^T(t,s,0)\right] \qquad \begin{array}{l} -\alpha_\delta \le r \le 0 \\ -\alpha_\delta \le s \le 0 \end{array} \tag{4.5.110}$$

$$\frac{\partial \mathbf{E}_3(t,s)}{\partial t} = \frac{\partial \mathbf{E}_3(t,s)}{\partial s} - \mathbf{A}_0^T\mathbf{E}_3(t,s) - \mathbf{E}_5(t,0,s) + \left[\mathbf{E}_0(t)\mathbf{B}_0 + \mathbf{E}_3(t,0)\right]$$

$$\times\, \mathbf{E}^{-1}\left[\mathbf{B}_0^T\mathbf{E}_3(t,s) + \mathbf{E}_4(t,0,s)\right] \qquad -\beta_\mu \le s \le 0 \tag{4.5.111}$$

$$\frac{\partial \mathbf{E}_4(t,r,s)}{\partial t} = \frac{\partial \mathbf{E}_4(t,r,s)}{\partial r} + \frac{\partial \mathbf{E}_4(t,r,s)}{\partial s} + \left[\mathbf{E}_3^T(t,r)\mathbf{B}_0 + \mathbf{E}_4(t,r,0)\right]$$

$$\times\, \mathbf{E}^{-1}\left[\mathbf{B}_0^T\mathbf{E}_3(t,s) + \mathbf{E}_4(t,0,s)\right] \qquad \begin{array}{l} -\beta_\mu \le r \le 0 \\ -\beta_\mu \le s \le 0 \end{array} \tag{4.5.112}$$

$$\frac{\partial \mathbf{E}_5(t,r,s)}{\partial t} = \frac{\partial \mathbf{E}_5(t,r,s)}{\partial r} + \frac{\partial \mathbf{E}_5(t,r,s)}{\partial s} + \left[\mathbf{E}_1^T(t,r)\mathbf{B}_0 + \mathbf{E}_5(t,r,0)\right]$$

$$\times\, \mathbf{E}^{-1}\left[\mathbf{B}_0^T\mathbf{E}_3(t,s) + \mathbf{E}_4(t,0,s)\right] \qquad \begin{array}{l} -\beta_\mu \le s \le 0 \\ -\alpha_\delta \le r \le 0 \end{array} \tag{4.5.113}$$

where $\mathbf{E}_0(t)$, $\mathbf{E}_1(t, s)$, and $\mathbf{E}_2(t, r, s)$ are $n \times n$ matrix functions; $\mathbf{E}_3(t, s)$ and $\mathbf{E}_5(t, r, s)$ are $n \times m$ matrix functions; and $\mathbf{E}_4(t, r, s)$ is an $m \times m$ matrix function. The boundary conditions on the delayed time variables, s and r are given by

$$\begin{aligned}
\mathbf{E}_1(t, -\alpha_\delta) &= \mathbf{E}_0(t)\mathbf{A}_1 \\
\mathbf{E}_3(t, -\beta_\mu) &= \mathbf{E}_0(t)\mathbf{B}_1 \\
\mathbf{E}_2(t, -\alpha_\delta, s) &= \mathbf{A}_1^T\mathbf{E}_1(t,s) \\
\mathbf{E}_4(t, -\beta_\mu, s) &= \mathbf{B}_1^T\mathbf{E}_3(t,s) \\
\mathbf{E}_5(t, -\alpha_\delta, s) &= \mathbf{A}_1^T\mathbf{E}_3(t,s) \\
\mathbf{E}_5(t, r, -\beta_\mu) &= \mathbf{E}_1^T(t,r)\mathbf{B}_1
\end{aligned} \tag{4.5.114}$$

The matrices $\mathbf{E}_2(t, r, s)$, $\mathbf{E}_4(t, r, s)$ have the property

$$\begin{aligned} \mathbf{E}_2^T(t, r, s) &= \mathbf{E}_2(t, s, r) \\ \mathbf{E}_4^T(t, r, s) &= \mathbf{E}_4(t, s, r) \end{aligned} \tag{4.5.115}$$

while the terminal conditions are

$$\begin{aligned} \mathbf{E}_0(t_f) &= \mathbf{S} \\ \mathbf{E}_1(t_f, s) &= \mathbf{0} \quad -\alpha_\delta \le s \le 0 \\ \mathbf{E}_2(t_f, r, s) &= \mathbf{0} \quad -\alpha_\delta \le s \le 0 \quad -\alpha_\delta \le r \le 0 \\ \mathbf{E}_3(t_f, s) &= \mathbf{0} \quad -\beta_\mu \le s \le 0 \\ \mathbf{E}_4(t_f, r, s) &= \mathbf{0} \quad -\beta_\mu \le s \le 0 \quad -\beta_\mu \le r \le 0 \\ \mathbf{E}_5(t_f, r, s) &= \mathbf{0} \quad -\beta_\mu \le s \le 0 \quad -\alpha_\delta \le r \le 0 \end{aligned} \tag{4.5.116}$$

In addition there are certain discontinuities which must be satisfied at α_i, β_j:

$$\begin{aligned} \mathbf{E}_1(t, -\alpha_a) &= \mathbf{E}_0(t)\mathbf{A}_a \\ \mathbf{E}_1(t, -\alpha_i^+) &= \mathbf{E}_1(t, -\alpha_i^-) + \mathbf{E}_0(t)\mathbf{A}_i \qquad i = 1, 2, \ldots, a-1 \\ \mathbf{E}_3(t, -\beta_b) &= \mathbf{E}_0(t)\mathbf{B}_b \\ \mathbf{E}_3(t, -\beta_j^+) &= \mathbf{E}_3(t, -\beta_j^-) + \mathbf{E}_0(t)\mathbf{B}_j \qquad j = 1, 2, \ldots, b-1 \\ \mathbf{E}_2(t, -\alpha_a, s) &= \mathbf{A}_a^T\mathbf{E}_1(t, s) \\ \mathbf{E}_2(t, -\alpha_i^+, s) &= \mathbf{E}_2(t, -\alpha_i^-, s) + \mathbf{A}_i^T\mathbf{E}_1(t, s) \qquad i = 1, 2, \ldots, a-1 \\ \mathbf{E}_4(t, -\beta_b, s) &= \mathbf{B}_b^T\mathbf{E}_3(t, s) \\ \mathbf{E}_4(t, -\beta_j^+, s) &= \mathbf{E}_4(t, -\beta_j^-, s) + \mathbf{B}_j^T\mathbf{E}_3(t, s) \qquad j = 1, 2, \ldots, b-1 \\ \mathbf{E}_5(t, -\alpha_a, s) &= \mathbf{A}_a^T\mathbf{E}_3(t, s) \\ \mathbf{E}_5(t, -\alpha_i^+, s) &= \mathbf{E}_5(t, -\alpha_i^-, s) + \mathbf{A}_i^T\mathbf{E}_3(t, s) \qquad i = 1, 2, \ldots, a-1 \\ \mathbf{E}_5(t, r, -\beta_b) &= \mathbf{E}_1^T(t, r)\mathbf{B}_b \\ \mathbf{E}_5(t, r, -\beta_j^+) &= \mathbf{E}_5(t, r, -\beta_j^-) + \mathbf{E}_1^T(t, r)\mathbf{B}_j \qquad j = 1, 2, \ldots, b-1 \end{aligned} \tag{4.5.117}$$

Notice that the first term in the feedback control law, Eq. (4.5.107), is analogous to the familiar form for systems without delay, while the additional terms account for the delays in the state and in the control. As would be expected, elimination of both state and control delays reduces the control law to the conventional type (Chap. 3), with Eq. (4.5.108) taking the form of the well-known Riccati equations for such systems.

Example 4.5.6* Let us now illustrate the application of linear quadratic controller design by recalling the class of problems represented by Eqs. (4.5.1) and (4.5.2), i.e., linear transfer function models having time delays. As an example, the exit temperature from a tubular heat exchanger $x(t)$ can be shown [76] to be related to the jacket temperature $u(t)$ by the transfer function

$$\bar{x}(s) = \frac{K_1\left[1 - K_2 e^{-\beta s}\right]}{(as+1)(bs+1)}\bar{u}(s) \tag{4.5.118}$$

Let us suppose we wish to control the exit temperature by adjusting the jacket temperature while minimizing the quadratic objective:

$$I = \tfrac{1}{2}\int_0^{t_f}\left[F(x - x_s)^2 + E(u - u_s)^2\right] dt \tag{4.5.119}$$

For this problem the differential-difference equation representation becomes

$$\begin{gathered} \dot{\mathbf{z}} = \mathbf{A}\mathbf{z} + \mathbf{B}_0 u(t) + \mathbf{B}_1 u(t - \beta) \qquad \mathbf{z}(0) = \mathbf{0} \\ x = z_1 \\ u(t) = 0 \qquad -\beta \le t < 0 \end{gathered} \tag{4.5.120}$$

where

$$\mathbf{A} = \begin{bmatrix} 0 & 1 \\ -\dfrac{1}{ab} & -\dfrac{(a+b)}{ab} \end{bmatrix} \qquad \mathbf{B}_0 = \begin{bmatrix} 0 \\ \dfrac{K_1}{ab} \end{bmatrix}$$

$$\mathbf{B}_1 = \begin{bmatrix} 0 \\ \dfrac{-K_1 K_2}{ab} \end{bmatrix} \qquad \mathbf{z} = \begin{bmatrix} z_1 \\ z_2 \end{bmatrix} \tag{4.5.121}$$

For the numerical computation we choose the parameters $F(t) = 2t^2$, $E = 20$, $K_1 = 1$, $K_2 = 0.5$, $\beta = 10$, $a = 40$, $b = 15$, $t_f = 80$, $x_s = 0.2$, $u_s = 0.4$ and apply the optimal feedback control law developed above. This becomes

$$\begin{aligned} u = u_s - (E)^{-1}\Big(&\left[\mathbf{B}_0^T \mathbf{E}_0(t) + \mathbf{E}_1^T(t,0)\right]\mathbf{y} \\ &+ \int_{-\beta}^{0}\left\{\left[\mathbf{B}_0^T \mathbf{E}_1(t,s) + E_2(t,0,s)\right]\left[u(t+s) - u_s\right]\right\} ds\Big) \end{aligned} \tag{4.5.122}$$

where

$$\mathbf{y} = \begin{bmatrix} x - x_s \\ \dot{x} \end{bmatrix} = \begin{bmatrix} z_1 - x_s \\ z_2 \end{bmatrix} \tag{4.5.123}$$

* This example is taken from [76] with permission of Pergamon Press Ltd.

and feedback controller parameters

$$\mathbf{E}_0 = \begin{bmatrix} E_{011} & E_{012} \\ E_{021} & E_{022} \end{bmatrix} \qquad \mathbf{E}_1 = \begin{bmatrix} E_{11} \\ E_{12} \end{bmatrix}$$

and E_2 are determined from the following Riccati differential equations:

$$\frac{d\mathbf{E}_0(t)}{dt} = -\mathbf{E}_0(t)\mathbf{A} - \mathbf{A}^T\mathbf{E}_0(t) + \left[\mathbf{E}_0(t)\mathbf{B}_0 + \mathbf{E}_1(t, 0)\right]E^{-1} \times \left[\mathbf{B}_0^T\mathbf{E}_0(t) + \mathbf{E}_1^T(t, 0)\right] - \mathbf{F}_0 \tag{4.5.124}$$

$$\frac{\partial \mathbf{E}_1(t, s)}{\partial t} = \frac{\partial \mathbf{E}_1(t, s)}{\partial s} - \mathbf{A}^T\mathbf{E}_1(t, s) + \left[\mathbf{E}_0(t)\mathbf{B}_0 + \mathbf{E}_1(t, 0)\right]E^{-1} \times \left[\mathbf{B}_0^T\mathbf{E}_1(t, s) + \mathbf{E}_2(t, 0, s)\right] \qquad -\beta \le s \le 0 \tag{4.5.125}$$

$$\frac{\partial E_2(t, r, s)}{\partial t} = \frac{\partial E_2(t, r, s)}{\partial r} + \frac{\partial E_2(t, r, s)}{\partial s} + \left[\mathbf{E}_1^T(t, r)\mathbf{B}_0 + E_2(t, r, 0)\right]E^{-1} \times \left[\mathbf{B}_0^T\mathbf{E}_1(t, s) + E_2(t, 0, s)\right] \qquad \begin{matrix} -\beta \le r \le 0 \\ -\beta \le s \le 0 \end{matrix} \tag{4.5.126}$$

where $\mathbf{F}_0$ is defined as

$$\mathbf{F}_0 = \begin{bmatrix} F & 0 \\ 0 & 0 \end{bmatrix}$$

The boundary conditions on the variables r, s are

$$\mathbf{E}_1(t, -\beta) = \mathbf{E}_0(t)\mathbf{B}_1$$
$$E_2(t, -\beta, s) = \mathbf{B}_1^T\mathbf{E}_1(t, s) \tag{4.5.127}$$

and the terminal conditions are

$$\mathbf{E}_0(t_f) = \mathbf{0}$$
$$\mathbf{E}_1(t_f, s) = \mathbf{0} \qquad -\beta \le s \le 0$$
$$E_2(t_f, r, s) = 0 \qquad -\beta \le r \le 0 - \beta \le s \le 0 \tag{4.5.128}$$

Even though these equations appear quite formidable, they can be precomputed off-line and the optimal feedback controller of the form

$$u = u_s - P_1(t)(x - x_s) - P_2(t)\dot{x} + \int_{-\beta}^{0} P_3(t, s)\left[u(t + s) - u_s\right] ds \tag{4.5.129}$$

implemented, where $P_1(t)$, $P_2(t)$, $P_3(t, s)$ are the obvious combination of terms in Eq. (4.5.122). For this case it is seen that the optimal feedback controller is a proportional-derivative controller with a memory of the control required over the interval $(t - \beta, t)$.

The feedback controller may be implemented by precomputing Eqs. (4.5.124) to (4.5.126) and forming the variable gains $P_1(t)$, $P_2(t)$, $P_3(t, s)$. The

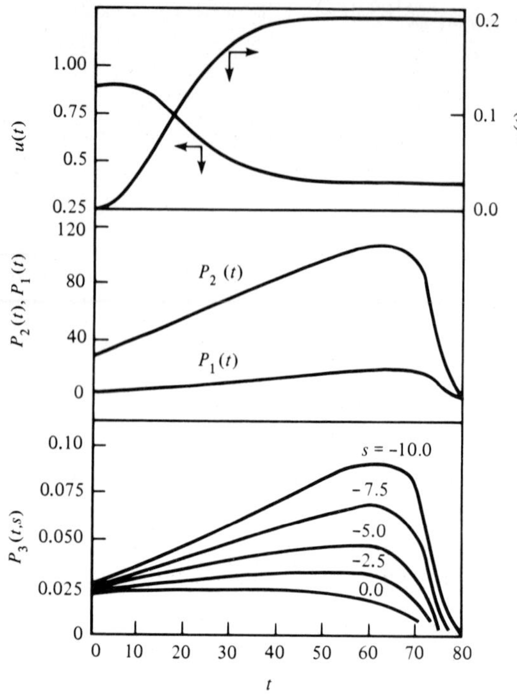

Figure 4.33 Optimal linear-quadratic feedback control of a tubular heat exchanger [76]. (*Reproduced with permission of Pergamon Press, Ltd.*)

results are plotted in Fig. 4.33 and show the controller gains as well as the state and control variables under optimal feedback control.

The linear quadratic formulation may be extended to nonlinear problems by linearization about a nominal open-loop trajectory. The feedback control law in this case and an example problem may be found in Ref. [77].

REFERENCES

1. Ray, W. H.: *Automatica* **14**:281 (1978).
2. Butkovsky, A. G.: *Distributed Control Systems*, Elsevier, Amsterdam, 1969.
3. Lions, J. L.: *Optimal Control of Systems Governed by Partial Differential Equations*, Springer-Verlag, 1971.
4. Ray, W. H., and D. G. Lainiotis: *Distributed Parameter Systems*, Marcel Dekker, New York, 1978.
5. Ray, W. H., and J. Szekely: *Process Optimization*, Wiley, New York, 1973.
6. Bird, R. B., W. E. Stewart, and E. N. Lightfoot: *Transport Phenomena*, Wiley, New York, 1960.
7. Friedly, J. C.: *Dynamic Behaviour of Processes*, Prentice-Hall, Englewood Cliffs, N.J., 1973, chap. 9.
8. Johnson, T. L.: *SIAM J. Control* **11**:119 (1973).
9. Russel, D. L.: *Proceedings 1975 World IFAC Congress*, Boston, paper 1.4.
10. Dennemeyer, R.: *Introduction to Partial Differential Equations and Boundary Value Problems*, McGraw-Hill, New York, 1968.

11. Gilles, E. D.: *Systeme mit verteilten Parametern*, R. Oldenbourg Verlag, Munich, 1973.
12. Gould, L. A.: *Chemical Process Control*, Addison-Wesley, Reading, Mass., 1969, p. 255.
13. Wang, P. K. C. *IEEE Trans. Auto. Control*, **AC-17**:552 (1972).
14. Sakawa, Y.: *Int. J. Control* **16**:115 (1972).
15. Ajinkya, M. B., M. Köhne, M. F. Mäder, and W. H. Ray: *Automatica* **11**:571 (1975).
16. Ince, E. L.: *Ordinary Differential Equations*, Dover, New York, 1926, p. 123.
17. Courant, R., and D. Hilbert: *Methods of Mathematical Physics,* Interscience, New York, 1953, p. 279.
18. Mäder, H. F.: *Regelungstechnik* **24**:347 (1976).
19. Erzberger, H., and M. Kim: *Inf. and Cont.* **9**:265 (1966).
20. Park, P. D.: *Recent Mathematical Developments in Control*, D. J. Bell (ed.), Academic, New York, 1973, p. 267.
21. Olivei, A.: *Int. J. Control* **20**:129 (1974).
22. Wylie, C. R.: *Advanced Engineering Math*, Wiley, New York, 1966, p. 356.
23. Wang, P. K. C.: *Advances in Control Systems*, vol. 1, Academic, New York, 1964.
24. Sakawa, Y.: *SIAM J. Control* **12**:389 (1974).
25. Amouroux, M., and J. P. Babary: *Proceedings 6th World IFAC Congress*, Boston (1975), paper 1.2.
26. Aidarous, S. E., M. R. Gevers, and M. I. Installe: *Int. J. Control* **22**:197 (1975).
27. Amouroux, M., G. DiPillo, L. Grippo: *Ricerche de Automatica* **11**: (1976).
28. Amouroux, M., and J. P. Babary: *Comp. Rendus* **A** (1976).
29. Amouroux, M., and J. P. Babary: *Podstawy Sterowania* **6**: (1976).
30. Sage, A. P.: *Optimum Systems Control*, Prentice-Hall, Englewood Cliffs, N.J., 1968.
31. Denn, M. M.: *Optimization by Variational Methods*, McGraw-Hill, New York, 1970.
32. Ogunye, A. F., and W. H. Ray: *AIChE J.* **17**:43, 365 (1971).
33. Ogunye, A. F., and W. H. Ray: *I & EC Proc. Des. Dev* **9**:619 (1970); **10**:410, 416 (1971).
34. Zahradnik, R. L., and L. L. Lynn: *Proceedings 1970 JACC*, paper 22E.
35. Bosarge, E.: *Proceedings 1st IFAC Symposium on the Control of Distributed Parameter Systems*, Banff, Canada (June 1971).
36. Brogan, W. L.: *Advances in Control Systems*, **6**: 222 (1960), Academic Press.
37. Butkovskii, A. G., A. I. Egorov, and K. A. Lurie, *SIAM J. Control* **6**:437 (1968).
38. *Proceedings 1st IFAC Symposium on the Control of Distributed Parameter Systems*, Banff, Canada (June 1971).
39. Robinson, A. C.: *Automatica* **7**:371 (1971).
40. *Proceedings 2d IFAC Symposium on the Control of Distributed Parameter Systems*, Coventry, England (July 1977).
41. Koppel, L., Y.-P. Shih, and D. R. Coughanowr.: *I & EC Fundamentals* **7**:287, 414 (1968).
42. Denn, M. M.: *I & EC Fundamentals* **7**:411 (1968).
43. Seinfeld, J. H., and K. S. P. Kumar: *Int. J. Cont.* **7**:417 (1968).
44. Koivo, A. J., and P. Kruh: *Int. J. Cont.* **10**:53 (1969).
45. Gilles, E. D., and M. Zeitz: *Proc. 1970 JACC*, Atlanta, p. 779.
46. Gilles, E. D., and M. Zeitz: *Regelungstechnik* **17**: 204 (1969).
47. Finlayson, B. A.: *The Method of Weighted Residuals and Variational Principles*, Academic, New York, 1972.
48. Crandall, S. H.: *Engineering Analysis*, McGraw-Hill, New York, 1956, p. 147.
49. Villadsen, John: *Selected Approximation Methods for Chemical Engineering Problems*, Tech. Univ. Denmark, Copenhagen, 1970.
50. Norrie, D. H. and G. deVries: *The Finite Element Method*, Academic, New York, 1973.
51. Stewart, W. E., and J. Sørensen: *Collocation and Parameter Estimation in Chemical Rxn. Eng.*
52. Finlayson, B. A.: *SIAM J. Num. Anal.* **8**:316 (1971).
53. Newman, C. P., and A. Sen: *Int. J. Control* **16**:539 (1972); **18**:1291 (1973).
54. Lynn, L. L., and R. L. Zahradnik: *Int. J. Control* **12**:1079 (1970), *Proc. 1970 JACC*, Atlanta, p. 590.
55. Bosarge, W. E., and R. S. McKnight: *SIAM J. Cont.* **11**:510 (1973).

56. Prabhu, S. S., and I. McCausland: *Proc. Inst. E.E.* **117**:1398 (1970).
57. Dwight, H. B.: *Tables of Integrals and Other Mathematical Data*, Macmillan, New York, 1961.
58. Ogunnaike, B. A.: Ph.D. Thesis, University of Wisconsin, 1980.
59. Yu, T. K., J. H. Seinfeld, and W. H. Ray, *IEEE Trans. Auto. Cont.* **AC-19**:324 (1974).
60. Koivo, H. N., and A. J. Koivo: "Control and Estimation of Systems with Time Delays," W. H. Ray and D. G. Lainiotis (eds.), in *Distributed Parameter Systems,* Marcel Dekker, New York, 1978.
61. Smith, O. J. M.: *Chem. Eng. Prog.* **53**:217 (1957).
62. Alevisakis, G., and D. E. Seborg: *Int. J. Control* **17**:541 (1973).
63. Alevisakis, G., and D. E. Seborg: *Chem. Eng. Sci.* **29**, 373 (1974).
64. Prasad, C. C., and P. R. Krishnaswamy: *Chem. Eng. Sci.* **30**:207 (1975).
65. Buckley, P. S.: *Techniques of Process Control*, Wiley, New York, 1964.
66. Tzafestas, S. G., and P. N. Paraskevopoulos: *Int. J. Control* **17**:405 (1973).
67. Ogunnaike, B. A., and W. H. Ray: *AIChE J.* **25**: 1043 (1979).
68. Moore, C. F., C. L. Smith, and P. W. Murrill: *Instruments and Control Systems* **43**(1):70 (1970).
69. Wood, R. K., and M. W. Berry: *Chem. Eng. Sci.* **28**:1707 (1973).
70. Shah, S. L., and D. G. Fisher: *Proc. 1978 Joint Automatic Control Conference*, Phila.
71. Meyer, C., D. E. Seborg, and R. K. Wood: *I&EC Proc. Des. Dev.* **17**:62 (1978).
72. Meyer, C., D. E. Seborg, and R. K. Wood: *AIChE J.* **25**:24 (1979).
73. Ray, W. H., and M. A. Soliman: *Chem. Eng. Sci.* **25**:1911 (1970).
74. Soliman, M. A., and W. H. Ray: *Int. J. Control* **15**:609 (1972).
75. Koivo, H. N., and E. B. Lee: *Automatica* **8**:203 (1972).
76. Soliman, M. A., and W. H. Ray: *Chem. Eng. Sci.* **27**:2183 (1972).
77. Soliman, M. A., and W. H. Ray: *Automatica* **7**:681 (1971).

PROBLEMS

4.1 Consider the chemical reaction $A \xrightarrow{k_1} B \xrightarrow{k_2} C$ described in Example 3.3.2, except that it is now carried out in a homogeneous tubular reactor. If the reactor has length L, mean velocity v, and a flat velocity profile, a possible model is

$$\frac{\partial c_1}{\partial t} = -v\frac{\partial c_1}{\partial z'} - k_1(T)c_1^2 \qquad \begin{matrix} 0 \le z' \le L \\ t > 0 \end{matrix}$$

$$\frac{\partial c_2}{\partial t} = -v\frac{\partial c_2}{\partial z'} + k_1(T)c_1^2 - k_2(T)c_2 \qquad \begin{matrix} 0 \le z' \le L \\ t > 0 \end{matrix}$$

$$z' = 0,\ c_1 = 1.0,\ c_2 = 0 \qquad \text{for all } t > 0$$

$$t = 0,\ c_1 = 1.0,\ c_2 = 0 \qquad \text{for all } z' \epsilon (0, L)$$

Suppose that the reactor tube is immersed in a well-agitated bath and the heat of reaction is sufficiently small that isothermal operation is possible at the bath temperature $T(t)$.

By defining $\theta = L/v$, the mean residence time, and $z = z'/L$, one obtains the model

$$\frac{\partial c_1(z,t)}{\partial t} = -\frac{1}{\theta}\frac{\partial c_1}{\partial z} - k_1(T)c_1^2 \qquad \begin{matrix} 0 \le z \le 1 \\ t > 0 \end{matrix}$$

$$\frac{\partial c_2(z,t)}{\partial t} = -\frac{1}{\theta}\frac{\partial c_2}{\partial z} + k_1(T)c_1^2 - k_2(T)c_2$$

Now it is desired to start-up the reactor in such a way that we maximize the production of species B, i.e.,

$$\max_{T(t)} \left\{ I = \int_0^{t_f} c_2(1,t)\,dt \right\}$$

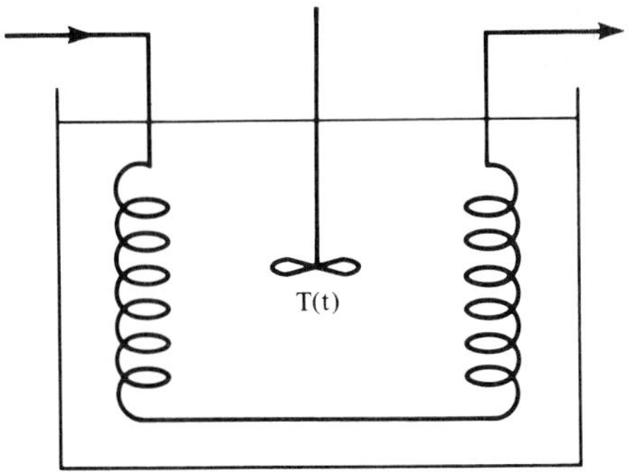

where the bath temperature is constrained by

$$T_* \le T \le T^*$$

(*a*) Derive the necessary conditions for optimality of $T(t)$.

(*b*) Describe in detail the control vector iteration procedure you would use to determine $T(t)$. List all the equations (including boundary conditions) needing solution. Describe your proposed numerical procedure.

(*c*) Carry out this control vector iteration procedure for the parameters given in Example 3.3.2 and with the additional parameters $\theta = 1$ h, $t_f = 2$ h.

4.2 In Sec. 4.3 the linear-quadratic optimal feedback control law has been derived for $\mathbf{A}_2$, $\mathbf{A}_1$, $\mathbf{A}_0$, $\mathbf{B}$ only functions of t. Rederive the equations for the case where $\mathbf{A}_2$, $\mathbf{A}_1$, $\mathbf{A}_0$, $\mathbf{B}$ all depend on the spatial variable z as well.

4.3 For the heated rod problem of Example 4.3.3, use modal analysis to decompose both the state and Riccati equations.

(*a*) Describe in detail the modal computational algorithm for $S(r, s, t)$ to be solved off-line.

(*b*) Describe how you would simulate the controlled system and how you would implement the feedback control law.

(*c*) Carry out the computations and show the response of the feedback controller for $F = 1$, $E = 0.25$, $x(z, 0) = \sqrt{2}\cos \pi z$, $t_f = 4$.

4.4 Consider the boundary control of a thin metal rod which has one end in a water bath at 25°C and the other end inserted into a steam chest. Air at 25°C is blowing transversely across the rod. The temperature of the right-hand end is assumed fixed at 25°C, while the temperature of the left-hand end may be controlled by adjusting the steam pressure. Thus the system may be modeled by

$$\rho C_p \frac{\partial T}{\partial t'}(z', t') = k\frac{\partial^2 T}{\partial z'^2} - h'(T - 25) \qquad \begin{matrix} 0 < z' < L \\ t' > 0 \end{matrix}$$

$z' = 0$ $\qquad T(0, t') = T_s(t')$

$z' = L$ $\qquad T(L, t') = 25$

where $T_s(t)$ is adjustable.

By using the dimensionless variables

$$x = \frac{T - 25}{25} \qquad u_0 = \frac{T_s - 25}{25} \qquad t = \frac{t'k}{\rho C_p L^2} \qquad \beta = \frac{h'L^2}{k} \qquad z = \frac{z'}{L}$$

we obtain the model

$$\frac{\partial x(z, t)}{\partial t} = \frac{\partial^2 x}{\partial z^2} - \beta x$$

$z = 0$ $\qquad x(0, t) = u_0(t)$

$z = 1$ $\qquad x(1, t) = 0$

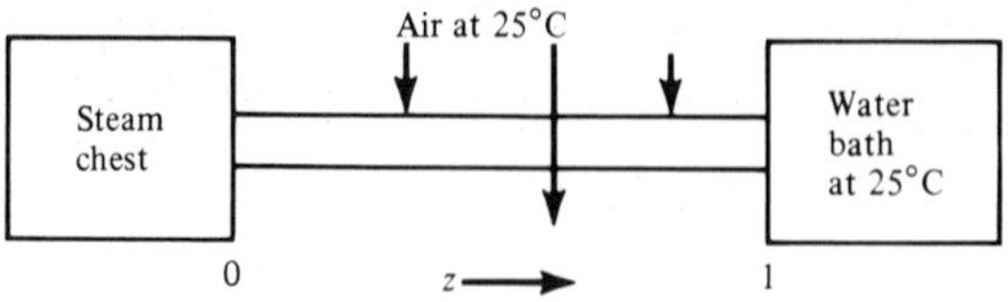

Now it may be more convenient for you to consider the equivalent form

$$\frac{\partial x}{\partial t} = \frac{\partial^2 x}{\partial z^2} - \beta x - \dot{\delta}(z) u_0(t)$$

with boundary conditions

$$z = 0, 1 \qquad x = 0$$

Note that $\dot{\delta}(z) \equiv d(\delta(z))/dz$ where $\delta(z)$ is the dirac delta function. Also note that for any continuous function $\phi_n(z)$,

$$\int_0^1 \dot{\delta}(z)\phi_n(z)\, dz \equiv -\int_0^1 \dot{\phi}_n(z)\delta(z)\, dz$$

Given this information:

(*a*) Solve the modeling equations through an eigenfunction expansion of the form

$$x(z, t) = \sum_{n=1}^{N} a_n(t)\phi_n(z)$$

and determine an orthonormal set $\phi_n(z)$ and the equations for $a_n(t)$.

(*b*) Determine if the system is *approximately controllable*.

(*c*) Develop the optimal linear-quadratic feedback control law, Riccati equations, and implementation scheme for this boundary control problem.

(*d*) Carry out the computations and show the response of the feedback controller for $F = 1$, $E_0 = 0.25$, $\beta = 3$, $x(z, 0) = \sqrt{2}\ \sin \pi z$, $t_f = 10$.

4.5 For the nonlinear system described in Example 4.4.3, develop a pseudo-modal feedback controller. In particular,

(*a*) Outline how one would implement such a controller.

(*b*) Simulate the system under feedback control using the described Galerkin procedure and computationally determine the number of "eigenfunctions" necessary to obtain reasonable convergence.

(*c*) Discuss the multivariable controller design problem arising from this pseudo-modal analysis.

4.6 Consider the heat exchanger control problem posed in Example 4.3.4. Show that this system in the Laplace transform domain has the same form as Example 4.5.6. Discuss the relationship between first-order hyperbolic partial differential equations and differential-difference equations. Compare the optimal feedback control law formulations for both forms of the problem.

4.7 For the distillation column discussed in Example 3.2.8 but for the case where $\mathbf{G}(s)$ contains time delays [i.e., $\mathbf{G}(s)$ given by Eq. (4.5.4)]:

(*a*) Determine the equation for the time-domain realization of $y_1(t)$, $y_2(t)$, $y_3(t)$ in response to $u_1(t)$, $u_2(t)$, $u_3(t)$.

(*b*) Calculate the open-loop response for step changes in the controls, $u_1 = 1.0$, $u_2 = 2.0$, $u_3 = 3.0$.

(*c*) Design a multidelay compensator to be included in a feedback control system where proportional controllers are used and the loop pairings are $y_1 \leftrightarrow u_1$, $y_2 \leftrightarrow u_2$, $y_3 \leftrightarrow u_3$. Develop all the necessary design equations.

(*d*) Simulate the performance of your multidelay compensator using the realization equations similar to those developed in part (*a*).

CHAPTER

FIVE

STATE ESTIMATION AND STOCHASTIC CONTROL

5.1 INTRODUCTION

Up to this point we have considered only the control algorithms for process control without much discussion of the problems of process measurement and random process disturbances. However, in most industrial processes the total state vector can seldom be measured and the number of outputs is much less than the number of states. In addition, the process measurements are often corrupted by significant experimental error, and the process itself is subject to random, unmodeled upsets. Thus without some consideration of these problems in the total control system design, the measurements used for feedback control will often be inadequate for acceptable control system performance. In this chapter we shall begin by discussing on-line *state estimation* techniques which may be used to provide acceptable estimates of all the state variables (even those not directly measured) in the face of measurement error and process disturbances. Following this, a brief introduction to *stochastic feedback control*, which is explicitly designed for systems with random disturbances and measurement errors, will be provided along with some illustrative applications. First we shall treat systems described by ordinary differential equations and then discuss methods for distributed parameter systems.

A full, rigorous treatment of these topics requires a thorough background in the theory of stochastic processes. However, very few process control engineers have this preparation, so the approach to be used here will be *operational*, the goal being to provide general, useful results for the engineer through formal plausible derivations of key results. For the reader who wishes a fuller treatment of the theory and alternative approaches, Refs. [1–7] are recommended.

State Estimation

In this chapter we are interested in state estimates which can be used with real-time control schemes; thus we shall consider only *sequential state estimation* algorithms in any detail. Nonsequential methods, which require a complete data base before computation begins, shall be mentioned only in passing. By *sequential estimation* we mean that initial *a priori* estimates of the process states are continually updated and the best current estimates used in the control application. State estimation algorithms may be classified into three categories as shown in Fig. 5.1:

1. *Smoothing*, in which estimates at time t are made from data taken both before and after time t. Thus, smoothing does not provide current estimates at time t, but only estimates of the state at some time $t_1 - t$ in the past. This is

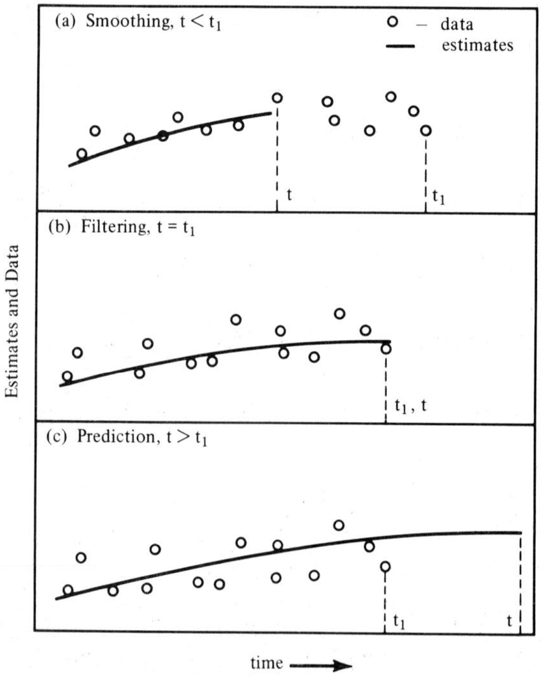

Figure 5.1 Three types of state estimation: (*a*) smoothing, (*b*) filtering, (*c*) prediction.

illustrated in Fig. 5.1*a*. Smoothing is basically a nonsequential technique and will not be discussed to any great extent here.

2. *Filtering*, in which estimates at time t are made from data up to time t, but not beyond. Thus, estimates are at $t = t_1$, the current time, as shown in Fig. 5.1*b*. Filtering is the most common estimation technique employed with feedback controllers because the most up-to-date state estimates are provided in a sequential fashion.
3. *Prediction*, in which estimates at time t are made from data up to time t_1, where $t > t_1$. This type of estimation, shown in Fig. 5.1*c*, is employed when one must extrapolate ahead of data measurements. This situation might arise when there are analysis delays in measurements of outputs such as concentration (e.g., in chromatographic analysis) or when the states themselves have time delays in them (e.g., as in flow-through piping).

In what follows we shall concentrate mainly on *filtering* and *prediction*.

Fundamentally, state estimation is the problem of determining the values of the state variables from only a knowledge of the outputs (data) and the inputs (controls, disturbances). Clearly, for this to be successful, this input-output information must provide a *unique state estimate*, which implies system *observability* (see Sec. 5.2 for a broader discussion of observability). For sequential estimation (filtering or prediction), the structure of the problem is shown in Fig. 5.2. One has available a process model corrupted by a noise process $\xi(t)$ due to either unknown disturbances or model error. In addition one has a corrupted

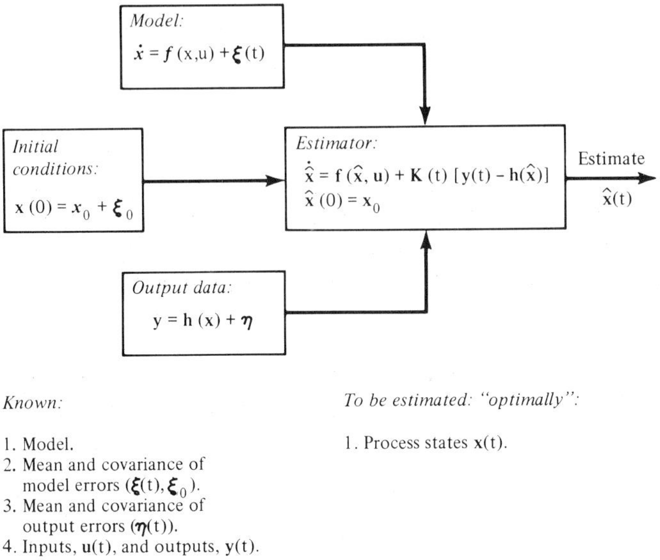

Figure 5.2 The structure of a sequential estimation device.

estimate of the initial conditions. Finally, output data, which are some combination of the state variables **h**(**x**), are measured with some error $\eta(t)$. Thus, **x**, **y** are random variables evolving in time. It is assumed that the statistics of the noise processes $\xi(t)$, $\eta(t)$ and the initial error ξ_0 are known (i.e., the form of the error distribution plus distribution moments are known). Given the statistics of ξ_0, $\xi(t)$, it is possible to envision a distribution of possible process states **p**(**x**, t) at each time resulting from the stochastic model. This distribution will evolve in time as shown in Fig. 5.3 for a single state variable. Notice that there are no data taken, and thus the predicted probability distribution widens considerably with time. If the measurements **y**(t) are available, then it is possible to consider the *conditional probability distribution* $p(x(t)|Y)$, which is the probability distribution of the state given the set of data $y(t')$, $0 \leq t' \leq t$ (denoted by Y). This distribution, plotted in Fig. 5.4, can be narrowed with time as shown so that the estimates improve with time due to the measured information. The degree of narrowing depends on the statistics of the process noise and measurement errors. The choice of the best estimate for the process state depends on the criterion used. If one wishes to minimize the *square of the deviation* between the estimate $\hat{x}(t)$ and the true state $x(t)$ (which is unknown), then the best estimate will be the *mean* of the distribution $p(x|Y)$, [i.e., $\hat{x}(t) = \bar{x}(t)$]. If, on the other hand, one wishes to maximize the *likelihood* that the estimate is the true state, then the peak in the distribution function $p(x|Y)$ would be the estimate [i.e., $x(t) = x_m(t)$]. In general these two criteria yield different estimates, though for some distributions (such as the Gaussian) they are identical.

The form of the estimation equations for a least squares criterion is shown in Fig. 5.2. The estimate can be determined by solving the differential equation for the mean of the state probability distribution. Notice that the evolution equation has two parts, one arising directly from the model and a second "feedback" term correcting the estimate for discrepancies between the actual

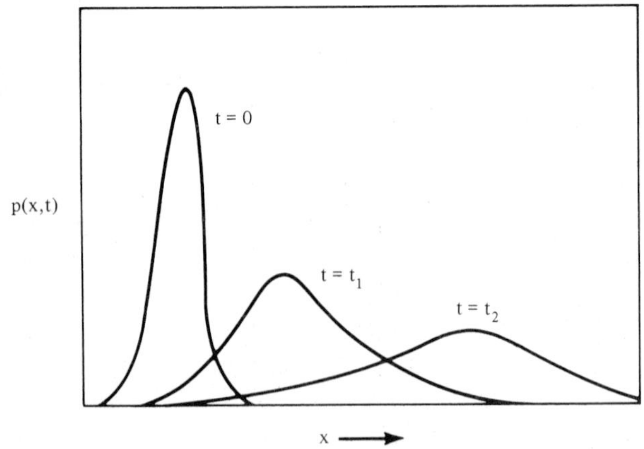

Figure 5.3 Evolution of the state probability distribution for a stochastic process without data.

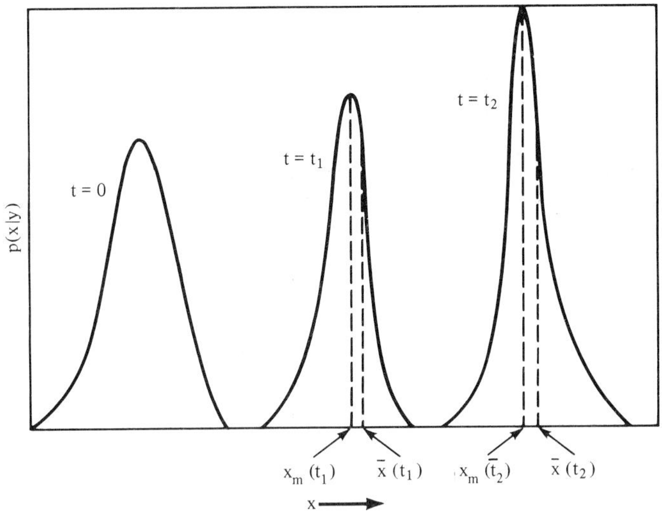

Figure 5.4 Evolution of probability distributions of system state conditional on the data. $\bar{x}(t)$ is the mean of the distribution, and $x_m(t)$ the mode or maximum likelihood value.

output data $\mathbf{y}(t)$ and the theoretical value of $\mathbf{y}(t)$ if the state estimates were correct, $\mathbf{h}(\hat{\mathbf{x}}(t))$. The magnitude of this feedback correction is controlled by a gain matrix $\mathbf{K}(t)$ which depends on the error statistics of the model and the output data. Generally speaking, $\mathbf{K}(t)$ will be large when the errors in the model are relatively larger than the errors in the data. Conversely, when the output data have a large relative error, the value of $\mathbf{K}(t)$ will be small. Thus the estimator naturally relies heaviest on the most precise information available to it. These very general concepts will be fleshed out with practical details in the ensuing sections.

Stochastic Feedback Control

Stochastic control is concerned with controller design when the measured outputs are random variables due to measurement errors and process noise. Secs. 5.4 and 5.7 below shall treat controller design for stochastic processes.

5.2 STATE ESTIMATION FOR LINEAR SYSTEMS DESCRIBED BY ORDINARY DIFFERENTIAL EQUATIONS

As in the case of feedback control, for state estimation a large body of powerful results are available for linear systems. Fortunately, a great many practical estimation problems are linear or nearly linear, so that linear state estimation techniques have both theoretical and practical importance. Although this class of system is now routinely discussed in standard references [1–7], one should note that Kalman and Bucy [8, 9] were the first to define the structure of the theory which follows.

Let us consider the system

$$\dot{\mathbf{x}} = \mathbf{A}(t)\mathbf{x} + \boldsymbol{\xi}(t) \tag{5.2.1}$$

$$\mathbf{y} = \mathbf{C}(t)\mathbf{x} + \boldsymbol{\eta}(t) \tag{5.2.2}$$

$$\mathbf{x}(0) = \mathbf{x}_0 + \boldsymbol{\xi}_0 \tag{5.2.3}$$

where $\mathbf{x}$ is an n vector of states, $\mathbf{y}$ is an l vector of continuous time outputs, $\boldsymbol{\xi}(t)$ is an n vector of random process noise, $\boldsymbol{\eta}(t)$ is an l vector of random measurement error, $\mathbf{A}(t)$ and $\mathbf{C}(t)$ are $n \times n$ and $l \times n$ time-varying matrices, $\mathbf{x}_0$ is an estimate of the initial state, and $\boldsymbol{\xi}_0$ is its random error. The variables $\mathbf{x}(t)$, $\mathbf{y}(t)$ are stochastic random variables having some probability distribution at any instant of time, and Eq. (5.2.1) is a stochastic differential equation. A mathematically rigorous analysis of such a system requires more sophisticated mathematics than is assumed here, and the reader is urged to consult [4, 5] for these details. In our treatment here, the results shall be developed through more formal means.

Observability

Let us now discuss the observability property in some detail. Roughly speaking, a system is *observable* if it is possible to determine all the state variables at some time t_0 based on a knowledge of the system output $\mathbf{y}(t)$ and control $\mathbf{u}(t)$ over some finite time interval. To be more precise, we can state that:

If every initial system state $\mathbf{x}(t_0)$ *can be determined through knowledge of the system control* $\mathbf{u}(t)$ *and system output* $\mathbf{y}(t)$ *over some finite time interval* $t_0 \le t \le t_1$, *then the system is completely observable.* Clearly it is also possible to have systems which are partially observable, i.e., in which only a subset of the state variables are observable.

Note that observability is independent of the noise processes $\boldsymbol{\xi}(t)$, $\boldsymbol{\eta}(t)$, $\boldsymbol{\xi}_0$ and is only a property of the deterministic model equations.

Conditions for observability have been derived for a number of classes of systems [1–11]. For example, for the linear system of Eqs. (5.2.1) and (5.2.2) having constant matrices **A**, **B**, **C**, it can be shown that the system is *completely observable* if and only if the rank of an $n \times nl$ "observability matrix" L_0 is n, where

$$\mathbf{L}_0 \equiv \left[\mathbf{C}^T \,\vdots\, \mathbf{A}^T\mathbf{C}^T \,\vdots\, (\mathbf{A}^T)^2\mathbf{C}^T \,\vdots\, \cdots \,\vdots\, (\mathbf{A}^T)^{n-1}\mathbf{C}^T\right] \tag{5.2.4}$$

In order to see how this condition arises, let us consider the system of Eq. (5.2.1) with zero control action and zero process noise. The solution to Eq. (5.2.1) in that case is

$$\mathbf{x}(t) = e^{\mathbf{A}t}\mathbf{x}_0 = \left(c_0\mathbf{I} + c_1 t\mathbf{A} + \cdots + c_{n-1}t^{n-1}\mathbf{A}^{n-1}\right)\mathbf{x}_0 \tag{5.2.5}$$

Now from Eq. (5.2.2),

$$\mathbf{y}(t) = \mathbf{C}\mathbf{x} = \left(c_0\mathbf{C} + c_1 t\mathbf{C}\mathbf{A} + \cdots + c_{n-1}t^{n-1}\mathbf{C}\mathbf{A}^{n-1}\right)\mathbf{x}_0 \tag{5.2.6}$$

Now for the system to be observable, one must be able to identify the initial conditions $\mathbf{x}_0$ from the data $\mathbf{y}(t)$. [For if $\mathbf{x}_0$ is known, then the model can provide all future estimates $\mathbf{x}(t)$.] Thus we must be able to construct a *pseudo-inverse* between $\mathbf{x}_0$ and $\mathbf{y}(t)$ in Eq. (5.2.6). One can show that by multiplying both sides of Eq. (5.2.6) by $\exp(\mathbf{A}t)^T$ and integrating from zero to t_f, one obtains

$$\mathbf{x}_0 = \left[\int_0^{t_f} (c_0\mathbf{C} + c_1t\mathbf{CA} + \cdots + c_{n-1}t^{n-1}\mathbf{CA}^{n-1})^T \right.$$
$$\left. \times (c_0\mathbf{C} + \cdots + c_{n-1}t^{n-1}\mathbf{CA}^{n-1})\, dt \right]^{-1}$$
$$\times \int_0^{t_f} (c_0\mathbf{C} + c_1t\mathbf{CA} + \cdots + c_{n-1}t^{n-1}\mathbf{CA}^{n-1})^T \mathbf{y}(t)\, dt \qquad (5.2.7)$$

and that this is the desired pseudo-inverse. Now for the pseudo-inverse to exist, it is required that the $n \times n$ matrix

$$\mathbf{M} = \int_0^{t_f} (c_0\mathbf{C}^T + c_1t\mathbf{A}^T\mathbf{C}^T + \cdots + c_{n-1}t^{n-1}\mathbf{A}^{T^{n-1}}\mathbf{C}^T)$$
$$\times (c_0\mathbf{C} + c_1t\mathbf{CA} + \cdots + c_{n-1}t^{n-1}\mathbf{CA}^{n-1})\, dt \qquad (5.2.8)$$

be nonsingular (i.e., have rank n). $\mathbf{M}$ may be written

$$\mathbf{M} = \int_0^{t_f} [\mathbf{C}^T \vdots\, \mathbf{A}^T\mathbf{C}^T \cdots \vdots\, \mathbf{A}^{T^{n-1}}\mathbf{C}^T] \begin{bmatrix} c_0\mathbf{I} \\ c_1t\mathbf{I} \\ \vdots \\ c_{n-1}t^{n-1}\mathbf{I} \end{bmatrix}$$
$$\times [c_0\mathbf{I} \,\vdots\, c_1t\mathbf{I} \cdots \vdots\, c_{n-1}t^{n-1}\mathbf{I}] \begin{bmatrix} \mathbf{C} \\ \mathbf{CA} \\ \vdots \\ \mathbf{CA}^{n-1} \end{bmatrix} dt$$

where $\mathbf{I}$ is an $l \times l$ identity matrix. This may be reduced to

$$M = [C^TA^TC^T \cdots \mathbf{A}^{T^{n-1}}\mathbf{C}^T] \int_0^{t_f} \mathbf{T}\, dt \begin{bmatrix} \mathbf{C} \\ \mathbf{CA} \\ \vdots \\ \mathbf{CA}^{n-1} \end{bmatrix} \qquad (5.2.9)$$

where the $nl \times nl$ matrix $\mathbf{T}$ has $l \times l$ blocks of diagonal elements $[c_kc_jt^kt^j]$, $k, j = 0, 1, \ldots, n-1$. By application of the fundamental laws of linear algebra, it is possible to show that $\mathbf{M}$ will have rank n if and only if the $n \times nl$ observability matrix given by Eq. (5.2.4) has rank n.

To generalize these results, Kalman [10] showed that the system of Eqs. (5.2.1) to (5.2.3) with time-varying **A**, **C** matrices will be completely observable at time $t_f > t_0$ if and only if

$$\mathbf{M}(t_0, t_f) = \int_{t_0}^{t_f} \mathbf{\Phi}(t, t_0)^T \mathbf{C}^T(t)\mathbf{C}(t)\mathbf{\Phi}(t, t_0)\, dt \tag{5.2.10}$$

is positive definite. Here $\mathbf{\Phi}(t, t_0)$ is the *fundamental matrix solution* defined by

$$\dot{\mathbf{\Phi}}(t, t_0) = \mathbf{A}(t)\mathbf{\Phi}(t, t_0) \qquad \mathbf{\Phi}(t_0, t_0) = \mathbf{I} \tag{3.3.12}$$

The proof of this result follows the same arguments as that for constant coefficient systems. The output is related to the initial conditions by

$$\mathbf{y}(t) = \mathbf{C}(t)\mathbf{\Phi}(t, t_0)\mathbf{x}_0 \tag{5.2.11}$$

so that by multiplying both sides by $\mathbf{\Phi}^T(t, t_0)\mathbf{C}^T(t)$ and integrating one obtains the inverse relation

$$\mathbf{x}_0 = \mathbf{M}(t_0, t_f)^{-1} \int_{t_0}^{t_f} \mathbf{\Phi}^T(t, t_0)\mathbf{C}^T(t)\mathbf{y}(t)\, dt \tag{5.2.12}$$

Now it is easy to see [2, 7] that the symmetric matrix $\mathbf{M}(t_0, t_f)$ must be nonsingular (and hence positive definite) for the inversion Eq. (5.2.12) to exist.

In the case where measurements are taken at discrete intervals of time t_i, so that Eq. (5.2.3) becomes

$$\mathbf{y}(t_i) = \mathbf{C}(t_i)\mathbf{x}(t_i) + \boldsymbol{\eta}(t_i) \qquad i = 1, 2, \ldots \tag{5.2.13}$$

the observability condition for h sampling points $t_1, t_2, \ldots, t_h$ is that the *discrete data observability matrix* $\mathbf{L}_{0d}$

$$\mathbf{L}_{0d} = \left[\mathbf{\Phi}^T(t_1, t_0)\mathbf{C}^T(t_1), \mathbf{\Phi}^T(t_2, t_0)\mathbf{C}^T(t_2), \ldots, \mathbf{\Phi}^T(t_h, t_0)\mathbf{C}^T(t_h)\right] \tag{5.2.14}$$

have rank n [11]. The proof of this result follows from the same approach as used above.

A weaker property than observability is *detectability*. *Detectability is the property that all unstable modes of the process are observable.*

Clearly any *observable* system is also *detectable*. The property of detectability is important for control because one may successfully design a control system for an unobservable but detectable system so as to estimate and control the unstable modes.

Let us now illustrate these results with some examples.

Example 5.2.1 Let us consider the CSTR system of Example 3.2.14 described by

$$\frac{dx_1}{dt} = -(1 + \mathrm{Da}_1)x_1 + u_1 \tag{3.2.123}$$

$$\frac{dx_2}{dt} = \mathrm{Da}_1 x_1 - (1 + \mathrm{Da}_3)x_2 + u_2 \tag{3.2.124}$$

where it is only possible to measure the concentration of species A:

$$y_1 = x_1 \tag{5.2.15}$$

In this case, the matrix $\mathbf{A}$ is given by Eq. (3.2.128) and

$$\mathbf{C} = [1 \quad 0]$$

so that the observability matrix is

$$\mathbf{L}_0 = [\mathbf{C}^T \,\vdots\, \mathbf{A}^T\mathbf{C}^T] = \begin{bmatrix} 1 & \vdots & -(1 + \text{Da}_1) \\ 0 & \vdots & 0 \end{bmatrix}$$

which has only rank 1. Thus the system is *not* observable. However, because all the eigenvalues of $\mathbf{A}$ are negative, there are no unstable modes and the system is *detectable.*

Example 5.2.2 If we change the output equation in Example 5.2.1 to

$$y_1 = x_2 \tag{5.2.16}$$

so that one is measuring species B, then

$$\mathbf{C} = [0 \quad 1]$$

and the observability matrix is

$$\mathbf{L}_0 = \begin{bmatrix} 0 & \text{Da}_1 \\ 1 & -(1 + \text{Da}_3) \end{bmatrix}$$

which has rank 2. Thus the system of Eqs. (3.2.123), (3.2.124), and (5.2.16) is *completely observable.*

There are important practical implications to the observability property which are illustrated for these problems. For the output $y_1 = x_1$ in Example 5.2.1, there is not sufficient information available to uniquely determine x_2, and thus *it is impossible to design an estimation scheme to estimate both x_1 and x_2* from x_1 measurements alone. Conversely, when $y_1 = x_2$ is chosen as an output, as in Example 5.2.2, there is enough information to determine x_1 uniquely, and one could devise an estimation scheme to do this. The physical reasons for this can be seen by noting that x_2 depends on x_1 and x_2, while x_1 is independent of x_2; therefore by measuring $x_2(t)$ and knowing $\mathbf{u}(t)$ in Eq. (3.2.124), $x_1(t)$ can be determined. Conversely, if we measure $x_1(t)$ and know $\mathbf{u}(t)$, $x_2(t)$ can take on any values and still satisfy the information constraints.

Example 5.2.3 To illustrate the observability conditions for nonautonomous linear systems, let us again consider the CSTR system from Example 3.2.14. The equations in the absence of control are

$$\frac{dx_1}{dt} = -(1 + \text{Da}_1)x_1 \tag{5.2.17}$$

$$\frac{dx_2}{dt} = \text{Da}_1 x_1 - (1 + \text{Da}_3)x_2 \tag{5.2.18}$$

Suppose we are interested in the system observability over the time interval during startup $0 < t < t_f$. Further, let us suppose that the temperature is increasing with time, causing k_1 and k_2 to increase with time. Thus for this problem

$$\mathbf{A}(t) = \begin{bmatrix} -[1 + \mathrm{Da}_1(t)] & 0 \\ \mathrm{Da}_1(t) & -[1 + \mathrm{Da}_3(t)] \end{bmatrix} = \begin{bmatrix} a_{11}(t) & 0 \\ a_{21}(t) & a_{22}(t) \end{bmatrix} \tag{5.2.19}$$

Let us further assume that our measuring device can measure x_1 or x_2 but not both simultaneously. If we assume a measuring device of the form

$$y(t) = \mathbf{C}(t)\mathbf{x}(t) \tag{5.2.20}$$

where $\mathbf{C} = [c_1, c_2]$ and

$$c_1(t) = \begin{cases} 1 & 0 \le t \le \dfrac{t_f}{2} \\ 0 & \dfrac{t_f}{2} < t \le t_f \end{cases}$$

$$c_2(t) = \begin{cases} 0 & 0 \le t \le \dfrac{t_f}{2} \\ 1 & \dfrac{t_f}{2} \le t \le t_f \end{cases} \tag{5.2.21}$$

then we sample $x_1(t)$ for the first half of the startup and $x_2(t)$ for the second half.

Applying the observability conditions, Eq. (5.2.8),

$$\mathbf{M}(0, t_f) = \int_0^{t_f/2} \mathbf{\Phi}(t, 0)^T \begin{bmatrix} 1 & 0 \\ 0 & 0 \end{bmatrix} \mathbf{\Phi}(t, 0)\, dt + \int_{t_f/2}^{t_f} \mathbf{\Phi}\left(t, \frac{t_f}{2}\right)^T \begin{bmatrix} 0 & 0 \\ 0 & 1 \end{bmatrix} \mathbf{\Phi}\left(t, \frac{t_f}{2}\right) dt \tag{5.2.22}$$

where

$$\mathbf{\Phi} = \begin{bmatrix} \phi_{11} & \phi_{12} \\ \phi_{21} & \phi_{22} \end{bmatrix}$$

is given by

$$\begin{aligned} \dot{\phi}_{11}(t, 0) &= a_{11}(t)\phi_{11}(t, 0) & \phi_{11}(0, 0) &= 1 \\ \dot{\phi}_{12}(t, 0) &= a_{11}(t)\phi_{12}(t, 0) & \phi_{12}(0, 0) &= 0 \\ \dot{\phi}_{21}(t, 0) &= a_{21}(t)\phi_{11}(t, 0) + a_{22}(t)\phi_{21}(t, 0) & \phi_{21}(0, 0) &= 0 \\ \dot{\phi}_{22}(t, 0) &= a_{21}(t)\phi_{12}(t, 0) + a_{22}(t)\phi_{22}(t, 0) & \phi_{22}(0, 0) &= 1 \end{aligned} \tag{5.2.23}$$

which immediately implies $\phi_{12}(t, 0) \equiv 0$. Thus

$$\mathbf{M}(0, t_f) = \int_0^{t_f/2} \begin{bmatrix} \phi_{11}(t,0) & \phi_{21}(t,0) \\ 0 & \phi_{22}(t,0) \end{bmatrix} \begin{bmatrix} 1 & 0 \\ 0 & 0 \end{bmatrix} \begin{bmatrix} \phi_{11}(t,0) & 0 \\ \phi_{21}(t,0) & \phi_{22}(t,0) \end{bmatrix} dt$$

$$+ \int_{t_f/2}^{t_f} \begin{bmatrix} \phi_{11}\left(t, \frac{t_f}{2}\right) & \phi_{21}\left(t, \frac{t_f}{2}\right) \\ 0 & \phi_{22}\left(t, \frac{t_f}{2}\right) \end{bmatrix} \begin{bmatrix} 0 & 0 \\ 0 & 1 \end{bmatrix} \begin{bmatrix} \phi_{11}\left(t, \frac{t_f}{2}\right) & 0 \\ \phi_{21}\left(t, \frac{t_f}{2}\right) & \phi_{22}\left(t, \frac{t_f}{2}\right) \end{bmatrix} dt \tag{5.2.24}$$

or

$$\mathbf{M}(0, t_f) = \int_0^{t_f/2} \begin{bmatrix} \phi_{11}(t,0)^2 & 0 \\ 0 & 0 \end{bmatrix} dt + \int_{t_f/2}^{t_f} \begin{bmatrix} \phi_{21}\left(t, \frac{t_f}{2}\right)^2 & \phi_{21}\phi_{22} \\ \phi_{21}\phi_{22} & \phi_{22}\left(t, \frac{t_f}{2}\right)^2 \end{bmatrix} dt \tag{5.2.25}$$

Now clearly the process is *not observable* for $0 \le t \le t_f/2$ because the first term is *not* positive definite. However, when the sampling device is changed to x_2 at $t = t_f/2$, the system can be observable, as shown by the second term of Eq. (5.2.25), which can be positive definite. The final conclusion has to be based on the specific values of $a_{11}(t)$, $a_{21}(t)$, $a_{22}(t)$.

Note that the second term in Eq. (5.2.25) has a singular matrix for an integrand, but the integral

$$\begin{bmatrix} \int_{t_f/2}^{t_f} \phi_{21}\left(t, \frac{t_f}{2}\right)^2 dt & \int_{t_f/2}^{t_f} \phi_{21}\left(t, \frac{t_f}{2}\right)\phi_{22}\left(t, \frac{t_f}{2}\right) dt \\ \int_{t_f/2}^{t_f} \phi_{21}\left(t, \frac{t_f}{2}\right)\phi_{22}\left(t, \frac{t_f}{2}\right) dt & \int_{t_f/2}^{t_f} \phi_{22}^2\left(t, \frac{t_f}{2}\right) dt \end{bmatrix}$$

is in general *not singular* and could be positive definite.

Optimal State Estimation

Let us now discuss the concept of *optimal estimation* and objective functionals for estimation. There are many possible objectives one could use in defining optimal state estimates (e.g., minimal least squares, maximum likelihood, minimum maximum error); however, in our discussion here we shall deal with the minimum least squares objective and shall phrase our presentation so that it may be most easily extended to nonlinear problems. The weighted least squares objective to be considered along with the system equations (5.2.1) to (5.2.3) is

$$I = \tfrac{1}{2}[\mathbf{x}(0) - \mathbf{x}_0]^T \mathbf{P}_0^{-1}[\mathbf{x}(0) - \mathbf{x}_0] + \frac{1}{2}\int_0^{t_f} \{(\dot{\mathbf{x}} - \mathbf{A}\mathbf{x})^T \mathbf{R}(t)(\dot{\mathbf{x}} - \mathbf{A}\mathbf{x})$$

$$+ [\mathbf{y}(t) - \mathbf{C}(t)\mathbf{x}(t)]^T \mathbf{Q}(t)[\mathbf{y}(t) - \mathbf{C}(t)\mathbf{x}(t)]\}\, dt \tag{5.2.26}$$

where the first term minimizes the squared error of initial condition estimates, the second term minimizes the integral squared modeling error, and the third term minimizes the integral squared measurement error. The weighting factors $\mathbf{P}_0^{-1}$, $\mathbf{R}(t)$, $\mathbf{Q}(t)$ are chosen based on the statistics of the problem (see the discussion to follow). Let us assume the noise processes $\boldsymbol{\xi}(t)$, $\boldsymbol{\eta}(t)$ in Eqs. (5.2.1) to (5.2.3) to be Gaussian and uncorrelated in time (i.e., *white* noise) as well as uncorrelated with the initial state. Also, we assume that the expected value relations

$$\mathcal{E}(\boldsymbol{\xi}(t)) = \mathbf{0} \qquad \mathcal{E}(\boldsymbol{\eta}(t)) = \mathbf{0} \qquad \mathcal{E}(\boldsymbol{\xi}(t)\boldsymbol{\xi}(\tau)^T) = \mathbf{R}^{-1}(t)\delta(t-\tau)$$

$$\mathcal{E}(\boldsymbol{\eta}(t)\mathbf{x}^T(0)) = \mathbf{0} \qquad \mathcal{E}(\boldsymbol{\xi}(t)\mathbf{x}^T(0)) = \mathbf{0} \qquad \mathcal{E}(\boldsymbol{\xi}(t)\boldsymbol{\eta}^T(\tau)) = \mathbf{0}$$

$$\mathcal{E}(\mathbf{x}(0)) = \mathbf{x}_0 \qquad \mathcal{E}([\mathbf{x}_0 - \mathbf{x}(0)][\mathbf{x}_0 - \mathbf{x}(0)]^T) = \mathbf{P}_0$$

$$\mathcal{E}(\boldsymbol{\eta}(t)\boldsymbol{\eta}(\tau)^T) = \mathbf{Q}^{-1}(t)\delta(t-\tau) \tag{5.2.27}$$

hold, where $\mathbf{P}_0$ is the covariance of the initial state errors, $\mathbf{R}^{-1}(t)$ is the covariance of the process noise, and $\mathbf{Q}^{-1}$ is the covariance of the measurement errors. Under these conditions one can show [1–7] that the stochastic process $\mathbf{x}(t)$ described by Eq. (5.2.1) has a Gaussian distribution at each point in time and the measurements $\mathbf{y}(t)$ given by Eq. (5.2.2) will also be Gaussianly distributed. Thus, the conditional probability distribution $p(x|Y)$ will also be Gaussian and the least squares estimate, the maximum likelihood estimate, and the minimum maximum deviation estimates are all the same.

There is a very elegant and powerful theory which applies to linear system state estimation. However, the scope is enormous and requires mathematical background not expected of the reader; thus Refs. [1–7] should be consulted for more theoretical details. We shall present key results in a formal way and concentrate on the applications of the theory.

We shall now proceed to derive state estimation algorithms which estimate $\mathbf{x}(t)$ such that the objective, Eq. (5.2.26), is minimized. This problem may be reformulated by defining $\mathbf{u}(t) = \dot{\mathbf{x}} - \mathbf{A}\mathbf{x}$, and rewriting the objective

$$I = \tfrac{1}{2}[\mathbf{x}(0) - \mathbf{x}_0]^T \mathbf{P}_0^{-1}[\mathbf{x}(0) - \mathbf{x}_0] + \frac{1}{2}\int_0^{t_f} \{\mathbf{u}(t)^T \mathbf{R}(t)\mathbf{u}(t) + [\mathbf{y}(t) - \mathbf{C}(t)\mathbf{x}(t)]^T$$

$$\times \mathbf{Q}(t)[\mathbf{y}(t) - \mathbf{C}(t)\mathbf{x}(t)]\}\, dt \tag{5.2.28}$$

Thus the estimation problem can be posed as a deterministic *optimal control problem*; i.e., select the control $\mathbf{u}(t)$ such that I in Eq. (5.2.28) is minimized subject to the constraints

$$\dot{\mathbf{x}}(t) = \mathbf{A}(t)\mathbf{x}(t) + \mathbf{u}(t) \tag{5.2.29}$$

$$\mathbf{x}(0) \text{ unspecified} \tag{5.2.30}$$

Note that after the optimal "control" $\mathbf{u}(t)$ is found, Eqs. (5.2.29) and (5.2.30) can be used to generate the optimal state estimates.

Applying the maximum principle (see Chap. 3) to this problem, one obtains

$$H = \tfrac{1}{2}\left[\mathbf{u}^T\mathbf{R}\mathbf{u} + (\mathbf{y} - \mathbf{C}\mathbf{x})^T\mathbf{Q}(\mathbf{y} - \mathbf{C}\mathbf{x})\right] + \boldsymbol{\lambda}^T(\mathbf{A}\mathbf{x} + \mathbf{u}) \tag{5.2.31}$$

and the condition $\partial H/\partial \mathbf{u} = \mathbf{0}$ yields

$$\mathbf{u}(t) = -\mathbf{R}^{-1}(t)\boldsymbol{\lambda}(t) \tag{5.2.32}$$

where

$$\dot{\boldsymbol{\lambda}}^T = -\frac{\partial H}{\partial \mathbf{x}} = \left[\mathbf{C}^T\mathbf{Q}(\mathbf{y} - \mathbf{C}\mathbf{x}) - \mathbf{A}^T\boldsymbol{\lambda}\right]^T \tag{5.2.33}$$

or

$$\dot{\boldsymbol{\lambda}} = -\mathbf{C}^T\mathbf{Q}\mathbf{C}\mathbf{x} - \mathbf{A}^T\boldsymbol{\lambda} + \mathbf{C}^T\mathbf{Q}\mathbf{y} \tag{5.2.34}$$

Because both $\mathbf{x}(0)$, $\mathbf{x}(t_f)$ are free, then there are two boundary conditions on $\boldsymbol{\lambda}$:

$$\boldsymbol{\lambda}(t_f) = \mathbf{0} \tag{5.2.35}$$

and

$$\mathbf{x}(0) = \mathbf{x}_0 - \mathbf{P}_0\,\boldsymbol{\lambda}(0) \tag{5.2.36}$$

By substituting Eq. (5.2.32) into Eq. (5.2.29), one obtains

$$\dot{\mathbf{x}} = \mathbf{A}\mathbf{x} - \mathbf{R}^{-1}\boldsymbol{\lambda} \tag{5.2.37}$$

Now Eqs. (5.2.34) to (5.2.37) form a two-point boundary value problem which can be solved for $\mathbf{x}(t)$, $\boldsymbol{\lambda}(t)$ and thus produce the optimal estimates. To make things more explicit, we shall denote $\hat{\mathbf{x}}(t|t_f)$, $\hat{\mathbf{u}}(t|t_f)$ as the optimal estimates and controls at time t, with data $\mathbf{y}(t)$ up to time t_f. Thus $\hat{\mathbf{x}}(t|t_f)$ is the estimate found from the two-point boundary value problem of Eqs. (5.2.34) to (5.2.37). We shall now make a transformation

$$\hat{\mathbf{x}}(t|t_f) = \mathbf{w}(t) - \mathbf{P}(t)\boldsymbol{\lambda}(t) \tag{5.2.38}$$

where the n vector $\mathbf{w}(t)$ and $n \times n$ matrix $\mathbf{P}(t)$ are to be determined. If we substitute Eq. (5.2.38) into Eq. (5.2.37), then one obtains for each side of the equation

$$\text{RHS} = \mathbf{A}(\mathbf{w} - \mathbf{P}\boldsymbol{\lambda}) - \mathbf{R}^{-1}\boldsymbol{\lambda} \tag{5.2.39}$$

$$\begin{aligned} \text{LHS} &= \dot{\mathbf{w}} - \dot{\mathbf{P}}\boldsymbol{\lambda} - \mathbf{P}\dot{\boldsymbol{\lambda}} \\ &= \dot{\mathbf{w}} - \dot{\mathbf{P}}\boldsymbol{\lambda} + \mathbf{P}\left[\mathbf{C}^T\mathbf{Q}\mathbf{C}(\mathbf{w} - \mathbf{P}\boldsymbol{\lambda}) + \mathbf{A}^T\boldsymbol{\lambda} - \mathbf{C}^T\mathbf{Q}\mathbf{y}\right] \end{aligned} \tag{5.2.40}$$

Collecting terms, one obtains

$$\dot{\mathbf{w}} - \mathbf{P}\mathbf{C}^T\mathbf{Q}(\mathbf{y} - \mathbf{C}\mathbf{w}) - \mathbf{A}\mathbf{w} = (\dot{\mathbf{P}} - \mathbf{P}\mathbf{A}^T - \mathbf{A}\mathbf{P} - \mathbf{R}^{-1} + \mathbf{P}\mathbf{C}^T\mathbf{Q}\mathbf{C}\mathbf{P})\boldsymbol{\lambda} \tag{5.2.41}$$

Now we can choose to define $\mathbf{w}(t)$, $\mathbf{P}(t)$ such that the coefficients in Eq. (5.2.41) vanish and choose the boundary conditions to satisfy Eqs. (5.2.35) and (5.2.36).

Thus we have

$$\dot{\mathbf{w}} = \mathbf{A}\mathbf{w} + \mathbf{P}\mathbf{C}^T\mathbf{Q}(\mathbf{y} - \mathbf{C}\mathbf{w}) \qquad \mathbf{w}(0) = \mathbf{x}_0 \tag{5.2.42}$$

$$\dot{\mathbf{P}} = \mathbf{P}\mathbf{A}^T + \mathbf{A}\mathbf{P}^T + \mathbf{R}^{-1} - \mathbf{P}\mathbf{C}^T\mathbf{Q}\mathbf{C}\mathbf{P} \qquad \mathbf{P}(0) = \mathbf{P}_0 \tag{5.2.43}$$

Note that the state estimates may be found by first solving Eqs. (5.2.42) and (5.2.43) forward in time to produce $\mathbf{w}(t)$, $\mathbf{P}(t)$, then solving backward in time using (5.2.35), (5.2.37), and (5.2.38) to find the optimal estimates $\hat{\mathbf{x}}(t|t_f)$. This estimate $\hat{\mathbf{x}}(t|t_f)$ is the minimal least squares estimate at t, conditional on all the data in the interval $0 \le t' \le t_f$. Thus, this is a *smoothed* estimate, *nonsequential*, and usually impossible to obtain in real time.

The *filtering estimate*, which is needed for online control, is $\hat{\mathbf{x}}(t_f|t_f)$, the minimal least squares estimate at t_f conditional on all the data up to time t_f. From Eq. (5.2.35) one sees that at the end of a data period $t = t_f$, $\boldsymbol{\lambda}(t_f)$ always vanishes. Thus for any t_f, Eq. (5.2.38) yields the result

$$\hat{\mathbf{x}}(t_f|t_f) \equiv \mathbf{w}(t_f) \tag{5.2.44}$$

Thus the filtered estimates are determined from the sequential real-time equation (5.2.42) where t is always the current time.

$$\dot{\hat{\mathbf{x}}}(t|t) = \mathbf{A}(t)\hat{\mathbf{x}}(t|t) + \mathbf{P}(t)\mathbf{C}^T(t)\mathbf{Q}(t)[\mathbf{y}(t) - \mathbf{C}(t)\hat{\mathbf{x}}(t|t)] \qquad \hat{\mathbf{x}}(0|0) = \mathbf{x}_0 \tag{5.2.45}$$

The $n \times n$ matrix function $\mathbf{P}(t)$ is given by Eq. (5.2.43).

Let us now investigate the statistics of these filtered estimates. The error between the true state $\mathbf{x}(t)$ and the filter estimate is given by the stochastic variable

$$\mathbf{e}(t) = \mathbf{x}(t) - \hat{\mathbf{x}}(t|t) \tag{5.2.46}$$

Making use of Eqs. (5.2.1) and (5.2.45), one obtains the stochastic error process

$$\dot{\mathbf{e}}(t) = [\mathbf{A}(t) - \mathbf{P}(t)\mathbf{C}^T(t)\mathbf{Q}(t)\mathbf{C}(t)]\mathbf{e}(t) + \boldsymbol{\xi}(t) - \mathbf{P}(t)\mathbf{C}^T(t)\mathbf{Q}(t)\boldsymbol{\eta}(t) \tag{5.2.47}$$

with the initial condition taken from Eq. (5.2.3) as

$$\mathbf{e}(0) = \boldsymbol{\xi}_0 \tag{5.2.48}$$

The expected value of the error process

$$\bar{\mathbf{e}}(t) = \mathcal{E}(\mathbf{e}(t)) \tag{5.2.49}$$

can be found by taking expectations of Eqs. (5.2.47) and (5.2.48)

$$\dot{\bar{\mathbf{e}}}(t) = (\mathbf{A} - \mathbf{P}\mathbf{C}^T\mathbf{Q}\mathbf{C})\bar{e}(t) \qquad \bar{\mathbf{e}}(0) = \mathbf{0} \tag{5.2.50}$$

The solution to this equation yields $\bar{\mathbf{e}}(t)$ identically zero, so the estimate has no bias. The covariance of the estimation error can be found from

$$\mathbf{Cov}(t, \tau) = \mathcal{E}(\mathbf{e}(t)\mathbf{e}^T(\tau)) \tag{5.2.51}$$

However, because of the statistical assumptions we have made, the estimates are uncorrelated in time and the covariance depends only on one time, i.e.,

$$\mathbf{Cov}(t, \tau) = \mathbf{Cov}(t) = \mathcal{E}(\mathbf{e}(t)\mathbf{e}^T(\tau)\delta(t-\tau)) = \mathcal{E}(\mathbf{e}(t)\mathbf{e}^T(t)) \tag{5.2.52}$$

Postmultiplying Eq. (5.2.47) by $\mathbf{e}^T(t)$ and taking expectations, one obtains

$$\frac{d\,\mathbf{Cov}(t)}{dt} = \mathcal{E}\left[\mathbf{e}(t)\dot{\mathbf{e}}^T + \dot{\mathbf{e}}(t)\mathbf{e}^T\right] = \mathcal{E}\left\{\mathbf{e}(t)\left[\mathbf{e}^T(\mathbf{A}^T - \mathbf{C}^T\mathbf{QCP}) + \boldsymbol{\xi}^T - \boldsymbol{\eta}^T\mathbf{QCP}\right]\right.$$
$$\left. + \left[(\mathbf{A} - \mathbf{PC}^T\mathbf{QC})\mathbf{e} + \boldsymbol{\xi} - \mathbf{PC}^T\mathbf{Q}\boldsymbol{\eta}\right]\mathbf{e}^T\right\} \tag{5.2.53}$$

Now formally it is possible to write down the solution to Eq. (5.2.47) as

$$\mathbf{e}(t) = \boldsymbol{\Phi}(t, t_0)\boldsymbol{\xi}_0 + \int_0^t \boldsymbol{\Phi}(t, \tau)\left[\boldsymbol{\xi}(\tau) - \mathbf{P}(\tau)\mathbf{C}^T(\tau)\mathbf{Q}(\tau)\boldsymbol{\eta}(\tau)\right] d\tau \tag{5.2.54}$$

where $\boldsymbol{\Phi}(t, \tau)$ is the transition matrix of the system. Because the noise is uncorrelated in time and $\boldsymbol{\xi}_0$, $\boldsymbol{\xi}$, $\boldsymbol{\eta}$ are uncorrelated, postmultiplying Eq. (5.2.54) by $\boldsymbol{\xi}^T(t)$ or $\boldsymbol{\eta}^T(t)$ gives

$$\mathcal{E}(\mathbf{e}(t)\boldsymbol{\xi}^T(t)) = \mathcal{E}\left(\int_0^t \boldsymbol{\Phi}(t, \tau)\boldsymbol{\xi}(\tau)\boldsymbol{\xi}^T(t)\, d\tau\right)$$
$$= \int_0^t \boldsymbol{\Phi}(t, \tau)\mathbf{R}^{-1}(t)\delta(t-\tau)\, d\tau = \tfrac{1}{2}\mathbf{R}^{-1}(t) \tag{5.2.55}$$

$$\mathcal{E}(\mathbf{e}(t)\boldsymbol{\eta}^T(t)) = \mathcal{E}\left(-\int_0^t \boldsymbol{\Phi}(t, \tau)\mathbf{P}(\tau)\mathbf{C}^T(\tau)\mathbf{Q}(\tau)\boldsymbol{\eta}(\tau)\boldsymbol{\eta}^T(t)\, d\tau\right)$$
$$= -\int_0^t \boldsymbol{\Phi}(t, \tau)\mathbf{P}(\tau)\mathbf{C}^T(\tau)\mathbf{Q}(\tau)\mathbf{Q}^{-1}(t)\delta(t-\tau)\, d\tau = -\tfrac{1}{2}\mathbf{P}(t)\mathbf{C}^T(t) \tag{5.2.56}$$

where the factor $\frac{1}{2}$ arises in Eqs. (5.2.55) and (5.2.56) because the delta function takes nonzero values at the upper limit of integration.

Substituting into Eq. (5.2.53), one obtains

$$\frac{d\,\mathbf{Cov}(t)}{dt} = \mathbf{Cov}(t)(\mathbf{A}^T - \mathbf{C}^T\mathbf{QCP}) + \tfrac{1}{2}\mathbf{R}^{-1} + \tfrac{1}{2}\mathbf{PC}^T\mathbf{QCP}$$
$$+ (\mathbf{A} - \mathbf{PC}^T\mathbf{QC})\mathbf{Cov}(t) + \tfrac{1}{2}\mathbf{R}^{-1} + \tfrac{1}{2}\mathbf{PC}^T\mathbf{QCP} \tag{5.2.57}$$

where $\mathbf{Cov}(0) = \mathbf{P}_0$. It is useful to notice that Eqs. (5.2.57) and (5.2.43) are identical if we let

$$\mathbf{Cov}(t) = \mathbf{P}(t) \tag{5.2.58}$$

Thus we see that $\mathbf{P}(t)$ is the filter *estimate covariance* and can be precomputed because it does not depend on the estimate $\hat{\mathbf{x}}(t|t)$ or the data $\mathbf{y}(t)$. To summarize our optimal estimator for linear systems, one has the following results:

1. *Smoothed estimates* $\hat{\mathbf{x}}(t|t_f)$ for the system of Eqs. (5.2.1) to (5.2.3) and (5.2.26) can be found by solving Eqs. (5.2.45) and (5.2.53) for the filtered estimates $\hat{\mathbf{x}}(t|t) = \mathbf{w}(t)$ and filter covariance $\mathbf{P}(t)$, then solving Eqs. (5.2.37) backwards,

which takes the form

$$\dot{\hat{\mathbf{x}}}(t|t_f) = \mathbf{A}(t)\hat{\mathbf{x}}(t|t_f) + \mathbf{R}^{-1}\mathbf{P}^{-1}[\hat{\mathbf{x}}(t|t_f) - \hat{\mathbf{x}}(t|t)] \tag{5.2.59}$$

where $\hat{\mathbf{x}}(t_f|t_f)$ is known from the filtering result.

By subtracting the true state $\mathbf{x}(t)$ from both sides of Eq. (5.2.38) it is possible to show that the smoothed estimate covariance

$$\mathbf{P}(t|t_f) \equiv \mathcal{E}\{[\hat{\mathbf{x}}(t|t_f) - \mathbf{x}(t)][\hat{\mathbf{x}}(t|t_f) - \mathbf{x}(t)]^T\} \tag{5.2.60}$$

can be related to the filtered covariance by

$$\mathbf{P}(t|t_f) = \mathbf{P}(t) - \mathbf{P}(t)\mathbf{\Lambda}(t)\mathbf{P}(t) \tag{5.2.61}$$

where

$$\mathbf{\Lambda}(t) = \mathcal{E}(\mathbf{P}^{-1}\mathbf{e}\boldsymbol{\lambda}^T + \boldsymbol{\lambda}\mathbf{e}^T\mathbf{P}^{-1} - \boldsymbol{\lambda}\boldsymbol{\lambda}^T) \tag{5.2.62}$$

If we note that Eq. (5.2.34) can be written

$$\dot{\boldsymbol{\lambda}} = -(\mathbf{A}^T - \mathbf{C}^T\mathbf{QCP})\boldsymbol{\lambda} + \mathbf{C}^T\mathbf{Q}\boldsymbol{\eta} + \mathbf{C}^T\mathbf{QCe} \qquad \boldsymbol{\lambda}(t_f) = \mathbf{0} \tag{5.2.63}$$

then substituting Eqs. (5.2.43), (5.2.47), and (5.2.63) into Eq. (5.2.62) yields

$$\dot{\mathbf{\Lambda}}(t) = -(\mathbf{A}^T - \mathbf{C}^T\mathbf{QCP})\mathbf{\Lambda} - \mathbf{\Lambda}(\mathbf{A} - \mathbf{PC}^T\mathbf{QC}) + \mathbf{C}^T\mathbf{QC} \qquad \mathbf{\Lambda}(t_f) = \mathbf{0} \tag{5.2.64}$$

Because $\mathbf{\Lambda}$ is positive definite, the covariance for the smoothed estimate is always as good as or better than the filtered estimate. An alternative equation for $\mathbf{P}(t|t_f)$ is [1]

$$\dot{\mathbf{P}}(t|t_f) = (\mathbf{A} + \mathbf{R}^{-1}\mathbf{P}^{-1})\mathbf{P}(t|t_f) + \mathbf{P}(t|t_f)(\mathbf{A}^T + \mathbf{P}^{-1}\mathbf{R}^{-1}) - \mathbf{R}^{-1} - \mathbf{PC}^T\mathbf{QCP} \qquad \mathbf{P}(t_f|t_f) = \mathbf{P}(t_f) \tag{5.2.65}$$

2. *Filtering estimates* $\hat{\mathbf{x}}(t|t)$ for the system of Eqs. (5.2.1) to (5.2.3) and (5.2.26) can be found by solving Eq. (5.2.45). The estimate covariance $\mathbf{P}(t)$ is computed from Eq. (5.2.43). Notice that the filter estimates may have covariances which increase or decrease with time depending on the noise covariances $\mathbf{R}^{-1}$, $\mathbf{Q}^{-1}$.
3. *Prediction estimates* $\hat{\mathbf{x}}(t|t_0)$ for the system of Eqs. (5.2.1) to (5.2.3) and (5.2.26) are estimates at time $t > t_0$ for a system having no data after time t_0. These arise directly from the filtering equations if we let $\mathbf{Q}(t) \to 0$ for $t > t_0$ in Eqs. (5.2.43) and (5.2.45). Thus the prediction equations are

$$\dot{\hat{\mathbf{x}}}(t|t_0) = \mathbf{A}\hat{\mathbf{x}}(t|t_0) \tag{5.2.66}$$

where $\hat{\mathbf{x}}(t_0|t_0)$ is the filter estimate at time t_0. The prediction covariances $\mathbf{P}(t|t_0)$ are given by

$$\dot{\mathbf{P}}(t|t_0) = \mathbf{P}(t|t_0)\mathbf{A}^T(t) + \mathbf{A}(t)\mathbf{P}(t|t_0) + \mathbf{R}^{-1} \qquad \mathbf{P}(t_0|t_0) = \mathbf{P}(t_0) \tag{5.2.67}$$

Note that the prediction equations yield estimates *not conditional on data*, and $\mathbf{P}(t|t_0)$ generally tends to increase with time.

Let us now review some important properties of the estimation equations. First, all covariance matrices are *symmetric* and *positive semidefinite*. Thus the calculation of the covariance matrix having n^2 elements

$$\mathbf{P}(t) = \begin{bmatrix} P_{11} & P_{12} & \cdots & P_{1n} \\ P_{21} & P_{22} & \cdots & P_{2n} \\ \cdots & \cdots & \cdots & \cdots \\ P_{n1} & \cdots & \cdots & P_{nn} \end{bmatrix}$$

requires only the solution of $(n^2 + n)/2$ ODE equations because $P_{ij} = P_{ji}$. Second, observe that the filtering equations can be written in the form

$$\dot{\hat{\mathbf{x}}}(t|t) = \mathbf{A}\hat{\mathbf{x}} + \mathbf{K}(t)[\mathbf{y}(t) - \mathbf{C}\hat{\mathbf{x}}(t)] \tag{5.2.68}$$

where

$$\mathbf{K}(t) = \mathbf{P}(t)\mathbf{C}^T(t)\mathbf{Q}(t) \tag{5.2.69}$$

so that the filter behaves like the process model except for the feedback correction terms coming from the data. Note how similar this is to the optimal linear-quadratic feedback control law seen in Chap. 3. The covariance equations are Riccati equations very similar to those for $\mathbf{S}(t)$ in feedback control problems. In fact there is a very precise *duality* relationship between these two problems (see [8, 9]).

There are a limited number of more general results available for linear systems. Estimation equations when the process and sampling noise are correlated, or when the errors are correlated in time (so-called *colored noise*), for example, have been developed. The reader is urged to consult [1–7] as well as the recent literature for a discussion of these cases. The situation when the noise is non-Gaussian is particularly difficult to analyze because higher moments of the process state must be treated. Thus it is usually desirable to assume Gaussian distributions for the noise because these are completely described by the first two moments. Practically speaking, a wide range of naturally occurring noise processes can be well approximated by Gaussian distributions due to the central limit theorem of statistics.

Before continuing our discussion of theoretical results, let us illustrate the application of the filter with an example problem.

Example 5.2.4 Let us consider the CSTR problem discussed in Example 5.2.1. The system is described by

$$\dot{x}_1 = -(1 + \mathrm{Da}_1)x_1 + \xi_1(t) \qquad x_1(0) = x_{10} + \xi_{10} \tag{5.2.70}$$

$$\dot{x}_2 = \mathrm{Da}_1 x_1 - (1 + \mathrm{Da}_3)x_2 + \xi(t) \qquad x_2(0) = x_{20} + \xi_{20} \tag{5.2.71}$$

Recall that we know from Example 5.2.2 that the deterministic system is observable if we measure $x_2(t)$; thus let us choose our measuring device as

$$y(t) = x_2(t) + \eta(t) \tag{5.2.72}$$

Now let us assume that the process noise processes $\xi_1(t)$, $\xi_2(t)$ (possibly due to flow variations, temperature variations, or other unmeasured process disturbances) are white, Gaussian at every t with mean zero and covariance $R^{-1}(t)$, i.e.,

$$\mathcal{E}(\xi(t)\xi^T(\tau)) = \mathbf{R}^{-1}(t)\delta(t-\tau) \tag{5.2.73}$$

where

$$\mathbf{R}^{-1} = \begin{bmatrix} \rho_{11} & \rho_{12} \\ \rho_{21} & \rho_{22} \end{bmatrix} = \begin{bmatrix} \mathcal{E}(\xi_1(t)^2) & \mathcal{E}(\xi_1(t)\xi_2(t)) \\ \mathcal{E}(\xi_2(t)\xi_1(t)) & \mathcal{E}(\xi_2(t)^2) \end{bmatrix} \tag{5.2.74}$$

Similarly we assume that $\eta(t)$ and ξ_0 are white Gaussian with zero mean and covariances

$$\mathcal{E}(\eta(t)\eta(\tau)) = Q^{-1}(t)\delta(t-\tau) \tag{5.2.75}$$

$$\mathcal{E}(\xi_0\,\xi_0^T) = \mathbf{P}_0 \tag{5.2.76}$$

where

$$\mathbf{P}_0 = \begin{bmatrix} P_{110} & P_{120} \\ P_{210} & P_{220} \end{bmatrix} = \begin{bmatrix} \mathcal{E}(\xi_{10}^2) & \mathcal{E}(\xi_{10}\xi_{20}) \\ \mathcal{E}(\xi_{20}\xi_{10}) & \mathcal{E}(\xi_{20}^2) \end{bmatrix} \tag{5.2.77}$$

Applying Eq. (5.2.45), the filter equations become

$$\dot{\hat{x}}_1 = -(1 + \text{Da}_1)\hat{x}_1 + P_{12}(t)Q(t)[y - \hat{x}_2(t)] \tag{5.2.78}$$

$$\dot{\hat{x}}_2 = \text{Da}_1\hat{x}_1 - (1 + \text{Da}_3)\hat{x}_2 + P_{22}(t)Q(t)[y - \hat{x}_2(t)] \tag{5.2.79}$$

where the precomputable covariance equations arise from Eq. (5.2.43) and take the form

$$\begin{aligned} \dot{P}_{11}(t) &= -2(1 + \text{Da}_1)P_{11} + \rho_{11} - Q(P_{12})^2 \\ \dot{P}_{12}(t) &= \text{Da}_1 P_{11} - (2 + \text{Da}_1 + \text{Da}_3)P_{12} + \rho_{12} - Q\,P_{12}P_{22} \\ \dot{P}_{22}(t) &= 2\text{Da}_1 P_{12} - 2(1 + \text{Da}_3)P_{22} + \rho_{22} - Q(P_{22})^2 \end{aligned} \tag{5.2.80}$$

where symmetry requires $P_{12}(t) = P_{21}(t)$.

To implement this state estimator, one must compute $\mathbf{P}(t)$ off-line and store it in the process control computer. Then $y(t)$ is fed to the estimator equations (5.2.78) and (5.2.79), which are numerically integrated in real time to yield current estimates of x_1 and x_2.

To demonstrate the performance of this estimation scheme, numerical computations were carried out for the parameter values

$$\text{Da}_1 = 3.0 \qquad \text{Da}_3 = 1.0 \qquad t_f = 2.0 \qquad x_{10} = 1.0 \qquad x_{20} = 0.0$$

$$\mathbf{P}(0) = \begin{bmatrix} 0.04 & 0 \\ 0 & 0.01 \end{bmatrix} \qquad Q^{-1} = 0.0025 \qquad \mathbf{R}^{-1} = \mathbf{0}$$

and the filter initial guesses were

$$\hat{x}_1(0) = 0.85 \qquad \hat{x}_2(0) = 0.15$$

Measurement errors having a zero mean and variance $\sigma = 0.05$ were simulated by a random number generator and added to the x_2 values to produce the sensor signals $y(t)$. The estimate covariances $P_{ij}(t)$ are plotted in Fig. 5.5. Because $\mathbf{R}^{-1} = \mathbf{0}$, all the P_{ij} decline to zero as $t \to \infty$. The "true" states x_1, x_2, the filter estimates $\hat{x}_1$, $\hat{x}_2$, and the measurement noise $\eta(t)$ are shown in Fig. 5.6. Note how the estimates converge toward the "true" values even with high measurement error and poor initial estimates.

This example problem serves to illustrate a shortcoming in the theoretical results we have presented so far. Our results require that the measuring device yield data continuously in time. However, for this example problem we are measuring a concentration in the reactor, and many composition measurements can only be made by sampling at discrete intervals in time (e.g., through on-line chromatography). Thus we need to extend our estimation results to include discrete time sampling.

Estimation with Discrete Time Data

For *samples discrete in time*, the output device should be modeled by

$$\mathbf{y}(t_k) = \mathbf{C}(t_k)\mathbf{x}(t_k) + \boldsymbol{\eta}(t_k) \qquad k = 1, 2, \ldots \tag{5.2.81}$$

where $\boldsymbol{\eta}(t_k)$ is Gaussian white (uncorrelated in time) noise with zero mean and covariance $\mathbf{Q}_k^{-1}$. It can be shown [12] that the proper estimation equations for

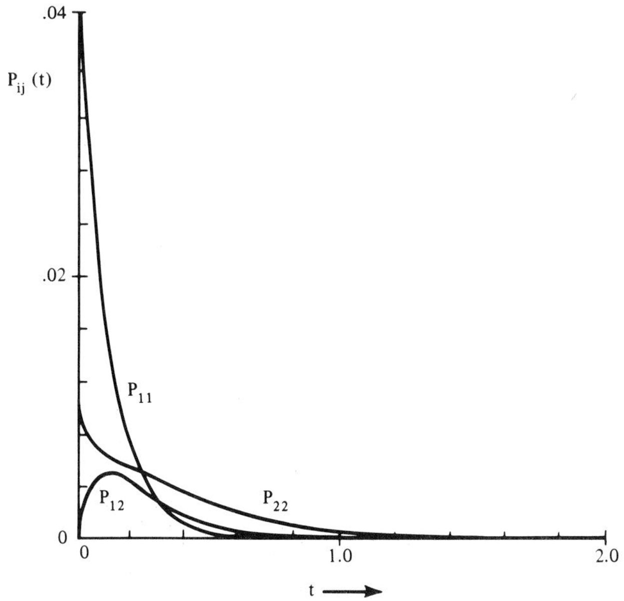

Figure 5.5 Estimate covariances for CSTR example with continuous data.

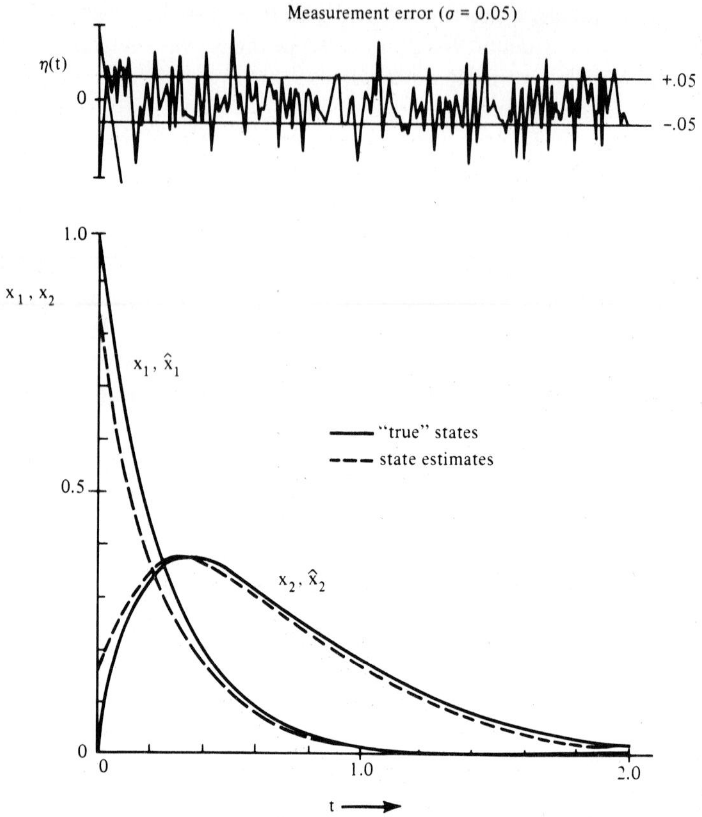

Figure 5.6 Comparison of "true" states and filter estimates for continuous data. $\eta(t)$ is the actual measurement error used ($\sigma = 0.05$).

discrete samples come directly from the continuous data results if we let $\mathbf{Q}_k = \mathbf{Q}(t_k)\,\Delta t_k$ and

$$\mathbf{Q}(t) = \sum_{k=1}^{M} \mathbf{Q}_k \delta(t - t_k) \tag{5.2.82}$$

in the continuous estimation equations. Here Δt_k is the sampling interval at sample k, and any time t_f can be represented by

$$t_f = \sum_{k=1}^{M} \Delta t_k$$

Substituting Eq. (5.2.82) into Eqs. (5.2.43) and (5.2.45), one obtains the following discrete time *filtering equations*. Between samples, $t_{k-1} < t < t_k$, one must use the prediction equations

$$\dot{\hat{\mathbf{x}}}(t|t_{k-1}) = \mathbf{A}(t)\hat{\mathbf{x}}(t|t_{k-1}) \tag{5.2.83}$$

$$\dot{\mathbf{P}}(t|t_{k-1}) = \mathbf{P}(t|t_{k-1})\mathbf{A}^T(t) + \mathbf{A}(t)\mathbf{P}(t|t_{k-1}) + \mathbf{R}^{-1}(t) \tag{5.2.84}$$

while at sampling points the updating equations

$$\hat{x}(t_k|t_k) = \hat{x}(t_k|t_{k-1}) + \mathbf{K}(t_k)[\mathbf{y}(t_k) - \mathbf{C}(t_k)\hat{\mathbf{x}}(t_k|t_{k-1})] \tag{5.2.85}$$

$$\mathbf{P}(t_k|t_k) = \mathbf{P}(t_k|t_{k-1}) - \mathbf{K}(t_k)\mathbf{C}(t_k)\mathbf{P}(t_k|t_{k-1}) \tag{5.2.86}$$

must be used. Here

$$\mathbf{K}(t_k) = \mathbf{P}(t_k|t_{k-1})\mathbf{C}^T(t_k)[\mathbf{C}(t_k)\mathbf{P}(t_k|t_{k-1})\mathbf{C}^T(t_k) + \mathbf{Q}_k^{-1}]^{-1} \tag{5.2.87}$$

Thus both the filter estimates and the covariance matrix have discontinuities at sampling points t_k. Example trajectories of the filter estimates and covariance for both continuous and discrete data are shown in Fig. 5.7. Note that in the continuous case the covariance tends to a positive steady-state value determined by the sampling and process noise levels. For the discrete case, the covariance tends to increase between samples and be reduced at sampling points.

We are now ready to summarize our results for discrete data estimation.

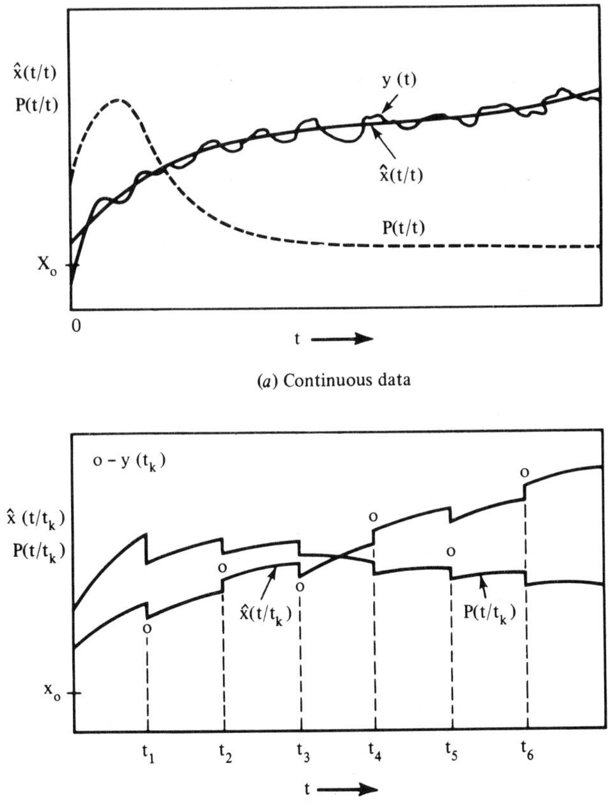

(*a*) Continuous data

(*b*) Discrete data

Figure 5.7 Typical filtering trajectories for (*a*) continuous data, and for (*b*) discrete data.

1. *For smoothing estimates*, one solves the filtering equations (5.2.83) to (5.2.87) forward in time and then uses Eq. (5.2.59) to generate the smoothed estimates $\hat{\mathbf{x}}(t|t_f)$. The covariance equation for the smoothed estimates can be found by substituting Eqs. (5.2.84) and (5.2.86) into Eq. (5.2.65) and integrating backward. Note that although the filtered estimates are discontinuous at sampling points, the smoothed estimates are continuous.
2. *For filtering estimates*, $\hat{\mathbf{x}}(t|t_{k-1})$, one solves the prediction equations (5.2.83) and (5.2.84) between samples and the updating equations (5.2.85) to (5.2.87) at the sampling points.
3. Since *prediction estimates* involve no data, the prediction equations are independent of the sampling device.

Note that just as in the continuous data case, the covariance equations can be precomputed off-line, so that only the filter equations need be solved in real time.

Let us illustrate the discrete data filter with an example problem.

Example 5.2.5 Let us again consider the CSTR filtering problem discussed in Example 5.2.4, with the exception that here the sampling device is discrete in time:

$$y(t_k) = x_2(t_k) + \eta(t_k) \tag{5.2.88}$$

The filtering equations between samples become

$$\dot{\hat{x}}_1 = -(1 + \mathrm{Da}_1)\hat{x}_1 \qquad t_{k-1} < t < t_k \tag{5.2.89}$$

$$\dot{\hat{x}}_2 = \mathrm{Da}_1\hat{x}_1 - (1 + \mathrm{Da}_3)\hat{x}_2 \tag{5.2.90}$$

and the updating equations at samples take the form

$$\hat{x}_1(t_k|t_k) = \hat{x}_1(t_k|t_{k-1}) + \frac{P_{12}(t_k|t_{k-1})}{P_{22}(t_k|t_{k-1}) + Q_k^{-1}} \times [y(t_k) - \hat{x}_2(t_k|t_{k-1})] \tag{5.2.91}$$

$$\hat{x}_2(t_k|t_k) = \hat{x}_2(t_k|t_{k-1}) + \frac{P_{22}(t_k|t_{k-1})}{P_{22}(t_k|t_{k-1}) + Q_k^{-1}} \times [y(t_k) - \hat{x}_2(t_k|t_{k-1})] \tag{5.2.92}$$

The covariance equations between samples, $t_{k-1} < t < t_k$, are

$$\dot{P}_{11}(t|t_{k-1}) = -2(1 + \mathrm{Da}_1)P_{11}(t|t_{k-1}) + \rho_{11} \tag{5.2.93}$$

$$\dot{P}_{12}(t|t_{k-1}) = \mathrm{Da}_1 P_{11}(t|t_{k-1}) - (2 + \mathrm{Da}_1 + \mathrm{Da}_3)P_{12}(t|t_{k-1}) + \rho_{12} \tag{5.2.94}$$

$$\dot{P}_{22}(t|t_{k-1}) = 2\mathrm{Da}_1 P_{12}(t|t_{k-1}) - 2(1 + \mathrm{Da}_3)P_{22}(t|t_{k-1}) + \rho_{22} \tag{5.2.95}$$

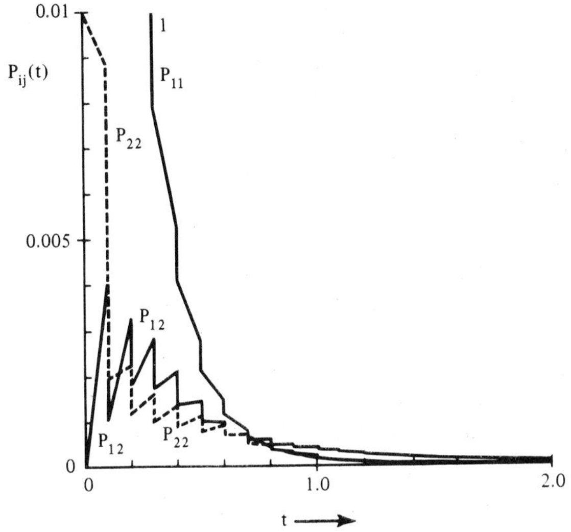

Figure 5.8 Estimate covariances for CSTR example with discrete data.

and the updating equations at samples are

$$P_{11}(t_k|t_k) = P_{11}(t_k|t_{k-1}) - \frac{[P_{12}(t_k|t_{k-1})]^2}{P_{22}(t_k|t_{k-1}) + Q_k^{-1}} \tag{5.2.96}$$

$$P_{12}(t_k|t_k) = P_{12}(t_k|t_{k-1}) - \frac{P_{12}(t_k|t_{k-1})P_{22}(t_k|t_{k-1})}{P_{22}(t_k|t_{k-1}) + Q_k^{-1}} \tag{5.2.97}$$

$$P_{22}(t_k|t_k) = P_{22}(t_k|t_{k-1}) - \frac{P_{22}(t_k|t_{k-1})^2}{P_{22}(t_k|t_{k-1}) + Q_k^{-1}} \tag{5.2.98}$$

In order to illustrate the estimator behavior, numerical calculations were carried out for the same parameters and conditions as in Example 5.2.4. However, in this case the data are obtained only at discrete times $t_n = n\,\Delta t$ where $\Delta t = 0.05$. The estimate covariances are plotted in Fig. 5.8, where one should note how the P_{ij} usually increase between samples and make a discontinuous improvement after each measurement point. The state estimates, which have the same type of discontinuous behavior, are shown in Fig. 5.9 when there is no measurement error. Even with intermittant measurements, the filter estimates converge rapidly to the true state.

Observers

Observers are estimators for the state variables of a deterministic system, i.e., a system without any significant process noise or measurement errors. Like filtering, observers are used to reconstruct the full-state vector for the system $\mathbf{x}(t)$ from the available outputs $\mathbf{y}(t)$. In this sense, the optimal estimators just

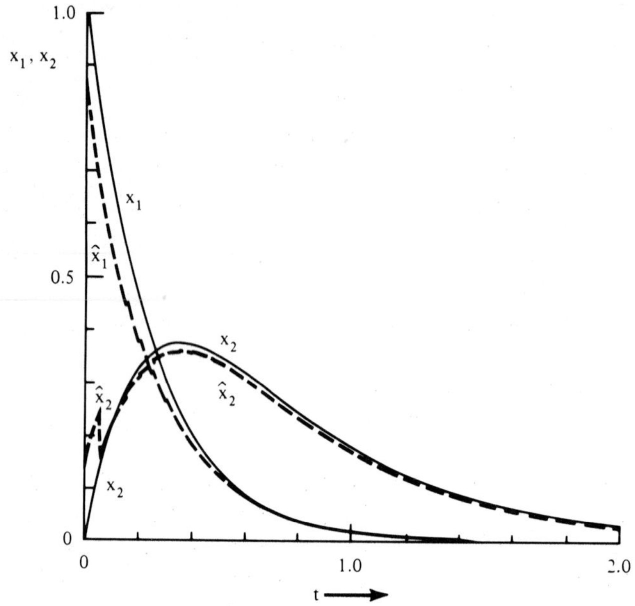

Figure 5.9 Comparison of "true" states and filter estimates for discrete data.

discussed may be considered as a type of optimal, stochastic observer. Observer theory [6, 13, 14] has been highly developed for linear systems. To illustrate the properties of observers, let us consider the linear deterministic system.

$$\dot{\mathbf{x}} = \mathbf{A}\mathbf{x} \tag{5.2.99}$$

$$\mathbf{y}(t) = \mathbf{C}\mathbf{x} \tag{5.2.100}$$

which has n states and l outputs. If the system is observable, then one can construct a deterministic observer in the following way. Let us define a new variable, $\mathbf{z}(t)$ of dimension $n - l$, which may be related to the state by the relation

$$\mathbf{z}(t) = \mathbf{T}(t)\mathbf{x}(t) \tag{5.2.101}$$

where the $(n - l) \times n$ matrix $\mathbf{T}(t)$ is chosen so that the $n \times n$ matrix

$$\begin{bmatrix} \mathbf{T}(t) \\ \text{------} \\ \mathbf{C}(t) \end{bmatrix}$$

is nonsingular. Then the full state vector may be expressed in terms of $\mathbf{z}$, $\mathbf{y}$ as

$$\mathbf{x} = \begin{bmatrix} \mathbf{T}(t) \\ \text{------} \\ \mathbf{C}(t) \end{bmatrix}^{-1} \begin{bmatrix} \mathbf{z}(t) \\ \text{-----} \\ \mathbf{y}(t) \end{bmatrix} \tag{5.2.102}$$

Now if $\begin{bmatrix} \mathbf{T}(t) \\ \hdashline \mathbf{C}(t) \end{bmatrix}^{-1}$ is partitioned as

$$\begin{bmatrix} \mathbf{T}(t) \\ \hdashline \mathbf{C}(t) \end{bmatrix}^{-1} \equiv [\boldsymbol{\Omega}_1 \,\vdots\, \boldsymbol{\Omega}_2] \tag{5.2.103}$$

where $\boldsymbol{\Omega}_1$ is an $n \times (n - l)$ matrix and $\boldsymbol{\Omega}_2$ is an $n \times l$ matrix, then

$$\mathbf{x}(t) = \boldsymbol{\Omega}_1\mathbf{z}(t) + \boldsymbol{\Omega}_2\mathbf{y}(t) \tag{5.2.104}$$

It now remains to determine $\mathbf{z}(t)$. Let us differentiate Eq. (5.2.101) to yield

$$\dot{\mathbf{z}} = \dot{\mathbf{T}}\mathbf{x} + \mathbf{T}\dot{\mathbf{x}} = \dot{\mathbf{T}}[\boldsymbol{\Omega}_1\mathbf{z}(t) + \boldsymbol{\Omega}_2\mathbf{y}(t)] + \mathbf{TA}[\boldsymbol{\Omega}_1\mathbf{z}(t) + \boldsymbol{\Omega}_2\mathbf{y}(t)] \tag{5.2.105}$$

or

$$\dot{\mathbf{z}} = (\mathbf{TA}\boldsymbol{\Omega}_1 + \dot{\mathbf{T}}\boldsymbol{\Omega}_1)\mathbf{z}(t) + (\mathbf{TA}\boldsymbol{\Omega}_2 + \dot{\mathbf{T}}\boldsymbol{\Omega}_2)\mathbf{y}(t) \tag{5.2.106}$$

where we note that from Eq. (5.2.103)

$$\boldsymbol{\Omega}_1\mathbf{T} + \boldsymbol{\Omega}_2\mathbf{C} = \mathbf{I} \tag{5.2.107}$$

and

$$\begin{bmatrix} \mathbf{T} \\ \hdashline \mathbf{C}(t) \end{bmatrix} [\boldsymbol{\Omega}_1, \boldsymbol{\Omega}_2] = \begin{bmatrix} \mathbf{T}\boldsymbol{\Omega}_1 & \vdots & \mathbf{T}\boldsymbol{\Omega}_2 \\ \hdashline \mathbf{C}\boldsymbol{\Omega}_1 & \vdots & \mathbf{C}\boldsymbol{\Omega}_2 \end{bmatrix} = \mathbf{I} \tag{5.2.108}$$

Thus

$$\mathbf{T}\boldsymbol{\Omega}_1 = \mathbf{I} \qquad \mathbf{T}\boldsymbol{\Omega}_2 = \mathbf{0} \qquad \mathbf{C}\boldsymbol{\Omega}_1 = \mathbf{0} \qquad \mathbf{C}\boldsymbol{\Omega}_2 = \mathbf{I} \tag{5.2.109}$$

From Eq. (5.2.107) one sees that

$$(\dot{\boldsymbol{\Omega}}_1\mathbf{T}) + (\dot{\boldsymbol{\Omega}}_2\mathbf{C}) = \mathbf{0}$$

and from Eq. (5.2.109),

$$\begin{aligned} \dot{\mathbf{T}}\boldsymbol{\Omega}_1 &= -\mathbf{T}\dot{\boldsymbol{\Omega}}_1 \\ \dot{\mathbf{T}}\boldsymbol{\Omega}_2 &= -\mathbf{T}\dot{\boldsymbol{\Omega}}_2 \end{aligned} \tag{5.2.110}$$

Thus Eq. (5.2.106) becomes

$$\dot{\mathbf{z}}(t) = (\mathbf{TA}\boldsymbol{\Omega}_1 - \mathbf{T}\dot{\boldsymbol{\Omega}}_1)\mathbf{z}(t) + (\mathbf{TA}\boldsymbol{\Omega}_2 - \mathbf{T}\dot{\boldsymbol{\Omega}}_2)\mathbf{y}(t) \tag{5.2.111}$$

and our observer takes the form

$$\dot{\hat{\mathbf{z}}} = (\mathbf{TA}\boldsymbol{\Omega}_1 - \mathbf{T}\dot{\boldsymbol{\Omega}}_1)\hat{\mathbf{z}} + (\mathbf{TA}\boldsymbol{\Omega}_2 - \mathbf{T}\dot{\boldsymbol{\Omega}}_2)\mathbf{y}(t) \tag{5.2.112}$$

$$\hat{\mathbf{x}}(t) = \boldsymbol{\Omega}_1\hat{\mathbf{z}} + \boldsymbol{\Omega}_2\mathbf{y}(t) \tag{5.2.113}$$

The estimate error may be found by subtracting the actual process, Eqs. (5.2.111) and (5.2.104), from the estimator equations (5.2.112) and (5.2.113) and noting that in general $\hat{\mathbf{z}}(0) - \mathbf{z}(0) \neq \mathbf{0}$ because we don't know the initial conditions. Thus the errors in $\mathbf{z}$, $\mathbf{x}$ are given by

$$\mathbf{e}_z = \hat{\mathbf{z}} - \mathbf{z}$$

$$\mathbf{e}_x = \hat{\mathbf{x}} - \mathbf{x}$$

and

$$\dot{\mathbf{e}}_z = (\mathbf{TA}\boldsymbol{\Omega}_1 - \mathbf{T}\dot{\boldsymbol{\Omega}}_1)\mathbf{e}_z \tag{5.2.114}$$

$$\mathbf{e}_x = \boldsymbol{\Omega}_1\mathbf{e}_z \qquad \mathbf{e}_z = \mathbf{T}\mathbf{e}_x \qquad \dot{\mathbf{e}}_x = \dot{\boldsymbol{\Omega}}_1\mathbf{e}_z + \boldsymbol{\Omega}\dot{\mathbf{e}}_z \tag{5.2.115}$$

or*

$$\dot{\mathbf{e}}_x = \left[\boldsymbol{\Omega}_1\mathbf{TA} - \boldsymbol{\Omega}_1\mathbf{T}\dot{\boldsymbol{\Omega}}_1\mathbf{T} + \dot{\boldsymbol{\Omega}}_1\mathbf{T}\right]\mathbf{e}_x \tag{5.2.116}$$

and the observer has an exponential rate of convergence with rate given by the eigenvalues of the matrix in square brackets.

By employing Eq. (5.2.110) it is possible to show that

$$\dot{\mathbf{e}}_x = (\boldsymbol{\Omega}_1\mathbf{TA} + \boldsymbol{\Omega}_1\dot{\mathbf{T}}\boldsymbol{\Omega}_1\mathbf{T} + \dot{\boldsymbol{\Omega}}_1\mathbf{T})\mathbf{e}_x \tag{5.2.117}$$

but applying $\boldsymbol{\Omega}_1\mathbf{T}\mathbf{e}_x = \mathbf{e}_x$ and Eq. (5.2.107) yields

$$\dot{\mathbf{e}}_x = \left[(\mathbf{I} - \boldsymbol{\Omega}_2\mathbf{C})\mathbf{A} + \boldsymbol{\Omega}_1\dot{\mathbf{T}} + \dot{\boldsymbol{\Omega}}_1\mathbf{T}\right]\mathbf{e}_x \tag{5.2.118}$$

or

$$\dot{\mathbf{e}}_x = (\mathbf{A} - \boldsymbol{\Omega}_2\mathbf{CA} - \boldsymbol{\Omega}_2\dot{\mathbf{C}} - \dot{\boldsymbol{\Omega}}_2\mathbf{C})\mathbf{e}_x \qquad \mathbf{e}_x(0) = \mathbf{e}_{x_0} \tag{5.2.119}$$

where $\mathbf{e}_{x_0}$ is the initial error in the state estimates. Note that one may control the rate of convergence of the observer by adjusting $\boldsymbol{\Omega}_2$ in Eq. (5.2.119).

One should realize that there are infinitely many transformations $\mathbf{T}$, $\boldsymbol{\Omega}_1$, $\boldsymbol{\Omega}_2$ which satisfy Eqs. (5.2.107) and (5.2.108); thus one has great freedom of choice. For systems having constant matrices $\mathbf{A}$, $\mathbf{C}$, one possible observer design procedure would be

1. Choose $\boldsymbol{\Omega}_2$ such that $\mathbf{A} - \boldsymbol{\Omega}_2\mathbf{CA}$ has the desired eigenvalues for convergence.
2. Choose some $\boldsymbol{\Omega}_1$,$\mathbf{T}$ such that Eq. (5.2.107) is satisfied.

Observers have also been developed for stochastic systems (e.g., [6, 15–18]), where there are fewer estimation equations to solve than for optimal state estimation because only $n - l$ states need estimation. However, the available experience suggests that observers are much less robust in the face of measurement and process noise than the optimal estimators. Thus observers should only be considered for implementation in control systems with small measurement and process noise.

Let us illustrate the application of an observer with an example problem.

* Note that Eq. (5.2.115) implies $\boldsymbol{\Omega}_1\mathbf{T}\mathbf{e}_x \equiv \mathbf{e}_x$ but *not* $\boldsymbol{\Omega}_1\mathbf{T} = \mathbf{I}$.

Example 5.2.6 Consider the state estimation problem for the CSTR discussed in Example 5.2.4 and apply an observer to the problem. If we measure x_2, then the equations are

$$\dot{x}_1 = -(1 + \mathrm{Da}_1)x_1$$
$$\dot{x}_2 = \mathrm{Da}_1 x_1 - (1 + \mathrm{Da}_3)x_2$$
$$y = x_2$$

Recall that we have already proved that this example is observable. Let us choose

$$z = \mathbf{T}\mathbf{x} = T_1 x_1 + T_2 x_2 \tag{5.2.120}$$

Thus

$$\begin{bmatrix} z \\ y \end{bmatrix} = \begin{bmatrix} T_1 & T_2 \\ 0 & 1 \end{bmatrix} \mathbf{x} \tag{5.2.121}$$

and by inversion,

$$\mathbf{x} = \begin{bmatrix} \dfrac{1}{T_1} & -\dfrac{T_2}{T_1} \\ 0 & 1 \end{bmatrix} \begin{bmatrix} z \\ y \end{bmatrix} = \begin{bmatrix} \dfrac{1}{T_1} \\ 0 \end{bmatrix} z + \begin{bmatrix} \dfrac{-T_2}{T_1} \\ 1 \end{bmatrix} y \tag{5.2.122}$$

so that

$$\Omega_1 = \begin{bmatrix} \dfrac{1}{T_1} \\ 0 \end{bmatrix} \qquad \Omega_2 = \begin{bmatrix} -\dfrac{T_2}{T_1} \\ 1 \end{bmatrix} \tag{5.2.123}$$

Now the observer error as given by Eq. (5.2.119) is

$$\dot{\mathbf{e}}_x = \begin{bmatrix} -(1 + \mathrm{Da}_1) + \dfrac{T_2}{T_1}\mathrm{Da}_1 & \dfrac{-T_2}{T_1}(1 + \mathrm{Da}_3) \\ 0 & 0 \end{bmatrix} \mathbf{e}_x \qquad \mathbf{e}_x(0) = \begin{bmatrix} e_{x10} \\ 0 \end{bmatrix} \tag{5.2.124}$$

Note that there is no error in the estimates of x_2 because they are directly measured. Also, the eigenvalue of the x_1 estimate is $-(1 + \mathrm{Da}_1) + (T_2/T_1)\mathrm{Da}_1$. Thus by choosing T_2/T_1 large and negative we can get rapid convergence of the observer.

The observer equations (5.2.112) then become

$$\dot{\hat{z}} = \left[-T_1(1 + \mathrm{Da}_1) + T_2\mathrm{Da}_1, \; -T_2(1 + \mathrm{Da}_3) \right] \begin{bmatrix} \dfrac{1}{T_1} \\ 0 \end{bmatrix} \hat{z}$$
$$+ \left[-T_1(1 + \mathrm{Da}_1) + T_2\mathrm{Da}_1, \; -T_2(1 + \mathrm{Da}_3) \right] \begin{bmatrix} \dfrac{-T_2}{T_1} \\ 1 \end{bmatrix} y$$

or

$$\dot{\hat{z}} = \left[-(1 + \mathrm{Da}_1) + \frac{T_2}{T_1}\mathrm{Da}_1\right]\hat{z}$$

$$+\left[T_2(1 + \mathrm{Da}_1) - \frac{T_2^2}{T_1}\mathrm{Da}_1 - T_2(1 + \mathrm{Da}_3)\right]y \qquad (5.2.125)$$

$$\hat{x}_1 = \frac{1}{T_1}\hat{z} - \frac{T_2}{T_1}y \qquad (5.2.126)$$

$$\hat{x}_2 = y \qquad (5.2.127)$$

In order to illustrate the performance of the observer for the conditions given in Example 5.2.4, one must choose T_1 and T_2. To aid this choice, note that the eigenvalue associated with the error in x_1 may be determined from Eq. (5.2.124) as

$$\lambda = \left[-(1 + \mathrm{Da}_1) + \frac{T_2}{T_1}\mathrm{Da}_1\right]$$

which for $\mathrm{Da}_1 = 3.0$ is

$$\lambda = -4 + 3\frac{T_2}{T_1}$$

Thus the rate of convergence can be made as fast as desired (in the absence of measurement and process errors) by adjusting T_2/T_1. As specific examples, Fig. 5.10 shows the rate of convergence when $T_1 = 1$, $T_2 = -4$,

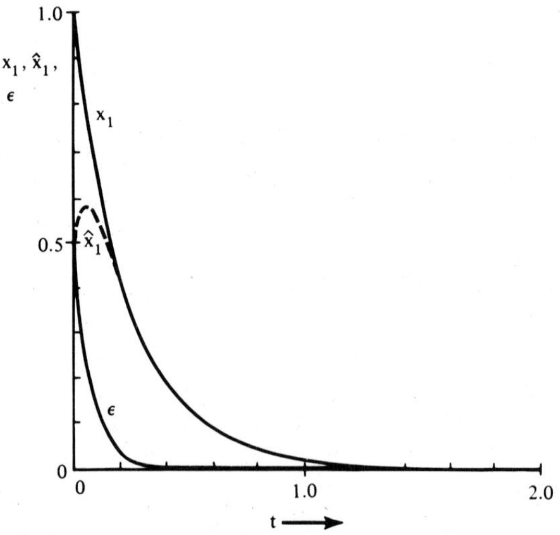

Figure 5.10 Observer performance for $T_1 = 1$, $T_2 = -4$, $\lambda = -16$, $\epsilon = x_1 - \hat{x}_1$.

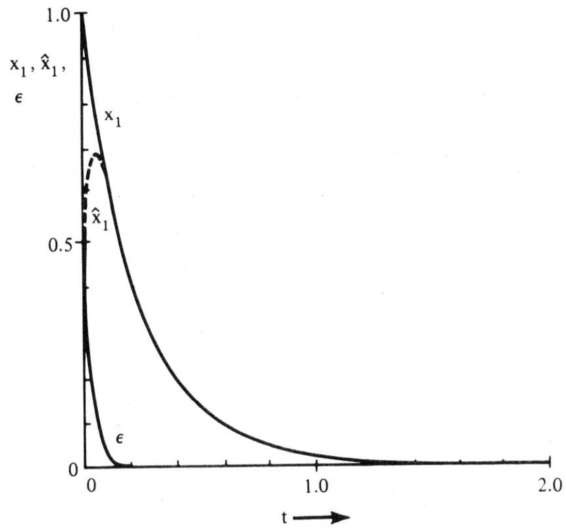

Figure 5.11 Observer performance for $T_1 = 1$, $T_2 = -8$, $\lambda = -28$, $\epsilon = x_1 - \hat{x}_1$.

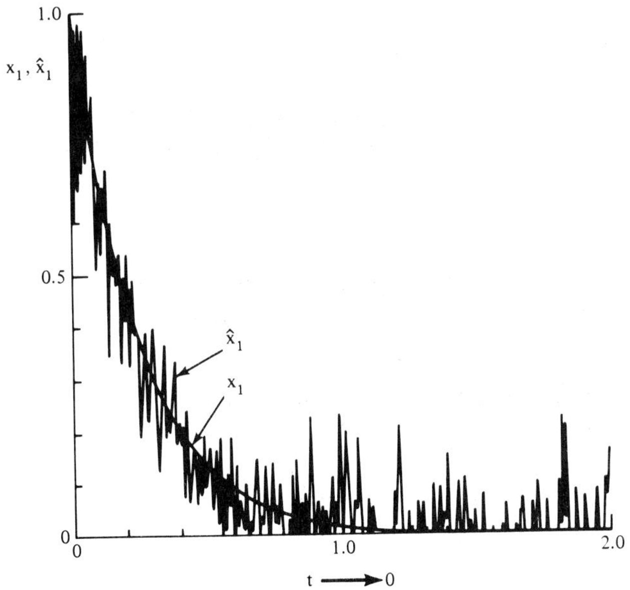

Figure 5.12 Observer performance for $T_1 = 1$, $T_2 = -8$, and random measurement error ($\sigma = 0.01$).

$\lambda = -16$, while Fig. 5.11 gives the observer performance when $T_1 = 1$, $T_2 = -8$, $\lambda = -28$. In both these cases the estimated initial condition for x_1 was $\hat{x}_1(0) = 0.5$, far from the true value of 1.0, and yet the observer converged quickly.

The difficulty observers have with measurement or process noise is illustrated in Fig. 5.12, where the random noise with standard deviation $\sigma = 0.01$ (five times smaller than the noise levels easily handled by the filter in Example 5.2.4) has been added to the x_2 measurements. The observer estimates are so bad as to be useless for control purposes. Thus observers are not recommended for estimation where noise is significant.

5.3 STATE ESTIMATION FOR NONLINEAR SYSTEMS DESCRIBED BY ORDINARY DIFFERENTIAL EQUATIONS

In this section we shall extend our treatment of state estimation to a broad class of nonlinear systems modeled *formally* by

$$\dot{\mathbf{x}}(t) = \mathbf{f}(\mathbf{x}, t) + \boldsymbol{\xi}(t) \tag{5.3.1}$$

$$\mathbf{x}(0) = \mathbf{x}_0 + \boldsymbol{\xi}_0 \tag{5.3.2}$$

$$\mathbf{y}(t) = \mathbf{h}(\mathbf{x}, t) + \boldsymbol{\eta}(t) \tag{5.3.3}$$

where Eqs. (5.3.1) and (5.3.2) represent the nonlinear system state equations, and Eq. (5.3.3) the nonlinear measuring device. The noise processes $\boldsymbol{\xi}(t)$, $\boldsymbol{\eta}(t)$ as well as the initial error $\boldsymbol{\xi}_0$ are assumed to have zero mean and unspecified distributions.

Unfortunately, for nonlinear systems the conditional probability distributions for the state evolving in time are not Gaussian even when $\boldsymbol{\xi}(t)$, $\boldsymbol{\eta}(t)$, and $\boldsymbol{\xi}_0$ are assumed to have Gaussian distributions. This means that an infinite number of moments are required to determine the distribution and that the moments are coupled in increasing order; i.e., the first moment depends on the second, the second on the third, etc. This structure of the statistics means that approximations must be made in order to obtain a computationally feasible filter.

Furthermore, a new type of differential calculus (e.g., the Ito calculus) must be used to rigorously treat these nonlinear time-varying probability distributions (see [4]). The Ito calculus would require, for example, that Eq. (5.3.1) be rewritten in differential form

$$d\mathbf{x} = \mathbf{f}(\mathbf{x}, t)\, dt + d\boldsymbol{\beta} \tag{5.3.4}$$

where $\boldsymbol{\xi}(t)$ is the formal definition of $d\boldsymbol{\beta}/dt$. These considerations carry us into deep mathematical waters and too far afield from our discussion of applications. Thus we urge the reader to pursue these developments independently [4]. In this chapter we shall proceed with formal derivations of nonlinear state estimators and where possible compare them with rigorously derived results.

Observability

In any discussion of estimation, observability must be a primary question. Unfortunately, the results available for nonlinear systems are more difficult to apply than the results for linear systems. Basically the approach that has been used is to linearize the nonlinear equations about some nominal trajectory $\bar{\mathbf{x}}(t)$ and apply the known results for linear, nonautonomous systems. Hwang and Seinfeld [19] have a good discussion of this approach.

To establish conditions for observability, let us linearize Eqs. (5.3.1) to (5.3.3) about a nominal trajectory $\bar{\mathbf{x}}(t)$ satisfying Eq. (5.3.1) and beginning at $\bar{\mathbf{x}}(0) = \bar{\mathbf{x}}_0$, and define

$$\delta\mathbf{x}(t) = \mathbf{x}(t) - \bar{\mathbf{x}}(t) \qquad \delta\mathbf{y}(t) = \mathbf{y}(t) - \bar{\mathbf{y}}(t)$$

$$\mathbf{A}(t) = \left.\frac{\partial \mathbf{f}}{\partial \mathbf{x}}\right|_{\bar{\mathbf{x}}(t)} \qquad \mathbf{C}(t) = \left.\frac{\partial \mathbf{h}}{\partial \mathbf{x}}\right|_{\bar{\mathbf{x}}(t)} \tag{5.3.5}$$

where we neglect the noise processes $\xi(t)$, $\eta(t)$, ξ_0 because observability is a property of the deterministic system. Then the linearized system is

$$\delta\dot{\mathbf{x}}(t) = \mathbf{A}(t)\delta\mathbf{x}(t) \qquad \delta\mathbf{x}(0) = \delta\mathbf{x}_0 \tag{5.3.6}$$

$$\delta\mathbf{y}(t) = \mathbf{C}(t)\delta\mathbf{x}(t) \tag{5.3.7}$$

We can now apply the results of the last section to provide the result: *The nonlinear system of Eqs.* (5.3.1) *to* (5.3.3) *is observable for all initial conditions in some neighborhood of* $\mathbf{x}_0$ *provided the matrix*

$$\mathbf{M}(0, t_f) = \int_0^{t_f} \mathbf{\Phi}(t, 0)^T \mathbf{C}^T(t)\mathbf{C}(t)\mathbf{\Phi}(t, 0)\, dt \tag{5.3.8}$$

is positive definite for $t_f > 0$, where, of course, $\Phi(t, \tau)$ is the fundamental matrix solution associated with the solution to Eq. (5.3.6). This result can be extended to the entire $\mathbf{x}$ domain by selecting a grid of initial conditions covering the entire domain.

In principle the application of this criterion could involve extensive calculation to map the entire domain of initial conditions in marginal cases. However, in practice one often finds that observability is determined by the problem structure and not dependent on $\mathbf{x}_0$ in a complex manner. Hence simple linearized observability tests are usually adequate for nonlinear problems. We shall illustrate these results with an example problem.

Example 5.3.1 Let us consider an adiabatic batch reactor in which the reaction $A \xrightarrow{k_1} B \xrightarrow{k_2} C$ is taking place. The modeling equations for the reactor take the form

$$\frac{dc_A}{dt'} = -k_1 c_A \qquad c_A(0) = c_{A_0} \tag{5.3.9}$$

$$\frac{dc_B}{dt'} = k_1 c_A - k_2 c_B \qquad c_B(0) = c_{B_0} \tag{5.3.10}$$

$$\frac{dT}{dt'} = J_1 k_1 c_A + J_2 k_2 c_B = -J_1 \frac{dc_A}{dt'} - J_2\left(\frac{dc_A}{dt'} + \frac{dc_B}{dt'}\right) \qquad T(0) = T_0 \tag{5.3.11}$$

where

$$J_i = -\Delta H_i/\rho C_p \qquad i = 1, 2$$

Now integrating the heat balance one obtains

$$T(t) = T_0 + (J_1 + J_2)(c_{A_0} - c_A) + J_2(c_{B_0} - c_B) \tag{5.3.12}$$

Thus if we know c_A, c_B, we can calculate T from Eq. (5.3.12). The velocity constants k_1, k_2 are Arrhenius functions of temperature, so that

$$k_i = A_{i0}e^{-E_i/RT} \qquad i = 1, 2 \tag{5.3.13}$$

and this provides the strongest nonlinearity in the problem. Now the question is, if one measures $c_B(t)$, will the nonlinear system be observable?

Let us put the equations in reduced form by defining

$$x_1 = c_A \qquad x_2 = c_B \qquad t = t'A_{10} \qquad p = \frac{E_2}{E_1}$$

$$\alpha_0 = \frac{R}{E_1}\left[T_0 + (J_1 + J_2)c_{A_0} + J_2 c_{B_0}\right]$$

$$\alpha_1 = \frac{R}{E_1}(J_1 + J_2) \qquad \alpha_2 = \frac{J_2 R}{E_1} \qquad \gamma = \frac{A_{20}}{A_{10}} \qquad \begin{bmatrix} x_{10} \\ x_{20} \end{bmatrix} = \begin{bmatrix} c_{A_0} \\ c_{B_0} \end{bmatrix} \tag{5.3.14}$$

then Eq. (5.3.12) is

$$\frac{RT}{E_1} = \alpha_0 - \alpha_1 x_1 - \alpha_2 x_2 \tag{5.3.15}$$

and the system becomes

$$\frac{dx_1}{dt} = -\exp\left(-\frac{1}{\alpha_0 - \alpha_1 x_1 - \alpha_2 x_2}\right)x_1 \qquad x_1(0) = x_{10} \tag{5.3.16}$$

$$\frac{dx_2}{dt} = \exp\left(-\frac{1}{\alpha_0 - \alpha_1 x_1 - \alpha_2 x_2}\right)x_1 - \gamma\exp\left(-\frac{p}{\alpha_0 - \alpha_1 x_1 - \alpha_2 x_2}\right)x_2$$

$$x_2(0) = x_{20} \tag{5.3.17}$$

Now let us see if the system is observable with the output*

$$y = x_2(t) \tag{5.3.18}$$

If we linearize about some nominal trajectory $\bar{x}$ with initial conditions $\bar{x}_{10}$, $\bar{x}_{20}$, then we get the linear perturbation equations:

$$\delta y(t) = \mathbf{C}\delta\mathbf{x}(t) \tag{5.3.19}$$

$$\delta\dot{\mathbf{x}} = \mathbf{A}(t)\delta\mathbf{x} \qquad \delta\mathbf{x}(0) = \delta\mathbf{x}_0 \tag{5.3.20}$$

* Note that the problem assumes a knowledge of α_0, which involves a linear combination of c_{A_0}, c_{B_0}. However, the value of α_0 could be known while c_{A_0} and c_{B_0} were individually unknown.

where

$$\mathbf{C} = [0 \quad 1] \tag{5.3.21}$$

and

$$\mathbf{A}(t) = \begin{bmatrix} a_{11} & a_{12} \\ a_{21} & a_{22} \end{bmatrix}$$

$$a_{11}(t) = -\exp\left(-\frac{1}{\alpha_0 - \alpha_1\bar{x}_1 - \alpha_2\bar{x}_2}\right)\left[1 - \frac{\alpha_1\bar{x}_1}{(\alpha_0 - \alpha_1\bar{x}_1 - \alpha_2\bar{x}_2)^2}\right] \tag{5.3.22}$$

$$a_{12}(t) = \frac{\alpha_2\bar{x}_1}{(\alpha_0 - \alpha_0\bar{x}_1 - \alpha_2\bar{x}_2)^2}\exp\left(-\frac{1}{\alpha_0 - \alpha_1\bar{x}_1 - \alpha_2\bar{x}_2}\right) \tag{5.3.23}$$

$$\begin{aligned} a_{21}(t) = {} & \exp\left(-\frac{1}{\alpha_0 - \alpha_1\bar{x}_1 - \alpha_2\bar{x}_2}\right)\left[1 - \frac{\alpha_1\bar{x}_1}{(\alpha_0 - \alpha_1\bar{x}_1 - \alpha_2\bar{x}_2)^2}\right] \\ & + \frac{\gamma p \alpha_1\bar{x}_2}{(\alpha_0 - \alpha_1\bar{x}_1 - \alpha_2\bar{x}_2)^2}\exp\left(\frac{-p}{\alpha_0 - \alpha_1\bar{x}_1 - \alpha_2\bar{x}_2}\right) \end{aligned} \tag{5.3.24}$$

$$\begin{aligned} a_{22}(t) = {} & \frac{-\alpha_2\bar{x}_1}{(\alpha_0 - \alpha_1\bar{x}_1 - \alpha_2\bar{x}_2)^2}\exp\left(\frac{-1}{\alpha_0 - \alpha_1\bar{x}_1 - \alpha_2\bar{x}_2}\right) \\ & - \gamma\exp\left(\frac{-p}{\alpha_0 - \alpha_1\bar{x}_1 - \alpha_2\bar{x}_2}\right)\left[1 - \frac{p\alpha_2\bar{x}_2}{(\alpha_0 - \alpha_1\bar{x}_1 - \alpha_2\bar{x}_2)^2}\right] \end{aligned} \tag{5.3.25}$$

Now since $\mathbf{C}^T\mathbf{C} = \begin{bmatrix} 0 & 0 \\ 0 & 1 \end{bmatrix}$, we see that

$$\mathbf{M}(0, t_f) = \int_0^{t_f} \begin{bmatrix} \phi_{11} & \phi_{21} \\ \phi_{12} & \phi_{22} \end{bmatrix} \begin{bmatrix} 0 & 0 \\ 0 & 1 \end{bmatrix} \begin{bmatrix} \phi_{11} & \phi_{12} \\ \phi_{21} & \phi_{22} \end{bmatrix} dt \tag{5.3.26}$$

where the transition matrix $\mathbf{\Phi}(t, 0)$ is the solution of

$$\dot{\mathbf{\Phi}}(t, 0) = \mathbf{A}(t)\mathbf{\Phi}(t, 0) \qquad \mathbf{\Phi}(0, 0) = \mathbf{I} \tag{5.3.27}$$

Thus

$$\mathbf{M}(0, t_f) = \int_0^{t_f} \begin{bmatrix} \phi_{21}^2 & \phi_{21}\phi_{22} \\ \phi_{21}\phi_{22} & \phi_{22}^2 \end{bmatrix} dt \tag{5.3.28}$$

can be positive definite (the actual situation depends on the parameters and nominal trajectory) and the system could be observable.

A simpler test could be made if the nominal trajectory chosen were constant, in which case **A** would become a constant and the observability condition, Eq. (5.2.4), could be used. This requires that

$$\mathbf{L}_0 = \left[\mathbf{C}^T \,\vdots\, \mathbf{A}^T\mathbf{C}^T\right] = \begin{bmatrix} 0 & a_{21} \\ 1 & a_{22} \end{bmatrix}$$

have rank 2. For a_{21} given by Eq. (5.3.24) this condition is clearly satisfied.

Optimal Nonlinear State Estimation

There have been a large number of different estimation schemes developed for nonlinear systems (e.g., [4]), so that we shall only discuss a few here. We shall show how these results may be derived for the case of a minimum least squares objective:

$$\begin{aligned} I = {} & \tfrac{1}{2}\left[\mathbf{x}(0) - \mathbf{x}_0\right]^T \mathbf{P}_0^{-1}\left[\mathbf{x}(0) - \mathbf{x}_0\right] \\ & + \tfrac{1}{2}\int_0^{t_f} \left\{\left[\dot{\mathbf{x}} - \mathbf{f}(\mathbf{x}, t)\right]^T \mathbf{R}(t)\left[\dot{\mathbf{x}} - \mathbf{f}(\mathbf{x}, t)\right]\right\} dt \\ & + \tfrac{1}{2}\int_0^{t_f} \left\{\left[\mathbf{y}(t) - \mathbf{h}(\mathbf{x}, t)\right]^T \mathbf{Q}(t)\left[\mathbf{y}(t) - \mathbf{h}(\mathbf{x}, t)\right]\right\} dt \end{aligned} \tag{5.3.29}$$

where the weighting matrices $\mathbf{P}_0^{-1}$, $\mathbf{R}(t)$, and $\mathbf{Q}(t)$ can be chosen to reflect the errors in the initial estimate, the process model, and the measuring device.

To derive the state estimation equations for nonlinear systems, we can proceed in a formal way, as in the last section, to solve the optimal smoothing problem and then extend the results to filtering and prediction. Thus let us define

$$\mathbf{u}(t) = \dot{\mathbf{x}} - \mathbf{f}(\mathbf{x}, t) \tag{5.3.30}$$

so that the smoothing problem may be stated as determining the control $\mathbf{u}(t)$ such that the objective

$$\begin{aligned} I = {} & \tfrac{1}{2}\left[\mathbf{x}(0) - \mathbf{x}_0\right]^T \mathbf{P}_0^{-1}\left[\mathbf{x}(0) - \mathbf{x}_0\right] \\ & + \tfrac{1}{2}\int_0^{t_f} \left\{\mathbf{u}^T(t)\mathbf{R}(t)\mathbf{u}(t) + \left[\mathbf{y}(t) - \mathbf{h}(\mathbf{x}, t)\right]^T \mathbf{Q}(t)\left[\mathbf{y}(t) - \mathbf{h}(\mathbf{x}, t)\right]\right\} dt \end{aligned} \tag{5.3.31}$$

is minimized subject to the constraints

$$\dot{\mathbf{x}} = \mathbf{f}(\mathbf{x}, t) + \mathbf{u}(t) \qquad \mathbf{x}(0) \text{ unspecified} \tag{5.3.32}$$

Applying the maximum principle, the Hamiltonian is

$$H = \tfrac{1}{2}\left[\mathbf{u}^T\mathbf{R}\mathbf{u} + (\mathbf{y} - \mathbf{h})^T\mathbf{Q}(\mathbf{y} - \mathbf{h})\right] + \boldsymbol{\lambda}^T(\mathbf{f} + \mathbf{u}) \tag{5.3.33}$$

and the condition $\partial H/\partial \mathbf{u} = \mathbf{0}$ yields

$$\mathbf{u}(t) = -\mathbf{R}^{-1}\boldsymbol{\lambda}(t) \tag{5.3.34}$$

where

$$\dot{\boldsymbol{\lambda}}^T = -\frac{\partial H}{\partial \mathbf{x}} = \frac{\partial \hat{\mathbf{h}}^T}{\partial \mathbf{x}}\mathbf{Q}(\mathbf{y} - \hat{\mathbf{h}}) - \frac{\partial \hat{\mathbf{f}}^T}{\partial \mathbf{x}}\hat{\boldsymbol{\lambda}} \tag{5.3.35}$$

subject to

$$\hat{\boldsymbol{\lambda}}(t_f) = \mathbf{0} \tag{5.3.36}$$

$$\hat{\mathbf{x}}(0) = \mathbf{x}_0 - \mathbf{P}_0\hat{\boldsymbol{\lambda}}(0) \tag{5.3.37}$$

Now upon substitution of Eq. (5.3.34) into Eq. (5.3.32) one obtains

$$\dot{\hat{\mathbf{x}}} = \mathbf{f}(\hat{\mathbf{x}}, t) - \mathbf{R}^{-1}(t)\hat{\boldsymbol{\lambda}}(t) \tag{5.3.38}$$

so that the nonlinear optimal smoothing problem can be found from the solution of Eqs. (5.3.35) and (5.3.36). Notice that this is an exact solution, with no approximations being necessary.

To produce the *filter* equations, let us again make use of the more explicit notation $\hat{\mathbf{x}}(t|t_f)$, $\hat{\boldsymbol{\lambda}}(t|t_f)$ denoting the optimal estimates and adjoint variables at time t, conditional on data up to time t_f. To derive the estimation equations we shall take advantage of the fact (see [20]) that there exists a decomposition of the estimation equations. If we recall that for *smoothing*, the estimates evolve by $\partial\hat{\mathbf{x}}(t|t_f)/\partial t_f$, the rate of change of the estimate at t with increasing data at time t_f, $t < t_f$, while for *prediction* we require $\partial\hat{\mathbf{x}}(t|t_f)/\partial t$, the rate of change of the estimate at time t with fixed data base, $t > t_f$, and for *filtering* the estimates are $d\hat{\mathbf{x}}(t_f|t_f)/dt_f$, the rate of change of the estimate at time t_f with both data base and estimate time changing together, it is straightforward to show that

$$\frac{d\hat{\mathbf{x}}(t_f|t_f)}{dt_f} = \left.\frac{\partial\hat{\mathbf{x}}(t|t_f)}{\partial t}\right|_{t=t_f} + \left.\frac{\partial\hat{\mathbf{x}}(t_f|T)}{\partial T}\right|_{T=t_f} \tag{5.3.39}$$

To show this, use the definition of a derivative

$$\begin{aligned}\frac{d\hat{\mathbf{x}}(t_f|t_f)}{dt_f} &= \lim_{\delta\to 0}\left[\frac{\hat{\mathbf{x}}(t_f+\delta|t_f+\delta) - \hat{\mathbf{x}}(t_f|t_f)}{\delta}\right] \\ &= \lim_{\delta\to 0}\left[\frac{\hat{\mathbf{x}}(t_f+\delta|t_f+\delta) - \hat{\mathbf{x}}(t_f|t_f+\delta)}{\delta} + \frac{\hat{\mathbf{x}}(t_f|t_f+\delta) - \hat{\mathbf{x}}(t_f|t_f)}{\delta}\right]\end{aligned} \tag{5.3.40}$$

which leads directly to Eq. (5.3.39).

We shall shortly make use of this decomposition property; however, first let us recognize that there exists a nonlinear transformation

$$\hat{\mathbf{x}}(t|t_f) = \hat{\mathbf{x}}\left[\boldsymbol{\lambda}(t|t_f)\right] \tag{5.3.41}$$

which is the solution to the two-point boundary value problem of Eqs. (5.3.35) to (5.3.38). Recall that for the linear problem, this transformation was linear and took the form of Eq. (5.2.38). However, for nonlinear systems a nonlinear transformation is required. By making use of the chain rule of calculus in Eq. (5.3.41), one obtains

$$\frac{\partial\hat{\mathbf{x}}(t|t_f)}{\partial t_f} = \frac{\partial\hat{\mathbf{x}}(t|t_f)}{\partial\hat{\boldsymbol{\lambda}}(t|t_f)}\frac{\partial\hat{\boldsymbol{\lambda}}(t|t_f)}{\partial t_f} \tag{5.3.42}$$

and one may define the matrix of "differential sensitivities"

$$\mathbf{P}(t|t_f) \equiv -\frac{\partial \hat{\mathbf{x}}(t|t_f)}{\partial \hat{\boldsymbol{\lambda}}(t|t_f)} \tag{5.3.43}$$

so that Eq. (5.3.42) becomes

$$\frac{\partial \hat{x}(t|t_f)}{\partial t_f} = -\mathbf{P}(t|t_f)\frac{\partial \hat{\boldsymbol{\lambda}}(t|t_f)}{\partial t_f} \tag{5.3.44}$$

Now making use of the decomposition property, Eq. (5.3.39), applied to $\hat{\boldsymbol{\lambda}}(t|t_f)$, one obtains

$$\frac{d\hat{\boldsymbol{\lambda}}(t_f|t_f)}{dt_f} = \left.\frac{\partial \hat{\boldsymbol{\lambda}}(t|t_f)}{\partial t}\right|_{t=t_f} + \left.\frac{\partial \hat{\boldsymbol{\lambda}}(t_f|T)}{\partial T}\right|_{T=t_f} \tag{5.3.45}$$

By considering the terminal condition, Eq. (5.3.36), on $\hat{\boldsymbol{\lambda}}(t_f|t_f)$,we see that the left-hand side of Eq. (5.3.45) must vanish. Let us now denote

$$\left.\frac{\partial \hat{\boldsymbol{\lambda}}(t|t_f)}{\partial t}\right|_{t=t_f} \equiv \hat{\boldsymbol{\lambda}}_t(t_f|t_f)$$

$$\left.\frac{\partial \hat{\boldsymbol{\lambda}}(t_f|T)}{\partial T}\right|_{T=t_f} \equiv \hat{\boldsymbol{\lambda}}_{t_f}(t_f|t_f) \tag{5.3.46}$$

with similar notation for $\hat{\mathbf{x}}(t|t_f)$ as well. Then the first term on the RHS of Eq. (5.3.45) is given by Eq. (5.3.35) with $t = t_f$. Thus

$$\hat{\boldsymbol{\lambda}}_{t_f}(t_f|t_f) = -\hat{\boldsymbol{\lambda}}_t(t_f|t_f) = -\mathbf{h}_x^T(\hat{\mathbf{x}}, t_f)\mathbf{Q}(t_f)\left[\mathbf{y}(t_f) - \mathbf{h}(\hat{\mathbf{x}}, t_f)\right] \tag{5.3.47}$$

If one substitutes Eq. (5.3.47) into Eq. (5.3.44) for $t = t_f$, one obtains

$$\hat{\mathbf{x}}_{t_f}(t_f|t_f) = -\mathbf{P}(t_f|t_f)\hat{\boldsymbol{\lambda}}_{t_f}(t_f|t_f) = \mathbf{P}(t_f|t_f)\hat{\mathbf{h}}_x^T\mathbf{Q}(\mathbf{y} - \hat{\mathbf{h}}) \tag{5.3.48}$$

and by evaluating Eq. (5.3.38) at $t = t_f$, the result

$$\hat{\mathbf{x}}_t(t_f|t_f) = \mathbf{f}(\hat{\mathbf{x}}(t_f|t_f), t_f) \tag{5.3.49}$$

is found. Now making use of the decomposition result, Eq. (5.3.39), one obtains the filter equations

$$\dot{\hat{\mathbf{x}}}(t_f|t_f) = \hat{\mathbf{x}}_t(t_f|t_f) + \hat{\mathbf{x}}_{t_f}(t_f|t_f)$$

or

$$\dot{\hat{\mathbf{x}}}(t_f|t_f) = \mathbf{f}(\hat{\mathbf{x}}, t_f) + \mathbf{P}(t_f|t_f)\mathbf{h}_x^T(\hat{\mathbf{x}}, t_f)\mathbf{Q}(t_f)\left[\mathbf{y}(t_f) - \mathbf{h}(\hat{\mathbf{x}}, t_f)\right] \tag{5.3.50}$$

Notice this has the same structure as the linear filtering equations—a predictive part coming from the modeling equations, and a "feedback" term incorporating the data. The decomposition result allows one to see these two contributions quite explicitly.

The initial condition for the filter arises by allowing $t_f \to 0$ and using Eq. (5.3.36) to see that

$$\hat{\boldsymbol{\lambda}}(0|0) = \mathbf{0} \tag{5.3.51}$$

so that Eq. (5.3.37) yields the initial filter estimate

$$\hat{\mathbf{x}}(0|0) = \mathbf{x}_0 \tag{5.3.52}$$

What remains now is to calculate the matrix of differential sensitivities $\mathbf{P}(t_f|t_f)$. If we differentiate Eq. (5.3.37) with respect to t_f, we obtain

$$\hat{\mathbf{x}}_{t_f}(0|t_f) = -\mathbf{P}_0\hat{\boldsymbol{\lambda}}_{t_f}(0|t_f) \tag{5.3.53}$$

Then letting t, $t_f \to 0$ in Eqs. (5.3.44) and (5.3.53), we see that

$$\mathbf{P}(0|0) = \mathbf{P}_0 \tag{5.3.54}$$

provides the initial value of the differential sensitivity.

To find the evolution equations for $\mathbf{P}(t_f|t_f)$, let us note that

$$\frac{\partial}{\partial t}\left[\hat{\mathbf{x}}_{t_f}(t|t_f)\right] \equiv \frac{\partial}{\partial t_f}\left[\hat{\mathbf{x}}_t(t|t_f)\right] \tag{5.3.55}$$

By evaluating the LHS using Eq. (5.3.44),

$$-\frac{\partial}{\partial t}\left[\mathbf{P}(t|t_f)\hat{\boldsymbol{\lambda}}_{t_f}(t|t_f)\right] = -\mathbf{P}_t(t|t_f)\hat{\boldsymbol{\lambda}}_{t_f}(t|t_f) - \mathbf{P}(t|t_f)\frac{\partial}{\partial t}\left[\hat{\boldsymbol{\lambda}}_{t_f}(t|t_f)\right] \tag{5.3.56}$$

however,

$$\frac{\partial}{\partial t}\left[\hat{\boldsymbol{\lambda}}_{t_f}(t|t_f)\right] = \frac{\partial}{\partial t_f}\left[\hat{\boldsymbol{\lambda}}_t(t|t_f)\right] = -\frac{\partial}{\partial t_f}\left[\hat{\mathbf{f}}_x^T\hat{\boldsymbol{\lambda}}(t|t_f) - \hat{\mathbf{h}}_x^T\mathbf{Q}(\mathbf{y}-\hat{\mathbf{h}})\right] \tag{5.3.57}$$

Now applying the chain rule of differentiation to Eq. (5.3.57),

$$\frac{\partial}{\partial t}\left[\hat{\boldsymbol{\lambda}}_{t_f}(t|t_f)\right] = -\left\{\hat{\mathbf{f}}_x^T\hat{\boldsymbol{\lambda}}_{t_f}(t|t_f) + \left[\hat{\mathbf{f}}_{xx}\hat{\boldsymbol{\lambda}}(t|t_f) + \hat{\mathbf{h}}_x^T\mathbf{Q}\hat{\mathbf{h}}_x^T - \hat{\mathbf{h}}_{xx}\mathbf{Q}(\mathbf{y}-\hat{\mathbf{h}})\right]\hat{\mathbf{x}}_{t_f}(t|t_f)\right\} \tag{5.3.58}$$

or

$$\frac{\partial}{\partial t}\left[\hat{\boldsymbol{\lambda}}_{t_f}(t|t_f)\right] = -\left\{\hat{\mathbf{f}}_x^T - \left[\hat{\mathbf{f}}_{xx}\hat{\boldsymbol{\lambda}}(t|t_f) + \hat{\mathbf{h}}_x^T\mathbf{Q}\hat{\mathbf{h}}_x - \hat{\mathbf{h}}_{xx}\mathbf{Q}(\mathbf{y}-\hat{\mathbf{h}})\right]\mathbf{P}(t|t_f)\right\}\hat{\boldsymbol{\lambda}}_{t_f}(t|t_f) \tag{5.3.59}$$

Thus the LHS of Eq. (5.3.55) becomes

$$\begin{aligned}\frac{\partial}{\partial t}\left[\hat{\mathbf{x}}_{t_f}(t|t_f)\right] = -\Big(\mathbf{P}_t(t|t_f) - \mathbf{P}(t|t_f)\Big\{\hat{\mathbf{f}}_x^T - \Big[\hat{\mathbf{f}}_{xx}\hat{\boldsymbol{\lambda}}(t|t_f) + \hat{\mathbf{h}}_x^T\mathbf{Q}\hat{\mathbf{h}}_x \\ -\hat{\mathbf{h}}_{xx}\mathbf{Q}(\mathbf{y}-\hat{\mathbf{h}})\Big]\mathbf{P}(t|t_f)\Big\}\Big)\hat{\boldsymbol{\lambda}}_{t_f}(t|t_f)\end{aligned} \tag{5.3.60}$$

The right-hand side of Eq. (5.3.55) may be written

$$\begin{aligned}\frac{\partial}{\partial t_f}\left[\hat{\mathbf{x}}_t(t|t_f)\right] &= \frac{\partial}{\partial t_f}\left[\mathbf{f}(\hat{\mathbf{x}}, t) - \mathbf{R}^{-1}(t)\hat{\boldsymbol{\lambda}}(t|t_f)\right] = \hat{\mathbf{f}}_x\hat{\mathbf{x}}_{t_f}(t|t_f) - \mathbf{R}^{-1}(t)\hat{\boldsymbol{\lambda}}_{t_f}(t|t_f) \\ &= -\left[\hat{\mathbf{f}}_x\mathbf{P}(t|t_f) + \mathbf{R}^{-1}(t)\right]\hat{\boldsymbol{\lambda}}_{t_f}(t|t_f)\end{aligned} \tag{5.3.61}$$

Upon comparing the RHS and LHS of Eq. (5.3.55), one sees that for the equation to hold for all $\hat{\boldsymbol{\lambda}}_{t_f}(t|t_f)$ the coefficients of $\hat{\boldsymbol{\lambda}}_{t_f}(t|t_f)$ must vanish, so that

$$\begin{aligned}\mathbf{P}_t(t|t_f) &= \mathbf{P}(t|t_f)\left[\hat{\mathbf{f}}_x^T - \hat{\mathbf{f}}_{xx}\hat{\boldsymbol{\lambda}}(t|t_f)\mathbf{P}(t|t_f)\right] \\ &\quad + \hat{\mathbf{f}}_x\mathbf{P}(t|t_f) - \mathbf{P}(t|t_f)\left[\hat{\mathbf{h}}_x^T\mathbf{Q}\hat{\mathbf{h}}_x - \mathbf{h}_{xx}\mathbf{Q}(\mathbf{y} - \hat{\mathbf{h}})\right]\mathbf{P}(t|t_f) + \mathbf{R}^{-1}(t)\end{aligned} \tag{5.3.62}$$

and when $t \to t_f$, Eq. (5.3.62) becomes

$$\begin{aligned}\mathbf{P}_t(t_f|t_f) &= \mathbf{P}(t_f|t_f)\hat{\mathbf{f}}_x^T + \hat{\mathbf{f}}_x\mathbf{P}(t_f|t_f) - \mathbf{P}(t_f|t_f)\left[\hat{\mathbf{h}}_x^T\mathbf{Q}\hat{\mathbf{h}}_x - \hat{\mathbf{h}}_{xx}\mathbf{Q}(\mathbf{y} - \hat{\mathbf{h}})\right]\mathbf{P}(t_f|t_f) \\ &\quad + \mathbf{R}^{-1}(t_f)\end{aligned} \tag{5.3.63}$$

However, remember that this is only part of the contribution because of the decomposition result:

$$\dot{\mathbf{P}}(t_f|t_f) = \mathbf{P}_t(t_f|t_f) + \mathbf{P}_{t_f}(t_f|t_f) \tag{5.3.64}$$

The first term on the RHS is given by Eq. (5.3.63), and the second term can be found by applying the chain rule to Eq. (5.3.43):

$$\mathbf{P}_{t_f}(t_f|t_f) = \frac{\partial \mathbf{P}(t_f|t_f)}{\partial \hat{\boldsymbol{\lambda}}(t_f|t_f)}\hat{\boldsymbol{\lambda}}_{t_f}(t_f|t_f) \tag{5.3.65}$$

If we define $\partial \mathbf{P}/\partial \hat{\boldsymbol{\lambda}}$ to be $\mathbf{P}'(t_f|t_f)$, then it will have the evolution equations

$$\dot{\mathbf{P}}'(t_f|t_f) = \mathbf{P}'_t(t_f|t_f) + \mathbf{P}'_{t_f}(t_f|t_f) \tag{5.3.66}$$

where

$$\mathbf{P}'_{t_f}(t_f|t_f) = \frac{\partial^2 \mathbf{P}(t_f|t_f)}{\partial \hat{\boldsymbol{\lambda}}^2(t_f|t_f)}\boldsymbol{\lambda}_{t_f}(t_f|t_f) \tag{5.3.67}$$

Thus the second terms in Eqs. (5.3.64) and (5.3.66) lead to an infinite set of upward-coupled moment equations which cannot be solved in closed form. This means that some approximation must be made to get a solution. The various nonlinear filters now in use differ only by the approximations made at this point.

The most commonly used nonlinear filter is a *first-order filter* which arises when one truncates the moments by setting $\mathbf{P}_{t_f}(t_f|t_f) = \mathbf{0}$. In this case the filter equations take the form

$$\dot{\hat{\mathbf{x}}}(t_f|t_f) = \hat{\mathbf{f}}(\hat{\mathbf{x}}, t_f) + \mathbf{P}(t_f|t_f)\hat{\mathbf{h}}_x^T\mathbf{Q}(t_f)\left[\mathbf{y}(t_f) - \mathbf{h}(\hat{\mathbf{x}}, t_f)\right], \qquad \hat{\mathbf{x}}(0|0) = \mathbf{x}_0 \tag{5.3.68}$$

and the differential sensitivities have the approximate solution

$$\begin{aligned}\dot{\mathbf{P}}(t_f|t_f) &= \mathbf{P}(t_f|t_f)\hat{\mathbf{f}}_x^T + \hat{\mathbf{f}}_x\mathbf{P}(t_f|t_f) \\ &\quad - \mathbf{P}(t_f|t_f)\left[\hat{\mathbf{h}}_x^T\mathbf{Q}\hat{\mathbf{h}}_x - \hat{\mathbf{h}}_{xx}\mathbf{Q}(\mathbf{y} - \hat{\mathbf{h}})\right]\mathbf{P}(t_f|t_f) + \mathbf{R}^{-1}(t_f) \\ &\qquad \mathbf{P}(0|0) = \mathbf{P}_0\end{aligned} \tag{5.3.69}$$

If in addition one assumes $\hat{\mathbf{h}}_{xx} = \mathbf{0}$, then Eqs. (5.3.68) and (5.3.69) represent the so-called *extended Kalman filter*.

Jazwinski [4] develops exact expressions for the estimates and covariance matrices for nonlinear problems having specific process noise and measurement error. However, these must be solved in some approximate manner as we have done here. The reader is referred to [4] for a variety of approximate filters.

One should note that, if desired, the present equations could be used to extend the solution to as high an order approximation as desired for $\mathbf{P}(t_f|t_f)$. The fact that first-order filters have been found to perform well in many applications means that these additional computations are often unnecessary.

As in the case of linear problems, the *prediction* equations only involve the properties of the model and take the form

$$\mathbf{x}_t(t|t_f) = \hat{f}(\hat{\mathbf{x}}(t|t_f), t) \qquad \begin{array}{l} \hat{\mathbf{x}}(0|0) = \mathbf{x}_0 \\ t > t_f \end{array} \tag{5.3.70}$$

Let us now make some general comments about non-linear estimation.

1. The optimal smoothing and prediction problems may be solved *exactly* with no approximations.
2. The filtering problem usually involves approximations in the differential sensitivity equations to provide a reasonable solution.
3. In general, *both* the filter equations and the differential sensitivity equations must be solved on-line (in real time) because both involve the current state estimates and possibly even the data. However, further approximations will allow these differential sensitivities to be precomputed off-line. Let us illustrate the performance of a nonlinear filter with an example.

Example 5.3.2* Consider the continuous stirred tank reactor (CSTR) shown in Fig. 5.13. Only the reactor temperature can be measured; thus state estimation is used to determine the reactant concentration c_A. The modeling equations take the form

$$V\frac{dc_A}{dt'} = (c_{AF} - c_A)F - Vk_0 \exp(-E_a/RT)c_A$$

$$V\rho C_p \frac{dT}{dt'} = F\rho C_p(T_F - T) - (\Delta H)Vk_0 \exp(-E_a/RT)c_A - hA(T - T_c)$$

* This example resulted from a term project carried out by Barry Freehill as part of the graduate course in Advanced Process Control at the University of Wisconsin.

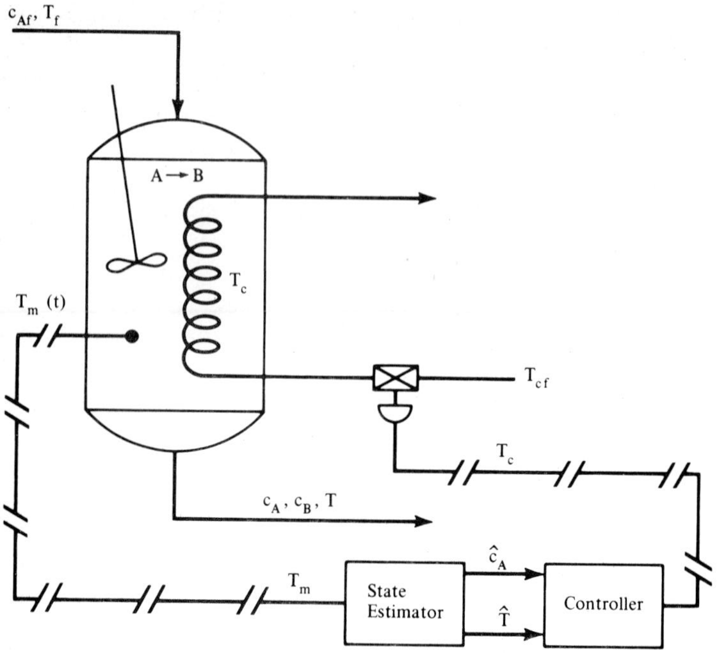

Figure 5.13 Nonlinear state estimator and controller for CSTR.

which may be put in dimensionless form by defining new variables

$$x_1 = \frac{c_{Af} - c_A}{c_{Af}} \qquad x_2 = \frac{T - T_f}{T_f}\gamma \qquad \beta = \frac{hA}{F\rho C_p} \qquad t = t'\frac{F}{V}$$

$$\gamma = \frac{E_a}{RT_f} \qquad \text{Da} = \frac{k_0 e^{-\gamma} V}{F} \qquad u = \frac{T_c - T_f}{T_f}\gamma \qquad H = \frac{(-\Delta H)c_{Af}\gamma}{\rho C_p T_f}$$

Hence the model becomes

$$\frac{dx_1}{dt} = -x_1 + \text{Da}(1 - x_1)\exp\left(\frac{x_2}{1 + x_2/\gamma}\right) + \xi_1(t)$$

$$\frac{dx_2}{dt} = -x_2(1 + \beta) + H\,\text{Da}(1 - x_1)\exp\left(\frac{x_2}{1 + x_2/\gamma}\right) + \beta u + \xi_2(t)$$

where $\xi_1(t)$, $\xi_2(t)$ represent random process disturbances with covariance matrix $\mathbf{R}^{-1}$.

The temperature measurement is given by

$$y(t) = x_2(t) + \eta(t) = \mathbf{C}\mathbf{x} + \eta(t)$$

where $\eta(t)$ represents zero mean random measurement error having covariance Q^{-1} and the output matrix is

$$\mathbf{C} = [0 \quad 1]$$

To begin, *observability conditions* can be checked by linearizing about the steady state of interest

$$\mathbf{f}_{\mathbf{x}_s} = \begin{bmatrix} \dfrac{\partial f_1}{\partial x_1} & \dfrac{\partial f_1}{\partial x_2} \\ \dfrac{\partial f_2}{\partial x_1} & \dfrac{\partial f_2}{\partial x_2} \end{bmatrix}_{ss} = \begin{bmatrix} \dfrac{-1}{1 - x_{1s}} & \dfrac{x_{1s}}{(1 + x_{2s}/\gamma)^2} \\ \dfrac{-Hx_{1s}}{1 - x_{1s}} & -(1+\beta) + \dfrac{Hx_{1s}}{(1 + x_{2s}/\gamma)^2} \end{bmatrix}$$

and testing the observability matrix

$$L_0 = \left[\mathbf{C}^T \,\vdots\, \mathbf{f}_{\mathbf{x}_s}^T \mathbf{C}^T\right] = \begin{bmatrix} 0 & \dfrac{-Hx_{1s}}{1 - x_{1s}} \\ 1 & -(1+\beta) + \dfrac{Hx_{1s}}{(1 + x_{2s}/\gamma)^2} \end{bmatrix}$$

which has rank 2 provided $Hx_{1s} \neq 0$. Thus the nonlinear system is expected to be *observable*.

The *extended Kalman filter* [Eqs. (5.3.68) and (5.3.69) with $\mathbf{h}_{xx} = \mathbf{0}$] was tested on this system by simulating the reactor on an analog computer and carrying out state estimation and feedback control from the digital computer (see Fig. 5.14). The parameters used were

$$\gamma = 13.4 \qquad H = 2.5 \qquad \mathrm{Da} = 1.0 \qquad \beta = 0.5 \qquad Q = 2500$$

$$\mathbf{R}^{-1} = \begin{bmatrix} 0 & 0 \\ 0 & 0.0001 \end{bmatrix} \qquad \mathbf{P}(0) = \begin{bmatrix} 1 \times 10^{-6} & 0 \\ 0 & 1.6 \times 10^{-7} \end{bmatrix}$$

The matrix $\mathbf{f}_{\mathbf{x}}$ resulting from linearization around the current estimate is

$$\hat{\mathbf{f}}_{\mathbf{x}} = \begin{bmatrix} \dfrac{\partial \hat{f}_1}{\partial x_1} & \dfrac{\partial \hat{f}_1}{\partial x_2} \\ \dfrac{\partial \hat{f}_2}{\partial x_1} & \dfrac{\partial \hat{f}_2}{\partial x_2} \end{bmatrix}$$

$$= \begin{bmatrix} -1 - \mathrm{Da}\exp\left(\dfrac{\hat{x}_2}{1 + \dfrac{\hat{x}_2}{\gamma}}\right) & \dfrac{\mathrm{Da}(1 - \hat{x}_1)\exp(\hat{x}_2/(1 + \hat{x}_2/\gamma))}{[1 + \hat{x}_2/\gamma]^2} \\ -H\,\mathrm{Da}\exp\left(\dfrac{\hat{x}_2}{1 + \hat{x}_2/\gamma}\right) & -(1+\beta) + \dfrac{H\,\mathrm{Da}(1 - \hat{x}_1)\exp(\hat{x}_2/(1 + \hat{x}_2/\gamma))}{[1 + \hat{x}_2/\gamma]^2} \end{bmatrix}$$

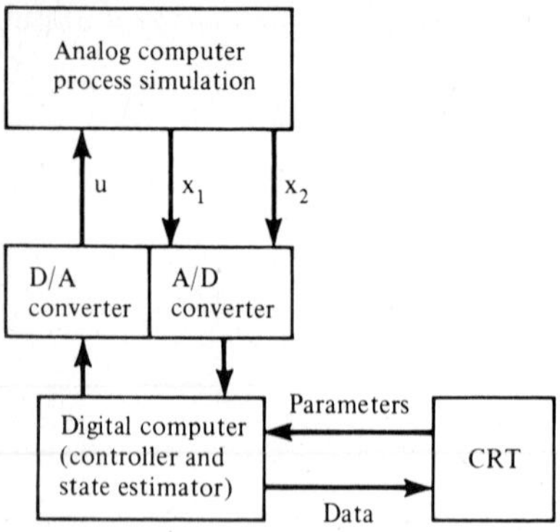

Figure 5.14 Simulation testing of the state estimation and control algorithm.

The filter equations then become

$$\dot{\hat{x}}_1 = -\hat{x}_1 + \mathrm{Da}(1 - \hat{x}_1)\exp\left(\frac{\hat{x}_2}{1 + \hat{x}_2/\gamma}\right) + P_{12}Q[y(t) - \hat{x}_2]$$

$$\dot{\hat{x}}_2 = -\hat{x}_2(1 + \beta) + H\,\mathrm{Da}(1 - \hat{x}_1)\exp\left(\frac{\hat{x}_2}{1 + \hat{x}_2/\gamma}\right) + \beta u + P_{22}Q[y(t) - \hat{x}_2]$$

while the covariance equations are

$$\dot{P}_{11} = 2\left(\frac{\partial f_1}{\partial x_1}P_{11} + \frac{\partial f_1}{\partial x_2}P_{12}\right) - Q(P_{12})^2$$

$$\dot{P}_{12} = \frac{\partial f_2}{\partial x_1}P_{11} + P_{12}\left(\frac{\partial f_2}{\partial x_1} + \frac{\partial f_2}{\partial x_2}\right) + P_{22}\frac{\partial f_1}{\partial x_2} - QP_{12}P_{22}$$

$$\dot{P}_{22} = 2\left(P_{12}\frac{\partial f_2}{\partial x_1} + P_{22}\frac{\partial f_2}{\partial x_2}\right) - Q(P_{22})^2 + R_{22}^{-1}$$

In this nonlinear problem both filter and covariance equations were solved on-line in real time.

The results when the state estimator is included in the feedback loop to provide estimates of conversion $\hat{x}_1$ are shown in Fig. 5.15. A single-loop PID controller

$$u = K_c\left(\epsilon + \frac{1}{\tau_I}\int \epsilon\, dt + \tau_d\frac{d\epsilon}{dt}\right)$$

was implemented. Here

$$\epsilon = x_{1d} - \hat{x}_1$$

is the deviation of the *estimated* conversion from the desired value. As can be seen in Fig. 5.15, the estimated and true values of $\hat{x}_1$ agree quite closely after a short transient, and the control loop, including the conversion

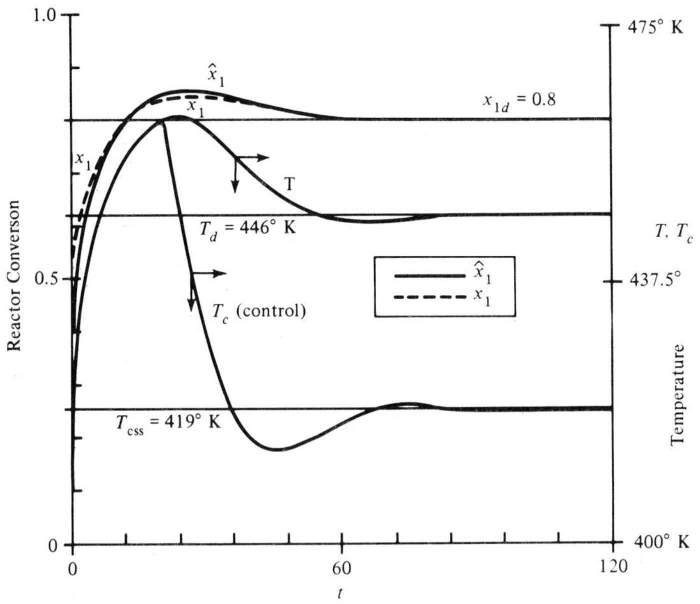

Figure 5.15 State estimator and feedback controller performance with temperature measurement only. $x_1(0)_{\text{actual}} = 0.5$; $\hat{x}_1(0) = 0.1$.

estimates, performed quite well. The variables T, T_c are plotted to show the reactor temperature and coolant temperature control action.

Nonlinear State Estimation with Discrete Time Data

For samples which are discrete in time the output device is

$$\mathbf{y}(t_k) = \mathbf{h}(\mathbf{x}(t_k), t_k) + \boldsymbol{\eta}_k \qquad k = 1, 2, \ldots \tag{5.3.71}$$

Although the estimation equation can be developed directly in this case (e.g., [4], p. 345), one may also use delta functions to obtain the equations from the continuous sampling case. Suppose in Eqs. (5.3.68) and (5.3.69) we let

$$\mathbf{Q}_k = \mathbf{Q}(t_k)\Delta t_k \tag{5.3.72}$$

and

$$\mathbf{Q}(t) = \sum_{k=1}^{M} \mathbf{Q}_k \delta(t - t_k) \tag{5.3.73}$$

where Δt_k is the sampling interval at time t_k and

$$t_f = \sum_{k=1}^{M} \Delta t_k \tag{5.3.74}$$

Then the discrete data nonlinear first-order extended Kalman filter is

$$\dot{\hat{\mathbf{x}}}(t|t_{k-1}) = \mathbf{f}(\hat{\mathbf{x}}, t) \tag{5.3.75}$$

$$\dot{\mathbf{P}}(t|t_{k-1}) = \hat{\mathbf{f}}_x\mathbf{P} + \mathbf{P}\mathbf{f}_x^T + \mathbf{R}^{-1}(t) \tag{5.3.76}$$

between observations $t_{k-1} < t < t_k$. At sampling points the updating expressions become [12]

$$\hat{\mathbf{x}}(t_k|t_k) = \hat{\mathbf{x}}(t_k|t_{k-1}) + \mathbf{K}(t_k)[\mathbf{y}(t_k) - \mathbf{h}(\hat{\mathbf{x}}(t_k|t_{k-1}), t_k)] \quad (5.3.77)$$

$$\mathbf{P}(t_k|t_k) = \mathbf{P}(t_k|t_{k-1}) - \mathbf{K}(t_k)\hat{\mathbf{h}}_x^T\mathbf{P}(t_k|t_{k-1}) \quad (5.3.78)$$

where

$$\mathbf{K}(t_k) = \mathbf{P}(t_k|t_{k-1})\hat{\mathbf{h}}_x[\hat{\mathbf{h}}_x\mathbf{P}(t_k|t_{k-1})\hat{\mathbf{h}}_x^T + \mathbf{Q}_k^{-1}]^{-1} \quad (5.3.79)$$

and $\hat{\mathbf{h}}_x$ is evaluated at $\hat{\mathbf{x}}(t_k|t_{k-1})$.

Nonlinear Observers

Just as for linear problems, observers may be constructed for nonlinear systems. However, because of the generality of the observation equations

$$\mathbf{y}(t) = \mathbf{h}(\mathbf{x}(t)) \quad (5.3.80)$$

for nonlinear problems, the theory is not nearly so neat and compact as for linear problems. The reader should consult Refs. [21, 22] for some results in special cases.

5.4 STOCHASTIC FEEDBACK CONTROL FOR SYSTEMS DESCRIBED BY ORDINARY DIFFERENTIAL EQUATIONS

Stochastic control is concerned with the problem of controlling systems described by stochastic differential equations. For example, the system

$$d\mathbf{x} = \mathbf{f}(\mathbf{x}, \mathbf{u}, t)\, dt + d\mathbf{v} \quad (5.4.1)$$

$$d\mathbf{w} = \mathbf{h}(\mathbf{x}, t)\, dt + d\mathbf{e} \quad (5.4.2)$$

is a set of nonlinear stochastic differential equations showing the response of the system state and output variables to random noise in the process $d\mathbf{v}$ and in the measuring device $d\mathbf{e}$. Here the variables $\mathbf{x}$, $\mathbf{w}$ are random variables and must be treated by special rules of stochastic calculus (e.g., the Ito or Stratonovich formulation). However, it is beyond the scope of this text to pursue these matters in depth, and thus we shall content ourselves with a formal treatment of the important results of interest. The interested reader should consult Refs. [4, 5, 7, 23–27] for more details of stochastic control.

The great bulk of useful results in stochastic control theory is for optimal stochastic feedback controllers [1–3, 5, 26, 27]. The basic design question is, "How should the stochastic controller differ from the deterministic controller in structure?" For linear systems, the answer is quite simple—there is usually very little difference. However, for nonlinear systems, the situation is a great deal more complex. To illustrate the linear case, let us treat the linear-quadratic problem in some detail.

For the case of additive white,* Gaussian process noise and measurement errors, and linear system and measurement equations, Eqs. (5.4.1) and (5.4.2) can be written

$$\frac{d\mathbf{x}}{dt} = \mathbf{Ax} + \mathbf{Bu} + \boldsymbol{\xi}(t) \tag{5.4.3}$$

$$\mathbf{y}(t) = \mathbf{Cx} + \boldsymbol{\eta} \tag{5.4.4}$$

where formally the noise processes $\boldsymbol{\xi}(t)$, $\boldsymbol{\eta}(t)$ are $\boldsymbol{\eta}(t) \approx d\mathbf{e}/dt$, $\boldsymbol{\xi}(t) \approx d\mathbf{v}/dt$, and $\mathbf{y}(t) \approx d\mathbf{w}/dt$ with statistics given by Eq. (5.2.27). For linear-quadratic optimal control, the quadratic objective must be written in terms of expectations,

$$\min_{\mathbf{u}(t)} \left\{ I = \mathcal{E}\left[\tfrac{1}{2}\mathbf{x}^T(t_f)\mathbf{S}_f\mathbf{x}(t_f) + \tfrac{1}{2}\int_0^{t_f}(\mathbf{x}^T\mathbf{Fx} + \mathbf{u}^T\mathbf{Eu})\,dt \right] \right\} \tag{5.4.5}$$

Now if $\boldsymbol{\xi}(t)$, $\boldsymbol{\eta}(t)$ are independent, zero-mean, white-noise processes, then they contribute no bias into the control law, and one can show [1–3, 5, 23–27] that the *stochastic* feedback control law is the same as the *deterministic* feedback control law, i.e.,

$$\mathbf{u}(t) = -\mathbf{K}(t)\mathbf{x}(t) \tag{3.2.81}$$

where

$$\mathbf{K}(t) = \mathbf{E}^{-1}\mathbf{B}^T\mathbf{S}(t) \tag{3.2.82}$$

$$\frac{d\mathbf{S}}{dt} = -\mathbf{SA} - \mathbf{A}^T\mathbf{S} + \mathbf{SBE}^{-1}\mathbf{B}^T\mathbf{S} - \mathbf{F} \qquad \mathbf{S}(t_f) = \mathbf{S}_f \tag{3.2.80}$$

Thus if complete state measurements are available, $\mathbf{C} = \mathbf{I}$, the optimal stochastic controller has the same structure as the deterministic controller.

In the event that there is incomplete state measurement, then the optimal stochastic feedback controller must be coupled in some way to a state estimator. Thus, if the initial state $\mathbf{x}(0)$ is uncorrelated with $\boldsymbol{\xi}(t)$, $\boldsymbol{\eta}(t)$ and is Gaussian with mean and covariance given by

$$\mathcal{E}(\mathbf{x}_0) = \hat{\mathbf{x}}_0 \tag{5.4.6}$$

$$\mathcal{E}\left((\mathbf{x}(0) - \hat{\mathbf{x}}_0)(\mathbf{x}(0) - \hat{\mathbf{x}}_0)^T\right) = \mathbf{P}_0 \tag{5.4.7}$$

then the optimal stochastic feedback controller is

$$\mathbf{u} = -\mathbf{K}(t)\hat{\mathbf{x}}(t) \tag{5.4.8}$$

$$\frac{d\hat{\mathbf{x}}(t)}{dt} = \mathbf{A}\hat{\mathbf{x}} + \mathbf{Bu} + \mathbf{PC}^T\mathbf{Q}(\mathbf{y} - \mathbf{C}\hat{\mathbf{x}}) \tag{5.4.9}$$

where $\mathbf{K}(t)$ is given by Eqs. (3.3.82) and (3.3.80) and

$$\frac{d\mathbf{P}(t)}{dt} = \mathbf{PA}^T + \mathbf{AP} - \mathbf{PC}^T\mathbf{QCP} + \mathbf{R}^{-1} \qquad \mathbf{P}(0) = \mathbf{P}_0 \tag{5.4.10}$$

Note that one simply uses the optimal estimates in the deterministic feedback control law. This *separation principle* or *certainty-equivalence principle* is a powerful result which means that the optimal controller and optimal estimator may be

* "White" noise contains all frequencies and is therefore totally uncorrelated in time.

completely separated in structure. Such separation principles apply to a rather broad class of linear systems [27], *but do not apply in general to nonlinear systems.* Thus the very neat theory for Gaussian, white-noise, linear systems is greatly complicated if:

1. The process is nonlinear.
2. The noise is colored (i.e., correlated in time) or non-Gaussian.

We shall not pursue these more complex cases here, but shall rely on certain approximations to allow suboptimal but acceptable controller designs for nonlinear stochastic processes. A practical discussion of these points may be found in [28].

Let us illustrate the results for linear systems with the following example problems.

Example 5.4.1 Let us consider the isothermal CSTR of Examples 3.2.5 and 5.2.4, in which the reaction $A \rightarrow B \rightarrow C$ is taking place. Let us assume that only x_2 (species B) is measured and that u_1 (the feed concentration of A) is the only control variable allowed. The modeling equations take the form

$$\frac{dx_1}{dt} = -(1 + \mathrm{Da}_1)x_1 + u_1 + \xi_1(t) \qquad x_1(0) = x_{10} + \xi_{10} \tag{5.4.11}$$

$$\frac{dx_2}{dt} = \mathrm{Da}_1 x_1 - (1 + \mathrm{Da}_3)x_2 + \xi_2(t) \qquad x_2(0) = x_{20} + \xi_{20} \tag{5.4.12}$$

$$y(t) = x_2(t) + \eta(t) \tag{5.4.13}$$

Now we know from Example 3.2.6 that the system is *completely controllable* with only $u_1(t)$ as a control. Similarly, in Example 5.2.2, we showed that the system is *completely observable* with only $x_2(t)$ as an output.

Now if we assume $\xi_1(t)$, $\xi_2(t)$, $\eta(t)$ are zero-mean, independent, Gaussian, white-noise processes and ξ_{10}, ξ_{20} are zero-mean, independent, Gaussian random variables, then the *separation theorem* applies and the optimal stochastic feedback controller can be broken into two parts: (1) a deterministic linear-quadratic feedback control law, and (2) an optimal least squares estimator for providing the state estimates. This structure may be seen in Fig. 5.16.

Therefore, if we wish to minimize the control objective

$$I_c = \mathcal{E}\left\{ \frac{1}{2} \int_0^{t_f} \left[\mathbf{x}^T(t)\mathbf{F}\mathbf{x}(t) + E u_1(t)^2 \right] dt \right\} \tag{5.4.14}$$

then the optimal stochastic feedback control law is

$$u_1(t) = -\mathbf{K}(t)\hat{\mathbf{x}}(t) = -K_1(t)\hat{x}_1(t) - K_2(t)\hat{x}_2(t) \tag{5.4.15}$$

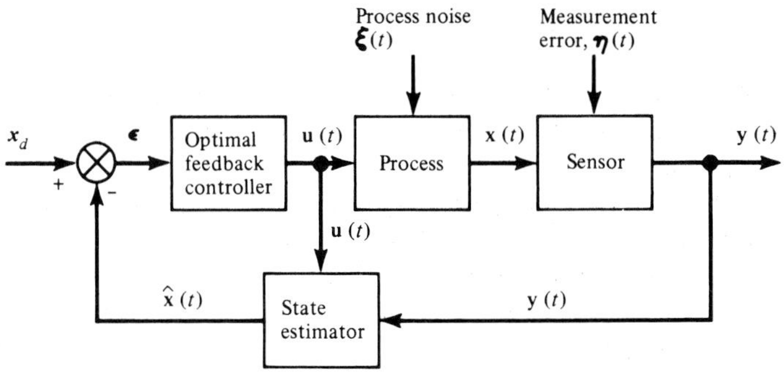

Figure 5.16 Structure of optimal stochastic controller.

where

$$\mathbf{K} = E^{-1}[S_{11}(t), S_{12}(t)] \tag{5.4.16}$$

or

$$K_1(t) = \frac{S_{11}(t)}{E} \qquad K_2(t) = \frac{S_{12}(t)}{E} \tag{5.4.17}$$

The parameters S_{ij} come from the solution to the Riccati equations

$$\dot{S}_{11} = 2S_{11}(1 + \mathrm{Da}_1) - 2S_{12}\,\mathrm{Da}_1 + \frac{1}{E}S_{11}^2 - F_{11} \qquad S_{11}(t_f) = 0 \tag{5.4.18}$$

$$\dot{S}_{12} = S_{12}(2 + \mathrm{Da}_1 + \mathrm{Da}_3) - \mathrm{Da}_1 S_{22} + \frac{1}{E}S_{11}S_{12} - F_{12} \qquad S_{12}(t_f) = 0 \tag{5.4.19}$$

$$\dot{S}_{22} = 2S_{22}(1 + \mathrm{Da}_3) + \frac{1}{E}S_{12}^2 - F_{22} \qquad S_{22}(t_f) = 0 \tag{5.4.20}$$

Thus one may precompute Eqs. (5.4.18) to (5.4.20) in order to obtain the optimal feedback controller gains.

The optimal estimates $\hat{x}_1(t)$, $\hat{x}_2(t)$ needed by the controller come from the filter equations, which are only slightly modified from Example 5.2.4, i.e.,

$$\dot{\hat{x}}_1 = -(1 + \mathrm{Da}_1)\hat{x}_1 + u_1(t) + P_{12}(t)Q(t)(y - \hat{x}_2) \tag{5.4.21}$$

$$\dot{\hat{x}}_2 = \mathrm{Da}_1\hat{x}_1 - (1 + \mathrm{Da}_3)\hat{x}_2 + P_{22}(t)Q(t)(y - \hat{x}_2) \tag{5.4.22}$$

where $u_1(t)$ is given by Eq. (5.4.15) and the estimate covariance may be precomputed from Eq. (5.2.80).

It is possible to combine state estimation and feedback control to produce proportional plus integral control. As an example [29], consider the system

$$\dot{\mathbf{x}} = \mathbf{Ax} + \mathbf{Bu} + \mathbf{Dv} \tag{5.4.23}$$

where v is a vector of "environmental disturbance" variables given by

$$\dot{\mathbf{v}} = \xi(t) \tag{5.4.24}$$

Here $\xi(t)$ represents some random disturbance. The system outputs are

$$\mathbf{y} = \mathbf{Cx} + \eta \tag{5.4.25}$$

Now the steady-state linear-quadratic controller for the desired steady state $\mathbf{x}_d = \mathbf{0}$, $\mathbf{u}_d = \mathbf{0}$ becomes

$$\mathbf{u} = -\mathbf{K}_1\hat{\mathbf{x}} - \mathbf{K}_2\hat{\mathbf{v}} \tag{5.4.26}$$

and the state estimates of $\mathbf{x}$ and $\mathbf{v}$ are given by

$$\dot{\hat{\mathbf{x}}} = \mathbf{A}\hat{\mathbf{x}} + \mathbf{Bu} + \mathbf{D}\hat{\mathbf{v}} + \mathbf{K}_{e1}(\mathbf{y} - \mathbf{C}\hat{\mathbf{x}}) \tag{5.4.27}$$

$$\dot{\hat{\mathbf{v}}} = \mathbf{K}_{e2}(\mathbf{y} - \mathbf{C}\hat{\mathbf{x}}) \tag{5.4.28}$$

where $\mathbf{K}_{e1}$, $\mathbf{K}_{e2}$ become constants for long estimation time.

Now substitution of Eq. (5.4.28) into Eq. (5.4.26) yields the optimal, proportional plus integral control law

$$\mathbf{u} = -\mathbf{K}_1\hat{\mathbf{x}} + \mathbf{K}_2\mathbf{K}_{e2}\mathbf{C}\int_0^t \hat{\mathbf{x}}\,dt - \mathbf{K}_2\mathbf{K}_{e2}\int_0^t \mathbf{y}(t)\,dt \tag{5.4.29}$$

Let us illustrate this with an example.

Example 5.4.2 Let us consider the heating of a fluid in a stirred heating tank. The inlet temperature T_f is raised to T at the exit by heat transfer with a steam jacket at temperature T_w. A heat balance in the process yields

$$\rho C_p V \frac{dT}{dt'} = F\rho C_p(T_f - T) - hA(T - T_w) \tag{5.4.30}$$

Now suppose we let

$$x = T \qquad u = T_w \qquad v = T_f \qquad t = \frac{t'}{\theta} \qquad \alpha = \frac{hA}{F\rho C_p} \qquad \theta = \frac{V}{F}$$

$$\frac{dx}{dt} = -(1 + \alpha)x + v + \alpha u \tag{5.4.31}$$

where v, the inlet temperature, is assumed subject to disturbances given by

$$\frac{dv}{dt} = \xi(t) \tag{5.4.32}$$

where $\xi(t)$ represents some type of disturbance process. Let us assume that only $x(t)$ can be measured; thus

$$y = x + \eta \tag{5.4.33}$$

is the output device. Now the steady-state, linear-quadratic, optimal feedback control law is

$$u = u_d - K_1(\hat{x} - x_d) - K_2\hat{v} \tag{5.4.34}$$

where x_d, u_d represent the steady-state controller set point on x and u.

The state estimation equations are

$$\dot{\hat{x}} = -(1+\alpha)\hat{x} + \alpha u + \hat{v} + K_{e1}(y - \hat{x}) \tag{5.4.35}$$

$$\dot{\hat{v}} = K_{e2}(y - \hat{x}) \tag{5.4.36}$$

This leads immediately to the proportional plus integral controller

$$u(t) = u_d - K_1(\hat{x} - x_d) - K_2 K_{e2}\int_0^t (y - \hat{x})\, dt' \tag{5.4.37}$$

Note that the second integral term is designed to compensate for disturbances v which are estimated by the filter.

5.5 STATE ESTIMATION FOR SYSTEMS DESCRIBED BY FIRST-ORDER HYPERBOLIC PARTIAL DIFFERENTIAL EQUATIONS

Let us consider the general class of systems described by

$$\frac{\partial \mathbf{x}(z,t)}{\partial t} = \mathbf{A}_1 \frac{\partial \mathbf{x}}{\partial z} + \mathbf{f}(\mathbf{x}(z,t), \mathbf{u}(z,t)) + \boldsymbol{\xi}(z,t) \tag{5.5.1}$$

$$\mathbf{x}(0,t) = \mathbf{B}_0 \mathbf{u}_0(t) \tag{5.5.2}$$

$$\mathbf{y}(t) = \mathbf{h}(\mathbf{x}(z_1^*, t), \mathbf{x}(z_2^*, t), \ldots, \quad \mathbf{x}(z_\gamma^*, t)) + \boldsymbol{\eta}(t) \tag{5.5.3}$$

where $\boldsymbol{\xi}$, $\boldsymbol{\eta}$ are additive, zero-mean noise processes. This is a very general class of equations, encompassing both linear and nonlinear systems and even systems with pure time delays. In what follows we shall consider conditions for *observability* and then discuss state estimation algorithms.

Observability

General conditions for *observability* for first-order hyperbolic systems have been discussed by Goodson and Klein [30], Yu and Seinfeld [11], and Thowsen and Perkins [31] and essentially require that every characteristic line intersect a measuring device and that a lumped parameter observability condition must be satisfied along these characteristic lines. To see this, consider the observation paths $w_i(t)$ in Fig. 5.17 beginning at $z = 1$ and moving across all characteristic lines in the domain R_α. Then we define outputs corresponding to the intersection of the characteristic lines and the observation paths:

$$\mathbf{y}_i(t) = \mathbf{C}_i \mathbf{x}(z,t)|_{z = w_i(t)} \qquad i = 1, 2, \ldots, \gamma$$

Finally one can apply a lumped parameter observability condition along the characteristics.

For illustration, we consider constant-coefficient linear systems having fixed sensors and only one set of characteristic lines. Equations (5.5.1) to (5.5.3) take

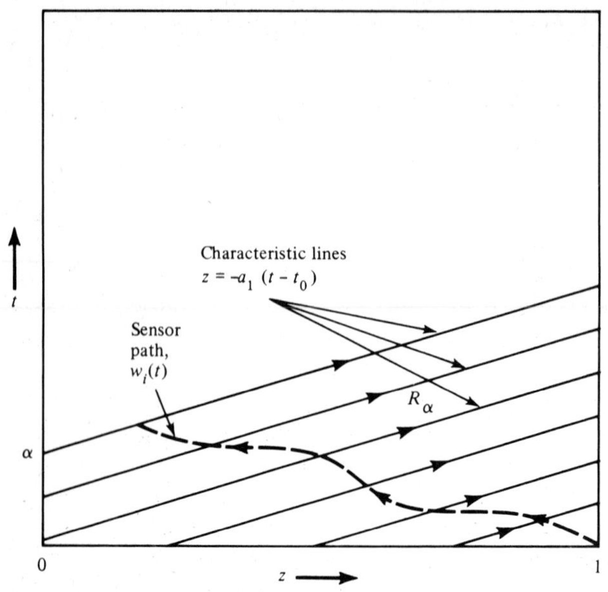

Figure 5.17 Characteristic lines and sensor path for first-order hyperbolic systems.

the form (where we suppress the controller for the moment)

$$\frac{\partial \mathbf{x}(z,t)}{\partial t} = a_1 \frac{\partial \mathbf{x}}{\partial z} + \mathbf{A}_0\mathbf{x} + \boldsymbol{\xi}(z,t) \tag{5.5.4}$$

$$\mathbf{y}(t) = \sum_{i=1}^{\gamma} \mathbf{C}_i \mathbf{x}(z_i^*, t) + \boldsymbol{\eta}(t) \tag{5.5.5}$$

where the solution takes the form

$$\left.\frac{d\mathbf{x}}{dt}\right|_0 = \mathbf{A}_0\mathbf{x} + \boldsymbol{\xi} \tag{5.5.6}$$

along the characteristic lines

$$z = -a_1(t - t_0) \tag{5.5.7}$$

where $a_1 < 0$ in general for flow processes. Now for a *fixed* sensor to intersect each characteristic line, it must be located at $z = 1$ (see Fig. 5.17); otherwise the portion of the initial conditions between any sensor location z_i^* and $z = 1$ *are not observable.*

Now applying the lumped parameter observability conditions along the characteristics, one has the following conditions for observability.

In order for the system [*Eqs.* (5.5.4) *and* (5.5.5)] *to be completely observable, it is necessary and sufficient that each characteristic line intersect a sensor and that the matrix*

$$\mathbf{L}_{od} = \left[\boldsymbol{\Phi}(t_1, 0)^T \mathbf{C}_1^T \vdots \dots \vdots \boldsymbol{\Phi}(t_\gamma, 0)^T \mathbf{C}_\gamma^T\right] \tag{5.5.8}$$

have rank n.

Here t_i is the time at which the particular characteristic line in question intersects the sensor at z_i^*. Thus

$$t_i = t_0 - z_i^*/a_1 \qquad i = 1, 2, \ldots, \gamma \tag{5.5.9}$$

The $n \times n$ matrix $\mathbf{\Phi}(t, 0)$ is the state transition matrix for the matrix $\mathbf{A}_0$.

Conditions for a wider class of first-order hyperbolic processes may be found in [11, 31].

Let us illustrate this result with an example.

Example 5.5.1 Let us consider the heat exchanger of Example 4.2.1 having fixed temperature sensors at

$$z_1^* = 0.25$$
$$z_2^* = 0.5$$
$$z_3^* = 0.75$$
$$z_4^* = 1.0$$

Recall that the modeling equations are

$$\frac{\partial x}{\partial t}(z, t) = -v\frac{\partial x}{\partial z} + a_0(x - u) \qquad x(0, t) = 0 \tag{4.2.25}$$

so that along the characteristic lines

$$t = t_0 + z/v \tag{5.5.10}$$

the solution is

$$\left.\frac{dx}{dt}\right|_0 = a_0 x - a_0 u \tag{5.5.11}$$

and

$$\Phi(t, 0) = e^{a_0 t} \tag{5.5.12}$$

with measuring device

$$\mathbf{y}(t) = \begin{bmatrix} y_1 \\ y_2 \\ y_3 \\ y_4 \end{bmatrix} = \begin{bmatrix} 1 \\ 0 \\ 0 \\ 0 \end{bmatrix} x(0.25, t) + \begin{bmatrix} 0 \\ 1 \\ 0 \\ 0 \end{bmatrix} x(0.5, t) + \begin{bmatrix} 0 \\ 0 \\ 1 \\ 0 \end{bmatrix} x(0.75, t) + \begin{bmatrix} 0 \\ 0 \\ 0 \\ 1 \end{bmatrix} x(1, t) \tag{5.5.13}$$

Thus the observability matrix becomes

$$\mathbf{L}_{od} = \left[e^{a_0 t_1} 000 \,\vdots\, 0 e^{a_0 t_2} 00 \,\vdots\, 00 e^{a_0 t_3} 0 \,\vdots\, 000 e^{a_0 t_4} \right] \tag{5.5.14}$$

which clearly has rank 1, and the system is observable.

Note that only z_4^* intersects all the characteristics, so the system is not *observable* without the outlet temperature sensor. If only z_2^* were used, for example, the shaded area in Fig. 5.18 bounded by $z = 1$, $t = 0$, and $t = (z - 0.5)/v$ would not be observable.

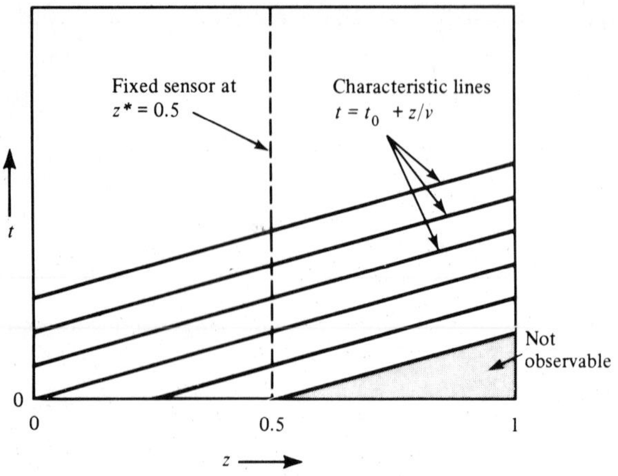

Figure 5.18 Characteristic lines and fixed temperature sensor at $z^* = 0.5$ for plug flow heat exchanger.

Note that from a practical feedback control point of view, the fixed sensor required for complete observability (i.e., at $z = 1$) is not very useful because one cannot take corrective control action. Thus state estimation of first-order hyperbolic systems is often directed at identifying inlet disturbances rather than at identifying the complete initial state. Therefore, partial observation of the process, concentrating on the section near the entrance (where identified disturbances can be compensated for by control action before the exit is reached), is often the practical goal. In this case sensors would be grouped toward the entrance, with perhaps only one sensor at $z = 1$ to allow a final check on the outlet condition (and satisfy the observability condition).

One should note that any time delay system can be represented by equations of the form of Eqs. (5.5.1) to (5.5.3). Explicit conditions for observability of time delay systems are discussed in [32].

State Estimation

Very general optimal state estimators for first-order partial differential equations have been developed and include a wide range of time delay and other hereditary systems as special cases [33]. In this section, however, we shall only present the results for systems of the form of Eqs. (5.5.1) to (5.5.3). The method of derivation follows closely the approach of Sec. 5.3 but requires considerably more algebra; therefore, we shall only present the results here and refer the reader to [33] for the derivation details.

The sequential state estimation algorithm which minimizes

$$I = \frac{1}{2}\int_0^{t_f}\Big\{(\mathbf{y} - \mathbf{h})^T\mathbf{Q}(t)(\mathbf{y} - \mathbf{h})\,dt + \frac{1}{2}\int_0^t\int_0^1\int_0^1\big[\mathbf{x}_t(r, t) - \mathbf{A}_1\mathbf{x}_r(r, t) - \mathbf{f}\big]^T$$

$$\times\,\mathbf{R}(r, s, t)\big[\mathbf{x}_t(s, t) - \mathbf{A}_1\mathbf{x}_s(s, t) - \mathbf{f}\big]\,dt\,dr\,ds\Big\} \tag{5.5.15}$$

is given by

$$\frac{\partial\hat{\mathbf{x}}(r, t)}{\partial t} = \mathbf{A}_1\frac{\partial\mathbf{x}}{\partial r}(r, t) + \hat{\mathbf{f}}(\hat{\mathbf{x}}(r, t), \mathbf{u}(r, t))$$

$$+ \sum_{i=1}^{\gamma}\mathbf{P}(r, r_i^*, t)\frac{\partial\hat{\mathbf{h}}}{\partial\hat{\mathbf{x}}(r_i^*, t)}\mathbf{Q}(t)\big\{\mathbf{y} - \hat{\mathbf{h}}\big[\hat{\mathbf{x}}(r_1^*, t), \ldots, \hat{\mathbf{x}}(r_\gamma^*, t)\big]\big\} \tag{5.5.16}$$

with boundary condition

$$\hat{\mathbf{x}}(0, t) = \mathbf{B}_0\mathbf{u}_0(t) \tag{5.5.17}$$

and initial condition

$$\hat{\mathbf{x}}(r, 0) = \hat{\mathbf{x}}_0(r)$$

The $n \times n$ differential sensitivity matrix $\mathbf{P}(r, s, t)$ is the solution of

$$\mathbf{P}_t(r, s, t) = \hat{\mathbf{f}}_x\mathbf{P} + \mathbf{P}\hat{\mathbf{f}}_x^T + \mathbf{A}_1\mathbf{P}_r + \mathbf{P}_s\mathbf{A}_1^T + \sum_{i=1}^{\gamma}\sum_{j=1}^{\gamma}\mathbf{P}(r, r_i^*, t)$$

$$\times\frac{\partial\big\{\big[\partial\hat{\mathbf{h}}/\partial\hat{\mathbf{x}}(r_i^*, t)\big]\mathbf{Q}(t)(\mathbf{y} - \hat{\mathbf{h}})\big\}}{\partial\hat{\mathbf{x}}(r_j^*, t)}\mathbf{P}(r_j^*, s, t) + \mathbf{R}_1^+(r, s, t) \tag{5.5.18}$$

$$\mathbf{P}(r, 0, t) = \mathbf{P}(0, s, t) = \mathbf{0} \tag{5.5.19}$$

$$\mathbf{P}(r, s, 0) = \mathbf{P}_0(r, s) \tag{5.5.20}$$

where for linear problems having white, Gaussian noise, $\mathbf{P}_0$ is the error covariance of the initial condition, $\mathbf{Q}^{-1}(t)$ is the covariance of the measurement error, and $\mathbf{R}_1^+(r, s, t)$ is the covariance of the process noise. For nonlinear problems, $\mathbf{P}_0$, $\mathbf{Q}^{-1}$, and $\mathbf{R}_1^+$ have no strict statistical significance and may be considered filter tuning parameters. Furthermore, $\mathbf{P}$ has no statistical significance and usually must be computed on-line in real time unless approximations are made. By contrast, for linear systems with white, Gaussian noise processes, the differential sensitivities $\mathbf{P}$ become true estimate covariances and may be precomputed off-line.

General results are also available for data taken at discrete time intervals; however, the reader should consult Ref. [34] for details. Also, work on observers for this class of systems has been reported [35].

Let us illustrate the application of this filtering result by considering an example problem.

Example 5.5.2 Let us consider the heat exchanger of the previous example where it is desired to estimate the temperature profile based on four fixed thermocouple sensors. Substituting Eqs. (4.2.25) and (5.5.13) into Eqs. (5.5.16) to (5.5.20), one obtains the estimation equations:

$$\frac{\partial \hat{x}(z,t)}{\partial t} = -v\frac{\partial \hat{x}(z,t)}{\partial z} + a_0(\hat{x} - u)$$

$$+ \sum_{i=1}^{4} P(r, r_i^*, t)\mathbf{C}_i^T\mathbf{Q}(t)\left[\mathbf{y} - \sum_{j=1}^{4} \mathbf{C}_j\mathbf{x}(r_j^*, t)\right] \tag{5.5.21}$$

$$\hat{x}(0,t) = 0 \qquad \hat{x}(r,0) = x_0(r) \tag{5.5.22}$$

$$P_t(r,s,t) = 2a_0P - v[P_r + P_s] + R_1^+(r,s,t)$$

$$- \sum_{i=1}^{4}\sum_{j=1}^{4} P(r, r_i^*, t)\mathbf{C}_i^T\mathbf{Q}(t)\mathbf{C}_jP(r_j^*, s, t) \tag{5.5.23}$$

$$P(r,0,t) = P(0,s,t) = 0 \qquad P(r,s,0) = P_0(r,s) \tag{5.5.24}$$

where $\mathbf{Q}^{-1}(t)$ is a 4×4 matrix of measurement error covariances, R_1^+ is a scalar process noise covariance, $P_0(r,s)$ is a covariance of the error in the initial state, and

$$\mathbf{C}_1 = \begin{bmatrix}1\\0\\0\\0\end{bmatrix} \qquad \mathbf{C}_2 = \begin{bmatrix}0\\1\\0\\0\end{bmatrix} \qquad \mathbf{C}_3 = \begin{bmatrix}0\\0\\1\\0\end{bmatrix} \qquad \mathbf{C}_4 = \begin{bmatrix}0\\0\\0\\1\end{bmatrix} \tag{5.5.25}$$

This is a linear problem, and if we assume the measurement and process noise to be white and Gaussian, then $P(r,s,t)$ is the distributed covariance of the error estimates, defined by

$$P(r,s,t) = \mathcal{E}\{[\hat{x}(r,t) - x(r,t)][\hat{x}(s,t) - x(s,t)]\} \tag{5.5.26}$$

and can be precomputed off-line. Only the estimator equation, (5.5.21), must be solved on-line in real time.

5.6 STATE ESTIMATION FOR SYSTEMS DESCRIBED BY SECOND-ORDER PARTIAL DIFFERENTIAL EQUATIONS

By far the most common type of model arising from heat, mass, and momentum balances is the second-order partial differential equation. These equations occur in heat conduction, diffusion, and pressure-driven flow processes. For these reasons, state estimation applied to this class of problems has particular practical importance.

The class of systems we shall consider explicitly in this chapter take the form

$$\frac{\partial \mathbf{x}(z,t)}{\partial t} = \mathbf{f}[\mathbf{x}_{zz}, \mathbf{x}_z, \mathbf{x}(z,t), \mathbf{u}(z,t)] + \boldsymbol{\xi}(z,t) \tag{5.6.1}$$

with boundary conditions

$$\mathbf{b}_0[\mathbf{x}_z, \mathbf{x}, \mathbf{u}_0(t)] + \boldsymbol{\xi}_0(t) = \mathbf{0} \qquad z = 0 \tag{5.6.2}$$

$$\mathbf{b}_1[\mathbf{x}_z, \mathbf{x}, \mathbf{u}_1(t)] + \boldsymbol{\xi}_1(t) = \mathbf{0} \qquad z = 1 \tag{5.6.3}$$

These equations are capable of representing most one-dimensional* PDE systems of process control interest. The measurements can be considered either continuous in time,

$$\mathbf{y}(t) = \mathbf{h}[\mathbf{x}(z_1^*, t), \mathbf{x}(z_2^*, t), \ldots, \mathbf{x}(z_Y^*, t)] + \boldsymbol{\eta}(t) \tag{5.6.4}$$

or discrete in time,

$$\mathbf{y}(t_k) = \mathbf{h}[\mathbf{x}(z_1^*, t_k), \mathbf{x}(z_2^*, t_k), \ldots, \mathbf{x}(z_Y^*, t_k)] + \boldsymbol{\eta}(t_k) \qquad k = 1, 2, \ldots \tag{5.6.5}$$

Equations (5.6.1) to (5.6.5) are defined for $t \geq 0$ and $0 < z < 1$, $\mathbf{x}(z, t)$ is an n vector, $\mathbf{y}$ is an l vector, while $\mathbf{b}_0$ and $\mathbf{b}_1$ are l_0 and l_1 vector functions, respectively. The functions $\boldsymbol{\xi}(z, t)$, $\boldsymbol{\xi}_0(t)$, $\boldsymbol{\xi}_1(t)$, $\boldsymbol{\eta}(t)$, $\boldsymbol{\eta}(t_k)$ represent zero-mean random processes with arbitrary statistical properties. The points $0 \leq z_1^* \leq z_2^* \ldots \leq z_Y^* \leq 1$ represent the sensor locations. The initial condition, $\mathbf{x}(z, 0)$ is generally unknown.

Before proceeding to state estimation algorithms, we shall consider the question of observability and the choice of sensor locations.

Observability and the Choice of Sensor Location

Just as in lumped parameter systems, conditions for observability are only well developed for linear systems and are usually "approximate observability" conditions which allow observation of the state to within an arbitrarily small error. In practice, this means that one uses modal analysis to analyze the system and observability conditions are stated in terms of the system eigenfunctions [30, 36–41]. In addition, just as the *controllability conditions* discussed in Chap. 4 were dependent on actuator position, the observability conditions depend strongly on the choice of sensor location.

To illustrate these points, let us consider the problem of the long, thin rod heated along its axis and having modeling equations

$$\frac{\partial x}{\partial t}(z, t) = \frac{\partial^2 x(z, t)}{\partial z^2} + u(z, t) \tag{5.6.6}$$

$$z = 0 \qquad \frac{\partial x}{\partial z} = 0 \tag{5.6.7}$$

$$z = 1 \qquad \frac{\partial x}{\partial z} = 0 \tag{5.6.8}$$

* Problems involving more space dimensions require straightforward extensions of these estimation equations. An illustrative example is given in Chap. 6.

Further, let us assume a measuring device of the form

$$y_i(t) = x(z_i^*, t) \qquad i = 1, 2, \ldots, l \tag{5.6.9}$$

i.e., there are thermocouple measurements at a finite number of discrete points. Now the question is, "*How many measurements are needed and at what location are measurements required to ensure observability?*" Let us begin with a single measurement and test for observability.

From Sec. 4.2 we recall that the solution to Eqs. (5.6.6) to (5.6.8) takes the form

$$x(z, t) = a_0(t) + \sqrt{2} \sum_{n=1}^{N} a_n(t) \cos n\pi z \tag{5.6.10}$$

$$u(z, t) = b_0(t) + \sqrt{2} \sum_{n=1}^{N} b_n(t) \cos n\pi z \tag{5.6.11}$$

where

$$\frac{da_n(t)}{dt} = -n^2\pi^2 a_n + b_n(t) \qquad n = 0, 1, 2, \ldots, N \tag{5.6.12}$$

and

$$y_i(t) = a_0(t) + \sqrt{2} \sum_{n=1}^{N} a_n(t) \cos n\pi z_i^* \qquad i = 1, 2, \ldots, l \tag{5.6.13}$$

If we define the $N + 1$ vector $\mathbf{w}(t)$, $(N + 1) \times (N + 1)$ matrix $\mathbf{A}$, and $N + 1$ vector $\mathbf{v}$ as

$$\mathbf{w} = \begin{bmatrix} a_0(t) \\ a_1(t) \\ \vdots \\ a_N(t) \end{bmatrix} \qquad \mathbf{A} = \begin{bmatrix} 0 & 0 & \cdots & 0 & 0 \\ 0 & -\pi^2 & \cdots & \cdots & 0 \\ \cdots & \cdots & -4\pi^2 & \cdots & \cdots \\ \cdots & \cdots & \cdots & \cdots & \cdots \\ 0 & \cdots & \cdots & \cdots & -N^2\pi^2 \end{bmatrix} \qquad \mathbf{v} = \begin{bmatrix} b_0(t) \\ b_1(t) \\ \vdots \\ b_N(t) \end{bmatrix} \tag{5.6.14}$$

the system takes the form

$$\dot{\mathbf{w}} = \mathbf{A}\mathbf{w} + \mathbf{v} \tag{5.6.15}$$

with output given by

$$\mathbf{y} = \mathbf{C}\mathbf{w} \tag{5.6.16}$$

where the $l \times (N + 1)$ matrix $\mathbf{C}$ is given by

$$\mathbf{C} = \begin{bmatrix} 1 & \sqrt{2}\cos \pi z_1^* & \sqrt{2}\cos 2\pi z_1^* & \cdots & \sqrt{2}\cos N\pi z_1^* \\ 1 & \sqrt{2}\cos \pi z_2^* & \sqrt{2}\cos 2\pi z_2^* & \cdots & \sqrt{2}\cos N\pi z_2^* \\ \cdots & \cdots & \cdots & \cdots & \cdots \\ 1 & \sqrt{2}\cos \pi z_l^* & \sqrt{2}\cos 2\pi z_l^* & \cdots & \sqrt{2}\cos N\pi z_l^* \end{bmatrix} \tag{5.6.17}$$

Now application of the approximate N mode observability conditions yields the condition that the $(N+1) \times (N+1)$ observability matrix $\mathbf{L}_0$ should have rank $N+1$, where

$$\mathbf{L}_0 = \left[\mathbf{C}^T \,\vdots\, \mathbf{A}^T\mathbf{C}^T \,\vdots\, \dots \,\vdots\, (\mathbf{A}^T)^N \mathbf{C}^T\right] \tag{5.6.18}$$

For the case of only a *single sensor* z_1^*, the observability condition takes the form

$$\mathbf{L}_0 = \begin{bmatrix} 1 & 0 & \cdots & 0 \\ \sqrt{2}\cos \pi z_1^* & -\pi^2\sqrt{2}\cos \pi z_1^* & \cdots & (-1)^N \pi^{2N}\sqrt{2}\cos \pi z_1^* \\ \sqrt{2}\cos 2\pi z_1^* & -4\pi^2\sqrt{2}\cos 2\pi z_1^* & \cdots & (-1)^N(4\pi^2)^N\sqrt{2}\cos 2\pi z_1^* \\ \cdots & \cdots & \cdots & \cdots \\ \sqrt{2}\cos N\pi z_1^* & -N^2\pi^2\sqrt{2}\cos N\pi z_1^* & \cdots & (-1)^N(N^2\pi^2)^N\sqrt{2}\cos N\pi z_1^* \end{bmatrix} \tag{5.6.19}$$

Thus $\mathbf{L}_0$ will have rank $N+1$ if and only if z_1^* is selected so that none of the eigenfunctions vanish, i.e.,

$$\cos n\pi z_1^* \neq 0 \qquad \text{for all } n = 1, 2, \dots, N \tag{5.6.20}$$

This is a fairly severe restriction; for example, in the event that

$$z_1^* = \begin{cases} \frac{1}{2}, \frac{1}{4}, \frac{1}{6}, \frac{1}{8}, \frac{1}{10}, \dots, & \frac{1}{2N} \\ \frac{3}{4}, \frac{3}{8}, \frac{3}{10}, \dots, & \frac{3}{2N} \\ \frac{5}{6}, \frac{5}{8}, \frac{5}{12}, \dots, & \frac{5}{2N} \\ \vdots \end{cases}$$

the system is *not observable*. In fact, Goodson and Klein [30] show that for increasing N the zeros of the eigenfunction move closer and closer to the external boundaries, as shown in Fig. 5.19. Thus one must place measurements to avoid these zeros. As N increases, the zeros within the envelope become more and more dense. There is, however, one significant advantage to this structure: *the surface measurement locations, which are the easiest to realize practically, always guarantee observability*. This is a consequence of the cosine eigenfunctions which arise because of the form of the boundary conditions, Eqs. (5.6.7) and (5.6.8). If instead the surface temperatures had been specified, the system would be unobservable at the external surface; however, a boundary heat flux measurement in this case would again make the system observable on the boundary.

In summary, we have the remarkable result that the heated rod is observable even with only a single temperature measurement if we avoid placing this sensor at the zeros of the eigenfunctions.

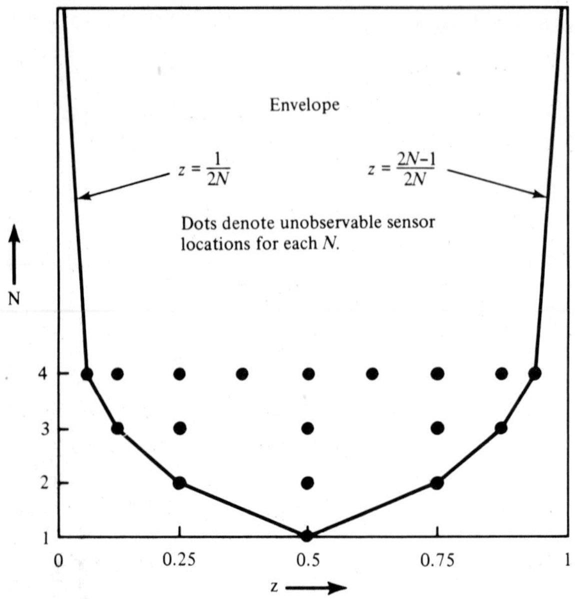

Figure 5.19 Influence of sensor location on observability of one-dimensional heated rod.

The choice of *optimal* sensor locations requires carrying the analysis a bit further, for there is an infinite variety of sensor locations satisfying the observability conditions. A number of computational algorithms have been proposed for determining the optimal sensor locations, and the reader is urged to consult the literature for a discussion of these [42–47].

For *nonlinear* problems, very few observability results exist, and one must be content with either linearizing the system and testing local observability or relaxing the nonlinearity and examining the observability of the related linear problem.

State Estimation

State estimation algorithms have been developed for a wide range of problems and by a wide variety of derivation methods. For linear problems having white, Gaussian noise, very complete rigorous results are available; however, for nonlinear problems or for problems with more complex noise processes, there are fewer rigorous results, but many general formal results. The reader is directed to a recent review [36] for a fuller discussion of these points and for a survey of practical applications.

In this section we shall present a very general nonlinear state estimator for the system of Eqs. (5.6.1) to (5.6.5). To begin, let us require that the state estimates minimize the error functional

$$I = \int_0^{t_f} (\mathbf{y} - \mathbf{h})^T \mathbf{Q}(\mathbf{y} - \mathbf{h})\, dt$$

$$+ \int_0^{t_f}\int_0^1\int_0^1 \left[\mathbf{x}_t(r, t) - \mathbf{f}(\mathbf{x}_{rr}, \mathbf{x}_r, \mathbf{x}, \mathbf{u})\right]^T$$

$$\times \mathbf{R}(r, s, t)\left[\mathbf{x}_t(s, t) - \mathbf{f}(\mathbf{x}_{ss}, \mathbf{x}_s, \mathbf{x}, \mathbf{u})\right] dr\, ds\, dt$$

$$+ \int_0^{t_f}\left[\left(\mathbf{b}_0^T \mathbf{R}_0 \mathbf{b}_0\right) + \left(\mathbf{b}_1^T \mathbf{R}_1 \mathbf{b}_1\right)\right] dt \tag{5.6.21}$$

where the matrices $\mathbf{R}_0$, $\mathbf{R}_1$, $\mathbf{Q}(t)$ are positive definite and symmetric. In the case of discrete time data, $\mathbf{Q}(t)$ is replaced by $\mathbf{Q}_d(t)$, where

$$\mathbf{Q}_d(t) = \sum_{k=1}^{M} \mathbf{Q}(t_k)\delta(t - t_k)\Delta t_k \tag{5.6.22}$$

and Δt_k is the sampling interval at time k. The quantity $\mathbf{R}(r, s, t)$ is defined by

$$\int_0^1 \mathbf{R}^+(r, \rho, t)\mathbf{R}(\rho, s, t)d\rho = \mathbf{I}\delta(r - s) \tag{5.6.23}$$

where $\mathbf{R}^+(r, s, t)$ is a positive definite, symmetric matrix function. There will be two cases to consider:

1. *Continuous time data.* For continuous time data, the state estimation equations take the form [34]

$$\frac{\partial \hat{\mathbf{x}}}{\partial t}(z, t) = \hat{\mathbf{f}}(\hat{\mathbf{x}}_{zz}, \hat{\mathbf{x}}_z, \hat{\mathbf{x}}, \mathbf{u}) + \sum_{i=1}^{\Upsilon} \mathbf{P}(z, z_i^*, t)\frac{\partial \hat{\mathbf{h}}}{\partial \hat{\mathbf{x}}(z_i^*, t)}\mathbf{Q}(t)\left[\mathbf{y}(t) - \hat{\mathbf{h}}\right] \tag{5.6.24}$$

with boundary conditions

$$\hat{\mathbf{b}}_0(\hat{\mathbf{x}}, \hat{\mathbf{x}}_z, \mathbf{u}_0) = \mathbf{0} \qquad z = 0 \tag{5.6.25}$$

$$\hat{\mathbf{b}}_1(\hat{\mathbf{x}}, \hat{\mathbf{x}}_z, \mathbf{u}_1) = \mathbf{0} \qquad z = 1 \tag{5.6.26}$$

where the differential sensitivities $\mathbf{P}(r, s, t)$ must satisfy

$$\mathbf{P}_t(r, s, t) = \frac{\partial \hat{\mathbf{f}}}{\partial \hat{\mathbf{x}}}(\hat{\mathbf{x}}_{rr}, \hat{\mathbf{x}}_r, \hat{\mathbf{x}}, \mathbf{u})\mathbf{P}(r, s, t) + \frac{\partial \hat{\mathbf{f}}}{\partial \hat{\mathbf{x}}_r}\mathbf{P}_r(r, s, t)$$

$$+ \frac{\partial \hat{\mathbf{f}}}{\partial \hat{\mathbf{x}}_{rr}}\mathbf{P}_{rr}(r, s, t) + \mathbf{P}(r, s, t)\frac{\partial \hat{\mathbf{f}}}{\partial \hat{\mathbf{x}}}(\hat{\mathbf{x}}_{ss}, \hat{\mathbf{x}}_s, \mathbf{x}, \mathbf{u})^T$$

$$+ \mathbf{P}_s(r, s, t)\frac{\partial \hat{\mathbf{f}}^T}{\partial \hat{\mathbf{x}}_s} + \mathbf{P}_{ss}(r, s, t)\frac{\partial \hat{\mathbf{f}}^T}{\partial \hat{\mathbf{x}}_{ss}}$$

$$+ \sum_{i=1}^{\Upsilon}\sum_{j=1}^{\Upsilon} \mathbf{P}(r, r_i^*, t)\frac{\partial\left\{\left[\partial \hat{\mathbf{h}}/\partial \hat{\mathbf{x}}(r_i^*, t)\right]\mathbf{Q}(t)(\mathbf{y} - \hat{\mathbf{h}})\right\}}{\partial \hat{\mathbf{x}}(r_j^*, t)}\mathbf{P}(r_j^*, s, t)$$

$$+ \mathbf{R}^+(r, s, t) \tag{5.6.27}$$

as well as the boundary conditions at

$r = 0$

$$\frac{\partial \hat{\mathbf{b}}_0}{\partial \hat{\mathbf{x}}}\mathbf{P}(r, s, t) + \frac{\partial \hat{\mathbf{b}}_0}{\partial \hat{\mathbf{x}}_r}\mathbf{P}_r(r, s, t) + \mathbf{R}_0^{-1}(t)\left(\frac{\partial \hat{\mathbf{b}}_0}{\partial \hat{\mathbf{x}}_r}\right)^{-1}\hat{\mathbf{f}}^T_{\mathbf{x}_{rr}}\delta(s) = \mathbf{0} \tag{5.6.28}$$

$r = 1$

$$\frac{\partial \hat{\mathbf{b}}_1}{\partial \hat{\mathbf{x}}}\mathbf{P}(r, s, t) + \frac{\partial \hat{\mathbf{b}}_1}{\partial \hat{\mathbf{x}}_r}\mathbf{P}_r(r, s, t) - \mathbf{R}_1^{-1}(t)\left(\frac{\partial \hat{\mathbf{b}}_1}{\partial \hat{\mathbf{x}}_r}\right)^{-1}\hat{\mathbf{f}}^T_{\mathbf{x}_{rr}}\delta(s - 1) = \mathbf{0} \tag{5.6.29}$$

$s = 0$

$$\mathbf{P}(r, s, t)\frac{\partial \hat{\mathbf{b}}_0^T}{\partial \hat{\mathbf{x}}} + \mathbf{P}_s(r, s, t)\frac{\partial \hat{\mathbf{b}}_0^T}{\partial \hat{\mathbf{x}}_s} + \left[\mathbf{R}_0^{-1}(t)\left(\frac{\partial \hat{\mathbf{b}}_0}{\partial \hat{\mathbf{x}}_s}\right)^{-1}\hat{\mathbf{f}}^T_{\mathbf{x}_{ss}}\right]^T\delta(r) = \mathbf{0} \tag{5.6.30}$$

$s = 1$

$$\mathbf{P}(r, s, t)\frac{\partial \hat{\mathbf{b}}_1^T}{\partial \hat{\mathbf{x}}} + \mathbf{P}_s(r, s, t)\frac{\partial \hat{\mathbf{b}}_1^T}{\partial \hat{\mathbf{x}}_s} - \left[\mathbf{R}_1^{-1}(t)\left(\frac{\partial \hat{\mathbf{b}}_1}{\partial \hat{\mathbf{x}}_s}\right)^{-1}\hat{\mathbf{f}}^T_{x_{ss}}\right]^T\delta(r - 1) = \mathbf{0} \tag{5.6.31}$$

Note that the differential sensitivities are symmetric [i.e., $\mathbf{P}(r, s, t) = \mathbf{P}(s, r, t)^T$] and reduce to estimate covariances when the system becomes linear with Gaussian, white-noise processes.

2. *Discrete time data.* The state estimation equations [34] for discrete time data take the following form between samples:

$$\frac{\partial \hat{\mathbf{x}}(z, t)}{\partial t} = \mathbf{f}(\hat{\mathbf{x}}_{zz}, \hat{\mathbf{x}}_z, \hat{\mathbf{x}}, \mathbf{u}) \qquad \begin{array}{c} t_{k-1} < t < t_k \\ k = 1, 2, \ldots \end{array} \tag{5.6.32}$$

with boundary conditions given by Eqs. (5.6.25) and (5.6.26). At sampling points t_k the estimates are updated by

$$\begin{aligned} \hat{\mathbf{x}}(z, t_k^+) = \hat{\mathbf{x}}(z, t_k^-) + \sum_{i=1}^{\gamma}\Bigg\{ & \mathbf{P}(z, z_i^*, t_k^-)\hat{\mathbf{V}}_i(t_k^-) \\ & + \tfrac{1}{2}\mathbf{P}(z, z_i^*, t_k^-)\sum_{j=1}^{\gamma}\hat{\mathbf{V}}_{ij}(t_k^-)\delta\hat{\mathbf{x}}(z_j^*, t_k) \\ & + \tfrac{1}{2}\left[\delta\mathbf{P}(z, z_i^*, t_k)\hat{\mathbf{V}}_i(t_k^-)\right]\Bigg\} \end{aligned} \tag{5.6.33}$$

The differential sensitivities $\mathbf{P}(r, s, t)$ are given by the following equation between samples:

$$\mathbf{P}_t(r, s, t) = \hat{\mathbf{f}}_{\hat{\mathbf{x}}}\mathbf{P} + \hat{\mathbf{f}}_{\hat{\mathbf{x}}_r}\mathbf{P}_r + \hat{\mathbf{f}}_{\hat{\mathbf{x}}_{rr}}\mathbf{P}_{rr} + \mathbf{P}\hat{\mathbf{f}}^T_{\hat{\mathbf{x}}} + \mathbf{P}_s\hat{\mathbf{f}}^T_{\hat{\mathbf{x}}_s} + \mathbf{P}_{ss}\hat{\mathbf{f}}^T_{\hat{\mathbf{x}}_{ss}} + \mathbf{R}^+ \qquad t_{k-1} < t < t_k \tag{5.6.34}$$

with boundary conditions determined by Eqs. (5.6.28) to (5.6.31). The updating of the differential sensitivities at the sampling points is given by

$$\mathbf{P}(r, s, t_k^+) = \mathbf{P}(r, s, t_k^-) + \sum_{i=1}^{\gamma}\sum_{j=1}^{\gamma}\Big\{\mathbf{P}(r, r_i^*, t_k^-)\hat{\mathbf{V}}_{ij}(t_k^-)\mathbf{P}(r_j^*, s, t_k^-)$$

$$+\tfrac{1}{2}\delta\mathbf{P}(r, r_i^*, t_k)\hat{\mathbf{V}}_{ij}(t_k^-)\mathbf{P}(r_j^*, s, t_k^-)$$

$$+\tfrac{1}{2}\mathbf{P}(r, r_i^*, t_k^-)\hat{\mathbf{V}}_{ij}(t_k^-)\delta\mathbf{P}(r_j^*, s, t_k)$$

$$+\tfrac{1}{2}\mathbf{P}(r, r_i^*, t_k^-)\left[\sum_{m=1}^{\gamma}\mathbf{V}_{ijm}(t_k^-)\delta\hat{\mathbf{x}}(r_m^*, t_k)\right]\mathbf{P}(r_j^*, s, t_k^-)\Big\} \tag{5.6.35}$$

In these equations,

$$\begin{aligned}
\delta\hat{\mathbf{x}}(z, t_k) &= \hat{\mathbf{x}}(z, t_k^+) - \hat{\mathbf{x}}(z, t_k^-)\\
\delta\mathbf{P}(r, s, t_k) &= \mathbf{P}(r, s, t_k^+) - \mathbf{P}(r, s, t_k^-)\\
\hat{V}(t_k^-) &= -(\mathbf{y} - \hat{\mathbf{h}})^T\mathbf{Q}_k(\mathbf{y} - \hat{\mathbf{h}})\\
\hat{\mathbf{V}}_i(t_k^-) &= \frac{\partial\hat{V}(t_k^-)}{\partial\hat{\mathbf{x}}(z_i^*, t_k^-)}\\
\hat{\mathbf{V}}_{ij}(t_k^-) &= \frac{\partial^2\hat{V}(t_k^-)}{\partial\hat{\mathbf{x}}(z_i^*, t_k^-)\partial\hat{\mathbf{x}}(z_j^*, t_k^-)}\\
\hat{\mathbf{V}}_{ijm}(t_k^-) &= \frac{\partial^3\hat{V}(t_k^-)}{\partial\hat{\mathbf{x}}(z_i^*, t_k^-)\partial\hat{\mathbf{x}}(z_j^*, t_k^-)\partial\hat{\mathbf{x}}(z_m^*, t_k^-)}
\end{aligned} \tag{5.6.36}$$

Example 5.6.1 Let us illustrate these results by applying them to the problem of a thin flat plate having heating $u(z, t)$ applied along the length and water cooling passed through the center of the slab. The system, as constructed by Mäder [48], is shown in Fig. 5.20. The mathematical model of the heated slab takes the form

$$\frac{\partial x(z, t)}{\partial t} = \alpha\frac{\partial^2 x(z, t)}{\partial z^2} - \beta x(z, t) + \gamma u(z, t) + \xi(z, t) \qquad \begin{matrix} t > 0 \\ 0 \le z \le 1\end{matrix} \tag{5.6.37}$$

$$z = 0, 1 \qquad \frac{\partial x}{\partial z} = 0 \tag{5.6.38}$$

with temperature sensors of the form

$$y_i(t) = x(z_i^*, t) + \eta_i(t) \qquad i = 1, 2, \ldots, l \tag{5.6.39}$$

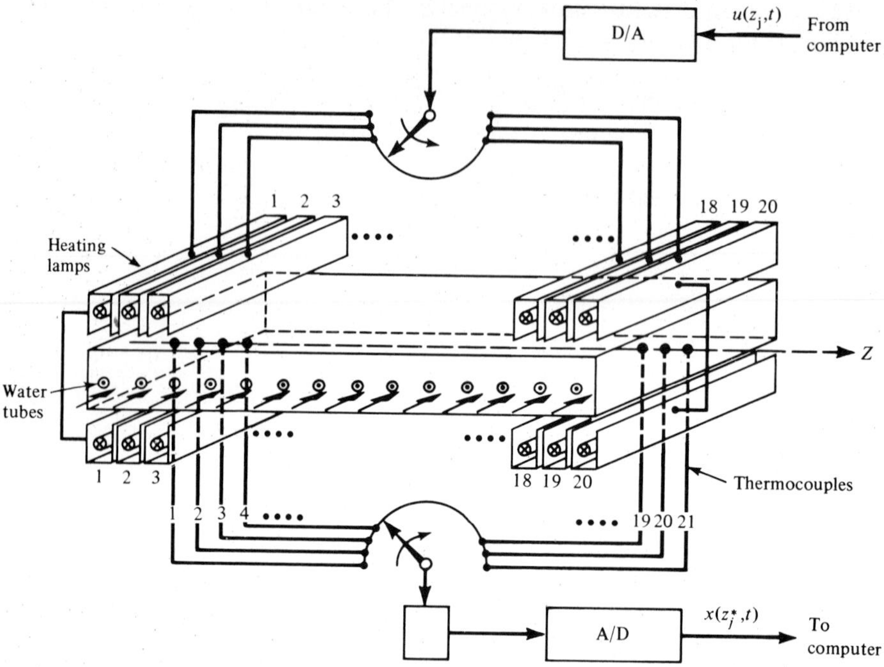

Figure 5.20 Experimental details of the heated slab [49]. *(Reproduced by permission of Pergamon Press Ltd.)*

Note that in Mäder's apparatus, there are 20 heating lamps which allow a good approximation to continuous heating $u(z, t)$. Also there are 21 thermocouples, so that the exact temperature profile may be known.*

First, it is easy to show that this system is observable if the thermocouples used by the state estimator do not all fall at the zeros of the system eigenfunctions, cos $n\pi z$. In particular, if one chooses $z_1^* = 0$ as the single sensor to be used by the state estimator, then the system is observable and the state estimation equations take the form

$$\frac{\partial \hat{x}(z, t)}{\partial t} = \alpha \frac{\partial^2 \hat{x}(z, t)}{\partial z^2} - \beta \hat{x}(z, t) + \gamma u(z, t)$$
$$+ P(z, 0, t)Q(t)[y(t) - \hat{x}(0, t)] \qquad (5.6.40)$$

with the boundary conditions of Eq. (5.6.38).

The problem is linear, and if one assumes $\xi(z, t)$, $\eta(t)$ to be Gaussian, white noise, then the differential sensitivities become estimate covariances of the form

$$P(z, z', t) = \mathcal{E}\{[x(z, t) - \hat{x}(z, t)][x(z', t) - \hat{x}(z', t)]\} \qquad (5.6.41)$$

* This example is taken from [49] with permission of Pergamon Press Ltd.

The covariance equations arise directly from Eqs. (5.6.27) to (5.6.31) and take the form

$$P_t(z, z', t) = -2\beta P(z, z', t) + \alpha[P_{zz}(z, z', t) + P_{z'z'}(z, z', t)] - P(z, 0, t)QP(0, z', t) + R^+(z, z', t) \tag{5.6.42}$$

with boundary conditions

$$\begin{aligned}
z = 0: &\quad P_z(0, z', t) + \alpha R_0^{-1}\delta(z') = 0 \\
z = 1: &\quad P_z(1, z', t) - \alpha R_1^{-1}\delta(z' - 1) = 0 \\
z' = 0: &\quad P_{z'}(z, 0, t) + \alpha R_0^{-1}\delta(z) = 0 \\
z' = 1: &\quad P_{z'}(z, 1, t) - \alpha R_1^{-1}\delta(z - 1) = 0
\end{aligned} \tag{5.6.43}$$

Now it is possible to use the eigenfunctions of the system

$$\begin{cases} \phi_0 = 1 \\ \phi_n = \sqrt{2}\cos n\pi z \qquad n = 1, 2, \ldots, N \end{cases} \tag{5.6.44}$$

to solve *both* the state estimation equations and the covariance equations. By making the substitutions

$$\hat{x}(z, t) = \sum_{n=0}^{N} a_n(t)\phi_n(z) \qquad u(z, t) = \sum_{n=0}^{N} b_n(t)\phi_n(z) \tag{5.6.45}$$

$$P(z, z', t) = \sum_{n=0}^{N}\sum_{m=0}^{N} P_{nm}(t)\phi_n(z)\phi_m(z') \tag{5.6.46}$$

one can reduce the state estimation equations to the form

$$\frac{d\mathbf{w}}{dt} = \mathbf{Aw} + \mathbf{P}(t)\mathbf{C}Q(t)(y - \mathbf{Cw}) + \mathbf{v} \tag{5.6.47}$$

$$\frac{d\mathbf{P}(t)}{dt} = \mathbf{AP} + \mathbf{PA} - \mathbf{PC}Q\mathbf{C}^T\mathbf{P} + \mathbf{D}(t) + \mathbf{D}_0(t) + \mathbf{D}_1(t) \tag{5.6.48}$$

where **w**, **v**, **C** are defined by Eqs. (5.6.14) and (5.6.17) and

$$\mathbf{D}_0 = \alpha^2\mathbf{\Phi}(0)\mathbf{R}_0^{-1}\mathbf{\Phi}^T(0) \tag{5.6.49}$$

$$\mathbf{D}_1 = \alpha^2\mathbf{\Phi}(1)\mathbf{R}_1^{-1}\mathbf{\Phi}(1)^T \tag{5.6.50}$$

Here **D** is the matrix of eigencoefficients d_{nm} of

$$R^+(z, z', t) = \sum_{n=0}^{N}\sum_{m=0}^{N} d_{nm}\phi_n(z)\phi_m(z') \tag{5.6.51}$$

and

$$\mathbf{\Phi}(z) = \begin{bmatrix} \phi_0(z) \\ \phi_1(z) \\ \vdots \\ \phi_N(z) \end{bmatrix}$$

$$\mathbf{A} = \begin{bmatrix} -\beta & 0 & \cdots & \cdots & 0 \\ 0 & -\beta - \pi^2 & \cdots & \cdots & 0 \\ 0 & \cdots & -\beta - 4\pi^2 & \cdots & 0 \\ \cdots & \cdots & \cdots & \cdots & \cdots \\ 0 & \cdots & \cdots & \cdots & -\beta - N^2\pi^2 \end{bmatrix} \tag{5.6.52}$$

Note that the $[(N + 1)^2 + (N + 1)]/2$ independent elements of the symmetric matrix $\mathbf{P}(t)$ may be precomputed off-line, while the $N + 1$ state estimation equations for $\mathbf{w}$ must be solved on-line.

These filter equations were implemented by Ajinkya et al. [49], and typical experimental results for the case of one thermocouple at $z = 0$ are shown in Fig. 5.21. Note that the filter converges to within 2°C of the exact profile in 1 min and to within 1°C in 3 min. More extensive experimental

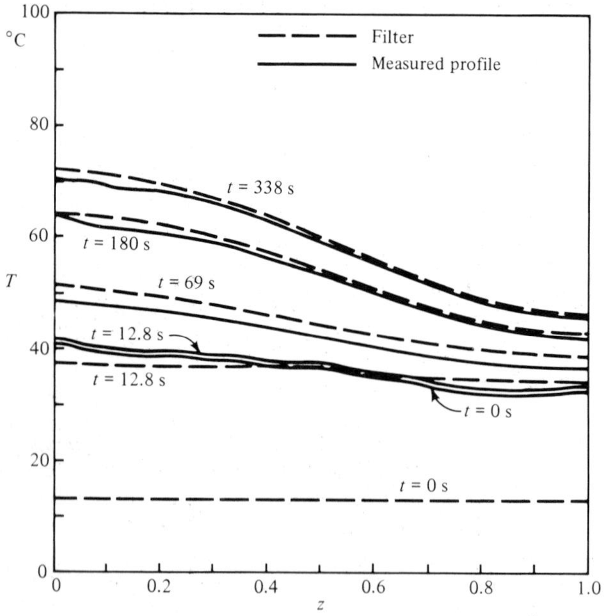

Figure 5.21 Open-loop filter performance with one measurement ($z = 0$). *(Reproduced by permission of Pergamon Press Ltd.)*

results may be seen in [49]. Only three eigenfunctions were used in this case ($N = 2$), so the covariance and state estimation equations together consist of nine ODEs. Even though the covariance equations were solved on-line in real time (for convenience), the total computations required less than $\frac{1}{2}$ percent of real time on the minicomputer.

Observers

State observers have been developed for distributed parameter systems (e.g., [50, 51]) and have the same basic properties as the lumped observers discussed in Sec. 5.2. As in the lumped parameter case, the purpose is to construct a deterministic estimator for unmeasured state variables. Let us illustrate the application of an observer to the example system described in Example 5.6.1.

Example 5.6.2 We shall neglect the noise in the equations for the heated slab so that the model becomes deterministic,

$$\frac{\partial x(z, t)}{\partial t} = \alpha \frac{\partial^2 x(z, t)}{\partial z^2} - \beta x(z, t) + \gamma u(z, t) \tag{5.6.53}$$

$$z = 0, 1 \qquad \frac{\partial x}{\partial z} = 0 \tag{5.6.54}$$

$$y_i(t) = x(z_i^*, t) \qquad i = 1, 2, \ldots, l \tag{5.6.55}$$

One may show [50, 51] that the structure of the observer is the same as for the optimal state estimator, i.e.,

$$\hat{x}_t(z, t) = \alpha \hat{x}_{zz} - \beta \hat{x} + \gamma u(z, t) + \mathbf{g}^T(z)[\mathbf{y}(t) - \hat{\mathbf{y}}(t)] \tag{5.6.56}$$

where

$$\hat{\mathbf{y}}(t) = \begin{bmatrix} \hat{x}(z_1^*, t) \\ \vdots \\ \hat{x}(z_l^*, t) \end{bmatrix} = \int_0^1 \mathbf{C}(z)\hat{x}(z, t)\, dz \tag{5.6.57}$$

The boundary conditions are given by Eq. (5.6.54), and $\mathbf{g}(z)$ is an l vector of observer gains which must be chosen. The observer error may be defined as

$$e(z, t) = \hat{x}(z, t) - x(z, t) \tag{5.6.58}$$

and must satisfy

$$e_t(z, t) = \alpha e_{zz} - \beta e - \mathbf{g}^T(z) \int_0^1 \mathbf{C}(z') e(z', t)\, dz' \tag{5.6.59}$$

$$z = 0, 1 \qquad e_z = 0 \tag{5.6.60}$$

Note that Eq. (5.6.57) requires

$$\mathbf{C}(z) = \begin{bmatrix} \delta(z - z_1^*) \\ \delta(z - z_2^*) \\ \vdots \\ \delta(z - z_l^*) \end{bmatrix} \tag{5.6.61}$$

Now let us expand Eq. (5.6.59) in the system eigenfunctions

$$e(z, t) = \sum_{n=1}^{N} \epsilon_n(t)\phi_n(z) = \mathbf{\Phi}^T(z)\boldsymbol{\epsilon}(t) \tag{5.6.62}$$

where

$$\epsilon_n(t) = \int_0^1 \phi_n(z)e(z, t)\,dz \tag{5.6.63}$$

$$\phi_n(z) = \begin{cases} 1 & n = 0 \\ \sqrt{2}\cos n\pi z & n = 1, 2, \ldots, N \end{cases} \tag{5.6.64}$$

Then Eq. (5.6.59) reduces to

$$\dot{\boldsymbol{\epsilon}}(t) = (\alpha\mathbf{\Lambda} - \beta\mathbf{I} - \mathbf{GC})\boldsymbol{\epsilon}(t) \qquad \boldsymbol{\epsilon}(0) = \boldsymbol{\epsilon}_0 \tag{5.6.65}$$

where

$$\mathbf{\Lambda} = \begin{bmatrix} 0 & & & & \\ & -\pi^2 & & & \\ & & -4\pi^2 & & \mathbf{0} \\ \mathbf{0} & & & \ddots & \\ & & & & -N^2\pi^2 \end{bmatrix}$$

$$\mathbf{C} = \begin{bmatrix} \phi_0(z_1^*) & \phi_1(z_1^*) & \cdots & \phi_N(z_1^*) \\ \phi_0(z_2^*) & \phi_1(z_2^*) & \cdots & \phi_N(z_2^*) \\ \cdots & \cdots & \cdots & \cdots \\ \phi_0(z_l^*) & \cdots & \cdots & \phi_N(z_l^*) \end{bmatrix} \tag{5.6.66}$$

and the elements of $\mathbf{G}$, g_{nm}, are given by

$$g_{nm} = \int_0^1 \phi_n(z)g_m(z)\,dz \tag{5.6.67}$$

The observer will converge from some initial estimate error $\boldsymbol{\epsilon}_0$ to zero error if and only if all the eigenvalues of the matrix

$$\mathbf{E} = \alpha\mathbf{\Lambda} - \beta\mathbf{I} - \mathbf{GC} \tag{5.6.68}$$

have negative real parts. The speed of convergence is controlled by the magnitude of these eigenvalues. Thus observer design consists of choosing the elements g_{nm} such that the real parts of all the eigenvalues of $\mathbf{E}$ are large and negative. Köhne [50, 51] suggests several techniques for making this choice.

Köhne [51] has applied this observer experimentally with three sensors

$$z_1^* = 0 \qquad z_2^* = 0.5 \qquad z_3^* = 1.0$$

and with the observer weighting functions chosen as

$$g_1(z) = 1 - 2z$$

$$g_2(z) = \begin{cases} 2z & z \in [0, 0.5] \\ 2(1 - z) & z \in [0.5, 1] \end{cases}$$

$$g_3(z) = 2z - 1$$

and reported excellent results. Typical results from an initial guess some 45°C in error are shown in Fig. 5.22. Note that the observer converges to within 1°C of the true profile in about 80 s.

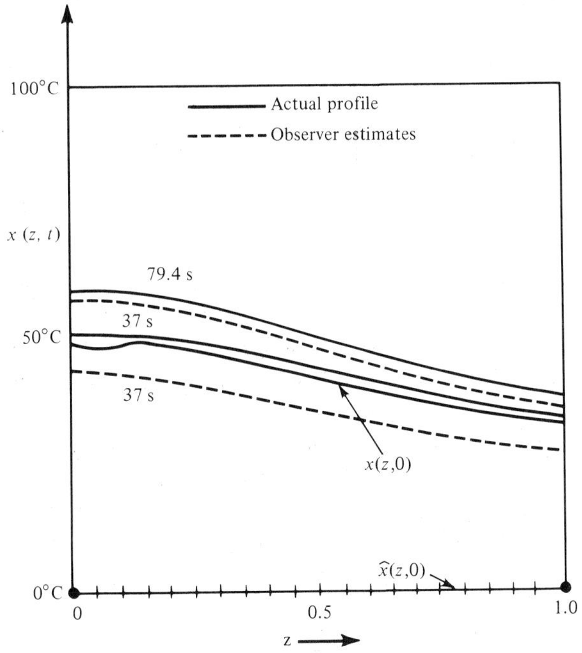

Figure 5.22 Observer performance with a heated slab plate [51]. *(Reproduced with permission of Springer-Verlag).*

5.7 STOCHASTIC FEEDBACK CONTROL FOR DISTRIBUTED PARAMETER SYSTEMS

Just as in the case of lumped parameter systems, distributed parameter stochastic feedback control is concerned with the control of systems having random disturbances in the process and in the measurements. The controller design involves choosing appropriate estimates of the states to be used in the control loop and to determine the best control structure. This is a relatively new and unexplored field for distributed parameter systems, but important results are known for linear systems. Good summaries of recent results may be found in Refs. [36, 52].

We shall illustrate the application of stochastic feedback control through an example problem.*

Example 5.7.1 Let us consider the heated slab shown in Fig. 5.20 and discussed in Example 5.6.1. The modeling equations are given by Eqs. (5.6.37) to (5.6.39), and it is desired to design a feedback control system for this stochastic process. One may show [36, 52] that for the white, Gaussian noise process $\xi(z, t)$, $\eta_i(t)$, $\xi_0(t)$, $\xi_1(t)$, the stochastic feedback controller which minimizes the expected quadratic objective

$$I = \mathcal{E}\left\{\frac{1}{2}\int_0^1\int_0^1 x(r, t_f)S_f(r, s)x(s, t_f)\,dr\,ds + \frac{1}{2}\int_0^{t_f}\int_0^1\int_0^1\left[x(r, t)F(r, s, t)x(s, t) + u(r, t)E(r, s, t)u(s, t)\right]dt\,dr\,ds\right\} \tag{5.7.1}$$

is the deterministic feedback control law

$$u(z, t) = -\gamma\int_0^1\int_0^1 E^*(z, s, t)S(s, \rho, t)\hat{x}(\rho, t)\,ds\,d\rho \tag{5.7.2}$$

where $\hat{x}(\rho, t)$ is the optimal least squares estimate found in the last section. The quantity E^* is a weighting factor defined by

$$\int_0^1 E^*(z, s, t)E(s, \rho, t)\,ds = \delta(z - \rho) \tag{5.7.3}$$

and the Riccati variables $S(s, \rho, t)$ are found just as in the deterministic case (see Sec. 4.3):

$$S_t(r, s, t) = -\alpha^2\left[S_{ss} + S_{rr}\right] + 2\beta S + \gamma^2\int_0^1\int_0^1 S(r, z, t)E^*(z, \rho, t)S(\rho, s, t)\,ds\,d\rho - F(r, s, t) \tag{5.7.4}$$

*This example is taken from Ref. [49] with the permission of Pergamon Press Ltd.

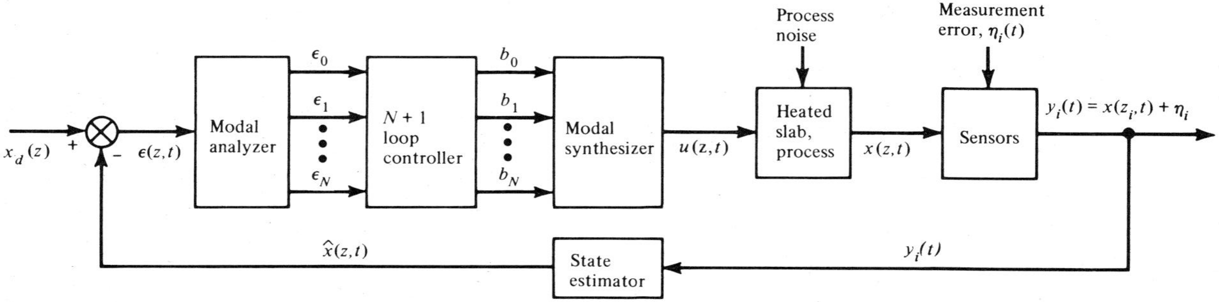

Figure 5.23 Structure of a stochastic modal feedback controller.

with boundary conditions

$$r = 0, 1 \qquad S_r = 0$$

$$s = 0, 1 \qquad S_s = 0 \tag{5.7.5}$$

and terminal condition

$$S(r, s, t_f) = S_f(r, s) \tag{5.7.6}$$

Thus just as in the lumped parameter case discussed in Sec. 5.4, the optimal linear-quadratic stochastic controller for distributed parameter systems is the *deterministic* feedback controller operating on the minimal least squares state estimates $\hat{x}(z, t)$. Hence, a *separation theorem* exists for this class of problems [52].

As an illustration of how a *suboptimal* stochastic feedback controller performs for this process, a simple modal stochastic feedback controller coupled to the optimal state estimator was tested experimentally [49]. The controller structure is shown in Fig. 5.23. The modal feedback controller consists of $N + 1$ single-loop controllers

$$\bar{b}_n(s) = g_n(s)\bar{\epsilon}_n(s) \qquad n = 0, 1, \ldots, N \tag{5.7.7}$$

In the present experimental example, the controllers were chosen to be proportional plus integral controllers, so that

$$\bar{b}_n(s) = K\left(1 + \frac{1}{\tau_I s}\right)\bar{\epsilon}_n(s) \tag{5.7.8}$$

The stochastic feedback controller performance can be seen in Fig. 5.24

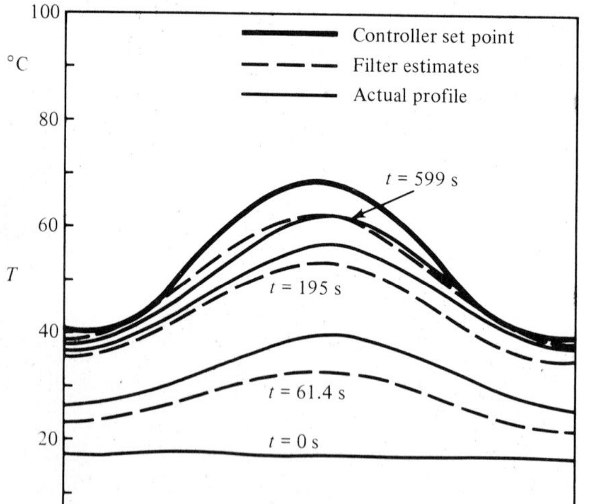

Figure 5.24 Closed-loop filter performance with one measurement ($z = 0$) and 8°C standard deviation added measurement errors [49]. *(Reproduced by permission of Pergamon Press Ltd.)*

when only one thermocouple at $z = 0$ is used and random errors of 8°C standard deviation are added to the thermocouple signal. Note that the filter converges rapidly and the stochastic feedback controller drives the temperature profile to the set point.

REFERENCES

1. Bryson, A. E., and Y. C. Ho: *Applied Optimal Control*, Halsted Press, New York,1976.
2. Meditch, J. S.: *Stochastic Optimal Linear Estimation and Control*, McGraw-Hill, New York, 1969.
3. Sage, A. P., and J. L. Melsa: *Estimation Theory*, McGraw-Hill, New York, 1971.
4. Jazwinski, A. H.: *Stochastic Processes and Filtering Theory*, Academic Press, New York, 1970.
5. Åström, K. J.: *Introduction to Stochastic Control Theory*, Academic Press, New York, 1970.
6. Gelb, A.: *Applied Optimal Estimation*, M.I.T. Press, Cambridge, Mass., 1974.
7. McGarty, T. P.: *Stochastic Systems and State Estimation*, Wiley, New York, 1973.
8. Kalman, R. E.: *J. Basic Eng.*, p. 35 (1960).
9. Kalman, R. E., and R. S. Bucy: *J. Basic Eng.*, p. 95 (1961).
10. Kalman, R. E.: *Bul. Soc. Math. Mex.*, 1961.
11. Yu, T. K., and J. H. Seinfeld: *IEEE Trans. Auto Control*, **AC-16**:495 (1971).
12. Ajinkya, M. B.: Ph.D. thesis, State University of New York at Buffalo, 1974.
13. Luenberger, D. G.: *IEEE Trans. Mil. Elec.*, **MIL 8**:74 (1964).
14. Luenberger, D. G.: *IEEE Trans. Auto. Control*, **AC-16**:596(1971).
15. Hostetter, G. H., and J. S. Meditch, *Automatica*, **9**:721 (1973).
16. Thau, F. E., and A. Kestenbaum: *Trans. ASME, J. Dyn. Sys. Meas. Cont.*, 454 (1974).
17. Bhattacharya, S. P.: *Proc. 1975 IFAC Congress*, Boston, paper 29.6.
18. Leondes, C. T., and J. F. Yocum: *Automatica*, **11**:61 (1975).
19. Hwang, M., and J. H. Seinfeld, *J. Opt. Theor. Appl.*, **10**:67 (1972).
20. Padmanabhan, L.: *Chem. Eng. J.*, **1**:232 (1970).
21. Gal'perin, Y. A.: *Engineering Cybernetics*, **10**:165 (1972).
22. Al'brekt, E. G., and N. N. Krasovskii: *Auto. Remote Control*, **25**:7 (1964).
23. Kushner, H. J.: *Stochastic Stability and Control*, Academic Press, New York, 1967.
24. Kushner, H. J.: *Intro to Stochastic Control*, Holt, Rinehart and Winston, New York 1971.
25. Parzen, E.: *Stochastic Processes*, Holden-Day, New York, 1962.
26. Aoki, M.: *Optimization of Stochastic Systems*, Academic Press, New York, 1967.
27. Wonham, W. M.: *SIAM J. Control*, **6**:312 (1968).
28. Seinfeld, J. H.: *AIChE J.*, **16**:1016 (1970).
29. Balchen, J. G., M. Fjeld, and T. O. Olsen: *Proc. 2d IFAC Symp. Multivariable Control*, paper 5.1.1 (1971).
30. Goodson, R. E., and R. E. Klein: *IEEE Trans. Auto. Control*, **AC-15**:165 (1970).
31. Thowsen, A., and W. R. Perkins: *IEEE Trans. Auto. Control*, **AC-19**:603 (1974).
32. Koivo, H. N., and A. J. Koivo: "Control and Estimation of Systems with Time Delays," in W. H. Ray and D. G. Lainiotis (eds.), *Distributed Parameter Systems*, Marcel Dekker, New York, 1978.
33. Yu, T. K., J. H. Seinfeld, and W. H. Ray: *IEEE Trans. Auto Cont.* **AC-19**:324 (1974).
34. Ajinkya, M. B., W. H. Ray, T. K. Yu, and J. H. Seinfeld: *Int. J. Systems Sci.* **6**:313 (1975).
35. Bhat, K. P. M. and H. N. Koivo: *IEEE Trans. Auto Control*, **AC-21**:266 (1976).
36. Ray, W. H.: "Some Applications of State Estimation and Control Theory to Distributed Parameter Systems," in *Control Theory of Systems Governed by Partial Differential Equations*, Academic Press, New York, 1977.
37. Sakawa, Y.: *SIAM J. Control* **13**:14 (1975).
38. Dolecki, S., and D. L. Russell: *SIAM J. Control*, **15**:185 (1977).
39. Triggiani, R.: *SIAM J. Control*, **14**:313 (1976).

40. Seidman, T. I.: *J. Math. Anal. Appl* **51**:165 (1975).
41. Seidman, T. I.: in *Calculus of Variations and Control Theory*, Academic Press, New York, 1976, p. 321.
42. Yu, T. K., and J. H. Seinfeld: *Int. J. Control*, **18**:785 (1973).
43. Chen, W. H., and J. H. Seinfeld: *Int. J. Control*, **21**:1003 (1975).
44. Caravoni, P., G. DiPillo, L. Grippo: *Proc. 1975 World IFAC Congress*, paper 8.3 (1975).
45. Aidarous, S. E., M. R. Gevers, and M. J. Installe: *Int. J. Control*, **22**:197 (1975).
46. Amouroux, M., G. DiPillo, L. Grippo: *Ricerche De Automatica*, **11** (1976).
47. Amouroux, M., J. P. Babary, and C. Malandrakis: *Proc. Rome IFIP Symp. Dist. Para. Systems*, 1976.
48. Mäder, H. R.: "Zeit optimale Steuerung und modale regelung eines praktische realisierten Wärmleitsystems," doctoral dissertation, Universität Stuttgart, 1975.
49. Ajinkya, M. B., M. Köhne, H. F. Mäder, and W. H. Ray: *Automatica*, **11**:571 (1975).
50. Köhne, M.: *Regelungstechnik*, pp. 277, 314 (1976).
51. Köhne, M.: "Implementation of Distributed Parameter State Observers," *Proc. IFIP Conference on Dist. Para. Sys.*, Rome, June 1976 (Springer-Verlag, 1977).
52. Bensoussan, A.: "Control of Stochastic Partial Differential Equations," in W. H. Ray and D. G. Lainiotis (eds.) *Distributed Parameter Systems*, Marcel Dekker, New York, 1978.

PROBLEMS

5.1 The following kinetic scheme is being carried out in an isothermal batch chemical reactor. The scheme is characteristic of partial oxidation reactions found in industry. If we wish to estimate all the concentrations, we must determine the minimal number of species to be measured and which ones should be chosen for measurement. Assume that the initial concentrations are *unknown*. Thus this is simply a question of *observability*.

$$\begin{array}{l} A \xrightarrow{k_1} B \xrightarrow{k_2} C \\ \downarrow k_3 \\ C \end{array}$$

The mathematical model is

$$\frac{dx_1}{dt} = -(k_1 + k_3)x_1$$

$$\frac{dx_2}{dt} = k_1x_1 - k_2x_2$$

$$\frac{dx_3}{dt} = k_3x_1 + k_2x_2$$

where

$$x_1 = [A] \qquad x_2 = [B] \qquad x_3 = [C]$$

(*a*) If continuous concentration measurements are available, determine the minimal set of measurements sufficient for observability.

(*b*) For discrete measurements at time t_k, $k = 1, 2, \ldots, N$, determine the minimal number of sample points N sufficient for observability. [Hint: Here $\mathbf{\Phi}(t, 0) = e^{\mathbf{A}t} = \mathbf{M}e^{\mathbf{\Lambda}t}\mathbf{M}^{-1}$, where $\mathbf{\Lambda}$ is a diagonal matrix of the eigenvalues of $\mathbf{A}$ and $\mathbf{M}$ is the matrix of corresponding eigenvectors.]

5.2 For the batch kinetic scheme shown in Prob. 5.1, a least squares state estimator is to be developed.

(*a*) Write out the filtering and covariance equations assuming that both x_2 and x_3 are measured continuously. Which equations must be solved online and which may be solved off-line?

(*b*) Repeat part (*a*) when only discrete time measurements of x_2 and x_3 are possible.
(*c*) Carry out estimation simulation for part (*a*) when

$$k_1 = 1 \quad k_2 = 2 \quad k_3 = 0.5 \quad x_1(0) = 1.0 \quad x_2(0) = x_3(0) = 0$$

$$\hat{x}_1(0) = 0.8 \quad \hat{x}_2(0) = 0.1 \quad \hat{x}_3(0) = 0.1 \quad \mathbf{Q}^{-1} = \begin{bmatrix} 0.0001 & 0 \\ 0 & 0.0001 \end{bmatrix}$$

$$\mathbf{R}^{-1} = \begin{bmatrix} 0 & 0 & 0 \\ 0 & 0 & 0 \\ 0 & 0 & 0 \end{bmatrix} \quad \mathbf{P}(0) = \begin{bmatrix} 0.005 & 0 & 0 \\ 0 & 0.0001 & 0 \\ 0 & 0 & 0.0001 \end{bmatrix}$$

Use the model to generate data $y_1 = x_2 + \eta_1, y_2 = x_3 + \eta_2$ where the measurement error is chosen from a random number generator having zero mean and a Gaussian distribution with standard deviation $\sigma = 0.01$.

(*d*) Repeat the computations in part *c* for the discrete data filter.

5.3 Let us consider a kinetic scheme similar to that in Prob. 5.1 except that two of the reactions are now second order. The mathematical modeling equations may be written in terms of the species $x_1 = [A]$, $x_2 = [B]$, $x_3 = [C]$. As in the previous case, the initial compositions are unknown.

$$\begin{array}{ccccc} 2A & \underset{k_1}{\rightarrow} & B & \underset{k_2}{\rightarrow} & C \\ k_3 \downarrow & & & & \\ C & & & & \end{array}$$

$$\frac{dx_1}{dt} = -2(k_1 + k_3)x_1^2$$

$$\frac{dx_2}{dt} = k_1 x_1^2 - k_2 x_2$$

$$\frac{dx_3}{dt} = k_1 x_1^2 + k_2 x_2$$

(*a*) By linearization and using an observability test, determine observability when both *B* and *C* are measured continuously. Repeat for the case when only *C* is measured.

(*b*) Write out the extended Kalman filter equations for this problem as well as the equations for the differential sensitivities. Assume both x_2 and x_3 are measured continuously. Which equations must be solved on-line? Explain.

(*c*) Repeat part (*b*) when only discrete measurements of x_2 and x_3 are possible.

5.4 (*a*) For the heat exchanger problem discussed in Example 5.5.2, carry out the filter computations for the parameters.

$$v = 0.2 \quad a_0 = -1.0 \quad r_1^* = 0.25 \quad r_2^* = 0.5 \quad r_3^* = 0.75$$

$$r_4^* = 1.0 \quad R_1^+ = 0 \quad P_0 = 0.0025\delta(r - s) \quad Q^{-1} = 0.0025$$

(*b*) Repeat the calculations with successively fewer sensors (i.e., three, two, and only one).

5.5 Consider the heating of a thin rod in a furnace with one end insulated and the other end ($z = 1$) inserted into a flowing liquid stream at constant temperature T_c. The modeling equations take the form

$$\rho C_p \frac{\partial T(z, t')}{\partial t'} = k \frac{\partial^2 T}{\partial z^2} + q(z, t') \qquad \begin{array}{l} t' > 0 \\ 0 < z < 1 \end{array}$$

$$z = 0 \qquad \frac{\partial T}{\partial z} = 0$$

$$z = 1 \qquad -k\frac{\partial T}{\partial z} = h(T - T_c)$$

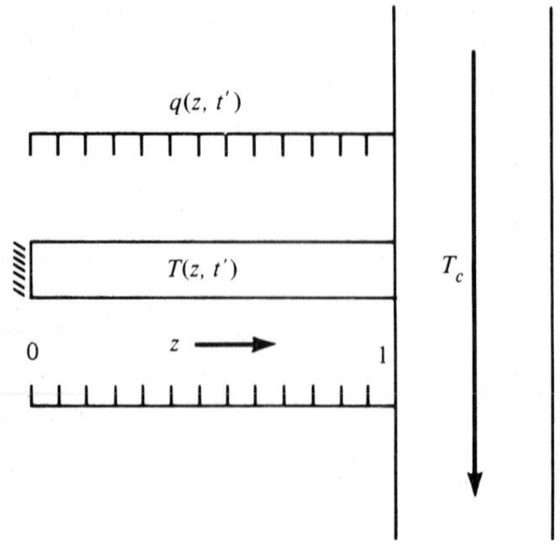

(*a*) Reduce the model to dimensionless form using the parameters

$$x = \frac{T - T_c}{T_c} \qquad u = \frac{q}{kT_c} \qquad t = \frac{t'k}{\rho C_p}$$

$$Bi = \frac{h}{k}$$

(*b*) Solve the modeling equations through an orthonormal expansion of the form

$$x(z, t) = \sum_{n=0}^{N} a_n(t)\phi_n(z)$$

$$u(z, t) = \sum_{n=0}^{N} b_n(t)\phi_n(z)$$

Determine $\phi_n(z)$ and the equations for $a_n(t)$.

(*c*) Determine the N-mode observability conditions for the case of only one sensor. For $N = 4$, determine which sensor locations must be avoided in order for one sensor to guarantee observability. Recommend a specific sensor location and justify your recommendation.

(*d*) Develop the state estimation equations for this problem given one sensor providing continuous temperature measurements. Which equations must be solved on-line and which ones may be solved off-line? Explain how you would use a modal decomposition to solve both the filter equations and the covariance equations.

(*e*) Carry out state estimation simulation with the following parameters: $Bi = 2.0$, u = constant $= 0.1$, $P_0 = 0.01\delta(r - s)$, $Q^{-1} = 0.0001$, $R^+ = 0$. Use one sensor location of your choice, and use modal decomposition to solve the filter and covariance equations. To obtain data, $x(r_1^*, t)$, use the model simulation and, if desired, add random measurement errors from a Gaussian random number generator having zero mean and $\sigma = 0.01$. Use $x(0) = 0$, $\hat{x}(0) = 0.1$ as actual and estimated initial conditions, respectively.

CHAPTER

SIX

CONTROL SYSTEM DESIGN CASE STUDIES

6.1 INTRODUCTION

This chapter is devoted to a series of case studies showing applications of modern control theory to chemical, petroleum, and metallurgical processes. For each problem, one or more of the techniques discussed in earlier chapters is used, and the performance of the resulting design is compared with more conventional approaches. It is hoped that this set of example problems will stimulate the reader to further applications in the real world of the process industries.

6.2 CONTROL OF A MULTI-SIDESTREAM DISTILLATION COLUMN*

The goal of this case study is to develop a control strategy for the multi-sidestream distillation column shown in Fig. 6.1. The compositions of the overhead and two sidestreams are the output variables y_1, y_2, y_3, and the drawoff rates of these streams constitute the manipulated variables u_1, u_2, u_3. Although one could formulate a very high-order time-domain model of the column involving concentrations and temperatures on every tray, this is not usually the best approach for process control design. As noted in Sec. 3.2, it is often possible to fit a linear

* This case study was carried out by Lance Lauerhass, Paul Noble, Larry Biegler, and Tunde Ogunnaike as a project in the graduate course in Advanced Process Control at the University of Wisconsin.

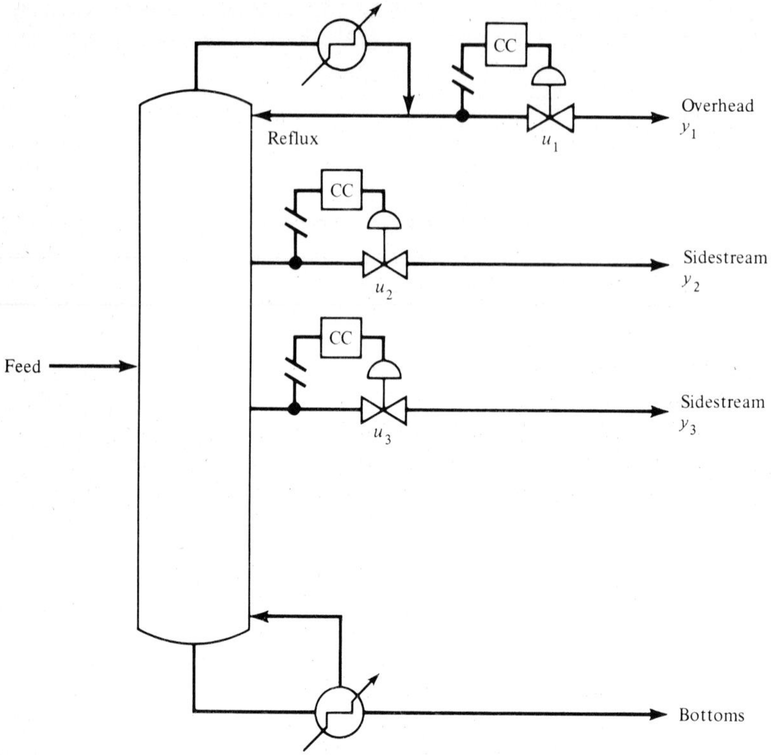

Figure 6.1 Distillation column schematic.

transfer function model to the observed sidestream composition dynamics through step- or frequency-response experiments. We shall assume this has been done in the present case, yielding the open-loop transfer function

$$\bar{\mathbf{y}}(s) = \mathbf{G}(s)\bar{\mathbf{u}}(s) \tag{6.2.1}$$

where

$$\mathbf{G}(s) = \begin{bmatrix} \dfrac{0.7}{1+9s} & 0 & 0 \\ \dfrac{2.0}{1+8s} & \dfrac{0.4}{1+6s} & 0 \\ \dfrac{2.3}{1+10s} & \dfrac{2.3}{1+8s} & \dfrac{2.1}{1+7s} \end{bmatrix} \tag{6.2.2}$$

Very often the experimentally determined transfer function $\mathbf{G}(s)$ includes pure time delays in some of the elements; however, we shall assume these are so small as to be negligible in the present case.

The present control scheme for the column consists of three single-loop controllers as shown in Fig. 6.2. For each loop, the composition y_i is measured and used in a PI controller to adjust the flow rate u_i. Experience has shown that

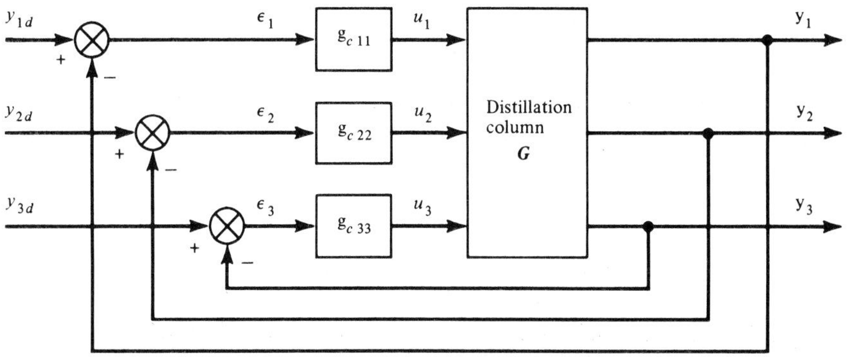

Figure 6.2 Multiple single-loop control for the distillation column.

there are two major operating difficulties with this present control system:

1. The response to disturbances is poor, yielding steady-state offset and oscillations.
2. Changing the set point in any one variable causes the other variables to go off specification and to oscillate.

To illustrate these problems, consider Fig. 6.3, which shows the response of three single-loop proportional controllers to set-point changes

$$\bar{\mathbf{y}}_d = \begin{bmatrix} 0.05 \\ -0.05 \\ 0.02 \end{bmatrix} \tag{6.2.3}$$

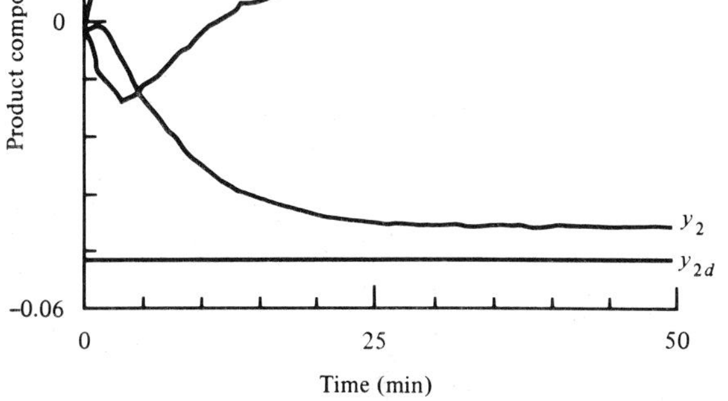

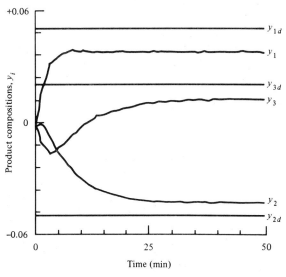

Figure 6.3 Product compositions after a set-point change (proportional control with $k_{c_{11}} = 5$, $k_{c_{22}} = 20$, $k_{c_{33}} = 20$).

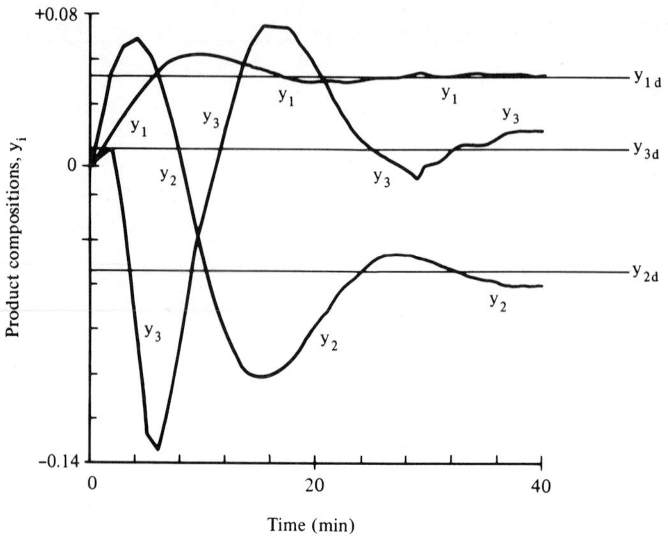

Figure 6.4 Product compositions after a set-point change (proportional plus integral control with $k_{c_{ii}} = 2$, $\tau_i = 2$).

while Fig. 6.4 illustrates the response with three proportional plus integral controllers. With only proportional control (Fig. 6.3), both set-point changes and disturbances cause large offsets. When integral action is added in an effort to prevent offsets, the three controllers fight one another, causing persistent oscillations (Fig. 6.4). In this case study, two control strategies designed to eliminate these difficulties shall be evaluated.

Set-Point Compensation

In some distillation towers with multiple products, the effect of disturbances is minor and the principal difficulties arise due to frequent set-point changes. As discussed in Chap. 3, the simple techniques of set-point compensation can correct many of these types of difficulties. Recall from Sec. 3.2 that the addition of set-point compensation modifies Fig. 6.2 to the control scheme shown in Fig. 6.5. The closed-loop transfer function becomes

$$\bar{\mathbf{y}} = (\mathbf{I} + \mathbf{G}\mathbf{G}_c)^{-1}\mathbf{G}\mathbf{G}_c\mathbf{S}\hat{\mathbf{y}}_d \tag{3.2.94}$$

where the controller matrix is

$$\mathbf{G}_c = \begin{bmatrix} g_{c11} & 0 & 0 \\ 0 & g_{c22} & 0 \\ 0 & 0 & g_{c33} \end{bmatrix}$$

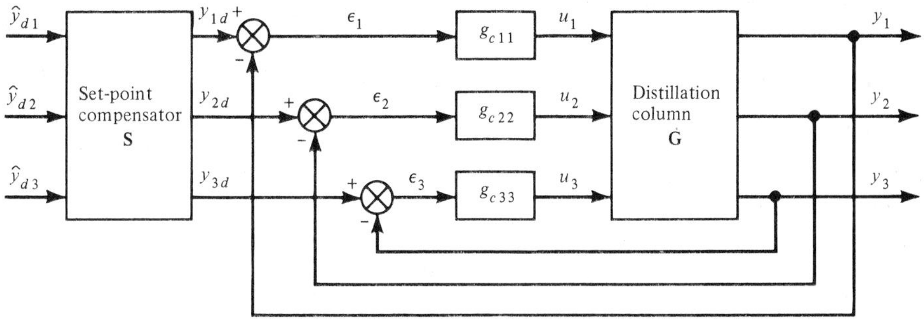

Figure 6.5 Set-point compensator added to multiple single-loop control.

and the set-point compensator

$$\mathbf{S} = \begin{bmatrix} S_{11} & S_{12} & S_{13} \\ S_{21} & S_{22} & S_{23} \\ S_{31} & S_{32} & S_{33} \end{bmatrix}$$

is to be chosen to make

$$(\mathbf{I} + \mathbf{G}\mathbf{G}_c)^{-1}\mathbf{G}\mathbf{G}_c\mathbf{S} = \mathbf{I} \tag{6.2.4}$$

at steady state. Thus, if the single-loop controllers are proportional controllers $g_{cii} = K_{cii}$, $i = 1, 2, 3$, then

$$\mathbf{S} = \begin{bmatrix} \frac{1.43}{K_{c11}} + 1 & 0 & 0 \\ -\frac{7.14}{K_{c22}} & \frac{2.5}{K_{c22}} + 1 & 0 \\ \frac{6.26}{K_{c33}} & -\frac{2.74}{K_{c33}} & \frac{0.48}{K_{c33}} + 1 \end{bmatrix} \tag{6.2.5}$$

satisfies Eq. (6.2.4). The performance of this compensator is discussed below.

Noninteracting Control

A second control strategy to be evaluated is multivariable noninteracting control, shown in Fig. 6.6. It may be implemented using single-loop controllers, but the signals from these controllers must be sent to decoupling operators to accomplish the noninteractive control. Recall from Chap. 3 that the closed-loop transfer function for the structure in Fig. 6.6 is

$$\bar{\mathbf{y}} = (\mathbf{I} + \mathbf{G}\mathbf{G}_I\mathbf{G}_c)^{-1}\mathbf{G}\mathbf{G}_I\mathbf{G}_c\bar{\mathbf{y}}_d \tag{3.2.81}$$

and $\mathbf{G}_I$ must be chosen to make

$$\mathbf{T} = (\mathbf{I} + \mathbf{G}\mathbf{G}_I\mathbf{G}_c)^{-1}\mathbf{G}\mathbf{G}_I\mathbf{G}_c \tag{3.2.82}$$

a diagonal matrix.

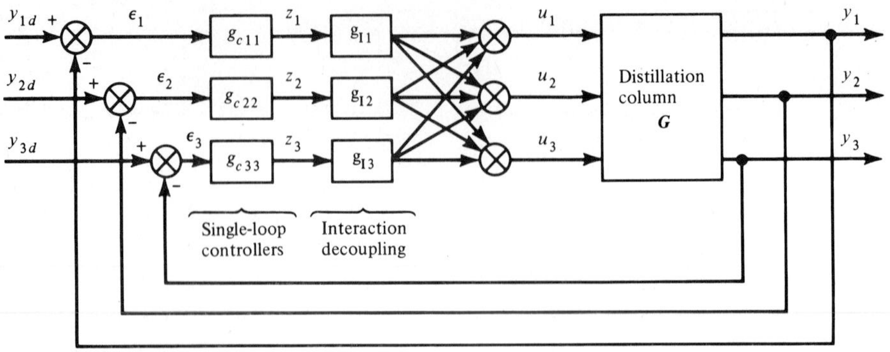

Figure 6.6 Noninteracting multivariable feedback control.

For the simple case of *steady-state compensation*, which eliminates steady-state interactions, one could choose to let

$$\mathbf{G}_I = (\mathbf{G}_{ss}^{-1})\text{diag } \mathbf{G}_{ss} \tag{3.2.85}$$

where

$$\mathbf{G}_{ss} = \lim_{s \to 0} \mathbf{G}(s) = \begin{bmatrix} 0.7 & 0 & 0 \\ 2.0 & 0.4 & 0 \\ 2.3 & 2.3 & 2.1 \end{bmatrix}$$

However, in this example, we shall be even more demanding and require that perfect steady-state compensation be accomplished; i.e., we must choose

$$\mathbf{G}_I = (\mathbf{G}^{-1})_{ss} = \begin{bmatrix} 1.43 & 0 & 0 \\ -7.14 & 2.5 & 0 \\ 6.26 & -2.74 & 0.48 \end{bmatrix}$$

Furthermore, we could pursue the even more ambitious goal of perfectly compensating for dynamic interactions. For this example, such a "perfect" dynamic compensator would take the form

$$\mathbf{G}_I = \mathbf{G}^{-1} = \begin{bmatrix} 1.43(1 + 9s) & 0 & 0 \\ \dfrac{-7.14(1 + 9s)(1 + 6s)}{(1 + 8s)} & 2.50(1 + 6s) & 0 \\ \left\{ \dfrac{7.82(1 + 9s)(1 + 6s)(1 + 7s)}{(1 + 8s)^2} - \dfrac{1.56(1 + 9s)(1 + 7s)}{1 + 10s} \right\} & \dfrac{-2.74(1 + 6s)(1 + 7s)}{1 + 8s} & 0.48(1 + 7s) \end{bmatrix} \tag{6.2.6}$$

This compensator may be implemented by noting that

$$\mathbf{u} = \mathbf{G}_I \mathbf{G}_c \boldsymbol{\epsilon} \tag{6.2.7}$$

determines the desired control action. If $\mathbf{G}_c$ represents an actual set of three controllers as shown in Fig. 6.6, then

$$z_1 = g_{c11}\epsilon_1 \qquad z_2 = g_{c22}\epsilon_2 \qquad z_3 = g_{c33}\epsilon_3 \tag{6.2.8}$$

and

$$\mathbf{u} = \mathbf{G}_I \mathbf{z} \tag{6.2.9}$$

is the operation which must be carried out to accomplish this dynamic decoupling. From Eq. (6.2.6), this operation requires that

$$u_1(s) = 1.43(1 + 9s)z_1(s) \tag{6.2.10}$$

$$u_2(s) = \frac{-7.14(1 + 9s)(1 + 6s)}{1 + 8s} z_1(s) + 2.50(1 + 6s)z_2(s) \tag{6.2.11}$$

$$u_3(s) = \left[\frac{7.82(1 + 9s)(1 + 6s)(1 + 7s)}{(1 + 8s)^2} - \frac{1.56(1 + 9s)(1 + 7s)}{1 + 10s}\right] z_1(s)$$

$$- \frac{2.74(1 + 6s)(1 + 7s)}{1 + 8s} z_2(s) + 0.48(1 + 7s)z_3(s) \tag{6.2.12}$$

Transforming these expressions to the time domain, one obtains

$$u_1(t) = 1.43\left[z_1(t) + 9\frac{dz_1(t)}{dt}\right] \tag{6.2.13}$$

$$u_2(t) = -7.14\left[6.75\frac{dz_1}{dt} + 1.03z_1 - 0.0039\int_0^t \exp\left(-\frac{t - \tau}{8}\right) z_1(\tau)\,d\tau\right]$$

$$+2.50\left[z_2(t) + 6\frac{dz_2}{dt}\right] \tag{6.2.14}$$

$$u_3(t) = 7.82\left[5.91\frac{dz_1}{dt} + 1.01z_1 - (0.000488 + 0.0000610t)\right.$$

$$\left.\times \int_0^t \exp\left(-\frac{t - \tau}{8}\right) z_1(\tau)\,d\tau + 0.0000610\int_0^t \exp\left(-\frac{t - \tau}{8}\right) \tau z_1(\tau)\,d\tau\right]$$

$$-1.56\left[6.3\frac{dz_1}{dt} + 0.97z_1 + 0.003\int_0^t \exp\left(-\frac{t - \tau}{10}\right) z_1(\tau)\,d\tau\right]$$

$$-2.74\left[5.25\frac{dz_2}{dt} + 9.69z_2 + 0.0022\int_0^t \exp\left(-\frac{t - \tau}{8}\right) z_2(\tau)\,d\tau\right]$$

$$+0.48\left[z_3(t) + 7\frac{dz_3}{dt}\right] \tag{6.2.15}$$

This integration and differentiation of the signal $z_i(t)$ can clearly be implemented either with analog circuitry or by a real-time digital controller. For the case of DDC, Eq. (6.2.8) would also be carried out by the digital computer.

Control System Performance Testing

In order to test the performance of these two control schemes when implemented on the process control digital computer, the distillation column was simulated on the analog computer and the control algorithms programmed to respond in real time on the digital computer. The information flow is shown in Fig. 6.7, and the analog circuit diagram representing the column is presented in Fig. 6.8.

Before proceeding further to test these algorithms, it is useful to investigate the *controllability* of the column. The transfer function model [Eq. (6.2.1)] may be easily put into the time domain to yield equations of the form

$$\frac{d\mathbf{x}}{dt} = \mathbf{Ax} + \mathbf{Bu} \tag{6.2.16}$$

$$\mathbf{y} = \mathbf{Cx} \tag{6.2.17}$$

where

$$\mathbf{x} = \begin{bmatrix} x_1 \\ x_2 \\ \vdots \\ x_6 \end{bmatrix}$$

$$\mathbf{A} = \begin{bmatrix} -0.111 & 0 & 0 & 0 & 0 & 0 \\ 0 & -0.125 & 0 & 0 & 0 & 0 \\ 0 & 0 & -0.167 & 0 & 0 & 0 \\ 0 & 0 & 0 & -0.1 & 0 & 0 \\ 0 & 0 & 0 & 0 & -0.125 & 0 \\ 0 & 0 & 0 & 0 & 0 & -0.143 \end{bmatrix}$$

$$\mathbf{B} = \begin{bmatrix} 1 & 0 & 0 \\ 1 & 0 & 0 \\ 0 & 1 & 0 \\ 1 & 0 & 0 \\ 0 & 1 & 0 \\ 0 & 0 & 1 \end{bmatrix} \qquad \mathbf{C} = \begin{bmatrix} 1 & 0 & 0 & 0 & 0 & 0 \\ 0 & 1 & 1 & 0 & 0 & 0 \\ 0 & 0 & 0 & 1 & 1 & 1 \end{bmatrix} \tag{6.2.18}$$

The output controllability matrix, which is

$$\mathbf{L}_y = [\mathbf{CB} \mid \mathbf{CAB} \mid \ldots \mid \mathbf{CA}^5\mathbf{B}] \tag{6.2.19}$$

clearly has rank 3 because

$$\mathbf{CB} = \begin{bmatrix} 1 & 0 & 0 \\ 1 & 1 & 0 \\ 1 & 1 & 1 \end{bmatrix} \tag{6.2.20}$$

is nonsingular; thus the column is *completely controllable*.

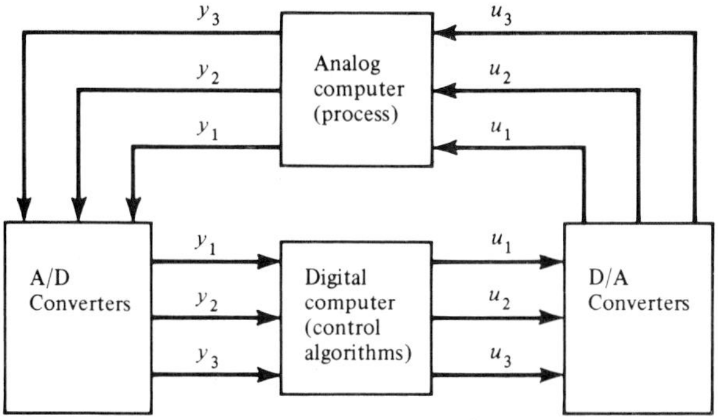

Figure 6.7 Digital computer control of the simulated process.

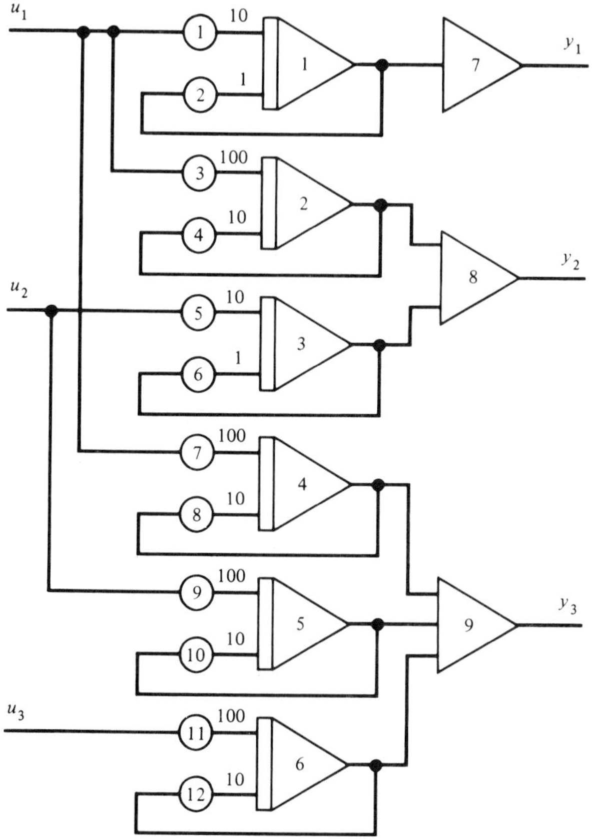

Figure 6.8 Analog circuit diagram.

The *set-point compensation* algorithm shown in Fig. 6.5 was applied for the same conditions as for Fig. 6.3 [i.e., with three proportional controllers and a set-point change given by Eq. (6.2.3)]. The dynamic response of the column, shown in Fig. 6.9, is much improved over the uncompensated case, showing rapid attainment of steady state, with very little offset and no oscillations. Further experiments confirmed that good performance for set-point changes

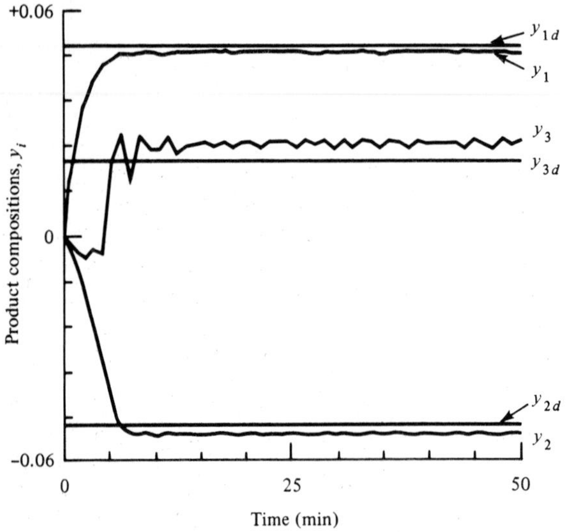

Figure 6.9 Product compositions after a set-point change (set-point compensator used with proportional controllers, same conditions as for Fig. 6.3).

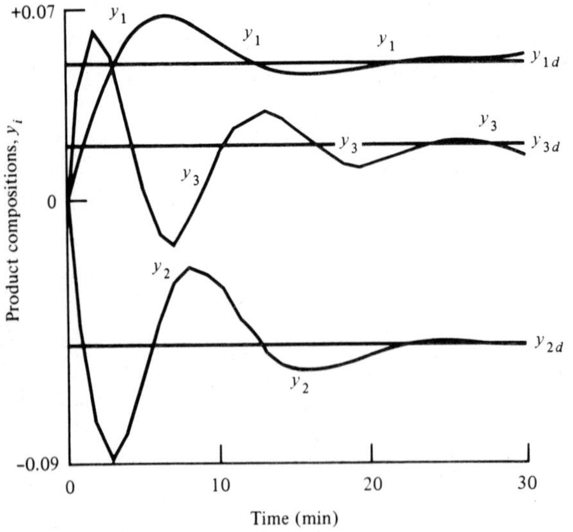

Figure 6.10 Product compositions after a set-point change (steady-state decoupling together with proportional plus integral controllers, $k_{c_{ii}} = 2.0$, $\tau_i = 2.0$).

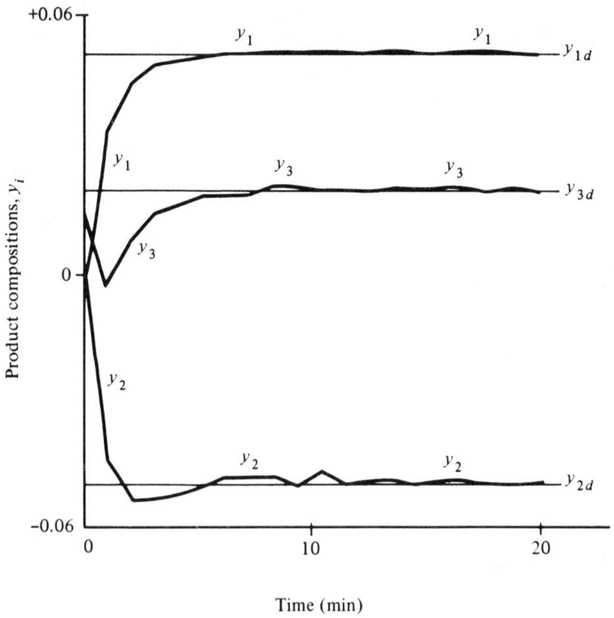

Figure 6.11 Product compositions after a set-point change (dynamic decoupling together with proportional plus integral controllers, $k_{c_{ii}} = 0.25$, $\tau_i = 0.5$).

should be expected with this control scheme. Unfortunately, the set-point compensator does not help in the case of disturbances because it is not contained in the feedback loop.

To improve the control system performance in the face of disturbances, both steady-state and dynamic noninteracting control schemes were tested. Figure 6.10 shows the effect of adding *steady-state compensation* for the conditions of Fig. 6.4. Notice that even though there are still some oscillations, they are smaller in amplitude and settle faster than the response shown in Fig. 6.4. By adding *dynamic compensation*, the response is improved even more dramatically, as shown in Fig. 6.11. The settling time without any compensation (Fig. 6.4) is on the order of 50 to 60 min, while for steady-state decoupling (Fig. 6.10) this drops to ~25 min. What is even more impressive is that the dynamic decoupling controller produces a settling time of only about 6 min—an order-of-magnitude improvement over multiple single-loop control.

Evaluation

Although all the new control schemes worked better than the multiple single-loop controllers, the dynamic noninteracting controller performed best and handled both disturbances and set-point changes. The set-point compensation algorithm is much simpler to implement and gives good response to set-point changes, but cannot respond to disturbances. Thus if one does not wish to

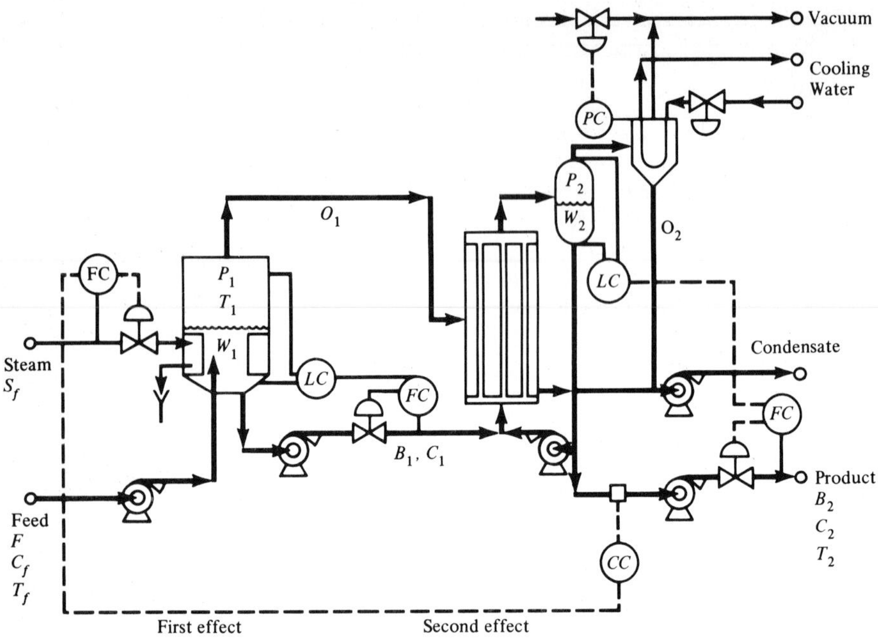

Figure 6.12 The pilot plant multiple-effect evaporator showing conventional single-loop controls. *(Reproduced from Proceedings 4th IFAC/IFIP Conference on Digital Computer Applications to Process Control,* 1974, *p.* 154, *by permission of Springer-Verlag.)*

implement the complicated dynamic noninteracting controller, then the steady-state noninteracting control scheme is preferred because it eliminates steady-state interactions for both set-point changes and disturbances.

6.3 THE CONTROL OF A MULTIPLE-EFFECT EVAPORATOR

As our second case study, we shall consider the computer control of the pilot plant multiple-effect evaporator shown in Fig. 6.12. A whole series of these case studies were carried out at the University of Alberta, Edmonton, Alberta, Canada by Professors Fisher and Seborg and their students through links to an IBM 1800 process control computer. In our discussion here we shall treat only a small part of their work and refer to their monograph [1] for the whole story. The goal of the present discussion is to illustrate the performance of several advanced process control algorithms when applied to this pilot plant process.

Modeling

The first step in this control study was to develop a simple yet reliable mathematical model of the process. The relevant variables and their steady-state values are given in Table 6.1. From Fig. 6.12 it is seen that the solution to be concentrated enters the first effect at feed rate F, solute concentration C_f, and

Table 6.1 Evaporator variables and steady-state values [1]

Variable	Feed	First Effect	Second Effect
B_1, B_2—bottoms flow rate (lb/min)	—	3.3	1.7
C_f, C_1, C_2—solute concentration (wt %)	3.2	4.85	9.64
F—feed flow rate (lb/min)	5.0	—	—
h_f, h_1—liquid enthalpy (Btu/lb)	1.62	194	—
S_f—steam flow rate (lb/min)	1.9	—	—
W_1, W_2—solute holdup (lb)	—	30	35
O_1, O_2—overhead vapor flow (lb/min)	—	1.7	1.6
T_f, T_1, T_2—temperature (°F)	190	225	160
P_1, P_2—pressure (psia)	—	<25	7.5

temperature T_f. For the present study the feed solution was triethylene glycol in water. Steam at rate S_f is injected into the first effect to vaporize the water, producing vapor stream O_1. The first-effect liquid effluent B_1 at concentration C_1 goes to the tube side of the second effect and is vaporized further under reduced pressure by condensation of the first-effect vapor stream on the shell side. The concentrated liquid B_2 from the second effect is the product at concentration C_2. The quantities W_1 and W_2 are the liquid holdups in each effect. A fifth-order nonlinear model of the evaporator was developed [1] under the following assumptions:

1. The heat capacitances of the steam chests, tube walls, etc., are all sufficiently small that they may be neglected.
2. The pressure controller on the second effect (see Fig. 6.12) is sufficiently powerful to hold the temperature in the second effect T_2 at steady state with negligible dynamic variations.
3. The solute concentration in the vapor leaving each effect of the evaporator is negligibly small compared with the amount of solute leaving in the liquid.

Under these conditions, total material, solute, and heat balances on the *first effect* may be written

$$\frac{dW_1}{dt} = F - B_1 - O_1 \tag{6.3.1}$$

$$W_1\frac{dC_1}{dt} = F(C_f - C_1) + O_1C_1 \tag{6.3.2}$$

$$W_1\frac{dh_1}{dt} = F(h_f - h_1) - O_1(H_{1v} - h_1) + Q_1 - L_1 \tag{6.3.3}$$

Similarly material balances on the *second effect* give

$$\frac{dW_2}{dt} = B_1 - B_2 - O_2 \tag{6.3.4}$$

$$W_2\frac{dC_2}{dt} = B_1(C_1 - C_2) + O_2C_2 \tag{6.3.5}$$

while a steady-state heat balance on the *second effect* yields

$$O_2\left(H_{2v} - h_2 + \frac{\partial h_2}{\partial C_2} C_2\right) = Q_2 - L_2 + B_1(h_1 - h_2) + \frac{\partial h_2}{\partial C_2} B_1(C_2 - C_1) \tag{6.3.6}$$

Here Q_1 and Q_2 are the heat inputs to each effect, given by

$$Q_1 = u_1 A_1 (T_s - T_1) = \lambda_s S_f \tag{6.3.7}$$

$$Q_2 = u_2 A_2 (T_1 - T_2) \tag{6.3.8}$$

The quantities L_1 and L_2 are the environmental heat losses from each effect; h_f, h_1, and h_2 are liquid enthalpies; H_{1v} and H_{2v} are the vapor enthalpies; and λ_s represents the heat of vaporization of the input steam at temperature T_s.

This set of equations constitutes a *fifth-order nonlinear model* of the process. By linearization of these equations around the steady state shown in Table 6.1, a *fifth-order linear model* may be obtained in the form

$$\dot{\mathbf{x}} = \mathbf{A}\mathbf{x} + \mathbf{B}\mathbf{u} + \mathbf{\Gamma}\mathbf{d} \tag{6.3.9}$$

$$\mathbf{y} = \mathbf{C}\mathbf{x} \tag{6.3.10}$$

where the state vector **x**, control vector **u**, disturbance vector **d**, and output vector **y** are

$$\mathbf{x} = \begin{bmatrix} W_1 \\ C_1 \\ h_1 \\ W_2 \\ C_2 \end{bmatrix} \quad \mathbf{u} = \begin{bmatrix} S_f \\ B_1 \\ B_2 \end{bmatrix} \quad \mathbf{d} = \begin{bmatrix} F \\ C_f \\ h_f \end{bmatrix} \quad \mathbf{y} = \begin{bmatrix} W_1 \\ W_2 \\ C_2 \end{bmatrix} \tag{6.3.11}$$

while

$$\mathbf{A} = \begin{bmatrix} 0 & -0.00156 & -0.1711 & 0 & 0 \\ 0 & -0.1419 & 0.1711 & 0 & 0 \\ 0 & -0.00875 & -1.102 & 0 & 0 \\ 0 & -0.00128 & -0.1489 & 0 & 0.00013 \\ 0 & 0.0605 & 0.1489 & 0 & -0.0591 \end{bmatrix}$$

$$\mathbf{B} = \begin{bmatrix} 0 & -0.143 & 0 \\ 0 & 0 & 0 \\ 0.392 & 0 & 0 \\ 0 & 0.108 & -0.0592 \\ 0 & -0.0486 & 0 \end{bmatrix}$$

$$\mathbf{C} = \begin{bmatrix} 1 & 0 & 0 & 0 & 0 \\ 0 & 0 & 0 & 1 & 0 \\ 0 & 0 & 0 & 0 & 1 \end{bmatrix}$$

$$\mathbf{\Gamma} = \begin{bmatrix} 0.2174 & 0 & 0 \\ -0.074 & 0.1434 & 0 \\ -0.036 & 0 & 0.1814 \\ 0 & 0 & 0 \\ 0 & 0 & 0 \end{bmatrix} \tag{6.3.12}$$

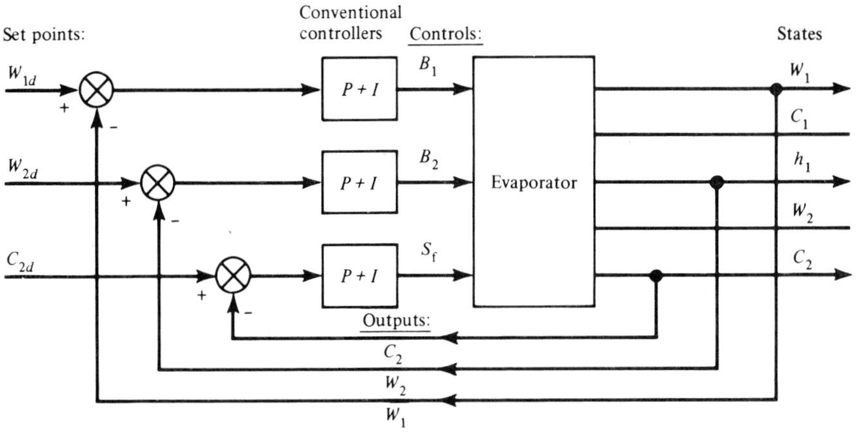

Figure 6.13 Block diagram for conventional control of the evaporator.

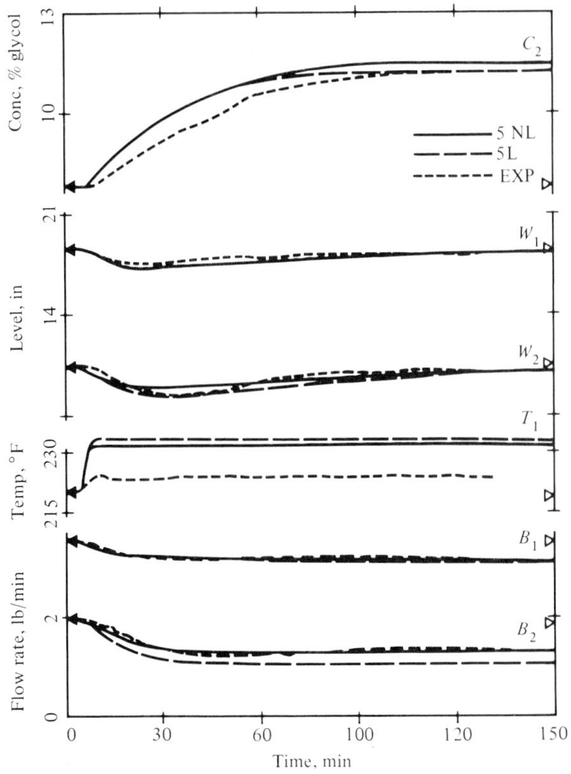

Figure 6.14 Comparison of fifth-order linear and nonlinear models with experimental data for the case of a 20% increase in stream feed rate. *(Reproduced with permission from I & EC Process Design Development* 11, 216 (1972). *Copyright by American Chemical Society.)*

The feedback relationship between controls **u** and outputs **y** under the conventional control scheme is shown in Fig. 6.13.

Figure 6.14 presents a typical comparison of both the nonlinear (5NL) and linear (5L) models with an experimental run under conventional control of W_1, W_2 for the case of a 20 percent increase in inlet steam flow-rate disturbance. Note that both models compare reasonably well with the experimental data except when predicting the temperature dynamics in the first effect. The model responds much more strongly than the experimental equipment, indicating that the thermal capacitance of the equipment itself should perhaps be included in Eq. (6.3.3).

Multivariable Control

Having developed a reliable linear model, we can now design multivariable control algorithms and compare these with the performance of the conventional single-loop control shown in Fig. 6.13. A large number of algorithms have been tested [1], but we shall only discuss the application of optimal multivariable feedback control algorithms here (see Chap. 3 to review the theory).

The standard optimal linear-quadratic multivariable controller design was modified to allow integral control action on the output variables. By defining a composite state vector $\hat{\mathbf{x}} = \begin{bmatrix} \mathbf{x} \\ \mathbf{z} \end{bmatrix}$, where

$$\dot{\mathbf{x}} = \mathbf{A}\mathbf{x} + \mathbf{B}\mathbf{u} + \mathbf{\Gamma}\mathbf{d} \tag{6.3.13}$$

$$\dot{\mathbf{z}} = \mathbf{y} - \mathbf{y}_d \tag{6.3.14}$$

$$\mathbf{y} = \mathbf{C}\mathbf{x} \tag{6.3.15}$$

and $\mathbf{y}_d$ is the set point of the output variables, one obtains the optimal feedback control law in the form (see Sec. 3.3)

$$\mathbf{u}(t) = -\mathbf{K}\hat{\mathbf{x}} = -\mathbf{K}_1\mathbf{x} - \mathbf{K}_2\mathbf{z} = -\mathbf{K}_1\mathbf{x} - \mathbf{K}_2\int_0^t (\mathbf{y} - \mathbf{y}_d)\, dt \tag{6.3.16}$$

thus yielding proportional and integral control. Recall that $\mathbf{K}_1$, $\mathbf{K}_2$ must be computed off-line from the solution of a Riccati equation. This controller, whose block diagram may be seen in Fig. 6.15, was implemented on the evaporator for the case where all five states were measured and optimal constant gains were used (corresponding to the infinite-time optimal control problem). Simulation results shown in Fig. 6.16 illustrate the superior performance of the optimal multivariable controller for both proportional and proportional plus integral action. An experimental comparison is seen in Fig. 6.17 and illustrates even more effectively the advantages of the optimal multivariable feedback control scheme over conventional control. Note that in both instances the conventional controller allowed significant upsets in the process dynamics, while the disturbances had almost no effect on the system under optimal multivariable control.

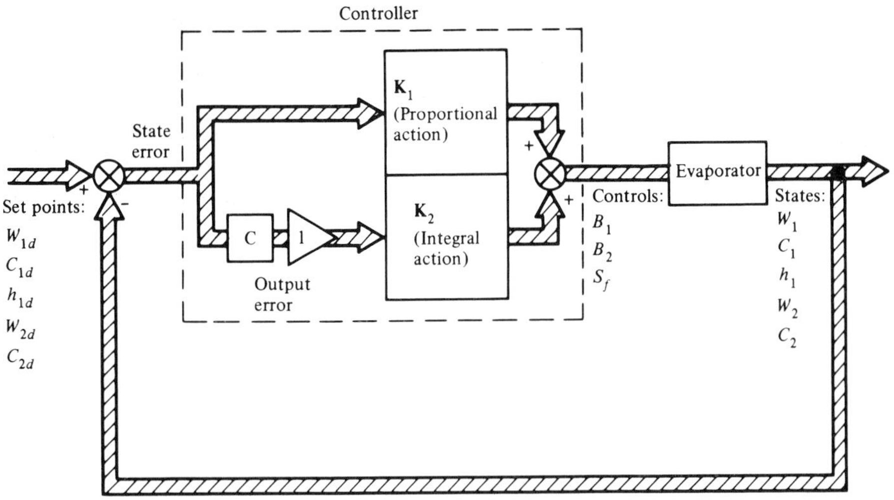

Figure 6.15 Deterministic optimal multvariable feedback control system having both proportional and integral action

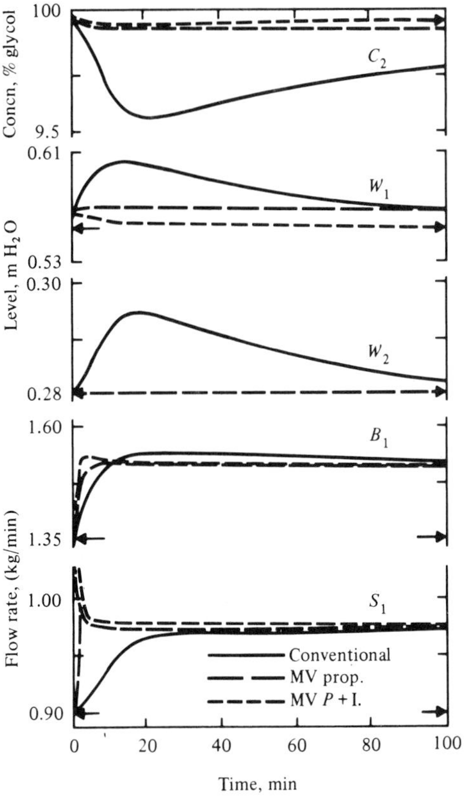

Figure 6.16 Simulation comparison of evaporator responses under optimal multivariable and conventional PI control. Disturbance: 10% increase in feed rate. *(Reproduced from Automatica* **8**, 247 (1972) *by permission of Pergamon Press Ltd.)*

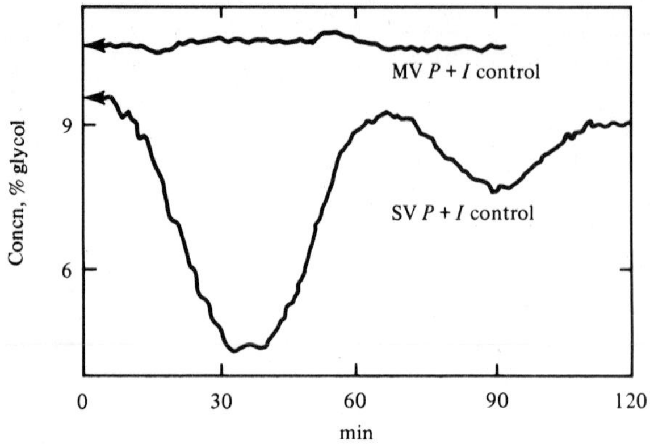

Figure 6.17 Comparison of experimental responses of evaporator product concentration using conventional PI controllers versus optimal multivariable control. Disturbance: 20% feed rate increase followed by decrease. *(Reproduced from Automatica* 8, 247 (1972) *by permission of Pergamon Press Ltd.)*

State Estimation and Stochastic Feedback Control

Fisher and Seborg [1] also carried out experimental evaluations of state-estimation and stochastic feedback control algorithms for the case when only W_1, W_2, and C_2 were available as outputs. A Luenberger observer and a Kalman filter (see Chap. 5) were implemented to estimate the state variables. Both of these were found to work well and give reliable estimates when properly tuned. These estimators were then coupled to the optimal multivariable feedback controller to form the stochastic feedback control system shown in Fig. 6.18.

When the observer was coupled to an optimal multivariable state feedback control scheme, the control system behavior may be seen in Fig. 6.19. These

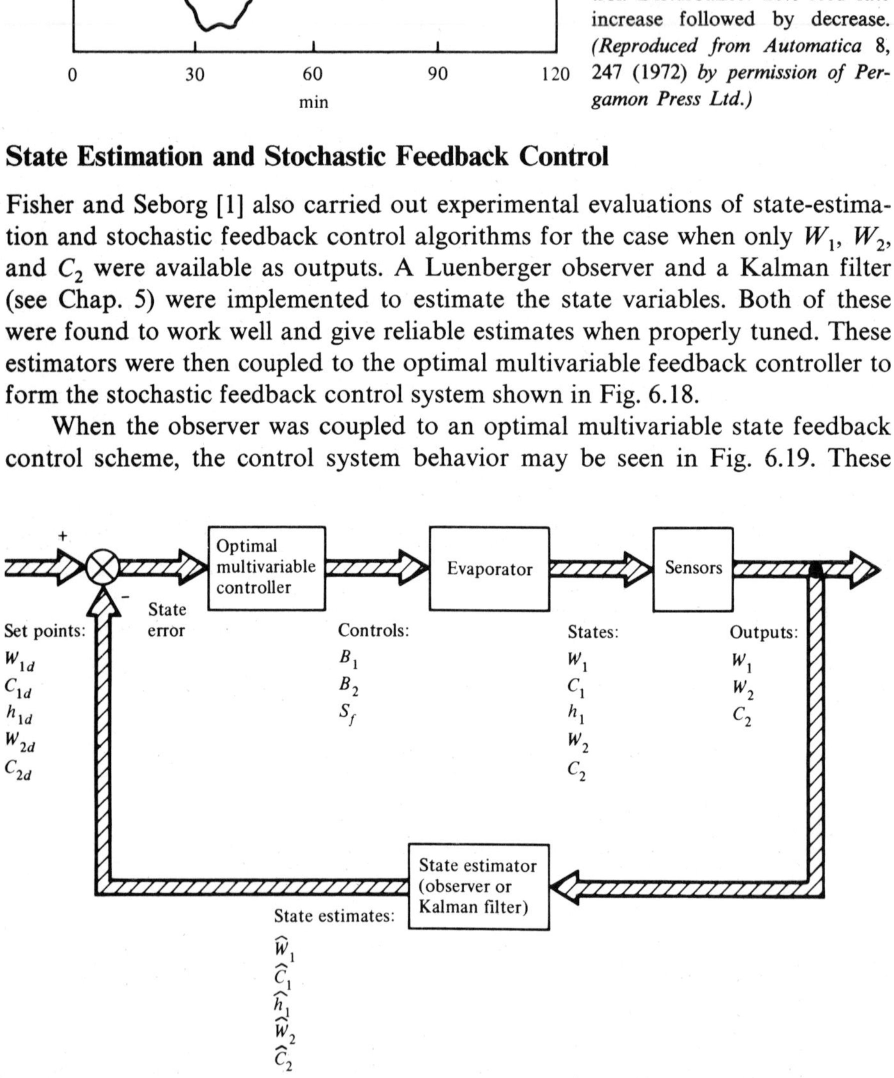

Figure 6.18 Stochastic optimal multivariable feedback control scheme utilizing an on-line state estimator.

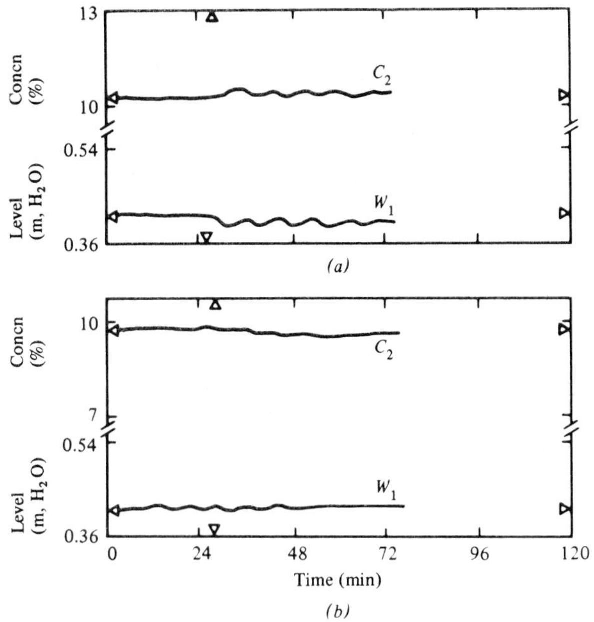

Figure 6.19 Optimal stochastic control system response with observer state estimates; disturbances: (*a*) single "unknown" 20% feed-rate decrease; (*b*) single "known" 30% decrease in feed solute concentration. *(Reproduced from Proceedings 4th IFAC/IFIP Conference on Digital Computer Applications to Process Control,* 1974, *p.* 154, *by permission of Springer-Verlag.)*

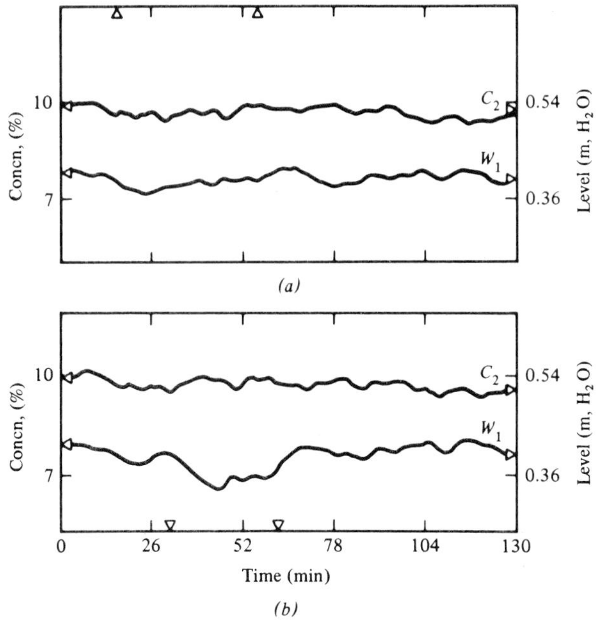

Figure 6.20 Optimal stochastic control system response with Kalman filter state estimates; disturbances: two 20% changes in feed rate at times denoted by ∇; (*a*) "known" disturbance, (*b*) "unknown" disturbance. *(Reproduced from Proceedings 4th IFAC/IFIP Conference on Digital Computer Applications to Process Control,* 1974, *p.* 154, *by permission of Springer-Verlag.)*

almost "bumpless" responses to rather large input disturbances are very impressive; however, the observer behavior was seen to deteriorate rapidly if the noise level of the data increased.

The Kalman filter, on the other hand, was found to be more robust in the face of noisy data. Some typical responses to feed-rate disturbances are shown in Fig. 6.20. Note that while the stochastic control system responds better to measured "known" disturbances, it also responds well to large "unknown" upsets.

Evaluation

The studies of Fisher and Seborg and their students [1] in applying advanced process algorithms to this pilot plant evaporator serve as a fine demonstration of computer control applied easily and profitably to an important chemical engineering process. Both the deterministic and stochastic multivariable feedback controllers performed well and proved to be a great improvement over the conventional control system.

6.4 A STRATEGY FOR STEEL MILL SOAKING PIT CONTROL

The soaking pit furnace is a major unit operation in the traditional steel mill. Large steel ingots which have been cast into molds and allowed to cool must be reheated in soaking pits to achieve a proper temperature distribution for rolling. Figure 6.21 shows the interior of a typical soaking pit. The ingots are placed in the furnace in a batchwise fashion, and some 6 to 12 h later they are removed for rolling in a rolling mill.

Unfortunately, the initial temperature distribution of the ingots is unknown, and the temperature distribution cannot be measured directly. Only furnace wall temperatures are routinely recorded, and these are augmented by sporadic optical pyrometric ingot surface temperature measurements. Thus it is difficult to determine how to control the furnace gas firing rate and to know when the ingots should be removed from the furnace. Too high a furnace firing rate will accelerate corrosion of the ingot surface (and can even cause surface melting), resulting in yield loss, while very low firing rates require excessive residence time in the furnace. Determining when the desired temperature distribution has been achieved (so that the ingots can be removed from the furnace) is even more of a problem. Removing ingots too soon results in poor rolling performance and requires the return of the ingot to the soaking pit for further heating. On the other hand, conservative, overlong heating cuts down the productivity of the process and increases production costs. In current steel mill practice, the furnace firing rate and ingot withdrawal time are based on certain "rules of thumb" and visual observations of an experienced operator, but steel industry figures indicate that this control scheme is not very reliable or effective.

Figure 6.21 Ingots in a soaking pit furnace. *(Reproduced from "A Visit to STELCO" by permission of Steel Co. of Canada.)*

The present case study, described in more detail elsewhere [2–4], is devoted to testing the feasibility of an advanced process control scheme capable of solving these practical problems. Specifically, the control scheme must:

1. Estimate in real time the temperature distribution in the ingots residing in the soaking pit.
2. Provide a feedback control law for furnace firing rate.
3. Determine precisely when the ingots have achieved the desired temperature distribution and should be removed from the furnace.

Clearly specifications (1) and (3) call for on-line state estimation, while (2) requires feedback controller design based on these estimates. Because the ingots are distributed in nature, having a nearly cylindrical shape with both axial and radial temperature variations, our control strategy must involve distributed parameter state estimation and control algorithms such as those discussed in Chaps. 4 and 5. The equations to be solved for such algorithms are multidimensional partial differential equations, and the real-time computations could be substantial. Therefore, the principal aim of the feasibility study is to investigate the control system performance on a pilot plant process and to determine if the required computations can be readily performed in real time.

The pilot plant ingot and furnace, shown in Fig. 6.22, consists of a stainless steel cylindrical ingot in a three-zone electrical furnace. A hole was drilled through the center of the ingot, through which cooling water could be passed. This allowed rapid cooling of the ingot after a test so that a new run could begin. Although only ingot surface temperatures were made available to the control algorithm (to emulate optical pyrometry measurements in an actual soaking pit), the actual ingot temperature distribution was measured by 32 thermocouples placed at 8 axial positions z_i, $i = 1, 2, 3, \ldots, 8$, and 4 radial positions r_j, $j = 1, 2, 3$, and 4, as shown in Fig. 6.23.

The ingot was modeled assuming angular symmetry, negligible heat losses at each end, and constant physical parameters. Under these conditions, the ingot model takes the form

$$\frac{\partial T}{\partial t'} = \alpha\left(\frac{\partial^2 T}{\partial r'^2} + \frac{1}{r'}\frac{\partial T}{\partial r'} + \frac{\partial^2 T}{\partial z'^2}\right) \qquad 0 \le z' \le L$$

$$r_0' \le r \le R$$

$$t' > 0 \tag{6.4.1}$$

where $\alpha = k/\rho C_p$ is the thermal diffusivity and the boundary conditions are given as

$$\frac{\partial T}{\partial z'} = 0 \qquad \text{at } z' = 0 \tag{6.4.2}$$

$$\frac{\partial T}{\partial z'} = 0 \qquad \text{at } z' = L \tag{6.4.3}$$

$$k\frac{\partial T}{\partial r'} = h(T - T_w) \qquad \text{at } r' = r_0' \tag{6.4.4}$$

$$k\frac{\partial T}{\partial r'} = q'(z', t') \qquad \text{at } r' = R \tag{6.4.5}$$

Figure 6.22 The experimental ingot and furnace system.

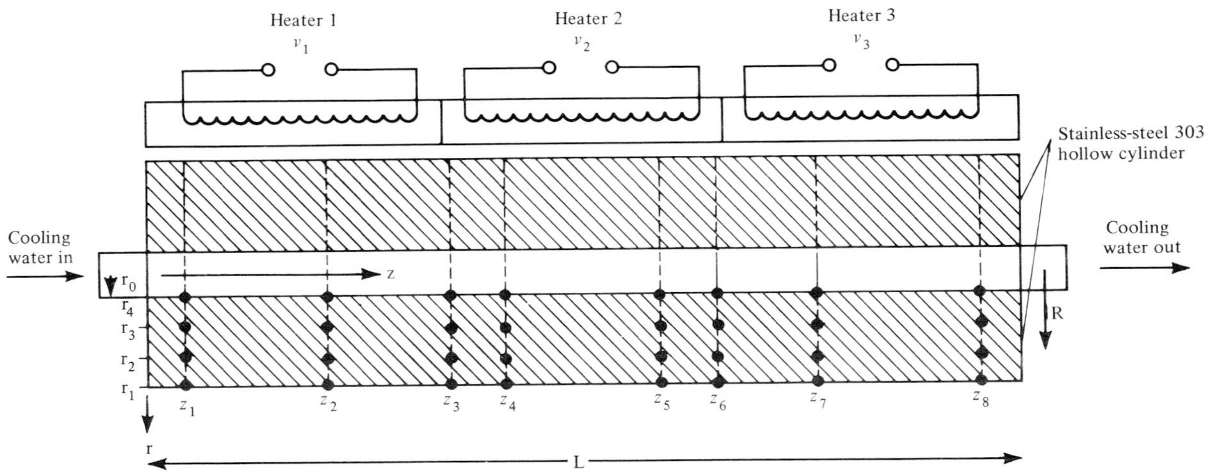

Figure 6.23 Axial cross section of the experimental apparatus.

Here k is the thermal conductivity, h is the experimentally determined overall heat transfer coefficient, T_w is the mean water temperature, and $q'(z', t')$ is the heat flux from the heaters at the outer surface into the cylinder. Let us define the following dimensionless quantities:

$$\theta = \frac{T - T_w}{T_w} \qquad z = \frac{z'}{l} \qquad r = \frac{r'}{R} \qquad r_0 = \frac{r'_0}{R}$$

$$t = \frac{\alpha t'}{R^2} \qquad \alpha' = \frac{R^2}{L^2} \qquad Bi = \frac{hR}{k}$$

$$q(z, t) = \frac{q'(z', t')R}{kT_w} = \mathbf{g}^T(z)\mathbf{v}(t) \tag{6.4.6}$$

where $g_i(z)$ is the spatial distribution of heat flux and $v_i(t)$ the heater power for the ith zone of the furnace. Then by inserting the heater input into the partial differential equations, in order to make the boundary conditions homogeneous, we obtain

$$\frac{\partial \theta}{\partial t} = \frac{\partial^2 \theta}{\partial r^2} + \frac{1}{r}\frac{\partial \theta}{\partial r} + \alpha' \frac{\partial^2 \theta}{\partial z^2} + \delta(r-1)\mathbf{g}^T(z)\mathbf{v}(t) \tag{6.4.7}$$

$$\frac{\partial \theta}{\partial z} = 0 \qquad \text{at } z = 0 \qquad \text{and} \qquad z = 1 \tag{6.4.8}$$

$$\frac{\partial \theta}{\partial r} = Bi\theta \qquad \text{at } r = r_0 \tag{6.4.9}$$

$$\frac{\partial \theta}{\partial r} = 0 \qquad \text{at } r = 1 \tag{6.4.10}$$

The temperature measurements are given by

$$y_{ik}(t) = \theta(r_i, z_k, t) + \eta_{ik}(t) \qquad \begin{array}{l} i = 1, 2, 3, 4 \\ k = 1, 2, \ldots, 8 \end{array} \tag{6.4.11}$$

where η_{ik} represents the measurement error.

State Estimation

The first step in the control system synthesis is to develop the state estimation equations. By extending the linear distributed parameter state estimation results of Chap. 5 to two space dimensions, one obtains

$$\frac{\partial \hat{\theta}(r, z, t)}{\partial t} = \frac{\partial^2 \hat{\theta}(r, z, t)}{\partial r^2} + \frac{1}{r}\frac{\partial \hat{\theta}(r, z, t)}{\partial r} + \alpha' \frac{\partial^2 \hat{\theta}(r, z, t)}{\partial z^2} + \delta(r-1)\mathbf{g}^T(z)\mathbf{v}(t)$$
$$+ \sum_{i=1}^{N_r} \sum_{j=1}^{N_r} \sum_{k=1}^{M_z} \sum_{l=1}^{M_z} P(r, r_i, z, z_k, t) Q_{ijkl}(t) \times \left[y_{jl}(t) - \hat{\theta}(r_j, z_l, t) \right] \tag{6.4.12}$$

which when solved with the boundary conditions of Eqs. (6.4.8) to (6.4.10) gives the estimated ingot temperature distribution, $\hat{\theta}(r, z, t)$.

The estimate covariance $P(r, s, z, u, t)$ is the solution of

$$\begin{aligned}\frac{\partial P(r, s, z, u, t)}{\partial t} &= \frac{\partial^2 P(r, s, z, u, t)}{\partial r^2} + \frac{1}{r}\frac{\partial P(r, s, z, u, t)}{\partial r} \\ &\quad + \frac{\partial^2 P(r, s, z, u, t)}{\partial s^2} + \frac{1}{s}\frac{\partial P(r, s, z, u, t)}{\partial s} + \alpha' \frac{\partial^2 P(r, s, z, u, t)}{\partial z^2} \\ &\quad + \alpha' \frac{\partial^2 P(r, s, z, u, t)}{\partial u^2} - \sum_{i=1}^{N_r} \sum_{j=1}^{N_r} \sum_{k=1}^{M_z} \sum_{l=1}^{M_z} P(r, r_i, z, z_k, t) Q_{ijkl}(t) \\ &\quad \times P(r_j, s, z_l, u, t) + R^+(r, s, z, u, t) \qquad \begin{aligned} r_0 &\le r \le 1 \\ 0 &\le z \le 1 \\ 0 &\le t \le t_f \end{aligned}\end{aligned} \tag{6.4.13}$$

with the boundary conditions

$$\frac{\partial P(r, s, z, u, t)}{\partial r} - BiP(r, s, z, u, t) + R_0^{-1}(t)\delta(s - r_0) = 0 \qquad \text{at } r = r_0 \tag{6.4.14}$$

$$\frac{\partial P(r, s, z, u, t)}{\partial r} - R_1^{-1}(t)\delta(s - 1) = 0 \qquad \text{at } r = 1 \tag{6.4.15}$$

$$\frac{\partial P(r, s, z, u, t)}{\partial z} + \alpha' R_2^{-1}(t)\delta(u) = 0 \qquad \text{at } z = 0 \tag{6.4.16}$$

$$\frac{\partial P(r, s, z, u, t)}{\partial z} - \alpha' R_3^{-1}(t)\delta(u - 1) = 0 \qquad \text{at } z = 1 \tag{6.4.17}$$

A similar set of boundary conditions holds for $s = r_0$, $s = 1$ and $u = 0$, $u = 1$.

Because the system is linear, both the filter and covariance equations may be solved by a modal decomposition of the form

$$\hat{\theta}(r, z, t) = \sum_{n=1}^{N} \sum_{m=1}^{M} \hat{a}_{nm}(t)\phi_n(r)\psi_m(z) \tag{6.4.18}$$

$$P(r, s, z, u, t) = \sum_{n=1}^{N_c} \sum_{k'=1}^{N_c} \sum_{m=1}^{M_c} \sum_{p=1}^{M_c} p_{nk'mp}(t)\phi_n(r)\phi_{k'}(s)\psi_m(z)\psi_p(u) \tag{6.4.19}$$

where N, M and N_c, M_c represent the number of terms in the eigenfunction expansion necessary for an adequate representation of the filter and covariance, respectively. Here the $\phi_n(r)$, $\psi_m(z)$ are eigenfunctions of the system [1–3] given by

$$\phi_n(r) = A_n\left[J_0(\sqrt{\mu_n}\, r) - \frac{J_1(\sqrt{\mu_n})Y_0(\sqrt{\mu_n}\, r)}{Y_1(\sqrt{\mu_n})}\right] \tag{6.4.20}$$

$$\psi_m(z) = \begin{cases} 1 & m = 1 \\ \sqrt{2}\cos(m-1)\pi z & m > 1 \end{cases} \tag{6.4.21}$$

The quantities A_n, μ_n may be determined from the solution to certain transcendental equations [2–4]. The time-dependent coefficients $\hat{a}_{nm}(t)$ and $p_{nk'mp}(t)$ are the solutions of

$$\frac{d\hat{a}_{nm}(t)}{dt} = -\lambda_{nm}\hat{a}_{nm}(t) + \sum_{k'=1}^{N_c}\sum_{p=1}^{M_c}\sum_{i=1}^{N_r}\sum_{j=1}^{N_r}\sum_{k=1}^{M_z}\sum_{l=1}^{M_z} p_{nk'mp}(t)$$
$$\times \phi_{k'}(r_i)\psi_p(z_k)Q_{ijkl}(t)\left[y_{jl} - \sum_{n'=1}^{N}\sum_{m'=1}^{M}\hat{a}_{n'm'}(t)\phi_{n'}(r_j)\psi_{m'}(z_l)\right] + u^*_{nm}(t) \tag{6.4.22}$$

$$\frac{dp_{nk'mp}(t)}{dt} = -\gamma_{nk'mp}p_{nk'mp}(t) - \sum_{n'=1}^{N_c}\sum_{l'=1}^{N_c}\sum_{m'=1}^{M_c}\sum_{p'=1}^{M_c}\sum_{i=1}^{N_r}\sum_{j=1}^{N_r}\sum_{k=1}^{M_z}\sum_{l=1}^{M_z}$$
$$\times p_{nl'mp'}(t)\phi_{l'}(r_i)\psi_{p'}(z_k)Q_{ijkl}(t)\phi_{n'}(r_j)\psi_{m'}(z_l)p_{n'k'm'p}(t)$$
$$+ r_{nk'mp}(t) + \sum_{i=0}^{3} r_{i_{nk'mp}}(t) \tag{6.4.23}$$

where

$$\lambda_{nm} = \mu_n + \alpha'[(m-1)\pi]^2 \tag{6.4.24}$$

$$u^*_{nm}(t) = \int_0^1 \phi_n(1)\psi_m(z)\mathbf{g}^T(z)\mathbf{v}(t)\,dz \tag{6.4.25}$$

The covariance equations (6.4.23) may be solved off-line, so that only the state estimator equations (6.4.22) must be solved in real time. The experimental testing of this state estimator and subsequent controller designs was accomplished using the communications and computing scheme shown in Fig. 6.24. Temperature measurements were transmitted to the computer, which carried out the estimation and control calculations necessary to determine adjustments to be made in the heater power to the three zones of the furnace.

Optimal Stochastic Feedback Control

In order to control the furnace heat input, a distributed linear-quadratic optimal stochastic feedback controller was developed and tested.* For this problem, the

* See Chaps. 4 and 5 to review the necessary theory.

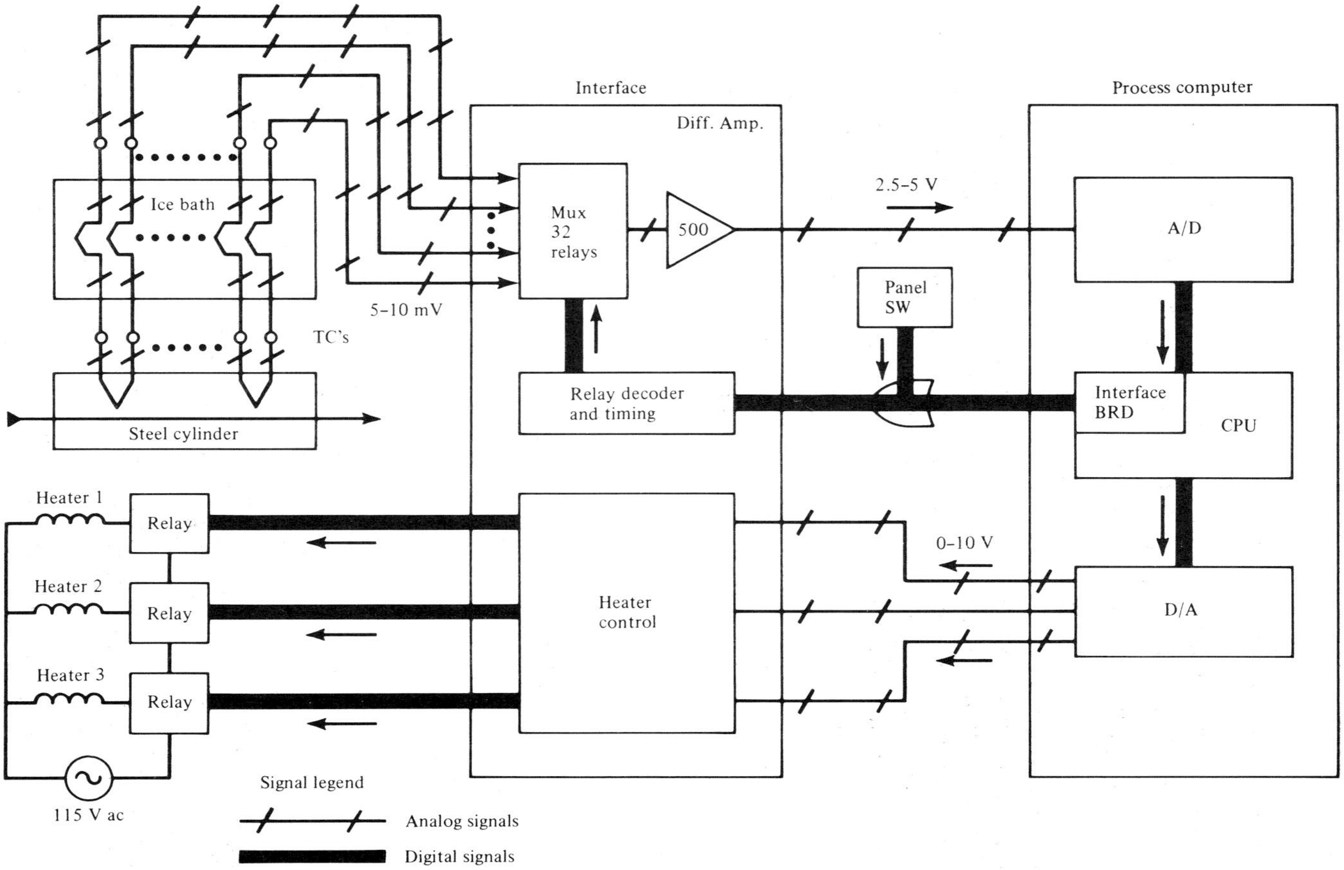

Figure 6.24 Communications for on-line testing of the ingot-furnace system.

control law takes the form [2–4]

$$\mathbf{v}(t) = \mathbf{v}^*(t) + \boldsymbol{\Gamma}_u^{-1}\int_0^1\int_0^1\int_{r_0}^1\int_{r_0}^1 R_c(r, r', z, z', t) \times \left[\theta_d(r', z', t) - \hat{\bar{\theta}}(r', z', t)\right]\mathbf{g}(z)\delta(r-1)\, dr\, dr'\, dz\, dz' \quad (6.4.26)$$

where θ_d is the desired temperature distribution set point, $\mathbf{v}^*(t)$ is the furnace heat flux which holds θ at θ_d, and R_c is found from the solution of

$$\frac{\partial R_c}{\partial t} = -\frac{\partial^2 R_c}{\partial r^2} + \frac{\partial}{\partial r}\left(\frac{1}{r}R_c\right) - \frac{\partial^2 R_c}{\partial r'^2} + \frac{\partial}{\partial r'}\left(\frac{1}{r'}R_c\right) - \alpha'\left(\frac{\partial^2 R_c}{\partial z^2} + \frac{\partial^2 R_c}{\partial z'^2}\right) + \gamma_d(r, r', z, z', t) - \int_0^1\int_0^1\int_{r_0}^1\int_{r_0}^1 R_c(r, \rho, z, \xi, t)\delta(\rho-1)\mathbf{g}^T(\xi)\boldsymbol{\Gamma}_u^{-1}\delta(\rho'-1)\mathbf{g}(\xi') \times R_c(\rho', r', \xi', z', t)\, d\rho\, d\rho'\, d\xi\, d\xi' \quad (6.4.27)$$

with boundary conditions being the adjoint of those given by Eqs. (6.4.14) to (6.4.17). Here $\boldsymbol{\Gamma}_u$ and γ_d are controller weighting parameters. The quantity R_c may be expanded in terms of the adjoint eigenfunctions to yield

$$R_c(r, r', z, z', t) = \sum_{n=1}^{N_R}\sum_{m=1}^{M_R}\sum_{k'=1}^{N_R}\sum_{p=1}^{M_R} r^c_{nk'mp}(t)rr'\phi_n(r)\phi_{k'}(r')\psi_m(z)\psi_p(z') \quad (6.4.28)$$

and $r^c_{nk'mp}(t)$ is the solution of

$$\frac{dr^c_{nk'mp}}{dt} = \gamma_{nk'mp}r^c_{nk'mp}(t) - \gamma^d_{nk'mp} + \sum_{n'=1}^{N_R}\sum_{m'=1}^{N_R}\sum_{l'=1}^{M_R}\sum_{p'=1}^{M_R} r^c_{n'k'm'p'}(t)\mathbf{b}^T_{n'm'}\boldsymbol{\Gamma}_u^{-1}\mathbf{b}_{l'p'}r^c_{nl'mp'}(t) \quad (6.4.29)$$

where

$$\mathbf{b}_{nm} = \int_0^1\int_{r_0}^1 r\phi_n(r)\psi_m(z)\mathbf{g}(z)\delta(r-1)\, dr\, dz \quad (6.4.30)$$

and

$$\gamma^d_{nk'mp}(t) = \int_0^1\int_0^1\int_{r_0}^1\int_{r_0}^1 \gamma_d(r, r', z, z', t)\phi_n(r)\phi_{k'}(r')\psi_m(z)\psi_p(z')\, dr\, dr'\, dz\, dz' \quad (6.4.31)$$

Finally, the feedback control law, Eq. (6.4.26), may be put in the simpler form

$$\mathbf{v}(t) = \mathbf{v}^*(t) + \boldsymbol{\Gamma}_u^{-1}\sum_{n=1}^{N_R}\sum_{k'=1}^{N_R}\sum_{m=1}^{M_R}\sum_{p=1}^{M_R} r^c_{nk'mp}(t)\mathbf{b}_{nm}\left(a^d_{k'p}(t) - \hat{a}_{k'p}(t)\right) \quad (6.4.32)$$

where $a^d_{k'p}(t)$ is the eigencoefficient of the temperature set point $\theta_d(r', z', t)$ given by the orthogonality relation

$$a^d_{k'p}(t) = \int_0^1 \int_{r_0}^1 \phi_{k'}(r')\psi_p(z')\theta_d(r', z', t)\, dr'\, dz' \tag{6.4.33}$$

and $\hat{a}_{k'p}(t)$ is the eigencoefficient of the state estimator determined previously. The Riccati equation (6.4.29) may be solved off-line, so that only the optimal feedback control law, Eq. (6.4.32), need be calculated in real time.

Case 1 As a first test of the state estimator alone, all eight ingot surface temperatures were provided to the estimator. These measurements were corrupted with Gaussian random errors having zero mean and $\sigma = 10°C$ and taken from a random number generator. The initial conditions, seen in Fig. 6.25, show the estimated temperature distribution as uniform and some 10 to 20°C below the actual distribution. For this case two radial and five axial eigenfunctions were used, so that the *off-line* solution of the covariance equations (6.4.23) consisted of integrating 45 differential equations. By contrast, the on-line solution of the estimator equations (6.4.22) required solving only 10 differential equations in real time. The results after 120 s show the filter tracking the actual temperature distribution quite well (Fig. 6.26), and it continues to provide good estimates as the ingot is heated further (Fig. 6.27).

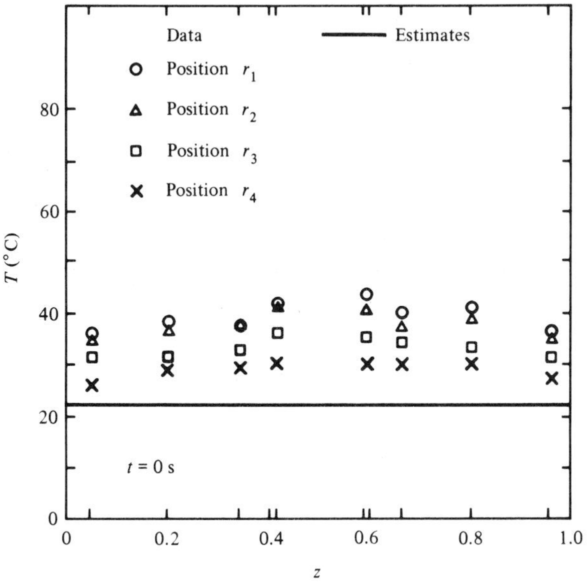

Figure 6.25 Initial estimates and data, Case 1.

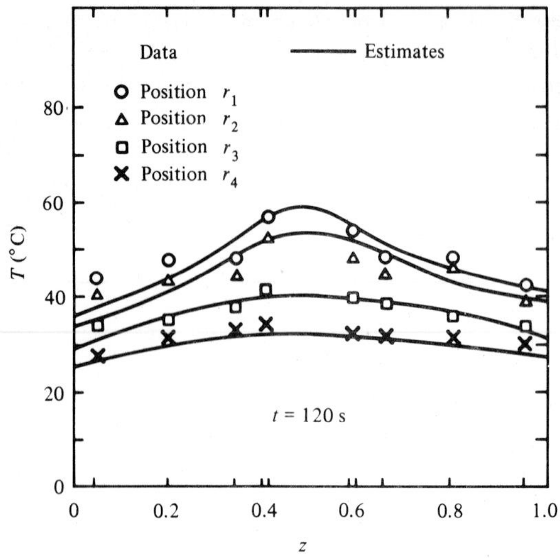

Figure 6.26 Filter estimates and data after 120 s, Case 1.

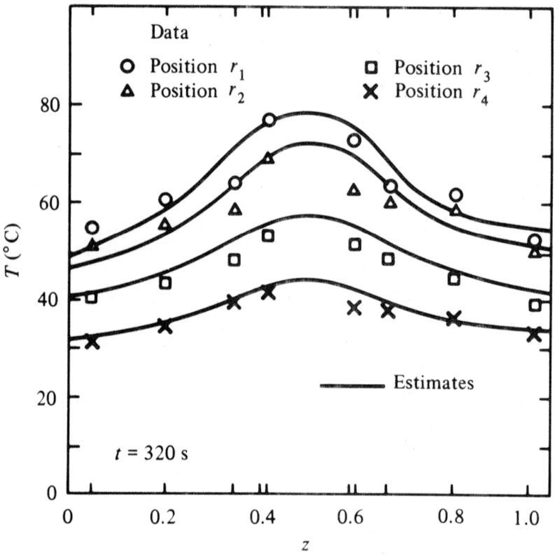

Figure 6.27 Filter estimates and data after 320 s, Case 1.

Case 2 As a test of what might prove to be the final control system design, only a single ingot surface thermocouple $\theta(r_1, z_3, t)$ was provided for the state estimator (see Fig. 6.28). The state estimates were then compared with the set-point value and the error fed to an optimal feedback controller which adjusts the furnace heat inputs. As in Case 1, zero-mean Gaussian measurement errors with $\sigma = 10°C$ were added to the actual temperature measurement to simulate very noisy steel mill conditions. The performance of the control scheme may be seen in Figs. 6.29 to 6.31. As shown in Fig. 6.29, the estimator initial condition is some 20 to 25°C below the actual ingot temperature distribution, and the temperature distribution set point is much different from the initial values. After 40 s (Fig. 6.30) the estimator is beginning to track the true temperature distribution, and by 320 s (Fig. 6.31) both the estimated and actual temperature distributions approximate the set point quite well.

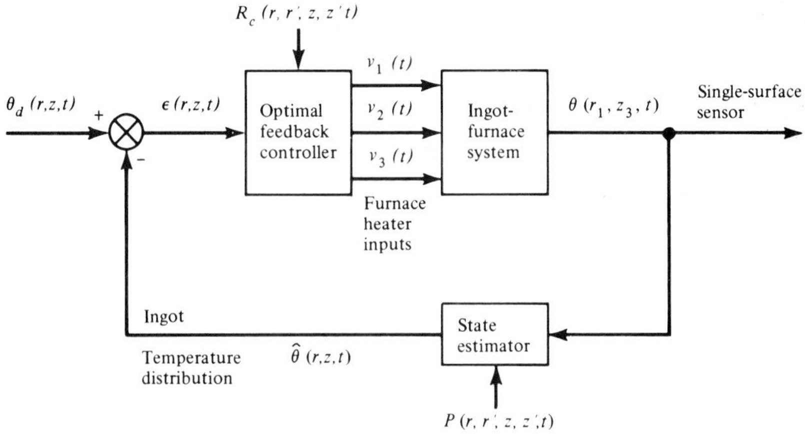

Figure 6.28 Estimator-controller for the soaking pit requiring only one surface temperature sensor.

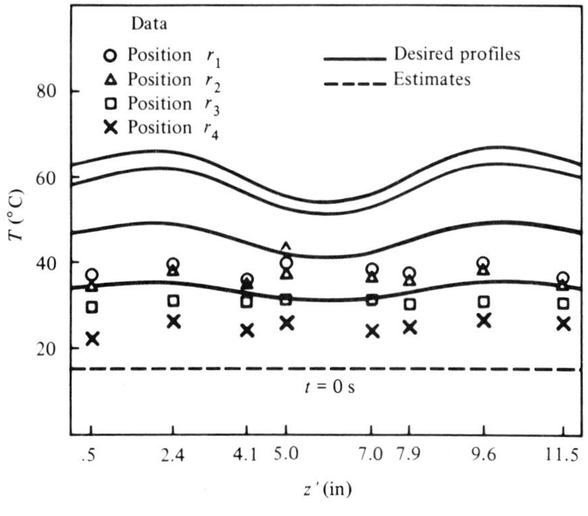

Figure 6.29 Stochastic feedback controller with one sensor.

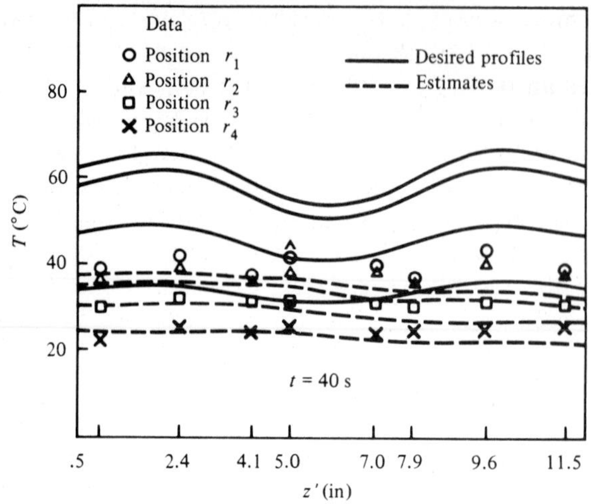

Figure 6.30 Stochastic feedback controller with one sensor; system evolution at 40 s.

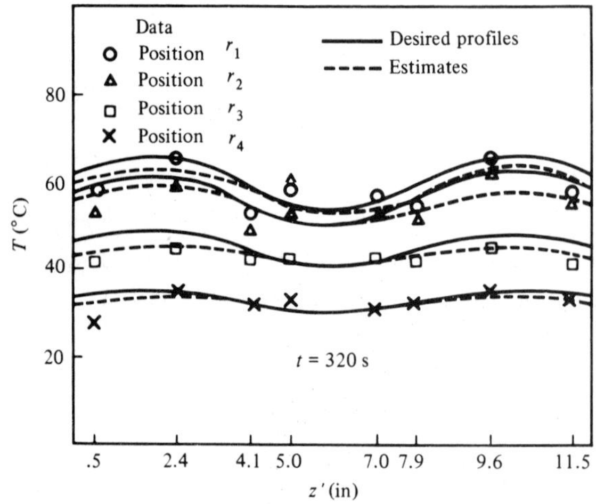

Figure 6.31 Stochastic feedback controller with one sensor; system evolution at 320 s.

Evaluation

The performance of the combined estimator/controller system, shown in Fig. 6.28, seems outstanding, allowing good control system performance when only one noisy temperature sensor is provided to the control system. The on-line computational requirements were less than 25 percent of real time for this pilot plant soaking pit having a principal time constant of about 5 min. This means that for industrial-scale soaking pits with time constants of 5 h or more, these computational requirements amount to less than $\frac{1}{2}$ percent of real time. This suggests that a hundred or more soaking pits could be controlled by the same computer in an actual steel mill.

This case study provides an important philosophical lesson for the control system designer. One should not be disheartened by control system designs involving formidable partial differential equations in many space dimensions [such as Eqs. (6.4.12) to (6.4.17), (6.4.26), and (6.4.27)] because it is often possible, as was done here, to reduce these to manageable proportions through judicious use of engineering judgment and numerical analysis. The effort is usually worthwhile because the resulting control system performance can be quite impressive, as was the case here.

6.5 CONTROL OF METALLURGICAL CASTING OPERATIONS

Another type of steel mill unit operation of great importance is casting. This process is carried out both batchwise in molds and continuously in continuous casting machines. Often it is important to control these casting processes so as to prevent excessive thermal stresses which lead to crack formation, and to prevent "breakout" of molten steel in the continuous process. The goal of the present case study is to develop and test the feasibility of a control system for a continuous casting machine.

The continuous casting of steel is an increasingly important part of modern steelmaking because it is a much more efficient route to steel slabs and billets than the conventional ingot casting-reheating-slab rolling operation. The process, sketched in Fig. 6.32, involves pouring molten steel at the top of a water-cooled mold and continuously drawing out a thin-walled steel slab or billet at the bottom. If the solid steel crust is too thin when it leaves the mold, either because of some process upset or because the withdrawal rates are too high, the molten steel core will "break out" and the casting machine must be shut down. By employing a distributed parameter filter to estimate the steel shell thickness in real time, one could operate at high average withdrawal rates while detecting potential breakouts before they occur and taking appropriate control action.

Although a very detailed model for this process has been developed [5, 6], the following simple model has been found to be adequate for the mold region. This idealized picture, illustrated in Fig. 6.33, approximates the two-phase "mushy" zone shown in Fig. 6.32 by an interface.

Assume that:

1. The solid at temperature $T_S(r', z', t')$ is moving downward at speed u_c while the liquid region is well mixed.
2. The physical properties are constant.
3. There is heat transfer to the mold wall with heat transfer coefficient h.

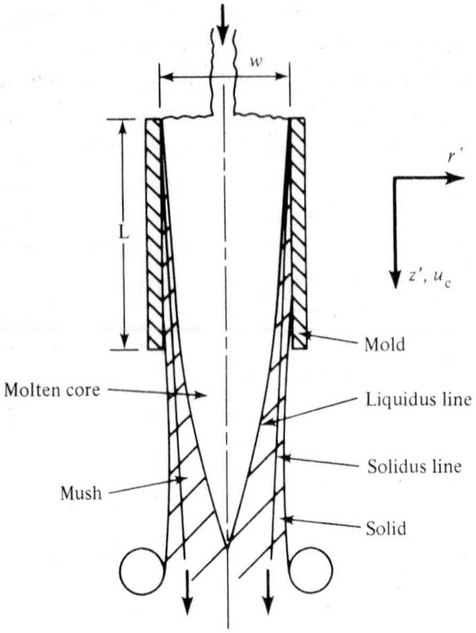

Figure 6.32 The continuous casting process.

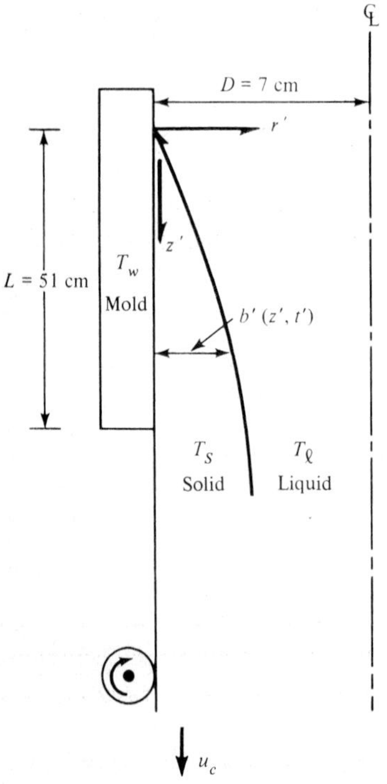

Figure 6.33 The mold region of a continuous casting operation.

4. There is heat transfer from the molten liquid to the solid at $r' = b'$ with heat transfer coefficient h_l and latent heat of solidification, $\mathfrak{L}$.
5. The solid-liquid interface is at the solidus temperature, T_{sol}.

Then the modeling equations take the form

$$\frac{\partial T_S(r', z', t')}{\partial t'} + u_c \frac{\partial T_S(r', z', t')}{\partial z'} = \alpha_s \frac{\partial^2 T_S(r', z', t')}{\partial r'^2} \tag{6.5.1}$$

with boundary conditions

$$z' = 0 \qquad T_S(r', 0, t) = T_l(t') \tag{6.5.2}$$

$$r' = 0 \qquad k_s \frac{\partial T_S}{\partial t'} = h[T_S(0, z', t') - T_w] \tag{6.5.3}$$

$$r' = b'(z', t') \qquad T_S = T_{sol} \tag{6.5.4}$$

and moving boundary condition

$$\frac{\partial b'(z', t')}{\partial t'} = \frac{k_s}{\mathfrak{L}\rho_s} \frac{\partial T_S}{\partial r'}\bigg|_{r' = b'(z', t')} + \frac{h_l}{\mathfrak{L}\rho_l}[T_S(b', z', t) - T_l(t')] \tag{6.5.5}$$

Equation (6.5.5) represents a heat balance over the moving interface and states that the net heat flux at $r' = b'$ is balanced by solidification.

It is possible to eliminate the variable z' from the model by noting that the vertical flow in the mold is along the characteristic lines

$$\frac{dz'}{dt'} = u_c \qquad z'(0) = z'_0 \tag{6.5.6}$$

Thus the solution along these characteristic lines may be determined from

$$\frac{\partial T_S(r', t')}{\partial t'} = \alpha_S \frac{\partial^2 T_S(r', t')}{\partial r'^2} \qquad 0 < r' < b'(t') \tag{6.5.7}$$

$$r' = 0 \qquad k_S \frac{\partial T_S}{\partial r'} = h[T_S(0, t') - T_w] \tag{6.5.8}$$

$$r' = b'(t') \qquad T_S = T_{sol} \tag{6.5.9}$$

$$t' = 0 \qquad T_S(r', 0) = T_l(t') \tag{6.5.10}$$

$$\frac{db'(t')}{dt'} = \frac{k_S}{\mathfrak{L}\rho_S} \frac{\partial T_S}{\partial r'}\bigg|_{r' = b'(t')} + \frac{h_l}{\mathfrak{L}\rho_l}[T_S(b', t') - T_l(t')] \tag{6.5.11}$$

These equations are nonlinear due to the moving boundary; thus we shall make some transformations which will convert the equations to a *fixed-boundary problem*. Let us define the variables

$$\theta_S = \frac{T_S - T_{\text{sol}}}{T_{\text{sol}}} \qquad r = \frac{r'}{b'(t')} \qquad b(t') = \frac{b'(t')}{D}$$

$$\theta_w = \frac{T_w - T_{\text{sol}}}{T_{\text{sol}}} \qquad H = \frac{hD}{k_S} \qquad \eta = \frac{k_S T_{\text{sol}}}{\rho_S \mathfrak{L} \alpha_S}$$

$$\theta_l = \frac{T_l - T_{\text{sol}}}{T_{\text{sol}}} \qquad K = \frac{h_l D}{\alpha_S \mathfrak{L} \rho_l} T_{\text{sol}} \qquad t = \int_0^{t'} \frac{\alpha_S}{b'(t'')^2}\, dt'' \tag{6.5.12}$$

By substituting Eq. (6.5.12) into Eqs. (6.5.7) to (6.5.11) and making the boundary conditions homogeneous through the use of a Dirac delta function, the model becomes

$$\frac{\partial \theta_S(r,t)}{\partial t} = \frac{\partial^2 \theta_S(r,t)}{\partial r^2} + r\frac{d \ln b(t)}{dt}\frac{\partial \theta_S(r,t)}{\partial r} - b(t)H(\theta_S(0,t) - \theta_w)\delta(r) \qquad 0 < r < 1 \tag{6.5.13}$$

$$\frac{d \ln b(t)}{dt} = \eta \frac{\partial \theta_S}{\partial r}\Big|_{r=1} - Kb(t)\theta_l(t) \tag{6.5.14}$$

$$r = 0 \qquad \frac{\partial \theta_S}{\partial r} = 0 \tag{6.5.15}$$

$$r = 1 \qquad \theta_S = 0 \tag{6.5.16}$$

In dimensionless form, the solid surface temperature measurements (obtained from thermocouples placed in the mold surface) take the form

$$y(t) = \theta_S(0, t) + \epsilon(t) \tag{6.5.17}$$

where $\epsilon(t)$ is a random measurement error.

In order to test the validity of the model, simulations were carried out for the conditions shown in Table 6.2 and compared with experimental data for the

Table 6.2

Property values used in the computation [4]

$T_{\text{sol}} = 1495°\text{C}$
$T_{\text{liq}} = 1523°\text{C}$
$C_{p_S} = C_{p_l} = 0.16\ \text{cal/(g)(°C)}$
$k_S = k_l = 7.02 \times 10^{-3}\ \text{cal/(cm)(s)(°C)}$
$T_l = 1525°\text{C}$
$h_l = 0.01355\ \text{cal/(cm}^2\text{)(s)(°C)}$
$u_c = 2.34\ \text{cm/s}$
$T_c = 21°\text{C}$
$h = 0.044\left(\frac{1 - 0.98z'}{100}\right)\text{cal/(cm}^2\text{)(s)(°C)}$ (z' is cm)
$\rho_S = \rho_l = 7.4\ \text{g/cm}^3$
$D = 7\ \text{cm}$

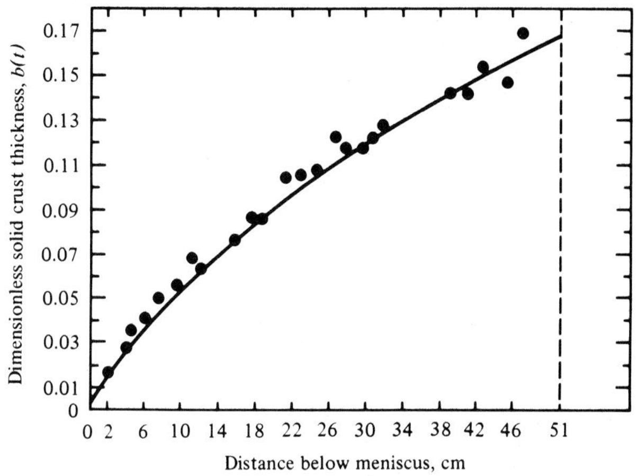

Figure 6.34 A comparison of the model predictions with experimental data.

same operating conditions. The model predictions for solid crust thickness versus time (or axial position), shown in Fig. 6.34, are in excellent agreement with the data; thus it appears that the model is representative of actual experimental operations, and we may proceed in confidence with the state estimation study.

State Estimation

The crux of the control scheme for the continuous caster is a state estimation algorithm which receives temperature data from thermocouples in the mold wall [Eq. (6.5.17)] and provides estimates of the solid crust thickness $b(t)$ as well as the solid temperature distribution $\theta_S(r, t)$. The optimal least squares state estimation equations [5, 6] take the form

$$\frac{\partial \hat{\theta}_S}{\partial t} = \frac{\partial^2 \hat{\theta}_S}{\partial r^2} + r \frac{d \ln \hat{b}(t)}{dt} \frac{\partial \hat{\theta}_S}{\partial r} - b(t) H\big(\hat{\theta}_S(0, t) - \theta_w\big)\delta(r)$$

$$+ P^{uu}(r, 0, t) Q(t)\big(y - \hat{\theta}_S(0, t)\big) \tag{6.5.18}$$

$$\frac{d\hat{b}(t)}{dt} = \eta \hat{b} \frac{\partial \theta_S}{\partial r}\Big|_{r=1} - K\hat{b}^2 \theta_l(t)$$

$$+ P^{ub}(0, t) Q(t)\big(y - \hat{\theta}_S(0, t)\big) \tag{6.5.19}$$

$$\hat{\theta}_S(1, t) = 0 \tag{6.5.20}$$

$$\frac{\partial \hat{\theta}_S(0, t)}{\partial r} = 0 \tag{6.5.21}$$

where $P^{uu}(r, s, t)$, $P^{ub}(r, t)$, and $P^{bb}(t)$ are the relevant differential sensitivities (i.e., nonlinear "covariances"), determined by

$$\begin{aligned}
P_t^{uu}(r, s, t) = {} & P_{rr}^{uu} + P_{ss}^{uu} - P^{bu}(s, t)\frac{r}{\hat{b}^2}\frac{d\hat{b}}{dt}\frac{\partial \hat{\theta}_S}{\partial r} + H\big(\hat{\theta}_S(0, t) - \theta_w\big)\delta(r) \\
& - P^{ub}(r, t)\frac{s}{\hat{b}^2}\frac{d\hat{b}}{dt}\frac{\partial \hat{\theta}_S}{\partial s} + H\big(\hat{\theta}_S(0, t) - \theta_w\big)\delta(s) \\
& - P^{uu}(r, 0, t)Q(t)P^{uu}(0, s, t) \\
& + P_s^{uu}(r, s, t)\frac{s}{\hat{b}^2}\frac{d\hat{b}}{dt} \\
& + P_r^{uu}(r, s, t)\frac{r}{\hat{b}^2}\frac{d\hat{b}}{dt} + R^{+}(r, s, t)
\end{aligned} \tag{6.5.22}$$

$$\begin{aligned}
P_t^{ub}(r, t) = {} & \left[\eta\frac{\partial \hat{\theta}_S}{\partial r}\Big|_{r=1} - 2\hat{b}\theta_l(t)K\right]P^{ub}(r, t) \\
& - P^{bb}(t)\left[\frac{r}{\hat{b}^2}\frac{d\hat{b}}{dt}\frac{\partial \hat{\theta}_S}{\partial r} + H\big(\hat{\theta}_S(0, t) - \theta_w\big)\delta(r)\right] \\
& + P_{rr}^{ub}(r, t) + P_s^{uu}(r, 1, t)\eta\hat{b}(t) \\
& + P_r^{ub}(r, t)\frac{r}{\hat{b}}\frac{d\hat{b}}{dt} - P^{uu}(r, 0, t)Q(t)P^{ub}(0, t)
\end{aligned} \tag{6.5.23}$$

$$\begin{aligned}
\frac{dP^{bb}}{dt} = {} & 2\left[\eta\frac{\partial \hat{\theta}_S}{\partial r}\Big|_{r=1} - 2\hat{b}\theta_l(t)K\right]P^{bb}(t) \\
& + \eta\hat{b}(t)P_r^{ub}(1, t) - P^{bu}(0, t)Q(t)P^{ub}(0, t) \\
& + \eta\hat{b}(t)P_s^{bu}(1, t) + R^{-1}(t)
\end{aligned} \tag{6.5.24}$$

with the symmetry condition

$$P^{ub}(r, t) = P^{bu}(r, t) \tag{6.5.25}$$

The boundary conditions are

$$\left.\begin{aligned} P_s^{uu}(r, s, t) + R_0^{-1}(t)\delta(r) &= 0 \\ P_s^{bu}(s, t) &= 0 \end{aligned}\right\} \quad s = 0 \tag{6.5.26}$$

$$\left.\begin{aligned} P_r^{uu}(r, s, t) + R_0^{-1}(t)\delta(s) &= 0 \\ P_r^{ub}(r, t) &= 0 \end{aligned}\right\} \quad r = 0 \tag{6.5.27}$$

$$\left.\begin{aligned} P^{uu}(r, s, t) &= 0 \\ P^{bu}(s, t) &= 0 \end{aligned}\right\} \quad s = 1 \tag{6.5.28}$$

$$\left.\begin{aligned} P^{uu}(r, s, t) &= 0 \\ P^{ub}(r, t) &= 0 \end{aligned}\right\} \quad r = 1 \tag{6.5.29}$$

where $R(r, s, t)$, $R(t)$, $Q(t)$, $R_0(t)$ are positive weighting factors.

These equations may appear intimidating, but it is possible to solve them through an eigenfunction expansion technique of the form

$$\hat{u}(r, t) = \sum_{n=1}^{\infty} A_n(t)\phi_n(r) \tag{6.5.30}$$

$$P^{uu}(r, s, t) = \sum_{n=1}^{\infty} \sum_{m=1}^{\infty} a_{nm}(t)\phi_n(r)\phi_m(s) \tag{6.5.31}$$

$$P^{ub}(r, t) = \sum_{n=1}^{\infty} B_n(t)\phi_n(r) \tag{6.5.32}$$

where the $\phi_n(r)$ are the eigenfunctions associated with the linear part of Eq. (6.5.18) and are the solution of

$$\ddot{\phi}(r) + \lambda_n^2\phi_n(r) = 0 \qquad 0 < r < 1 \tag{6.5.33}$$

$$\begin{aligned} \dot{\phi}_n(0) &= 0 \\ \phi_n(1) &= 0 \end{aligned} \qquad n = 1, 2, \ldots \tag{6.5.34}$$

which yields

$$\begin{aligned} \phi_n(r) &= \sqrt{2}\ \cos \lambda_n r \\ \lambda_n &= (2n - 1)\frac{\pi}{2} \end{aligned} \qquad n = 1, 2, \ldots \tag{6.5.35}$$

Applying Galerkin orthogonality conditions to the equations for $\hat{\theta}_S$, P^{uu}, and P^{ub} yields the eigencoefficient equations

$$\dot{A}_n(t) = -\lambda_n^2 A_n(t) + c_n(t) \tag{6.5.36}$$

$$\dot{a}_{nm}(t) = -\lambda_{nm}^2 a_{nm}(t) + D_{nm}(t) \tag{6.5.37}$$

$$\dot{B}_n(t) = -\lambda_n^2 B_n(t) + E_n(t) \tag{6.5.38}$$

where $\lambda_{nm} = \sqrt{\lambda_n^2 + \lambda_m^2}$ and c_n, D_{nm}, and E_n are given by

$$c_n(t) = -\sqrt{2}\ H\hat{b}(\hat{\theta}_s(0, t) - \theta_w) - 2\frac{d \ln \hat{b}}{dt} \sum_{m=1}^{N} A_m(t)\lambda_m I_{nm}$$

$$+ \sqrt{2}\ Q(t)(y - \hat{\theta}(0, t)) \sum_{m=1}^{N_c} a_{nm} \tag{6.5.39}$$

$$D_{nm}(t) = B_n\left[-2\sqrt{2}\, H(\hat{\theta}_S(0,t) - \theta_w) + \frac{2}{\hat{b}^2}\frac{d\hat{b}}{dt}\left(\sum_{j=1}^{N} \lambda_j A_j I_{jm}\right)\right]$$

$$+ B_m\left[-2\sqrt{2}\, H(\hat{\theta}_S(0,t) - \theta_w) + \frac{2}{\hat{b}^2}\frac{d\hat{b}}{dt}\left(\sum_{k=1}^{N} \lambda_k A_k I_{kn}\right)\right]$$

$$-2\frac{d\ln\hat{b}}{dt}\left(\sum_{k=1}^{N_c} a_{km}\lambda_k I_{mk} + \sum_{j=1}^{N_c} a_{nj}\lambda_j I_{nj}\right)$$

$$-2Q(t)\sum_{k=1}^{N_c} a_{nk}\sum_{j=1}^{N_c} a_{jm} + \frac{2R^{+}(-1)^{m+1}(-1)^{n+1}}{\lambda_m\lambda_n}$$

$$+ R_0^{-1}\left(\frac{(-1)^{n+1}}{\lambda_n} + \frac{(-1)^{m+1}}{\lambda_m}\right) \qquad (6.5.40)$$

$$E_n(t) = \frac{2}{\hat{b}^2} P^{bb}(t)\frac{d\hat{b}}{dt}\sum_{j=1}^{N} A_j\lambda_j I_{jn} - \sqrt{2}\, P^{bb} H(\hat{\theta}_S(0,t) - \theta_w)$$

$$-2\frac{d\ln\hat{b}}{dt}\sum_{k=1}^{N_c} \lambda_k B_k I_{kn}$$

$$-\left(\sqrt{2}\,\eta\sum_{m=1}^{N} \lambda_m A_m(-1)^{m+1} + 2\hat{b}\theta_l K\right)B_n - 2Q(t)\sum_{k=1}^{N_c} B_k\sum_{m=1}^{N_c} a_{nm} \qquad (6.5.41)$$

The variables $\hat{b}(t)$ and $P^{bb}(t)$ may be determined from

$$\frac{d\hat{b}}{dt} = -\eta\hat{b}\sqrt{2}\sum_{m=1}^{N}(-1)^{m+1}\lambda_m A_m(t)$$

$$-\hat{b}^2 K\theta_l + \sqrt{2}\left(\sum_{k=1}^{N_c} B_k\right)Q(t)\left(y - \hat{\theta}_S(0,t)\right) \qquad (6.5.42)$$

$$\frac{dP^{bb}}{dt} = -2P^{bb}\left[\eta\sqrt{2}\sum_{m=1}^{N}(-1)^{m+1}\lambda_m A_m(t) + 2\hat{b}\theta_l K\right]$$

$$+2\sqrt{2}\,\eta\hat{b}\sum_{k=1}^{N_c}(-1)^{k+1}\lambda_k B_k(t)$$

$$-\left(\sum_{i=1}^{N_c} B_i(t)\right)Q(t)\left(\sum_{j=1}^{N_c} B_j(t)\right) + R^{-1}(t) \qquad (6.5.43)$$

Here N is the number of eigenfunctions required for the filter estimates, while N_c is the number of eigenfunctions used to represent the differential sensitivities. The state estimation algorithm then consists of solving $N + 1$ ordinary differential equations for the filter [Eqs. (6.5.36) and (6.5.42)] and

$1 + N_c + (N_c^2 + N_c)/2$ ordinary differential equations for the differential sensitivities [Eqs. (6.5.37), (6.5.38), and (6.5.43)]. Although it would be possible to solve both the filter and sensitivity equations in real time, in practice it is more practical to solve the sensitivity equations in an approximate way off-line for a nominal state trajectory so that only the $N + 1$ filter equations need be integrated in real time. In this way the state estimator is easily implemented in real time on presently available process control computers. In the present study, it was found (after some adjustments in the computational procedure [6]) that $N = 4$ was sufficient to provide a good solution to the filter equations and $N_c = 3$ sufficed for adequate filter performance. Thus the filter required the solution of five ordinary differential equations in real time. In order to provide an initial test of the filter in the face of large measurement errors, a number of simulations were performed. The steel surface temperature measurement "data" were provided by a simulation of the model in which the resulting surface temperatures $\theta_S(0, t)$ were corrupted by adding zero-mean white Gaussian noise from a random number generator having a specified standard deviation σ.

A selection of results may be seen in Figs. 6.35 to 6.38 for the filter parameters given in Table 6.3. As can be seen, this nonlinear filter performs well, converging from extremely poor initial guesses in a very short time even in the face of 100°C standard deviation measurement error.

Evaluation

Although the state estimation algorithm developed here has been tested only through simulation, these tests show that minimal real-time computations are required for implementation and indicate that the solid steel crust thickness can be adequately tracked by the estimator. Further experimental testing of the estimator and evaluation of feedback controllers for casting operations is reported elsewhere [6, 7].

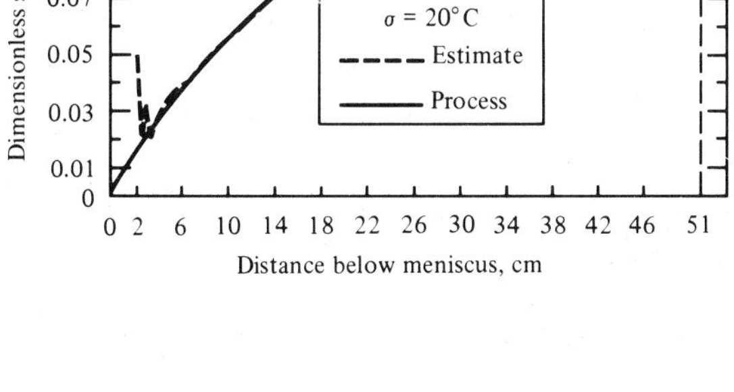

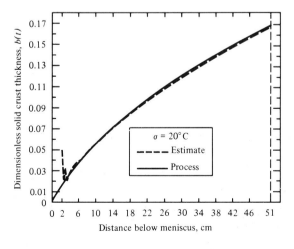

Figure 6.35 Filter estimates and process behavior for the solid crust thickness, σ = 20°C.

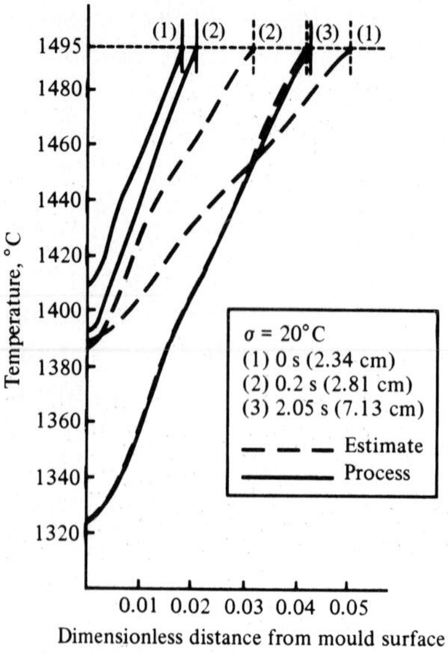

Figure 6.36 Filter estimates and process behavior for the temperature profile in the solid crust, $\sigma = 20°C$.

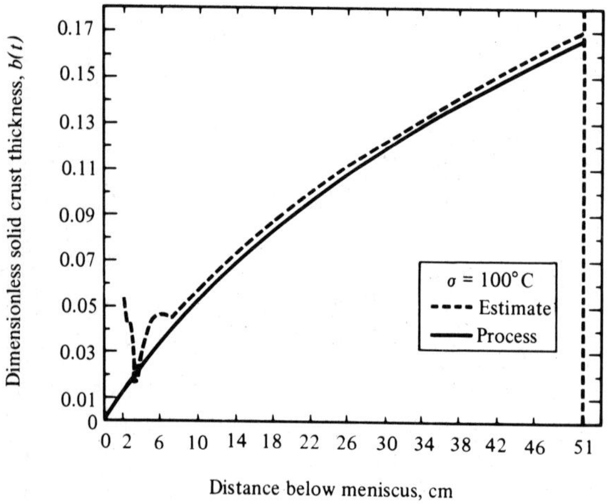

Figure 6.37 Filter estimates and process behavior for the solid crust thickness, $\sigma = 100°C$.

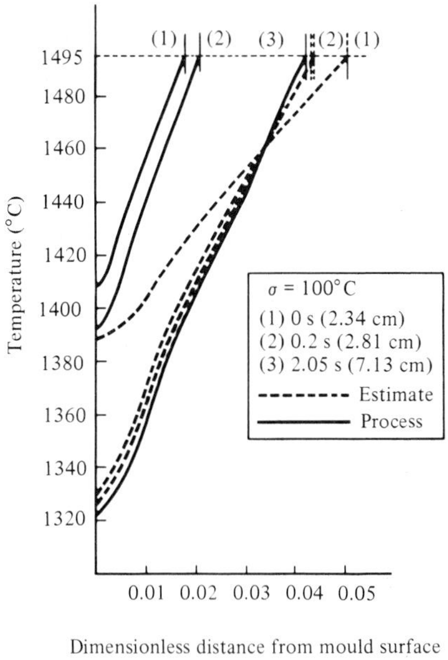

Figure 6.38 Filter estimates and process behavior for the temperature profile in the solid crust, $\sigma = 100°C$.

Table 6.3 Filter parameters

Figure no.	σ	$Q(t)$	$P^{bb}(0)$
6.35–6.36	20°C	1.96	0.001
6.37–6.38	100°C	0.0784	0.007

For all runs: $\hat{b}(0) = 0.05$, $R^{-1} = R_0^{-1} = R^+ = 0$, $B_n(0) = 0$, $D_{nm}(0) = 1.02/\lambda_n\lambda_m$.

6.6 FURTHER CASE STUDIES

A number of other case studies which have appeared in the literature recently illustrate the application of modern process control to industrial scale or pilot plant processes. These include studies on distillation column control, chemical reactor control, paper mill control, steel mill control, and a wide range of other process control problems [8–12]. The reader is urged to consult these references and the current journal literature for further examples.

REFERENCES

1. Fisher, D. G., and D. E. Seborg: *Multivariable Computer Control—A Case Study*, American Elsevier, New York, 1976.
2. Lausterer, G. K., W. H. Ray, and H. R. Martens: *Automatica*, **14**:335 (1978).
3. Lausterer, G. K., and W. H. Ray: *IEEE Trans. Auto. Control*, **AC-24**:179 (1979).

4. Lausterer, G. K., Ph.D. thesis, State University of New York at Buffalo, 1977.
5. Greiss, F. K., and W. H. Ray: *Proc. IFAC Symp. New Trends Sys. Anal.*, Springer-Verlag, 1977.
6. Greiss, F. K.: Ph.D. thesis, University of Wisconsin, 1978.
7. Greiss, F. K., and W. H. Ray: *Automatica*, **16** (1980).
8. Foss, A. S., and M. M. Denn: "Chemical Process Control," AIChE. Symposium Series 72 (1976).
9. *Proc. Joint Autom. Control Conf.*, 1976–1979.
10. Lemke, H., R. Van Nauta, and H. B. Verbruggen (eds.): *Digital Computer Applications to Process Control*, North-Holland, Amsterdam, 1977.
11. Ray, W. H.: *Automatica*, **14**:281 (1978).
12. Ray, W. H., and D. G. Lainiotis (eds.): *Distributed Parameter Systems*, Marcel Dekker, New York, 1978.

APPENDIX

SOME COMPUTER-AIDED DESIGN PROGRAMS

A number of educational and research institutions have devoloped computer-aided design programs for interactive computer-aided control system design [1]. Some of the more comprehensive design packages are listed in the table below. These computer programs are usually available for a fee. Further information may be obtained directly from the sources given.

Program	Capabilities	Source
1. CYPROS, DAREK	For linear and nonlinear lumped parameter systems: 1. Optimal and suboptimal multivariable feedback control 2. Process identification 3. State estimation 4. Simulation	Division of Engineering Cybernetics Technical University of Norway Trondheim, Norway
2. UMIST COMPUTER-AIDED CONTROL-SYSTEM DESIGN SUITE	For linear lumped parameter systems: 1. Optimal and suboptimal multivariable feedback control 2. State estimation 3. Simulation	Control Systems Centre University of Manchester Institute of Science and Technology Manchester, England
3. CAMBRIDGE LINEAR ANALYSIS DESIGN PROGRAMS	For linear lumped parameter systems: 1. Multivariable feedback control 2. Simulation	Control Engineering Dept. Cambridge University Cambridge, England
4. GEMSCOPE	For linear lumped parameter systems: 1. Optimal and suboptimal feedback control 2. State estimation 3. Simulation	Data Acquisition and Control System Center Dept. of Chemical Eng. University of Alberta Edmonton, Alberta Canada

REFERENCE

1. Lemmens, W. J. M., and A. J. W. Van den Boom: *Automatica*, **15**:113 (1979).

INDEXES

AUTHOR INDEX

SUBJECT INDEX